THE PRACTICAL HANDBOOK OF CLINICAL GERONTOLOGY

THE PRACTICAL HANDBOOK OF CLINICAL GERONTOLOGY

LAURA L. CARSTENSEN, PH.D.
BARRY A. EDELSTEIN, PH.D.
LAURIE DORNBRAND, M.D.
EDITORS

SAGE Publications
International Educational and Professional Publisher
Thousand Oaks   London   New Delhi

For information address:

SAGE Publications, Inc.
2455 Teller Road
Thousand Oaks, California 91320
E-mail: order@sagepub.com

SAGE Publications Ltd.
6 Bonhill Street
London EC2A 4PU
United Kingdom

SAGE Publications India Pvt. Ltd.
M-32 Market
Greater Kailash I
New Delhi 110 048 India

Printed in the United States of America

Library of Congress Cataloging-in-Publication Data

Main entry under title:

The practical handbook of clinical gerontology / editors, Laura L.
    Carstensen, Barry A. Edelstein, Laurie Dornbrand.
        p.   cm.
    Includes bibliographical references and index.
    ISBN 0-8039-5237-6 (cloth)
        1. Geriatrics—Handbooks, manuals, etc.   I. Carstensen, Laura L.
    II. Edelstein, Barry A., 1945-   .   III. Dornbrand, Laurie.
    IN PROCESS
    618.97—dc20   96-9986

This book is printed on acid-free paper.

96 97 98 99 00 01 10 9 8 7 6 5 4 3 2 1

Sage Production Editor: Vicki Baker
Sage Typesetter: Andrea D. Swanson

Contents

I

General Issues in the Treatment of the Elderly

1

Psychological Perspectives on the Normal Aging Process

Susan Krauss Whitbourne

That the aging process is, fundamentally, "normal" is one of the undeniable facts of human life. Yet the definition of *normal aging* is far less clear. In this chapter, I will describe a set of physical and cognitive changes in later adulthood that are considered to be the result of the normal aging process. Although it is true that as individuals age, they are at greater risk of developing chronic health problems such as arthritis, cardiovascular disease, diabetes, and sensory impairments, these conditions are not inherent in the aging process. This distinction between normal aging and disease is important for mental health providers to be able to recognize for the purposes of both diagnosis and treatment. Symptoms of depression and anxiety related to the presence of disease may be lifted when the underlying disease is treated. Normal age-related changes may also contribute to psychological distress, and even though these changes may not be reversible, compensatory measures can be taken to improve the individual's emotional well-being.

Relevant to these points is that fact that there are wide individual differences in reactions to aging as well as differences in the rates of aging. Many effects

3

vary tremendously in the rates at which they occur, both from person to person and within the same person, from one bodily system or psychological function to another. The rate of aging is determined in part by genetic factors and in part by the individual's behavior to compensate for or accelerate the aging process. In many cases, "bad habits," such as cigarette smoking, inactivity, and poor diet, can increase the individual's vulnerability to disease or deleterious effects of aging. By contrast, it is often the case that taking advantage of the "use it or lose it" principle, involving exercise and other attempts to maintain functioning, can help slow or offset the physical and psychological consequences of aging.

Personality and self-concept clearly play interactive roles in understanding physical and cognitive aging processes (Whitbourne, 1987). It is useful to conceptualize the individual's reaction to aging in terms of the meaning that specific age-related changes have for sense of competence, mastery, and sense of the self as continuous over time as well as the ability to adapt to the environment. For certain individuals, changes in particular aspects of functioning may prove extremely threatening to identity because these changes involve loss of particularly valued abilities or characteristics. Individuals may react defensively to these changes, either pretending that they have not in fact occurred or attempting to overcompensate by engaging in a series of desperate measures to prevent any further deterioration. Other age-related changes not as central to identity may be perceived and reacted to in a more neutral, dispassionate manner. In developing therapeutic interventions, it is essential to understand the meaning of a particular age-related change for the individual in terms of lifelong patterns of activity, behavior, interests, and personality. Within this context, suggestions can be made to help the individual by adapting coping strategies and other cognitive interventions for reducing stress (Folkman, Lazarus, Gruen, & DeLongis, 1986; Lazarus & Folkman, 1984). For example, the individual can be helped to compensate for certain changes using a variety of problem-focused coping strategies, such as planful problem solving. If the availability of compensatory measures is limited, the clinician can help the individual accommodate to these changes through, for example, positive reappraisal and other emotion-focused forms of coping. In this chapter, I will outline the major physical and cognitive changes associated with the aging process and present suggestions for compensatory measures that can be incorporated into such intervention strategies for older adult clients.

Normal Age-Related Changes
in Physical Functioning

The physiological changes associated with the aging process occur as the result of an inexorable process that moves the individual ultimately toward death. The cause of aging is not yet known, and there are many theories that attempt to address the underlying mechanism that manifests itself in the aging of the body. Yet it is clear that the human body is remarkable in its ability to maintain its functional competence and integrity over time despite deleterious physiological changes. Rather than simply deteriorating until the end of life, the body actively attempts to integrate the deleterious changes in its tissues into new levels of organization to preserve life and functioning for as long as possible. As I review the changes in the body with age, it is important to keep this point in mind, as the aging of the body is not synonymous with the aging of a machine (Whitbourne, 1986). In each of these areas, I will develop the themes of the interaction of physical aging with psychological processes and the ways that individuals can affect the physical aging process through their own behaviors.

APPEARANCE

The signs of aging are most apparent in the aging of the individual's appearance. Contributing to the aging of appearance are changes in the skin, hair, facial structures, and body build. For the most part, the effect of these changes is cosmetic; however, there are ramifications of the aging of these structures for the individual's overall physical functioning.

Skin. The development of creases, discoloration, furrows, sagging, and loss of resiliency are the most apparent changes in the skin. The processes responsible for these changes have a negative effect on the skin's protective functions as well as its appearance. There is less insulation provided against extremes of temperature and less of a barrier against environmental agents that can irritate the skin and cause dermatitis (Grove, 1989). Dryness, sagging, and wrinkling of the skin on the face and body can also lead to discomfort (Kligman, 1989). There are also alterations in the immune responsiveness of the skin and, along with a diminished blood supply to the skin, the immune system's response to surface inflammation is reduced (Balin & Pratt, 1989).

Hair. With increasing age in adulthood, for both men and women, the hair on the head and body loses its pigmentation and becomes white due to decreased melanin production in the hair follicles. The extent to which a person's hair begins to appear gray depends on the rate at which colored hairs turn white and the original hair color into which the white hairs become mixed. For both men and women, hair on the face becomes coarser and longer, and men may develop long hairs on the external canal of the ear (Whitbourne, 1986).

Face. Changes in the appearance of the face represent changes already discussed in the skin and hair as well as changes in the bones of the face comparable to bone changes throughout the body. The structure of the face changes as the nose and ears become longer and broader and the jaws lose bone causing them to shrink in size. Changes in the teeth occur, including tooth loss, discoloration, and chipping. The need to wear eyeglasses, due to changes in vision, may lead to a striking change in appearance. Wrinkling, puffiness, and deepening of pigmentation around the eyes cause the eyes to appear more sunken. In addition, the cornea loses brightness and translucency.

Body Build. It is well established that over the course of adulthood, there is a consistent pattern of a reduction in standing height, occurring at a greater rate after the 50s and particularly pronounced in women (Adams, Davies, & Sweetname, 1970; Shephard, 1978). Not only is there a height decrease, but there are changes in the overall shape of the body due to altered distribution of body fat starting in middle age. Based primarily on cross-sectional studies but also consistent with clinical experience, it is well documented that weight increases from the 20s until the mid-50s, after which total body weight declines. Body fat distribution also changes over the course of adulthood, with subcutaneous fat decreasing in the extremities and increasing in the abdominal area for both men and women (Shephard, 1978).

Psychological Interactions

As the individual's appearance changes in later adulthood, the potential exists for his or her identity to change in corresponding ways, some of them negative. Comparisons of present appearance with pictures or memories of early adulthood can be damaging to self-esteem to people who valued their youthful image (Fenske & Albers, 1990; Kleinsmith & Perricone, 1989). At the same time, others may be repulsed by the wrinkles, discolorations, and white hair of the older person, causing the aged individual to feel rejected and isolated (Kligman, 1989). These changes involve primarily the face but can also include changes in exposed areas of the body. With regard to body build, changes in body fat and muscle tone that lead to the appearance of a sagging or heavier body shape can result in increased identification of the self as moving away from the figure of youth. The development of "middle-aged spread" is one of the first occurrences to trigger recognition of the self as aging, even before the first gray hairs have become fully evident.

Compensatory Measures

Short of cosmetic surgery, there are many steps that older individuals can take to slow, compensate for, or correct the changes in appearance caused by aging of the skin. The primary method of prevention, which must be started early in life, is for fair-skinned people to avoid direct exposure to the sun and to use sunblock when exposure cannot be avoided (Gilchrest, 1989). Cigarette smoke can also be harmful to the skin.

There are many possible ways for the individual to compensate for age-related changes in the skin once they have become manifest. To counteract the fragility, sensitivity, and dryness of the skin, the individual can use sunscreens, emollients, and fragrance-free cosmetics. As it is traditional for women to use facial cosmetics, the proper choice of color and coverup techniques can enhance the individual's appearance (O'Donoghue, 1991). Changes in body build can be compensated, often remarkably so, by regular involvement in activities and exercise that maintain muscle tone and reduce fat deposits under the skin.

MOBILITY

The ability to move about through one's physical surroundings is a function of the smooth coordination of the body's joints and muscles and the associated tendons and ligaments. Movement is also made possible by the bones, which must be both strong and resilient. The normal aging process results in changes in all these structures, leading to the possibility that the individual will become limited in the ability to carry out desired movements and actions.

Muscles. There is little reduction in muscle strength until at least age 40 or 50 years, a 10% to 20% decrease thereafter until about age 50 or 60 years, and a 30% to 40% decrease by the 70s and 80s. Loss of muscle strength is more pronounced in the legs than the hands and arms (McArdle, Katch, & Katch, 1991).

Bones. The overall pattern of bone development in adulthood is a progressive loss of bone strength, due primarily to a loss of bone mineral content as the rate of resorption exceeds that of new bone apposition. The decrease in various measures of bone strength ranges from 5% to 12% per decade from the 20s through the 90s (McCalden, McGeough, Barker, & Court-Brown, 1993). In part, bone density and the loss of bone mass in the later years of adulthood may be a function of genetic factors (Dargent & Breart, 1993; Kelly et al., 1993). Lifestyle also seems to play a role, however, including factors such as physical activity, smoking, alcohol use, and diet, which can account for 50% to 60% of the variation in bone density (Krall & Dawson-Hughes, 1993). There are also hormonal influences on bone mass, as indicated by the observation that bone mineral loss in women proceeds at a higher rate in postmenopausal women, who are no longer producing estrogen in monthly cycles

(Nuti & Martini, 1993). In addition to a total loss of bone mineral content, the bones become more brittle and porous so that they are less resistant to stress and more likely to undergo serious fracture than the bones of younger persons (Whitbourne, 1986).

Joints. Age-related losses have been documented to occur in every structural component of the joints, including the tendons, ligaments, synovial membranes, synovial fluid, and arterial cartilage (Brooks & Fahey, 1984). Joint functioning peaks in efficiency in the 20s and decreases continuously thereafter (Bortz, 1982) with accelerating decreases after the 60s (Bassey, Morgan, Dallosso, & Ebrahim, 1989; Vandervoort et al., 1992).

Psychological Interactions

Degenerative changes in the muscles and joints, whether due to disease or the normal aging process, have many pervasive effects on the individual's life and are a major source of disability (Hughes, Cordray, & Spiker, 1984; Hughes, Edelman, Singer, & Chang, 1993). Restriction of movement in the upper limbs rules out many enjoyable leisure activities and can make it difficult for the individual to perform occupations that require finely tuned motor skills and repetitive movements of the hand and arm. Pain and lack of flexibility in the legs and feet can slow the individual's pace when walking. Restricted movement of the hip leads to a number of restrictions, such as limping, difficulty climbing stairs, and rising from a chair or sofa. Involvement of the knee adds to these difficulties. Degenerative changes in the spine, in addition, often result in back pain that, if not restrictive in and of itself, has the constant potential to detract from the individual's enjoyment of both occupational and recreational activities. This restriction of activities, combined with the experience of pain, may lead the individual to suffer from clinical symptoms of depression (Williamson & Schulz, 1992a). In part, the effects of mobility loss can be attributed to the enforced reliance on others that is created, leading to other deleterious processes, such as being treated like a dependent child (Whitbourne & Wills, 1993).

One of the most deleterious outcomes of reduced muscle strength, bone strength, and joint mobility is the heightened susceptibility of older individuals, particularly women, to falls and to serious consequences resulting from falls (Kelsey & Hoffman, 1987; Lord, Clark, & Webster, 1991a). Community survey estimates of the prevalence of falling range from 32% (Tinetti, Speechley, & Ginter, 1988) to 42% (Downton & Andrews, 1990) to 53% (Walker & Allen, 1991). Over 250,000 patients are hospitalized each year in the United States for treatment of fractured hips (Allegrante, MacKenzie, Robbins, & Cornell, 1991). There are a number of interacting age-related processes that operate to increase the older adult's likelihood of suffering from a disabling fall, including musculoskeletal changes and sensory losses (Woollacott, 1993) and an increased likelihood of tripping over obstacles (Chen, Ashton-Miller, Alexander, & Schultz, 1991). Those elderly who are most at risk of falling include people who suffer, in addition to bone loss, from visual impairment, neurological deficits, gait disturbance, loss of muscle strength and coordination, and health problems requiring certain medications (Craven & Bruno, 1986; Felson et al., 1989; Kelsey & Hoffman, 1987; Lipsitz, Jonsson, Kelley, & Koestner, 1991; Lord, Clark, & Webster, 1991; Maki, Holliday, & Topper, 1991; Morse, Tylko, & Dixon, 1987; Nevitt, Cummings, & Hudes, 1991). Weakness and limitations in range of movement of the ankles and knees play an important role in heightening the risk of a fall due to the individual's inability to avoid obstacles (Whipple, Wolfson, & Amerman, 1987). Cognitive impairments, particularly those associated with Alzheimer's disease, contribute further to heightened risk of falling (Morris, Rubin, Morris, & Mandel, 1987; Spar, LaRue, Hewes, & Fairbanks, 1987; Tinetti et al., 1988). Psychological factors, such as anxiety and depression, also increase the older individual's risk of falling (Tinetti, Richman, & Powell, 1990). Disability and a history of smoking are two final contributing risk factors (Vetter & Ford, 1989).

The experience of a fall can lead to a vicious cycle in which one fall leads the individual to become fearful of more falls, and as a result, to walk less securely and confidently. This loss of a sense of security can serve to increase the risk that older persons will lose their balance and actually make them more likely to fall in the future. The experience of falling can also lead individuals to develop low self-efficacy about themselves as being unable to avoid a fall, further impairing their balance and gait (Downton & Andrews, 1990; Tinetti et al., 1990). Apart from the physical risk factors that increase the likelihood of falling, there exist psychological variables related to elderly persons' attitudes toward their abilities and senses of security (Tinetti & Powell, 1993). Even without actual bone fracture, then, the older adult may experience some of the psychological consequences associated with lessened mobility. Furthermore, necessary daily activities that were previously conducted with little concern, such as descending a steep flight of stairs or walking on icy pavement, may create fear and hence avoidance. The experience of falling, in this sense, might precipitate rapid realization of aging regarding the fragility of the bones and lead to a loss of autonomy and sense of competence.

Compensatory Mechanisms

Counteracting the picture of inevitable decline in muscle strength is evidence, accruing from the 1970s, showing that a regular program of exercise can help the middle-aged and older adult compensate substantially for the loss of muscle fibers. Although there is nothing that can be done to stop the loss of muscle cells, the remaining fibers can be strengthened and work efficiency increased through exercise training, even in persons as old as 90 years (Fiatarone et al., 1990; Grimby & Saltin, 1983; see also Chapter 2, this volume). Inactivity is a bad habit that can accelerate the loss of muscle strength, and the same is true of bone loss. It appears that older individuals can benefit from resistance training exercises that, within limits, increase the stress placed on the bone (Dalsky, 1988; Rikli & McManis, 1990; Smith, 1981). Although degenerative changes in the joints are not reversible, it is nevertheless possible for older individuals to benefit from exercise training, particularly if it is oriented toward promoting flexibility (Jirovec, 1991); strengthening the muscles that support the joints; increasing the circulation of blood to the joints, thereby promoting the repair of injured tissues (Brooks & Fahey, 1984); and decreasing risk of injury (Stamford, 1988).

CARDIOVASCULAR FUNCTIONING

Age-related changes in the heart and arteries have the effect of reducing the amount of blood available to the cells of the body, but under ordinary conditions, this is not particularly pronounced or noticeable. The effects of aging of the circulatory system are most apparent when the individual is engaging in aerobic exercise, when there is a reduction both in maximum oxygen consumption (aerobic capacity) and the maximum attainable heart rate (Lakatta, 1987; Morley & Reese, 1989). The decrease in maximum oxygen consumption occurs in a linear fashion throughout the adult years so that the average 65-year-old individual has 30% to 40% of the aerobic capacity of the young adult (McArdle, Katch, & Katch, 1991). Other functional variables that decrease to a commensurate degree include stroke volume (the amount of blood pumped at each beat of the heart) (Weisfeldt & Gerstenblith, 1986) and cardiac output per minute (heart rate times the stroke volume). As a result of these decreases in the functional capacity of the heart, less oxygen reaches the muscles during exercise, and the individual is more likely to suffer from temporary ischemia. These functional changes appear to be attributable to reduced pumping capacity of the heart due to a variety of changes affecting the structure and function of the heart muscle walls, particularly in the area of the left ventricle (Kitzman & Edwards, 1990; Weisfeldt & Gerstenblith, 1986). Changes in the heart and arteries can account, in part, for the observation that older individuals have higher levels of systolic and diastolic blood pressure, both at rest and during exercise; however, this is not a consistent finding and may be confounded by the presence of individuals with hypertension in the older populations that are tested (Whitbourne, 1986).

Psychological Interactions

The adequacy of the cardiovascular system is reflected in the individual's ability to engage in a range of physical activities, including walking outside, moving about the house, carrying heavy objects, and engaging in strenuous exercise. Reductions in the cardiovascular system's functioning therefore contribute importantly to changes in the structures underlying movement to reduce, potentially, the individual's mobility in the physical environment. In addition, although not as apparent in its effects on identity as appearance, the functioning of the cardiovascular system is an important influence on the individual's feelings of well-being and identity. All adults know that the efficiency of the cardiovascular system is essential to life so that threats to the integrity of this system are perceived as highly dangerous. Awareness of reduced cardiovascular efficiency can therefore serve as reminders of one's own personal mortality.

Compensatory Mechanisms

Given the importance of cardiovascular functioning to the overall health and longevity of the individual, there has been a wealth of research pointing to the effectiveness of exercise in slowing or reversing the effects of the aging process on the system (Stamford, 1988). Much of the original research in this area was conducted in Sweden, due to the popularity of endurance sports, such as cross-country skiing and long-distance running. Many of the participants in this early research were lifelong exercisers. With the growth of the fitness industry in the United States, however, contemporary research includes respondents with recent interest in aerobic exercise who may constitute a more representative group than do long-term fitness fanatics.

The major dependent variable in research on the effectiveness of exercise training is aerobic capacity and, secondarily, maximum attainable heart rate. The results of research on the effectiveness of exercise training have consistently revealed improved functioning in long-term endurance athletes, master athletes who remain active, long-term exercisers, and previously sedentary adults who enroll in short-term training programs (McArdle, Katch, & Katch, 1991; Whitbourne, 1986). The main advantage that exercise seems to hold as a means of retaining a higher level of cardiovascular functioning is that it provides a continued potent stimulus for the muscle cells of the heart to undergo strong contractions so that they retain or gain contractile power. The greater strength of the myocardial muscle improves the functioning of the left ventricle and as a result, more blood can be ejected from the left ventricle during the systolic phase of the cardiac cycle (Ehsani, Ogawa, Miller, Spina, & Jilka, 1991). The other advantage of exercise training is that it makes it possible for the individual to "save" energy during aerobic work that is less than maximal by fulfilling the demands of the workload but placing less stress on the heart (Morey et al., 1991; Poulin, Paterson, Govindasamy, & Cunningham, 1988). Due to the fact that more blood is ejected with each cardiac muscle contraction, the same output of blood can be pumped per minute but at a lower heart rate. The effects of training on cardiac functioning under submaximal conditions are of interest in that these performance situations are closer to the conditions under which people exert themselves in their daily lives. Exercise training also has favorable effects on the body's performance by increasing the efficiency of metabolism in the working muscles (Meredith et al., 1989).

In addition to the benefits that exercise training has for the cardiovascular system, it is well established that adults who become involved in aerobic activities experience a variety of positive effects on mood, anxiety levels, and particularly feelings of mastery and control, leading to enhanced feelings of self-esteem (Hill, Storandt, & Malley, 1993; McAuley, Lox, & Duncan, 1993; Sidney & Shephard, 1976). Questions remain, however, regarding the causal linkages in this relationship between exercise and well-being (Brown, 1992). Although some researchers have demonstrated there to be positive effects of exercise on cognitive functioning (Chodzko-Zajko, Schuler, Solomon, Heinl, & Ellis, 1992; Stevenson & Topp, 1990), this effect is not consistently observed (Hill, Storandt, & Malley, 1993). Nevertheless, the finding is consistently observed that older adults who enter exercise training programs "feel better," and this improvement in mood can be clinically useful for many aging clients.

RESPIRATORY SYSTEM

Structures in the respiratory system are responsible for the process of gas exchange between the blood and air so that the body's cells receive adequate support for their metabolic activities. The major effect of aging is to reduce the quality of gas exchange in the lungs so that less oxygen from the outside air reaches the blood (Kenney, 1989). There are also age-related reductions in vital capacity, the amount of air that is moved into and out of the lungs at maximal levels of exertion (Reddan, 1981).

Psychological Interactions

Age changes in respiration can lead to feelings of dyspnea and fatigue associated with exertion, sensations that can be extremely distressing and have the potential to arouse panic (McConnell & Davies, 1992). Dyspnea (shortness of breath) will be more likely to occur at lower degrees of activity than was true when the individual was younger, such as trying to catch a bus or crossing the street before the light changes (Cunningham, Nancekievill, Paterson, Donner, & Rechnitzer, 1985). Such experiences can lead the aging individual to avoid strenuous activities, a consequence that would further impair the individual's cardiovascular and respiratory efficiency. Because both of these functions are so crucial to life and because shortness of breath is such an anxiety-provoking state, the individual might be prematurely frightened into thinking that death is soon to follow.

Compensatory Mechanisms

The effects of exercise training on respiratory functioning are encouraging (Blumenthal et al., 1989), but the specific effects of exercise on respiratory functioning are not as dramatic as are the effects on the cardiovascular system. Equally, if not more, beneficial to the respiratory function is the avoidance of cigarette smoking (Hermanson et al., 1988; Webster & Kadah, 1991).

EXCRETORY SYSTEM

With increasing age in adulthood, the efficiency of the excretory process is reduced such that the kidneys are generally able to function under normal conditions but become inefficient when there are wide fluctuations in fluid levels within the body (Danzinger, Tobin, Becker, Lakatta, & Fleg, 1990). Reduced functioning of the kidneys in older adults also results in a slower rate of excreting drugs from the body so that relatively low dosages of medication can accumulate to toxic levels in the bloodstream (Rowe, 1982). Unless the dosage is adjusted to take into account this lower rate of tubular transport, the drugs may have adverse effects instead of their intended benefits (Lamy, 1988; Montgomery, 1990).

The most significant effect of changes with age in the bladder is on patterns of urinary incontinence. The prevalence of incontinence among the population 60 years and older is estimated to be 19% for women and 8% for men (Herzog, Diokno, Brown, Normolle, & Brock, 1990) but can reach as high as 36% among community-dwelling elderly with dementia (Ouslander, Zarit, Orr, & Muira, 1990). Women are more likely to suffer from stress incontinence, which refers to loss of urine at times of exertion, such as when laughing, sneezing, lifting, or bending. This condition is the result of weakness of the pelvic muscles. Urge incontinence is more prevalent in men and involves urine loss following an urge to void or lack of control over voiding with little or no warning (Diokno, Brock, Brown, & Herzog, 1986). For men, incontinence is related to prostatic hypertrophy, prostate disease, or incomplete emptying of the bladder.

Psychological Interactions

The aging of the excretory system is unlikely to have a discernible effect on everyday functioning. However, age-related changes in the bladder can present significant problems. Such changes can be highly disruptive to the older individual's everyday life, causing subjective distress and embarrassment in social situations (Ouslander & Abelson, 1990; Wyman, Harkins, & Fantl, 1990; Yu, 1987). Fear of becoming incontinent may also increase the individual's general anxiety about problems in urination, further exacerbating these difficulties.

Compensatory Mechanisms

The effects of aging on the kidney and the bladder are not amenable to compensation; though, once identified, behavioral methods have proven effective for the treatment of incontinence. Techniques ranging from biofeedback to very simple exercises (such as the "Kegel" exercise in which a woman contracts and relaxes the pelvic muscles) can hold the problem in check if not reverse it (Baigis-Smith, Smith, Rose, & Newman, 1989; Burgio & Engel, 1990; Burns et al., 1993). Thus, although the psychological damage is potentially very high from changes in urinary functioning, this can be offset by the individual's experience of success in learning new forms of behavioral management. (See also Chapter 16, this volume.) Prostate symptoms have also been shown to respond to treatment.

EATING AND DIGESTION

Although a great deal of attention is given by advertisers and the popular media to the inefficient digestive processes of older adults, the documented effects of aging are of far less significance. There are numerous gastrointestinal diseases that interfere with the efficiency of digestion and must be ruled out before considering the possibility that a particular problem or symptom is the result of aging. Furthermore, the fact that individuals vary so much in digestive habits further complicates the analysis of aging effects. There are a host of psychological, cultural, and economic factors whose cumulative effects on diet over a lifetime interact with whatever changes are intrinsic to the aging process.

Early investigations in salivary functioning yielded evidence of diminished secretions by the parotid glands (Kamocka, 1970). These investigations failed to exclude participants with diagnosed medical problems, however, and they were based exclusively on cross-sectional data. When healthy individuals only are studied and are followed over time, there is no diminution reported to occur in salivary gland flow (Ship, Patton, & Tylenda, 1991; Wu, Atkinson, Fox, Baum, & Ship, 1992) or in the antibacterial function of saliva secreted by the parotid gland (Fox et al., 1987). Therefore, the healthy elderly person should not experience symptoms such as dry mouth or difficulty swallowing. Some investigators have described as a normal function of aging the condition called *presbyesophagus*, literally meaning "old" esophagus, defined as a diminution of primary peristalsis and increase in secondary peristalsis. Researchers studying the healthy elderly have found that primary peristalsis remains intact in old age. However, secondary peristalsis does seem to be negatively affected by aging, as indicated by reduced intensity of the peristaltic wave propelling food into the stomach and a higher resting esophageal pressure (Khan, Shragge, Crispin, & Lind, 1977). Aging appears to affect the secretion of gastric juice, with estimates of its decrease amounting to approximately 25% by the time a person reaches the age of 60 years (Bernier, Vidon, & Mignon, 1973). The reduction in gastric juice secretion has several effects on the digestion of specific nutrients. Protein, iron, calcium, and Vitamin $B_{12,}$ folic acid are less completely digested, and there is in addition increased bacterial growth in the intestinal tract (Bowman & Rosenberg, 1983).There are some structural changes in the small intestine that have the potential to impair the absorption process (Minaker & Rowe, 1982); however, these changes have little functional effect because the epithelial cells turn over so rapidly that they do not "age." Nevertheless, there appear to be some notable age-related changes, including reduction in the absorption of fats, calcium, Vitamin $B_{12,}$ folic acid, iron, and Vitamin B_6 (Eastell et al., 1991; Hsu & Smith, 1984; Lynch, Finch, Monsen, & Cook, 1982; Minaker & Rowe, 1982). These changes are exacerbated by the lack of compliance shown by many older adults with maintaining adequate dietary intakes of magnesium, vitamins A and E, calcium, and zinc (Costello & Moser-Veillon, 1992; Ryan, Craig, & Finn, 1992). There is no evidence that apart from some changes in the lining of the large intestine and atrophy of muscles responsible for moving fecal material through it (Yamagata, 1965), age changes in the functioning of this organ are minimal (Brauer, Slavin, & Marlett, 1981; Brocklehurst, 1978; Minaker & Rowe, 1982). When constipation occurs in the elderly individual, it is more likely to be caused by factors related to diet and lifestyle, as will be discussed. Fecal incontinence, the loss of control over anal sphincters, is more likely to occur in women after the age of 50 compared to men, perhaps related to estrogen changes associated with the menopause (Haadem, Dahlstrom, & Ling, 1991).

Psychological Interactions

Changes in the digestive system at the physiological level due to aging are minimal in terms of their effects on the individual's adaptation. Inaccurate conceptions communicated through the media, however, may lead older persons to misuse laxatives, avoid roughage, and become overly preoccupied with minor digestive upsets (Minaker & Rowe, 1982). What originates as a temporary bout of indigestion or constipation can thereby come to have a more prolonged course. Laxative use in the elderly may be more of a generational than an age-related issue, however. More important than constipation, dyspepsia, and reduced sensory capacities for enjoying food are the beliefs that people hold as communicated through the media, the social context in which food is eaten, and other physical and cognitive deficiencies (Fischer & Johnson, 1990; Holt, 1991; Minaker & Rowe, 1982).

Equally serious is the potential for reductions in the quality of the individual's food intake due to age-related changes in other bodily systems. It is well established that apart from the disease diabetes mellitus, glucose tolerance is impaired in older adults (Davidson, 1982). Reductions in mobility make it more difficult for the older adult to push a shopping cart, carry groceries into and from a bus or automobile, and reach for items on high shelves in the supermarket or at home (Wantz & Gay, 1981). Sensory losses may reduce the individual's ability to read shopping lists, grocery advertisements, and prepare good-tasting food. Problems with teeth and dentures are another source of possible loss of eating pleasure and, ultimately, nutritional deficiencies (Posner, Jette, Smigelski, Miller, & Mitchell, 1994). In the cognitive domain, memory problems and difficulties processing information can make it more difficult for the older individual to take the necessary steps for healthy and satisfying food preparation. Changes in family patterns, particularly the loss of a spouse, can cause older individuals to lose the incentive to cook, and the emotional associations to family mealtimes of the past that no longer can take place may lead to depression and disinterest in eating (Rosenbloom & Whittington, 1993). Men living alone are particularly vulnerable to poor nutrition (Davis, Murphy, & Neuhaus, 1988; Davis, Randall, Forthofer, Lee, & Margen, 1985). Adverse economic circumstances also can play a major role in affecting patterns of eating because the individual may be working with such a limited budget that only the minimal, and perhaps unappetizing, necessities can be acquired.

Compensatory Mechanisms

The avoidance of bad habits is a crucial compensatory strategy. Perhaps the greatest obstacle for the individual to overcome in this process is the mountain of publicity heaped on the adult population by pharmaceutical companies, warning them of the dangers of not being "regular."

To overcome changes in the context in which food is bought, prepared, and eaten, older adults may find that they need to change their lifelong habits in favor of strategies that will be more realistic given their income, changes in other areas of physical functioning, and social relationships. They may need to learn new ways to budget their food expenditures, find recipes that do not involve extensive preparation, and seek out companionship during mealtimes. In some cases, the individual may need assistance in shopping and reeducation in food preparation techniques, both of which demand considerable motivation and effort.

AUTONOMIC NERVOUS SYSTEM (ANS)

There are discernible effects of aging in important functions that are controlled by the ANS; two in particular have a considerable effect on the individual's daily life: bodily temperature control and sleep patterns.

It is well established both through population health statistics and experimental studies that individuals over the age of 65 years have impaired adaptive responses to extremely hot and cold environmental temperatures (Phillips, Bretherton, Johnston, & Gray, 1991; Tankersley, Smolander, Kenney, & Fortney, 1991). The diminished response of the elderly to cold appears to be due to diminished feedback that the core body temperature is low and to an impaired ability to raise core temperatures when the body's peripheral temperature becomes lowered. Responses to extremes of heat are impaired due to decreased secretion by the sweat glands in the skin. Paradoxically, some older adults report feeling cold even when others in the environment feel uncomfortably warm; this effect does not appear to be linked to normal aging processes but instead reflects diminished cardiovascular functioning (Whitbourne, 1985).

Older adults spend more time in bed relative to time spent asleep due to longer time taken to fall asleep, more periods of wakefulness during the night, and time spent lying awake before arising in the morning. In old age, the primary causes of sleep disturbance include sleep apnea (Ancoli-Israel & Kripke, 1991), periodic leg movements, heartburn, and frequent needs to urinate (Friedman et al., 1992; Whitbourne, 1986; see also Chapter 18, this volume). Electroencephalograph sleep patterns show some corresponding age alterations, including a rise in Stage 1 sleep (drowsiness without actual sleep) and a large decrease in Stage 4 sleep (slow wave or heavy sleep). By the 60s and 70s, REM sleep starts to diminish as well, as do the observable behaviors associated with REM sleep (Prinz, Vitiello, Raskind, & Thorpy, 1990).

Psychological Interactions

The changes in the regulatory efficiency of the ANS can create another set of difficulties in a range of everyday activities. The ability to adjust blood circulation, body temperature, and sleep habits to meet the particular needs of the situation are critical for engaging in pleasurable recreational activities, such as traveling, exercising, and socializing, as well as for adapting to changes in climates, demands for exertion, and sleep schedules. Recognition of the body's reduced efficiency may lead to a reduced sense of independence because the individual can no longer engage spontaneously in some activities.

Compensatory Mechanisms

Changes in the ANS occur largely outside the individual's control. The individual can avoid exacerbating these changes or causing them to become life threatening or disruptive to flow of ordinary daily activities, however. With regard to body temperature control, the aging individual needs to be aware of the fact that perception of temperature extremes (particularly cold) is likely to be diminished. Careful attention must be given to weather conditions, particularly wind chill levels in the winter and heat-humidity indexes in the summer, and the individual should be aware of what precautions will be needed in these instances.

Altered sleep patterns can also be compensated for by taking steps to avoid daytime naps and follow good sleep habits. One of the most damaging effects on sleep is anxiety over insomnia, a condition that might well develop in individuals who have believed all their lives that 8 hours of sleep is the normal human need rather than the 7 hours that the average adult actually sleeps. The longer the time spent in bed awake, the harder it is for the individual to develop a normal nightly rhythm based on this more realistic sleep requirement. If these strategies are ineffective, behavioral methods such as stimulus control can be used (Morin & Azrin, 1988).

REPRODUCTIVE SYSTEM

The feelings connected with sexuality, both in terms of reproduction and the expression of sexual drives, are important contributors to the adult's overall well-being and form an important component of intimate relationships with other adults. In addition, the individual's identity may be influenced in part by his or her self-evaluation of sexual attractiveness, responsiveness, and capacity to produce offspring.

Female Reproductive System

Throughout her 40s, a woman's reproductive capacity becomes gradually reduced until, by the age of 50 to 55 years, it ceases altogether. This transitional time, the climacteric, ends in the menopause. Associated with the ending of the monthly phases of ovulation and menstruation is a diminution of estrogen and progesterone, the hormones produced by the ovary and uterus (Sherman, West, & Korenmann, 1976).

Other changes in sexual functioning occur due to aging of the tissues in other bodily systems. For example, sagging of the breasts and wrinkling of the skin in the torso occurs as the result of decreased elasticity of the skin. Subcutaneous fat accumulates in the torso, especially around the waist, leading to uneven bulges. These changes add to those in body build, facial structure, and the skin on the face to alter progressively the woman's appearance in old age.

The appearance and functioning of the genital organs also change after the menopause (Schiff & Wilson, 1978). The pubic hair on the mons veneris and around the vulva becomes thin and coarser. The labia majora and minora become thinner and wrinkled, the skin in the vulva atrophies, and the surface mucosa of the vaginal wall becomes thin, dry, pale, and smooth. The vagina also becomes narrower and shorter so that it is less able to accommodate an inserted penis. These changes are significant not only for their effects on sexual functioning but for their effects on the woman's enjoyment of sexual intercourse. The older woman may experience discomfort during prolonged intercourse due to changes in the vagina and vulva, and the rhythmic contractions of the uterus may become painful.

Despite changes in the reproductive system, the conclusion reached by Masters and Johnson nearly 30 years ago is still generally accepted—that older women are limited in their potential to achieve sexual gratification more by their attitudes, values, and accessibility to partners than they are by the physical changes involved in the aging process. The sexual response cycle might be slowed down somewhat in the older woman, but the possibility of achieving orgasm is not reduced (Masters & Johnson, 1966). There appears to be minimal functional impairment in sexual functioning as women age.

Male Reproductive System

Just as women gradually lose reproductive capacity throughout the middle years of adulthood, men experience a climacteric of sorts in which there is a gradual reduction in the number of viable sperm they produce due to degenerative changes in the seminiferous tubules of the testes. Although men retain the ability to father children into old age, the reduction of viable sperm results in a steady decrease of fertilization potential through the later years of adulthood (Harman, 1978).

With increasing age in adulthood, men may experience changes in the prostate gland that lead to a reduction of the volume and pressure of semen expelled during ejaculation. Age-related changes also include overgrowth or hypertrophy of the glandular and connective tissue in the parts of the prostate that surround the prostatic urethra. This condition, called *benign prostatic hypertrophy,* is found with increasing prevalence in men past the age of 50 years, becoming almost universal in old age (Harman & Talbert, 1985). The adjacent penile urethra may become constricted due to this overgrowth, and urinary retention may ensue. Discomfort and embarrassment may result from difficulties in urination and from the occurrence of involuntary penile erections (Masters & Johnson, 1966). If urinary retention becomes a chronic condition, kidney problems may develop, leading to more serious health threats.

A physiological index of reproductive function that has a decidedly noticeable effect on the older man's sense of his own sexuality is that of penile erectility. It is well documented that older men experience fewer nightly episodes of penile erections compared to younger males (Karacan, Williams, Thornby, & Salis, 1975). By contrast, there are inconsistencies in the findings regarding an increase in penile circumference during erection, with some decreases noted across age groups by some researchers (Solnick & Birren, 1977), and in other research, no age differences are observed (Schiavi & Schreiner-Engel, 1988).

As is true for aging women, there is a general slowing down in aging men of the progression through the phases of the human sexual response cycle, from excitement through resolution. Compared to young adult men, orgasm is shorter, involving fewer contractions of the prostate and ejection of a smaller amount of seminal fluid (Masters & Johnson, 1970). These findings are consistent with the physiological data on changes in the male reproductive system and carry some negative implications for the aging male's sexual relations. However, the gains for the older man's ability to enjoy sexuality are also compelling. He may feel less driven toward the pressure to ejaculate, be able to prolong the period of sensual enjoyment prior to orgasm, and have the control to coordinate his pleasure cycle to correspond more to his partner's.

A man's pattern of sexual activity in the earlier years of adulthood is by far the best predictor of his sexual activity in old age (George & Weiler, 1985). The sexually active middle-aged man, given good health, has the potential to remain sexually active well into his later years.

Psychological Interactions

The effect of reproductive changes in later adulthood depends heavily on how the individual interprets the significance of this transition. The menopause may be met with relief or it may serve as a reminder of the inevitability of aging and one's own mortality. Age-related changes leading to a slowing of sexual response may have a negative effect on the individual's enjoyment of sexual relations. The man may write himself off as a sexual partner, believing that his masculine prowess has failed. Furthermore, the changes in sexual functioning may serve as signs that one's body is deteriorating and death is around the corner. As is true regardless of age, depression, heavy alcohol use, or late-life career pressures may also interfere with the ability to enjoy sexual relations in later adulthood. Conversely, feelings of self-worth and a sense of competence can promote sexual relations among older adults (Marsiglio & Donnelly, 1991). Illness, particularly cardiovascular disease, can be another important factor causing the older individual to feel the need to discontinue sexual activity (Persson & Svanborg, 1992).

Compensatory Mechanisms

If the aging individual is distressed about changes in appearance, he or she can use various strategies, including the creative use of clothing, to disguise or compensate for them. However, changes in one's sexual appearance that are visible only to oneself or one's intimate partner may constitute a different set of challenges. It may be embarrassing for the aging person to seek the emotional support and reassurance of a partner or same-sex peers about the changing appearance of the body. On the other hand, as the partners in a relationship age together, seeing the changes that both undergo as a result of the aging process may provide a sense of comfort and companionship.

Difficulties in adjusting to age changes in the sexual response cycle may present a problem if the partners are unfamiliar with the fact that sexual responsiveness naturally becomes altered in later adulthood. The individual may worry about loss of orgasmic capacity because it takes longer to become aroused, excited, and stimulated. Adding to these concerns may be the belief that it is wrong and unnatural for older people to harbor sexual desires and that it is inappropriate for them to maintain an interest in sexual relations (Weg, 1983). If one's partner is infirm, or if one is widowed, the older individual in current society, raised during a sexually more conservative period of history, is unlikely to seek other outlets of sexual stimulation such as masturbation, homosexual partnerships, or liaisons outside the marriage (Croft, 1982). Increasingly, the individual may come to view himself or herself as an asexual creature when, in fact, he or she possesses a considerable reserve of potential sexual enjoyment. Educational programs that inform the older individual or couple about normal age-related changes in sexual functioning can help break what would otherwise be a negative cycle of loss of sexual interest and capacity (Goldman & Carroll, 1990).

CENTRAL NERVOUS SYSTEM

In the nervous system, as in the other major organ systems, changes with age that are due to disease alone are difficult to separate from changes that are the result of disease processes (Morris & McManus, 1991). For example, neurofibrillary tangles, amyloid plaques, and granulovacuolar degeneration are deleterious changes that are observed in the brains of people with Alzheimer's disease but are also found, albeit to a lesser extent, in normal aging (Price, Davis, Morris, & White, 1991). Decreases in acetylcholine levels in the hippocampus and a decline in the number of neurons in the hippocampus are thought to be associated with aging but are also well-known correlates of Alzheimer's disease (Mann, 1991). Similarly, decreased amounts of dopamine in the substantia nigra-basal ganglia pathway are regarded as age-related changes but are also observed in the case of Parkinson's disease. It is not clear whether these losses occur normally in later life and are exaggerated in the case of disease or whether they constitute discrete phenomena.

Keeping in mind the distinction between normal aging and disease processes, there is documentation that areas of the brain are differentially affected by neuronal loss in later adulthood. There appears to be significant loss of neurons from the hippocampus, the area affected by Alzheimer's disease and involved in short-term memory (Mouritzen Dam, 1979). There is also significant loss of cells from the cerebellum (Hall, Miller, & Corsellis, 1975), the structure that regulates refined motor patterns. Age-related losses in these subcortical areas, however, are considered relatively minor compared to losses (as high as 50%) in the areas of the cerebral cortex responsible for processing sensory information, including the primary visual cortex (Devaney & Johnson, 1980), the primary somatosensory region (Henderson, Tomlinson, & Gibson, 1980), and the secondary auditory cortex, which loses between one third to one half of its total number of neurons over the adult years (Brody, 1955; Henderson, Tomlinson, & Gibson, 1980). Cells in the motor cortex show comparable losses of between 20% to 50%, and these losses are thought to be a contributing factor to muscular stiffness, slowness, and joint pain (Scheibel, 1982). In contrast to these somewhat dramatic losses of neuron density is the relative stability in the prefrontal region of the cortex (Higatsberger, Budka, & Bernheimer, 1982; Huttenlocher, 1979). The stability of neurons in this region of the cortex is important because these are the parts of the nervous system involved in judgment, abstract thinking, and the ability to plan. Such patterns map well onto findings of differential loss of cognitive abilities valued in intelligence.

Psychological Interactions

Aging of the central nervous system has direct effects on a variety of sensory, motor, and cognitive capacities and behaviors. Aging appears to affect a number of specific functions served by the central nervous system, including perception, short-term memory, fine motor coordination, and large muscle control. These changes in the brain contribute a central integrative component to the losses that occur within the specific sensory and motor systems of the peripheral nervous system.

Compensatory Mechanisms

The view of the aging brain as a degenerating system does not take into account what is known about the compensatory processes of redundancy and plasticity. The effect of these processes is most likely to occur in the association areas of the cerebral cortex, where higher-order abstract thinking processes are mediated. In fact, these abilities may improve in the later years of adulthood as individual stores of experiences are incorporated into long-term memory and on which decisions and judgments are based. As will be discussed later, by maintaining an active and inquisitive lifestyle through exposure to stimulating environments, the older individual can optimize the aging brain's potential for plasticity and compensation

Normal Age-Related Changes in Sensory Functioning

The psychological significance of having adequately functioning sensory systems can hardly be overemphasized. The abilities of sight, hearing, touch, taste, and smell contribute in a variety of ways to the individual's adaptation to the physical and social environment and to the individual's sense of personal competence. Deleterious age-related changes in any of these systems can detract from the individual's ability to enjoy a variety of sensory experiences, move about in the environment, and participate in social interactions without feeling awkward or uncomfortable.

VISION

Structural changes in the eye associated with the aging process result in a number of important changes in visual perception. These conditions include alterations in refractive power leading to hypermetropia (farsightedness). Presbyopia is another significant change, developing in adults past the age of 40 years, in which the individual has difficulty focusing on near objects. There is a general reduction in visual acuity that is especially severe at low levels of illumination, such as driving at night and when tracking moving objects (Panek, Barrett, Sterns, & Alexander, 1977; Richards, 1977). Dark adaptation is reduced so that older adults have greater difficulty adjusting to movement from bright to dim lighting and have lower absolute levels of ability to see in the dark (McFarland, Domey, Warren, & Ward, 1960). Difficulties in dark adaptation can heighten the older adult's vulnerability to falls (McMurdo & Gaskell, 1991). There is also a reduction in the individual's ability to react to scotomatic glare, or sudden exposure to bright light, such as a flashbulb or the headlights of an oncoming car at night (Wolf, 1960; Wolf & Gardiner, 1965). Although there are only minimal data on depth perception, there appear to be reductions in stereopsis, the perception of three-dimensional space, resulting from the varying input that reaches the two eyes (Bell, Wolf, & Bernholtz, 1972).

Many, if not all, age effects on visual functions can be explained in terms of the effects of normal aging on the optical structures (Scheie & Albert, 1977; Weale, 1963). One major set of changes pertains to the clarity of the visual image reaching the retina. The image reaching the retina is clouded by increased density and opacity of the lens (Spector, 1982) and by the formation of opacities in the vitreous, the clear gelatinous matter that fills part of the eyeball between the retina and the lens. Adding to these structural changes are changes in the retina itself, including declines in the number of photoreceptors (rods and cones) (Ordy, Brizzee, & Johnson, 1982), the accumulation of debris in the outermost layer of the retina (Marmor, 1980), and the detachment of the vitreous from the surface of the retina (Scheie & Albert, 1977; Weale, 1963). The amount of light reaching the retina is diminished by the condition known as *senile miosis,* the reduction in the size of the pupil due to atrophy of the iris dilator (Carter, 1982).

In addition to these changes that reduce the quality of the visual image on the retina are changes in the lens that decrease its capacity to accommodate to necessary changes in focus as objects move closer or farther away from the individual, leading to presbyopia. In addition to becoming denser, the lens fibers become harder and less elastic (Fisher, 1969; Paterson, 1979). The loss of accommodative power of the lens due to these changes is referred to as presbyopia, and it is a condition that typically requires correction between the ages of 40 to 50 years. By the age of 60 years, the lens is completely incapable of accommodating to focus on objects at close distance (Moses, 1981). The lens also becomes yellowed due to an accumulation of yellow pigment, and as a result, the older adult is less able to discriminate colors in the green-blue-violet end of the spectrum (Weale, 1963).

Psychological Interactions

Age-related changes in the functioning of the eye can have a range of effects on the individual's functioning in everyday life and range from difficulties in visual processing speed, light sensitivity, near vision, visual search, and the ability to adjust to varying distances. These changes influence the ability to read, engage in hobbies, recognize objects, sort colors, react to glare, and see objects at night (Kosnik, Winslow, Kline, Rasinski, & Sekuler, 1988). An important consequence of these changes for the individual's ability to maintain independence are those changes that affect driving abilities for older adults who have access to an automobile, particularly in communities with limited public transportation. The loss of the ability to drive constitutes a significant psychological event in the older person's life. A range of activities of daily living are also affected by vision loss, including housekeeping, grocery shopping, and food preparation (Branch, Horowitz, & Carr, 1989). Although perhaps less significant, altered color perception can interfere with the appreciation of works of art, movies, and other forms of visual stimulation.

Compensatory Measures

Although there are no practical measures that individuals can take to overcome the effects of age on the structures of the eye, there are compensatory steps available to help the older person overcome some of the effects of aging on visual sensation. Appropriate increases in ambient lighting that increase the availability of illumination without increasing glare can help offset age effects on retinal illumination. Increasing the available light is especially important in areas that tend to be dimly lit, such as halls, stairways, entrances, and landings. Yellowish light is preferable for these purposes because bluish light is scattered more by the lens (Richards, 1977; Weale, 1963). Errors in depth perception, when they occur, are particularly deleterious because they can lead to accidental falls (Tobis, Nayak, & Hoehler, 1981). Familiarizing an older adult with a new setting can help reduce the likelihood of falls due to faulty depth perception. Improvements in visual functioning as the result of surgery or other corrective measures can have important ramifications in a number of areas of everyday life due to the increased autonomy these changes make possible (Brenner, Curbow, Javitt, Legro, & Sommer, 1993). Apart from these measures, most older adults seem to adapt spontaneously to visual problems in driving caused by changes in visual perception, either by reducing their driving overall, avoiding night driving, becoming more cautious or by relying on their many years of driving experience (Owsley, Ball, Sloane, Roenker, & Bruni, 1991).

HEARING

Presbycusis, the general term used to refer to age-related hearing loss, actually includes several specific subtypes reflecting different changes in the auditory structures. The most common form of hearing loss reduces sensitivity to high-frequency tones earlier and more severely than sensitivity to low-frequency tones (Van-Rooij & Plomp, 1990). The loss of high-frequency pitch perception is particularly pronounced in men (Lebo & Reddell, 1972).

Speech perception, which is a major concern when considering the effects of aging on hearing in everyday life, is affected both by the various forms of presbycusis operating at the sensory level and by changes in the central processing of auditory information at the level of the brain stem and above (Van-Rooij & Plomp, 1992). As mentioned earlier, the most common effect of presbycusis is a reduction in sensitivity to high-frequency tones. Translated into speech discrimination, this means that older adults suffering from presbycusis have greater difficulty perceiving sibilants, which are consonants that have frequencies in the upper ranges of 3,000 to over 6,000 Hz. The sibilants include the underlined phonemes in these words: plus, xerox, ship, azure, wrench, and drudge. The English language is rich in these phonemes, particularly the s used in plurals so that loss of the ability to hear these sounds can have a particularly damaging effect on everyday speech.

In addition to the effects of aging on speech discrimination due to the loss of high-pitched tone sensitivity are the effects of aging on the ability to hear under conditions of interference or distraction. Age effects begin to appear even as early as 40 years in the understanding of sentences under a variety of distorting conditions, particularly when the speech signal is interrupted (Bergman, 1971; Bergman et al., 1976). Other conditions known to impair speech perception in the aged include higher rate of presentation, deletion of parts of the message, competition from background noise or competing messages, and reverberation (Neils, Newman, Hill, & Weiler, 1991; Whitbourne, 1986).

Psychological Interactions

Deficits in hearing make it particularly difficult for the older individual to communicate in a variety of social settings. Although empirical investigation does not support the long-held belief that hearing loss contributes to psychological disorder in later life, these changes in communication ability can lead to strains in interpersonal relationships and greater caution on the part of the older person who wishes to avoid making inappropriate responses to uncertain auditory signals. There is also some evidence linking significant hearing loss to impaired physical functioning (Bess et al., 1989) and psychological difficulties, including loneliness (Christian, Dluhy, & O'Neill, 1989) and depression (Kalayam et al., 1991). Depression is not consistently found to be related to hearing loss (Norris & Cunningham, 1981; Powers & Powers, 1978).

BALANCE

The effects of age on the vestibular organs involve both the sensory structures and the links to the higher levels of the nervous system. The hair cells degenerate and are reduced in number, particularly in the saccule (Johnsson & Hawkins, 1972; Rosenhall & Rubin, 1975). The vestibular nerve fibers begin to degenerate in response to accumulation of bony material in the inner ear structures that encase them (Krmpotic-Nemanic, 1969). Adding to these changes at the level of the sensory structures are reductions in the numbers of Purkinje cells in the cerebellum (Hall, Miller, & Corsellis, 1975), which could result in the lowering of reflexive abilities to adjust the body's posture to changes in position.

These changes in the vestibular system can result in increased dizziness and vertigo in older adults (Toglia, 1975). Not only are these sensations unpleasant, but they can increase the likelihood of accidental falls (Maki, Holliday, & Topper, 1994). Consistent with findings in studies of nystagmus across age groups of adults is a decrease in this response after the age of 70 years (Bruner & Norris, 1971; DiZio & Lackner, 1990), reflecting the cumulative loss of sensory receptors over the adult years. Although it might be expected that dizziness and vertigo would negatively affect the individual's ability to maintain a static posture, compensation is possible through training that involves the positional receptors in the somesthetic system (Babin & Harker, 1982; Lord, Clark, & Webster, 1991b) and the postural muscles (Hu & Woollacott, 1994a, 1994b).

TASTE AND SMELL

Because they are continuously replenished from their surrounding epithelial cells, the number of taste buds shows no appreciable decline over the adult years (Engen, 1982). Nevertheless, the detection thresholds for all four primary tastes are significantly higher for many adults over the age of 60 years (Grzegorczyk, Jones, & Mistretta, 1979; Moore, Nielsen, & Mistretta, 1983), particularly for bitter tastes (Murphy & Gilmore, 1989). Cross-sectional observations also indicate a decrease in the ability to identify foods and flavors in foods among middle-aged and older adults (Cain, Reid, & Stevens, 1990; Schiffman, 1977; Stevens, Cain, Demarque, & Ruthruff, 1991) and preference for higher concentrations of flavoring in certain kinds of food (DeGraaf, Polet, & VanStaveren, 1994). The discrepancy between anatomical and perceptual data on taste perception might be accounted for by undetected age changes in the regeneration of taste buds, the possibility that laboratory measures of taste exaggerate the effects of aging, and that factors other than age, such as smoking history or the presence of dentures, accentuate age effects in the cross-sectional studies reported in the literature (Chauhan, 1989; Stevens, 1989; Zallen, Hooks, & O'Brien, 1990). There is also considerable redundancy among taste receptors so that the loss of one area of taste reception may be compensated by the increased activity of other receptors (Bartoshuk, 1989). The possibility that these findings may reflect cohort differences rather than intrinsic aging changes has not been ruled out.

Corresponding to a reduction in olfactory receptors are cross-sectional reports of diminished sensitivity to odors among older adults (Cain & Stevens, 1989; Murphy, 1983; Stevens & Cain, 1987); however, there is wide variation among the over-60 population based in large part on health status (Doty et al., 1984), and it appears that a variety of diseases can interfere with smell thresholds (Doty, 1989; Weiffenbach & Bartoshuk, 1992). Contributing to age effects on basic smell sensitivity may be difficulties in labeling rather than smelling (Schemper, Voss, & Cain, 1981). As is true with taste, there may be many lifestyle variations and cognitive factors that contribute to apparent cross-sectional age effects in smell sensitivity.

Psychological Interactions

The main psychological effect of age changes in taste and smell are in food enjoyment. Reduced sensitivity to flavors in food may lower the individual's motivation to eat or lead to unhealthy addition of seasonings such as salts and sugars. In addition, age losses in smell sensitivity may have adverse effects on the individual's ability to detect the odors of dangerous toxins or the presence of a fire. A reduced sensitivity to bodily odors might also make the individual less fastidious in personal grooming habits so that others avoid close personal contact. Although these undesirable outcomes form a possible scenario, it is also important to point out that age differences in taste and smell are not found consistently and that when they do exist, may be relatively insignificant in daily life as compared to the laboratory.

Compensatory Mechanisms

The major forms of compensation for age losses in taste and smell involve the avoidance of bad habits, particularly smoking, starting in adulthood. Adequate dental care also plays a role in preserving taste sensitivity. Apart from these preventive measures, adults can compensate for the effect of any age losses in taste and smell on food enjoyment by using flavor enhancers (Schiffman & Warwick, 1989; Weiffenbach & Bartoshuk, 1992) and by using other sensory cues, particularly for avoiding exposure to dangerous fumes or toxins.

Normal Age Changes in Cognitive Functioning

Just as changes in the body's appearance and functioning require adaptation to the environment and self-concept via compensation, similar processes can be examined regarding changes in cognitive abilities.

INFORMATION PROCESSING

One overall finding to emerge from research on information processing is a general slowing down with age in reaction time, particularly when complex decisions are required (Salthouse, 1985). Part of this slowing can be accounted for by less efficient attentional processes. Older adults have greater difficulty integrating information, both in laboratory tasks involving visual display information (Plude & Doussard-Roosevelt, 1989) and in simulated driving situations (Brouwer, Waterink, Van-Wolffelaar, & Rothengatter, 1991). They are less able to ignore or inhibit their processing of irrelevant information (McDowd & Filion, 1992) and are at a disadvantage when they must divide their attention among two or more complex tasks at once (Plude & Doussard-Roosevelt, 1990). It takes older adults longer to make a decision, particularly when the task involves complex choices (Cerella, Poon, & Williams, 1980; Salthouse & Somberg, 1982). Increased difficulty in preparing a response adds further to the slowing of response speed, particularly when the expected response is not clearly indicated (Stelmach, Goggin, & Garcia-Colera, 1987). Last, when a complex response is demanded, such as using both hands simultaneously, older adults show a disproportionate loss of speed compared to younger adults (Light & Spirduso, 1990; Stelmach, Amrhein, & Goggin, 1988).

The underlying reason for slowing of response time with age is a reduction in the efficiency and effectiveness of information processing in the central nervous system of the older adult (Hartley, 1992). The effect of neuronal loss might occur through a direct one-to-one link between information loss and a reduction in neuron number (Myerson, Hale, Wagstaff, Poon, & Smith, 1990). A more complex proposal is that as individual neurons are lost, the connecting pathways in the brain's neural network become less efficient (Cerella, 1990).

Psychological Interactions

The individual's ability to monitor and pace reactions to speeded tasks depends not only on the integrity of the central nervous system but on the ability to work on problems without distractions from extraneous information or from negative affective states. According to one view of aging's effects on response times, increasing age brings with it a diminished ability to screen out irrelevant details, a greater tendency to make erroneous interpretations of the stimuli presented to them, and heightened sensitivity to thoughts unrelated to the task at hand (Hasher & Zacks, 1988). Concern about increased time necessary to complete a task may further interfere with performance, creating a vicious cycle. In addition to whatever changes occur at the neural level, these changes in control processes may have a wide-ranging effect on daily life activities (Park, 1992). Conversely, greater experience and knowledge of a problem area can enhance the speed of performance of older adults when they are being tested in areas of expertise (Hoyer, 1985).

Compensatory Mechanisms

There is growing evidence that people who are in better physical condition in terms of cardiovascular functioning do not experience the same degree of change in reaction time as those whose physical fitness is poor (Baylor & Spirduso, 1988; Chodzko-Zajko, 1991; Chodzko-Zajko et al., 1992; Milligan, Powell, Harley, & Furchtgott, 1984; Spirduso, 1980). Along the same lines, as noted earlier, involvement in exercise training programs may improve a variety of cognitive functions in the older individual, although the effects may be limited in individuals who have maintained an active life style throughout adulthood (Madden, Allen, Blumenthal, & Emery, 1989). Training specific to improving response time can also be effective for older adults (Salthouse, 1990b). In addition to training and physical activity as a way of maintaining cognitive and psychomotor functioning, individuals can find other ways to compensate for age-related slowing in response time. One way is to monitor the rate as well as accuracy of responses on particular tasks so that not all tasks are performed with the same accuracy if accuracy varies in importance from task to task. Second, the individual can develop automaticity in frequently performed tasks to reduce the central processing demand. Third, the individual can become aware of the role that anxiety plays in reaction time and learn to reduce distractions from concern over how one's performance looks to others. All of these techniques involve developing conscious control mechanisms that monitor performance so that the individual gains greater ability to adjust the rate of performance to the situation. Finally, the individual may "compensate" by not becoming overly concerned about slight delays in response time. Age-related losses in the laboratory are not necessarily reflected as important decrements in the performance of tasks in real-life situations (Schaie, 1988).

MEMORY

There is general agreement among researchers in cognition that aging brings with it a decline in the efficiency of *working memory,* the component of memory that is activated when the individual holds information in the mind to address a particular problem or situation. Working memory is thought to be distinct from *primary memory,* which involves a more passive set of short-term memory processes as, for example, is used in a digit-span task (Craik, 1992). It has been fairly well established that pure measures of primary memory, such as Digit Span Forward, are relatively unimpaired in older adults (Craik & Rabinowitz, 1984), although a recent large reanalysis of published studies has called this conclusion into question (Verhaeghen, Marcoen, & Goossens, 1993). It is believed that, as was true for age effects on attention, the greater the complexity of the task, the greater the observed working memory deficit (Salthouse, Babcock, & Shaw, 1991). Some of the explanations used to account for age deficits in working memory include reduced storage capacity, less efficient and slower processing of information, or greater susceptibility to distractions and irrelevant information (Babcock & Salthouse, 1990; Hasher & Zacks, 1988; Salthouse & Coon, 1993). There are, however, important individual differences in memory performance among older adults, with longitudinal studies revealing the importance of such predictors of memory performance in old age as reasoning, working memory capacity, speed, verbal ability, and education (Zelinski, Gilewski, & Schaie, 1993). The effect on the aging individual of diminished working memory, whatever the cause, is greater difficulty in spoken and written language (Stine & Wingfield, 1990; Zacks & Hasher, 1988).

Looking to the recall of newly acquired events and information, such as memory for the name of a person one met the evening before or the title of a book recommended by a friend, there is again solid evidence of a decline in performance across age groups of individuals (Kausler, 1982). Explanations for this effect are diverse, ranging from focus on the stages of memory (viz., sensory, short-term, long-term) to the processes involved in the encoding and retrieval of information. According to levels of processing theory, the "deeper" the information is processed the more durable the trace is formed in memory (Craik & Tulving, 1975). Deep processing involves forming rich, elaborate, and distinctive associations to the material and to place the material in context. One approach to explaining age differences in event memory is that older adults fail to take advantage of deeper levels of processing because the deleterious effects of aging on the central nervous system limit the resources that the older individual has to use in performing cognitive operations. Limited processing capacity affects not only the encoding of new information but also the retrieval of this information when it is needed at a later time (Craik, 1992).

Psychological Interactions

The *processing deficiency* explanation of memory changes in later life is based on a limited resource model of aging in which age-related cognitive changes occur as an inevitable result of physiological and anatomical changes in the brain. By contrast, a *production deficiency* model emphasizes the ways that individuals control their memory performance. Hence, this model offers some insights into the relationship between psychological and cognitive factors in the aging of the memory system.

The production deficiency hypothesis proposes that older adults fail to use the more effective memory strategies involving deeper levels of processing because they are not aware of the strategies they could use that could potentially benefit their encoding and retrieval of information. This production deficiency hypothesis holds out more hope to individuals who are concerned about memory loss with age because it suggests ways to compensate for what might otherwise be perceived as an inevitable feature of aging (Whitbourne, 1986).

Evidence germane to the production deficiency hypothesis comes from the area of metamemory research, which captures a set of related concepts pertaining to what individuals know about memory, including how to take advantage of memory strategies, their own knowledge of their memory capacity, and what predictions they can make about their memory performance on future tasks (Dixon, 1989; Hertzog, Dixon, Schulenberg, & Hultsch, 1987; Lovelace & Marsh, 1985). In support of the idea that lack of awareness of memory strategies contributes to age declines in memory is the finding that aged individuals do not monitor their memories effectively or make good use of their capacities (Lachman, Lachman, & Thronesberry, 1979). They may also fail to use spontaneously the encoding and retrieval strategies that could otherwise help their performance (Perlmutter & Mitchell, 1982). Affective factors can also play a role in metamemory, and the more distressed the older person becomes about poor memory performance or the more anxious the individual is about a memory task, the less able he or she will be to take advantage of useful strategies. There is evidence that affective factors such as these do in fact play a role in memory performance (Cavanaugh & Poon, 1989). In terms of predicting performance, another component of metamemory, there are some interesting relationships between age and task familiarity. When given information about the characteristics of the memory task, older and younger adults are equivalent in predicting their performance, but older adults overestimate their performance when they are not told specifically about the nature of the task (Cavanaugh, 1989).

Compensatory Mechanisms

The production deficiency explanation of memory loss in the aged has obvious implications for modes of compensation for age-related deficits in working and long-term memory. Another source of compensation for impaired abilities to retain relatively new material in later adulthood is the functioning of the semantic memory system—the memory for words and their meanings. Semantic memory does not show appreciable age losses in later adulthood (Light, 1992). Furthermore, older adults show no deficits in being able to recall factual knowledge and historical events, even from the recent past (Perlmutter, Metzger, Miller, & Nazworski, 1980). By the same token, the memory of older adults for events from the remote past is no better than that of young adults, in contrast to popular beliefs that long-term memory improves with age (Herzog & Rodgers, 1989; Rabbitt & McInnis, 1989). What these findings indicate is that older individuals may be able to make up for deficits in the processing of new information by their enriched base of accumulated experiences. To the extent that this knowledge is assessed in experimental or clinical tasks of memory performance, performance and presumably self-efficacy, will be maximized.

INTELLIGENCE

The abilities of reasoning, judgment, problem solving, and decision making are incorporated into the broad construct of *intelligence*. Theories of intelligence differ from one another in the proposed components of intelligence as well as the extent to which intelligence is reflected in day-to-day activities of the individual. In terms of research on aging, the approach to intelligence that has gained the most popularity involves the distinction between crystallized and fluid intelligence. It is reasonably well established from both cross-sectional and longitudinal studies that crystallized intelligence, which reflects experience and education in specific areas of expertise, shows consistent gains over the years of adulthood and into old age. By contrast, fluid intelligence, conceptualized as the processing of new information, peaks in early adulthood and shows a consistent decline thereafter (Horn & Donaldson, 1980). Overall, the pattern of intellectual development across the life span is one of general stability until the late 60s with more pronounced decrements occurring by the early 80s. There is wide variability in terms of individual patterns of change during these years, however, and the magnitude of these decrements does not necessarily have large practical significance (Hertzog & Schaie, 1986; Schaie, 1988).

Psychological Interactions

Research on intelligence in older adults has historically been marked by methodological concerns, particularly those pertaining to the confounding effects of the "environment" on intelligence test scores (Schaie, 1990). When comparing the intellectual functioning of an aged individual to that of a younger person, it is important to take into account the differential educational experiences the two people have had as well as their exposure to differing health and nutritional benefits during their early years of development. Health and lifestyle factors in old age are equally important to consider; cardiovascular disease in particular appears to contribute to severe intellectual decline in the late adult years as does a lack of stimulation from the environment in the individual's daily life. Personality, as indexed by attitudinal rigidity, also appears to play a role in influencing the pattern of age effects on intelligence. Individuals with a rigid personality style are less likely to take advantage of health and lifestyle changes that could maximize their physical and intellectual functioning (Cooney, Schaie, & Willis, 1988).

Compensatory Mechanisms

The effects of aging on intelligence can be compensated for in measurable ways, either through spontaneous strategies used by the individual or through involvement in organized educational training programs (Baltes & Lindenberger, 1988; Willis & Schaie, 1994). Furthermore, as a result of their greater life experiences, older adults can develop the quality of wisdom (Baltes, Smith, & Staudinger, 1992) that serves as a major compensating factor for whatever losses they experience in the ability to manipulate symbols or puzzle pieces.

Summary

In this brief review of the psychology of normal aging, I have attempted to provide information on expectable changes in later life and to suggest ways that physical and cognitive age-related changes can interact with other psychological processes. I have also focused on compensatory mechanisms and ways that clinicians can maximize the potential for positive functioning in later life. From this review, several main points have emerged that cut across the specific areas, and these will be summarized here.

First, it is apparent that there are important interactions between age changes in various systems and the individual's interpretation of these changes. Age-related losses in important areas of functioning may be viewed with great unhappiness, leading to a reciprocal process in which anxiety over these losses contributes to further deterioration of those very functions. Conversely, if the individual is challenged to find ways to prevent further losses or to reverse those that are amenable to change, then the processes of aging can be significantly altered. Here again, though, extreme anxiety can be detrimental so that the harder the individual works, the more performance deteriorates due to heightened self-consciousness. The point is that the individual does have some control over the rate and effects of the aging process.

A second point is that many age-related changes can be compensated by following the "use it or lose it" principle or by finding ways to substitute functions that are efficient with those that are on the decline. By the same token, the avoidance of bad habits, particularly cigarette smoking, a sedentary lifestyle, and overuse of alcohol, can help maintain higher levels of functioning in many bodily and cognitive systems.

Last, from a clinical perspective, knowledge of the aging process is extremely vital to a wide range of mental health practitioners. At the simplest level, education can provide aging clients with normative information about the aging process to counteract harmful myths and stereotypes. The recommendation of specific ways to compensate for age-related losses can be even more beneficial, along with support and encouragement in what may be a difficult process to initiate. Clinicians who work with clients with elderly relatives can also benefit from knowledge of aging, as aging family members can present issues that are of concern to younger adults seeking psychological services.

Many mental health professionals, when contemplating the prospect of treating the elderly, look on the enterprise as difficult, depressing, and of limited value given the broad scope of age-related declines. The information presented in this chapter suggests that there is remarkable flexibility and resiliency in older peoples' response to decremental change, underscoring the potential of intervention.

2

Prevention, Nutrition, and Exercise in the Aged

Walter M. Bortz II
Sharon Stewart Bortz

It is unlikely that scientific discoveries will ever allow the perpetual blossoming of early life. Moreover, even if it were possible, the result would constitute arrested development. Aging is not a disease but the normal course of the human condition, and its prevention is neither desirable nor realistic. In this chapter, we give an overview of our conceptualization of the aging process and review ways in which people can influence this process through proper exercise and nutrition.

Order out of Disorder

Aging consists fundamentally of the interplay of three elements: energy, matter, and time. As the second law of thermodynamics states, any isolated system will, over a period of time, tend toward greater disorder. Such a disordered state is termed *entropy* and is ultimately the result of the irreversibility of most chemical reactions due to the nonrecapturability of the heat generated in their reactions. Hot things cool, moving objects become still, orderly systems and objects become disorderly, all because of loss of energy as heat from the system. The human condition is not immune from this cosmic imperative. We, too, progressively become disordered.

There is one critical qualifier, however, concerning the ordering effect that energy can offer (Bortz, 1986). Namely, progressive decay applies only to isolated systems in which there is no interchange of participating matter and energy flow with the environment. In contrast, living creatures contribute to an active interplay with their surroundings, an observation physicist Morowitz (1987) termed the *fourth law of thermodynamics*. Exploration of this dynamic lies in the new field of nonlinear thermodynamics explicated by Nobelist Ilya Prigogine and others (Prigogine & Stengers, 1984) whose insights have led to the concept of *order out of chaos,* in which the form of matter is rendered intact by the ordering effect of energy flow.

In our view, the aging of an organism is the net product of the entropically driven dissipative structural and functional change observable as irreversible free radical chemical reactions and the counterentropic, form-restoring effects of a modulated flow of energy on matter. In algorithmic form, Aging = Second law – Fourth law.

Developmental biology teaches us that the form of an organism is highly dependent on the effects of energy in various forms—mechanical, thermal, biochemical, radiant—on the genome early in life and throughout its duration. When such energy flow is disrupted by intent or dereliction, the entropic aspect of aging predominates and frailty ensues. When viewed from this thermodynamic perspective, then, aging and its frequent partner, frailty, are associated with one another. More important, however, it also points to preventive strategies that can enable lives to be lived to their fullest.

Aging Is Not a Disease

Our entire view of aging has been distorted by equating it with disease and disuse. In current times, virtually no one lives long enough to die of "natural causes." Rather, people die precociously from conditions that are largely preventable given available knowledge. Subsequently, what we view as normal and usual, is not. What is "average" is badly skewed toward negative outcomes influenced by potentially reversible disease processes.

Conceptualizing aging in terms of disease is also scientifically unappealing because the age-disease link is a moving target. At the beginning of the 20th century, eight of the leading causes of death were infections that have since been virtually eliminated. There is little doubt that 100 years from now, our contemporary killers will have been labeled as artifacts of our historical period, not part of the natural human condition.

Of course, aging and death would occur even in the absence of accidents and disease. What, then, are the natural causes of age-related change? In thermodynamic terms, they are the effects of the environment on organized matter. For a canyon, it is erosion; for an automobile, it is corrosion. For living creatures, it is the effect of metabolism on tissue. The central element in metabolism is oxygen. Its shuttle between plants and animals enables life. In addition to its life-giving property, however, oxygen creates mischief by its chemical tendency to create unstable molecules, called *free radicals.* Dean (1995) refers to these compounds as "molecular terrorists." Free radicals occur when oxygen is reduced, particularly in mitochondria. The resulting compounds are highly chemically reactive due to an unpaired electron in the outermost orbit of the molecule. Denaturation of protein, alteration in membrane permeability, and disruption of nucleic acids all result from the generation of free radicals (Harman, 1956). Free radical generation is the principal component of the "wear and tear" theory of aging (Gavrilov & Gavilova, 1991).

The fundamental process of oxygen metabolism does not go unchallenged, however, due to counteractive mechanisms in the body. Several classes of enzymes bind with reactive molecules, for example. Various nutrients, including vitamins C, E, and beta carotene, similarly abet the antioxidative effect[1]. Exercise and rest also influence oxygen metabolism. Subsequently, certain processes associated with age-related biological deterioration can be remedied or reversed.

In short, we argue that it makes better sense to define normal human aging in terms of basic processes rather than diseases. Such a conceptual shift is not a hollow exercise in semantics. Instead, it leads to an active approach with immense practical implications. For one, it suggests that the old age that individuals experience is influenced importantly by their knowledge, perspectives, and actions. Armed with an abundance of scientific findings that have accrued over the last 20 years, people can increasingly construct and live out their lives by design rather than by accident.

More important than sophisticated medical breakthroughs have been scientific findings about three simple principles related to positive health: exercise, nutrition, and rest (Belloc & Breslow, 1972; Breslow & Somers, 1977). These are the shaping forces that enable or deny us the opportunity to live the last stages of life with individual integrity and capacity. When any one of them is deprived, it ensures an abbreviated life course.

Exercise

In our view, exercise is the most important contributor to healthful aging. Exercise for younger people is an option; exercise for older people is imperative. Physical exercise provides the energy flow that ensures the physical vitality of the older organism. Blair et al. (1989) studied 13,000 men and women, ranked into quintiles according to fitness, for an average of 8 years. Not surprisingly, people who were the most fit survived longest. More interesting was the finding that the greatest differential was not between people who were moderately fit and most fit. The greatest differential was between those who did nothing and those who did a little. In other words, the most important step was the first one.

The second major finding from Blair et al.'s (1989) work was that the older we become, the more important fitness is to survival. By age 70, there was a sevenfold difference in survival between those who were least fit and those who were most fit, whereas this advantage was only marginal in younger adults. Perhaps this should have been intuitive—for the 40-year-old, fitness probably does not afford much protection against killers at that life stage—but as the years go by, physical fitness achieves ever greater predictive power in morbidity and mortality.

How does exercise benefit us? When we consider the body en mass, it is clear that most of our tissue contributes to movement—the muscles and bones do so directly and the heart, lungs, and circulatory and peripheral nervous systems, more indirectly. During movement, blood is diverted preferentially to the limbs and skin and away from the visceral organs serving digestive, reproductive, and excretory functions.

The older we become, the less we move (although bidirectional causality may be more to the point). Certainly, muscle power decreases as we age. Branch, Katz, Kniepman, & Papsidero (1984) examined results from the Framingham study and observed that only 42% of women and 66% of men over the age of 75 years were still able to perform heavy household work. Forty-two percent of women over 75 years cannot stand for over 15 minutes, 20% are unable to climb stairs, and 33% cannot lift a weight over 10 pounds (i.e., they cannot hold a newborn grandchild).

Such functional limitations are, for many people, a hallmark of old age. Approximately 12% of all people over 65 years, 16% of people between 75 and 84 years, and 44% of community-dwelling people 85 years and older endure some functional limitations. Functional dependency also increases risks of institutionalization and its consequences (see also Horgas, Werner-Wahl, & Baltes, Chapter 3, this volume). The portion of our lives that is lived robustly, without dependency, was coined *active life expectancy* by Katz and his colleagues (Katz et al., 1983). By and large, this tends to be several years less than the total life span. The older we become, the greater the proportion that is lived dependently. It does appear, however, that as a population, U.S. citizens are remaining healthier longer (Manton, 1982). Disability and institutional prevalence rates for the elderly population have declined in recent years even as life expectancy has increased. Similar findings have been reported in France (Robine, Labbe, Serouss, & Colvez, 1989) and Sweden (Svanborg, 1988), and significant improvements in functional status have been observed in Britain (Bebbington, 1988). Manton, Cordero, and Stallard (1993) credit improved economic status and increased knowledge with these improvements.

Perceptions of functional status are even more important than clinical diagnoses in predicting mortality. Whereas certain people without any clinical diagnoses feel they cannot walk around a city block, others diagnosed with diabetes, benign prostatic hypertrophy, coronary artery disease, or degenerative arthritis run marathons. Deficits in activities of daily living (i.e., the ability to carry on basic activities such as dressing, toileting, bathing, etc.— see also, Mosqueda, Chapter 21, this volume), have been linked to morbidity and mortality. Bortz (1990) found that approximately 50% of 97 elderly patients who died suffered from major functional limitations. In a study of 7,607 people over the age of 65 years who died in Glasgow, Scotland, Issacs, Gunn, McKecham, McMillan, and Neville (1971) reported that 60% were immobile, 36% incontinent, and 29% demented before death. Declines in functional status are not inevitable. Branch et al. (1984) reported that 30% of community-dwelling 85-year-olds retained full functionality over 6 years, as did 59% of the group aged 75 to 84 years.

Although it is widely assumed that physical illness leads to functional limitations, the causal relationship can be the other way around. Bortz (1984) coined the term *disuse syndrome*—a set of six conditions commonly seen in older people—which he argues derives from lack of body vigor due to disuse. The disuse syndrome includes cardiovascular vulnerability, musculoskeletal fragility, immunologic susceptibility, obesity, depression, and premature aging. Earlier, Kraus and Raab (1961) coined the phrase *hypokinetic disease* to reflect a similar concept that they felt represented the net product of insufficient exercise.

It is likely that for 99.9% of our species life on the planet, humans were extremely active throughout life. But modern culture has seduced us into a lifestyle in which physical exercise is demeaned and neglected. If anything, the situation is getting worse (see Baxter Institute, 1993).

CARDIOVASCULAR VULNERABILITY

Physical exercise provides strong protective benefits against every level of the elaborate chain of pathogenetic events eventuating in coronary artery disease. Blood pressure, serum lipids, blood coagulability, cardiac reserve, and the dimensions of the arteries are all directly benefited by exercise.

Paffenbarger, Hyde, Wing, and Steinmetz's (1984) multidecade longitudinal study of Harvard alumni suggests that physical exercise (measured in any variety of ways) acts prophylactically against clogged arteries.

MUSCULOSKELETAL FRAGILITY

Studies of osteoporosis and its attendant vertebral and hip fractures, often considered another hallmark of old age, have shown that such bone thinning is limited to the civilized world. That is, skeletal examinations of hunter-gatherers suggest that precivilized humans did not get the disease (Ruff, Trinkhaus, Walter, & Larsen, 1993). Because the robustness of bone is directly related to the stress applied to bone, it is not surprising that a sedentary lifestyle is related to osteoporosis. Two weeks in bed is equivalent to 1 year's worth of calcium loss in active people—a 50-fold acceleration.

Evans and Rosenberg (1991) coined the term *sarcopenia* to connote the loss of muscle tissue seen in older people. Age is not the primary determinant, however; rather, it is underusage of muscles. Fiatarone, Marks, Ryan, and Evans (1992) recruited a group of very frail 90-year-old nursing home residents to join an exercise program. At baseline, muscle size and strength, balance, and mobility suggested great fragility. Yet after a few weeks of participation in the program, muscle size and strength had improved by as much as 174%. Walking was also improved and the tendency toward falls was reduced. In another study (Evans & Rosenberg, 1991), a 3-month exercise program resulted in a doubling to tripling of muscle strength of 12 men aged 60 to 72 years.

IMMUNOLOGIC SUSCEPTIBILITY

Although a number of researchers have concluded that aging is associated with decreased immune responsiveness, it remains unclear whether decreased immunocompetence is due to aging or to disuse. Many studies have tested the improved immune surveillance noted in fit persons. T-cell levels, immunoglobulin assays, incidence of infection, and allergy are all superior in fit persons (Christ, McKinnon, Thompson, Atterbom, & Egan, 1989).[2]

Cancer also may be associated with disuse. There is general consensus that malignancies of the female reproductive tract are fewer in fit women (Bernstein, Ross, Lobo, Hanisch, & Henderson, 1987). This has been tied to the lower sex hormone levels in sedentary women. Similarly, Lee, Paffenbarger, and Hsieh (1992) reported a 40% decrease in the incidence of prostate cancer in their relatively fit Harvard alumni and hypothesized that this could result from lower testosterone level associated with physical activity. The lower colon cancer rates observed in exercisers is thought to be due to the shortened gastrointestinal transit time associated with physical activity (Bartram & Wynder, 1989).

OBESITY

In our view, the epidemic obesity we see in Western countries stems from cultural sedentariness more than gluttony. Dietary approaches alone do not reduce weight in overweight persons (Wood, Stefanich, Williams, & Haskell, 1991). Unless dieting is combined with exercise, substantial and sustained weight loss does not occur.

It appears that the brain's eating center is not down-regulated by inactivity. Mayer (1953), after several studies, concluded that the lack of exercise plays a central role in obesity. One key study showed that caloric intake and expenditure were tightly linked when animals were allowed ad lib movement. When they were restrained, however, they continued to eat the same amounts as they did when they were active. Consequently, they gained weight. Similarly, Mayer showed that obese children moved less during a game of tennis than did their nonobese counterparts (Mayer, 1968). In other words, there appears to be a forward feedback loop in the maintenance of obesity, with obesity leading to inactivity and inactivity leading to further obesity.

DEPRESSION

Numerous studies attest to the positive psychological benefits of exercise. Psychologists commonly incorporate physical exercise into the therapeutic approach to treatment, which contributes to well-established alterations in the neurotransmitters such as adrenalin, noradrenalin, dopamine, and beta endorphin. The catechols, of course, are the principal biochemical modulators of the manyfold physiologic responses that occur during exercise—cardiovascular, respiratory, neuromuscular, metabolic, and thermoregulatory. These compounds are decreased in the brains of depressed persons; thus, the administration of antidepressant drugs can be likened to giving insulin to a diabetic or dopamine to a Parkinson's disease patient (Bortz, 1984). Interestingly, however, exercise has a similar effect.

PRECOCIOUS AGING

Taken in the aggregate, most of the changes commonly attributed to aging—such as decreased cardiac output and function, hypertension, increased thrombotic events, osteopenia and sarcopenia, decreased immune competence, increased body fat, increased depression and frailty—can be linked to disuse (Bortz, 1982, 1987). This is a hopeful message.

An immediate extension of this reasoning, then, is that not only will a physical fitness program prevent major diseases and extend total life expectancy, more important, it will extend active life expectancy. The ideal, of course, is to compress morbidity to its shortest possible course (Fries, 1983). Indeed, it is unlikely that nature would operate any other way. To extend life without a concomitant extension of vigor is a bad bargain indeed (Fries & Crapo, 1981).

PRACTICAL RECOMMENDATIONS

Exercise is clearly important for health. We review different types of exercise and their appropriateness for older adults.

Aerobics

Physical fitness plays a central role in oxygen transport. Because oxygen delivery is the ultimate determinant of life itself, its competence is clearly our single most vital physiologic function. An age-related decline in the VO_2 max—the reference term for oxygen transport capacity—has been well established (Dehn & Bruce, 1972; Hodgson, 1971; Kasch, Boyer, Van Camp, Swerty, & Wallace, 1990; Pollak, Foster, Knapp, Rod, & Schmidt, 1987). Once again, however, the rate of the decline is highly dependent on physical fitness.

Although most studies of fitness are cross-sectional, one notable exception was reported by Kasch et al. (1990). They followed aerobically fit and unfit individuals longitudinally for more than 20 years. Their findings indicate that VO_2 max declines at one third the rate in fit as compared to unfit individuals.

To achieve aerobic fitness, it is necessary to push the workload. The gauging of appropriate exercise intensity is commonly guided by indexing the maximum pulse rate—computed by subtracting age from 220. The training-sensitive pulse rate for aerobic training is commonly thought to be 70% to 90% of the maximum pulse rate. Recent studies, however, have indicated that lower levels of intensity are also valuable, suggesting that the dose response curve of intensity and benefit has not yet been established (Katch & Katch, 1991).

Notable, too, is the specificity of the form of exercise to the training effect. Benefits obtained by walking versus biking do not carry over to swimming and vice versa (Katch & Katch, 1991). But generally, forms of exercise that are rhythmic and sustained contribute most directly to aerobic fitness. Once a level of fitness has been attained, the amount of effort that is required to sustain that level of fitness is less than that required to achieve it in the first place.

Interval training, which involves short bursts of high aerobic effort, has been emphasized by elite athletes to improve their aerobic condition. It is unlikely that this high intensity effort is appropriate for older individuals, although further inquiry is needed.

Aerobic training results in a wide variety of structural and functional improvements. Lean body mass increases. Body fat decreases. Cardiac vitality improves. Mitochondrial number and size increase. Blood vessels dilate, capillary density increases, and blood becomes less coagulable.

The number of aerobic training sessions required per week to achieve optimal benefits appears to be three, for a minimum of 20 minutes per session, cumulatively or consecutively. More frequent expenditures probably increase fitness more, but they do so at the risk of orthopedic injury. It is perhaps not just coincidence that three times per week is the average that the Bushmen hunted (Bortz, 1985). This optimal frequency may derive from a long genetic history.

Detraining, such as after an injury or sickness, occurs rapidly when a person stops exercising. In one study, 3 weeks of bed rest led to a 25% reduction of VO_2 max or approximately 1% per day (Saltin & Grimby, 1968). Such observation is critical to the understanding that prior physical fitness and athleticism does not confer a long-lasting benefit.

From a practical standpoint, we feel that older people should maintain a level of physical activity that ensures high oxygen transport capability. It is important to remember that it is never too late to start. In his classic report, DeVries (1970) initiated an aerobic training program with a group of 70-year-olds and found that they could substantially increase their VO_2 max in just a number of weeks. The capacity for renewal in the older body is one of its basic wonders.

Safety of Aerobic Exercise. The risk involved with aerobic exercise is very small. A few basic questions should be addressed, however, concerning chest pain, undue shortness of breath, and profound weakness. If patients do acknowledge any of these symptoms, they should consult their physicians prior to embarking on an exercise program. In the absence of affirmative answers to these questions, exercise is probably safe. To provide a more objective sense of risk, one group of investigators found that there was one death per 396,000 person-hours of running or one per 7,620 joggers per year (Thompson, 1979).

Muscle Strengthening. Certainly, one of the most compelling insights into the health of older persons emerged with the recognition of the clear need to maintain body strength with age. As mentioned, a large percentage of older people are unable to climb stairs, lift even 10 pounds, or rise from a chair unassisted (Branch et al., 1984). Although these problems are correlated with age, they are not caused by age alone. In the widely cited work by Fiatarone et al. (1992) in which a group of frail institutionalized nonagenarians increased their muscle size and strength and experienced improvements in walking and balance posttreatment, gains correlated directly with increased muscle strength. As quoted by Evans and Rosenberg (1991), one 93-year-old participant stated the following:

> I feel as though I were 50 again. Now I get up in the middle of the night and I can get around without using my walker or turning on the light. This program gave me strength that I didn't have before. Every day I feel better, more optimistic. Pills won't do for you what exercise does. (p. 22)

There are innumerable techniques to reclaim lost muscle power. Fundamentally, they involve lifting free weights or using resistance equipment. Free weights can be either standard barbells or improvised weights, such as cans of vegetables wrapped in socks. As with aerobics, strength training is specific to the muscle groups involved in the exercise. Training the arms does not increase leg strength and vice versa. The program involves intensity and duration, commonly referred to as numbers of repetitions. For older people, it makes sense to use a weight that is 50% to 80% of the maximum that can be lifted one time. Repetitions will increase as muscle strength increases, so constant adaptation is necessary. In general, the person should perform three sets of eight repetitions each of six to eight different exercises designed to strengthen the upper and lower limbs and the torso and back. The program should be followed three times a week. Many manuals are available that provide specific instructions for these regimens.

Any strengthening program will invariably result in some muscle soreness. It should be self-limited and last no more than 3 days. If it lasts longer than this, it means that the program is excessive and should be reduced. Mild analgesics, ice, and heat are useful adjuncts to muscle soreness. Benefits of muscle strengthening extend beyond muscles to include bone strengthening as well. Although there is little evidence that muscle strengthening can add major amounts of calcium to bones that already have been depleted, there is no question that weight training has a positive effect on the diminution of the progression of osteoporosis.

Flexibility Training. Best combined with strength training is a consecutive effort to ensure continued plasticity of our moving parts. Some membrane and soft-tissue stiffening is an intrinsic part of the aging process due to increased chemical cross-linking of many tissue bridges by free radical bombardment. However, the majority of stiffness is due to nonuse. Stretching before, during, and after aerobic or muscle strengthening sessions both increases the freedom of the body to move and improves coordination and agility. Stretching lengthens the muscles, tendons, and ligaments and thus helps them relax.

Once again, there is a variety of stretching exercises that can be learned from numerous manuals available in most bookstores. In essence, each body part should be stretched, with specific attention given to the particular muscle group being exercised. Stretching should be done slowly and evenly and not overdone. If significant discomfort occurs, too much stretching was done and the amount should be adjusted.

Balance Training. A principal invocation to older patients is, "Don't fall down." The tendency for older people to fall is a major cause of medical expense, morbidity, and mortality. Of the 250,000 hip fractures that occur each year, upward of 40,000 deaths per year are directly connected to falls. Many more deaths are indirectly related. The increased tendency to fall with age is overdetermined. Visual, vestibular, musculoskeletal, circulatory, and peripheral neural factors contribute. Each should be addressed specifically in the older person who falls. The integrity of aerobic exercise, muscle strength, and flexibility alone are insufficient to guarantee adequate balance. For this reason, balance training in and of itself should be incorporated into regular activity as we age.

Balance training requires no equipment. Merely standing on one leg alone and then on the other, with and without eyes closed and with or without chair support, is a start. With body weight on one foot, the person draws the alphabet with the large toe of the other foot. Standing near a wall and bending toward the wall in each direction is also helpful. Walking a straight line, toe to heel, backward and forward, helps steady gait. Balance training can result in 50% improvement in overall balance with a consequent diminution in the risk of falling.

The hope, of course, with all of these efforts is that years of life will not only be lengthened, but a substantial improvement to the quality of life will result as well. As Robert Butler, the former head of the National Institute of Aging, has said many times, "If we had a pill that contained all the benefits that exercise confers, the whole world would be on it." Barriers to exercise, physical and psychological, emerge as critical research topics. One burning question, for example, is "If exercise is so good for us, why do so few of us do it?"

Nutrition

Because the study of aging is still in its infancy so too is our knowledge of the nutritional needs of older people. The common habit has been, once again, to extend maxims about sound dietary needs of younger people to older people regardless of adequate support for the extension. Our collective lack of knowledge about some of the most basic questions concerning nutrient needs in older people is no less than alarming. Even the basic nutritional guidelines, the recommended daily allowances (RDAs), make no discrimination between 50-year-olds and 90-year-olds.

The relationship of nutrition to longevity was rendered graphic by the landmark studies of McCay (1935), recently elaborated on by Masoro (1993), which indicated that caloric restriction leads to longer life, at least in rodents. A major effort to extend this basic protocol to primates is under way. The relevance of this observation to daily clinical issues is not entirely clear at this point but may come to be of immense importance.

Obesity

Even if there is uncertainty about the positive benefits that caloric restriction may have on longevity, there is near perfect agreement about the adverse effects that obesity has on life length and quality. Obesity is an epidemic in Western countries. Hypertension, diabetes, and degenerative arthritis compose the central triad that frequently accompanies obesity, each of which threatens length and quality of life. Furthermore, obesity correlates with high rates of cardiovascular disease and certain malignancies.

One of the stated hallmarks of aging is an increasingly higher percentage of body fat. One must recognize, however, that this percentage is a function of the reciprocal decline in lean body mass along with an absolute increase in body fat, both of which are extremely sensitive to the effect of physical exercise. Too often as we age, our physical activity patterns diminish, and with this behavioral change, our muscles wither, basal metabolic rate declines, and calories are shunted to fat formation. The diminished glucose tolerance of older people due to fewer insulin binding sites is also a reflection in part of decreased physical conditioning in the later years (Litwak & Whedon, 1959).

If the obese person can avoid these pitfalls, however, then he or she may not be at much increased risk. Andres, Elahm, Tobin, Muller, and Brant (1985) have emphasized the inaccuracy of "desirable" weight tables. Rather, mortality decreases with increased body mass indices as we age. They stress that high mortality in very lean people is clearly evident in older people as well. Terminal cachexia—the accelerated weight gain before death—complicates these interpretations. There are many obese older people. It is even possible that obesity may act, unintentionally, as a tool for cardiovascular conditioning by providing "internal weights." One of the premiere threats posed by obesity at all ages, but particularly in the later years, is the likelihood of reduced mobility that occurs in result.

The proper assessment of obesity is computed using the body mass index (BMI). BMI involves height and weight measurement and their comparison with the standard nomogram (viz., desirable weight-height tables). BMI correlates well with increased mortality at both ends of the BMI. The BMI does not, however, reflect the percentage of body fat. In fact, the total amount of fat may not be as important as where it is stored. People with fat above the waist (apples) have higher disease rates than those whose fat is predominantly below the waist (pears). The waist-to-hip ratio is a convenient way to assess risk. For men, a ratio below 0.8 is good; for women, the ratio is 0.7.

Caloric Need and Aging

Numerous studies show decreased caloric intake with aging (Exton-Smith, 1977). This decrease places people at risk for malnourishment. Many reasons underlie the lowered caloric intake: dental problems; economic, social, and psychological influences; decreased appetite due to lower physical activity; certain medications; digestive problems; and sensory changes are the most prominent (American Dietetic Association, 1987). As noted, the RDAs for older people have been derived by simple extrapolation of those norms established for younger people and may be incorrect. Caloric need is determined ultimately by expenditure. If lean body mass is maintained by a persistent physical activity program, the caloric need will not decrease due merely to age (Mitchell, 1982). So, once again, exercise is important. In addition, exercise generally increases appetite and leads to increased consumption of important nutrients.

Protein Need

Protein is particularly sensitive to age. The serum albumin level is a semisensitive indicator of protein nutrition adequacy. The Baltimore Longitudinal Study of Aging found a progressive decrease in the grams of protein consumed per kilogram of body weight from ages 28 years (1.35) to 80 years (1.1) (Shock et al., 1984). The average percentages of total calories provided by protein (approximately 13%) did not increase over the life span. The current RDA for protein is 0.8 grams per kilogram of body weight for middle-aged people. Recent findings from the Tufts group indicate that this figure is probably insufficient for older people because the amount of lean body mass diminishes, particularly in regard to frailty (Evans & Rosenberg, 1991). We expect that the protein intake of the elderly should not be lower than that of younger adults and that they may require more dietary protein per unit of body weight to maintain nitrogen equilibrium at the customary level of energy intake (Young, Munro, & Fukayama, 1989). This domain needs more research because protein intake is particularly important for older people, especially those with low body weight. Economic issues, dental problems, and ease of food preparation are prominent concerns. Generally two to three protein servings per day are advised. One-serving equivalents are 2 to 3 ounces of cooked meat, 2 eggs, 1 cup of dry beans, 4 tablespoons of peanut butter, or a half cup of nuts.

CARBOHYDRATE INTAKE

As with younger people, carbohydrates constitute the most abundant source of calories for older people. It is crucial to emphasize that a diversity of carbohydrates is essential to health in older people. Grains, vegetables, and fruits are superior foodstuffs because they supply not only calories but other necessary nutrients, minerals, and vitamins. Carbohydrate foodstuffs supply most of the fiber content of the diet, which is critical in older people who are prone to various forms of immobility and altered gastrointestinal motility. Chronic constipation also can be a cause of undernutrition.

Fat Intake

The Committee on Diet and Health of the Food and Nutrition Board, as well as the American Heart Association, recommends that fat calories represent no more than 30% of total daily calories, with less than 10% supplied by saturated fats (U.S. Department of Health and Human Services, 1988). Dietary fat restriction derives largely from the causative role that dietary fat, particularly saturated fat, plays in the promotion of high cholesterol levels and coronary artery disease. The bottom line is that people should limit dietary fat, especially fat found in meat and dairy products. Recommendations proposed by Jolliffe (1963) over 30 years ago, shown in Table 2.1, remain appropriate today.

Cholesterol and Aging

Popular lore holds that if you haven't died of coronary disease by the time you are 70 years old, your chances are less that you will after that age. Health statistics do not support such pacifism. Serum cholesterol values do tend to fall with advancing age, but coronary artery death rates continue to rise (National Institutes of Health Consensus Development Conference, 1985). Another common view is that alteration of dietary patterns to lower serum cholesterol is not warranted after age 70 years because there is no evidence of benefits. Some contend that further dietary restriction may be dangerous to a frail person whose caloric intake is already marginal. Until definitive answers are known, fatalism is unwise at best. Atherosclerosis represents a

Table 2.1   Jolliffe's Dietary Recommendations

Foods to Avoid

Lean beef or lamb: eat no more than four times per week.
Replace pork or pork products with fish and skinless chicken.
Replace whole milk or whole milk products, such as cheese, butter, or ice cream, with oils,
    margarine, or sherbets.
Eat no more than four eggs per week.

Foods to Eat

Eat six servings of bread or cereal per day.
Eat two servings of lean meat per day.
Eat two servings of low-fat dairy products per day.
Eat seven servings of vegetables or fruits per day.

SOURCE: Adapted from Jolliffe (1963).

dynamic process in which cholesterol plays a role. Thus, lowering cholesterol levels regardless of age seems reasonable at this time.

Hydration

Dehydration is a common cause of acute diarrhea, confusion, and fever in older people. Roughly 1.5 quarts of noncaffeinated fluid is recommended daily. Individually computed, the recommended amount is one cup of nondehydrating fluids per 20 pounds of body weight. Water is the primary source of fluid.

Thirst response decreases in older people, which can result in insufficient fluid intake (Leaf, 1984), and failing to ingest adequate amounts of fluids can place several body systems at risk. Because of caffeine's diuretic effect, it is important to point out to older patients that large amounts of caffeine also can have dehydrating effects.

Vitamins

Forty percent of U.S. citizens take vitamin supplements. The optimum amount of supplementary vitamins that older people should take remains unclear, however. Virtually all nutritionists agree that given an adequate balanced diet, extra vitamins are unnecessary (Schneider, Vining, Handley, & Farnum, 1986). Unfortunately, many surveys indicate that a large percentage of elderly people consume less than two thirds of the RDA of vitamins. Vitamins A and D, as well as several B vitamins, are frequently deficient in the diets of older adults.

Vitamin inadequacy is related to poverty and social isolation, both of which are relevant to the elderly population (Morly, Silver, Fiatarone, & Mooradian,

1986). When people eat alone, diets tend to become marginal. Convenience foods predominate, resulting in a reduction in complex nutrional intake. An added complicating feature involves nutrient-drug interactions, which can increase certain vitamin and mineral needs.

Appropriate RDAs for older people living under diverse, and often deprived, social and economic conditions are simply unknown. The prudent course is to advocate a multiple daily vitamin and mineral supplement to all older people whose diets may be deficient.

Minerals

A similar story describes dietary calcium and phosphorus. The need for vigilance in dietary calcium has been sounded loudly (Marcus, 1982). It appears that men and women alike have inadequate calcium intake throughout life. Although supplemental calcium will do little to repair bones after the age of 70, continued attention to calcium intake is important to treat osteoporosis and its complications. Calcium needs of older people are complicated further by intestinal lactose intolerance, a frequent occurrence in older people. Because milk and its by-products are the most common source of dietary calcium, lactose intolerance makes the ingestion of the recommended intake of 1.5 mg per day even more difficult.

Antioxidants

No discussion of aging and nutrition is complete without an acknowledgment of the increasing interest in the role of peroxidative processes in the aging process. Harman's (1956) free radical theory of aging is generally acknowledged as at least one of the causes of age-related decline in living organisms. Clearly, any dietary practices that offset such change are tremendously important. Several potentially ameliorative candidates emerge. Vitamin E and beta carotene are prime among them. Evans and Rosenberg (1991) have shown convincingly that supplementary Vitamin E improves immunocompetence in older people. Cataract development may be related to low intake of ascorbic acid. Findings from the Baltimore Longitudinal Study suggest that Vitamin C intake actually increases over the years. On average, at 80 years of age, participants in this study were taking 10% more Vitamin C than when they were 28 years old (Shock et al., 1984).

Coffee and Alcohol Intake

Our cultural love of coffee and alcohol is pervasive. Nutritionally, however, these substances have virtually nothing to recommend them. They provide none of the necessary nutrients. Current evidence suggests that coffee consumption in normal amounts poses few, if any, health risks. However, indirect effects of insomnia (see also Bootzin, Epstein, Engle-Friedman, & Salvio, Chapter 18, this volume) and dehydration may be problematic.

Alcohol presents a more complex profile. Several reports now indicate that modest alcohol intake may actually provide a health benefit by way of increasing "good" high density lipoprotein cholesterol levels, stimulating appetite, and encouraging social intercourse. These findings do not warrant a blanket approval of alcohol use, however, because for many people, including elderly people, alcohol abuse is a major health risk (see also Liberto, Oslin, & Ruskin, Chapter 15, this volume).

Rest and Recreation

Rest and recreation complete the positive health triad. Because Chapter 18 (Bootzin et al., this volume) covers sleep extensively, we will limit our comments herein. We underscore these authors' observation, however, that even though it is clear that older people sleep differently than younger people, it remains unclear whether such changes are directly due to age or, alternatively, to behavioral patterns commonly associated with age.

Older people nap more, have more fragmented sleep, are more easily aroused from sleep, and show a different diurnal pattern compared to their younger counterparts. Sleep patterns are highly dependent on two variables, however: light exposure and exercise. Light and activity keep us awake. Darkness and inactivity facilitate sleep. The critical factor combatting prolonged sleep loss is probably physical fitness. Almost no degree of sleeplessness cannot be helped by vigorous exercise (Dement, 1986).

Recreation is the cousin of sleep. It too allows renewal opportunities. We know that U.S. adults work longer hours and take fewer vacations than citizens of most other industrialized nations. Yet as we age, time often becomes more available. Newly found availability of time late in life allows a rebalancing of priorities and an embracement of new opportunities. Leisure time can allow us to be whole rather than an otherwise disconnected series of staccato movements.

Summary

As the process of aging is redefined in terms of the natural culmination of events and accepted as a legitimate developmental period in life, it will become increasingly distanced from its disease status. Emphasis on the positive aspects of health and continued growth is the appropriate context for the study of aging. Adequate physical exercise, appropriate nutritional support, and sufficient rest and recreation are the three essential elements that contribute to good health across the life span. Their use is simple, cheap, and effective and there are no substitutes, medical or otherwise.

Notes

1. We note, however, that even though intense efforts to extend life through the therapeutic use of dietary supplements have been made, extending life through dietary supplements is not supported by scientific evidence (Schneider & Reed, 1985).

2. One important qualifier is necessary, there appears to be a curvilinear function to this effect. People in the midst of very intense physical training actually show impaired resistance to infection.

3

Dependency in Late Life

Ann L. Horgas
Hans-Werner Wahl
Margret M. Baltes

Dependency in older adults is a familiar concept, with relevance for practitioners, researchers, policy makers, and lay people. Many people, particularly those who work with older adults, have firm conceptions of what the term means and what it "looks like" in practical, everyday terms. Our main goal of this chapter is to challenge unidimensional understandings of dependency among older adults and to show that it may be more complicated than it first seems. Specifically, we focus on *behavioral dependency* in late life, which is defined as actively or passively asking for help or accepting help from others beyond the level needed to meet basic physical and psychological needs. This

AUTHORS' NOTE: Ann Horgas was supported by an individual postdoctoral National Research Service Award (Grant #1 F32 H00077-01), which was funded by the Agency for Health Care Policy and Research and sponsored by Margret M. Baltes. Dr. Hans-Werner Wahl was a research associate on the German dependency projects described herein from 1984 to 1988 and funded during that time by the Stiftung Volkswagenwerk. During the writing of this chapter, he was a research fellow of the German Research Foundation (Wa 809/1-2).

definition is particularly relevant to caregiving situations in which elderly persons rely on others for assistance or help.

There are a number of factors that can contribute to behavioral dependency in late life. These include physical, psychological, and contextual conditions, such as physical frailty, mental health, medication use, environment, and social interactions. Each of these possible antecedents are discussed later in this chapter. An appreciation of the many possible causes of behavioral dependency is fundamental to an understanding of the potential and limits of interventions to modify it.

This chapter draws on life span developmental psychology, a perspective that provides a framework for understanding behavioral dependence in late life and can aid practitioners in evaluating and modifying this behavior. Thus, the first part of the chapter briefly presents some of the theoretical assumptions of this perspective as they pertain to late life dependency.

The following sections will focus on describing, assessing, interpreting, and modifying behavioral dependency in late life. First, some conceptual issues regarding the measurement and prevalence of dependency in general are presented. Second, some of the biological, psychological, and environmental antecedents of behavioral dependence among older adults are discussed. Third, our research program on behavioral dependency is described in some detail and interpreted with respect to different theoretical models. Finally, behavioral interventions to modify dependency among older adults are described and discussed.

A Life Span Developmental Perspective on Behavioral Dependency

Until recently, aging was seen primarily as a process of decline and deterioration in many domains of functioning, all of which are likely to increase physical dependency. In contrast to this unidimensional view of late-life loss, the life span perspective provides a broader understanding of aging as a developmental process from childhood to very old age that incorporates both gains and losses (P. Baltes & M. Baltes, 1990). Behavioral development is believed to result from the interactive effects of biological, psychological, and social influences (P. Baltes, Reese, & Lipsitt, 1980; see also P. Baltes, 1987; P. Baltes & M. Baltes, 1990).

With regard to dependency in late life, three theoretical concepts of the life span developmental perspective are particularly relevant: multidimensionality, multicausality, and multifunctionality.

Multidimensionality. Multidimensionality refers to the fact that dependency can occur in multiple domains (e.g., mental, physical, economic dependence, or a combination of these) and can be analyzed on different levels (e.g., behavioral, personal, situational, and interpersonal dependency), depending on the theoretical and methodological approach used. Thus, it is important to recognize that dependence is not a unitary phenomenon and that individuals may exhibit a unique configuration of one or more types of dependency, depending on their context. The focus of our work, and thus the focus of this chapter, is on understanding and modifying behavioral dependency in late life.

Multicausality. Multicausality refers to the fact that dependency is not necessarily synonymous with old age. Rather, dependency is the potential outcome of many different factors. Biological status, for instance, is an important influence on physical dependency, a fact that is reflected in a large body of literature pertaining to the frail elderly (Bortz, 1993; Hadley, Ory, Suzman, Weindruch, & Fried, 1993). In addition, sociocultural, economic, and environmental conditions all play roles in the development and maintenance of dependence. Similarly, the absence of socioeconomic resources may play a role in dependency, especially in terms of the lack of a social network to provide support for physical or emotional dependency when it is needed or the absence of economic resources that may lead to financial dependency. Psychological factors, especially dependent personality traits (Bornstein, 1993), are also important considerations. All of these factors, both separately and combined, can contribute to late-life behavioral dependency and will be described in more detail throughout this chapter.

Multifunctionality. Multifunctionality, the third life span concept important for understanding dependence, suggests that dependency can have multiple purposes or goals. Though dependency is generally considered undesirable in Western societies, there are some instances in which it can have an important adaptive function. For instance, during childhood or illness, dependence may facilitate growth and development or physical or psychological healing. During late life, dependence may also play an important adaptive role, an assertion to which we will return later.

In sum, behavioral dependency among elderly adults is a complex phenomenon that can be characterized as multidimensional, multicausal, and multifunctional. Furthermore, the development and maintenance of dependency in general, and behavioral dependency in specific, is the outcome of the interaction of biological, psychological, and contextual influences. Thus, from the perspective of life span developmental psychology, the study of behavioral dependency among older adults requires careful consideration of a number of different factors. Before addressing these factors in more detail, we turn now to a brief discussion of some conceptual issues in defining and measuring dependency and some background information about the prevalence of late-life dependence.

Underlying Issues in Dependency Research

CONCEPTUALIZING AND MEASURING DEPENDENCY

In general, one might wonder about the magnitude of dependence among elderly persons. For instance, are the majority of older adults dependent? Are there differences between old persons living in private households and those living in institutions? As with any construct, the answer to these questions depends on the way the term is operationalized and the manner in which it is measured.

The different types of dependency notwithstanding, the global term of *dependence* can be studied from different levels of analysis and from both quantitative and qualitative methods. Each approach asks different questions and provides different answers. For instance, on a macro level of analysis, the term dependency can be used to characterize global social and demographic structures of societies. A quantitative macroperspective might address the dependency ratio or the rate of institutionalization in the elderly population; a more qualitative macrolevel analysis might ask whether modern social welfare states produce dependent behaviors among their citizens, thus representing structural dependency (M. Baltes & Silverberg, 1994). On a meso level of analysis, dependency can describe circumscribed societal subsystems, a quantitative example of which would be the proportion of people with pronounced basic care needs (e.g., physical dependency) within old-age institutions (see M. Baltes, 1995, for a review). A more qualitative analysis on this level might address the comparative dependency-inducing power of different institutional philosophies (e.g., Moos, Lemke, & David, 1987). Finally, based on a microlevel of analysis, the concept of dependency can be used to characterize the behavior of elderly people interacting with their immediate social environment. The amount of dependent behavior that residents exhibit in interactions with nursing home staff may serve here as a prototypical example to illustrate a quantitatively oriented, micro-analytic approach. Qualitative interpretations of dependency are also possible on this level, such as the identification of different interaction patterns that foster or hinder dependent behaviors of elderly adults.

Our own program of research has focused on a microlevel analysis of dependence as a function of the social interactions between elderly persons and their social environments. In so doing, both qualitative and quantitative methods have been used to describe the amount and the nature of socially induced behavioral dependency. This research will be described in detail later in this chapter. At this point, however, it is important to consider that different approaches to studying this construct exist, all of which answer different questions and provide potentially different answers regarding the prevalence of dependency.

PREVALENCE ESTIMATES

Most estimates of the prevalence of dependency have relied on macrolevel assessments, such as sociological data on the dependency ratio and service use as well as epidemiologic data on physical dependency measured by activity of daily living limitations. Although this reflects a different approach to the study of dependence from the one emphasized in our own research, a summary of these findings will provide some background information regarding late-life dependency in general and some rationale for the expectation of dependency in the social environments of elderly persons.

The magnitude of dependency in old age is often described in terms of the *dependency ratio*. This term reflects the proportion of the population that is employed and available to support those who are out of the labor force. Statistical trends show that dependency ratios are rising in Western societies, due in large part to an increased life expectancy that has raised the proportion of the population over age 65. This measure of dependency, however, represents only a crude estimate of the needs of dependents because it is based solely on labor force participation and does not address the specific needs or dependencies of unemployed persons regardless of their age group.

Other estimates of the prevalence of dependency have generally focused on two areas: institutionalization rates and activity of daily living limitations that reflect the need for care. With regard to institutionalization, it has been widely reported that about 5% of persons over the age of 65 live in long-term care facilities (Brock, Guralnik, & Brody, 1990). This cross-sectional estimate may be misleading, however, because the lifetime risk of nursing home institutionalization for individuals is actually roughly five times higher (Bickel, 1989; Kastenbaum & Candy, 1973). In addition, the use of nursing homes increases with age, with 22% of those over 85 years of age in the United States residing in long-term care facilities (Hing, 1987). Thus, institutionalization rates vary considerably according to measurement but still suggest considerable physical dependency among elderly adults.

The most common estimates of dependency are based on epidemiologic measurements of limitations in *activities of daily living*—those activities that are generally accepted as essential components of daily life (ADLs as coined by Katz, Ford, Moskowitz, Jackson, & Jaffe, 1963). ADLs include activities such as eating, dressing, and bathing, whereas the *instrumental activities of daily living* (IADLs as labeled by Lawton & Brody, 1969) include items such as shopping, banking, and using public transportation. According to data from the 1987 U.S. National Medical Expenditure Survey, more than half (58.8%)

of elderly nursing home residents had difficulties in four or more domains of functioning, most notably in bathing, dressing, toileting, and transferring from a bed or chair (Lair & Lefkowitz, 1990).

Among noninstitutionalized adults, it is estimated that roughly between 5% and 8% of those over the age of 65 years in the United States and Germany show ADL dependency (Guralnik & Simonsick, 1993; Wahl, 1993). In addition, the results of epidemiologic studies in several Western societies indicate three consistent findings. First, there is a strong positive correlation between dependence and age. For instance, it has been reported that 1.7% of persons 65 to 69 years old needed regular assistance in basic ADL, whereas 26.3% of those 85 years of age and older required help (Schneekloth & Potthoff, 1993). Second, estimates of functional limitations are higher among the old-old when IADLs are considered. In Germany, for example, 28.2% of those 85 and over required IADL assistance, indicating that about 55% of the oldest-old showed some type of physical dependency (Schneekloth & Potthoff, 1993). These findings are similar to those reported in the United States (Brock et al., 1990) and in Sweden (Zarit, Johansson, & Berg, 1993). Third, there are significant gender differences in the extent of both ADL and IADL limitations. Women generally show higher rates of physical dependency than men, especially after age 75 years (M. Baltes, Horgas, Klingenspor, Freund, & Carstensen, 1996; Guralnik & Simonsick, 1993; Verbrugge, 1989). Thus, the epidemiologic findings suggest that many older adults are physically dependent for ADL and IADL assistance but that considerable heterogeneity among older adults still exists, especially in relation to age and sex.

These global perspectives provide some useful information for social and health planning purposes about the prevalence of one aspect of late-life dependency, namely physical dependency. Unfortunately, this is one dimension of dependency that has been generalized to all old people. Although we recognize that physical dependency among older adults genuinely increases with age and may be an important precursor to behavioral dependency that remains even after the physical need for help is gone, there are other antecedents of dependency as well. Thus, we turn now to a discussion of the multiple causes of behavioral dependency in late life.

Behavioral Dependency as a Multicausal Construct

Behavioral dependency in late life can have many causes. In keeping with our developmental perspective, biological, psychological, and contextual factors all contribute to the etiology and maintenance of dependent behaviors among older adults. This section will provide an introduction to some of these etiologic factors and is intended to challenge the reader to consider the many possible antecedents of behavioral dependency. Recall that we emphasize behavioral dependency in late life, which is considered to be actively or passively asking for help or accepting help from others beyond the level needed to meet basic physical and psychological needs.

PHYSICAL HEALTH AND PHYSICAL DEPENDENCY AS AN ANTECEDENT OF BEHAVIORAL DEPENDENCY

Physical Frailty

Much recent attention has focused on physical frailty as a significant cause of late-life disability and ensuing dependency. Defined as severely impaired strength, mobility, balance, and endurance, physical frailty is associated with reduced capacity to perform ADL and IADL activities and often leads to accidents or injuries such as falls (Hadley et al., 1993). Many aspects of frailty are associated with normal age-related decline in the functioning of the musculoskeletal, sensory, cardiovascular, and neurological systems (Pendergast, Fisher, & Calkins, 1993). Musculoskeletal changes are particularly relevant for maintaining functional independence (Czaja, Weber, & Nair, 1993). The ability to modify biological decline varies across domains, but it has been suggested that the ability to delay, prevent, and even reverse age-related functional losses has been highly underestimated (Rowe & Kahn, 1987). Indeed, a growing body of literature supports multiple benefits of physical exercise training for older adults (Goldberg & Hagberg, 1990), especially in improving physical strength (Pendergast et al., 1993; see also Bortz & Bortz, this volume). Carefully prescribed interventions of this type may improve physical functioning and thus reduce physical dependency that can be a precursor to behavioral dependency.

Chronic Physical Disease

Undoubtedly, physical illness and chronic disease contribute significantly to the high rates of functional disability and physical dependency among older adults. About 80% of community-dwelling elderly adults in the United States have at least one chronic disorder, a figure that is likely to be even higher among those residing in long-term care institutions (Harper, 1990; Hing, 1987). Chronic physical diseases such as osteoarthritis, osteoporosis, cardiovascular disease, and stroke are often associated with mobility restrictions or chronic pain and are likely to contribute to behavioral dependencies. In addition, multimorbidity in late life is the norm rather than the exception, with many elderly adults suffering from more than one chronic disease or an acute illness superimposed on an underlying chronic condition.

Furthermore, sensory limitations, especially hearing and vision loss, also increase with advanced age and can compound the debilitating effects of illness. Among community-dwelling elders, about 12% have significant self-reported hearing loss or deafness and almost 14% report blindness or poor eyesight: Both of these sensory deficits are significantly associated with functional decline (LaForge, Spector, & Sternberg, 1992). In a nursing home sample, audiological evaluations revealed that 69% of residents have moderate to severe hearing loss (Ciurlia-Guy, Cashman, & Lewsen, 1993). One or all of these physical factors can contribute to functional losses and, thus, to behavioral dependency in late life.

Medication Use

Given the prevalence of the physical disorders described, high rates of prescription medication use among older adults are not surprising. In a large epidemiologic study, between 60% to 78% of community-dwelling men and women over the age of 65 years were found to use at least one prescription drug (Chrischilles et al., 1992). In nursing homes, the rates of prescription drug use are even higher, with more than half (56%) of residents ordered five or more prescription medications (Inspector General, 1989). This high rate of polypharmacy places elders at risk for potentially serious adverse drug reactions and drug-drug interactions (Avorn, 1990; Burke, Jolson, Goetsch, & Ahronheim, 1992; Hartshorn & Tatro, 1991; Ray, Griffin, & Shorr, 1990; Vestal, 1990). The behavioral manifestations of adverse drug effects among elderly adults include depression, confusion, sedation, and functional and cognitive impairments (Callahan, 1992; Larson, Kukull, Buchner, & Reifler, 1987), all of which can increase physical dependency and contribute to behavioral dependency. These drug outcomes are associated with many of most commonly used drugs, thus emphasizing the need for cautious prescribing and monitoring of even routine medication use among older adults (Vestal & Dawson, 1985). In U.S. geriatric long-term care settings, much of this responsibility falls on nurses due to their more autonomous role in determining the need for medications; their continuous contact with the residents, which enables them to observe behavior more closely; and the less prominent role of physicians in this caregiving context (Kolcaba & Miller, 1989). For a more detailed exposition of the issue of medications and the elderly, an excellent summary is provided in a volume edited by Rowe and Ahronheim (1992).

MENTAL HEALTH AND PERSONALITY
ANTECEDENTS OF BEHAVIORAL DEPENDENCY

Mental Health Disorders

Mental health disorders, especially dementia and depression, can contribute significantly to functional limitations and dependency in late life. Dementia, as a general class of organic brain disorders, affects over 15% of those 65 years of age and older, 5% of whom are severely demented and require full-time caregiving (Horvath & Davis, 1990). Senile dementia of the Alzheimer's type is the most common form of dementia and accounts for 55% to 65% of all dementia cases (Fisher & Carstensen, 1990; Horvath & Davis, 1990). Dementia manifests itself in progressive declines in cognitive functions, including memory, attention, judgment, and verbal ability, as well as behavioral changes, such as loss of self-care ability. These changes in mental and behavioral status are major contributing factors in late-life dependency, especially when they occur concomitantly with other physical and mental health disorders. It is important to recognize that there are many causes of dementia other than Alzheimer's disease, including multiple cerebrovascular infarcts, metabolic and nutritional deficits, brain lesions, and infections (Horvath & Davis, 1990). Unlike Alzheimer's disease, which is not reversible, some types of dementia can be treated and even reversed, with potentially positive effects on functional status and dependency.

Similarly, among mental health disorders in late life, depression is common (Anthony & Aboraya, 1992) and is often underrecognized and undertreated among older adults (Blazer, 1989b; Borchelt, Horgas, & Steinhagen-Thiessen, 1993; LaRue, Dessonville, & Jarvik, 1985). The exact prevalence of depression in late life, however, is unclear because reports vary widely depending on the definition and methodology used (Staudinger, Marsiske, and Baltes, 1993). For instance, Blazer (1982a) reported that between 11% and 44% of elderly adults, or about 20% on average, had symptoms of depression. Less than 1% of older adults, however, have a diagnosed depressive disorder (Blazer, Hughes, & George, 1987; George, Blazer, Winfield-Laird, Leaf, & Fischbach, 1988). Nonetheless, depressive symptoms and disorders are associated with social withdrawal, isolation, physical complaints, and functional decline (Cohen, 1990), all of which can contribute to physical and behavioral dependency.

Among nursing home residents, the prevalence of mental health disorders is considerably higher than among community-dwelling elders (Parmalee, Katz, & Lawton, 1989, 1992). Thus, long-term care facilities in the United States have essentially become de facto treatment sites of mentally impaired older adults (Beers et al., 1988; Smyer, 1989). The reported rates of mental illness in nursing homes, most notably dementia with or without concomitant disorders, vary widely, from about 40% to 94%, again depending on the assessment strategy used (German, Shapiro, & Kramer, 1986; Lair & Lefkowitz, 1990; Rovner, Kafonek, Filipp, Lucas, & Folstein, 1986). Depression among nursing home residents is also common, with some symptoms reported by 70% to 80% of residents (Browning, 1990). Thus, the potential for physical dependency associated with mental health disorders is particularly high among nursing home residents.

Personality

Personality influences are another important aspect of dependency in late life. Traditionally, dependency has been considered a personality disposition, and much has been written about the nature and development of dependent personality traits (see Zank & Baltes [in press] and Bornstein [1993] for a complete discussion). The role of personality is important in the etiology and maintenance of dependency in late life because it suggests that individual differences developed as early as childhood are carried into old age. As such, dependent personality characteristics may contribute to differences in independence versus dependence in specific social environments and interactions across the life span. In addition, having a dependent personality orientation may increase the risk of physical and mental health disorders (Greenberg & Bornstein, 1988a, 1988b). Thus, dependent personality characteristics may have both direct and indirect effects on late-life behavioral dependency: direct effects as a result of life span continuity and indirect effects through their association with physical dependency.

CONTEXTUAL ANTECEDENTS OF BEHAVIORAL DEPENDENCY

Physical Environment

The role of the physical environment in relation to functional limitations and dependency has been examined in both community and institutional settings. Czaja et al. (1993) reported that functional limitations in performing ADL and IADL tasks at home are often magnified by the physical nature of the task and the physical structure in which they take place. Meal preparation at home, for instance, requires physical stamina for standing, muscle strength for lifting and leaning, and grip strength for manipulating utensils (Czaja et al., 1993). Without a supportive environment or assistive devices, deficits in these domains of functioning can contribute to behavioral dependency.

Within the nursing home setting, Hussian and Brown (1987) focused on physical features of the facility, especially the effect of perceived barriers on residents' behavior. For instance, two-dimensional grid patterns on floors were perceived by older adults with cognitive decline as raised barriers that prevented walking. These grid patterns may occur intentionally (i.e., as an intervention to reduce wandering) or unintentionally, through nonskid bathtub patterns, tile designs, or carpeting. In addition, the lack of environmental stimuli can also contribute to dependent walking behaviors, especially when there are no visual signs to provide residents with directional cues that can facilitate way-finding (Fisher & Carstensen, 1990; Hussian & Brown, 1985), and may lead to behavioral dependency.

Moos and Lemke (1985) have examined the benefits of residential care facilities on the well-being and functioning of older adults on a more multi-dimensional level. They provide an integrated framework that examines the influences of environmental and personal characteristics on residents' health and psychological outcomes and consider the importance of cognitive appraisal and coping style in the relationship. In general, the fit between personal need factors (e.g., in terms of physical and social functioning and locus of control) and facility characteristics is important in positive adaptation and well-being. This fit is considered important at both the macrolevel, in terms of facility characteristics, and at the microlevel, in terms of interpersonal interactions. In this view, the lack of person-environment fit can contribute to negative outcomes such as behavioral dependency.

Social-Psychological Environment

In addition to physical contextual factors, Kayser-Jones (1992) has focused on the organizational culture as an important aspect of the social-psychological environment of nursing homes. Shared beliefs, norms, and behavioral patterns within nursing homes are especially important in relation to the use of physical and chemical restraints. In 1988, it was reported that an average of 41% of nursing home residents in the United States were physically restrained to beds or chairs (Health Care Financing Administration, 1988). Physical restraint has been associated with a range of negative physical and psychological consequences, including sensory deprivation, loss of self-image, confusion, withdrawal, and dependency (Evans & Strumpf, 1990; Hussian, 1981).

In addition, the social environment in nursing homes fosters dependency in other ways—namely, through individual interactions between residents and staff. This aspect of environmental etiologies of behavioral dependency has been the focus of our program of research and thus will be described more thoroughly in the next section.

Social Interaction Patterns as Antecedents of Behavioral Dependency

To date, there are two theoretical paradigms, supported by a sizable body of empirical research, that address the social environmental conditions of behavioral dependency in old age. Both models, the model of *learned helplessness* by Seligman (1975) and the model of *learned dependency* by M. Baltes (1982, 1988) are grounded in social learning theory and treat behavioral dependency as a socially induced phenomenon. Theoretically, they differ in their specifications of the sources of dependency (e.g., noncontingent versus contingent) and their evaluations of the resulting outcomes (i.e., dependency as only loss or also as gain). The noncontingency between behavior and environmental response is at the root of learned helplessness theory (Seligman, 1975); differential contingency is the basis of the learned dependency model (M. Baltes, 1988, 1995; Baltes & Skinner, 1983). Thus, learned-helplessness-based dependency is defined by loss (i.e., loss of control over contingencies or responses), whereas learned dependency is defined by a dynamic between gains and losses (i.e., loss of some control over contingencies but gain of some control over others; see also Baltes & Skinner, 1983). Thus, these two paradigms differ in terms of reasons for dependency and have practical implications for the nature of the intervention (i.e., whether to intervene and in which direction to intervene). For this reason, we now take a somewhat closer look at both of these models, particularly the learned dependency model, to understand their respective implications for intervention more clearly.

LEARNED HELPLESSNESS: A SITUATION OF LOSS

The major focus of dependency from the learned helplessness model is on noncontingent environments. Seligman (1975) and his collaborators have demonstrated that in the case of a lack of systematic, predictable connections between behavior and environmental responses, animals and humans learn that their behaviors have no differential consequences (i.e., responses are not contingent on individuals' actions). This situation has been described by Seligman and colleagues as *noncontingency*. Given repeated experiences with noncontingency, negative outcomes result, such as cognitive deficits or lack of performance, motivational deficits or passivity, and emotional deficits or depression. Later reformulations of the original model added attributional perspectives (Abramson, Seligman, & Teasdale, 1978) that suggest that noncontingency can lead to the experience of lack of control and subsequently to learned helplessness and dependency. The learned helplessness model, in effect, says that depriving individuals of the chance to control their environments may actually teach them that attempts to exercise control are futile. The consequence of this learned helplessness may be manifested in behaviors such as being passive and emotionally withdrawn, which characterize behavioral dependency. Nursing homes, in particular, have long been discussed as control-depriving environments that lead to dependency (Rodin & Langer, 1977; Smyer, Cohn, & Brannon, 1988).

LEARNED DEPENDENCY: GAINS AND LOSSES

Similar to Seligman's original model, the main aspect of M. Baltes's research has focused on environmental conditions involved in the maintenance and development of dependent behaviors. In contrast, however, the model of learned dependency (M. Baltes, 1982, 1988) with regard to aging assumes differential environmental contingencies for dependent versus independent behaviors as well as differential (or multifunctional) outcomes of dependency. To analyze the social environmental systems producing dependency, M. Baltes and her collaborators employed three convergent methodological strategies: an experimental, a sequential observational, and an ecological intervention approach (see also Baer, 1973).

In experimental work (M. Baltes & Lascomb, 1975; M. Baltes & Zerbe, 1976a, 1976b), the modifiability of even chronic dependent behaviors in institutionalized elderly persons was demonstrated. For instance, through the implementation of the behavioral techniques of stimulus control and reinforcement, elderly persons were able to relearn to eat by themselves, to dress themselves, and to perform other similar self-care behaviors. Such evidence of the modifiability of dependent behaviors among elderly people was rather novel in the mid-70s (for review, see M. Baltes & Barton, 1979) but was consistent with a growing view of substantial plasticity, or modifiability, in aging (e.g., P. Baltes, 1987). The important conclusion from this early experimental work for the present discussion is that it is not always lack of competence due to physical or mental impairment that is at the root of behavioral dependency; environmental factors may also be responsible for its development and maintenance (see also Mosher-Ashley, 1986/87 for a review).

The second research strategy, a sequential observation approach, established the effect of social environmental consequences on dependent behaviors in everyday life. In particular, the interactive stream of behavior between elderly persons and their social partners during self-care was examined. This research was conducted in a variety of living environments, including long-term care institutions and private dwellings. In this research, it was demonstrated that the dominant interactional pattern in these microsocial systems is one in which dependent behaviors of elderly persons are immediately attended to, whereas independent behaviors are ignored. In other words, it was dependent behavior rather than independent behavior on the part of the elderly that produced social responses. Dependent behaviors of elderly adults, more than any other actions in their behavioral repertoire, resulted in immediate and positive reactions from others in their social environment. Dependent behaviors initiated and maintained social contact (for review, see M. Baltes, 1988; M. Baltes, Neumann, & Zank, 1994; M. Baltes & Reisenzein, 1986; M. Baltes & Wahl, 1987, 1992). At the same time, these observations imply that elders' independent behaviors, when they occur, do not initiate social responses. In fact, independent self-care behaviors were mostly ignored, and constructively engaged behavior was reinforced only 25% of the time.

The observed patterns relating to dependent and independent behaviors of older adults are highly robust and replicable across cultures (e.g., Germany and the United States), nursing homes, gender, length of institutionalization, and health status. Because of the high predictability and the robustness of this finding, we have labeled it the *dependency-support script* that dictates social interactional patterns.

The generalizability of the dependency-support script beyond institutional settings was confirmed by observations of interactions between elderly persons and their partners in private dwellings (M. Baltes & Wahl, 1992). At the same time, however, there was greater diversity in interaction patterns in this setting. Aside from the dominant support for dependent behaviors, independent behavior also had contingencies, albeit more ambivalent ones; independent actions were sometimes followed by independence-supportive behaviors, though they were followed more often by dependence-supportive behaviors.

To obtain further evidence for the conclusions about the generality and typicality of the dependency-support script in the world of elderly adults, sequential observational research was conducted with children and their social partners both in institutions and private dwellings (M. Baltes, Reisenzein, & Kindermann, 1985; Kindermann, 1986). The outcome of this research suggests that a major part of the dependency-support script seems to be old-age specific. The social world of children seems to be directed toward the development and autonomy of the child, whereas the social world of elderly adults is geared toward assistance and the fostering of dependency.

In our view, these observational findings contain a clear message concerning the model of learned helplessness as a paradigm for dependency in the old. Although we acknowledge that learned helplessness does exist in old age and that it may also contribute to some dependent behaviors, our research strongly supports a contingent rather than a noncontingent view of dependency. The contingency view is predominantly represented by the concept of the dependency-support script. Dependent behaviors are instrumental in securing social consequences: attention and contact—that is, in exerting control over the social world. This control, albeit passive, seems to fulfill a very important compensatory function in gaining social contact. In this sense, dependent behaviors are highly functional and adaptive. They represent not only a loss (e.g., reduced autonomy) but also a gain in the form of control over social contact.

Social expectations about old persons are very likely to be a major factor in the production of a dependency-support script. For the most part, the social environment accepts dependent behavior on the part of the elderly as appropriate and consistent with normative expectations. Reichert (1993) was able to confirm this suggestion in a laboratory study comparing nurses and educators as they interacted with elderly people in problem-solving situations; they found significant differences. Nurses' interactions with elders were characterized by more direct and immediate helping behaviors, a tendency that can be attributed to the medical model in which responsibilities are taken over by the medical environment and the caregivers. Thus, the dependency-support script describes an environment that is excessively responsive, thereby fostering dependent behaviors at the cost of independent behaviors. This overly responsive and overly protective environment is insensitive to the old person's remaining strengths and presumes that dependency is inherent to aging.

This view is further confirmed by the attributional styles held by elderly persons and their social partners with regard to dependent and independent behaviors. When confronting elderly couples with their respective observed behaviors, Wahl (1991) found that the partners ascribed responsibility for dependent behaviors to the elderly person but attributed independent behavior to their own actions. In contrast, elderly persons ascribed independent behavior to themselves and dependent behavior either to illness or to their environment, including the behavior of their social partners.

Thus, this program of research has documented that dependent behaviors can be caused by the social environment in which they take place. That is, social partners in both institutional and community-dwelling settings contribute to dependent behaviors by ignoring independent actions and reinforcing dependent actions through social contact and assistance. Thus, individuals learn that being dependent provides a means of gaining other desired objectives. These findings support the theory of learned dependency (M. Baltes, 1982) rather than the theory of learned helplessness because dependent behaviors experience contingencies and are instrumental acts to gain social contact.

Behavioral Dependency in Old Age as a Contributor to Successful Aging

These observations have led us to consider the larger behavioral system of adaptation within which dependency in old age can be located. Any given case of dependency must also be considered as a component of the adaptive strategy that elderly persons use to manage their own aging process (P. Baltes & M. Baltes, 1990). In this vein, we have recently argued for a third paradigm for behavioral dependency—namely, *self-regulated dependency* (M. Baltes, Wahl, & Reichert, 1991). In this sense, dependency becomes an integral part of successful aging. Recently, a model of successful aging called *selective optimization with compensation* has been proposed in which dependency or other forms of performance reductions are considered to have positive, adaptive value (P. Baltes & M. Baltes, 1990). With regard to behavioral dependency, the elderly person faced with increasing losses in reserves and strength has several choices: (a) to give up the domains and activities hampered by functional loss, (b) to compensate for them by searching for the means to maintain activities, or (c) to become increasingly dependent in those weakened or threatened domains to free energy for the pursuit of other activities that have higher personal priority. In the latter strategy, the person acknowledges losses and delegates control to others as a form of proxy control.

The model of selective optimization with compensation (P. Baltes & M. Baltes, 1990) highlights the possible adaptive potential of lowered performance of which behavioral dependency is one example. This model argues that effective coordination of three processes—selection, compensation, and optimization—ensures successful aging despite the losses encountered and a reduction in reserve capacities. It is important to highlight that this model is meant to describe general adaptive processes across the life span. These adaptive processes are particularly applicable in late life when adaptation to losses becomes increasingly important. *Selection* is based on the argument that age-related losses mandate both a reduction of the range of activities and domains of functioning and a concentration on those that remain. These remaining domains take high priority and involve a convergence of environmental demands, individual motivations, skills, and biological capacities. The second component—*compensation*—becomes operative when life tasks require a level of capacity beyond the current performance potential. Losses and reductions of behavioral capacities are experienced by older adults, particularly in regard to situations or goals that demand high levels of physical or mental functioning for adequate performance. The third component, *optimization,* is derived from the argument that it is also possible to maintain high levels of functioning in old age in some selected domains through practice and acquisition of new bodies of knowledge and technology. Consideration of this model of successful aging with its emphasis on increased selection and compensation in late life provides a third perspective on dependent behaviors. In this case, behavioral dependency may not represent helplessness, lack of control, dysfunction, or passive control of social contact via contingent reinforcement of dependency. Rather, dependent behaviors can be self-selected and the outcome of active selection and compensation.

Thus, in addition to the models of learned helplessness and learned dependency, there is at least a third perspective by which to consider behavioral dependency. In this model, dependency is viewed as an active, adaptive strategy for dealing with late-life losses in functioning. In contrast to dependency as a socially induced phenomenon, this theoretical perspective suggests that dependency in late life, in some instances, may be self-induced.

Interventions With Behavioral Dependency

Thus far, behavioral dependency in old age has been described from several different perspectives. First, possible biological, psychological, and contextual antecedents were described. Second, a body of research documenting behavioral dependency as a learned response to social interactions was presented. Third, dependency as a selected, adaptive behavioral process was discussed. These diverse perspectives have important implications for interventions with behavioral dependency that will be addressed in the following section. We will first present a brief overview of the behavioral approach for modifying behavior among older adults. Our intervention program focusing on behavioral dependency will then be discussed. Finally, some general intervention issues of when and when not to intervene in behavioral dependency will be addressed.

BEHAVIORAL INTERVENTION STRATEGIES

The assumption underlying the use of a behavioral approach to the treatment of any disorder is that environmental factors influence behavior (Fisher & Carstensen, 1990). Because a number of environmental issues, including interpersonal interactions, have been discussed herein as contributing to late-life dependency, behavioral strategies are likely to be effective interventions. Basically, behavioral interventions involve recognizing and changing the antecedents of the behavior and using reinforcement to reward and maintain the desired behavioral response. These strategies have been effectively used among older adults with several different behaviors, including incontinence (Burgio, Engel, McCormick, Hawkins, & Scheve, 1988; Colling, Ouslander, Hadley, Eisch, & Campbell, 1992; Schnelle, 1990), ambulation (Burgio, Burgio, Engel, & Tice, 1986), wandering (Hussian, 1981) and depression (Gallagher & Thompson, 1982). In addition, behavioral techniques have been applied successfully with other behaviors associated with dementia, such as eating and self-care deficits and inappropriate sexual behavior (Fisher & Carstensen, 1990).

Despite these reports of success, behavioral techniques are less routinely used with older adults in general (Carstensen, 1988) and nursing home residents in particular (Smyer, Cohn, & Brannon, 1988). Recent attention, however, has focused on the ability to train caregiving staff to use behavior management strategies to work more effectively with problem behaviors among nursing home residents. This is especially important because nursing assistants (i.e., relatively untrained caregivers) provide 80% to 90% of all direct care in nursing homes. Recent research in this area has documented that nursing assistants can learn to use behavioral strategies to work more effectively with depressed, disoriented, and agitated behaviors among their residents (Cohn, Horgas, & Marsiske, 1990). Others have focused on aggressive behaviors and again documented success in educating nursing assistants in behavioral approaches (Feldt & Ryden, 1992). Most intervention programs in this domain have targeted behaviors that are disruptive or particularly disturbing to the staff.

A SOCIAL ECOLOGICAL INTERVENTION
WITH BEHAVIORAL DEPENDENCY

On the basis of the research findings previously described in detail, an intervention program was initiated to modify behavioral dependency. This program involved ecological interventions in the social world of elderly adults and, in particular, the social world of institutions (M. Baltes, Neumann, & Zank, 1994; Neumann, Zank, Tzschätzsch, & Baltes, 1993). The goal was to change the behavior of social partners (i.e., the caregiving staff) in the direction of increased responsiveness to autonomy and independence and to evaluate the consequences of such a change in interactional style. A training program was implemented that provided skills to the social partners that focused on how to increase independence-supportive behaviors. The training program consisted of both a theoretical and a practical component; that is, skills were taught in the first part and then applied in the second part. Skills covered included the following: (a) current, factual knowledge of the aging process, (b) communication with residents and other staff, and (c) behavior management, or behavior modification, principles. Results based on a pretest-posttest control group design demonstrated the intended effect. Caregivers systematically exhibited more independence-supportive behaviors in response to independent behaviors of the elderly as well as in response to dependent behaviors of the elderly. As a consequence of the increase in independence-supportive staff behaviors, independent behaviors among elderly nursing home residents increased. Thus, it is possible to alter the prevalent "dependence-support and independence-ignore" script of the social world of the elderly in institutions. The resulting environment is one that continues to be responsive to dependency when it is appropriate and necessary but becomes more differentiated in terms of stimulating and fostering independence where possible.

THE DECISION TO INTERVENE
IN BEHAVIORAL DEPENDENCY

In making the decision about when and how to intervene in behavioral dependency, one must carefully consider the multidimensional, multicausal, and multifunctional nature of late-life dependency. Comprehensive evaluation of the behavior and its context must be conducted to intervene appropriately and realistically. In addition, behavioral assessment may reveal instances in which dependency should not be changed, especially in light of our previous discussion of the multiple functions that dependency can have.

Given the multidimensionality of dependency, it is important to recognize that several types of dependencies, such as physical, emotional, and structural, may occur simultaneously. Once again, we direct our discussion to interventions with behavioral dependency. In so doing, many factors that can contribute to behavioral dependency must be considered, including the important role of physical factors. Assessment and subsequent intervention must first address the underlying roots of the behavior whenever possible. Treatment of physical and mental illness, chronic pain, sensory impairments, and mobility restrictions may reduce some of the physical dependencies that can lead to or exacerbate behavioral dependency. In addition, medication regimens should be scrutinized for their potentially negative consequences on dependency. Last, physical and social environments must also be assessed. At the same time, attention should focus on the function of behavioral dependency as highlighted in this chapter—namely, dependency as a learned behavior or as a self-selected phenomenon in successful aging. Each of these aspects of dependency has different implications for the question of whether or not to intervene in these behavioral patterns.

Given these differing perspectives, there are at least two conditions under which dependent behaviors should not be changed: (a) when there is true biological decline or physical illness and associated physical limitations that require assistance and (b) when the dependent behavior is the result of an active choice or selection by the elderly person to maintain optimal functioning in other, higher priority domains of functioning. In the first case, any intervention to change the social environmental conditions so as not to support dependent behavior would be detrimental in terms of loss of self-efficacy and personal control as well as in possible physical pain and suffering. In the second case, intervention to change dependent behaviors that result from personal choice and selection would not be appropriate unless dependency can be reduced through new or different resources or technologies without placing additional demands on the individual.

On the other hand, intervention is warranted when dependent behaviors are the result of conformity to social stereotypes and prejudices or an underestimation of either one's resources or the responsiveness of the environment. That is to say, dependency that results from or is intensified by the dependency-support script often merits intervention to alter the pattern of social interactions. In addition, intervention may be warranted in situations where dependent behaviors cause personal harm to the elderly person, such as disuse that exacerbates physical decline and the loss of remaining abilities. This potential for personal harm, however, must be carefully evaluated in relationship to the person's true physical and mental capabilities and strengths. In this vein, Parmalee and Lawton (1990; see also Wahl & Baltes, 1990) have argued for an environment that is fitted to both the strengths and the weaknesses of the elderly individual, thus creating a balance between security (dependence-support) and autonomy (independence-support) that allows as much security as necessary and as much autonomy as possible. Because of the incurring losses with age, there is often little doubt that some support is needed and that some dependency is realistic. Under no circumstances should caregiving assistance be denied when it is truly needed.

For practitioners who work with elderly persons and seek to change dependency, the following three questions may help to distinguish between the many causes and functions of behavioral dependency. These questions are adapted from an intervention program for dealing with depressed, disoriented, and agitated behaviors (Cohn, Smyer, & Horgas, 1994) but applicable to dependent behaviors as well.

Is the dependent behavior a problem? If so, for whom is it a problem—for the individual or for others (e.g., caregivers, family)? Unlike other kinds of problem behaviors among older adults, such as wandering, aggressiveness, or incontinence, behavioral dependency may be considered less problematic by others. In institutional settings, dependent behaviors may be interpreted as compliance, considered a time-saving measure in completing personal care tasks, and welcomed in comparison to other, more active or disruptive behaviors. In this setting, the challenge may be for caregiving staff to recognize the physical and emotional costs to the individual that are associated with behavioral dependency. In noninstitutional settings, dependency may be considered a more pressing problem, because one social partner is likely to carry the caregiving burden that dependency induces. Thus, behavioral dependency in the community may have an even greater effect for elderly persons and their social partners and caregivers than in institutions.

What are the antecedents of the behavioral dependency? Consider biological, psychological, and contextual factors. Are there any physical or mental illnesses or medications that can be changed? Have there been any unusual events, such as bereavement or hospitalization, that have triggered the dependent behavior? What is the context for the behavior? Does it occur in a particular place or with a particular person? Consider other peoples' behavior—do caregivers automatically offer help and assistance or do they offer verbal and physical prompts to encourage more independent behaviors? Evaluate the possible antecedents to understand the dependency more fully and to recognize specific factors that can be changed or eliminated.

What are the consequences of behavioral dependency? The outcomes of behavioral dependency can provide important clues as to whether the dependency-support script is operating, thus supporting the perspective of learned dependency, or whether dependency is the result of a self-selected process. How do others such as caregivers or family respond to dependency—with immediate efforts to provide assistance or with encouragement and reinforcement for independent behaviors? What are the consequences of the dependency for the individual's other domains of functioning? Does dependency and help in one activity free the person's physical and mental resources to do other activities that are more personally important? Consideration of these questions will help the practitioner to decide when and how to intervene.

When planning and implementing interventions, there are two important underlying principles. First, interventions must be developed in conjunction with the individual, especially if it presupposes that the elderly person will change his or her behavior. That is, the plan to reduce dependent behavior must be made collaboratively so that the intervention is aimed at working with, rather than working on, the person. Second, the goal of the intervention must be clearly defined and realistic. The most appropriate goal in most cases is to reduce the frequency of dependent behaviors in one specific activity domain, because complete elimination of dependent behaviors is unlikely. For example, interventions might focus on self-care behaviors in the morning, eating behaviors, or walking behaviors singly or sequentially, rather than simultaneously. Intervention goals must be sensitive to the individual's remaining strengths because unrealistic or inappropriate plans could have negative consequences for his or her personal dignity and self-efficacy. Furthermore, unrealistic goals for change may have detrimental consequences for the staff as well in terms of disappointment, job dissatisfaction, and reinforcement of negative stereotypes of elderly adults.

Summary

In this chapter, the concept of behavioral dependency among older adults has been examined from the perspective of life span developmental psychology. As such, dependency has been considered as a multicausal, multidimensional, and multifunctional concept, all of which have important implications for understanding the physical, psychological, and contextual causes of dependency. In addition, our body of research documenting the role of social interactions in inducing and maintaining dependency, such as the dependency-support script, has been described. Furthermore, the model of learned dependency has been juxtaposed with the model of learned helplessness as well as with the model of selective optimization with compensation. Finally, intervention issues with dependency have been outlined, including the effectiveness of behavioral interventions, a description of our training intervention program and its results, and some conceptual, etiological, practical, and ethical issues pertaining to the process of intervention.

Thus, attention to dependency in late life seems highly worthwhile because it is an issue that many older individuals, their partners and families, and their paid caregivers will face. With that said, dependency is not inevitable in old age nor is it irremediable. Instead, it is a complex phenomenon that requires careful and systematic intervention to change the behavior of the individual as well as the context in which he or she lives.

4

Clinical Intervention
With Ethnic Minority Elders

Jeanne L. Tsai
Laura L. Carstensen

In addition to the well-documented increase in the number of individuals who will live into old age, our nation faces a second, less noted demographic trend that promises to shape its future—specifically, the disproportionate growth of ethnic minority elders within the older population. By the year 2040, approximately 40% of the population over 65 years will be composed of ethnic minorities (Markides & Mindel, 1987). Across all ethnic minority groups, the growth rate of elders is higher than the average for all ages within each group (U.S. Bureau of the Census, 1993a). This demographic trend ensures that clinicians will treat an increasing number of ethnic minority elders. As the makeup of the elderly population changes, so do the needs change. In anticipation of these changing needs, we propose clinical recommendations regarding the treatment of ethnic minority populations.

Rather than make specific recommendations about the treatment of ethnic minority elders that have the potential to perpetuate inaccurate stereotypes, we present different ways clinicians might regard ethnicity in their work with the elderly. Specifically, we discuss how differences across ethnic minority groups (e.g., their historical experiences in the United States) may come to influence the experience of old age and what implications these differences may have for clinical work with ethnic minority elders. We also note possible sources of within-group variation (e.g., acculturation, place of residence, role of ethnicity) that have received minimal attention in the existing literature. We focus on various Asian American, African American, Hispanic American, and Native American populations.[1]

Following a brief definition of *ethnicity,* we begin with thumbnail sketches of the demographics and service needs of particular subgroups of ethnic minority elders. As we show, the backgrounds and the issues these subgroups face may be as different from one another as from mainstream European Americans, attesting to the dubiousness of considering minority elders as one group. Next, we overview the cultural, political, and social circumstances that brought these peoples to the United States, factors that continue to influence the current needs and values of different subgroups and that may influence the type of problems individuals present in mental health and medical settings. We end the chapter with a section on the influence that ethnicity may have on the experience of old age as well as aspects of the therapeutic process. Our goal is not to prescribe specific approaches for specific subgroups, which we argue would only perpetuate stereotypic beliefs, but to highlight special problems (and offer possible solutions) that arise in working with older members of ethnic minority groups in the United States.

What Is Ethnicity?

We define *ethnicity* as membership in a subgroup that views itself and is viewed by others as distinct from the majority culture in history, language, religion, physical characteristics, ancestral homeland, or any combination of these (Yinger, 1986). Specific components of ethnicity range from relatively concrete aspects of daily life (e.g., holidays, customs, traditions, religious practices) to more abstract, intangible components, such as social expectations, patterns of emotional response, and identification with minority group status. We stress that individuals within an ethnic group vary in the degree to which they identify with and adhere to the particular norms and values of their group. Clearly, the concrete components are easier to discern than the abstract ones. Both must be considered in clinical work with the elderly.

In this chapter, we focus on ethnic minority elders in the United States— members of ethnic groups that have been traditionally underserved, marginalized, and underrepresented by mainstream U.S. culture. This includes groups that fall under the broader ethnic categories of African American, Asian American, Hispanic American, and Native American.

Today's Ethnic Minority Elders

As we will document, minority elders constitute a vastly heterogeneous group bringing very different life experiences to bear on old age. Perhaps the main similarity across ethnic minority groups is their shared experience of discrimination. Within each group lies tremendous variation. In this section, these differences will become obvious as we briefly introduce each group of ethnic minority elders by covering their basic demographic information and current service needs.

AFRICAN AMERICANS

Of the ethnic minority groups discussed in this chapter, African Americans are the largest, comprising 8% of today's elders (compared with European Americans, who constitute 87% of the elderly). By the year 2050, the percentage of aged African Americans is expected to increase to 10% of the elderly population, whereas the percentage of European Americans will decrease to 67% (U.S. Bureau of the Census, 1993a). Currently, the majority of African American elders are 75 years and older.

There is tremendous heterogeneity within the African American population. One such aspect is geographic residence. Often in the literature, African Americans from the southern regions of the United States are distinguished from those from the Northern regions; more than half of today's African American elders reside in the South (Davis & Fuller, 1991; U.S. Bureau of the Census, 1993a). Another source of individual variation is the degree to which individuals identify with Black culture (Helms, 1990).

Most of the existing literature contrasts African Americans with their European American counterparts. Although this is common practice in the literature regardless of ethnic subgroup, it is especially so for African Americans because, unlike immigrant groups such as Chinese Americans and Mexican Americans, the distinction between African American and mainstream American culture is less clear.

Compared to European American populations, as a group, African American elders are disadvantaged in a number of ways. In general, functional old age occurs at an earlier chronological age for African Americans than for European Americans (e.g., 55 years vs. 65 years of age) because of higher rates of disability and the accumulated effects of low education and financial disadvantages (Jackson, 1988). Although African Americans constitute the poorest of the poor and have relatively low literacy rates and levels of education compared to the majority European American group (Bell, Kasschau, & Zellman, 1976; Jackson, 1988; Richardson, 1990), 65% of African

American elders are not at all or only mildly limited in everyday functioning (Jackson, 1988). African Americans also have earlier onsets of most chronic diseases as well as higher rates of severe impairment compared to their European American counterparts. It is interesting to note that this trend reverses during the later stages of old age. By the age of 80, African American elders have lower mortality and morbidity rates than their European American counterparts. The cause of this crossover effect is unknown, but several hypotheses have been proposed, including (a) selective survival (i.e., African Americans who survive to age 80 may be the strongest of both African American and European American groups), (b) hardships of life in the United States result in the development of coping skills that ease the transition to old age, (c) cultural practices indigenous to the African American community protect elders from external stresses in old age, or (d) a combination of these (Jackson, 1988).

Stereotypes of African Americans in the United States often obscure the strengths of this group. For example, African American elders are stereotyped as suffering from unstable home and family environments, whereas in actuality, older African Americans have more frequent contact with and receive higher levels of social support from family members than their European American counterparts (George, 1988; Taylor, 1988). Compared to their European American counterparts, older African Americans are also more likely to live with their own children and relatives (other than their spouses) (George, 1988). In part, this appears to be due to the considerable exchange of financial and child care support between elders and younger family members (Taylor, 1988). With the increased migration of young African Americans to urban areas, however, this familial source of support may be on the decline, forcing elders to rely on other resources, such as friends and religious organizations (Bell et al., 1976; Faulkner, Heisel, & Simms, 1975; Richardson, 1990; Taylor, 1988).

ASIAN AMERICANS

Currently, Asian American elders account for 7.3% of Asian/Pacific Islanders of all ages and 1.6% of all Americans 65 years of age and older. As mentioned earlier, these percentages are steadily increasing, and it is expected that Asian Americans will constitute 8% of the elderly in 2050 (U.S. Bureau of the Census, 1993a). The ethnic category, "Asian American," refers to any of 20+ different Asian ethnic groups that include Chinese, Filipinos, Japanese, Koreans, and Southeast Asians (Morioka-Douglas & Yeo, 1990). Although these groups share some characteristics and values (e.g., the importance of family), there are significant differences between the groups that may affect

Asian American elders. Most obvious are the different historical backgrounds, reasons for immigrating to the United States, and experiences in the United States (described in the following sections). In addition to differences across various Asian American ethnic groups, numerous differences between individuals exist, including the degree of acculturation—namely, the extent to which individuals have adopted the values, norms, and traditions of a majority culture (Szapocznik et al., 1978).

Although 81% of Asian elders were born outside of the United States, many have spent the majority of their lives in the United States, predominantly in urban cities in California, Hawaii, and New York (Morioka-Douglas & Yeo, 1990; U.S. Bureau of the Census, 1993a; Yeo & Hikayeda, in press). Despite the length of time they have spent in the United States, most Asian American elders are relatively unacculturated to mainstream U.S. ways. They have resided in highly structured ethnic enclaves, such as Chinatowns and Japantowns, in which their customs and traditions have been staunchly maintained (Morioka-Douglas & Yeo, 1990). This explains why the vast majority (75%) of Asian American elders speak only in their native tongue (Morioka-Douglas & Yeo, 1990).[2]

Two commonly held stereotypes regarding Asian Americans are that they are the model minority group and that they "take care of their own" (Kalish & Moriwaki, 1973). The model minority myth depicts Asian Americans as a group of well-educated, upper-middle-class individuals who have succeeded in achieving the American dream. Such stereotypes, however, reflect a minority of the Asian American population that is primarily young. In actuality, the socioeconomic status of the majority of Asian Americans is similar to that of other ethnic minority groups. For example, although Asian Americans have a higher median income than other ethnic minority groups, the prevalence of poverty is comparable to the others. Ethnic enclaves, in which most Asian Americans reside, are really impoverished ethnic ghettos. Also contradicting prevailing stereotypes, a large percentage of Asian American elders are uneducated (Morioka-Douglas & Yeo, 1990). Clearly, the stereotype of affluence does not apply to a large percentage of Asian American elders, many of whom are in dire need of services; however, this stereotype may contribute to the fact that Asian American elders receive lower levels of poverty assistance and welfare than the general population (Lee, 1986; Sakayue, 1992).

Service providers often erroneously attribute relatively low rates of mental health service use among Asian American elders to stereotypic portrayals that Asian elders are cared for by their families. Indeed, allocation of mental health service funds to Asian American elders is low relative to other ethnic minority groups (Lee, 1986; Lum, Cheung, Cho, Tang, & Yau, 1980; Morioka-Douglas & Yeo, 1990; Sakayue, 1992). Some recent research, however, suggests that the low rates of mental health service use are due to the reluctance of Asian

Americans to seek outside help and the cultural insensitivity of the mental health services themselves more than a lack of need (Sue, 1977). Thus, low rates of mental health service use tell us little about the care Asian American elders may need and are receiving. In the worst case, many Asian American elders may be suffering in silence and isolation.

HISPANIC AMERICANS

Approximately 22.4 million Hispanic Americans—persons of Spanish descent from Central America, Latin America, Mexico, Cuba, and Puerto Rico—currently reside in the United States (Leslie, 1992; U.S. Bureau of the Census, 1993a), not including the vast number of undocumented immigrants. Recently, Hispanic Americans have come to compose one of the largest ethnic minority groups residing in the United States (U.S. Bureau of the Census, 1993b).

The elderly currently compose about 7.8% of the Hispanic population; as with other ethnic minority groups, this figure is expected to increase as a result of declining birthrates and increasing life expectancies (Sanchez, 1992; U.S. Bureau of the Census, 1993a). Of the elderly in the United States, 4% are of Hispanic descent. Although there are great similarities across Hispanic ethnic groups in culture and language, there are differences across subgroups (Maldondo, 1975; Sanchez, 1992). For example, whereas most Mexican Americans came to the United States desiring improved economic status, the majority of Cuban Americans immigrated for political and religious freedom (Boswell & Curtis, 1983). Hispanic ethnic groups also differ in their service needs. For example, the Puerto Rican elderly may have lower health status and income than the Cuban elderly, placing them in greater need for social and health services. Thus, it is not surprising that for the Puerto Rican elderly, the need for services is the greatest predictor of service use, whereas for Cuban elderly, knowledge of services is the greatest predictor of use (Starrett, Todd, & DeLeon, 1989). Within each Hispanic ethnic group, individual differences in levels of acculturation to U.S. culture and language proficiency exist. In most cases, the two are strongly correlated; those who speak Spanish primarily are often the least acculturated to U.S. culture (Marin, Sabogal, Marin, Oter-Sabogal, & Perez-Stable, 1987). Despite these differences across Hispanic subgroups, much of the literature has either not distinguished between groups or has focused primarily on Mexican American elders.

Among the minority elderly, the Hispanic population has the second highest illiteracy rate and receives twice as high a proportion of income below the poverty line than do European Americans (Sanchez, 1992). In addition, many Hispanic elders do not have any form of health insurance, rendering many health care services inaccessible (Sanchez, 1992).

As with Asian American elders, stereotypes about Hispanic culture persist regarding the family's role in caring for the elderly. Although the family plays an important role in caregiving, it is becoming increasingly more difficult for younger relatives to care for older members. As a result, many Hispanic elders are in greater need for formal, outside services (Mahard, 1989).

NATIVE AMERICANS

We know remarkably little about Native Americans as a group and even less about Native American elders in particular (Bell et al., 1976; Cuellar, 1988; Gelfand & Baressi, 1987). This may be because, given their previous experiences with the U.S. government, Native American tribes are extremely suspicious of outsiders, making it considerably difficult for non-Native Americans to conduct research on Native American populations (Gelfand & Baressi, 1987). As a result, much of the research on Native American elders is described in unpublished reports or presented at Native American community centers (American Association of Retired Persons, no date).

Currently, approximately 1.9+ million individuals are Native American (U.S. Bureau of the Census, 1993a). No doubt, however, this figure is a gross underestimate because it excludes the large number of Native Americans who have less than 25% Native American ancestry and who are not officially recognized as Native Americans by the U.S. government (Bell et al., 1976).[3] Approximately 9% of the Native American population is composed of individuals 60 years of age or older, and Native Americans compose approximately 3% of the elderly (U.S. Bureau of the Census, 1993a).

As with the other groups, Native Americans are a heterogeneous group comprising 500+ separate tribes, including the Navajo, Cherokee, Sioux, Chippewa, Laguna Pueblo, and Hopi (Bell et al., 1976; McCabe & Cuellar, 1994). Another source of distinction is place of residence. Thirty-five percent of Native Americans live on reservations and other areas allocated for Native Americans, whereas others live in urban areas, primarily in California (U.S. Bureau of the Census, 1993b). Although there appears to be a constant flux of Native Americans who move from reservations to urban areas, at some time during the course of their lives, approximately 40% of Native Americans return to the reservations (Sue & Sue, 1990). The extent of urban migration varies by tribe. Urban and reservation-dwelling Native American elders differ along multiple dimensions, including financial status, nature and degree of social contact, proximity to friends, life satisfaction, subjective health status, and patterns of assistance (John, 1985).

Most Native Americans live in impoverished conditions. Housing is poor and rates of infectious diseases are high (Bell et al., 1976). Moreover, in education and health, Native Americans rank far below other minority populations (Bell et al., 1976). For example, according to Mick (1983), Indian communities may be as much as 10 to 15 years behind the general population with respect to the availability of nursing homes.[4] In terms of economic, social, and health status, reservation-dwelling Native Americans over 45 years of age and urban-dwelling Native Americans over 55 years of age are comparable to members of the general population over 65 years of age (National Indian Council on Aging, 1981). For members of the Navajo tribe, however, there is a crossover effect; before age 65, Navajos have higher mortality rates than non-Native American populations; after age 65, they have lower mortality rates, particularly among women (Kunitz & Levy, 1989).

Stereotypes regarding Native Americans surround their need for services. With the existence of the Bureau of Indian Affairs, many health care providers assume that Native American physical and mental health care is completely provided for. However, there are many urban Native Americans who reside in communities that lack the services they need and who are not eligible for services because they do not reside on the reservation (Bell et al., 1976).

Historical Sketches

Clinicians need to have contexts in which to place their ethnic minority clients. Becoming informed about the historical experiences of ethnic minority elders is one step in this direction. These historical experiences have important clinical implications. For example, they may influence how these elders interpret their surrounding environments; they may be related to daily life stresses; and they may be the source of discomfort with and suspicion of mental health services. In fact, these historical experiences have been used to explain ethnic differences and similarities in other aspects of mental health, including life expectancies and prevalence rates of mental illness.

One systematic difference across ethnic minority groups concerns the historical circumstances under which individuals came to the United States. In addition, individuals' experiences in the United States differ. Being familiar with an ethnic minority elder's historical background may be important when assessing that elder's mental status, identifying the source(s) of symptomatology, understanding the elder's concerns, and providing a context for treatment (Yeo & Hikoyeda, 1992). Toward this aim, we present historical sketches of the four ethnic minority groups described earlier and certain subgroups within them. Although these are obviously not comprehensive accounts, we intend to illustrate how life circumstances have been different for these groups and may influence physical and mental health.

AFRICAN AMERICANS

The majority of today's African American elders are descendants of people who were brought involuntarily to the United States as slaves. African American history is marked by efforts to be recognized fully as Americans by their European American counterparts and to reclaim their ethnic heritage.

African Americans were and continue to be victims of intense discrimination. At the same time, African American culture is distinguished by impressive strength and resolve. In Giovanni's (1994) words,

> Throughout these centuries, Black Americans have been breaking open doors that others would close, opening lands that others stumbled through, finding emotional strength to carry on when a lesser people would have capitulated. Emmett Till found the strength to put his socks on before he was carried out to be brutally murdered; his mother found the strength to open his casket. Rosa Parks found the strength to stay seated; Martin Luther King found the words to define a movement. (p. 92)

Today's African American elders were born in the early 1900s and raised during a time when both African American achievements and discrimination were on the rise. At the same time that Booker T. Washington started the Tuskagee Institute for African American students, "Jim Crow laws," the "separate but equal" doctrine, and massive racial violence continued. In the early 1900s, the Ku Klux Klan brutally violated African Americans by lynching them and burning their homes and schools. In response to this violence, the National Association for the Advancement of Colored People was established in 1909 by a group of African Americans and European Americans. One of the founders was sociologist Dr. W.E.B. DuBois, the first African American individual to graduate from Harvard University (Yeo & Hikoyeda, 1992).

From 1910 to 1920, there were large migrations of African Americans from the rural South to the urban North. When World War I broke out, many African Americans joined the military to fight for the United States overseas and accumulated various military honors and accolades. When they returned to the United States, however, many were attacked and beaten by errant European American mobs (Yeo & Hikoyeda, 1992). By the 1920s, Ku Klux Klan membership rose to 5 million and demonstrated its strength in 1925 when 400,000 members marched through Washington, D.C. At this time, Marcus Garvey encouraged African Americans to return to Africa, where they "would have freedom and receive just treatment" (Yeo & Hikoyeda, 1992, p. 20). Although few African Americans actually moved to Africa, Garvey's message instilled a greater sense of racial-cultural pride, which promoted the exploration of their cultural roots. During the Harlem Renaissance, African Americans were formally recognized for their outstanding achievements in the arts, music, and sports (Yeo & Hikoyeda, 1992).

During the Great Depression of the 1930s, African Americans were harder hit than their European American counterparts. In response to these difficult times, African Americans increased their political influence by organizing labor unions, which led to legislation that racially integrated labor. African American figures such as Robert C. Weaver and Mary McLeod Bethune served as advisers to Presidents Roosevelt and Truman. In 1941, Executive Order 8802 outlawed racial discrimination in all national defense contract plants (Yeo & Hikoyeda, 1992). During World War II, African Americans demonstrated their valor once again and received numerous honors and distinctions for their military performance. Despite these advances, however, the armed forces did not become truly integrated until 1948.

In the 1950s, the Civil Rights Movement took a series of steps toward racial integration. The Supreme Court ruling that racially segregated schools were not equal, Rosa Parks's refusal to sit in a segregated section of a public bus, and the subsequent bus boycott led to the passage of legislation prohibiting segregation in schools and public transportation. As a result of the efforts of numerous civil rights leaders, including Dr. Martin Luther King, Jr., the Civil Rights Movement culminated with the passage of the Civil Rights Act in 1965, which completely integrated public facilities and schools. Although racial-ethnic prejudice and discrimination continue today, the Civil Rights Movement, spearheaded by many African American groups, has had significant consequences for the promotion of rights of all ethnic minority groups in the United States, including the relaxation of immigration restrictions (Yeo & Hikoyeda, 1992). These historical successes continue into current times as African American contributions pervade all aspects of American life.

Clearly, today's African American elders have lived through a time of tumultuous change. Many are now confronted with an additional set of concerns. A large-scale drug epidemic has hit younger generations of African Americans and subsequently, numerous elders have assumed primary care-taking responsibilities for young grandchildren and great grandchildren (Burton, 1992). Increases in rates of teenage pregnancies, out-of-wedlock births, and the premature deaths of adult children, often due to homicide and drugs, present further challenges to this group of older Americans.

ASIAN AMERICANS

Chinese Americans

From 1854 to the 1870s, approximately 12,000 to 15,000 Chinese entered the United States each year. Most of these sojourners were men who intended to return to China with the riches they had accumulated in the United States.

They settled on the West Coast and began their lives in the United States as indentured servants, or *coolies,* contracted to work in the gold mines or on railroads. By the year 1870, 100,000 Chinese immigrants had arrived (Bell et al., 1976). Because they intended to stay in the United States only temporarily, they resided in ethnic enclaves and made few efforts to adopt American ways. These enclaves protected Chinese laborers from the racism and discrimination that they received from European Americans. With the onset of the Sino-Japanese war in 1894, however, their plans to return to China were thwarted, and these Chinese were essentially stranded in the United States (Bell et al., 1976).

Chinese sojourners were further isolated from their relatives and mother country by a series of discriminatory acts that severely curtailed immigration. In 1882, the Chinese Exclusion Act excluded laborers from coming to the United States for work. Only sons of naturalized citizens were allowed to immigrate to the United States (Yeo & Hikoyeda, 1992). Because few Chinese males were actually granted citizenship, this legislation only reinforced already severe quotas. In 1906, however, an earthquake destroyed a substantial set of immigration records, allowing many Chinese to bring their "paper sons," or relatives into the United States via false documentation. A few families also entered the United States under immigration laws that allowed merchants and their families to immigrate. Many of these people, however, were detained for weeks on Angel Island, until two "credible" non-Chinese witnesses testified that they were legitimate merchants and not laborers. These families typically ran Chinese restaurants, laundromats, grocery stores, and other businesses that did not conflict with the interests of local European Americans. When witnesses did not arrive, families were sent back to China. In 1924, another exclusion act entirely outlawed the immigration of Chinese single women, wives, and families.

A bachelor society of Chinese laborers emerged and developed *tongs,* or family associations, which functioned primarily to support and protect Chinese laborers. Tongs also ran gambling, prostitution, and drug rings in Chinatown communities. Other sources of support included *fongs* and *clans,* which played important roles in maintaining Chinese traditions and values (Takaki, 1989).

Around World War II, the United States began to open its doors to the Chinese. In 1943, all exclusion acts were repealed; by 1946, although quotas remained rigid, wives were allowed to immigrate. In 1965, the immigration act that accompanied the passage of the Civil Rights Act substantially relaxed quotas. At this time, the majority of Chinese immigrants were either relatives of earlier Chinese immigrants or Chinese with professional and entrepreneurial skills.

Today's Chinese American elders compose 30% of the Asian American elderly (U.S. Bureau of the Census, 1993a) and are a diverse group of individuals with different levels of acculturation to mainstream U.S. culture. For example, the Chinese bachelors are considered "geriatric orphans" (Kalish & Moriwaki, 1973), who have spent the majority of their lives in the United States, speak little English, have few financial or educational resources, live in crowded one-room apartments, and lead relatively isolated lives. Other Chinese elders have only recently arrived in the United States to join their children; 35% have immigrated since 1970 (Yeo & Hikayeda, in press). They also speak little English and are unaccustomed to American ways (Yeo & Hikayeda, 1992). Still others are well-educated and highly acculturated, corresponding closely to the stereotypic view of Chinese Americans as a model minority group.

Filipino Americans

Today's Filipino elders share some experiences with Chinese American elders and differ in others. There have been three main waves of Filipino immigration to the United States. The first occurred shortly after the Philippines became a U.S. protectorate in 1898. Approximately 2,700 Filipinos, called *pensionados,* received pensions to study in the United States. Most pensionados did not complete their degrees but settled permanently in the United States.

The second wave, *pinoys,* came to the United States to work on sugar plantations in Hawaii and in mines and farms in Washington and California. In 1934, the Tydings-McDuffie Act limited immigration to 50 Filipino immigrants per year. Immigration steadily dwindled until 1946, when the Philippines became an independent nation. Filipinos were then permitted to apply for citizenship, which allowed family members to join relatives already residing in the United States. As with Chinese Americans, immigration quotas were relaxed a little more in 1965. This gave way to the third wave of immigration, which has been composed primarily of female professionals and health care providers (Yeo & Hikoyeda, 1992).

Unlike other Asian American groups, Filipino Americans were considered *Malays* rather than *Mongolians*—they were thought to be of different racial ancestry than other Asian Americans. This afforded them rights that other Asian groups did not have. For example, except in California, although they were still targets of much racism and discrimination, Filipino Americans were legally allowed to intermarry with other ethnic groups, including European Americans. In addition, they were allowed to serve in the American military forces (Fong, 1992). As a result, compared to other Asian groups, Filipino Americans, on the average, are more acculturated to American culture.

Filipino Americans compose 24% of the Asian American elderly (U.S. Bureau of the Census, 1993a). As with Chinese American elders, some

Filipino American elders are bachelors who lead relatively isolated lives in the United States; others have only recently immigrated to the United States to join their children. The majority of today's Filipino American elders, however, are quite unlike their Chinese American counterparts. They tend to speak English, and many are war veterans and have extensive family networks in the United States (Yeo & Hikoyeda, 1992).

Japanese Americans

Like the Chinese sojourners, the first wave of Japanese immigrants (called *Issei*) were men in search of wealth who intended to return to Japan after amassing financial riches. In many ways, however, the experiences of the Japanese were different from those of the Chinese. First, these men were primarily second sons who were forced by the Japanese primogeniture system to establish their own sources of income. Second, because these Japanese immigrants arrived after the Chinese, they anticipated potential ethnic conflicts. The Japanese government was fully aware of the discrimination waged against the Chinese sojourners by Americans. Attributing it to the "ignominious conduct and behavior" and "inferior character" of the Chinese, the Japanese believed that if they "behaved" and assimilated to U.S. culture, they would be welcomed by U.S. citizens and escape the discrimination suffered by their Chinese predecessors. As a result, Japanese immigrants were carefully selected, closely monitored, and held responsible for "maintaining Japan's honor" by the Japanese government (Takaki, 1989). Third, the Japanese immediately sent women and families to the United States; as a result, the Japanese immigrants were able to establish families and communities in addition to institutions that regulated business and maintained religious and cultural traditions (Bell et al., 1976; Fong, 1992; Takaki, 1989). By 1900, 90,000+ Japanese had settled in Hawaii and the United States mainland.

It is not surprising that the efforts of the Japanese to evade U.S. discrimination were futile. Part of the discrimination waged against Japanese Americans was in response to their agricultural success. Most of the Japanese immigrants were skilled farmers in Japan and pursued this work in the United States. Their success quickly surpassed that of their European American competitors. In retaliation, U.S. farmers lobbied for legislation that limited Japanese American agricultural success by denying them citizenship and land-ownership rights. To circumvent this discriminatory legislation, Japanese Americans purchased land in the names of their children who were American citizens by birth (Bell et al., 1976; Takaki, 1989).

In addition to severe discriminatory agricultural legislation, strict quotas were placed on Japanese American immigrants. In 1907, under the Gentlemen's Agreement, the immigration of Japanese was severely curtailed; in

1924, the Immigration Exclusion Act completely restricted immigration of the Japanese along with other Asian groups. The curtailment of immigration, however, had a different effect on the Japanese than it did on the Chinese. Because a relatively high percentage of Japanese immigrants already living in the United States were women and families, the quotas did not preclude the emergence of a substantial second generation of Japanese Americans (called *Nisei,* or second generation).

As American citizens, the Nisei grew up less isolated than their predecessors and Chinese American counterparts. As a result, they readily adopted American ways as their own. Ironically, they were the victims of the worst discrimination waged against Japanese Americans. In 1942, Executive Order 9066 interned 120,000 Japanese (66% of whom were American citizens) because of their potential threat to the welfare of the United States during World War II (Yabusaki, 1993). The internment not only stripped Japanese Americans of their possessions (including their land) but also tore apart families. After the war, many Japanese Americans attempted to reconstruct their lives, but few were able to achieve their preinternment economic success, and many lost contact with family members entirely. In 1989, Congress appropriated $20,000 to each internment survivor to compensate for these gross injustices. Little attention has been paid to the psychological effect of the internment on today's Japanese elders (Yabusaki, 1993).

Given the maltreatment of Japanese Americans by the federal government, it is not surprising that the immigration act in 1965 did not result in a large influx of Japanese to the United States. Currently, Japanese Americans compose 24% of the Asian American elderly. Most of today's Japanese American elders are U.S. natives or have spent the majority of their lives in the United States and, compared to other Asian Americans, are highly acculturated to mainstream American culture (Fong, 1992; Kalish & Moriwaki, 1973).

Korean Americans

In the early 1900s, the first Koreans immigrated to the United States from Japan. They accompanied Japanese laborers to the sugar cane plantations of Hawaii and were sometimes misidentified as Japanese immigrants (Fong, 1992). Because many of the opportunities in Hawaii were less "golden" than expected, many moved to the mainland (Takaki, 1989). Other Koreans, predominantly political exiles and students, immigrated directly to the U.S. mainland from Korea.

Like the Chinese and Japanese, Korean Americans experienced severe discrimination, and soon, a bachelor society of men emerged (Takaki, 1989). The Korean American experience, however, was distinct from those of Chinese and Japanese groups in several ways. First, Koreans in the United States were a relatively unknown group. Because Korea was formally annexed by Japan in 1910, Korean Americans were represented by the Japanese Council. As a result, few Americans were aware that Korea was a separate nation with its own set of norms and traditions, and instead, misidentified Koreans as Japanese. Second, the small number of Korean Americans in the United States made it virtually impossible to develop ethnic neighborhoods or supportive community networks comparable to the Chinatowns and Japantowns. The majority of Korean immigrants, however, were Christians, and churches became the centers of political resistance movements to extricate their homeland from Japanese domination (Fong, 1992).

Eight percent of Asian American elders are Korean (U.S. Bureau of the Census, 1993a). Many Korean American elders, in order to return to their homeland, actively participated in the movement to liberate their country. These Korean elders are only beginning to reconcile the fact that they will probably never return to Korea. In addition, many Korean American elders have only recently immigrated to the United States to join their children, who immigrated to the United States several years prior (G. Yeo, personal communication, January 11, 1995). Currently, the Korean American population is growing, and the number of Korean American ethnic enclaves is increasing. Korean Americans have recently also become the most visible targets of ethnic conflict, particularly since the Los Angeles Rodney King riots, during which the conflict between Korean Americans and African Americans erupted in brutal violence.

Southeast Asian Americans

The most recent Asians to arrive in the United States are refugees from the Southeast Asian countries of Vietnam, Cambodia, and Laos. Before 1975, Southeast Asian immigrants in the United States were well-educated, young urban students or married couples. Since 1975, one million Southeast Asians have arrived in the United States. The majority are refugees who have only narrowly escaped political and social persecution and turmoil (Ying, 1993). Although most Southeast Asian Americans are young (i.e., between the ages of 20 to 30 years), a substantial proportion of Southeast Asian elders in the United States have experienced similar trauma.

After the Vietnam war and subsequent Communist takeover, the first waves of South Vietnamese came to the United States in 1968. These Vietnamese were relatively well-off and often had connections with U.S. military personnel or government officials. In 1975, however, after the fall of Saigon, hordes of "boat people" fled to the United States, as well as other countries. The flight of these less fortunate Vietnamese was more chaotic. For example, the small, overcrowded fishing boats often left Vietnam without the food or equipment necessary to provide for its passengers, and disease and pestilence were rampant. Boats fled Vietnam with no clear final destination and were often ransacked by pirates or sunk. Families were often separated; women and children were regularly raped and beaten (Gordon, 1980).

From 1978 to the mid-1980s, the majority of refugees were Cambodian. When the Communist Khmer Rouge gained control of the government, most of these refugees fled to miserable, pestilence-ridden camps in Thailand before arriving in the United States (Sughandabhirom, 1986). Most Cambodian refugees have lost at least one family member, either in Cambodia or en route to the United States. Thus, it is no surprise that of Southeast Asian refugee groups, the Cambodians are the most traumatized.

Laotians are the most recent arrivals to the United States from Southeast Asia. Within Laotians, there are ethnic groups that differ both historically and culturally (Luangpraset, 1989). Half of Laotians are the ethnic Lao who lived in relatively large villages in the lowlands of Laos. Two hillside tribal groups, the Hmong and Mien, compose the other half. Although two separate tribes, the Hmong and Mien are culturally similar. They were both self-sufficient, relatively small groups that existed through slash-and-burn farming in the mountain regions of Laos. During the Vietnam War, the Hmong were employed by the CIA to fight against the Communist Lathet Lao. When the Communists took over Laos, about 100,000 Hmong fled for their lives to refugee camps in Thailand and ultimately settled in the United States (McInnis, 1991).

Among the Asian elderly, 4% are Vietnamese, 0.8% are Cambodian, 0.8% are Laotian, and 0.6% are Hmong (Yeo & Hikayeda, in press). Despite the different histories behind the journeys of Vietnamese, Cambodians, and Laotians to the United States, in general, Southeast Asians are a population of refugees who are under intense emotional, psychological, and physical strain. Among what appears an endless list of sources of stress, the majority of Southeast Asian Americans have lost family members, friends, possessions, and their homelands; are socially isolated in an alien culture; experienced severe migratory stress; and must adjust to drastic changes in social and economic status. Not surprisingly, the majority of refugees suffer from both posttraumatic stress and depressive disorders (Mollica & Lavelle, 1988) as well as chronic adjustment or acculturation disorders (Cerhan, 1990). In addition, Southeast Asian elders must also accept tremendous losses in status and the shattering of their expectations for a peaceful old age. Many recent immigrants from Southeast Asia are elders who have followed their children to the United States (G. Yeo, personal communication, January 11, 1995).

In addition to the Asian American subgroups that we have discussed, there are others that deserve attention but who have received minimal attention in the literature (Yeo & Hikoyeda, in press). They include Asian Indians, who compose 5% of the Asian American elderly, and Pacific Islander groups, who compose 3.2% of the Asian elderly (U.S. Bureau of the Census, 1993a; Yeo & Hikayeda, in press).

HISPANIC AMERICANS

Central Americans

As we have mentioned, most literature on Hispanic American elders focus on Mexican American populations. Central Americans compose a much smaller percentage of the Hispanic elderly (G. Yeo, personal communication, January 11, 1995). As a result, Central Americans are often overlooked, despite the fact that Mexican Americans and Central Americans differ in ways that may influence physical and mental health.

Unlike most Mexican Americans, who came to the United States primarily for economic reasons, most Central Americans fled their homelands to escape religious and political persecution. The U.S. government does not recognize this difference, and instead, places Central Americans in the same immigration category as Mexican Americans. As a result, despite the severe trauma they experienced before they arrived and the tenuousness of life in the United States, Central Americans are not eligible for services provided to refugees (Leslie & Leitch, 1989).

Because the government classifies Central Americans with Mexican Americans, little is known about Central Americans in the United States in general, and Central American elders in particular. It is estimated that 3% of Central Americans in the United States are over the age of 65; however, the percentage of elders in each of the specific Central American groups (e.g., Salvadorans, Hondurans) is unknown.

Although there are no exact figures of the number of immigrants or refugees from particular Central American countries (Carrillo, 1990), it is estimated that Salvadorans alone constitute a significant percentage of the population. Approximately one half million Salvadorans entered the United States in the 1980s (Leslie, 1992). The majority of Salvadorans left their homeland to escape the intense human rights violations of the Salvadoran military (Lopez, Bocellari, & Hall, 1988). Psychologically, the war had profound effects on Salvadorans, creating feelings of vulnerability, exacerbated alertness, loss of control, and an altered sense of reality (Lira, as cited in Martin-Buro, 1989). This is perhaps just a hint of the types of issues that may concern Central American elders.

Cuban Americans

As with most of the ethnic minority groups discussed in this chapter, an integral part of Cuban American history revolves around the migratory experiences of Cubans to the United States. Immigration from Cuba began between 1959 and 1962, when Fidel Castro overthrew the Batista government and dramatically changed Cuba's social, political, and economic systems. The "Golden Exiles"—215,000 Cubans, most of whom were members of the upper-middle-class—fled to escape political imprisonment, harassment, and persecution. More than half of the immigrants were women and children sent by their husbands and fathers for safety and protection. Although most of the immigrants were members of the upper-middle-class, a substantial proportion were also members of the working class. Many settled in New York and Florida and were forced to take unskilled jobs; however, many of these immigrants were able to improve their socioeconomic situation rapidly. For the most part, U.S. citizens were sympathetic to the plight of these Cuban exiles and therefore, they were well-received (Boswell & Curtis, 1983).

Castro's affiliation with the Soviet Union and the identification of Cuba as a socialist state led to the break of diplomatic relations with the United States in 1961. That same year, the unsuccessful Bay of Pigs invasion and the Cuban Missile Crisis heightened tensions between the United States and Cuba (Boswell & Curtis, 1983).

Between 1962 and 1965, despite Castro's formal cessation of immigration to the United States, 56,000 Cubans arrived, either directly or via another country. Between 1966 and 1972, Castro allowed immigration to the United States once again; during this time, 297,318 Cubans left on "Freedom Flights"—airlifts between Miami and Havana. The majority of these immigrants were the elderly or individuals who already had family in the United States. Restrictions were placed on young males of military age as well as skilled workers, making it difficult for them to leave Cuba (Boswell & Curtis, 1983).

From 1973 to 1980, there was a temporary hiatus in immigration to the United States; despite this, 38,000 people immigrated at this time, most of whom were imprisoned criminals. In 1980, Castro opened the immigration doors once more, allowing only Cuban "undesirables," such as prisoners and the disabled, to leave. Of the 124,779 Cubans who left at this time, 26,000 had prison records. Because crime rates increased significantly in Dade County, Florida, where many of these immigrants settled, for the first time, Cuban immigrants were viewed negatively, and there was a strong tension between "old" and "new" Cubans. Since 1980, there has been a steady decline of Cuban emigration (Boswell & Curtis, 1983).

Among elders, Cuban Americans are the second largest Hispanic subgroup, composing 15% of the Hispanic elderly (U.S. Bureau of the Census, 1993a).

Many Cuban elders are babysitters of their grandchildren. Because many Cuban elders are keepers of Cuban traditions and customs, they are often the ones who pass Cuban culture onto the younger generations. This often creates intergenerational conflict and stress between younger Cuban Americans who are assimilating rapidly to mainstream American culture and Cuban elders who are not (Boswell & Curtis, 1983).

Mexican Americans

Much of Mexican American history revolves around labor relations between Mexican immigrants and the U.S. government. In the mid-1800s, the United States annexed most of northern Mexico; as a result, movement across the Mexican-U.S. border (into California, Arizona, and Texas) was relatively informal and relaxed until the early 1900s. Like the Chinese, most Mexicans came to the United States in search of economic gains. Mexicans also faced widespread discrimination in employment, housing, and education. The Texas Rangers committed atrocities against Mexicans that were comparable to those of the Ku Klux Klan (Yeo & Hikoyeda, 1992).

In 1910, many Mexicans, mainly from the upper and middle classes, immigrated to the United States to escape the Mexican Revolution, uncertain whether they would ever return to Mexico. Another wave of immigration occurred between 1920 and 1928, when quotas preventing the entrance of Chinese and Japanese laborers allowed thousands of Mexicans to enter the United States to fill agricultural labor and domestic service needs. However, the number of Mexicans who immigrated far outweighed the existing quotas, and border patrols were established to curb illegal Mexican immigration. In the 1930s, many Mexicans were hit hard by the Great Depression. U.S.-born Mexican Americans were either forced to repatriate or became migrant workers living under substandard conditions. Because many Mexican Americans were uprooted during this time, few were able to attend school regularly; as a result, most elder Mexican Americans are illiterate (Yeo & Hikoyeda, 1992).

During World War II, again due to a labor shortage, Mexicans were allowed to enter the United States as *braceros,* or temporary workers. In addition, many Mexican Americans valiantly fought for the United States in World War II. Despite these contributions to the war effort, Mexican Americans continued to be victims of harsh discrimination. In response, the G.I. Forum was formed, which became the foundation for the Mexican American civil rights movement (Yeo & Hikoyeda, 1992).

In the 1970s, wives and families of Mexican domestic workers were allowed to immigrate to the United States again to meet the increasing need for female domestic workers. Due to declines in agricultural work, many

Mexican Americans moved to cities in the midwestern, eastern, and north-western United States. At the same time, Mexican Americans became more politically active, creating organizations such as the Mexican American Political Association and the United Farm Workers, which fought for social, economic, and educational reforms (Yeo & Hikoyeda, 1992).

Mexican Americans comprise 49% of the Hispanic elderly (U.S. Bureau of the Census, 1993a). Many of today's Mexican American elderly came to the United States as braceros but settled permanently in the United States. Others have only recently immigrated to join their children (G. Yeo, personal communication, January 11, 1995). Twenty percent to 30% live in poverty (G. Yeo, personal communication, January 11, 1995), and over 60% have low levels of education and literacy. Despite advancements made in Mexican American civil rights in the past 20 years, many Mexican American elders, especially the oldest-old, do not consider themselves Americans.

Puerto Ricans

Puerto Rico was freed from Spanish control and became a U.S. possession in the Treaty of Paris after the Spanish-American War. Until 1900, a U.S. military government ruled Puerto Rico and initiated many civil works projects that improved sanitation, established an education system, and built highways. In 1900, the Foraker Act replaced the military government with a two-house civil government, of which Puerto Ricans were allowed to elect the lower house. Due largely to the efforts of Luis Munoz Rivera, the Jones Act in 1917 granted Puerto Ricans U.S. citizenship, and Puerto Rico became a U.S. territory. Many mainland-U.S. businesses built factories and developed farmland; however, few Puerto Ricans reaped rewards from U.S. investments. In 1930, devastating hurricanes and the Great Depression virtually wiped out Puerto Rico's economy, and it soon became the "Poorhouse of the Caribbean" (Larsen, 1973).

The economy improved immensely in 1933, with the establishment of the Puerto Rico Emergency Relief Administration and the Puerto Rico Recon-struction Administration, which provided clothing, food, and training pro-grams for Puerto Ricans and reestablished failed industries. In 1948, Puerto Ricans were allowed to elect their own governor. They chose Muñoz Marin, the son of Luis Muñoz Rivera, who was committed to improving the economy under Operation Bootstrap, a program whose goals included industrialization, improved health and education, slum clearance, agricultural expansion, and land redistribution. With World War II, Operation Bootstrap experienced severe setbacks. During this time, many Puerto Ricans moved to the U.S. mainland in search of jobs. By 1955, 675,000 Puerto Ricans lived in the United States, and 500,000 of them were in New York City. In 1950, Public

Law 600 gave Puerto Rico the right to draft its own constitution, and in 1965, federal acts that prevented non-English-speaking citizens from voting were repealed, allowing Puerto Ricans to vote. In 1967, Puerto Rico voted on the future of its political status; 60% voted to continue its status as a commonwealth of the United States. At this time, Operation Bootstrap was successful, creating less of a need for employment on the U.S. mainland; as a result, many returned to Puerto Rico (Larsen, 1973).

Of the Puerto Ricans who remained on the U.S. mainland, most had limited knowledge of English, had low-income jobs, and lived in the inner-city slums of Spanish Harlem—"El Barrio." Women usually had an easier time finding work than their husbands, which often created marital conflict; this breaking of traditional gender norms often led to high rates of divorce (Larsen, 1973) and may explain why many of today's Puerto Rican elderly women are divorced or separated (Mahard, 1989). Intergenerational conflict due to different rates of acculturation between parents and children was also common. Because many parents did not understand their Americanized children, gangs of Puerto Rican adolescents emerged (Larsen, 1973). Today's second generation Puerto Ricans are considerably better off than their predecessors.

Currently, Puerto Rican elders residing on the U.S. mainland comprise 12% of the elderly Hispanic population (U.S. Bureau of the Census, 1993a). Physical disabilities, homesickness, and acculturation stress due to language difficulties are common problems among the elderly. Even though the majority of the elderly were born in Puerto Rico and immigrated after World War II, most are relatively unacculturated and speak only Spanish. Many rely on their children, primarily adult daughters, to be their translators and primary sources of emotional support (Sanchez-Ayendez, 1989). Many Puerto Rican elders also consider themselves Puerto Ricans rather than Americans and often express wishes to return to Puerto Rico, although few have actual plans to do so (Mahard, 1989).

NATIVE AMERICANS

Most of the conflicts between Native Americans and European American have revolved around land struggles. When European settlers first arrived in America, they viewed Native American uses of the land as "inefficient and incapable," (Olson & Wilson, 1984, p. 21) and therefore, felt justified in taking land from the Native Americans. Year after year, the U.S. government moved Native Americans to less and less valuable land (Olson & Wilson, 1984). The tribes were promised permanent control over these lands, but this promise was continually revoked.

Throughout the 19th century, Native Americans continued to be at the political mercy of European Americans. Two political attitudes about Native

Americans prevailed at the time. On the one hand, there were assimilationist political groups who espoused the "protection" of Native Americans from their own "savage" culture by transforming them into "law abiding farmers who believed in property and Jesus Christ" (Olson & Wilson, 1984, p. 23). On the other hand, there were "Indian haters," who saw Native Americans as "blood thirsty savages" (Olson & Wilson, 1984, p. 23) that needed to be expelled from society. Ultimately, both groups advocated the eventual decimation of Native American culture.

By the late 19th and early 20th centuries, the assimilationist camp prevailed and enacted a series of programs aimed to "civilize" Native Americans. For example, the Dawes Act of 1887, the Curtis Act of 1898, the Dead Indian Land Act of 1902, and the Burke Act of 1906 took a total of over 90 million acres of land from Native Americans and then attempted to turn Native Americans into family farmers. Consistent with other policies, most Native Americans lost their land and received nothing in return.

During World War I, thousands of Native Americans fought for the United States. In 1924, Native Americans were granted citizenship. However, this did little to address economic problems or acknowledge Native American culture. In 1934, the Indian Reorganization Act attempted to restore tribal authority, but in actuality, it only replaced direct with indirect supervision of Native American affairs by the federal government. After World War II, the U.S. government renewed efforts to assimilate Native Americans into the rest of American society by implementing urban relocation and training programs. Similarly, civil rights activists tried to rally for Native American integration into mainstream American society. Both movements only contributed to existing Native American resentment that these activists assumed that they wished to relinquish their culture. The relationship between Native Americans and non-Native Americans continues to be fragile, "marked by mutual suspicion and enormous cultural differences" (Olson & Wilson, 1984, p. 25).

Little is known about the status of Native American elders. One current concern is the mass exodus of young Native Americans to urban areas. Many of the older Native Americans are left on reservations with poor services and care (Murdock & Schwartz, 1978), lack of housing, and high crime rates (Twiss et al., 1989). Those who follow their younger relatives to the cities often have difficulty adjusting to urban life (Bell et al., 1976).

The Influence of Ethnicity on Old Age

To provide a general context within which to view individuals who seek treatment, we have considered the backgrounds and cultures of various ethnic minority elders and the circumstances under which they immigrated (or were forcibly brought) to the United States. Next we consider how ethnicity may influence the presentation of problems and the therapeutic process. Wherever possible, we suggest ways that professionals might enhance their work with ethnic minority elders. Because we know of no systematic studies comparing different styles and approaches, our suggestions are derived largely from clinical experience or inferred from empirical findings in the literature. We cannot emphasize enough the need for more empirical work.

ATTITUDES TOWARD AGING
AND ETHNIC IDENTITY

Aging is viewed differently by the various groups we review in this chapter. Indeed, the timing of old age varies by subgroup (Freed, 1992). The Hmong consider old age to start at 40 years old (Hayes, 1987). Mexican Americans and African Americans consider old age to begin at 59 years and 63 years, respectively, compared to the 70 year average at which European Americans demarcate entry into old age (Bengtson, 1979). European Americans have traditionally related old age with retirement, due to its association with eligibility for social security and pension income. For many ethnic minority elders, this association is less meaningful. Many are not eligible for retirement income because of lifetime employment in low-paying occupations without benefits and, thus, must continue to work. Instead of retirement, these sub-groups associate old age with other factors, many of which are represented by more gradual change, such as health impairment. In addition to functional health, factors include the acceptability of aging, aging milestones (such as grandparenthood) and life expectancy (Gibson, 1988). For example, for African Americans, their view of the life cycle may be influenced by grand-parenthood at 40 to 50 years of age, lowered life expectancy, an earlier age of widowhood, and poor functional health (Burton, 1992).

INTERGENERATIONAL SUPPORT
AND ETHNICITY

Although we have noted throughout this chapter ways in which minority status may systematically disadvantage ethnic minority elders, in other ways, ethnic identification and cultural values of ethnic groups may also contribute positively to the aging process. Among the Navajo, for example, life and death are viewed as part of a continuous process and thus, aging is relatively less threatening (Shomaker, 1981). Ethnographic and anthropological investiga-tions also suggest that aging may be viewed more positively among other ethnic subgroups than in mainstream U.S. culture. In a comparison of African Americans, Mexican Americans, and European Americans, for example, Bengtson (1979) found that, of the three groups, African Americans held the most positive views toward aging. Quite possibly, survival itself, in the face of tremendous racial discrimination, represents a major accomplishment in the African American community. It is interesting to note that Mexican Americans reported the most negative views.

It is widely believed that many ethnic subgroups provide better intergenerational support than European Americans (Kalish & Moriwaki, 1973; Sanchez-Ayendez, 1989). This portrayal, however, may be overly simplistic and contrasts with European Americans may not be as large as one might expect. It is important to stress that regardless of ethnicity, most of the care that older people in the United States receive is provided by family members. Nevertheless, there are some interesting differences in interpersonal relationships and social support as well as nursing homes across ethnic subgroups. Mexican Americans, for example, are more likely to receive care from families and report greater closeness to families than either African American or European American elders (Bell et al., 1976)

Among Chinese Americans, the situation appears to be more stressful. Of all ethnic minority subgroups, Chinese Americans are the most likely to live with their children (Raskind & Peskind, 1992). Yet compared to other groups, Chinese Americans report that they have the least contact with their children (Lubben & Becerra, 1987). Differing expectations by younger and older cohorts may contribute to this apparent paradox. Many Asian American elders grow old expecting to be surrounded and cared for on a daily basis by daughter-in-laws and younger relatives; the reality they face is often quite different from these expectations (Kalish & Moriwaki, 1973; Kobata, Lockery, & Moriwaki, 1990). For the many who do not live with relatives (even if they receive financial support from them), a deep sense of abandonment may occur. Even those who live with younger relatives may feel that they do not receive the respect they are due. Contributing further to intergenerational conflict are different levels of identification with ethnic culture. Elder relatives often see their role as cultural expert or advisor, whose function is to preserve cultural values. Among younger generations of Asian Americans, however, assimilation to Western culture is often a primary goal, which can seriously threaten the self-esteem of Chinese American elders and cause considerable intergenerational conflict.

Compared to their European American counterparts, African American elders interact more frequently with family members and report higher levels of support from them. In addition, African Americans include in their extended social networks *fictive kin,* namely, nonblood relatives who assume roles similar to family members (Markides & Mindel, 1987). Intergenerational conflict is also common, however, particularly among poor African American families who have been seriously affected by the drug epidemic of the past 20 years. Many older African Americans have lost their adult children to drugs or crime. Many have assumed primary caretaking responsibilities for grandchildren at a time in life where their own physical health makes this a particularly burdensome task (Burton, 1992). For the current cohort of African American elders who endured lifelong fights for civil rights during their lives and saw each decade bring them closer to equality with mainstream America, this experience has been devastating.

Intergenerational support is also affected by migration trends among younger relatives. Increasingly, younger cohorts of Native Americans are relocating to urban areas where ties to the ethnic community are threatened. And yet, sociocultural marginality in older Native Americans, often brought about by accompanying relocation, is associated with negative self-concept and even physical health (Wiebel-Orlando, 1989).

ETHNIC TIES

Strong ties to ethnic communities appear to affect psychological and physical health in several ways. Ethnic communities appear to provide elders with greater access to informal information sources about available services. For example, Cuban elders with greater contact with children and other relatives were more aware of and more likely to use available social services (Starrett, Decker, Araujo, & Walters, 1989). In addition, many ethnic communities instill a sense of purpose in elders. Many Native American elders see their purpose in life as transmitting cultural values to younger generations (Red Horse, 1980). Serbian American elders also identify strongly with their designated role of preserving their ethnic heritage (Simic, 1987), similar to the roles that Meyerhoff (1987) described for ethnic Jews and Luborsky and Rubenstein (1990) described for Irish, Italian, and Jewish widowers. In the latter study, ethnic identification played a crucial role in adjustment to widowhood. An awareness of the strength with which ethnic minority elders identify with their heritages is important for clinicians in assessing and devising treatment plans. The elder who identifies strongly with his or her ethnic heritage may respond well to treatments oriented around it.

LIFE EXPECTANCY AND MENTAL HEALTH

Ethnic elders vary in their average life expectancies and mortality rates. Compared to European Americans, Native Americans and African Americans have shorter life expectancies. The average age of death for European Americans is 76.6 years old; for African Americans, 70.4 years old; for Asian Americans, 82.9 years old; and for Hispanic populations, 79.0 years old (U.S. Bureau of the Census, 1993a). The average life expectancy for Native Americans appears to have changed dramatically over the years. In 1979, Native Americans were expected to live to 46 years of age (Varghese & Medinger, 1979); however, according to the 1993 U.S. Bureau of the Census, at birth, Native Americans are expected to live until 76.9 years of age. This change may be due to improved health services and fewer deaths due to infectious diseases such as tuberculosis and gastroenteritis (McCabe & Cuellar, 1994). It is interesting to note that African Americans demonstrate a crossover effect during later old age. Asian Americans and Hispanic Americans, on the other hand, have lower mortality rates than European Americans at all ages of the life span (Markides & Mindel, 1987; Sakayue, 1992). More and more, this appears to be the case for Native American elders as well (U.S. Bureau of the Census, 1993a).

Ethnic elders also vary in their prevalence rates of mental illness. In many cases, ethnic minority groups have higher rates of mental illness compared to European Americans. Older Hispanic women are at a higher risk for depression (Cuellar, 1988), alcohol abuse, phobias, and cognitive impairment compared to European American older women (Stanford & DuBois, 1992). Kemp, Staples, and Lopez-Aqueres (1987) examined 700 older Hispanics residing in Los Angeles County and found that more than 26% met the diagnostic criteria for major depression or dysphoria. Most of these depressions were related to physical health complications. In addition, socioeconomic status, health behavior, and family variables were related to these Hispanic elders' affective states (Kemp et al., 1987). Older African Americans report higher levels of psychological distress than old European Americans (Fillenbaum, Hughes, Heyman, George, & Blazer, 1988). Similarly, elderly Chinese American and Japanese American women have higher rates of suicide than their European American counterparts (Morioka-Douglas & Yeo, 1990).

These ethnic differences in prevalence rates may be a function of differences in socioeconomic resources and advantages rather than ethnic differences per se. In fact, when socioeconomic status is controlled for, many ethnic differences in prevalence rates disappear. Markides, Martin, and Sizemore (1980) showed that elderly Mexican American and European Americans did not differ in the number of psychological symptoms of distress; African American and European American elders demonstrate similar rates of depression (Stanford & DuBois, 1992). In the Kemp et al. (1987) study described earlier, only 5.5% (compared with a total of 26%) of the Hispanic elders studied suffered from depressions that were not related to concomitant physical problems.

In some cases, however, ethnic differences in psychopathology prevail even after controlling for differences in socioeconomic status. In a community sample, Raskind & Peskind (1992) found that even after controlling for socioeconomic status, European American elders showed more psychopathology and reported more somatic complaints than Chinese Americans. Ironically, European Americans were also more socially competent than Chinese Americans. Chinese Americans had more problems with memory but performed better overall on gross mental status exams.

As this review illustrates, life expectancies and prevalence rates of mental illness often distinguish between the groups, and therefore, no general statements regarding life expectancies and prevalence rates of mental illness can be made across ethnic minority groups. These differences may stem from the various historical experiences of each of the groups. For example, higher mortality rates of Native Americans and African Americans compared to European Americans may be the aftermath of tremendous discrimination, slavery, and genocide (Richardson, 1990). They may also reflect differences in the availability of resources, which also may be related to different historical experiences and treatment (e.g., economic and political disparities). It is also possible that differences in prevalence rates are a function of the more abstract components of ethnicity (e.g., belief systems). For example, in community samples, normal European American elders may have reported more somatic symptoms because they felt more comfortable disclosing their psychological distress to researchers than would Chinese American elders, who were influenced by the stigma of mental illness in Chinese culture.

Awareness of ethnic differences in prevalence rates of mental illness is critical in planning treatments, assessing the prognosis of ethnic minority elders, and placing the illness of the elder in context. Historical experiences, socioeconomic disparities, and beliefs and customs may all influence ethnic differences in life expectancies and rates of mental illness. Unfortunately, research on the influence of within-group differences (such as acculturation levels) on life expectancies and mental illness has yet to be conducted.

THE THERAPEUTIC PROCESS

Clinicians need to be sensitive to the expectations of ethnic minority elders about appropriate communication styles and the clinician-patient relationship. In many cases, establishing rapport determines whether or not patients return after the first session (Sue & Sue, 1990). Communication styles should be adjusted according to the degree of acculturation. Among foreign-born elders for whom language differences create a barrier, nonverbal communication, such as interpersonal space and body movements, may be particularly important, whereas among fluent English speakers, the content of conversation may be more critical (Sue & Sue, 1990).

We recommend that surnames be used in the default and that explicit permission be obtained when more informal address seems to be desired by the patient. We also recommend that clinicians use terms used by their patients (e.g., "hot" and "cold" to describe emotional states) rather than school patients in more mainstream terminology. In addition, depending on their ethnic background, patients may expect more or less involvement of family members in the therapeutic process. In some cases, failure to involve the family may signify a lack of serious commitment on the part of the therapist to ameliorate problems. It is very important, however, not to assume that such preferences exist. We believe strongly that clinicians explicitly ask patients about their desires for family involvement. They should be told that confidentiality will be maintained unless they desire otherwise. If they do expect that family members will be involved, clinicians should be ready to pursue family approaches.

We recommend that clinicians unfamiliar with their patients' cultural backgrounds inquire about them directly in a respectful and interested manner, placing the ethnic minority elder in a teaching role. Allowing sufficient time for this purpose may serve to inform clinicians, provide an opportunity for the clinician to empathize with the patient, and help to establish a trusting working relationship.

Finally, almost all ethnic minority elders have encountered severe discrimination and prejudice in the United States. Many may be dealing with the psychological consequences of discrimination without adequate assistance but may be reluctant to seek assistance because they are suspicious of mental health agencies and the largely European American health care system (Sue & Sue, 1990). For example, today's Japanese American elders continue to carry the ghosts of the internment inside themselves (Yabusaki, 1993). Native American elders also suffer from fears that they will be exploited by the U.S. government yet again. Thus, perhaps the most critical aspect of the therapeutic process is building a trusting relationship with the ethnic minority elder.

ACCEPTABILITY OF TREATMENT

Ethnic patients may also have different views of mental and physical illness, regarding their causes, medication, and specific culture-bound syndromes. For example, many Asian and Hispanic cultures embrace holistic views of health in which the mind-body dichotomy is nonexistent. In these cultures, the key to health is balance (between hot and cold, yin and yang, or other life forces; Morioka-Douglas & Yeo, 1990). Different views of physical and mental health may influence the ways in which symptoms are presented. For example, Chinese patients may somatize their symptoms; somatization is the expression of emotional, psychological, or social distress through bodily complaints in primarily medical settings (Kleinman, 1986). An awareness of the patient's views of health and illness may improve clinicians' understanding of their ethnic minority patients as well as how much these patients comply with prescribed treatments (Baker et al., 1990).

For example, some ethnic minority elders believe that once symptoms subside, the illness is gone; therefore, despite instructions to do otherwise, they erroneously assume that their medication is no longer necessary. Similarly, for groups that view health in terms of a balance between hot and cold, Western medicines are often considered too hot and therefore, are not taken at regularly recommended dosage levels. In some cases, usually for biological rather than cultural reasons, an actual adjustment in dosage based on ethnicity may be appropriate. For example, some studies suggest that Asian Americans require only half the dosage of medication given to European Americans (Lin, Poland, & Lesser, 1986).

In addition, ethnic minority elders often combine Western with traditional treatments. Clinicians' lack of appreciation for traditional treatments may result in clients' discontinuation of Western treatments rather than traditional ones. Moreover, these traditional treatments may contain substances that counteract or significantly alter the effects of Western medications (Hikoyeda & Grudzen, 1991).

Many ethnic minority elders may also suffer from culture-bound syndromes—disorders known in other cultures that have no recognizable Western analogs. For example, in Southern China, Hong Kong, and Taiwan, *frigophobia* is an excessive fear and intolerance of the cold in temperature and foods. African American elders may experience *falling out,* which has been presented as a disorder of the central nervous system or a metabolic abnormality with a sudden onset and of brief duration during an emotionally intense situation (Richardson, 1990). For some Hispanic Americans, *susto*—a constant state of anxiety and fear—occurs when a person is frightened by a traumatic event (e.g., witnessing an accident, being frightened by a snake). For the Oglala Sioux, *wacinko* is a form of reactive depression that may also require more traditional healing approaches (Lewis, 1975).

Many of these culture-bound syndromes are often thought to have supernatural causes; therefore, Western medications may be ineffective. As a result, different types of folk healing may be invoked. For example, *curanderismo* is a type of Indian folk healing that uses prayers, messages, and herbs to treat *susto* and *mal puesto*—a hex placed on one by his or her enemies (Comas-Diaz, 1989; Martinez, 1988). Clinicians should be aware that these traditional forms of healing may be in use.

Conclusion

Our goal in this chapter has been to make the general recommendation that clinicians familiarize themselves with the different ways in which ethnicity may affect their patients as well as to be aware of differences between and within ethnic groups. We have discussed a range of ways in which ethnicity may have an effect on clinical work with ethnic minority elders. Historical experiences, life expectancies, and prevalence rates of mental illness are characterized, for the most part, by group differences across the three ethnic minority groups. Ethnic groups also differ in the more abstract aspects of old age, such as attitudes toward aging, perceptions of old age, and milestones of old age. We have also emphasized that within-group differences may be as strong as between-group differences. Acculturation and ethnic identity are two sources from which within-group differences may stem.

We believe that by seriously considering the different ways by which ethnicity may influence clients and treatment efficacy, clinicians will be best prepared to work with ethnic minority elders. Implementing stereotyped ways of interacting with members of different ethnic minority groups can some-times suggest ethnic insensitivity rather than ethnic sensitivity by obscuring the ways in which the elder differs from his or her ethnic group. Ultimately, it is most important that clinicians view all of their patients as individuals, some of whom are highly influenced by their ethnic heritages and some of whom are less so. In many ways, the quality of care that the ethnic minority elder receives depends on the willingness of clinicians to appreciate the complexity of ethnicity and its relationship to their patients' lives. Further-more, clinicians must also be willing to tackle and question their own assumptions, biases, and values; to examine how these may carry over to their clinical work; and to determine how accurate or appropriate they are for their ethnic minority patients. For example, our biases and assumptions may occur at the most basic of levels and may cause us to impose our own notions of ethnicity, aging, and mental health onto our patients.

Working with ethnic minority elders, especially those whose backgrounds are vastly different from one's own, is a challenging but rewarding task. As this chapter has illustrated, the multitude of ways in which ethnicity may influence aging renders simple answers virtually irrelevant. However, this is what, in the end, will continue to make work with these groups so interesting and rewarding. We have much to learn from these ethnic minority elders, whose lives are a rich montage of traditions, experiences, and beliefs. Although a daunting task, it is one that we look forward to as our contact with ethnic minority elders increases in the years to come.

Notes

1. We use the term *European American* for non-Hispanic White populations with European ancestors, who are also commonly referred to in the literature as Anglo Americans and Caucasians.

2. In much of the literature, a distinction has been made between Asian Americans living in Hawaii and those who live on the U.S. mainland (Takaki, 1989). In this chapter, we will be primarily discussing the latter group of Asian Americans.

3. This percentage is relatively arbitrary and is used, along with the requirement that Native Americans live on a reservation, as an eligibility criterion for federal aid from the Bureau of Indian Affairs (Bell et al., 1976).

4. Although there is much debate over whether nursing homes are appropriate for Native American elders, we use this example to illustrate the lack of services available to them (Lustig, Ross, Davis, & Old Elk, 1979).

5

The Significance of Gender in the Treatment of Older Adults

Susan Turk-Charles
Tara Rose
Margaret Gatz

This chapter highlights biological and socially constructed differences between older women and men. Some of these factors begin in old age, whereas others represent cumulative effects that have persisted throughout life. The most fundamental of these differences between men and women—and one that relates to many subsequent differences—involves mortality. At birth, the average life expectancy for men is 73 years and for women, 80 years (U.S. Bureau of the Census, 1992a). Healthy women in the United States who celebrate their 65th birthdays will, on average, live an additional 20 years, with 16 of those years independent and in good health. Men, at age 65, are expected to live for 15 more years, with 13 of those years in good health (Suzman, Willis, & Manton, 1992). These statistics vary by ethnicity, but the absolute difference between men and women remains (U.S. Bureau of the Census, 1992a, 1992c).

Researchers examining sex and gender differences commonly compare the average older man to the average older woman. When working with older adults on a personal level, however—such as in psychotherapy or in a medical consultation—individual differences must be considered. An older woman who has remained single and held a job most of her life may have more in common with an older man with a similar work history from the same geographical region than with another older woman who never worked for a salary and lived in a different area of the country. Therefore, mental health professionals should be cautious when generalizing findings about these sex differences to individual men and women.

The chapter focuses on several areas of research where gender and sex differences have been found. Although men and women may be similar on a number of factors, the focus of this chapter will be differences highlighted in the literature. We begin by defining sex and gender. The following sections focus on differences for older adults in biological, psychosocial, and economic realms. First, biological differences are addressed, regarding both physical health and sexuality. Second, gender differences in psychosocial issues are examined, including social networks, older gays and lesbians, caregiving, and bereavement. We then discuss the economic status of men and women. Finally, we highlight therapy issues for both older men and women, including a discussion of age and sex bias in mental health delivery, the epidemiology of psychological disorders among men and women, and interventions that take gender roles into account. Despite discrete sections, it should be kept in mind that none of the issues reviewed in this chapter can be considered in isolation; they interact with each other to produce gender differences in old age. For example, economic status influences access to health care, and living alone affects social activity.

Sex and Gender

Genes determine sex. Many people limit sex differences to those related directly to hormones and reproductive differences between men and women. Men and women vary in other biological respects as well, however, and these differences are present throughout the life span. For example, gender differences in mortality appear before birth, with female fetuses having a greater chance of survival compared to male fetuses (Smith & Warner, 1989). Some physical differences appear in later life. For instance, more older men suffer from hearing loss than older women, and older women have higher rates of osteoporosis compared to older men (U.S. National Center for Health Statistics [NCHS], 1994). Environmental influences can interact with genetic or physiological processes to increase or decrease sex differences. For example, exercise and vitamin supplements may slow loss of bone mass, which is seen more often in women than men (Herzog, 1989). Subsequently, when women engage in these preventive measures, the gender gap with regard to this physical condition is narrowed.

In contrast to the term *sex, gender* refers to the social construction of differences between women and men. Gender differences vary according to a number of factors, including the society and the time period in which the individual has lived (Hendricks, 1992; Huyck, 1990). For example, today's older American woman was born during a time when, in many social classes, she was not expected to work to support her family financially. Women who did work outside of the home typically were limited to a few gender-specific occupations, such as nursing, teaching, or domestic services. When a woman was married, it was with the admonishment to obey her husband and to be the homemaker. In contrast, a younger woman in today's society is told that she should assert herself in her relationship with her husband and that women should have an equal say in household affairs. She sees that more women than men now attend college and that the percentage of single-parent families with women as the head of the household has increased in her lifetime (U.S. Bureau of the Census, 1992b). Over time, women have had to adjust to changing expectations concerning how a girl, woman, and elderly woman should behave (Gutmann, 1987; Sinnott, 1977).

Men also have experienced a change in gender roles (Gutmann, 1987; Sinnott, 1977). Today's older American man was raised to believe that he was the head of his household, solely responsible for the financial well-being of the family. In the extreme, he was taught not to express his emotions and that any sign of weakness, physical disability, or emotionality was unconscionable. Over the years, he experienced social changes, such as the women's movement, and witnessed many women sharing the financial responsibilities of a household. He also has been encouraged to express his emotions. In old age, he may have had to admit to physical limitations. These changes have led many men to question their identity and to alter their gender roles. Both men and women have had to question their changing gender roles throughout their life span (Gutmann, 1987). This questioning might be integrated into a new self or, conversely, might lead to role confusion and identity crises that are often expressed in therapy.

Gender is not divided into two categories, one for men and one for women. Rather, gender runs along a continuum, anchored by the prototypical female role on one end and the prototypical male role on the other. Although the average woman may differ from the average man, much overlap exists between both sexes in regards to social roles.

Physical Differences

Men and women differ with regard to basic physiological processes of aging. Some of these changes occur in both sexes, such as graying and thinning of hair and the decreasing weight of the vital organs. Many of these changes occur to a greater extent in one or the other sex, such as the thinning of the hair for men and loss in bone mass for women. One of the greatest gender differences involves chronic illness. Chronic illness is so prevalent in the older adult population that many therapists and physicians equate old age with illness. In fact, 80% of older adults suffer from at least one chronic condition (Ory, Abeles, & Lipman, 1992). Women suffer from a higher prevalence rate of chronic disease than men. Women living in the United States who are 75 years and older have two to three times the prevalence rate of spinal degeneration and deformity, colitis, anemia, migraines, bladder infection, and varicose veins compared to same-aged men; high blood pressure and stomach ulcers also are more likely in women over 75 than same-aged men (NCHS, 1994). Compared to men, older women also report more insomnia that cannot be explained by concurrent reports of mental or physical illness (Brabbins, Dewey, Copeland, Davidson, & McWilliam, 1993). The top five chronic illnesses for men aged over 65 years are, in order, hearing impairments, heart conditions, arthritis, hypertension, and chronic sinusitis. For women aged over 65, the top five chronic illnesses are arthritis, hypertension, hearing impairment, heart conditions, and orthopedic problems (NCHS, 1994). Men have higher rates of hearing impairments and heart conditions than women, but for every other chronic illness in the mentioned lists, including sinusitis, women have higher prevalence rates. Several less prevalent diseases (e.g., diabetes and hernias) are seen equally in older men and women, but the majority of chronic diseases in old age have a higher prevalence rate in women (NCHS, 1994).

Researchers have speculated about possible reasons for the higher rates of chronic diseases in women. One possibility is that there are no sex differences, and the problem stems in report bias, with men failing to either recognize or report physical symptoms (Herzog, 1989). Verbrugge (1990) suggests another possibility. She states that differences in prior social and personal histories have been responsible for the higher rates of disease in women than men, offering five psychosocial factors that may contribute to gender differences in chronic illness. These factors are (a) less paid employment, (b) higher emotional stress, (c) fewer time constraints, (d) less strenuous physical activity, and (e) a greater feeling of vulnerability to illness. In addition, poverty and educational differences often have been the focus for gender inequities in health. Older women are more likely to live in poverty, a factor that is linked to negative health outcomes for older adults (Shahtahmasebi, Davies, & Wenger, 1992). Besides past history and sociodemographic variables, differences in exercise between men and women may also contribute to higher rates of disease for women (Herzog, 1989). Exercise is beneficial for the older adult (see Bortz & Bortz, Chapter 2, this volume) and today's older men are more likely to have a history of exercising and a more positive attitude about it than today's older women. Older men report exercising more often than older women (Wingard, 1982). Furthermore, when older adults were asked to rate how appropriate exercise is for people their own age, they reported that all activities, except ballet, were more appropriate for men then women (Ostrow & Dzewaltowski, 1986).

Although women suffer from multiple chronic illnesses at a higher rate than same-aged males, men have a shorter life span. Thus, although women's lives are longer, they live more of their life with health problems—a questionable advantage for women. The gender difference in mortality occurs along the entire life span, beginning at conception and continuing into old age. Various theories have proposed explanations for the higher survival rates of women. These theories include the XX chromosome formation being stronger than the XY formation, sex hormones managing cholesterol, differences in immune system functioning, differences in vulnerability to environmental hazards, and health practices (Smith, 1990, 1992). Solomon (1981) posits that gender roles affect the mortality rates of men. He states that the male gender role—expecting men to fit the stereotype that includes the ideal man as one who is "the big wheel" and takes "no sissy stuff"—does not prepare men for the stresses of old age, which can include retirement, loss of a spouse, and illness. As a result, men have higher rates of homicide, suicide, accidents, and terminal illness compared to same-aged women throughout the life span. Solomon (1981) further writes that a more androgynous society may eliminate sex differences in life expectancy. This explanation does not fully explain the greater gender differences in longevity for other ethnicities. In the United States, Hispanic and African American males have a shorter life span than Caucasian males. These minorities also have a wider gender mortality gap, thus creating a greater disproportion of women over men in these minority groups. This gap exists throughout their life spans but widens in old age. The gender gap differs in other countries, ranging from 3 years in Kuwait to 9.1 years in Russia, but it always favors women (World Health Organization, 1988). For additional information about physical changes with age, see Whitbourne (Chapter 1).

Sexuality and Intimacy

Our society often views older adults as asexual, disinterested in sex, or incapable of sexual intimacy (Leiblum & Segraves, 1989); this perception is particularly vivid for older women. Although the rates of sexual activity for both women and men drop with age and certain normal physiological changes become noticeable in later years (see Whitbourne, Chapter 1), older adults do remain sexually active (Renshaw, 1988). Moreover, frequency of sexual activity alone does not explain adequately the importance of older adults' sexuality, intimacy, and sensuality (Starr, 1985; Weg, 1991).

SEXUALITY IN OLDER WOMEN

Menopause is often seen as a marker of aging because it entails obvious physical changes. Levels of sex hormones—progesterone and estrogen—are reduced after menopause (Cutler, Garcia, & McCoy, 1987). Decreased levels of estrogen are the primary reason for physiological changes in women's sexual functioning (described in Whitbourne, Chapter 1). Older women have several options that may help them to accommodate these changes, including hormone replacement therapy (HRT). This treatment is controversial, as endometrial cancer risk increases with continued use of unopposed estrogen, and data concerning estrogen with progesterone are conflicting (Grady, Gebretsadik, Kerlikowske, Ernster, & Petitti, 1995). In addition, HRT can accelerate the growth of estrogen-dependent cancer in women with this disease. However, many researchers are convinced that HRT has advantages that outweigh its potential costs. HRT counters many of the changes that interfere with sexual functioning, such as vaginal dryness. In addition, HRT has been found to be a protective factor for other physical conditions, such as coronary heart disease and bone fractures (Cauley et al., 1995; Stampfer & Colditz, 1991). Women interested in this treatment should see a physician specializing in menopause and HRT to discuss their treatment options (Goldman & Tosteson, 1991). For women where HRT is not recommended, lubricants and moisturizers can compensate for the decrease in vaginal lubrication commonly experienced after menopause (Notelowitz, 1990).

Researchers have found several behavioral and psychological factors that influence women's sexuality. Women who remain more sexually active through intercourse or masturbation experience milder vaginal changes overall (Leiblum & Bachman, 1987). Additional behavioral factors that influence a woman's sexual functioning include nutrition, exercise, and substance abuse (Leiblum & Bachman, 1987). Besides behavioral factors, psychological issues also affect sexual functioning in older women. Society generally holds a negative view of older women's sexuality, and as a result, older women may feel uncomfortable expressing their sexuality. The disproportionate number of women compared to men over the age of 65 further complicates the situation. Most men 75 years and older are married, whereas over half of same-aged women are divorced, widowed, or single (U.S. Bureau of the Census, 1992b), creating a shortage of male partners for heterosexual women.

Older women often are hesitant to discuss their sexual concerns, and when they do bring up these issues, therapists have fewer well-studied treatment options to offer their women clients as compared to their older male clients or to younger women (Crose & Drake, 1993). Alternatives to traditional sexual intercourse include masturbation, use of lotions and perfumes, bubble baths, and formation of new, interesting romantic or platonic relationships (Butler & Lewis, 1993; Crose & Drake, 1993). Whatever the issue, it is important to ask about sexual history and interests. Intimacy, sensuality, and sexuality come in many forms for older women (Weg, 1991).

SEXUALITY IN OLDER MEN

The changes in men's sexual response cycle involve modifications of intensity and duration of erectile response (see Whitbourne, Chapter 1). Many of the most common physical disorders among older men stem from problems involving the prostate gland, including benign and prostatic hypertrophy and malignant tumors. Older men may be affected psychologically by society's reaction to their sexuality as well as by their own reactions to physical changes. Although men may be less stigmatized for their sexuality in old age compared to women, men may have some strong psychological reactions to their physiological changes. Failure to achieve an erection often creates anxiety for men. Men also suffer from many of the same psychological factors affecting women, including history of sexual abuse and performance anxiety (Thienhaus, 1988). Many men may need to explore the meaning of sexuality and intimacy in their later years.

Older men and couples that include men should be informed that changes in sexual functioning are normal and not a sign of impotence or a reason to become anxious and cease sexual activity. A man's changes in erectile functioning may require different sexual techniques to achieve mutual orgasm (including additional stimulation). These changes often make men more dependent on their partners for physical and emotional support, possibly heightening intimacy. When a man and his partner understand these functional changes, the new patterns in his response cycle can have little or no effect on his enjoyment of sexual expression (LoPiccolo, 1991).

SEXUAL ISSUES AFFECTING
BOTH OLDER MEN AND WOMEN

A number of diseases and surgical procedures can cause side effects that interfere with sexual performance and sensual experience for both men and women. For example, diabetes and vascular disease are the leading organic causes of impotence in men (Butler, 1989). It is suggested that no male patient be referred to psychotherapy for sexual dysfunction unless he has had a medical workup, including a careful history taking, a test measuring hormone levels, and a sleep test monitoring nocturnal penile tumescence. A number of diseases and their respective medications are capable of producing erectile disorders, including prostatitis and blood pressure medications. There are also a number of diseases whose treatments can lower sexual interest and a sense of well-being in either sex (e.g., breast cancer, treated through radiation or chemotherapy; Leiblum & Seagraves, 1989). There is some controversy over the potential changes in women's sexual experience after hysterectomy, although it seems that women's experiences vary, with some experiencing losses in orgasmic ability (Cutler et al., 1987) and others experiencing no loss (Dennerstein & Burrows, 1982; Schover & Jensen, 1988).

Nursing homes also can present barriers to sexual expression and have been criticized for explicitly employing antisexual prejudice and practices in response to the sexual needs of the residents (Schmall & Pratt, 1989). For example, researchers have found that administrators resist programs focusing on sexuality (Starr & Weiner, 1981). Salamon and Charytan (1984) showed that a sexuality workshop series in the nursing home produced an improvement in the quality of life for both male and female residents. Workshop participants were more knowledgeable and better able to discuss their sexual needs. Crose and Drake (1993) suggest group discussions about sexuality for older women at care facilities, both in workshops and in ongoing groups.

To summarize, women and men's sexuality and intimate experiences change as they get older and each sex faces different issues associated with the process of aging. Whereas there has been a focus on physiological or anatomical sex differences, there are also psychological differences to consider. Clinicians must recognize the interaction between the older clients' physical components of sexuality and their feelings of intimacy. Both men and women need information on how their bodies are changing and the implications for sexual functioning. Providing basic education about sexuality, intimacy, and sensuality for men and women can be some of the most important work completed in therapy (LoPiccolo, 1991).

Social Networks

Mental health professionals need to be aware of social networks when working in both family and individual therapy situations. Social relationships are integral to well-being for people of all ages (Carstensen, 1991). For older adults, social support is a significant predictor of health (Kiecolt-Glaser et al., 1985), psychological well-being (Antonucci & Jackson, 1987), and mortality (Berkman & Syme, 1979; Blazer, 1982b; Silverstein & Bengston, 1991).

Gender differences exist with regard to social contact for older adults, some of which reflect patterns existing throughout the life span (Carstensen, 1991). At very young ages, girls and boys show different patterns of social support; boys have many acquaintances whereas girls have fewer, but more intimate, friendships (Kraft & Vraa, 1975; Maccoby, 1988). This pattern continues into old age, with women experiencing a greater intimacy with their social contacts than men (Candy, Troll, & Levy, 1981). Indeed, older women report more confidants than men, although older men report more acquaintances (Vaux, 1985).

Although family ties are rated as important for both older men and women, gender differences exist regarding both the amounts of contact with and the acts of confiding in their children. Both men and women are equally likely to name their children as confidants, and this tendency increases with age for both sexes (Kendig, Coles, Pittelkow, & Wilson, 1988). However, women report more contact, stronger bonds, and more emotional exchanges with their children and grandchildren than do men (Connidis & Davies, 1992; Depner & Ingersoll-Dayton, 1988; Field, Minkler, Falk, & Leino, 1993; Thomas, 1986). The mother-daughter bond is the strongest relationship in the family network, although it is not invulnerable to family stresses, such as marriages and illness of the parent (Troll, 1987). Gender differences in the topics of conversations among family members also have been found. The grandfather-father-son relationship is characterized by conversations of influence, advice, and opinions concerning career and nonfamily topics. In the grandmother-mother-daughter line, communication focuses on advice on intrafamilial and other personal matters (Troll, 1987). Size of the family has an effect on gender differences; older men and women who are part of a large family network covering many generations look more similar than those in a smaller family network (Antonucci & Akiyama, 1991).

Siblings serve as important social contacts for older adults. Not surprisingly, both men and women who do not have children are closer to their siblings than those who do have children (Connidis & Davies, 1992). The quality of the sibling relationship, however, varies according to the gender of the sibling. Older men and women who have sisters report less depression and higher levels of well-being than those who have either no siblings or who have only brothers (Cicerelli, 1989).

Older heterosexual men and women differ in marital status and marital satisfaction. Most older men are married, whereas most older women are single or widowed. For men aged 75 years and older, 70% are married, 24% are widowed, and the remaining are either single (3%) or divorced (3%). For women aged 75 years and older, 26% are married, 65% are widowed, and the rest are either single (5%) or divorced (4%; United States Bureau of the Census, 1992b). Men report confiding in their wives more than wives report confiding in their husbands (Kendig et al., 1988). Furthermore, at all ages, men report higher levels of satisfaction in marriage than women (Skolnick, 1986). Besides reporting greater satisfaction, men also report fewer health problems compared to women. In marriages with low rates of self-reported satisfaction, both middle-aged (40 to 50 years old) and older-aged (60 to 70 years old) wives reported more psychological and physical health problems than their husbands (Levenson, Carstensen, & Gottman, 1993). The authors contend that part of the explanation for this gender difference in health could be tied to gender differences in physiological arousal. Levenson et al. (1994) found that husbands' negative affect in a laboratory interaction with their spouses was highly correlated with their physiological arousal, whereas the wives' physiological arousal was not connected to their ratings of negative affect. In addition, men tended to withdraw, whereas women continued to engage during conflictive spousal interactions (Gottman & Krokoff, 1989), and both middle-aged and older-aged women were more emotionally expressive than their husbands (Carstensen, Gottman, & Levenson, 1995). As a result, women may remain in a heightened state of arousal much longer than their husbands. Levenson et al. (1994) posit that over a long period of time, this sustained autonomic arousal may play a role in disease etiology, thus linking lower marital satisfaction with greater health problems for women.

Friends, in addition to family, serve as important social contacts for the older adult. Women have a greater number of confidants and feel a greater intimacy with friends than their same-aged male counterparts (Candy et al., 1981; Connidis & Davies, 1992; Depner & Ingersoll-Dayton, 1988; Vaux, 1985). Women also report more continuity of their friendships than do men (Roberto & Kimboko, 1989). For widowed women, ability to remain in contact with friends surpasses that of married women and men and widowed men (Roberto & Kimboko, 1989). In addition, older men generally have fewer same-sex friends than women, possibly because women have a longer life span than men (Field & Minkler, 1988).

Overall, relationships with family and friends are important for both older men and women. Gender differences are mixed regarding family relationships, however; across all relatives—spouses, offspring, siblings—men report enjoying the general family network more than women (Field et al., 1993). Yet when specific family relationships are identified, women report greater satisfaction in their relationships with their grandchildren and children than men (Connidis & Davies, 1992; Thomas, 1986). With respect to nonfamilial relationships, women report greater satisfaction with friends and a greater number of confidants (Connidis & Davies, 1992). Unfortunately, the greater amounts of social support women receive in their earlier years can have negative consequences in very old age. Social support decreases in very old age for both men and women, and women feel more isolated than men as a result of the diminishing social network (Depner & Ingersoll-Dayton, 1988; Miller & Ingham, 1976). The same pattern has been found to occur in African American populations as well as Caucasian ones, with women becoming more depressed when faced with decreases in social contacts with friends and relatives in very old age compared to same-aged men (Husaini, Moore, Castor, Neser, Whitten-Stovall, 1991).

Older Lesbians and Gay Men

A number of authors have discussed older gays and lesbians in the context of diversity of the aged; however, older gays and lesbians are often placed together as one group, and the differences between these two populations are often overlooked. As a result, mental health professionals working with older adults know relatively little about either population (Rothblum, 1994). This oversight may stem partly from the fact that older gays and lesbians do share some similarities. This section begins by addressing the similarities as well as the differences between gays and lesbians. Next, we consider differences between heterosexuals and homosexuals and then explore stereotypes, myths, and issues unique to gay men and lesbians. Last, we offer guidance to therapists and clinicians working with these populations.

SIMILARITIES AND DIFFERENCES
BETWEEN GAYS AND LESBIANS

Both gay men and lesbians have received only recently some moderate protection and rights as citizens; however, there is still no legal, and very little social recognition of or support for gay and lesbian relationships (Hunter, Michaelson, & Stoddard, 1992). Prejudices are also apparent in the scarcity of institutional policies, the neglect by social service agencies, and the lack of appropriate attention by the medical community (Berger, 1982). As a result, both gays and lesbians have developed family structures distinct from those of heterosexuals (Garnets & Kimmel, 1993). Despite this similarity, differences between gays and lesbians exist, most notably because they represent two distinct subcultures (Kline, 1991). Kehoe (1989) found that 42% of her sample of 100 older lesbians had previously been in a heterosexual union; Berger's (1982) sample of 112 gay men revealed that 29% of the men had been in a heterosexual marriage. This gender difference could be explained in part by the stronger social and economic pressures on women to marry. In current friendships, one study found that over half the older lesbians reported that most of their closest friends were lesbians, whereas 27% of the older gay men reported that their closest friends were gay men (Quam & Whitford, 1992). Sixty-five percent of the gay men and only 38.5% of the lesbians described their network of close friends as a mixture of homosexual and heterosexual men and women. Another difference between gay men and lesbians stems from the AIDS epidemic, which has killed a vast number of gay men, but a much smaller percentage of lesbians. Thus, the disease has had differing effects on gay men's and women's relationships and culture.

COMPARISON BETWEEN
HETEROSEXUALS AND HOMOSEXUALS

Research literature tends to characterize "older adults" as individuals 65 years and older, but homosexuals over 50 years old tend to be characterized as "older" in studies of aging gays and lesbians. Another difference is that, unlike heterosexual relationships, in homosexual unions, the sex difference in longevity is not an issue. Furthermore, because older gay men and lesbians may have previously been in heterosexual marriages, comparisons between same-sex and opposite-sex couples may be blurred by inaccurate divisions between the groups. Some homosexuals spend their entire lives in heterosexual unions and are almost entirely invisible to researchers (Berger & Kelly, 1986).

STIGMA, STEREOTYPES, AND
HOW GAY MEN AND LESBIANS COPE

Gay men and lesbians suffer from similar stigmas and stereotypes resulting from homophobia and heterosexism that are exacerbated with age. For example, nursing home staff members are even less likely to feel comfortable allowing sexual intimacy or partnerships with gay and lesbian residents than with heterosexual couples. This policy is particularly unfortunate because 62% of gay men and lesbians would be interested in living in gay or lesbian retirement communities (Quam & Whitford, 1992).

Negative stereotypes about homosexuals' views of aging also exist, with gay men being targeted as people who are obsessed with youth (Berger, 1992). Research has found gay men to be more preoccupied with aging than heterosexual men; however, both groups have a negative outlook on aging (Goldfarb, 1985). It is suggested that greater social support and self-acceptance may help to ease the concerns gay men have about aging (Friend, 1987; Goldfarb, 1985). In contrast, lesbians tend to adapt well to aging with positive attitudes and self-images (Kehoe, 1986; Raphael & Robinson, 1980; Tully 1983).

Despite the difficulties that many older gays and lesbians face in this society compared to heterosexuals, researchers have found that these difficulties have fostered coping skills that may be beneficial in old age. In a study of older gay men, all participants felt "they had travelled a long and tortuous road toward self-acceptance" (Berger, 1982, p. 187). In another survey, both gays and lesbians reported that being homosexual had helped in the aging process (Quam and Whitford, 1992). Older gay men and lesbians often have a sense of competence from early life crises surrounding the coming out process, either coming out to themselves or to others. They also display greater gender flexibility compared to heterosexuals and have relatively strong friendship networks (Friend, 1987).

CLINICAL ISSUES

When working with older gay and lesbian clients, clinicians must challenge myths and misconceptions held by themselves and their clients with accurate information. Suggesting gay-affirming literature (Friend, 1987) and directed bibliotherapy can be useful tools for educating clients. In addition, therapists should be open to understanding their own reactions to gays and lesbians (Greene, 1994). Clinicians working with this population should be familiar with many issues specific to the homosexual population that may arise in therapy. These issues include attitudes about homosexuality, the effects of stigmatization, gay lifestyles and the process of coming out, and the meaning of a lesbian identity as compared to a gay male identity. In addition, legal issues often arise in therapy, such as property ownership, insurance, and employment. Legal issues can be especially important to know about prior to working with a client because these issues often arise in times of crisis and can compound a grieving period. For example, a surviving partner may not have been included in the discussions about health care decisions and can be barred from any involvement in funeral arrangements and disposition of property, leading to considerable psychological distress.

Mental health providers also should be aware of community services that are offered specifically to gay and lesbian clientele. There are also a growing number of service providers targeting only lesbians or only gay men, due to the difference in those communities' needs. For example, SAGE, Senior Action in a Gay Environment, in New York City offers services to over 3,500 gay men and women and has two programs that are at the heart of a wide range of services: the Assessors program and the Friendly Visitors program. The Assessors program is composed of mental health professionals who make referrals and offer case management to older gays and lesbians. The Friendly Visitors program provides regular visitations to older lesbians and gay men who may be homebound or need some assistance (Gwenwald, 1984). In summary, clinicians must acknowledge that gays and lesbians have issues that are distinct from each other and from the heterosexual majority.

Caregiving

The role of caregiver for older family members is predominantly filled by women (see Thompson & Gallagher-Thompson, Chapter 6). Women tend to marry older men, and women have longer life expectancies. As a result, husbands are more likely to need care earlier in the relationship than wives, resulting in greater involvement by elderly wives in caregiving compared to elderly husbands (Reiss & Lee, 1988). In caregiving for an elderly parent, gender disparity is even more pronounced; a greater number of daughters than sons are involved in caring for infirm parents (Dwyer & Coward, 1992). One reason for the greater number of daughters is that adult children are more likely to care for a parent of the same gender (Lee, Dwyer, & Coward, 1993). This gender consistency partially explains the greater amounts of women caregivers than men because most people who require caregiving outside of marriage are older widowed mothers.

At the same time, cultural and socialization factors have also been suggested. Lee (1992) discusses the parallels between women's roles in their families and as caregivers insofar as both are domestic labor that involve nurturance and kinship behavior. Similarly, Abel (1991) and Walker (1992) suggest that gender differences in numbers of caregivers can be explained by the fact that nurturance is a more central aspect of women's self-concept than that of men's; thus, women should be expected to express stronger feelings of obligation.

TYPES OF SUPPORT

Types of assistance provided by caregivers vary depending on the gender of the adult children performing the caregiving. Daughters visit and telephone their parents more often than sons (Spitze & Logan, 1989). Men provide intermittent assistance with occasional tasks and less frequently undertake routine household chores as compared to women (Stoller, 1990). Sons are also more likely to rely on the assistance of their own spouses and provide less overall direct help to their own parents. A further factor that may lead to underestimating the involvement of men in caregiving is that the types of help provided by women are more readily classified as caregiving, whereas assistance by men falls into more ambiguous categories that are harder to recognize, such as handling paperwork. Moreover, there appears to be a shift toward greater involvement by female caregivers as older adults' functional capacity decreases over time (Stoller, 1990).

CAREGIVING STRESSORS
AND CAREGIVER BURDEN

Gender differences in caregiving stressors and caregiver burden also have been examined (see review by Thompson & Gallagher-Thompson, Chapter 6). A meta-analysis of 14 descriptive studies found that women caregivers were more likely to report greater caregiver burden than men (Miller & Cafasso, 1992), whereas there were no significant differences based on functional impairment of the frail care recipient, total intensity of caregiver involvement in care, or involvement in money management tasks. The sexes provide different types of support and experience different levels of caregiving stress and burden. As a result, different issues may emerge and may need to be addressed in working with women and men caregivers.

Bereavement

Women are more likely to experience the loss of a spouse than men. Two related factors account for this occurrence: Women generally marry men who are 5 to 7 years older than themselves (Watkins, Menken, & Bongaarts, 1987), and women have a greater longevity, with an estimated life expectancy of about 7 years longer than men, regardless of ethnicity (World Health Organization, 1988). The life expectancy differential between the sexes has not changed despite the fact that longevity has increased for both men and women during this century. This increase in longevity, however, has affected the population of both men and women who have lost a spouse; today, widows and widowers are generally older than were bereaved individuals in the past.

Whether the loss of a spouse affects men more or whether the event is equally stressful for both sexes is still a debatable topic. Early literature suggested that men had a higher mortality rate immediately after the death of a spouse than women (Gerber, Rusalem, Hannon, Battin, & Arkin, 1975). These men all suffered from chronic illness, and one plausible explanation for their higher death rate is that women were instrumental in preparing nutritious meals and ensuring that medicine was taken properly. Other research also suggests excess mortality for widowers compared to widows (Mellstrom, Nilsson, Oden, Rundgren, & Svanborg, 1982). Another, more recent, study found that widowed men reported more depression than women (Umberson,

Wortman, & Kessler, 1992). However, the researchers caution that men in this study were bereaved for a shorter period of time compared to women, a common artifact in research using bereaved samples (Umberson et al., 1992). Another study examined stressors that individuals face after the loss of a spouse and found that men, in comparison to women, more often experienced additional unrelated stressors that could increase their vulnerability, such as the loss of another family member (Blieszner, 1993).

Nevertheless, similarities outnumber differences between the sexes (Gallagher, Breckinridge, Thompson, & Peterson, 1983; Lund, Caserta, & Dimond, 1986). Lund et al. (1986) followed recently bereaved men and women, aged 50 to 93 years, from an average of 3 weeks to 2 years after the loss of their spouses. At all time periods, men and women looked similar on variables such as emotional shock, coping, depression, and life satisfaction. A more recent study, in contrast, found that women reported more depression but that men and women expressed grief similarly (Thompson, Gallagher-Thompson, Futterman, Gilewski, & Peterson, 1991). Another similarity in the experience of the bereaved pertains to self-reported interest in mental health services; 38% of men reported that they were interested in support groups, which was almost the same as the proportion of women who showed interest (Lund et al., 1986).

Gender differences exist regarding the impact of bereavement; however, these differences do not signal that bereavement is the same experience for both men and women, differing only in severity of emotional distress. Specific stressors differ for each gender (Blieszner, 1993; Umberson et al., 1992) For women, especially minorities, financial stressors are more pronounced, as their spouses' pensions may have no survivor benefits and social security benefits can decrease when their spouse dies (Blieszner, 1993). Because women have historically earned less than men and have less consistent work histories both from changing jobs and absence from work during child rearing, their retirement incomes are smaller (or absent) compared to those of men, which makes finances a major strain. In the area of household chores, bereaved men and women both report difficulty in learning the responsibilities that had once been completed by their spouses. Consistent with traditional responsibilities, the chores women report having to learn include settling bills and household repairs. Many men have to take up cooking and cleaning for the first time (Blieszner, 1993; Umberson et al., 1992).

Economic Status

Medicare, social security, and government employees' retirement plans have helped many older adults from falling under the poverty line in the past several decades. Unfortunately, older adults represent a heterogeneous group, and public policy benefits are spread unequally between men and women (Quadagno & Meyer, 1993). Women compose 63% of the elderly population and 73% of the elderly poor (Commonwealth Fund Commission, 1987). Twenty-five percent of older Caucasian women, unmarried and married, are poor, and over half of both the African American and Hispanic female populations fall below the poverty level. In fact, Dressel (1988) argues that examining poverty only along gender lines hides the huge discrepancy between ethnicities. Unmarried African American men more often fall below the poverty line (64%) than unmarried Caucasian women (49%; Dressel, 1988). Examining minority populations reveals that the situation is much worse for men and women alike, with minority widows suffering the most.

Lifetime patterns of economic disparity between men and women provide the basis for differences in lifestyles in old age (Holden, 1989). Working women of all ages have generally earned less compared to men, with women earning on average 31% less than men throughout their lifetime (Grambs, 1989). Their jobs are often of lower status, often pay less when the work is equal, and often do not include pensions. This pattern of lower wages and status does not appear to be changing. Although more women are entering the workforce, they still earn less than men, and women at and below the poverty level are still predicted to outnumber men in the future (Carstensen & Pasupathi, 1993). In addition, a woman's retirement is more contingent on external events, such as a spouse's illness or a spouse's retirement, than is an older man's retirement decision; this difference results in a decrease in pension benefits and lower social security benefits for women compared to men (Szinovacz & Washo, 1992).

Women who spend most of their adult lives raising children and caregiving for older relatives do not benefit from pension plans or social security of their own. They also are more likely than men to care for their ill spouse, a task that requires not only energy and time but frequently the depletion of life savings. When spouses die, husbands' pensions do not always include survivor's benefits, and the social security that the widows receive based on their own earning history is much less than they had received when their husbands were living (Davis, Grant, & Rowland, 1992). Women are also more likely to live alone than men, which increases living expenses: 42% of older women compared to 16% of older men (U.S. Bureau of the Census, 1992b). Despite the fact that social security benefits are generally lower for women than men, they more often serve as the sole income for women than for men.

Lower income levels affect older adults in several ways. People living in poverty often cannot afford proper medical care and are less likely to seek care as a result. The poor have greater rates of mortality and morbidity than people who live above the poverty level. In addition, poverty exacerbates problems for those who live alone. They cannot afford activities that foster companionship, housecleaning services, and taxi services that are available to more financially secure individuals.

Therapy Issues

EPIDEMIOLOGY OF MENTAL
DISORDERS IN OLDER ADULTS

Older adults have a lower prevalence rate than younger adults for mental disorders other than organic mental disorders such as dementia. Researchers examined age differences in 1-month prevalence rates of disorders using the diagnostic interview schedule from the Epidemiological Catchment Area Survey based on five catchment area sites (Regier et al., 1988). They found that rates of functional psychiatric disorder were 15.4% for people aged from 18 to 24 years and 17.3% for people aged 18 to 24, compared to 13.3% for people aged 45 to 64 and 12.3% for those aged 65 and older (Regier et al., 1988). Among younger adults, sex differences are evident for several disorders. For example, four to five times as many younger men than women are diagnosed with antisocial personality disorder and drug dependence, whereas women are more likely to suffer from depression and anxiety (Anthony & Aboraya, 1992; Regier et al., 1988). The disorders that are defined heavily by biological processes, such as schizophrenia and severe mental retardation, have few prominent sex differences (Myers et al., 1984)

For older cohorts, differences between men and women in overall rates of mental disorders tend to disappear (Blazer et al., 1985; Myers et al., 1984). Men have higher prevalence rates of alcoholism in old age than older women, however, and are more likely to die from cirrhosis. Although women report more affective and anxiety disorders at younger ages than men, this sex discrepancy disappears between older men and women. Researchers speculate that this decrease stems from lower levels of depression in older women than in younger women (Travis, 1988). Because diagnostic criteria are largely unnormed for older populations (George, 1992), however, the picture of the prevalence rate and gender breakdown for the disorders remains equivocal. For cognitive impairment from disorders such as strokes and dementia, prevalence rates are roughly the same for older women and men, although more older women are affected due to their longer life span and because they live longer with this disease compared to men (Anthony & Aboraya, 1992; Bachman et al., 1993).

One indicator of psychological distress that increases with age is suicide, with rates highest among the oldest old—people aged over 85 years. The rate of suicide in the United States is 12.4 for every 100,000 people in the population, including older adults. For adults 65 and older, the rates are 21.4 for every 100,000 older adults. Of the 83 suicides per day, 17 are committed by older adults (McIntosh, 1992). Even these relatively high numbers may represent an underestimate due to reporting problems, especially among women who tend to use more passive methods, such as drug overdose (McIntosh, 1992). Both starvation and failure to take medicine occur in the older population, but it is unclear whether these causes of death are actual suicides. If these methods are suicidal acts, the rates of suicide may be much higher than are currently recorded (McIntosh, 1992). At all ages, reported numbers reveal that men commit suicide more often than women, and this difference increases with age. The rates of suicide for women of all ethnicities peak in middle age but remain fairly steady throughout old age. The incidence for Caucasian men increases linearly with age, thus increasing the gender gap. Non-Caucasian males have incidence rates that peak in young adulthood and decrease in old age. Their rates are still higher than non-Caucasian females at every age, however. Besides being male, risk factors include living alone, being depressed, living in a low-income area, and being divorced or widowed. Of course, the vast majority of people who meet this profile do not commit suicide.

   Both older men and women who suffer from psychological disturbances do not seek mental health treatment as often as younger adults (Burns & Taube, 1990). When older adults do seek treatment, both sexes seek help for psychological and psychiatric disorders most often from their primary care physician (Burns & Taube, 1990). The tendency to visit a general physician rather than a mental health professional is less pronounced among older men than older women (Shapiro et al., 1984). Compared to men, however, women are more likely to seek treatment for psychological disorders in general. Ironically, although older women compared to men will use their primary care physician more often than a mental health professional, researchers have found that women seek treatment more often than men because they are more likely to recognize depression and low general well-being as signs of emotional disturbances (Kessler, Brown, & Broman, 1981).

BIAS IN THE MENTAL HEALTH COMMUNITY

   Therapists working with older adults must be aware of not only the changing social roles for their older clients but also the gender bias within the mental health community. A now classic study by Broverman, Broverman, Clarkson, Rosenkrantz, and Vogel (1970) first pointed out that therapists perceive women as less healthy than men. In fact, the definition of mental health conforms to the qualities used to define middle-aged men, such as active, independent, self-confident, and decisive, and not to those stereotypically used to describe women, such as dependent and unassertive (Westbrook & Mitchel, 1979). In addition, several researchers have suggested that sex bias exists within the diagnostic criteria for psychological disorders such as antisocial personality disorder and borderline personality disorder (Ford & Widiger, 1989; Tavris, 1992). Bias is complex, leading to both overestimation and underestimation errors (Lopez, 1989). For instance, Rosenfield (1982) showed that disorders that run counter to the gender stereotype are regarded as more severe: Men who complained of neuroses and depression were more likely to be hospitalized than women who complained of the same problems. The belief that women were less mentally healthy presumably led to minimizing their disorder.

Besides sex bias, age bias and lack of knowledge enter into the diagnoses of older men and women. Both mental health professionals and older adults themselves may discount physical and emotional symptoms as being expected, age-related changes, thus underreporting symptoms and underdiagnosing the disorder (Knight, 1978-1979; Teri, 1982). In addition, health professionals may lack the knowledge to diagnose older adults accurately and often overestimate Alzheimer's disease as an explanation for the older adult's behavior (Gatz & Pearson, 1988). Sex bias, age bias, and lack of information can occur in every facet of the socialization process, affecting both individuals and entire social systems within a community. People and organizations within the mental health sector are not exceptions. This bias is damaging for both men and women and is often so subtle and pervasive that the health care professional may not realize that he or she plays a role in the perpetuation of these beliefs.

THERAPY WITH OLDER ADULTS

Psychotherapy for both older women and older men begins with a thorough understanding of the problem. For the therapist, an appreciation of life span developmental psychology may help in formulating a picture of the client. In addition, an appreciation of gender roles for both men and women is necessary to understand psychosocial change over the life span (Gutmann, 1976). Sinnott (1977) was one of the earliest researchers to discuss the possibility that older adults who have been able to synthesize different psychological, social, and cultural perspectives on role demands are considered to have aged more successfully. At the center of the ability to synthesize different perspectives is the adoption of an androgynous gender role—that is, an integration of both masculine and feminine traits (Sinnott, 1977). The masculine stereotype has been blamed for the greater mortality rates in men (Solomon, 1981), and the feminine stereotype, such as dependent and permissive, conforms to current definitions of mental illness (Westbrook & Mitchel, 1979). Androgyny represents flexibility in the older adult and an ability to adopt a variety of roles that life demands (Sinnott, 1977). Some researchers have come to believe that crossover or blurring of gender roles for people who have survived to old age is a naturally occurring phenomenon (Feinson, 1987; Rossi, 1986). Women discover their agentic qualities, and men recognize their nurturing abilities and interests (Rossi, 1986).

INTEGRATING FEMINIST PERSPECTIVES INTO THERAPY

In traditional psychotherapy, gender roles have often been ignored. There are a couple of contemporary approaches that do consider gender differences. For example, sex therapy obviously takes into account the different physiological processes and social needs of men and women. Another approach that takes gender differences into account is feminist therapy, which was specifically designed to accommodate the needs of women, although it can be used success-fully with men as well (Hare-Mustin & Marecek, 1990). In particular, old age for both men and women often is associated with loss of power and status. A cornerstone of feminist therapy is empowerment, and the basic assumption is that ideology, social structure, and behavior are inextricably interwoven. A feminist perspective can be used in conjunction with a variety of validated treatments (Chaplin, 1988), providing a framework for discussing topics relevant to aging, such as menopause, body image, physical frailty, age biases, and assertiveness (Watson & Williams, 1992). Feminist therapists work with older women, com-bining a supportive stance of the life choices women have made with a sensitivity to clients' feelings of possible anger and frustration regarding past social roles (Rush, 1985). Therapy incorporating a feminist perspective may offer women support to discuss problems they have been silent about all of their lives. In short, taking gender issues and sociopolitical context into account may be particularly helpful to older women clients.

Conclusion

Both men and women experience changes in many aspects of their lives as they age. These changes include losses as well as gains. Aging individuals experience a decline in physical functioning, from bone loss to the experience of chronic illness. With increasing age, older adults often experience the death of friends and spouses. With greater longevity in the population, older adults must face the responsibility of caregiving for parents, spouses, and other family members. At the same time that they experience these losses, they also benefit from life experiences that appear to strengthen their coping abilities. For example, many older adults have found great intimacy in lifelong friends and companions, have a greater self-knowledge, and can look back on life achievements.

Some have called aging "The Great Equalizer," for unless people die, they must all face old age, regardless of economic, gender, or other differences. However, this chapter has highlighted gender and sex differences that often make aging a qualitatively different experience for men and women. People experience losses with age, but these losses are not the same nor do older adults experience them equally, as often, or as intensely, depending on the issue and whether the older person is male or female. By virtue of longer lives, women are more likely to face age-related disadvantages than men. They often carry additional burdens of caregiving, chronic diseases, widowhood, and poverty. Men, compared to women, face fewer disadvantages in other areas. Men may lack the close friendship ties women enjoy. In addition, they often experience more severe sexual changes as compared to women.

The greater disadvantage experienced by the current group of older women is not a unique experience of old age. Historically, these women lived during a period where gender inequities were widely accepted and practiced. Older men and women were socialized to fulfill specific gender roles throughout their life span. In a changing world, differences between men and women may vary for future generations. Gender and sex differences are likely to exist always, but social, political, and medical advances will continually shape the nature of these differences.

Summary

Although older men and older women may be similar on a variety of factors, this chapter focused on both gender and sex differences between elderly men and women. We began by defining biologically based sex distinctions and socially constructed gender roles as bases for differences between men and women. Later sections reviewed gender differences for older adults in biological, psychosocial, and economic realms. First, biological differences were addressed, regarding both physical health and sexuality. Second, gender differences in psychosocial issues were examined, including social networks, caregiving, and bereavement. Within the psychosocial topics, we included a section on older gay men and lesbians, two populations that are often ignored in discussions of older adults. We then considered the economic status of men and women and how it differs in this society. Finally, we highlighted therapy issues for both older men and women, including age and sex bias in the mental health sector, the epidemiology of psychological disorders among men and women, and interventions that take gender roles into account.

6

Practical Issues Related to Maintenance of Mental Health and Positive Well-Being in Family Caregivers

Larry W. Thompson
Dolores Gallagher-Thompson

Marie is a 67-year-old slightly obese but otherwise reasonably healthy woman with a high school education who has been caring for her father-in-law over the past 6 years and her husband, the past 2 years. Her father-in-law was diagnosed as having Alzheimer's disease at age 79 years and soon thereafter was moved to Marie's home that he might receive closer care and supervision. Three years later, her husband, at age 63, suffered a stroke resulting in left-sided weakness, which required that he retire from his work. He became increasingly depressed over the next 6 months but was still able to perform

AUTHORS' NOTE: This work was supported in part by grants #AGO-4572 from the National Institute on Aging and grants #MH-37196 and #MH-47407 from the National Institute of Mental Health.

most instrumental activities of daily living and needed little of Marie's attention. However, within the same year, he suffered multiple strokes resulting in hemiparesis and substantial cognitive impairment. His condition has been stable over the past 2 years, but he now requires considerable care and supervision. Marie has two adult children, one of whom lives in the area and the other in a neighboring city 2 hours away by car. Neither provide assistance to their mother in the caregiving tasks, but this is more by Marie's choice than their reluctance to do so. Marie doesn't want to bother them. She affirms emphatically every time the issue is raised by a health care professional, "They have their own lives to live and their own families to look after!"

The burden of caregiving for Marie is immense, and at times she becomes so overwhelmed with duties and responsibilities that she just wants "to shut the door and run away, and never come back." She knows that wouldn't solve anything, however, and that if she "just keeps plugging away, taking one thing at a time, somehow or another, things will get done and she'll get through this." Many nights she is so sad about her husband's condition and her own plight for the future, she cries herself to sleep. But then the sleep is fitful, because the interruptions for care are numerous and must be handled. This leaves her exhausted most of the time but determined to do the very best she can for her husband and her father-in-law. "They would do the same for me," she claims. When the possibility of placement is discussed with her, she becomes very distressed.

> After all they've done for me, I couldn't think of putting either one of them away. That would be horrible! As long as I'm able, I'm going to do it, and that's the way it's going to be. You know, being a caregiver has its good points. It's just part of life. Everybody has to do it. You just have to make the best of it.

Like so many other caregivers, Marie actively searches the community for resources to aid her with her burdensome tasks. She attends support groups. She has sought out financial aid and other formal supports, such as day care, brief in-home respite, assistance with heavy housecleaning, legal advice on power of attorney and conservator issues, and so forth. She also has remained active in a number of organizations that are trying to change public policy and implement new assistance programs for family caregivers. Marie is particularly concerned about maintaining her own health and support systems so that she can continue in the role of caregiver as long as necessary.

Marie came to our attention when she responded to an announcement for our anger management classes. She was very concerned about her irritability with her husband and her father-in-law. She felt guilty that she got angry and knew that this impaired her effectiveness. It was just at such times that she would lose hope and begin to feel that she couldn't go on. She also had read that the anger she sometimes felt might be detrimental to her physical health, and she might become too ill to carry out her responsibilities. She found our course useful because it helped her recognize when she was becoming angry and that she could do something to minimize its effect. She reported the most helpful thing was the understanding that in many situations evoking anger, she actually believed it was her fault and therefore, her responsibility to prevent them. Developing an appreciation that this was not true most of the time seemed to aid her in constructive problem solving.

Marie's situation highlights a number of important issues and questions for the clinician and researcher interested in caregivers and their problems. For example, the amount of work and complexity of the day-to-day life problems appear horrendous to many who are not confronted with this challenge. Is this the perception of actual caregivers? If so, does the sustained stress of caregiving result in high levels of psychopathology? What is the likelihood that caregivers might develop increased physical disorders as well? How are people in Marie's predicament able to cope and maintain suitable functioning given the sustained nature of their distress and burden? What role do attitudes and belief systems play? How do past characteristic strategies for coping help the caregiver? Does the community provide important support resources that ensure their successful coping? Should there be special treatments developed for caregivers? What treatment programs have been developed with the caregiver in mind? Can these available interventions increase caregivers' abilities to function? Can they reduce the caregivers' symptoms? What should interested professionals be doing to develop improved programs and provide better services? Although this manuscript does not answer all of these questions, a cursory analysis of the relevant literature, along with impressions culled from our own clinical and research experience address some of them from a practical perspective. Many await research investigation. We hope that our presentation here will interest others in developing even more definitive solutions for the problems of the family caregiver.

Who Are the Family Caregivers?

The person most likely to become a primary caregiver for a disabled family member is the husband, wife, or daughter of the care recipient (Stone, Cafferata, & Sangl, 1987). Other relatives, such as daughter-in-laws, may become involved either as secondary caregivers or when a spouse or adult daughter is not available. According to data obtained in a 1984 National Long-Term Care Survey, of the 4.2 million active caregivers in the United States at that time, 1.6 million were spouses. Furthermore, it was the spouse group that was far more likely to be primary caregivers. Future projections indicate that spouses will become even more prominent as caregivers, because elders in general are expected to live longer. This increases the possibility that more men will function in the role of spouse caregivers than is currently the case. However, because many of the couples will themselves be quite old and frail, it is also possible that they will both be impaired and unable to provide extensive assistance to each other without regular help from either their adult children or from a formal health care system.

At the present time, the health care system depends heavily on the informal family network for care of the frail elder in the home setting and less on institutional support or other health care systems. The majority of this burden falls in the hands of women, but this pattern may change in future years, particularly for daughters. It is also the case that more and more women are becoming single heads of households. Given this trend of increasing employment combined with increasing household responsibility, the middle-aged daughter as primary caregiver may be far less common in the year 2020 than is true today. If this trend holds, then other resources will have to be diverted to accommodate the increasing needs formerly met by this informal means.

HOW DO CAREGIVERS EXPERIENCE
THE ROLE OF CAREGIVING?

A great deal has been written over the past 15 years about the stress and burden commonly reported by informal family caregivers. Zarit coined the term *burden* to describe the subjective experience of distress that caregivers reported. Over time, the definition of this construct has evolved to become far more multidimensional, with an awareness that burden may be social, emotional, financial, psychological, or physiological (Given et al., 1992). In other words, the responsibility of providing extensive day-to-day care for a disabled family relative has an effect on many aspects of the individual's life, not simply their intrapsychic experience.

At the same time, however, it has become increasingly recognized that caregivers maintain their role partly for the benefits that they derive from it (Genevay, 1994). Thus, the extent to which caregiving is a stressor versus a positive experience lies in how the caregiving role is defined. For some, caregiving means a series of tasks (including the provision of care such as help with feeding, dressing, bathing, and toileting) that require considerable time, energy, and emotional investment. For others, caregiving refers to a less extensive range of helping behaviors (such as assistance with balancing the checkbook, transportation, and food shopping and preparation). For still others, caregiving is primarily an emotional experience that involves their giving back to the parent or spouse in gratitude for the life that they have lived together. Finally, for some, caregiving can be a combination of all of these.

In an effort to bring some clarity to the diverse publications on this topic, researchers have developed several models to describe relationships among so-called objective and subjective burden and various psychological resources, such as the caregiver's degree of self-esteem, ability to use active cognitive and behavioral coping strategies, and the presence of an adequate social support network. *Objective burden* in this case refers to the actual amount of care required by the care receiver, and *subjective burden* refers to how stressful the tasks of caregiving are perceived. In general, these models have been derivations of the basic stress and coping model of Lazarus and Folkman (1984) in which an individual's reaction to a stressful event is thought to be mitigated by the appraisal of the extent of threat associated with the event as well as the ability to cope with the event itself. Pearlin and colleagues (Pearlin, Mullan, Semple, & Skaff, 1990), for example, have emphasized that secondary strains, such as conflicts with other family members, and intrapsychic strains, such as low self-esteem, can affect outcome through their effects on the caregiver's coping strength and support network. Similarly, Vitaliano and colleagues (Vitaliano, Maiuro, Ochs, & Russo, 1989) developed a model in which distress was regarded as the outcome of the relationship between the objective stressor and the psychological, social, and emotional resources of the caregiver. Such models have been helpful in accounting for the far-reaching and varied effects of caregiving and in providing useful frameworks for continued research.

The relationship of the caregiver to the care receiver is an important aspect of how the caregiving process is experienced. A caregiver who has had a long-term negative relationship with the care recipient is likely to experience the process more negatively than one who has had a positive relationship with the care recipient. Similarly, children are likely to experience caregiving more negatively than are spouses. Conflicts often occur between caring for a parent and other responsibilities, such as child care and employment, which has led to the designation of the *sandwich generation* for middle-aged women (Brody, 1981). Gender may also affect the caregiver experience. For example, husbands tend to report less emotional distress than wives (Anthony-Bergstone, Zarit, & Gatz, 1988; Barusch & Spaid, 1989), and sons report lower rates of distress than daughters (Brody, Hoffman, Kleban, & Schoonover, 1989; Horowitz, 1985). However, this trend may be influenced by the fact that females are more likely to report negative emotions than are males (Nolen-Hoeksema, 1987).

However one may choose to define caregiving, the demands made on caregivers fluctuate with the course of the care recipients' condition, thus requiring them to adapt to continually changing responsibilities. As this process unfolds over time, others in the family often begin to perform different caregiving activities, and the primary caregiver may come to view the role quite differently after being in it for 10 years versus at the outset. Caregivers who continue in this role over an extended period of time, say a decade or more, may be more committed, hardier, better at coping, or different in any number of ways that might significantly affect the physical and emotional distress that they experience, when compared to those who end their caregiving careers in a briefer interval (Montgomery & Kosloski, 1994). Perhaps these long-term caregivers experience less burden because they develop a perspective on caregiving over time that enables them to view their tasks as somewhat easier, less offensive, and more rewarding than in the early days of assuming that role. Viewing caregiving as a long-term process, with a highly fluctuating course, can be a helpful perspective for the development of interventions.

WHAT IS THE EVIDENCE FOR
CLINICAL DISORDERS IN CAREGIVERS

There can be little doubt about the negative effect of caregiving on primary caregivers, regardless of the type of disability experienced by the care receiver (Schulz, Visintainer, & Williamson, 1990). A substantial number of caregivers report significant symptoms associated with psychopathology, which is described later. On the other hand, the literature supporting the negative effects of caregiving on physical health of the caregivers has been less convincing (Schulz et al., 1990) because the majority of the studies have relied on self-report measures of health rather than objective evidence. We examined the physical health status of 102 women, aged 50 to 80 years, who were caring for a parent or a spouse with dementia (Koin et al., 1994) and a subsample of 38 caregivers with a sample of matched controls (Gallagher-Thompson et al., 1994). In agreement with Schulz et al. (1990), caregivers rated both their psychological and physical health negatively, but physical examination and laboratory studies, including a 12-lead electrocardiogram, revealed them to be in relatively good health when compared to normal population values for their ages. Calculation of cardiovascular and stroke risk, using the multivariate risk equations from the longitudinal Framingham Heart Study (American Heart Association, 1990; Anderson, Wilson, Odell, & Kannel, 1991; Wolf, D'Agostino, Belanger, & Kannel, 1991) also showed no differences between the subsample of caregivers and their matched controls. Furthermore, there were no differences between the two groups in use of nonpsychotropic medications, but caregivers were much more likely to report the use of psychotropic medications than control participants.

Returning to the report of psychological problems, the intense level of distress expressed by many caregivers has led numerous researchers to focus on the nature and prevalence of affective disorders commonly experienced by family caregivers. Gallagher, Rose, Rivera, Lovett, and Thompson (1989), for example, found that over 40% of 200 caregivers interviewed met diagnostic criteria for either a major or minor depressive disorder. Other researchers have also documented a high level of either depressive symptoms or depressive disorder among family caregivers (Coppel, Burton, Becker, & Fiore, 1985; Drinka, Smith, & Drinka, 1987). Intense anger may even be a more common occurrence than depression (Gallagher et al., 1989). Anthony-Bergstone et al. (1988) also found hostility to be higher among caregivers than among a matched sample of community control subjects at the time. These negative affects can, in turn, cause further psychological distress. Depression increases the likelihood of negative thinking or distortions about oneself, one's life situation, and what the future holds in store (Beck, 1972). Depression also decreases activity and behavioral functioning, which serves to decrease pleasant and increase unpleasant activities in one's life (Lewinsohn, Sullivan, & Grosscup, 1982). It's understandable that both of these could lead to further increased depression and anxiety, which in turn further negatively affects thinking and activities in a vicious downward-spiral-like manner. Anger can also lead to immense guilt and other serious negative consequences because the experience of anger and its expression have been heavily admonished in our society for many years, particularly for women.

Interventions to Support and Maintain Mental Health

Numerous interventions are available that can reduce emotional disorders common in caregiving and increase families' ability to cope with the ever changing demands of the caregiving situation. One must recognize, however, that caregiving is essentially a family affair and that interventions aimed specifically at the primary caregiver may be only partially effective. The context of caregiving and the need to view caregiving as occurring within a total family system are important. At present, few clinical investigations have focused on the development of techniques that employ family system strategies. Attention to this perspective in future research, to embrace the context within which caregiving activities occur, should lead to productive advances for assisting caregivers in coping with intense psychological distress.

WHAT TYPES OF INTERVENTIONS ARE AVAILABLE FOR CAREGIVERS?

The wide range of services, which address some of the negative outcomes of caregiving, can be divided into programs geared more toward environmental management (i.e., improving the situation of the frail elder) and those that are more oriented toward directly addressing caregivers' mental health and psychosocial functioning (Gallagher-Thompson, 1994b). The first category includes case management services, modification of the frail elders' actual living environment, and day or overnight respite programs. Respite programs are most likely to have an indirect effect on caregivers' mental health through the relief that they provide from the ongoing rigors of the role. The second category includes interventions such as support groups, psychoeducational programs, counseling, and psychotherapeutic services of various kinds. A recent meta-analysis of psychosocial treatments has shown the efficacy of these procedures in reducing distress in caregivers (Knight, Lutzky, & Macofsky-Urban, 1993). For the remainder of this chapter, we will focus on the more direct mental-health-oriented programs.

The question is often asked, "What characteristics of the caregiver or of his or her profile of symptoms and living arrangements might suggest one type of intervention over another to be maximally effective?" As noted earlier (Pearlin et al., 1990), caregivers have careers that can change over time. Therefore, interventions that might be appropriate at one phase of the disorder may be less needed at another phase, at which time a different kind of intervention may be more appropriate. This may also, of course, vary according to the nature of the disability of the care receiver as well as available social and family resources, although again, research data are lacking to elucidate critical factors. There are, however, some suggestions regarding the application of specific interventions that will be discussed after a description of the more common mental health services currently used.

Support Groups

These are a very popular form of intervention program. They are widely available throughout the United States and exist for just about every form of chronic illness, such as Alzheimer's disease, strokes, Parkinson's disease, cancers of various kinds, sensory impairments, and diabetes. Typically, the "parent" organization schedules meetings and arranges for speakers and the like, and participants attend according to their needs. The support groups are open-ended and tend to meet monthly, although there is great variability in how support groups are actually structured in terms of the number of participants, the frequency of meetings, and the meeting location. Generally, support groups are led by peers, but some are facilitated by professionals or by people with specialized training in the particular disease or disability. Participants are free to speak or not as they see fit at the time, and they may reveal as much or as little as they wish about their own situation and private feelings.

Support groups are perceived as most helpful in two areas: information sharing and peer support. In one of the few studies evaluating their effectiveness, Gonyea (1989) reported that 75% of the participants endorsed the group as very helpful but only about one third said that the support group had been helpful in reducing specific negative psychological feelings such as guilt or anger, and even fewer (about 25%) said they felt the group was very helpful in teaching them how to take care of their own needs. Thus, support groups clearly do not meet all the emotional needs of some participants, possibly due to the structure, the infrequent nature of contact, and the types of information that are presented and discussed at the meetings.

Educational Programs

Presentation of educational programs to family caregivers is a similar type of intervention but one that focuses less on sharing emotionally laden material. Caregivers' need for information falls in six general categories: (a) understanding the relative's condition, (b) improving coping skills, (c) dealing with family issues, (d) communicating effectively with the frail elder, (e) knowing appropriate community resources, and (f) long-term planning (e.g., legal and financial). Programs designed to convey information in one of these categories can be extremely valuable to caregivers, but they frequently precipitate intense emotional reactions, particularly when caregivers are faced with difficult decisions. Thus, educational programs need to recognize and validate feelings and provide for a certain level at least of interaction and sharing among participants (Schmall & Pratt, 1989). In fact, much caregiver education often can be effectively interwoven into the fabric of the monthly support group meetings sponsored by national organizations for caregiving. On a practical level, it does appear that the combination of being exposed to useful information and having the opportunity to process it at least to some degree on an emotional level is more helpful to family caregivers than the sterile delivery of facts and procedures in a classroom setting.

Psychoeducational Classes

The *psychoeducational* model is a more intense intervention focusing on the personal needs of the caregiver in dealing with the stresses confronted in caregiving. According to the cognitive-behavioral framework from which most psychoeducational interventions were developed, participants are presented not only with new information and given the opportunity to share feelings and reactions but are also expected to develop skills to enhance their coping abilities. This skill development occurs through active participation in the learning process (for example, through the use of role playing and demonstrations). Most psychoeducational programs have a built-in "homework" component, which refers to assigned activities between meetings that participants are expected to follow through on to deepen their knowledge and understanding of the material and to enhance their skill-building efficacy. Psychoeducational programs are time limited, usually for 8 to 12 sessions, and have specific goals to be achieved over the course of the program. They incorporate elements of group therapy as well as the presentation of information and an opportunity for sharing. They typically have a small number of members (often 8 to 12) to provide individual attention and the opportunity for individually oriented discussion for those who might require it.

Several models for psychoeducational interventions have appeared in the literature in the past several years, often in the context of a research program for which participants have been recruited. Their effectiveness has been demonstrated in a number of studies (Gallagher-Thompson, 1994a; Gallagher-Thompson & DeVries, 1994; Gallagher-Thompson, Lovett, Rose, & Futterman, 1994; Greene & Monahan, 1989; Lovett & Gallagher, 1988; and Whitlatch, Zarit, & von Eye, 1991, with a reanalysis of data in Zarit, Anthony, & Boutselis, 1987). Two other projects reported less positive results in terms of symptom change, but participants in both reported high levels of satisfaction with the classes and indicated that they were better able to deal with interpersonal concerns that arose in typical caregiver problems (Haley, Brown, & Levine, 1987; Toseland, Rossiter, & Labrecque, 1989).

We have found the psychoeducational approach to be extremely effective in working with caregivers. As others have noted, the decrease in the actual symptoms of psychological distress as a result of class participation may sometimes be unremarkable, but on follow-up, a substantial majority of participants report that their experience in the class has been immensely helpful to them in dealing with the myriad problems they encounter. The consistent announcements across studies by caregivers reflecting the beneficial nature of these structured group experiences should challenge us to focus more carefully on what might be reasonable and important outcomes for treatments used with this population. For example, the level of symptom distress is highly variable in caregivers, and many who participate in studies to evaluate these interventions have minimal or no evidence of severe distress at the outset. Therefore, one shouldn't necessarily expect substantive changes in symptoms in all cases. Furthermore, the plight of the caregiver often is a life filled with numerous heart-wrenching events, which occur in a seemingly random fashion, independent of treatments. This being the case, improvements in level of distress might often be temporarily obliterated, even though important changes in ways of coping and other behavioral functioning are either clearly in evidence or are in their formative stages.

Because depression and anger are frequently the two most prevalent negative emotions experienced by caregivers, we have focused on the development of two psychoeducational programs to help caregivers deal with them. The

Table 6.1   "Coping with the Blues"—A Class Format

Sessions 1 through 3
  Present the cognitive-behavior model and treatment rationale.
  Identify pleasant activities and events.
  Monitor pleasant activities and events daily to establish baselines.
  Monitor and graph mood daily.
  Examine the relationship between mood level and frequency of engaging in pleasant
    activities.
  "Aha!" experience number one: understanding the relationship of pleasurable activity and
    mood change.
Sessions 4 through 6
  Target certain pleasant events to increase.
  Examine obstacles to doing this.
  Develop and implement nine-step self-change program to increase pleasant activities.
  Continue monitoring and recording frequency of pleasant events and mood level.
  "Aha!" experience number two: understanding that the amount of pleasure experienced in
    one's life is, to some degree, under one's control.
Sessions 7 and 8
  Continue self-change planning: selecting a second target for change and repeating the
    nine-step program.
  Continue monitoring to evaluate the effects.
  Develop a "survival guide" to help maintain gains.
Sessions 9 and 10 (Booster Sessions)
  Review progress for successes and problems.
  Highlight reasons for successes.
  Determine what went wrong, if anything, when problems developed.
  Review techniques learned, and problem solve how to implement or modify them to avoid
    problems.

class focusing on depression is variously called "Coping with the Blues, Improving Life Satisfaction," or "Controlling Your Depression," depending on the circumstances under which it is being offered. The class designed to reduce anger is called "How to Control Your Frustration" or "How to Control Your Anger." Recent post hoc analyses of data from several studies in our laboratory, which include information from over 300 caregivers, show a differential effect of the two types of classes depending on the participants' initial levels of depression or anger. Those participants who had a higher level of anger than depression respond more positively to the anger management class, whereas participants who were higher in depression respond more positively to the depression control class. We also developed and evaluated a class that focuses strictly on problem-solving skills, but this program does not seem to be as effective as the depression and anger classes.

A brief description of the content of each of these two intervention programs can be found in Tables 6.1 and 6.2. Participant and leader instruction

Table 6.2   "Coping with Frustration: Anger Management"—A Class Format

Sessions 1 through 3
    Present the cognitive-behavioral model and treatment rationale.
    Discuss sources of frustration and anger in the caregiving situation and typical ways people respond. For example, let it all out or hold it in versus appropriate expression.
    Relaxation training and starting relaxation logs for monitoring.
Sessions 4 through 6
    Focus on cognitive techniques, such as self-talk and active listening to prepare for, and deal with, daily stressors.
    Each individual develops a series of self-statements that work for them in coping with frustration.
    Continue relaxation logs; add a log of situations that were anger-provoking along with techniques used to cope.
Sessions 7 and 8
    Focus on behavioral techniques for assertiveness (e.g., "Broken Record" technique).
    Practice assertion techniques with group and with family and friends outside the group setting.
    Begin to apply techniques with persons relevant to the caregiving situation.
    Develop "survival guides" to help maintain gains.
Sessions 9 and 10 (booster sessions)
    Review progress for successes and problems.
    Highlight reasons for successes.
    Determine what went wrong, if anything, when problems developed.
    Review techniques learned and problem solve how to implement or modify them to avoid problems.

manuals for these programs are available from the authors. A different set of cognitive-behavioral skills is taught in each class. In the "Coping with the Blues" class, a great emphasis is placed on learning how to both monitor and then increase the frequency of engagement in pleasurable activities. Individuals are also taught to develop a self-change plan to increase pleasant activities or decrease unpleasant activities and then to carry it out, with appropriate rewards on accomplishment of the goal. In the "Coping with Frustration" class, caregivers are taught systematic relaxation principles along with methods for challenging their negative thoughts that might influence how they are responding in the caregiving situation. They also learn assertion skills and how to apply them in dealing with care recipients at times when they are being uncooperative or difficult. Most caregivers report that these skills are also useful in dealing with difficult family members as well as professionals working for cumbersome health care systems.

Support groups, education programs, and psychoeducational programs may not be sufficient or appropriate for all caregivers. For example, some individuals are experiencing such distress that they need one-on-one time to talk extensively about their problems to better understand their feelings and options. Other individuals are too disruptive on an interpersonal level to really contribute to a class or group setting and therefore need to be ruled out at the beginning. Still others may have significant problems and not realize it until they have begun a program such as we have been describing. Once they are comfortable in the class or group setting and begin to share much more about their problems, the magnitude of their pain and suffering or their inability to apply the material being presented may often lead to a referral for individual counseling or psychotherapy.

Individual Psychotherapy

There are few studies describing the application of psychotherapy to extremely distressed caregivers. However, it appears that even relatively brief interventions, such as 4 to 6 weeks of therapy, can be extremely helpful in enabling the caregiver to become "unstuck" and proceed with their lives (Baum & Gallagher, 1985). Some individuals may then be able to benefit more from a group participation program, either by itself or in combination with continued therapy. As mentioned earlier, the optimal psychotherapy for a given caregiver may change depending on contextual features of the actual caregiving process. For example, we found that overall, brief psychodynamic and cognitive-behavioral therapy had a comparable beneficial effect on caregivers who were diagnosed as suffering from major depressive disorder. Those patients who were caregivers for less than 44 months, however, responded much better to the psychodynamic therapy, whereas those who were caregivers for longer than that responded best to the cognitive-behavioral approach (Gallagher-Thompson & Steffen, 1994). In attempting to explain this interaction, we noted that permission to grieve was an integral component in the particular model of short-term psychodynamic therapy that we used, which may be a particularly important process in the early stages of caregiving when the individual caregiver is coming to grips with the loss of the person that they once knew as well as the loss of many future possibilities and plans. The long-term caregivers, on the other hand, may have benefited more from a cognitive-behavioral approach because its emphasis on practical problem solving in the here and now may have increased their self-efficacy perceptions and their hope and expectancy for more effective coping, thus making it possible to function with less distress in their roles.

No matter what type of intervention we use to treat emotional distress in caregivers, we have found, as you might suspect, that any strategy that improves the caregiver's sense of efficacy in dealing with behavioral problems posed by the care recipient or actually improves the care recipient's functioning invariably has a positive effect on the caregiver's level of psychological distress. In this regard, modifications of more specialized behavioral therapy approaches, often used in long-term-care settings where a variety of behavioral problems are encountered, can be extremely effective. These rely heavily on the antecedent-behavior-consequence model for understanding and changing specific behaviors. This model emphasizes that specific behaviors typically have both an antecedent condition and one or more consequences, and that one must understand the antecedents and consequences of a behavior in question to change it. In a comprehensive review of behavioral therapy as applied to frail elders, Fisher and Carstensen (1990) found that techniques such as the use of clear and explicit reinforcement schedules along with individualized rewards or reinforcers were among the most effective behavioral methods for linking the behavior of dementia patients in ways to reduce excess functional disability. Pinkston and Linsk (1984) were among the first to apply this approach systematically with family caregivers. They developed specific sets of procedures designed to teach behavioral management skills to family caregivers. Intervention training occurred in the caregiver's home for an average of 10 to 15 sessions so that principles such as contracting and reinforcement-based interventions could be taught along with techniques for establishing a baseline and counting behaviors to monitor change. Teri and Uomoto (1991) have extended this work by incorporating behavioral principles into the treatment of depression in Alzheimer's patients. A key aspect of their program is the identification of pleasant activities that either the Alzheimer's victim could do alone or the patient and caregiver could do together. Teri and Logsdon (1991) developed a special questionnaire outlining 53 activities likely to still be in the repertoire of moderately to severely demented patients (such as listening to music, singing, recalling and discussing past events, etc.). This measure can be helpful in developing an individualized activity profile, which the caregiver can then implement in the home setting through the use of a systematic approach along with reward and reinforcement. There is a significant inverse relationship between depressed mood and duration of pleasant events when this strategy is applied. Although variations of behavioral therapy can be extremely effective with some caregivers in helping them deal with day-to-day problems, others are unable to keep the program going on a daily basis and still others are unwilling or unable to take the time needed to organize and supervise their relative in this particular program. Unfortunately, as is the case with so many patients, there is no foolproof way of predicting precisely who among distressed caregivers will apply these principles systematically until you actually try them. In our experience, however, once a caregiver realizes that behavioral strategies are actually cost-effective in terms of time and energy spent, they are much more likely to apply this model in dealing with new problems as they arise.

Family Therapy

As noted earlier, caregiving is a family affair, and although traditional family therapy approaches have been found to work with the elderly (Herr & Weakland, 1979; Qualls, 1988), there is very little in the literature on how best to do family therapy with elderly couples or family systems that have been assaulted with the recent stress of extended caregiving for a frail elder. Concerns such as the desirability of including the impaired relative, the number of family members to be present, the focus of such meetings, what the goals of treatment would be, and issues around confidentiality and privacy have not been addressed systematically in either the clinical or research literature. Our experience has been that involving family members in providing increased support to a primary caregiver is nearly always useful and often has made the difference in delaying or avoiding long-term hospitalization of the care recipient. For this to occur successfully, however, it is frequently necessary to deal not only with the fears and practical concerns of the individual family members but also with interpersonal and family issues that are rooted in past family interactions and significant family events. Development and evaluation of strategies for dealing with family systems in this context hold great promise for improving the lot of family caregivers.

WHAT ARE THE DECISION RULES
FOR SELECTING INTERVENTIONS?

The problem of deciding what interventions are most appropriate for a given caregiver client has not been addressed in any great detail in the professional literature. Past clinical experience and clinical "lore" are often the only available resources for developing a clinical program to assist a distressed caregiver. Some decisions are fairly obvious, however, and can be made with minimal concerns about their effectiveness in ameliorating caregiver distress. For example, if a major clinical diagnosis, such as dysthymic disorder or generalized anxiety disorder, can be made and the person is seeking help, a referral to a mental health professional is clearly appropriate. We have found that short-term psychotherapy is usually helpful with such patients, and their progress can sometimes be facilitated with a combination of therapy and psychotropic medications (Thompson & Gallagher-Thompson, 1991). Medication alone, however, is not usually the treatment of choice for severely distressed caregivers. Most often, their psychological problems have been precipitated by the stresses of caregiving, and they need to develop the psychological resources to cope with the problems that continually arise.

The psychotherapy modality to use may vary, not only across patients but also within patients, depending on how long they have been in the caregiving role and how their available support system might have changed. In the first few years of caregiving, issues concerning loss and grief may need as much or more attention than concerns about coping with the problems being confronted. Therapies designed to integrate grief work along with other techniques tend to be maximally effective. In later years, many caregivers have actually done a lot of anticipatory grief work, and their attention is more focused on how to deal with the immense and ever-increasing burdens of caregiving and how to maintain their own physical and emotional stability while confronting a seemingly ceaseless course of hassles and upheavals occurring usually in the context of sequentially dwindling material and interpersonal support systems. Caregivers in this predicament often become impatient with therapy modalities focusing on grief work or transference issues and seem to respond more positively to structured approaches that focus more on the acquisition of coping mechanisms (Gallagher-Thompson & Steffen, 1994).

With regard to individual differences, distressed caregivers who seem to have adequate resources to provide respite and some pleasurable experiences for themselves and their care recipients may benefit more if the primary focus is on the negative cognitions that they have about themselves, their situations, and their futures. For example, the caregiver may have unrealistic expectations about his or her responsibility for the care recipient's well-being or may be distorting life events by "all or none" thinking. The caregivers might believe, for example, that their happiness is dependent solely on the condition of the persons for whom they are caring, "The only way I could ever be happy again is for John to be well," or, "Life will never have meaning for me without sharing things with George, and I mean sharing so that he understands." Cognitive therapy can aid caregivers in modifying such beliefs as well as identifying ways in which they might be distorting events to support irrational belief systems. If the caregiver has few financial and social resources to provide for some modicum of pleasure for themselves, then a useful first step in therapy is to help them find ways within their means to increase their levels of pleasure and relaxation while maintaining the caregiver role. This can involve a wide range of behavioral techniques, from teaching them how to be assertive in recruiting family and other community resources for assistance to learning covert techniques for quick relaxation in the face of acutely stressful events or acquiring improved skills for time use. Often, caregivers may have ample resources for making their situation more comfortable but may be living by a rule of "fairness," such that engaging in pleasurable activities for one's own enjoyment is not acceptable when their loved one has to suffer. "Donald's needs, not mine, must always come first." This problem is sometimes easily overcome if the caregiver can gain the perspective that it is important for them to take care of themselves so that they can be maximally effective in caring for the person that needs their assistance. As one patient put it, "I see now. You know it's like they say in the airplane drill. Put on your oxygen mask first so that you'll be OK, and then you can help the child put on theirs."

Although help-seeking may well be the rule rather than the exception among caregivers, most who are looking for help do not identify themselves as patients in need of mental health services. Referrals of these individuals for psychiatric or psychological assistance tend not to work out, even though their symptoms might be consistent with a diagnosable illness. They either do not follow through, or they often drop out after a few sessions. They may use psychotropic medications as needed, but these are usually prescribed by their regular physician. Many of these individuals, however, will participate in programs that are less identified with serving psychiatric patients. For example, they might consider attending a series of classes on how to control frustration or how to chase away the blues (manuals for these psychoeducational programs are available from the authors). Programs offering practical information on problematic issues, such as wandering, incontinence, durable power of attorney, and so on, are extremely popular, as are periodic support groups that include such educational materials. Caregivers should be encouraged to participate in any of these programs. About the only exclusionary criteria to consider would be the presence of characterological features that might be significantly disruptive to the group, severe psychopathology associated with decompensation or a concern that sharing information in a group setting might precipitate decompensation in a marginally adjusted person, or concern that attendance might in some way interfere with the delivery of appropriate care to the recipient, such as the caregiver needing to leave a recipient unattended in a potentially harmful situation while participating in the program.

Many of the interventions available to caregivers can complement one another and, if available, could be offered simultaneously or interspersed sequentially. Indeed, left to their own devices, caregivers often are inclined to use as many and varied services as their limited time and financial resources will permit. We have found the support group and psychoeducational classes to be particularly effective when offered sequentially. Particularly after attending support groups where they have had an opportunity to share their concerns with others and gain some information about resources available, caregivers begin to have some realization that they need more than just the support of others in similar predicaments. As a result, they require less socialization into a group format and appear open and receptive to learning new techniques to help them alleviate their burdens. This in turn improves time use and effectiveness of the classes, which are typically time-limited and brief.

As noted earlier, caregiver satisfaction with such programs is high, and many feel that their functional capabilities are maintained or enhanced by virtue of their participation. Appropriate summative evaluations of many caregiver interventions to determine their effect on health care costs, timing of institutionalization of care recipient, and quality of life for family members are generally not available. In view of what is known about the burden of caregiving and the caregiver's continuing use of available services, however, one might reasonably expect these effects to be positive.

In our experience, a pivotal feature in making the decision to institutionalize a family member revolves around a deterioration in medical or psychological health status, in either the caregiver or care recipient, to such a degree that the caregiver feels it is no longer possible to provide adequate care in the family setting. In addition to the objective changes contributing to the caregiver's perception, subjective factors such as the caregiver's sense of adequacy and control in the situation and willingness to engage in new problem-solving behaviors to overcome the negative changes also play an important part. Furthermore, these subjective factors are influenced heavily by negative emotions, such as depression and anxiety. Thus, the more depressed or anxious the caregiver becomes, the less their sense of efficacy in dealing with stressful events, and the less they may be willing to continue their role as a family caregiver. Amelioration of negative emotions, then, is likely to have a positive effect on the caregiver's perception of their ability to function as a caregiver and thereby their willingness to continue in this role. Testimony of numerous caregivers in our work suggests that the psychoeducational class format has a definite positive effect on quality of life indicators and may have beneficial effects concerning health costs and time of placement as well. The case example to follow illustrates the magnitude of the effect that often occurs as a result of a simple 8-week class on improving life satisfaction:

Betty, a 51-year-old married female, lives with her husband, daughter, son-in-law, and 74-year-old mother who is suffering from Alzheimer's disease. She has been the primary caregiver for the mother over the past 4 years but receives some assistance from her children in supervising the mother when she is required to leave the home. The family owns a small business in which all members are employed, which enables Betty to work in the home and permits her some flexibility in the hours that she works. She also assumes responsibility for preparing meals and keeping the house in order. The mother's dementia has progressed to a moderate level. She has become very demanding on Betty's time and attention. Although she has lived with the family for 4 years, she thinks she has been a guest there for only a short period and therefore is entitled to be pampered by her daughter. In social gatherings, such as meal times or entertaining guests, if she is ignored for any length of time, she becomes angry and runs off to her room. At the time Betty entered the class, she would react to her mother's emotional outbursts by becoming extremely distressed and guilty and would run after her to console her. In every social gathering she would constantly focus on her mother and attempt to work her into the conversation in some way to prevent a problem from arising, but of course, this strategy repeatedly failed because of the mother's limitations. Betty's relationships with other family members was becoming strained, particularly with her husband, and she noted that she was constantly in need of a doctor's care. Dreadful as it was, she had begun to think about placement of her mother because she was fearful that the strained relationship with her husband might lead to a separation or divorce. She had actually visited a nursing home to work out the details, but the agony of this decision was becoming increasingly detrimental to her level of functioning.

Content and homework assignments in the Life Satisfaction Class provided Betty with objective data that she was engaging in virtually no pleasant activities, and she was doing nothing in her daily life with her own interests in mind. The rationale presented in class for increasing pleasurable activities, in combination with the encouraging support of the class, motivated Betty to evaluate the effect of increasing the frequency of pleasant activities in her life. The results were remarkable. The comfort she experienced by the increase in pleasurable activities provided credibility for the principles outlined in the course and set the stage for her to examine her reaction to her mother's irrational demands. Through class discussions, she accepted the realization that she was not responsible for her mother's problems and therefore did not have to feel guilty or put her mother's interests before her own. This led to a self-change plan of ignoring her mother's outbursts. The plan was successful, which enabled Betty to feel much more in control of the relationship with her mother. She subsequently became more relaxed. Her relationship with her husband improved immensely. She became more assertive in asking for help from the children in the home. She was enjoying life again and still able to care for her mother. At our 6-month follow-up, plans for the mother's placement had been dropped, doctor's visits had stopped, and she described her relationship with her husband as like a second honeymoon.

In Betty's case, the outcome of her plight would probably have been more negative without intervention. She was considering placement; the family system was disrupted and becoming more disorganized; health costs were increasing. Placement might actually have led to even greater strain in the family because her emotional state would probably have continued to deteriorate due to the guilt. However, her attendance in the class delayed placement and clearly gave her an increased sense of how to deal with her many seemingly insurmountable problems in caring for her mother.

Progress and Prospects in
Caregiving Research and Practice

Reflecting on the literature related to caregiving, several conclusions can be drawn.

First, it is clear that the burden of caregiving can be, at times, almost beyond comprehension. It truly is a "36-hour day" for some, and this may go on for years with little expectation of more than just temporary respite from the burdensome duties. There are, however, some positive aspects to caregiving, and this feature is often overlooked. What are these positive features and how can we capitalize on these to improve the plight of the caregiver?

Second, many caregivers are able to function capably in this role for unbelievably long periods. The thought of relinquishing their responsibilities is taken seriously only when there is a transition in health status of themselves or their care recipient that renders it no longer feasible for them to provide responsible, high-quality care. What are these danger signals, and what can we do to minimize their occurrence in the lives of caregivers?

Third, caregivers can experience incredible psychological distress, and in a sizable proportion, their symptoms may actually warrant a diagnosis of psychopathology. Yet in the face of high distress levels, they manage to function and cope with the day-to-day tasks inherent in the role. Caregiving is often viewed as a naturally occurring process in the life cycle, and therefore, serious stresses and strains are to be expected and dealt with as part of life's trials and tribulations. Thus, although symptoms of an emotional disorder may be manifest, conceptualizing the problem in a framework of psychopathology may not be the most productive strategy for the researcher or the practitioner. The development of useful models would greatly facilitate basic and clinical research efforts.

Fourth, although there is an increase in mental health problems in caregivers, there is some question as to whether they have more physical health problems than noncaregivers with the same age and socioeconomic status. This raises the questions of whether our measurements of physical health are not sensitive enough to detect change, whether enough time has elapsed in the caregiving for physical health problems to be manifest, or whether physical health changes are likely to occur only in those individuals who are taxed beyond the availability of their internal and external resources. These issues deserve particular attention in subsequent research.

Fifth, caregivers are in need of increased resources, and for the most part, they actively seek assistance both from formal and personal support systems. It's not all that clear, however, as to what resources might be maximally effective and how they should be adapted to the special needs of caregivers. This chapter highlights some of the interventions currently available to help caregivers address their mental health needs and to help them achieve a better quality of life. Many caregivers are using these available services, but the lack of an organized approach to research in this field has limited our ability to understand which interventions would be most appropriate for which caregivers at which stages of their caregiving careers.

Sixth, some studies have shown that structured group interventions designed specifically with the caregiver in mind are helpful, but others have reported no difference between these and general support groups. Furthermore, changes in emotional symptoms have been modest at best, although the majority of caregivers who participated in specific treatments report that the interventions have been extremely helpful. Several methodological problems were suggested earlier that may account for these equivocal findings. In our judgment, one of the most important problems pertains to the types of measures considered as indices of outcome efficacy. Our traditional models for outcome research stem from the study of psychopathology, and understandably call for the measurement of psychological distress and diagnosis of psychiatric disorder as primary indicators of efficacy, with less emphasis being placed on the measurement of adaptive functional behaviors. Careful consideration of the caregiving process raises some question concerning the appropriateness of a "disease" model and its typical measurement procedures. Caregiving and the stresses inherent in this process are generally part of the life cycle and may, therefore, be better understood if studied using models that reflect the problems of adaptation to transitions and perturbations that occur during the normal course of development. Such models would be likely to place greater emphasis on adaptive functioning and coping strategies rather than on symptoms associated with emotional disorders. On the basis of the limited data currently available, interventions appear to have greater effect on measures of adaptive functioning than on changes in levels of emotional symptoms. Continued exploration of other models and measures is clearly warranted, which should attempt to address a number of issues raised earlier: for example, the interface between physical and mental health factors in caregivers, changing needs of caregivers for mental health services over time, and how individual caregivers balance the demands of the situation with their emotional responses. Careful study of those who have adapted well to caregiving is needed to provide a more balanced view of the positive attributes associated with this role.

Seventh, there have been few outreach efforts specifically devoted to the needs of subgroups, such as the identification of male caregivers and development of programs to meet their particular needs. Some years ago, Davies, Priddy, and Tinklenberg (1986) described some of the qualitative differences that they noted in running a support group for male caregivers versus running one that was predominately attended by women. Men wanted more practical help, such as how to do the cooking and cleaning and the bathing and dressing of the frail elder, with very little discussion of their feelings and little sharing of feelings with other group members. This is one of the few reports in the literature that could guide clinicians in setting up clinical research programs to address the situation of elderly male caregivers.

Last, the specific needs of ethnic minority elders and their families have been largely unmet by the current service delivery system. Yet their proportion in the population will continue to grow in the years ahead and so it would be prudent to plan ahead and learn as much as one can about the relevant cultures to develop specific programs that truly reflect the communities and the peoples whom they are intended to serve. Similarly, little attention has been paid to the needs of ethnic minority caregivers. It is only recently that attention has been focused on the desirability of establishing special programs for minority groups that are tailored to fit in with some of the language and cultural expectations. For example, support groups run in Spanish have been reported in the literature (Henderson, Gutierrez-Mayka, Garcia, & Boyd, 1993) and more community-based interventions to increase informal support have also been reported (Valle, 1989). Yet these efforts are few and far between, especially when one considers the fact that ethnic minorities are increasing in their proportions in the population, particularly among the elderly. Our own experience working with professionals who treat Hispanic families and their caregivers suggests that ethnic minorities are lacking in much basic information about the various diseases of old age and are often uncomfortable with the formats for services such as we have been describing. Issues such as shame, family pride, and "taking care of ones' own" may be strong barriers to their accessing currently available services. It may be that new models need to be designed that specifically meet the needs of individual ethnic minority groups.

Summary

The purpose of this chapter is to describe characteristics of family caregivers of frail elders, to point out the kinds of stress and negative affects that they typically experience in the role of caregiver, and to review a variety of intervention strategies designed to improve their mental health and well-being. Also, the issue of caregiving as a family affair is addressed. The chapter closes by raising a number of issues to be addressed in future clinical research, such as the development of interventions specifically for male caregivers and for ethnic minorities.

II

Special Issues
in Assessment

7

Interviewing Older Adults

Barry A. Edelstein
Elizabeth M. Semenchuk

Interviews are two-person conversations with a purpose of obtaining information (Cannell & Kahn, 1968-1969). The *clinical* interview is the most frequently employed clinical assessment method in health settings (Edelstein & Berler, 1987; Haynes & Jensen, 1979) and is typically considered the "backbone of all mental health professions" (Shea, 1990, p. 283). Shea described a 1982 survey of 482 psychiatric teachers and practitioners conducted by Langsley and Hollender (1982) that revealed that 99.4% ranked the conduct of an interview as an important requirement for a psychiatrist. He also determined that 7 of the top 10 of 32 ranked skills were directly related to interviewing techniques. Similarly, a survey of clinical psychologists by Norcross, Prochaska, and Gallager (1989) revealed that the clinical interview was used by 96% of those surveyed and comprised 39% of their assessment.

The initial interview is typically the first contact between the clinician and the client and the first critical step in a process that can range from screening to intervention. Moreover, its importance is considerable in terms of the conceptualization of the problem and the establishment of rapport with the client. The interview is often the principal initial assessment method and is further used as an evaluative tool for interventions. For the purposes of this chapter, we will focus on the initial clinical assessment interview, with the understanding that the interview process is likely to continue over several interview periods. The interview will be approached as an assessment method and subject to the same general validity and reliability issues as any other assessment method. We will begin with a consideration of the psychometric properties of clinical interviews, followed by discussions of interview structure, structured and semistructured interviews, the interview process, ageism as a potential bias, and practical considerations for conducting an interview.

Psychometric Considerations

Regardless of the specific objectives of a particular interview or set of interviews, the overarching goal is to obtain accurate, reliable, and valid information. Psychometric concepts of most relevance to the general clinical interview are *content validity, temporal (test-retest) reliability, accuracy* (White & Edelstein, 1991), and *incremental validity.* A content-valid interview must contain questions that elicit information regarding all of the behavioral, cognitive, affective, historical, and social factors that are relevant to the problem(s) under consideration.

Temporal reliability is determined by the extent to which the data obtained at one point in time are consistent with that obtained at another point in time. One must assume, of course, that what is being measured has some temporal reliability or stability over time. In contrast, one cannot expect measures of mental status, physical activity, or mood to be temporally reliable for individuals whose mental and physical status varies significantly over time. One might expect great temporal stability of personality, person preferences, and intellectual variables. Consequently, the temporal reliability of an interview must be considered in the context of the stability of phenomena under examination.

The accuracy of an assessment instrument has also been termed *internal validity* (Haynes, 1991) and *sensitivity* (Cone, 1981, 1988; Haynes, 1991). The accuracy of an interview (the assessment instrument) is determined by the precision with which it captures the important qualities of clients' behaviors. If one is to assess the accuracy of an interview, it must have well-articulated rules for its use and agreed-on criteria by which to judge the data obtained. It is unfortunate that, with the exception of some very structured interviews, no agreed-on rules and procedures exist for conducting an initial interview.

Incremental validity refers to the increase in validity of information when new information is added to existing data (e.g., biographical information, results of testing). One might ask whether the validity of the assessment is increased when the interview information is added to that obtained via other methods. Because the interview is the most frequently employed initial assessment method, one is more likely to question the incremental validity of other assessment methods that follow (e.g., standardized testing). Nevertheless, incremental validity is important and should be addressed regardless of the nature of the assessment methods and instruments used. Unfortunately, little sound research has been conducted on the incremental validity of clinical interviews. Of the handful of studies reviewed by Garb (1984), only one (Sines, 1959) relates to the assessment of client characteristics or psychopathology. Sines found that interview information increased the accuracy of clinician judgments when the information was used in conjunction with that obtained from a biographical data sheet and results of Rorschachs and MMPIs. In summarizing his review of the literature, Garb (1984) noted that "the incremental validity paradigm has never been used to study structured interviews or behavioral rating scales and has never been used in two of the fastest growing areas in clinical psychology: health psychology and geriatric psychology" (Garb, 1984, p. 649). Garb's statement continues to hold true. With the exception of structured and semistructured interviews (e.g., Diagnostic Interview Schedule—Robbins, Helzer, Croughan, & Ratcliff, 1981; Schedule for Affective Disorders and Schizophrenia—Spitzer & Endicott, 1977; Structured Clinical Interview for DSM-III-R—Spitzer, Williams, Gibbon, & First, 1992; Comprehensive Assessment and Referral Evaluation Interview Schedule—Gurland et al., 1977), virtually no research has addressed the psychometric properties of the clinical interview. This is problematic because unstructured interviews are used with greater frequency and are subject to more threats to reliability and validity than more structured interviews. The flexibility that contributes to this vulnerability is both the strength and the weakness of the unstructured clinical interview. The lack of empirical support for the reliability and validity of interview practices is particularly unfortunate because clinicians frequently make interview-based decisions that are every bit as consequential as those made on the basis of assessment instruments with established reliability and validity. Though there is an absence of empirical support for many of our interviewing practices, this should not lead to the conclusion that such data should not be obtained or that the clinician should discontinue use of the interview. Rather, the paucity of psychometric information points to a need for caution in drawing conclusions from interview data and suggests the use of multiple assessment methods and retrieval of information from multiple sources.

RELIABILITY AND ACCURACY OF SELF-REPORTS BY OLDER ADULTS

Self-reports are subject to the same environmental influences as other verbal behavior. They are shaped by the reinforcement contingencies operative in the setting in which they are made. Moreover, they are vulnerable to influences arising from cognitive deficits that are often present among older adults who suffer from dementia, physical illnesses, medication side-effects, or any combination of these. Clinicians must be aware of the many factors that can influence self-reports of older adults (Edelstein, Northrop, Staats, & Packard, 1996). Sager et al. (1992) suggest that responses to interviewer inquiries can be altered by affective response to acute illness, changes from previous levels of physical functioning occurring during hospitalization, and the presence of acute or chronic cognitive impairment. For example, Kuriansky, Gurland, and Fleiss (1976) reported that affectively impaired older adults may underestimate their abilities.

The accuracy of self-reports may also be influenced by increases in cognitive impairment, as one might expect. Clients with severe dementia may not be able to comprehend questions or the nature of requested information. Older adults with dementia who deny memory loss also tend to deny the presence of other symptoms (Feher, Larrabee, & Crook, 1992). Feher et al. (1992) assert that accurate self-reporting of recent mood requires only minimal memory ability, suggesting that individuals with mild to moderate dementia can be accurate in responding to questions requiring minimal memory ability.

Response sets can influence responses to questions with older adults, much as they can with younger adults. However, there are some reported response biases that may be even more characteristic of older adults. Older adults may tend to be more cautious (Okun, 1976) and experience greater anxiety than younger adults regarding receipt of negative feedback and engage in risk-avoiding behavior when anticipating evaluative information (Poon, Rubin, & Wilson, 1986). Older adults are more likely than younger adults to respond to questions in a socially desirable fashion (Campbell, Converse, & Rodgers, 1976). Chronically ill older adults are also more likely than younger adults to skip questions when responding to questionnaires (Sherbourne & Meredith, 1992).

Accuracy of self-reported estimates of functional ability has been questioned by researchers although the findings are mixed. Myers and Huddy (1985) found that institutionalized older adults inaccurately reported current activities of daily living (ADL), physical ability, and estimates of functional capabilities in activities they no longer performed. Sager et al. (1992) found that older adults both under and overestimated their abilities to complete ADLs compared to performance-based measures. Rubenstein, Schairer, Weiland, and Kane (1984) supported at least some of the Sager et al. (1992) findings in their study where geriatric patients overestimated their functional ability. Last, Sager et al. (1992) found that self-reported ADLs performed in home settings were accurate when compared with more objective measures.

The accuracy of older adults' self-reports of memory impairment has also been questioned (e.g., Perlmutter, 1978; Rabbitt, 1982; Sunderland, Watts,

Baddeley, & Harris, 1986; Zelinski, Gilewski, & Thompson, 1980) although some found that older adults are no less accurate than younger adults when queried about survey-type information (e.g., Rodgers & Herzog, 1987).

Linguistic and semantic differences between generations (Kaszniak, 1990), genders, and ethnicity must be considered when evaluating responses to interview questions. Differences in what is considered socially desirable across generations may yield differences in responses to questions. For example, older adults often respond with less frankness to questions regarding sexuality than do younger adults (Yesavage, 1986).

RELIABILITY AND ACCURACY
OF REPORTS BY OTHERS

Staff, family members, and other individuals can be rich sources of primary and supplementary information. Reports by others are particularly helpful when the client is denying information suspected to be true, apparently overreporting symptoms, refusing to talk with a stranger (the interviewer), or unable to participate fully in the interview due to cognitive or physical impairment. The limitations and threats to accuracy and reliability are similar to those of self-reporting and direct observation. In addition, when multiple reports are involved, there is always the issue of which report constitutes the incontrovertible standard. The reliability and accuracy of such reports have been investigated with a variety of informants across a spectrum of content areas, yielding a mixture of findings.

Rubenstein et al. (1984) found that accuracy of functional status was greater with reports from a child, a relative, or a friend than with reports from a spouse. They also found that nurses and community proxies tended to rate patients as more dysfunctional than suggested by more objective indices.

Silverman, Breitner, Mohs, and Davis (1986) found high levels of agreement between multiple informants from the same family when reporting the time of dementia onset for a relative. Similarly, Kukull and Larson (1989) found that retrospective accounts of the symptoms of dementia could be recalled by close relatives of a deceased patient over an average of 2.9 years with reasonable accuracy, although the specificity for symptoms of primary degenerative dementia was only modest.

Last, LaRue, Watson, and Plotkin (1992) examined the reliability of relatives' accounts of dementia symptoms by comparing current reports with those obtained retrospectively. Moderately reliable correlations were obtained between retrospective and initial ratings by relatives over a period of a few months. Relatives recalled patients having fewer psychiatric symptoms in their retrospective accounts when compared with the initial reports, however.

When retrospective reports were examined by the type of relationship (spouse versus younger relative), younger relatives reported higher levels of impairment of demanding functional skills, cognition, mood, and thought disturbance than did spouses.

Though there is evidence from the foregoing studies that reports by others can be accurate, sufficient evidence exists to warrant caution when using only single-source reports regarding the behavior of the client. Perhaps the best model of information gathering is one that includes as many sources as possible so that a convergence of information is accumulated.

Interview Structure

Interviews vary in their structure and function from completely unstructured, free flowing conversations to carefully sequenced and branching questions leading to psychiatric diagnoses. At one end are the highly structured adult diagnostic interview schedules, which specify all questions and probes to be used and may include a response classification or symptom-scoring system by which to rate the client's responses. Diagnostic interview schedules are typically characterized by (a) a list of questions, behaviors, symptoms, and areas of inquiry, (b) a procedure or set of rules for conducting the interview, and (c) a procedure or rules for recording or rating the client's responses (Edelstein, Alberts, & Estill, 1988). Less structured interview schedules provide statements, probes, or outlines for questioning at the option of the interviewer. As interviews decrease in structure, they also tend to increase in the amount of skill and clinical inference required of the interviewer.

We lack sufficient space to cover all available interviews of relevance to older adults or even those developed specifically for older adults. Consequently, a few representative interviews will be briefly discussed for illustrative purposes. Diagnostic and more general structured interviews will be described first, followed by mental status examinations developed as cognitive screening instruments.

STRUCTURED INTERVIEWS

The Structured Clinical Interview for DSM-III-R (SCID; Spitzer et al., 1992) is an example of a semistructured diagnostic interview developed for a wide range of age groups and that may be used with older adults. The structure of the SCID allows several diagnostic hypotheses to be tested successively, with items grouped by diagnosis and criteria. For economy of time, a branching system allows the interviewer to skip items that are of no diagnostic significance for the client. The SCID also allows follow-up questions to clarify responses and obtain additional information that can ostensibly increase the validity of the interviewer's ratings. Two forms of the SCID are available. The SCID-P (Patient) is used with adult psychiatric patients. The SCID-NP (Nonpatient) is used with individuals who have not been identified as psychiatric patients. The semistructured nature of the SCID is both a strength and a weakness. Each opportunity to skip questions or probe with greater or less aggressiveness is a potential source of error that can influence reliability and validity. These errors can be diminished by thorough training in the use of the SCID, which is essential in clinical research.

The Geriatric Mental State Schedule (GMS; Copeland et al., 1976) is a semistructured interview for examining the mental state of older adults. The GMS comprises items from the eighth edition of the Present State Examination (Wing, Birley, Cooper, Graham, & Isaacs, 1967) and the Present Status Schedule (Spitzer, Fleiss, Burdock, & Hardesty, 1964). The authors established good reliability among trained raters, recommending that a person undertake 20 joint interviews with an instructor to establish adequate reliability.

The GMS formed the backbone for the psychiatric section of the Comprehensive Assessment and Referral Evaluation (CARE; Gurland et al., 1977-78). In constructing CARE, the GMS items were rewritten in a simplified form. Additional items were also added from a variety of other instruments to create a new one that addresses physical, social, and mental functioning of community-dwelling individuals. CARE comprises 22 scales with 314 items. According to Gurland and Wilder (1984), it permits one to determine

(a) the presence and severity of specific psychiatric, physical or social/environmental problems, (b) their etiological associations, (c) the severity of their personal or social effects, (d) the availability of assets and supports to the individual, (e) the effects of problems on the use of supports and services, (f) the changes that occur in problems over time, and (g) whether the person is at risk for developing new problems, or for deterioration, institutionalization or death. (p. 130)

The authors have reported good interrater reliability, internal consistency, concurrent validity, and predictive validity (Teresi, Golden, & Gurland, 1984). The SHORT-CARE is a briefer version of CARE that measures three content areas—depression, dementia, and disability—with good interrater reliability and internal consistency. It contains 143 items that form 6 of the 22 indicator scales from CARE.

The Cambridge Mental Disorders of the Elderly Examination (CAMDEX; Roth et al., 1986) is another example of a multielement assessment instrument that includes an interview component. It comprises three sections: (a) a structured clinical interview for obtaining family history and present and past history of the present problem(s), (b) a small battery of neuropsychological tests, and (c) a structured interview for a relative or other informant that addresses family history and present and past history of the present problem(s). The CAMDEX focuses on the diagnosis of dementia, particularly in its early stages. Administration requires approximately 80 minutes, including 60 minutes for the client and 20 minutes for the informant.

Each of the foregoing interviews can be of benefit to the clinician. The advantages of such interviews are that they force one to consider issues and factors that might be overlooked if one were interviewing in an unstructured fashion and that they can lead to more reliable conclusions than one might reach with less structure. Structured interviews can serve as excellent guides for students and less experienced clinicians. The principal disadvantages of structured and semistructured interviews are the significant amounts of time and training required to administer them.

MENTAL STATUS EXAMINATIONS

The mental status examination (MSE) is typically a semistructured interview that may also contain other performance measures (e.g., figure drawing). MSEs vary in depth and breadth of coverage. Content extends from minimal coverage of cognitive functioning (e.g., cognitive screening instruments) requiring only 10 minutes for assessment to more comprehensive coverage of cognitive and psychodiagnostic status requiring over an hour. The comprehensiveness of the MSE one employs is often a function of the question at hand, the sophistication and training of the examiner, and the setting (e.g., bedside, examination room, office) in which the examination is to be conducted. Results of the MSE can form the basis for more extensive assessment or the decision to forego standard assessment procedures due to the level of functioning of the client. The MSE can also serve as a pretest for cognitive status, permitting periodic reexamination that enables one to track the general mental status of an individual throughout the course of progressive dementia, before and after surgery, and so forth. Though the MSE has much to recommend it, it is limited by the cognitive-language status of the individual being interviewed. Moreover, the reliability of the MSE can vary with the amount of structure and standardization. Standardized administration and scoring procedures exist for a variety of the briefer cognitive screening instruments that fall under the rubric of MSEs. However, few of the more comprehensive MSEs are available in standardized form (i.e., with normative data, standard instructions, standard scoring procedures).

Cognitive screening instruments typically have been developed for detecting moderate to severe cognitive impairment. The advantages of such instruments are their brevity, ease of administration, and standardized forms. Their disadvantages include insensitivity to mild cognitive impairment (e.g., Appelgate, Blass, & Williams, 1990), susceptibility to influence by educational level, and their emphasis on language skills. These disadvantages become somewhat less significant as one moves from the briefest instruments to instruments of greater breadth and depth.

As with structured interviews, detailed discussion of the mental status examination is beyond the scope of this chapter. The interested reader is referred to Strub and Black's (1993) very thorough discussion of the mental status examination in neurology, Hodges's (1994) excellent coverage of cognitive assessment, and Mandell, Knoefel, and Albert's (1994) MSE for use with older adults. Albert (1994) has also provided a relatively complete analysis of the more popular brief cognitive screening instruments. For illustrative purposes, three different types of MSEs will be briefly described: one for general screening, one for screening of severely impaired individuals, and one for administration over the telephone.

Of the brief mental status examinations, the Mini-Mental State Examination (MMSE; Folstein et al., 1975) is probably the most widely used (Albert, 1994) and requires only approximately 10 minutes to administer. Domains assessed include memory, language, spatial ability, and set shifting. The MMSE has good 24-hour test-retest reliability ($r = .83$ to .89; Folstein et al., 1975). Sensitivity has been estimated to be 83% with individuals with moderate to severe dementia. Little training is required to administer the MMSE. Scores of 23 or lower are considered indicative of cognitive impairment, although higher and lower cutoffs have been established for individuals with multiple sclerosis (Beaty & Goodkin, 1990), lower education (Anthony, LeResche, Niaz, Von Korff, & Folstein, 1982) and different ages (Bleecker, Bolla-Wilson, Kawas, & Agnew, 1988).

The Severe Impairment Battery (SIB) (Saxton, McGonigle-Gibson, Swihart, Miller, & Boller, 1990), which requires 20+ minutes to administer, offers an alternative to the MMSE and other brief assessment instruments for individuals whose severe cognitive impairment can yield a floor effect with other screening measures. The SIB measures six domains: attention, orientation, language, memory, visuoperception, and construction. Social skills and praxis are also assessed in a very limited fashion. Scores, which range from 0 to 152, are correlated with those of the MMSE ($r = .74$) and have shown good stability over time ($r = .85$).

The Telephone Interview for Cognitive Status (TICS; Brandt, Spencer, & Folstein, 1988) is an 11-item, telephone-administered test of cognitive status designed primarily with an eye to research. The instrument requires approximately 10 minutes to administer and taps the following dimensions: orientation, immediate recall, information, language, concentration and set shifting, and concept formation (word opposites). Scores range from 0 to 40 and are strongly correlated with those on the MMSE ($r = .94$). Test-retest reliability is excellent ($r = .97$). An obvious advantage of the TICS over the MMSE and other instruments is that one may follow the cognitive status of individuals in the community without the expense of time and money associated with in-person interviews.

All of the foregoing assessment instruments can be helpful in the assessment of older adults although none is without limitations. Scores on the cognitive screening instruments are subject to influence by age, education, severity of cognitive deficit, location of focal cognitive deficits, racial background (Albert, 1994), physical condition, and familiarity of the assessor with test administration. Moreover, with the possible exception of the Strub and Black (1993) MSE, none of the other measures should be construed as providing a thorough evaluation of cognitive functioning. On the more positive side, scores on these instruments provide convenient means for quantifying the general cognitive status of individuals and baselines against which cognitive function can be repeatedly compared. They also function as screening instruments to alert the examiner to a need for more thorough cognitive testing, neurological evaluation, or both.

Interview Process

Little empirical support exists to guide the unstructured interview process. Much of the interview behavior of experienced clinicians is guided by repeated reflection on what has and has not worked in similar contexts and by moment-to-moment changes in the client's behavior. Both the client and the clinician bring histories of interactions to the clinical setting that influence at least their initial responses to each other. As the interview progresses, client and therapist exert reciprocal control over each other's behavior in a cybernetic fashion (e.g., Edelstein & Berler, 1987; Edelstein & Yoman, 1991). There are a variety of paths to successful interviews; no particular approach has been demonstrated to be most effective, particularly for unstructured interviews.

The initial element of an interview is establishment of rapport or a therapeutic relationship. The therapeutic relationship may be conceptualized as the collaboration between client and clinician in the interview tasks (cf. Frieswyk et al., 1986). Therefore, one can view the function of the relationship in the interview as the facilitation of the assessment process. The goal of the clinician is to gain the collaboration of the client and ultimately arrive at a reliable and valid analysis.

It is difficult to imagine the interview progressing without certain client collaborative behaviors (e.g, self-disclosure). Gaining the collaboration of the client is a complex process of social influence that requires much of the same social competence required in ordinary dyadic conversations. To achieve the collaborative relationship between client and clinician, the clinician may have to perform a procedure whereby the client's behavior is shaped into a collaborative role with the clinician.

CLIENT ROLE BEHAVIOR

The client's goal is to obtain professional services and not other personal or intimate contacts from the clinician (Zwick & Attkisson, 1984; Kanfer & Schefft, 1988). The client is expected to participate actively and collaboratively (Orne & Wender, 1968; Heitler, 1976). This can be accomplished by sharing responsibility with the clinician for the interview process (Kanfer & Schefft, 1988). This sharing includes the client stating personal goals and wishes, reporting concerns and complaints pertaining to a presenting problem, making decisions about the scope and course of treatment if needed, and openly discussing concerns about the treatment and clinician (Orne & Wender, 1968; Strupp & Bloxom, 1973; Zwick & Attkisson, 1984). Discussion of treatment concerns may involve disagreeing with the clinician and making specific requests. The client can also participate actively by offering his or her own problem solutions rather than seeking advice from the clinician (Orne & Wender, 1968; Zwick & Attkisson, 1984). Similarly, the client may generate consequences and value judgments for personal courses of action rather than eliciting them from the clinician.

The client must self-disclose to participate effectively in the interview (Kanfer & Schefft, 1988; Orne & Wender, 1968; Strupp & Bloxom, 1973; Zwick & Attkisson, 1984). This may entail tolerating discomfort, strong emotional reactions, or both from the content disclosed. Clients also learn to take responsibility for their problems in living (cf. Strupp & Bloxom, 1973) by discussing problems in terms of their own behavior. Self-disclosure, particularly of sensitive information, requires trust. Indeed, the client's perception that the therapist is trustworthy has been noted to be one of the most critical features of effective helping relationships (e.g., Cormier & Cormier, 1991).

Though no agreement exists as to what constitutes trustworthy behavior, Alberts (1991) has gleaned five classes of therapist behavior from the literature on client trust that various authors have argued convey a sense of trust to the client. These are

(a) That the therapist is genuinely concerned about the welfare of the client and is motivated solely by this concern to benefit the client, (b) that the therapist respects and does not judge the client despite the client's present inability to adjust to demands of his/her life circumstance, (c) that the therapist is understanding and comprehends the nature of the client's concerns and needs, (d) that the therapist credibly communicates his/her capacity to assist the client in improving his/her situation and is optimistic about a positive outcome, and (e) that the therapist is honest, reliable, and can be depended on to do what he/she says. (pp. 11-12)

Though these behavior categories may offer the therapist some guidance, they do not refer to specific therapist behaviors associated with trust. To address that void in the literature, Alberts and Edelstein (1992) developed a 20-item trust behavior assessment scale that could be used to measure the extent to which therapists emitted trustworthy behaviors. A factor analysis of this instrument revealed three principal factors: (a) positive regard or interest, (b) incompetence or disrespect, and (c) directive or structuring. Items that loaded significantly on these factors are as follows: A plus sign indicates a positive item and a minus sign indicates a negative item.

When the therapist first sees me, he or she generally smiles and is warm. +
The therapist makes decisions that affect me without asking for my input. −
The therapist holds his or her eye contact when talking to me. +
The therapist remembers and brings up things that I have talked about before. +
If something is bothering me, the therapist lets me talk about it and get it off my chest. +
The therapist takes time to think about the things I say before answering me. +
The therapist indicates that he or she won't judge me or criticize me no matter what I say. +
The therapist indicates that he or she respects me despite the problems I have. +
The therapist talks so much that I don't get a chance to say as much as I would like. −
The therapist gives me wrong information. −
The therapist is easily distracted and loses his or her train of thought. −
The therapist hurries our conversations along as if he or she was impatient with me. −
The therapist misstates things that I have said. −
The therapist indicates that my concerns or problems are silly. −
The therapist tells me his or her view of my problems and what it will take for me to feel better. +
The therapist gives me advice or suggestions about how to deal with my problems. +
The therapist indicates that I should ask questions if what he or she says is not clear. +
The therapist tells me what I should do if I need help in an emergency. +
The therapist indicates that for therapy to work, we need to trust each other. +

Use of the positively valenced behaviors and avoidance of the negatively valenced behaviors should increase the likelihood that the clinician will gain the trust of the client in the initial interviews. Unfortunately, we have no rules for determining the most effective points in an interview to use these strategies.

Shaping Client Role Behavior

The first step in accomplishing this is for the clinician to recognize that the interview process is one of mutual influence between the clinician and the client (Cormier & Cormier, 1991; Edelstein & Berler, 1987; Ferster, 1979). As Ferster (1979) noted, "the patient's speech is sustained by the way it influences the therapist" (p. 30). The clinician, therefore, must regulate his or her reactions to the client's verbal behavior to influence that behavior. Among the implications of this are that the clinician's listening responses, empathic responses, and statements of positive regard are made contingently and not unconditionally (Hamilton, 1988). For example, the clinician may cease minimal verbal responses (e.g., "uh huh," "good") when a client perseverates in describing a past event to the exclusion of a current topic of more immediate importance. An overriding concern in this endeavor is to keep the interview sufficiently reinforcing for the client to continue to participate collaboratively in the interview (Edelstein & Yoman, 1991).

Listening Behavior

If the interview requires reciprocation, then listening is an essential ingredient of the clinician's repertoire. Potter (as quoted in Cormier & Cormier, 1991) said, "Listening is the other half of talking. Listening well is no less important than speaking well and it is probably more difficult." Four important listening responses that the clinician may find effective for a variety of functions are *clarification, paraphrasing, reflection,* and *summarization* (Cormier & Cormier, 1991).

Clarification. This involves questioning the client regarding the content of a recent response. It is used to encourage clients to elaborate on what has been said, establish the accuracy of what one has heard, or to clarify confusing statements (e.g., "Are you saying that you don't know how you are going to face your responsibilities now that you have lost the ability to get around without assistance?").

Paraphrasing. This involves rephrasing the content of a client's message and is used to help the client focus on the content of the message or to focus on content rather than affect.

Reflection. This involves rephrasing the affective component of the client's statement(s). Reflection is used to encourage clients to express affect, express it with greater intensity, help the client acknowledge and manage affective responses, and help the client discriminate between different types of affective responses (Cormier & Cormier, 1991).

Summarization. This involves two or more paraphrases or reflections that pull together statements the client has made over a period of time. In addition to distilling the client's statements, summarization can also be used to identify a common theme or pattern, interrupt excessive rambling, or review the progress of the interview session (Cormier & Cormier, 1991).

The following vignette will be used to illustrate each of these listening responses:

An 80-year-old woman recently lost her husband to an unanticipated heart attack, leaving her at home alone to dwell on his loss and to struggle with the many daily tasks that her husband performed independently of her. She states,"I don't know what I am going to do now. My whole life centered around my husband. I never was much good at handling our financial affairs or taking care of little problems that occurred. I can't sleep, I can't concentrate, and I don't know where to begin with making sense of our financial situation."

Clarification—"Are you saying that you are having a difficult time not only dealing with the loss of your husband but also dealing with all the financial and other affairs that he handled all those years?"

Paraphrasing—"You seem to have lost the most important element of your life and are having trouble knowing how to deal with that loss and with all your new responsibilities that were previously handled by your husband."

Reflection—"You seem to be feeling anxiety and despair over how to cope with the loss of your husband and the assumption of his responsibilities."

Summarization—"Let me see if I can pull together what you have just discussed with me. With the loss of your husband, you are experiencing emotional problems associated with his loss and some very immediate practical problems associated with everyday affairs and your need to assume his financial responsibilities."

Through practice and experience, one can learn to use these listening techniques with considerable facility. For a more comprehensive discussion of these and other very helpful counseling techniques, the reader is referred to Cormier and Cormier (1991).

Interview Stress

Be mindful that the assessment interview can be a very stressful undertaking for an older adult for a variety of reasons. A few of these might be the physical energy required to complete a lengthy interview, the sharing of intimate information with a stranger, the risk that one will lose one's autonomy in decision making as a result of the interview, the frustration resulting from the inability to answer certain questions, and the realization that one's memory is becoming impaired. Reducing stress can lead to greater client cooperation, more complete exploration of presenting problems, a lower likelihood of exacerbating problems associated with cognitive impairment (e.g., apparent disorientation or memory impairment), and a greater likelihood that the interview will be completed.

Anxiety reduction can be accomplished in a variety of manners. The clinician can begin by informing the client that he or she will be asking many questions, some of which may seem to be unrelated to each other. The client can be encouraged to stop the clinician at any time to ask questions about the interview in general or about individual questions. Merely informing the client of his or her role in the interview process can often alleviate some anxiety. Apprehensiveness or anxiety can be reduced by telling the client that some of the questions will be more difficult than others, that he or she should not to worry if all the questions are not answered correctly, and (when true) that there are no right or wrong answers. When a client fails to correctly answer or provide an answer to a standardized assessment question, one can often obtain relevant information and reduce some of the client's concern over failure by asking related questions that address much of the same content but without the difficulty or complexity of the standardized questions.

A client's overall relaxed state can be attained through relaxation techniques (e.g., diaphragmatic breathing). This state can be paired with successively more threatening aspects of the interview (Edelstein & Yoman, 1991). Exposure techniques can also be used to increase the likelihood that the client will continue despite growing anxiety. For example, when the client changes the topic from a difficult problem to an off-task one, the clinician might persistently but supportively bring the client back on task until the problem topic had been thoroughly discussed.

Perhaps the best advice for the novice or less experienced clinician is to treat the interview as a situation in which problems can arise and interventions can be employed. Anxiety, for example, can be addressed in the context of the interview in much the same fashion as it would be with a client seeking help for anxiety. Similarly, problem-solving techniques are just as effective with interview process problems as they are with the presenting problems of clients. The clinician's goal is to develop a collaborative relationship with the client and obtain information necessary for making decisions. Forays into brief interventions during the interview process can often turn an apparently hopeless interview into a very productive and lasting relationship.

Although the foregoing process strategies can be very effective, one's efficiency and effectiveness will also rest on an appreciation of one's own biases that are brought to the interview setting.

Interview Biases: The Example of Ageism

Perhaps the most important of the potential biases that one can bring to the older-adult interview is *ageism*. The term was first described by Butler (1969) as the system of false assumptions and beliefs regarding older adults. Ageism includes socially accepted negative attitudes, erroneous beliefs, stereotypes, and discriminatory behaviors and practices toward older adults (Rodeheaver, 1990). Lack of knowledge about older adults can produce such a set of false beliefs, which can profoundly influence behavior toward older adults. Among the false beliefs are the following:

> (1) Aging brings an end to productivity; (2) The aged naturally desire to disengage from society; (3) Older people are inflexible, set in their ways; (4) Senility is a normal part of aging; and (5) The aged are (or should be) serene and accepting of these changes. (Rodeheaver, 1990, p. 7.1-7.2)

Ageism can influence the behavior of the clinician by encouraging discriminatory practices and fostering a higher recall of negative traits than of positive ones (Perdue & Gurtman, 1990). Moreover, Dupree and Patterson (1985) argue thusly:

> Views associated with professional ageism (particularly those noting that mental illness in old age is inevitable, untreatable, disabling, and irreversible) become a self-fulfilling prophecy, leading to a lack of prevention and treatment, which in turn tends to confirm the original belief. (p. 10)

Problems of older adults may be incorrectly labeled as senility, and the psychosocial concerns of older adults may be minimized or discussed less (Greene, Adelman, Charon, & Hoffman, 1986). These problems in professional ageism are compounded in older women because of sexism and the tendency to view them stereotypically as sick and alone. Investigators have noted that clinicians working with older adults tend to dominate the interview, are less respectful, less patient, and less engaged (Greene et al., 1986). Likewise, mental health professionals recommend drugs more frequently than psychotherapy and give poorer prognoses to older as compared to younger patients (Gatz & Pearson, 1988).

Suggestions for clinicians to employ to prevent the negative effect of ageism on the interview process include learning about the aging process, having greater exposure to older adults, and examining one's own personal feelings about aging and how they affect one's professional performance (Dupree & Patterson, 1985). It is particularly important to appreciate that ageism can even influence client behavior, as older adults adopt these attitudes themselves.

The foregoing recommendations should be complemented by knowledge of how physical changes sometimes associated with aging can influence the interview process. Knowledge and consideration of these factors can determine whether one achieves a successful interview or an incomplete or compromised one.

Physical Changes and Problems

During the initial interview, any physical problems of the client that might require further investigation or that could compromise the adequacy of the interview should be considered. Past medical history and present physical status should be considered and a current inventory of prescribed medications reviewed. In particular, sensory domains should be evaluated early in the interview.

HEARING

Hearing loss is a frequent problem among older adults and is more prevalent in men than in women. It has been estimated that more than 50% of the 27 million Americans over age 65 are affected by hearing impairment (Pfeifer, 1980; Vernon, 1989). Accordingly, health professionals should be aware of clues to possible hearing impairment: a history of ear infections, loud speech, requests for the clinician to repeat statements, the inability to distinguish figure-ground sounds in a group, and the tendency to watch a speaker's mouth intently (Vernon, 1989).

As the amount of background noise increases, older adults with hearing problems are particularly affected. This phenomenon, known as *masking,* highlights the need to minimize ambient background noise when interviewing older adults (Storandt, 1994). Hearing difficulties also increase at higher tone frequencies; therefore, older adults may experience difficulty distinguishing certain consonants (Ordy, Brizzee, Beavers, & Medart, 1979). Female clinicians with high-pitched voices should be sensitive to the fact that difficulty in hearing high frequencies may pose special communication problems with older adults and may need to consider lowering the pitch of their voices (Storandt, 1994). Causes of hearing deficits include presbycusis (loss of

auditory acuity associated with aging), drugs and allergies, circulatory disorders, central organic impairments, and occupational and recreational noise
(Pfeifer, 1980; Storandt, 1994).

Further communication problems may result as individuals with hearing
loss pretend to understand what is being said during the interview. More
critical consequences of hearing loss include denial (Vernon, Griffin, &
Yoken, 1981), isolation (Vernon, 1989), depression (Solomon, 1982), misleading diagnoses (Mindel & Vernon, 1987), and paranoid reactions (Zimbardo, Anderson, & Kabat, 1981).

Practical Recommendations

Interview the client in a quiet setting and minimize distractions; do not attempt
to compete with background noise. Behaviors that interfere with lipreading
include exaggerated or rapid speech, poor lighting, and anything that covers the
speaker's mouth (e.g., pencil, gum, moustache). Make certain there is good
lighting on your face. Sit facing the client so that he or she can take advantage of
your facial expressions. Speak slowly and distinctly. Do not overexaggerate your
mouth movements. Use facial expressions to emphasize a point. Try not to
exaggerate speech or speak too loudly, as this will distort speech. Take frequent
breaks if the client is having to read your lips to completely understand your
questions. Such a task is demanding for an older hearing-impaired person.

If you determine that the client cannot understand you using a face-to-face
seating arrangement and you have reason to believe that the client has better
hearing in one ear than another, you might attempt to talk directly into the
good ear or offer the client a sound amplification device. Such devices are
now inexpensive and readily available. Last, be aware of neutral responses
and head nodding, and if necessary, turn to written communication.

Edelstein, Northrop, Staats, & Packard (1996) have offered the following
additional recommendations with regard to hearing-impaired individuals:

> Do not necessarily rely on the results of audiograms obtained in quiet environments
> if one is really interested in an examinee's ability to comprehend the examiner's
> speech. A hearing (speech perception) check should ideally be performed under
> the conditions of assessment and perhaps in public settings if hearing is suspected
> of contributing to psychosocial problems.
>
> Do not overarticulate, which can distort speech and facial gestures.
>
> Be vigilant for selective (i.e., functional) hearing impairment characterized by
> hearing losses associated with task demands, poor motivation, and perhaps fear
> of performance failure.
>
> Failure to answer a question could result from, among other things, failure to hear
> or inability to understand (comprehend) the question.

VISION

Although 80% of older adults have fair to adequate vision (Pfeifer, 1980), many of those with visual problems have partial blindness, are unemployed, and are women. Types of common visual impairments include decreases in visual acuity, depth perception, peripheral vision, adaptation to light change, tolerance for glare, accommodation, convergence, and ability to look up (Heckheimer, 1989). Cataract, or clouding of the lens of the eye, is another common problem among older adults that can cause problems with glare in brightly lit areas.

Most individuals with significant visual impairment rely on methods of communication such as tape cassettes and lipreading (Shindell, 1989). The majority of such individuals are not completely blind and do not use braille.

Practical Recommendations

Visually impaired older adults may have trouble with nonverbal communication such as facial expressions. Do not assume individuals with visual problems are hard of hearing. Ask for permission before giving physical assistance. When offering physical guidance to an interview setting, give specific suggestions for guiding, determine whether the client has a preference, or both. Place the visually impaired person's hand on your arm just above the elbow. Lead but do not pull or push. Explain changes in the environment as they are encountered.

Once you begin the interview, ask about the client's preferred means of communication. Do not assume the examinee's preferred means of communication. Ask the client to describe their vision problem or any idiosyncrasies involving color, contrast, or field deficits (Shindell, 1989). Ask the examinee to describe any problems with lighting in the assessment room such as glare or insufficient lighting. If glare is a potential problem, make sure that the interview setting is sufficiently illuminated without being so bright as to cause unnecessary glare (Storandt, 1994). Avoid using high-gloss paper for self-report inventories, visual aids, and figure-drawing tasks. Limit nonverbal directions, rely more heavily on verbal or kinesthetic cueing (Shindell, 1989), and use multimodal (say and do) directions when possible. Last, be careful when interpreting the behavior of severely visually impaired examinees. For example, the examinee may arrive early for an assessment session or have rigid scheduling requirements that may be more a function of available transportation than resistance (Shindell, 1989).

MOTOR DISORDERS

Motor-impaired older adults have their own set of distinctive psychological circumstances requiring knowledge and understanding. One must consider the type, severity, and duration of a motor disability as well as the client's reaction and adaptation to such disabilities. Some of the more common motor disorders that might influence the interview assessment process and overall case conceptualization include Parkinsonism, essential familial or senile tremor, senile chorea, apraxia, peripheral neuropathies, muscle weakness (myopathy), and the side effects of various medications (e.g., neuroleptics) (Schlenoff, 1989).

Practical Recommendations

The clinician may have to modify interview procedures depending on the particular motor or perceptual-motor problems presented by the client. For example, some physically disabled individuals may tire easily. The clinician may want to schedule rest periods or use several short interview sessions (Storandt, 1994; Storandt, Siegler, & Elias, 1978). In another case, a client may exhibit a severe speech impairment resulting from a stroke. To adjust for this problem, the clinician may ask the client to write answers to questions. If the client is unable to respond verbally or in writing, questions may be posed in such a way that only a nod of "yes" or "no" is required.

COGNITIVE FUNCTIONING IMPAIRMENT

Memory loss is the most common complaint of the aged (Schear, 1984). Normal aging involves some complaints of memory loss often characterized by a mild increase in or awareness of normal forgetting. Older individuals tend to make errors of omission rather than commission. Recall of material with little association value suffers the most with increasing age, in contrast to material with greater association value and tasks requiring recognition rather than recall. Working memory also appears to suffer with increasing age (Morris, Craik, & Glick, 1990).

Some older adults may also have increasing difficulty with abstraction and flexibility as they age (Salthouse & Prill, 1987). Similarly, some older adults may experience difficulties working with abstract concepts that require significant attention and memory demands (e.g., Hess & Slaughter, 1986).

Practical Recommendations

Cognitively impaired individuals can find an interview particularly difficult and frustrating, leading to fatigue and confusion. Cueing can help with the encoding and retrieval process when questioning older adults with some apparent memory impairment. One may also follow open-ended questions with multiple-choice questions to assist an individual who experiences recall difficulties but is still competent at recognition. When working memory deficits are encountered, written questions can be provided so that the client may repeatedly revisit the information required for decision making. One may also present simpler, shorter, and less complex questions to reduce the demands of working memory and sustained attention. The clinician should be cautious of using too many words or using abstract concepts. Pronouns can be avoided in favor of nouns, to maximize the clarity of sentences. When possible, tasks can be broken into components and the client's success on each component can be praised.

The clinician should pace the interview so that the client is given the opportunity to provide complete information. Good active listening skills (e.g., reflecting, summarizing) can often be helpful when the client experiences difficulty responding to questions in a reasonable amount of time. Most important, the clinician must be patient and careful not to rush through an interview (Pfeifer, 1980; Storandt, 1994; Zeiss, 1992).

Conclusion

The clinical interview can be a very effective method for obtaining information from older adults and significant others. Though it has significant limitations in its most unstructured form, it also affords the clinician the opportunity to engage in an interactive, iterative process of hypothesis testing. The interview can be a rich source of information, but its limitations must be considered because conclusions are drawn from it and other assessment methods.

8

Assessment of Competence to Make Medical Decisions

Marshall B. Kapp

Mental health professionals who work with older adults regularly confront a wide variety of issues related to legal and functional competence. Questions about competence frequently pertain to individuals' abilities to engage in activities necessary to function in everyday life. At other times, questions involve retrospective assessments: for example, whether or not a target person was able to enter competently into a binding agreement, such as a legal will disposing of personal property, that was executed at a previous time. Still other questions relate to an older criminal defendant's competency to stand trial. And finally, on an ongoing basis, mental health professionals treating patients must determine, at least implicitly, whether or not their own patients are competent to accept or refuse the treatments they recommend to them.

The focus of this chapter is on the role of the mental health professional (MHP) as a consultant to legal representatives or treating physicians regarding the mental competence of a patient to make legally and ethically valid medical decisions. Much of the material discussed in the chapter is relevant to competency determinations in general, however. After overviewing the importance of competency assessment in this arena, the chapter considers basic conceptual guidelines, competing definitions of competence, strengths and weaknesses of available standardized assessment tools, possibilities for and limitations of the MHP's role as a competence consultant, and opportunities for research and education in the field.

Before proceeding, a word on nomenclature is necessary. First, because focus in this chapter is on assessment of potential consumers of medical services, the term *patient* is used to refer to the elderly person.

Second, the terms *competence* and *capacity* require definition. In everyday parlance, these terms are used interchangeably. Technically, however, there exists a significant distinction. Competence represents a legal status concerning an individual's right to make life decisions and engage in a variety of transactions with others. Competence can be determined conclusively only by a court with appropriate jurisdiction. In most states, this is a probate or other equity court. Capacity, in contrast, refers not to authoritative judicial determinations but instead to the working assessments of patients' cognitive and emotional abilities that treating clinicians make in everyday practice. Usually, capacity determinations are made relatively informally (Mahler & Perry, 1988).

The overwhelming majority of patients, even those with obvious deficits in abilities, never proceed to formal judicial adjudication regarding competence in the context of a guardianship proceeding. Thus, as a practical matter, the MHP's assessment of a patient's decision-making abilities is ordinarily a major, if not determinative, influence on the extent to which care providers will recognize and respect the patient's own medical choices, particularly when the patient and treating physician disagree. Because this chapter has a predominantly legal leitmotif, the term competence will be employed primarily.

The Importance and Consequences of Legal Competence Assessment

The assessment of competence assumes central importance as a result of the legal and ethical primacy in the medical care context of the doctrine of informed consent. Under the doctrine of informed consent, medical interventions (diagnostic, therapeutic, or experimental) may not be carried out without an adult individual's voluntary, informed, and competent consent, with limited exceptions, such as life-threatening emergencies (President's Commission, 1982). This legal doctrine embodies the fundamental ethical principle of personal autonomy or self-determination, including the individual's right to make bad or even foolish choices.

A formal adjudication of incompetence conducted by a court in response to a guardianship proceeding carries with it profound legal consequences; it disempowers the patient from making particular types of decisions. An adjudication of incompetence does not negate the medical provider's obligation to obtain valid consent before conducting a medical intervention. Rather, it shifts the decision-making authority from the patient to a surrogate or proxy appointed by the court. The surrogate is referred to as a *guardian* or *conservator,* depending on the jurisdiction in which the judicial proceeding is taking place and the surrogate's specific responsibilities.

When patients' cognitive and emotional problems limit their ability to make valid decisions and there is no court involvement, providers often rely on available family members or significant others to make decisions on the patient's behalf. The authority of surrogate decision makers may be conferred by statutes such as a state's family consent statute (Areen, 1987) or by a durable power of attorney instrument executed earlier by the patient when still decisionally capable (Annas, 1991). In many situations, providers turn to nonjudicially appointed surrogates as a matter of long-standing, traditionally accepted custom and convenience, even in the absence of explicit legal authority to do so.

For most medical patients, working clinical assessments of capacity are conducted exclusively by the treating physician, sometimes with input from nursing staff members (Weiler, 1991). For some patients, however, the treating physician will request a formal consultation by a mental health practitioner, typically a psychiatrist or clinical psychologist. These requests usually occur when a patient refuses to follow medical recommendations (Grisso, 1986; Melton, Petrila, Poythress, & Slobogin, 1987).

The consultation request may occur for several reasons. The treating physician may have a sincere feeling of uncertainty and discomfort about the patient's decision-making capacity and may value the opinion of a professional who is presumed to have particular expertise in evaluating cognitive and emotional capacity. Much of the time, however, concern about potential legal consequences underlies the consultation request. The treating physician may wish to respect a patient's decision to refuse a particular form of treatment but is concerned that a family member or other patient representative may later fault the physician for withholding or withdrawing an intervention. A mental health consultation may be requested in such a case to bolster documentation in support of respecting the patient's choice. Conversely, the treating physician who objects to a patient's noncompliance with medical recommendations may call in mental health consultants to convince the patient to reconsider and consent, or failing that, to support the appointment of a surrogate decision maker.

Basic Conceptual Guidelines

There is no magical "competence meter" that produces definitive, objective answers to questions of competence. The process is inevitably subjective and highly value laden (see the discussion to follow). However, several basic conceptual parameters guide competence assessments.

First, assessments begin with a clear presumption that adults who have not been otherwise adjudicated are competent to make decisions for themselves. Thus, the burden of proof rests with the party who is disputing the person's competence and must be established by clear and convincing evidence (Mishkin, 1989). A mere preponderance of proof (i.e., 51%) of the evidence ordinarily is insufficient for a finding of incompetence.

Second, competence reflects the individual's functional abilities or capacities. It should not be determined by a patient's medical decision itself or by the diagnosis the patient carries (Grisso & Appelbaum, 1991). Although, in practice, clinicians may resort to outcome tests (i.e., "Do I agree with the patient's decision?"; Abernethy, 1984), such tests of competence have been thoroughly rejected in legal and ethical thinking. When a patient's decision seems manifestly inappropriate, it should be viewed as a red flag signaling the possible need for further evaluation of the patient's capacity, not as a test of capacity itself. Also rejected is the notion that clinical diagnoses can be equated with decision-making capacity (e.g., a patient diagnosed with paranoid schizophrenia should not automatically be presumed to be unable to make competent decisions about medical care). Health care providers should remember that clinical diagnoses are arrived at for therapeutic purposes, not competency determination. Patients with dementia or psychiatric illness possess widely varying cognitive and emotional capacities. Although a patient's diagnosis may suggest the need for further investigation, it does not predetermine the outcome of competence decisions.

Third, there has been a clear retreat from earlier conceptualizations of competence as a global, all-or-none construct. Until about 20 years ago, both the medical and legal systems assumed that individuals were either completely competent, in which case they retained all decision-making prerogatives, or completely incompetent, such that all choices concerning that person were delegated to a surrogate. At present, competence is understood as decision specific in nature. Both clinicians and attorneys recognize that different types of decisions affecting the patient's well-being may entail different types and levels of cognitive and emotional abilities (Silberfeld, Nash, & Singer, 1993). The patient who is able to decide competently about undergoing a yearly mammogram test may be quite incompetent to decide about amputation of a gangrenous limb. Recognition of this principle is embodied in the recent wave of state guardianship statute amendments establishing partial or limited appointment of a surrogate decision maker, with the surrogate's authority delimited strictly to those areas in which the individual is incapacitated, as a less restrictive or intrusive alternative to complete or plenary guardianship (Hommel, Wang, & Bergman, 1990). That is, competence involves a relative, as opposed to an absolute, degree of cognitive and emotional capacity to make a particular decision. Assessment of competence, hence, should be focused narrowly on the issue of whether the particular individual is sufficiently capable to make a particular decision at a particular time under particular circumstances.

The Context of Competence

Perhaps the most important conceptual point about competence and medical decision making is that it must be viewed within the context of a particular patient and a particular set of circumstances. One of the law's great failings is that it treats competence as an essentially static condition or characteristic. In contrast, health care professionals are more likely to recognize competence as part of a dynamic process occurring over a period of time and involving an interplay of factors, including the patient's cognitive capacity, relationship to the treatment environment and personnel, and the nature of the decision at hand (Altman, Parmelee, & Smyer, 1992).

A patient's cognitive and emotional state may fluctuate over time, in response to either underlying mental pathology or environmental factors, ranging from seasonal changes in climate to the waxings and wanings of available social support. For this reason, repeated examinations conducted under varying circumstances are desirable for the most accurate assessment of competence.

The manner in which information concerning a specific medical decision is expressed to a patient may affect the patient's ability to comprehend and rationally consider that information. An examiner conducting a competency assessment should not assume automatically that the patient has received a substantive, understandable presentation of pertinent information prior to declining consent to the physician's recommendation. A refusal of recommended treatment may be due to insufficient, ineffective communication between provider and patient. The patient may be able to comprehend the choice—and, indeed, be willing to consent to intervention—once adequate explanation has been provided (Altman, Parmelee, & Smyer, 1992).

Similarly, a consulting MHP should consider the interpersonal relationships between the treating physician, other members of the treatment team, and the patient in assessing the causes of a patient's refusal of treatment. Educational, cultural, religious, ethnic, or linguistic barriers to effective communication may interfere with rational decision making. Such factors should be recognized and addressed before noncompliance is blamed on the patient's lack of capacity (Saks, 1991). Treatment professionals and their interactions with the patient can, in some cases, be changed to facilitate patient compliance. In extreme situations, even a change in the treating physician may be in order.

A patient's apparent incompetence may represent a transient reaction to a physical illness rather than the result of a continuing mental disease or defect. In such cases, effective treatment of the physical ailment will enhance the ability to make future decisions. Medical treatments that are intended to improve the patient's own eventual ability to make autonomous choices are much easier to justify on legal and ethical grounds than interventions that bring about no change in competency status.

Similarly, aspects of ongoing patient treatment, especially side effects of drug therapy, may produce diminished cognitive or emotional ability. This is particularly likely in older patients. In these situations, manipulating the drug regimen, at least until an accurate competence assessment has been made, is preferable to ignoring the patient's expressed wishes.

As important as contexts can be in assessing competence, it is just as important to acknowledge that context is also not a sufficient basis on which to judge competence. In other words, it is important to avoid the bias that all people within a particular treatment setting (e.g., an intensive care unit; Cohen, McCue, & Green, 1993) or who have received a particular treatment modality (e.g., pain relieving medications) are incompetent. Within any specific medical setting or modality, the level of patients' cognitive and emotional functioning differs enormously. Consequently, there is no substitute for careful individual assessment (Grisso & Appelbaum, 1991).

Once these kinds of contextual impediments to competent decision making, as well as possible assessment biases, have been recognized, addressed, or ruled out, the MHP can be more confident that an appropriate assessment has been made.

Definitions of Competence

A multitude of approaches to the task of defining competence to make medical decisions have been introduced into the health sciences, and to a lesser extent the legal, literature over the past several decades. Many of these constructs are reviewed in Kapp (1990, 1992). These proposals are variations on the following basic questions (Gutheil & Appelbaum, 1991; Roth, Meisel, & Lidz, 1977):

Can the person make and express choices concerning his or her life?

Can the person offer reasons for the choices made?

Are the reasons underlying the person's choices rational (i.e., based on factually plausible suppositions rather than delusions)?

Is the person able to understand the personal implications of the choices that are made?

Are the person's choices authentic; that is, do they appear to be consistent with the person's previously known values and preferences rather than aberrations resulting directly from an illness? (Hipshman, 1987)

All of these questions can be encompassed under two general categories (Beck, 1987): (a) Does the individual have the capacity to assimilate the relevant facts, and (b) can the patient appreciate or rationally understand his or her own situation as it relates to the medical facts? A mentally disordered person has the capacity to refuse treatment if he or she is aware of having a mental disorder, has sufficient factual knowledge about the proposed treatment, and does not base refusal on delusional beliefs.

Capacity criteria, according to Beck (1987), require that patients are knowledgeable and aware of pertinent facts. They do not require that the patient agree with the clinician's interpretation of those facts. Put differently, the patient who says in effect, "I know what you say, but I do not agree," usually possesses decisional capacity.

Beck argues that a patient may deny having an illness correctly because, in fact, there is no illness, or incorrectly because the patient does not understand his or her own situation. Only denial of a real illness signals decisional incapacity; consequently, the consulting MHP's first task in this formulation is to verify the existence of an actual illness. Moreover, Beck asserts that delusions produce decisional incapacity only if they relate to treatment refusal. The MHP consultant should probe whether even the delusional patient's choice rests on a realistic foundation.

Despite intellectually sophisticated constructs of competence outlined in the professional literature, legal determinations of individuals' competence often have been based on extremely vague guidelines. Most state guardianship statutes (Frolik & Brown, 1992; Strauss, Wolf, & Shilling, 1990) are patterned after the general wording of the definition of *incapacitated person* appearing in the Uniform Probate Code (Chapter 5, § 1-207[7]) and the Uniform Guardianship and Protective Procedures Act, both of which are model acts written by the National Conference of Commissioners on Uniform State Laws:

[One] who is impaired by reason of mental illness, mental deficiency, physical illness or disability, advanced age, chronic use of drugs, chronic intoxication, or other cause (except minority) to the extent of lacking sufficient understanding or capacity to make or communicate responsible decisions.

After thoroughly surveying the limited body of reported case law on the subject, legal scholar Elyn R. Saks (1991) concluded that courts, on the whole, have been remarkably nonspecific and imprecise about the criteria on which they base competence in medical treatment scenarios. Once the legal jargon has been cleared away, she suggests, most judicial determinations boil down to a general application of the "understanding and belief" test proposed in the literature. Under a typical formulation of this approach, a patient to be considered competent must have "sufficient mind to reasonably understand [his] condition, the nature and effect of the proposed treatment, attendant risks in pursuing the treatment, and not pursuing the treatment" (In re Schiller, 1977).

Tests of Competence

A number of standardized tests for measuring mental functioning in the elderly (Grisso, 1986), as well as other populations such as patients with HIV infection (Jones, Teng, Folstein, & Harrison, 1993), have been developed and disseminated widely. Silver (1987) recently proposed a triad of tests, including the Alzheimer's Disease Assessment Scale, Wechsler Adult Intelligence Scale, and the Wechsler Memory Scale. Baker (1989) examined the relative merits of the Folstein Mini-Mental State Examination, Kahn's Mental Status Questionnaire, Cognitive Capacity Screening Examination, Mattis Dementia Rating Scale, and Kokmen Short Test of Mental Status. Baker argues that the standardization and quick administerability by nurses are benefits of these tests but admits that they are only preliminary screening instruments, not the final word on a patient's capacity. Even the developers of these instruments acknowledge that they merely indicate the need for further inquiry, especially when they have been designed for patient management purposes and not particularly for use in resolving forensic (i.e., legal) questions (Jones et al., 1993). As the designers of one new quantitative screening test for competence have stated, "This test does not determine legal competency but rather is an aid to the clinician in forming an opinion about clinical competency" (Janofsky, McCarthy, & Folstein, 1992).

Even though there is some evidence suggesting a high rate of agreement between intuitive, "gut" judgments and more formal assessments of competence using standardized instruments (Cohen et al., 1993), standard psychological tests have been criticized because they usually were not constructed specifically for the older age cohort, are of suspect reliability, lack ecological validity, and are incapable of resolving the problem of differential diagnosis in the elderly (Altman et al., 1992). These criticisms are especially pointed when the older person is institutionalized (Altman & Parmelee, 1992).

Moreover, in clinical practice, competence assessments conducted by mental health professionals often diverge from the sophisticated theoretical constructs found in the literature because of the tendency to rely too heavily on available standardized, quantitative testing devices as opposed to functional assessments. Consistent with the conceptual guidelines reviewed earlier, it is important that the choice of instrument vary depending on the aspect of the patient's mentation that is in question, such as orientation, memory, cognitive processing, or neurological functioning.

As useful as standardized tests may be in establishing competence, they do not supplant the need for functional assessment of the mental and behavioral skills involved in the particular decision-making process in question. Standardized tests should form but one component of the assessment package that mental health professionals share with physicians, attorneys, and the courts. It is essential that test results be synthesized with other available data. It is especially important, in keeping with the discussion of context, to assess the functional capacity of an individual to engage in the cognitive and emotional processes required to address the particular issue at hand.

Functional assessments focus on the person's ability to perform everyday tasks and make decisions closely relevant to the decision in question. Information about functioning can be obtained by asking the patient directly or interviewing family members about the patient's abilities. In both cases, reports should be considered tentative due to potential representational biases that either exaggerate or minimize difficulties.

Grisso and Applebaum (1991; see also Grisso, 1994) outline four abilities that should be assessed in decision-making assessments: (a) Can the patient express a choice? (b) Does the patient understand treatment information disclosed in an informed consent procedure? (c) Does the patient appreciate the personal significance of the problem and the treatment? and (d) Can the patient process this information rationally? A structured interview in which patients are presented information about the disorder and treatment and questioned about their understanding of the information can be an excellent way to assess decisional capacity (Edelstein, Nygren, Northrop, Staats, & Pool, 1993).

The Role of the Mental Health Professional

As noted, physicians and attorneys request formal consultations from MHPs concerning the competence of an older individual for a variety of reasons. The following discussion concentrates on the MHP's role when asked to assist in a determination about the older person's ability to make autonomous medical and daily living choices when judicial appointment of a surrogate decision maker is also a viable option.

A number of commentators (Hull, Holmes, & Karst, 1990) have suggested broad input from an array of health and social service providers who bring complementary perspectives to a holistic evaluation of patients' abilities and the environmental conditions that support or impinge on functional capacity. Reform guardianship legislation enacted in the past few years in several states (e.g., Florida, Michigan, New Mexico) encourages and in some cases requires the involvement of MHPs, in addition to the treating physician, in evaluating a proposed ward's functional capacity (Hommel et al., 1990). A number of recent state statutes provide for the appointment of a "visitor," whose role it is to meet the proposed ward and prepare a report for the court that supplements the formal assessment and provides more information bearing on the ward's living situation and potential effects of changes proposed by the petitioner for guardianship. These developments suggest that functional assessment of an older person for possible guardianship purposes is likely to become increasingly more interdisciplinary. Indeed, a comprehensive functional assessment of an older person (Nolan, 1984, 1990) virtually demands the active input of community health nurses, social workers, occupational and physical therapists, gerontological specialists, psychologists, and psychiatrists in addition to the attending physician.

There is a multiplicity of separate but interconnected factors that the conscientious MHP should consider in formulating a recommendation for the most beneficial resolution of the needs of the impaired older person. As a starting point, a comprehensive psychological history and examination of the individual is needed. A complete and orderly competency assessment should include, minimally, the following elements: (a) an evaluation of the patient's orientation to person, place, time, and situation; (b) a test of recent and remote memory and logical sequencing; (c) an assessment of intellectual capacity—that is, ability to comprehend abstract ideas and to make a reasoned judgment based on that ability; (d) an assessment of mood and affect, noting particularly suicidal ideation; (e) an examination of the content of thought and perception for delusions, illusions, and hallucinations; (f) an inspection of visible behavior, noting agitation and anxiety as well as appetite, eating habits, and sleeping patterns; and (g) a review of past history for evidence of a psychiatric disturbance that might affect the patient's current judgment (Jonsen, Siegler, & Winslade, 1992). Findings derived from the MHP evaluation must be correlated with functional tests of capacity to understand, assimilate, and use information (discussed earlier) relevant to the specific type of decision facing the patient (Alexander, 1988).

The MHP must also account for the frequently fluid or transient nature of competence by considering (Appelbaum & Roth, 1981): (a) psychodynamic elements in the patient's personality, (b) the accuracy of the historical information conveyed by the patient, (c) the accuracy and completeness of the information disclosed to the patient, (d) the stability or consistency of the patient's mental status over time (Gottlieb & Reisberg, 1988), and (e) the effect of the setting in which the observations are being made. Communication barriers (e.g., language limitations, lack of education, aphasia, speech disorders) between health care professional and patient must be considered (Goodenough, 1988).

An ideal capacity evaluation includes not only multiple sessions with the patient but contact with other persons (e.g., friends, relatives, employer, clergy) who know the individual well enough to assess the authenticity of the patient's present expressed choices. The effect of the testing site should be considered; there is some evidence that in-home assessment may reveal the optimal cognitive function of geriatric patients (Ward et al., 1990). The American Bar Association (1989) is on record in this area: "Whenever possible, proposed wards should be assessed in their usual environment and with all due consideration given to their privacy and dignity" (pp. 17). Other important possible variables affecting functional test behavior are the use of alcohol and other drugs, dietary reactions, changes associated with underlying disease processes, and fatigue and anxiety associated with a clinic visit or hospital admission and the concomitant change in ordinary routine (leading to disorientation).

Once the MHP has arrived at an opinion concerning the patient's capabilities and deficiencies, that opinion ordinarily is presented in the form of a written report. If the consultation was requested by the treating physician, it should be written in medically comprehensible terms but with an eye toward potential introduction of the report into evidence in a guardianship proceeding. The treating physician might call the consulting MHP for clarification of particular assertions in the report; the report should be written cogently enough to stand on its own and make most such inquiries unnecessary. If the treating physician's initial request for a consultation contained ambiguities, the consulting MHP should contact the requester for precise clarification before commencing the assessment and certainly before writing the report.

In the guardianship context, the MHP's written report generally will be introduced into evidence in court. There is a growing trend for states to specify by statute, regulation, or court administrative rule the precise form that a report submitted to the court must take and the specific content it must include (Anderer, 1990). This trend toward specificity represents an attempt to deal with the prevalent problem of MHP and other medical reports to the courts in guardianship proceedings that are too vague, sketchy, and conclusory. Such requirements place a burden on the MHP to be much more detailed, focused, and discerning in the preparation of reports for judicial consumption. The MHP should be sure not to release reports to anyone but the patient (or his or her legal counsel) without prior assurance that considerations of confidentiality and privileged information have been addressed and resolved (e.g., under a court or a statutory grant of immunity).

Ordinarily, the MHP's live testimony in court will be required in addition to any prepared written report. The courts tend to show strong deference toward presumed expertise regarding matters such as mental competence

(Krasik, 1989), in essence turning the problem over to MHPs (Mahler & Perry, 1988). If a guardianship petition is not seriously contested (and relatively few of them are), there is a real likelihood of the judge simply ratifying the MHP's conclusory opinion without any rigorous probing of its basis or accuracy. Although MHP testimony ordinarily will not determine what criteria the court will use in making a judgment about competence, it almost always supplies the evidentiary hook on which the court may hang its legal hat.

As Pleak and Appelbaum (1985) comment, this places a heavy moral responsibility on the MHP to ensure the accuracy of the report, testimony, or both. They argue that an MHP who is asked to sign an affidavit or to testify about a patient's incompetence should do so only after a thorough personal examination of the patient in which the patient's functional capacity for the task at hand is directly assessed. These authors convincingly suggest that the clinical basis on which the MHP infers a patient's incompetence should be stated straightforwardly to permit and perhaps even to stimulate cross-exami-nation (American Bar Association, 1990) and judicial review because the courts ordinarily cannot be depended on to reject inappropriate guardianship petitions.

Vital in this aspect of forensic medicine—the application of clinical exper-tise and experience to help resolve legal issues—are the clinician's notes in the patient's record (Farnsworth, 1989). Gutheil and Bursztajn (1986) counsel their psychiatric colleagues to anticipate the possibility that a patient's mental competence may become a legal issue and to document thoroughly the clinical determinants (i.e., the facts) supporting the clinician's view regarding com-petence or incompetence. Communications concerning the patient with fam-ily, other treatment or forensic specialists, and other professional staff who have contact with the patient also should be documented in the patient's chart.

Some commentators have called for special geriatric training for experts who testify in guardianship cases (Scogin & Perry, 1986). Although this may represent the ideal, the MHP who is requested to be an expert witness at least should insist on being sufficiently briefed and prepared by the attorney desiring the testimony in advance of the hearing date. There should be a clear idea of what questions might be asked on both direct and cross-examination. One cannot and should not be expected to take the witness stand "cold." The MHP should demand that parameters to the testimony be set and emphasize to the attorney that the MHP cannot offer a definitive opinion about the ultimate question of the patient's competence.

In addition, as with written reports, there should be the assurance that any difficulties with confidentiality or the release of privileged information have been satisfactorily worked out. At a minimum, the MHP should insist on personal delivery of a subpoena before appearing in court to testify for either side. Also, it should be possible to negotiate with the attorney and judge the exact time that testimony will be taken so that the court appearance need not be excessively time-consuming and disruptive to scheduling.

The value of positive clinician-attorney collaboration on difficult competence assessment cases cannot be overemphasized (Appelbaum & Grisso, 1988; Murphy, 1991). According to leading forensic MHPs, the attorney as an advocate focusing on short-term rights and the clinician as an expert investigator and therapist concentrating on long-term benefits make a powerful and constructive team (Gutheil, Bursztajn, Kaplan, & Brodsky, 1987). Moreover, the MHP has an important role in educating attorneys and the courts about clinical issues and in the presentation of clinically probative evidence (Gutheil & Bursztajn, 1986).

Research and Education

Further research and educational efforts will be integral to achieving continual improvement in the quality of MHP interaction with treating physicians, attorneys, and the courts regarding competence assessments. Although a reasonable body of literature has been produced concerning the theoretical dimensions of the competence concept, very little research has been conducted on either the processes or the substantive standards that MHPs, other health care professionals, attorneys, or the courts actually use in practice in making competence assessments. For example, do the elegant theoretical constructs make much of a difference in how key actors really behave and therefore how patients are treated? There is a need for researchers familiar with law, mental health, and health services research methodology to carry out experimental, empirical, and ethnographic studies examining such issues in a variety of settings and with an array of patient populations.

Bringing theory and practice in this area into harmony will require extensive training and instruction concerning the competence issue in graduate and continuing education. Because physicians and legal representatives often turn to MHPs for assistance in assessing competence, it is essential that educational programs for MHPs validate that confidence by equipping MHPs with special expertise and practice skills that reflect underlying conceptual principles and emphasize functional assessment.

Many relevant interprofessional organizations regularly sponsor educational programs and publications of potential interest to MHPs who wish to learn more about the interface of law, ethics, and mental health generally and the theoretical underpinnings and practical techniques of competence assessment in particular. Among the most prominent are the American Academy of Psychiatry and Law; American Society of Law, Medicine & Ethics; Hastings

Center; American Bar Association Commission on Mental and Physical Disability; and American College of Legal Medicine.

Summary

This chapter focuses on the MHP's role as a consultant in assessing patient competence for purposes of making medical decisions. The discussion includes the reason that competence is an important legal and ethical issue, basic conceptual guidelines, competing definitions of competence, strengths and weaknesses of available assessment tools, and possibilities and limitations of the MHP as a consultant both to treating physicians and to the legal system regarding the competence question. The chapter concludes with comments on opportunities for needed research and education in this realm.

For additional information, the reader is referred to the leading journals in this area, which include *Bulletin of the American Academy of Psychiatry and Law; Journal of Psychiatry and Law; Behavioral Sciences and the Law; Law and Human Behavior; Mental and Physical Disability Law Reporter; Journal of Law, Medicine & Ethics; American Journal of Law and Medicine; Hastings Center Report; Journal of Legal Medicine; Journal of Health Politics, Policy & Law;* and *Journal of Ethics, Law, and Aging.*

9

Screening for
Neuropsychological Impairment

Michael D. Franzen
Roy C. Martin

Clinical neuropsychological assessment attempts to describe individuals' cognitive and emotional functioning and relate that functioning to brain dysfunction. Although neuropsychological assessment has a long history, most work in this area has focused on younger adults. Yet research indicates that neuropsychological functioning continues to change across the life span, and these changes present specific issues in the application and interpretation of performance (Franzen & Rasmussen, 1990).

Early research portrayed aging as a process of accumulated neurocognitive deficits. That is, as people age, the combined effects of minor head injuries, strokes, and disease processes would result in progressive impairment of cognitive processes (Reitan, 1967). However, early on, research began to indicate that the age-associated decline was not uniform across all aspects of cognitive functioning. For example, performance on subtests of the Halstead-Reitan Neuropsychological Battery (HRNB)—a collection of test procedures designed to tap organic aspects of cognitive operations—reveals a reliable profile of deterioration that affects some areas of functioning more than others. Problem solving in novel situations and fluid intelligence were shown to be particularly affected by the aging process, and these same functions were also more sensitive to subtle forms of brain impairment. Some tests, including the Block Design subtest of the Wechsler Adult Intelligence Scales (WAIS), the Category Test, the Tactual Performance Test, and the Trailmaking test (Reed & Reitan, 1963) are particularly sensitive to normal and abnormal changes that occur with age.

Early research that found little difference between older individuals and younger neurologically impaired individuals was limited by relatively insensitive clinical neuropsychological assessment instruments as well as by the conceptualizations of the researchers. Later, clinical neuropsychological researchers recognized the differential effects of aging on various neuropsychological functions as well as the need to study aging as a complex set of interacting variables, including physical health, emotional well being, and cognitive development. In addition, later studies investigated the older individuals in cohorts and not just as a single monolithic group of all subjects over the age of 55 years, as had been done previously. Bak and Greene (1980) evaluated the effects of aging on performance on the HRNB and added the methodological improvement of considering two groups of older subjects, those between the ages of 50 and 62 years and those between the ages of 67 and 86 years. Using a different set of tests, Benton, Eslinger, and Damasio (1981) followed up this idea with an investigation of aging effects by decade in a group of subjects between the ages of 65 and 84 years. Both of these later studies indicated that the effects of aging are differential across skill areas and that some skills are retained even into the ninth decade of life. In general, there is decline on timed tasks, on memory tasks, on tasks of active problem solving, and on tasks of perceptual processes with relative sparing in other areas.

Neuropsychological Correlates of Normal Aging

Within the behavioral sciences, a wealth of empirical data has been collected over the past 3 decades investigating the ramifications of growing old. Neuropsychologists have been particularly intent on understanding the effect that physiological aging has on cognitive, emotional, and behavioral functioning and to what extent primary and secondary aging processes affect neuropsychological functioning (Albert & Moss, 1988; van Gorp, Satz, & Mitrushina, 1990). Obviously, understanding manifestations of "normal aging" processes versus disease processes has important implications for appropriate identification and intervention for the aged population. Especially critical within neuropsychological investigations has been the development of methods to identify and distinguish cognitive effects associated with normal aging from degenerative dementing diseases (Malec, Ivnik, & Smith, 1993).

Although this review is not intended to present an exhaustive compilation of the physiological influence of aging (for a detailed discussion, see Birren & Schaie, 1990), general statements can be made regarding overall psychophysiological changes present within normal aging processes. Visual and auditory functioning are altered with advanced age and have been shown to account for a great deal of the variance in cognitive changes associated with age (Lindenberger & Baltes, 1994). Notable decreases in visual acuity and accommodation are evident, as are attenuated auditory thresholds (Fozard, 1990). Using electrophysiology, scientists have demonstrated reduced frequency and an abundance of alpha wave activity along with slower delta and theta wave activity that may relate to the increased nighttime wakefulness and impaired sleep maintenance in old age (Prinz, Dustman, & Emmerson, 1990). In the periphery, reduction in muscle fiber size and number contribute to the loss of muscle mass, especially after the age of 70 (Prinz et al., 1990).

Albert and Kaplan (1980) assert that morphological changes within prefrontal and subcortical brain regions are part of the normal aging process that lead to many of the declines in cognitive functioning evidenced on neuropsychological performance. Pathological and radiological evidence has supported this notion (Gur, Gur, Obrist, Skolnick, & Reivich, 1987; Haug et al., 1983). A prominent theoretical position holds that with advancing age, there develops a slowing in central nervous system processing (e.g., Birren & Schaie, 1990; Salthouse, 1991), which has a detrimental effect on cognitive speed and, in turn, produces a decline in a variety of cognitive functions.

The effect that cognitive speed plays in the older person is illustrated well in changes seen on tests of general intelligence. Probably the most widely cited notion of normal aging on psychometric test data is the "classic aging pattern" by which elderly subjects show relative decline in measures of performance skills as compared to verbal skills on tests of general intelligence such as the Wechsler Adult Intelligence Scale-Revised (WAIS-R; Wechsler, 1981). Theoretical descriptions of this relationship have been discussed in terms of the sparing of crystallized abilities (i.e., practiced, overlearned verbal skills) and in terms of the decline of fluid abilities (i.e., novel problem-solving skills) (Horn, 1982, 1988). A confounding variable in the interpretation of these tests in the aged involves the fact that whereas the verbal subtests are not timed, the performance subtests are timed. Age-associated slowing may therefore be partly responsible for their changes. Age trends reveal that verbal performances tend to be relatively stable until the 8th decade of life, whereas performance test scores steadily decline after the 4th decade of life (Botwinick, 1977). Educational attainment significantly moderates the mild decline in verbal functioning, whereas no such effect is present on performance subtests.

Examining the components of neuropsychological performance, van Gorp et al. (1990) investigated the effects of aging in an elderly sample (aged 57-85 years) across three primary factors: a verbal factor, a speed of processing factor, and a nonverbal factor, with the speed of processing factor showing the greatest sensitivity to age, especially after the 7th decade for the processing speed tasks. Neither the verbal nor nonverbal factors were affected by age of subject, suggesting relatively less susceptibility to decline in memory processes in the absence of systemic illness. Performance on tests of immediate auditory memory span may be most resistant to the effects of advancing age, whereas immediate and delayed visual memory are more affected by age (Farmer et al., 1987). Educational level moderates the decline for tasks of abstract conceptualization, generative fluency, and verbal memory. Despite the multiplicity of variables affecting decline, a few general statements can be made about general trends in certain skill areas.

PERCEPTION

The active selection and integration of sensory stimulation refers to perceptual processing. With increasing age, there is a reduction in the speed and capacity to process auditory and visual information (Kausler, 1991). The ability to process perceptual features of stimuli, however, appears to be consistently moderated by the familiarity that one has with the perceived stimulus (Kausler, 1991). Elderly persons continue to do well on tasks that require pattern recognition of familiar visual and auditory stimuli but evidence decline in processing less familiar sensory stimuli. Many of the declines present on tasks of color and depth perception are functions of the deteriorating sensory function. Central mechanisms appear to influence more complex processing of speech and form patterns, however. Therefore, an older individual who demonstrates or reports declines in sensory acuity may not be as likely to be experiencing a pathological decline as an individual who presents declines in speech or pattern recognition. However, it is more likely that the individual with self-observed changes in acuity will approach a health care professional with his or her concerns. The type of deficits associated with pathological changes (speech and pattern recognition) may be detected only on formal testing and therefore are frequently not noticed by the individuals, partly due to their lack of familiarity with the test stimuli.

ATTENTION

Attention refers to the cognitive processes responsible for focusing an organism's limited processing capacities on particular stimuli (Kausler, 1991).

Attention is typically measured by tasks of immediate visual and auditory repetition and tasks requiring sustained performance over time (i.e., vigilance). Performance on attentional tasks incorporating minimal memory demands (i.e., digit span tasks, continuous performance tasks) remains intact well into old age (e.g., Ardila & Rosselli, 1989; Farmer et al., 1987), but as the task becomes more complex and places higher demands on attentional capacity, age-related performance declines (e.g., Roman, Edwall, Buchanan, & Patton, 1991; Salthouse, Rogan, & Prill, 1984). Frequently, clinical assessment of attention is accomplished by asking the patient to repeat digits in a forward and backward modality, and the score on the two procedures is combined. This type of score is relatively insensitive both to the types of changes seen in normal aging and to the types of changes associated with all but the most advanced forms of dementia. The clinician who relies on digit repetition procedures to evaluate complaints of attentional problems may not be tapping the skill area noticed by the individual. Performance on the backward repetition may provide greater information, however. In addition, the clinician should be aware that performance on tasks that require attending to multiple sources of information may be adversely affected by age.

VISUOSPATIAL ABILITY

Visuospatial ability refers to a constellation of cognitive processes that incorporate motor, perceptual, spatial, and memory processes and allow for navigation of the spatial environment, identification of visual information (i.e., faces, maps), and manipulation of objects into appropriate spatial relationships (drawing, model constructing) (Benton & Tranel, 1993). Visuospatial ability declines with advancing age (Ogden, 1991). Notable performance declines on tasks of block construction, integration of pictorial fragments, and clock drawing are frequently found (Ardila & Rosselli, 1989; Plude & Hoyer, 1986). The clock drawing procedure has become popular especially among medical professionals, but care should be taken in the interpretation of results, with greater confidence possible for the interpretation of extremely disordered performance than for intact or borderline performance. Construction and drawing tasks are difficult to interpret due to their multidimensional nature, which incorporates motor, processing speed, memory, and visual functions (Ogden, 1991).

Malec et al. (1993) showed that tasks involving novel visuospatial problem-solving skills are age-sensitive, with performance declines evident prior to age 65 years. Visuospatial abilities are thought to be primarily right hemisphere mediated (Kolb & Whishaw, 1985). Age-related declines on the performance subtests of the WAIS and preserved verbal scores have been interpreted by some researchers as reflecting differential aging of the right hemisphere (Klisz, 1978), although evidence is equivocal (e.g., Malec et al., 1993; Mittenberg, Seidenberg, O'Leary, & DiGiulio, 1989). It is unlikely that the hemispheres show differential effects of aging, and performance on these tasks is better interpreted with a view toward the effects of aging on underlying skills.

LANGUAGE

"Language skills last, new memories pass" reflects the traditional view that language abilities in older adults are relatively well preserved, whereas the ability to learn and retain new information gradually fades. WAIS and WAIS-R verbal subtests remain stable until the very late stages of life (e.g., Farmer et al., 1987; Malec et al., 1993), and healthy elderly people do not demonstrate language disorders typically associated with cerebral damage (i.e., aphasias) (Bayles & Kaszniak, 1987). The distinction between aging and disease effects on language could be an important discriminator in determining whether an individual is demonstrating a pathological decline. Light (1988) has argued, however, that the view of unchanging linguistic functioning is only partially correct, and although the functional capacity of language skills remains stable, performance factors attenuate production and comprehension capabilities. Several key language functions will be discussed as they pertain to normal aging.

Word Knowledge. The ability to generate definitions for words holds throughout adulthood years (Bayles & Kaszniak, 1987). Tests of vocabulary show minimal age effects through the 9th decade of life (Malec et al., 1993), although other studies measuring longitudinal change have demonstrated modest declines in this ability (Storandt, 1991). Education appears to moderate this trend (Schaie, 1990).

Naming Skills. Confrontational naming ability is relatively well-preserved until age 70 years, where gradual decline is observed (Albert, 1988). Typically, errors on naming tests involve a greater proportion of circumlocutions—that is, the individual may describe the object or talk about its use rather than supply the actual name of the object (Bayles & Kaszniak, 1987). Education level appears to play a large role in maintaining naming performance in old age (Huff, 1991). For example, Spreen and Strauss (1991) report that in an older population, performance on the Boston Naming Test may be ten points lower than average when the subject has less than 8 years of education.

Speech Comprehension. With increased age comes a somewhat decreased ability to comprehend spoken language. Short-term memory deficits appear to play a large role in observed age effects (Light, 1988). Age-related declines are found to be minimal when immediate memory capacity is not exceeded (Emery, 1985). Age effects are also found when speed of response is recorded, showing older adults to be slower in processing orally presented verbal information (Bayles & Kaszniak, 1987).

Fluency Skills. Elderly adults have a decreased ability to generate linguistic output (Bayles & Kaszniak, 1987). Tasks of discourse production, letter and animal fluency, and verbal descriptions of pictorial material all show gradual declines after the age of 60 (Huff, 1991; Storandt, 1991). Qualitative aspects of elderly speech production include more errors of reference, fewer generated prepositions, and fewer units of information produced (Bayles & Kaszniak, 1987). However, verbal intelligence has been shown to be a strong predictor of generative fluency performance in elderly adults (Bolla, Lindgren, Bonaccorsy & Bleecker, 1990).

MEMORY

Memory decline is probably the most frequent complaint and concern of the elderly (Dobbs & Rule, 1987). Given the prominence of memory dysfunction in a variety of neurological diseases, it is critically important to understand age-related memory performance and its relationship to neurological disease.

Research has consistently demonstrated that primary memory (sometimes referred to as short-term memory) is relatively well preserved into old age (Albert, 1988). Tasks of digit span, word span, and visual span each show minimal age effects (Poon, 1985), yet age effects are evident on tasks of secondary memory (sometimes referred to as explicit memory), which are usually measured by tasks of recall and recognition for verbal and visual materials (Davis & Bernstein, 1992). Memory tasks that demand deliberate recall of information, such as word list recall, prose passage recall, and learning word pairs, are especially difficult for elderly adults (Verhaeghen, Marcoen, & Goossens, 1993). Age-related differences are reduced when providing older subjects with cues or recognition assistance, suggesting that the basic problem involves information retrieval rather than encoding (Albert, 1988).

The clinical description of "normal" memory loss in the elderly has been commonly referred to as benign senescent forgetfulness, indicating a nondementing aging process (Kral, 1958). However, recent work by a National Institute of Mental Health (NIMH) work group has updated this concept by listing quantifiable standards to accompany a definition of memory performance in the elderly (Crook et al., 1986). This new term, called *age-associated memory impairment,* is associated with several specific quantifiable criteria, including the absence of medical conditions that could contribute to memory impairment, a standardized secondary memory test performance at least one standard deviation below the mean of young adults, and subjective memory complaints (Crook et al., 1986). Blackford and LaRue (1989) offered further refinement of these criteria by considering age-appropriate memory impairment and late-life forgetfulness to be two conditions along a broad spectrum of memory functioning that ranges from *age normal* to *severe organic-based impairment.* Recent concerns have been voiced regarding this classification scheme, however. There is potential unreliability of the term due to the use of differentially sensitive test measures as well as concerns about labeling normal aging process as impairment (Malec et al., 1993). Recent criticisms are directed at improving the criteria and reducing the negative connotations of the label (Caine, 1993; Ratcliffe & Saxton, 1994). As a result of the controversy, the category of age-associated memory impairment was not added to the *Diagnostic and Statistical Manual of Mental Disorders* (*DSM-IV;* American Psychiatric Association [APA], 1994) as a diagnostic category, but it was added under "Other Conditions That May Be a Focus of Clinical Attention." Clearly, this is an issue that has not yet been resolved. Although the implication in the term *age-associated memory impairment* is that memory has somehow declined with age, it appears that there is stability of performance on tests of everyday memory across a period of 4 years in older individuals who meet the NIMH criteria for age-associated memory impairment (Youngjohn & Crook, 1993b).

Although experimental and clinical memory tests have repeatedly revealed age-related declines in the area of explicit memory (Poon, 1985; Verhaeghen et al., 1993), there has been increasing concern that clinical age-associated memory impairments may not reflect accurately the memory processes needed for adaptation to the natural environment (Poon, Rubin, & Wilson, 1989). Neuropsychological tests have recently been developed that measure aspects of everyday memory function and attempt to explain age-related performances on tasks considered more ecologically and face valid tests of memory (Crook & Larrabee, 1988; Larrabee & Crook, 1989). Age declines have been described across a variety of everyday domains, including name-face association, object misplacing, telephone dialing, grocery list recall, and simulated driving skills (Crook, Youngjohn, Larrabee, & Salama, 1992). However, familiarity with, and difficulty of, the everyday tasks are considered important factors moderating performance on these tasks (West, 1986).

Although the clinical literature has shown concern only with everyday memory, the experimental literature has investigated ecologically valid tasks in other domains (e.g., Willis, Jay, Diehl, & Marsiske, 1992). Incorporating this general approach into the clinical assessment of other skills in older individuals may be fruitful.

HIGHER-ORDER COGNITIVE PROCESSING

Thinking encompasses cognitive processes of problem solving, conceptualization, reasoning, and planning, which affect how individuals adapt and function within their natural environments. Laboratory studies of "higher level" cognitive functioning often demonstrate age-related declines in tasks involving thinking skills, whereas paradoxically, elderly adults can still function successfully in their day-to-day surroundings (Salthouse, 1990a). Tasks drawing on abilities to form concepts and shift cognitive sets in response to corrective feedback (i.e., Wisconsin Card Sorting Test, Category Test) are age-sensitive and reflect relatively poor abstraction and reduced concept flexibility (Cronin-Golomb, 1991). Tasks of problem solving are also found to be poorly performed by elderly adults, but considerable variability of performance is seen, given the multicomponential systems involved (Cronin-Golomb, 1991).

Evidence suggests that on tasks of more everyday problem-solving skills, elderly adults perform as well as or better than young adults (Cornelius & Caspi, 1987), highlighting the distinction between cognitive ability and cognitive competence when examining age-related performance on higher-level cognitive processes (Salthouse, 1990a). Gains in cumulative experience and differential evaluation standards of performance may contribute to the discrepancies seen on laboratory versus everyday thinking tasks (Salthouse, 1990a).

Overall, the normal aging process is associated with changes in clinic-based instruments that tap abstraction, problem-solving skills, and cognitive flexibility. These changes are moderate in comparison to the decrements associated with disease processes. In contrast, everyday measures of the same constructs do not always show the same declines associated with aging. The difference may be due to the amount of experience with the tasks, but this difference highlights the importance of using tasks with ecological validity when examining the effects of aging on cognitive processes.

Disorders in the Elderly With Neuropsychological Correlates

PSYCHIATRIC DISORDERS

Substantial numbers of elderly persons experience disability due to psychiatric impairment. Kermis (1986) reports that upward of 25% of all elderly persons experience some degree of mental health difficulties. In addition, certain populations are particularly at risk. Nearly 70% of institutionalized elderly persons will have psychiatric disorders (Cohen, 1990). Although a large portion of mental health disorders reflect manifestation of degenerative brain disease (i.e., Alzheimer's), it is important to rule out psychiatric disorders such as depression, anxiety, and substance abuse (Cohen, 1990).

The prevalence of the depressive spectrum in elderly populations, whether a major depressive disorder or display of some depressive symptoms, has ranged from a low of 1% to upward of 15% (Koenig & Blazer, 1992a). Recurrence of affective disorder in late-life is not uncommon, but first-time incidence after age 65 accounts for approximately 40% of cases of late-life depression (Alexopoulos, Young, Meyers, Abrams, & Shamoian, 1988). Relative to younger cohorts, older people appear to experience less major depression but more dysthymia (McGuire & Rabins, 1994). It is important to note that the incidence of depression in the elderly varies with the setting. Between 15% and 25% of older individuals who are inpatients in acute care settings may meet diagnostic criteria for major depression, and between 12% and 25% of nursing home residents meet such criteria (LaRue, 1992).

There exists complex relationships between neurological disease, cognitive dysfunction, and depression (e.g., Kramer & Reifler, 1992; Lamberty & Bieliauskas, 1993; Sweet, Newman, & Bell, 1992). Extensive attention has been devoted to the concept of *pseudodementia* in which cognitive deficits seen in depressive disorders appear to mimic dementia. Uncritical acceptance of the term is under increasing challenge, given the "diagnostic and therapeutic nihilism" surrounding its use (Kramer & Reifler, 1992, p. 290). Sizable percentages of depressed elderly with pseudodementia later exhibit cognitive deficits consistent with Alzheimer-type dementia. Lamberty and Bieliauskas (1993) have recently presented one of several (also see Folstein & Rabins, 1991) alternative conceptualizations to the dichotomization of dementia and depression in which these terms are being considered within a broader clinical spectrum of affective-cognitive dysfunction. Depressive symptomatology is considered along with cognitive dysfunction and imaging findings on a continuum of normal-mild-moderate-severe levels of impairment, reflecting the complex interactions of affective, cognitive, and physiological variables. A recent review (Nussbaum, 1994) suggests that the presence of leukoariaosis might represent a biological marker for the development of depressive affective features and associated cognitive impairment in some older individuals.

Neuropsychological research has described a number of characteristic patterns of performance differentiating nonneurologically diseased depressed elderly patients from healthy elderly and patients with a degenerative disease (Lamberty & Bieliauskas, 1993). Depressed patients typically present a middle range of performance across a variety of cognitive domains, between that of normal and dementing elderly. Depressed elderly patients can display mild attentional dysfunction, psychomotor slowing, and less efficient encoding of new information, with more profound deficits when psychosis, cerebrovascular history, or lower education status are present (Lamberty & Bieliauskas, 1993; Sweet et al., 1992). This pattern of dysfunction is viewed as reflecting the worsened motivation, arousal, and cognitive processing inherent in the depressive disorders (Weingartner, 1986). Depressed patients are less likely to present language or visuospatial dysfunction. The relationships between type or severity of depression and the extent of memory impairment is uncertain; however, it appears that degree of memory impairment is associated with the length of illness in depressed older individuals (LaRue, Goodman, & Spar, 1992). There may be some qualitative differences in the memory performance of depressed individuals versus individuals with Alzheimer's Dementia (AD). For example, Hill, Stoudemire, Morris, Martino-Saltzman, and Markwalter (1993) report that although overall scores on memory tests were similar for subjects with AD and subjects with reversible dementia secondary to depression, the subjects with AD were more likely to make intrusive errors on a serial word list learning task.

LATE-ONSET SCHIZOPHRENIA

To date, the neuropsychological status of late-onset schizophrenia has not been well documented, although initial investigations have suggested similar performance profiles compared to younger schizophrenic patients (Cullum, Heaton, & Nemiroff, 1988). Correlations between neuropsychological functioning and radiological findings have not produced consistent results, and when found, correlations are usually only modest (Randolph, Goldberg, & Weinberger, 1993). Attentional dysfunction in all forms of schizophrenia is a prominent feature that includes a diversity of dysfunction in the areas of immediate attention span, reaction time, and in selective and sustained attention. The attentional dysfunction may manifest prior to the onset of formal psychiatric symptoms (Randolph et al., 1993). Studies of memory functioning in schizophrenic patients of all age ranges have found deficits, relative to normal controls, for nonmodality or non-material-specific encoding, retrieval, and recognition memory components (Randolph et al., 1993). Performance on tasks measuring abstraction, novel problem-solving skills, set shifting, and word generation fluency are consistently found to be impaired for schizophrenic patients.

ALZHEIMER'S DISEASE AND RELATED DEMENTIAS

Dementia, as defined by the *DSM-IV* (APA, 1994), is the presentation of demonstrable impairment in memory functioning associated with other cognitive or personality changes that interfere with daily activities and social relationships. This definition does not specify etiological factors nor does it imply prognostic outcome. There are over 30 separate medical conditions ranging from Alzheimer's disease to chemical substance abuse to endocrine disorders that can manifest as a dementia syndrome (Mace, 1990). Similarly, not all of the medical conditions presenting as dementia are irreversible; some are amenable to treatment and eventual recovery. The most common type is AD (APA, 1994; Hart & Semple, 1990; Price, 1986). However, as La Rue (1992) points out, it can be difficult to diagnose vascular dementia on either pathological or clinical grounds, and the prevalence of vascular dementia may be underestimated. Be that as it may, the usual estimates of prevalence indicate that AD may account for as much as 50% of all dementias, and vascular dementia may account for as much as 30% of all dementias. Clearly, the irreversible dementias constitute the majority of cases occurring in older people.

Numerous studies have demonstrated that impaired ability to recall information is the best discriminator in identifying cases of mild AD from normal aging processes, whereas other neurocognitive deficits are less frequently seen early in the disease course (Christensen, Hadzi-Pavlovic, & Jacomb, 1991; Welsh, Butters, Hughes, Mohs, & Heyman, 1992). Neuropsychological deficits that appear in the early stages of AD are problems with visuospatial skills, word-finding difficulties, and poor performance when simultaneous attention to two tasks is required. As the disease progresses, however, a global amnesiac condition develops, encompassing all aspects of memory function (i.e., episodic, semantic, implicit), as well as deficits of aphasia, agnosia, apraxia, verbal fluency, visuospatial construction, and abstract problem-solving skills (Zec, 1993; see Table 9.1).

Although not as widely emphasized as cognitive deficits, problems in adaptive behavioral responses are commonly exhibited in AD (Maletta, 1988). Although the true prevalence is not known, surveys indicate that a majority of AD patients exhibit at least some type of behavioral disturbance (Gilley, 1993; Rabins, Mace, & Lucas, 1982). For example, Bozzola, Gorelick, and Freels (1992) profiled 80 AD patients for behavioral and personality changes and found that all patients in this sample exhibited at least one type of behavioral change, including diminished initiative (61% of sample), increased rigidity (41%), lack of regard for others (39%), diminution of subtle affect functioning (36%), and stereotyped or repetitive behaviors (29%). These behavioral displays were as likely to be present early in the disease course as during the late stages of the disease and were not entirely attributable to intellectual impairment. These behavioral deficits can affect both the informal and formal assessment of cognitive skills and therefore should be a focus of the clinical evaluation. In addition, family report of these problems may precede complaints of cognitive decline and should therefore be seen as possible prodromal signs.

Table 9.1   Characteristic Clinical Features of Cognitive Decline Between Early Stage
Alzheimer's Disease and Normal Aging

	Alzheimer's Disease	*Normal Aging*
Psychomotor speed	minimal	minimal
General cognitive slowing	moderate to severe	mild
Attention-concentration	mild to moderate	mild
Visual-spatial construction	moderate to severe	mild
Spatial orientation	mild to moderate	minimal
Naming skills	moderate to severe	minimal
Generative fluency	moderate	mild
Immediate recall	moderate to severe	minimal to mild
Delayed recall	moderate to severe	mild
Recognition memory	mild to moderate	minimal to mild
Remote memory	mild	minimal to mild
Abstract reasoning	mild	minimal to mild
Calculation skills	mild	minimal

PARKINSON'S DISEASE

Although the physical symptoms of tremor, akinesia, rigidity, and loss of postural reflexes are the most prominent features of this disease, anywhere from 15% to 50% of patients with Parkinson's disease develop some level of neuro-cognitive impairment beyond the effects of depression (Mahurin, Feher, Nance, Levy, & Pirozzolo, 1993). Common neuropsychological impairments seen in Parkinson's patients include those in the skill areas of psychomotor speed, information processing speed, visual and verbal memory, procedural memory, generative fluency, and executive functions (Mahurin et al., 1993). Relatively spared functions are found for most language functions, including confrontation naming, word knowledge, new learning, and recognition memory (Knight, 1992). There is disagreement as to whether there are actually dementing changes in Parkinson's or whether the cognitive changes seen in some Parkinson's patients are the result of a coexisting dementing disease. Table 9.2 presents a comparison of commonly impaired and spared skills in Parkinson's disease.

VASCULAR DEMENTIA

Vascular dementias are second only to Alzheimer's disease as the leading cause of dementia in the elderly. The term *vascular dementia* is used to represent the cognitive and behavioral changes that occur following strokes, either single or multiple. Epidemiological information surveyed by Roman et al. (1993) indicates that incidence of vascular dementia steadily increases with

Table 9.2   Patterns of Cognitive Function in Parkinson's Disease

Impaired	*Spared*
Motor speed	Language
Information processing speed	New learning
Recall memory	Recognition memory
Procedural memory	
Executive functions	

age, with males being at much higher risk than females across most age groups.

Roman et al. (1993) outlined several diagnostic criteria that would suggest vascular dementia. They include (a) presence of diminished cognitive ability in memory along with two or more other cognitive areas that occur within 3 months following a stroke, (b) stepwise cognitive deterioration, (c) focal neurological signs (e.g., unilateral hemiparesis), and (d) radiologically detected areas of cerebral infarction. Classification efforts have begun, describing the clinical presentation of the vascular dementias within a framework of cortical and subcortical processes (Brown & Hachinski, 1989). Attempts to differentiate subcortical and cortical vascular dementia have provided evidence for distinctive clinical presentations and pathologic disease processes (Metter & Wilson, 1993). Neuropsychological research has not resulted in a composite profile of the vascular dementia processes, given the shear number of potential infarction sites. However, several clinical syndromes are readily apparent with relatively localized damage and will be discussed in the cerebrovascular disease section.

Neuropsychological presentation of cortical forms of vascular dementia will usually produce area-specific focal neurologic signs, including dominant hemisphere deficits of language (i.e., fluent and nonfluent forms of aphasia) and verbal memory. Unilateral frontal region damage can produce pronounced hemiparetic findings contralateral to the lesion site, whereas nondominant parietal lobe damage can produce left spatial and body neglect.

Many of the subcortical forms of dementia, including subcortical forms of vascular dementias, frequently show the so-called "frontal lobe personality" changes, which may reflect cortico-thalamic disconnection of white matter tracts (Bornstein & Kelly, 1991). Neuropsychological profiles of the subcortical dementias reveal considerable heterogeneity in the intensity of cognitive impairment displayed, with leukoaraiotic changes viewed on a clinical continuum from mild asymptomatic radiologic changes, with little to no neuropsychological manifestations, to profuse subcortical changes accompanying a dementia presentation (Rao, 1993). Slowing of information processing is a

Table 9.3   Patterns of Cognitive Function in Vascular Dementia, Normal-Pressure Hydrocephalus, and Diabetes Mellitus

Condition	Impaired	Spared
Vascular Dementia[a]	Language fluency	—
	Unilateral motor skills	—
	Recall memory	—
Normal-Pressure	Memory	Language skills
Hydrocephalus	Speed of thought	Reading and writing
	Abstraction	Comprehension
Diabetes Mellitus	Visual-spatial skills	Motor speed
	Simple attention	Complex or divided attention
	Memory	—

a. There will be variability due to site of lesion.

prominent early cognitive sign that is usually more extensive than that seen in cortical dementias (i.e., Alzheimer's). Memory disturbances are present but are primarily retrieval-based problems and are less pronounced than in AD. Recognition memory is relatively preserved, and language and semantic-based knowledge remain relatively insensitive to subcortical deterioration (Metter & Wilson, 1993). Although there is great variability in manifest cognitive impairment in vascular disorders, Table 9.3 presents the more commonly found patterns of cognitive functions.

NORMAL-PRESSURE HYDROCEPHALUS

It is estimated that normal-pressure hydrocephalus (NPH) represents between 6% to 12% of all dementia cases (Strub & Black, 1988), with onset most frequent after the age of 60 years. There has been much interest in this form of dementia because shunting procedures result in improvement in upward of 50% to 60% of patients. Thus, in contrast to other forms of dementia, NPH is treatable (Stambrook et al., 1988). Idiopathic NPH is the most common etiology of cerebrospinal fluid disorder in the elderly, although subarachnoid hemorrhage, infection, tumor, and cerebral trauma may also result in similar circulatory conditions (Stambrook, Gill, Cardoso, & Moore, 1993). Compression of subcortical structures and connective white matter tracts contribute to the classic clinical triad often seen in NPH (gait ataxia, urinary incontinence, and memory disturbance). Symptom onset is usually a rather rapid onset over a period of days, with gait problems often appearing first (Adams & Victor, 1993).

Stambrook et al. (1993) concluded that prominent early neuropsychological changes include reductions in cognitive speed and sustained attention as well as notable behavioral changes, including loss of initiative (abulia), depressed mood, and apathy. As the condition worsens, cognitive changes include deficits in memory functioning, psychomotor speed, abstraction and problem solving, frontal lobe release signs of perseveration, verbal and behavioral intrusiveness, and also visuoperceptual problems. In other words, the person will appear to be grossly dementing with accompanying behavioral disturbances. In contrast to dementias involving cortical sites, NPH typically does not substantially affect linguistic abilities (i.e., graphic or reading skills, comprehension, word naming). However, Stambrook et al. (1993) point out that variability in symptom presentation is not uncommon. Table 9.3 presents the more frequently seen pattern of cognitive performance. Considerable resolution of cognitive impairments can be observed following successful shunting procedures.

DIABETES MELLITUS

Adults with diabetes mellitus (DM) are known to exhibit a number of neuropsychological problems (Ryan, 1990) that may be due to dysregulation of the insulin-glucose balance with cognitive deficits expressed during periods of hypoglycemic or hyperglycemic states (Holmes, 1990). Neuropsychological status correlates moderately with metabolic regulation of the glycemic state both within and between episodes of glycemia dysregulation. Reaven and Thompson (as cited in Perlmuter, Goldfinger, Shore, & Nathan, 1990) found that tasks measuring simple attention and motor speed did not differentiate DM patients with poorer disease control from aged-matched controls. Abstract reasoning and verbal learning tasks along with visuospatial tasks were more poorly performed by the DM group, however, even when controlling for the presence of hypertension and cardiovascular disease. In general, DM patients perform comparably to healthy peers on measures of overlearned material and on tasks of simple attention and reaction time. However, performance discrepancies do emerge on more complex tasks of attention, memory, problem solving and mental flexibility, and visuospatial analysis (Perlmuter et al., 1990). Table 9.3 presents a comparison of relatively impaired and spared skills in diabetes.

SUBSTANCE ABUSE DISORDERS

Recent findings presented from the NIMH's Epidemiological Catchment Area studies show that alcoholism rates in noninstitutionalized elderly populations may be as high as 14% in males and 1.5% in females (Helzer & Burnam, 1991). Alcohol has both acute and chronic neurobehavioral effects on the aging central nervous system (Adams & Victor, 1993). Neuropsychological research has focused on determining the residual neurobehavioral effects of alcoholism as well as recovery of function (Parsons & Nixon, 1993).

Researchers have investigated two primary groups of alcoholics: chronic abusers without neurological disorder and patients with neurologic impairment (e.g., alcohol dementia, Wernicke-Korsakoff syndrome). The neuropsychological condition of the neurologically intact chronic alcoholic following several weeks to months of abstinence has been identified as an intermediate-duration organic mental disorder (Grant, 1987), with deficits in new learning, perceptual-motor skills, visuospatial processing, problem solving, and abstraction. Cognitive dysfunction often subsides over a period of months but usually not to levels of age-matched nonalcoholic controls (Parsons & Nixon, 1993; Salmon, Butters, & Heindel, 1993). Radiologic imaging data suggest that alcohol-related cerebral atrophic changes and ventricular enlargement may gradually reverse following prolonged alcohol abstinence (Grant, 1987). Although neuropsychological and neuropathological recovery is common, the elderly alcoholic is more vulnerable to the toxic effects of alcohol on other systemic function (i.e., liver function), which also influences eventual neuropsychological outcome (Parsons & Nixon, 1993).

Alcoholic dementia involves a pervasive cognitive deterioration across multiple neuropsychological domains. Damage is permanent and results in impairment in usual occupational and social functioning (APA, 1994). Alcohol dementia patients exhibit severe impairments in memory functioning and marked changes in personality (i.e., apathy) (Salmon et al., 1993), but the more prominent feature is deterioration in global cognitive abilities (Salmon et al., 1993). Typically, in alcoholic dementia there is relative sparing of language functions. In particular, the paraphasic changes seen in AD are unlikely in alcoholic dementia, even though memory and constructional skills may be similarly impaired in both types of disorders. Table 9.4 lists the more frequent patterns of cognitive impairment and sparing found in alcoholic dementia.

THE EFFECTS OF PSYCHOTROPIC DRUGS

Many of the commonly prescribed medications for use with the elderly have psychotropic properties. Therefore, determining whether changes in mental status are related to drug use is an important diagnostic question with implications for treatment and prognosis. The elderly adult has a decreased physiological capacity to tolerate medications, resulting in an increased potential for adverse central nervous system (CNS) effects (Salzman, 1990b). Combi-

Table 9.4   Pattern of Cognitive Functions in Alcohol Abuse

Impaired	*Spared*
New learning	Language (naming, comprehension)
Perceptual-motor	Motor speed, strength
Construction	—

nations of over-the-counter drugs and prescription drugs increase the probability for oversedation and potential mental status changes. Therefore, it is very important to note any use of medication when interpreting the results of cognitive testing. (See Chapter 22 for a more complete discussion of the effects of psychoactive medication.)

NEUROPSYCHOLOGICAL CORRELATES OF HYPERTENSION

Hypertension affects nearly 45% of the U.S. Caucasian population and 60% of the African American population above the age of 65 years. Hypertension represents a major health risk for the development of cardiovascular disease and stroke (Wenger, 1992). Neuropathological changes resulting from hypertension typically consist of multiple lacunar infarcts to small arterial vessels, most prominently in subcortical brain regions (Metter & Wilson, 1993). Early alterations in CNS functioning are largely unrecognized by radiologic and electrographic instruments (Waldstein, Manuck, Ryan, & Muldoon, 1991).

Neuropsychological assessment has been shown to distinguish between groups of large community-based samples of normal and hypertensive elderly (Elias, Robbins, Schultz, Pierce, 1990; Farmer, Kittner, Abbott, Wolz, & White, 1990). Although performance differences are not always found across studies, in general, hypertensives do perform relatively more poorly on tests of complex attention, memory, and abstract reasoning, even controlling for demographic, health, and medication variables (Waldstein et al., 1991). Evidence has been presented for poorer performances by hypertensives on tasks of perceptual-motor skills, psychomotor speed, and visuospatial construction, although these changes may be clinically insignificant. In their comprehensive review of the literature, Waldstein et al. (1991) point out that although the performance differences are not of a magnitude that is usually considered clinically impaired, "small neuropsychological decrements may be early indicators of target organ involvement secondary to hypertension; such effects may thus be meaningful in predicting overt CNS sequelae, even if behavioral functioning is not overtly compromised" (p. 463). The changes will accumulate and increase, especially if the hypertension is left untreated.

In a notable study of aging and blood pressure effects on cognitive performance, Elias et al. (1990) found that although age-related changes in cognitive performance occurred, blood pressure (even nonhypertension ranges) was a significant predictor of performance on tasks of visual-motor speed and spatial memory. Blood pressure appears to have a smaller effect on older hypertensive adults, however, than on their younger counterparts (Elias et al., 1990). Use of medication, of any type, in the elderly may have CNS effects. Performance enhancement has been reported following initial administration of antihypertensive medications, although longer-term use may have less beneficial properties for cognitive abilities (Elias et al., 1990).

CEREBROVASCULAR DISEASE

Stroke is the third leading cause of death in adults, with the proportion of incidence and mortality rates steadily increasing with advancing age (Kurtze, 1985). Significant risk factors predisposing to stroke include hypertension, diabetes mellitus, and cardiac disease as well as lifestyle variables (i.e., smoking, diet) (Bornstein & Kelly, 1991).

Broadly based, the classification of cerebrovascular disease can be described as either occurring via ischemic or hemorrhagic events, with ischemic brain injury accounting for approximately 85% of total incidence of stroke (Starkstein & Robinson, 1992). Infarction of brain tissue results when blood supply is occluded to brain tissue through thrombotic or embolic processes. Cerebral embolisms produce rapid onset of focal neurologic signs, usually without precipitating symptoms and proportionately affecting small arterial branches of the middle cerebral artery (Adams & Victor, 1993). Transient focal neurological deficits, lasting a few hours to a few days, will often precede thrombotic events (Adams & Victor, 1993). Anterior arterial circulation blockage may result in unilateral visual disturbance, dysarthria, limb weakness, tingling or numbness, and mild aphasic symptoms, whereas posterior blockage may produce primarily transient diplopia, swallowing difficulty, bilateral weakness, and confusion (Funkenstein, 1988).

Disruption of blood flow to specific brain regions often produces focal neuropsychological deficits dependent on lesion location, size, age of insult, and acuteness of injury (Funkenstein, 1988). For example, strokes occurring in the anterior distribution of the middle cerebral artery (MCA) often produce motor and sensory disturbances in the contralateral body side (arm and face showing greater effects than the leg), whereas minimal motor-sensory impairment is noted with more anterior lesions of this arterial distribution (Brust, 1989). Dominant hemisphere stroke to anterior portions of the MCA (affecting frontal lobe regions) can produce multiple disturbances of language (most prominently those of expressive linguistic skills), and executive control and planning functioning. The language deficits of the Wernicke's type, memory impairment for verbal material, acalculia, and agnosia are frequently present following dominant hemisphere stroke to posterior regions of the MCA distribution (Funkenstein, 1988). Nondominant hemisphere lesions to MCA distributions can cause a variety of visuoperceptual problems, including hemispatial neglect and inattention, visual-construction deficits, anosognosia, impairment of nonverbal memory, and aprosodia (defect in the nonverbal aspects of speech and communication, such as gesture and vocal intonation) (Funkenstein, 1988).

Neuropsychological evaluations can be very helpful by delineating the cognitive and emotional problems associated with the structural infarcts. Cognitive and emotional problems can be variable both in type and degree. Even knowing the location of the stroke will not predict the psychological effects with sufficient specificity to allow adequate treatment planning. Knowing the location of the stroke can help plan the evaluation, however. For example, knowing that a stroke has occurred affecting the left middle cerebral artery distribution can alert the neuropsychologist to the need for a thorough evaluation of language, motor, and memory functions. However, only the results of that evaluation will provide information sufficient to make a decision regarding whether a return to home, placement in a skilled-care facility, or transfer to an acute rehabilitation setting would be beneficial. The neuropsychological evaluation can also be helpful in determining the need for psychological interventions for any emotional difficulties.

Neuropsychological Assessment Instruments

Earlier, we stated that neuropsychological function changes across the life span. This change tends to accelerate after the age of 60 years (Albert & Heaton, 1988). This point is particularly important because much of the change involves a gradual decline in some, but not all, skill areas. As well as changes in achievement scores on a test, there may be changes in qualitative aspects of performance that are normal in older individuals but pathologic in younger ones. For example, the rate of semantic paraphasic errors tends to increase with age. These same paraphasic errors are also associated with Alzheimer's dementia. Thus, it is inappropriate to interpret tests based on younger peoples' norms. Comparing an older subject's error rate to norms from younger subjects would result in faulty conclusions.

Some tests have age-related norms. For example, some of the most frequently used tests of general intelligence and memory, the WAIS-R and the Rey Auditory Verbal Learning Test, now have norms for older individuals based on a sample of healthy individuals living in Minnesota (Ivnik et al., 1992a, 1992b, 1992c). Other tests, such as the Randt Memory Test (Randt & Brown, 1979) and the Kendrick Cognitive Test (Gibson & Kendrick, 1982), were designed especially for older individuals, and normative information on this age group was collected as part of the standardization process. It is not the purpose of the following section to provide a comprehensive list of neuropsychological assessment methods for use with the aged. Other texts such as LaRue (1992) and Lovell and Nussbaum (1994) do so admirably. Rather, we review some of the most commonly used tests for which norms are available for the aged subject.

TESTS OF MEMORY

The Randt Memory Test (Randt & Brown, 1979) was designed to provide a reliable assessment of memory across both visual and verbal modalities. It assesses both immediate recall (new learning) and retrieval from long-term storage. The Randt consists of subtests that include a paragraph memory task, a selective reminding word learning task, a picture word association task, and a digit repetition task. Norms are available for ages 20 to 80 years. Five alternate forms exist to allow repeated assessments but reliability information is available only for Forms A and B (Franzen, Tishelman, Smith, Sharp, & Friedman, 1989). As another example, Youngjohn, Larrabee, and Crook (1993) provided both age and education corrections for the Benton Visual Retention Test, which requires the subject to draw a series of simple geometric forms after a 10-second exposure to each stimulus.

The Fuld Object Memory Test (Fuld, 1977) is based on Bushke's selective reminding procedure. There are norms available for ages 70 to 89 years. The memory items are actual household objects that the subject is allowed to manipulate, thus obviating visual or auditory limits that subjects may have. Although this appears to be a promising procedure for use with older subjects, there are limited data available regarding its diagnostic utility. The Object Memory Test has been used increasingly in clinical trials of new medications because of its similarity to ecological tasks.

The Kendrick Cognitive Test for the Elderly, formerly the Kendrick Battery for the Detection of Dementia in the Elderly (Gibson & Kendrick, 1982), is a short screening test that has been used more frequently in Great Britain than in the United States. It involves two tasks: The first involves a task of memory for pictures and the second involves a timed digit-copying task. By comparing performance on the two tasks to a set of age-related norms, decisions regarding the presence of dementia or pseudodementia can be made. The norms are based on a sample of 188 individuals across three age groups: 55 to 64 years old, 65 to 74 years old, and 75 years and older. The general notion is that by using two tasks, both of which are sensitive to cognitive decline, there can be greater confidence in the results.

TESTS OF INTELLECTUAL FUNCTIONING

One of the most frequently used tests either for clinical neuropsychological evaluations or general psychological evaluations is the WAIS-R (Wechsler, 1981). One of the limitations in using the WAIS-R with older populations had been the fact that the standardization sample ranged from age 16 years to 74 years. This problem was partly remedied by the work of Heaton (1992) who published a set of normative data based on a total sample of 1,680 subjects (1,260 subjects in the base sample and 420 subjects in the validation sample). Of this total sample, 160 subjects were in the group aged 65 to 69 years and 160 subjects were in the group aged 70 to 74 years. The subjects were additionally stratified by gender and by level of education to allow more precise demographic corrections. Although the overall sample size was quite impressive, by the time the divisions into gender and educations were made, the cell sizes are quite small. Therefore, the *T* scores based on the demographic corrections should be interpreted with some caution. And even here, the subjects were somewhat young, with a maximal age of 74 years.

Ivnik et al. (1992b) have also published normative information for the WAIS-R for a group of 512 older individuals. These researchers have extended the age groups from the age of 56 years to the age of 97 years. However, standard WAIS-R scores are available only for the group aged 56 to 74 years and tend to represent a high level of functioning. The average IQ values of these subjects indicates limitations in the use of these corrections in evaluating individuals with average or lower IQs. However, the availability of even limited normative data for individuals up to 97 years of age is certainly a welcome addition to the clinical neuropsychology literature.

NEUROPSYCHOLOGICAL BATTERIES

The HRNB is one of the most frequently used collections of neuropsychological assessment instruments. The original normative sample was quite limited, especially in its application to older individuals, and early research indicated that significant age effects exist. To expand the normative base, Heaton, Grant, and Matthews (1991) provided information for the HRNB as well as for the Boston Naming Test, the Thurstone Word Fluency Test, the Wepman Aphasia Screening Test, the Wisconsin Card Sorting Test, the

Complex Ideational Material subtest of the Boston Diagnostic Aphasia Exam, the Digit Vigilance Test, the Seashore Tonal Memory Test, and the Grooved Pegboard and Dynamometer as well as for Reitan's Story Memory and Figure Memory tests. The size of the normative sample varied across tests. Standardized T scores are available for subjects based on gender, education, and age. For the present purposes, the most important information is that T score transformations are provided for subjects up to the age of 80 years in 4-year increments. Unfortunately, the total sample size is only 480 subjects for the WAIS and HRNB and fewer numbers of subjects for the other tests. As a result, the cells based on gender, education, and age have limited sizes. (The manual does not provide precise information regarding the cell sizes.)

The Luria-Nebraska Neuropsychological Battery (LNNB; Golden, Purish, & Hammeke, 1985) uses a somewhat different approach to control for the effects of age and education. Rather than establishing norms separately for different age and education groups, age and education level are entered into a multiple regression formula to predict the score beyond which an individual might reasonably be expected to perform when some form of organic deficit is present. This cutoff score is known as the critical level. There are two alternate forms available for the LNNB. The range of ages in the standardization sample for Form I is not reported, but the average age was 42.0 years with a standard deviation of 14.8 years. The range of ages in the standardization sample for Form II was 19 to 88 years. Although the sample of older individuals was somewhat limited in the standardization sample, later normative data were provided by Spitzform (1982) and MacInnes et al. (1983). The entire battery can be somewhat lengthy to administer to an elderly person. Therefore, McCue, Goldstein, and Shelly (1989) investigated the use of a short form of the LNNB and reported that there was a high degree of discriminability of depressed elderly from Alzheimer's patients.

OTHER NEUROPSYCHOLOGICAL TESTS

Other neuropsychological test instruments also have normative information based on older samples. Ivnik et al. (1992a) have provided normative information for the Wechsler Memory Scale-Revised (WMS-R; Wechsler, 1987), and the Rey Auditory Verbal Learning Test (Ivnik et al., 1992a) based on the same sample discussed earlier in the context of the WAIS-R. The WMS-R is a battery of subtests that measure the ability to reproduce simple geometric designs, recall a paragraph narrative, learn word-word associations and color-design associations, repeat digits forward and backward, and recognize simple designs. For some of the subtests such as the paragraph recall and design drawing tasks, there are both immediate recall conditions and delayed recall conditions. The Rey Auditory

Verbal Learning Test evaluates the ability of an individual to learn a list of 15 unrelated words across five trials. The subject is then given a second list of words to learn and then asked to recall the first list, thereby assessing interference effects. There is also a recognition procedure for the first list.

The Boston Naming Test (Kaplan, Goodglass, & Weintraub, 1983) was specifically designed to detect deficits in naming skills in subjects with symptoms of aphasia. In this test, the subject is presented with a series of 60 line drawings of common objects and is asked to name the objects. The Boston Naming Test has aroused considerable interest among clinicians who evaluate older individuals because of the deficits in semantic relations demonstrated by individuals with Alzheimer's disease. As a result, there is normative information for this test based on samples composed of aged subjects (LaBarge, Edwards, & Knesevich, 1986; van Gorp, Satz, Kiersch, & Henry, 1986; Villardita, Cultrera, Cupone, & Meija, 1985).

The Wisconsin Card Sorting Test (Heaton, Chelune, Talley, Kay, & Curtis, 1993) has a newly published set of norms that includes subjects up to the age of 89 years, although it should be pointed out that the norms included only 22 subjects above the age of 80 years. The Wisconsin Card Sorting Test requires the subject to sort cards on the basis of color, shape, or number of objects but the subject is not told the underlying principle. Instead, the subject is given feedback of "correct" or "incorrect" following each sort and is to use this feedback to solve the sorting principles. There have also been modifications suggested, partly due to the frustration that impaired individuals sometimes experience with the instrument. Axelrod, Jiron, and Henry (1993) have reported normative information on an abbreviated form of the Wisconsin Card Sorting Test that uses only half the number of items. In their sample, there were 20 individuals in their 70s and 20 in their 80s.

Neuropsychological Screening Instruments

Screening instruments fall into two general classes; those that tap a variety of skills but with only one or two items each (broad but shallow) and those procedures that tap a single collection of skills but with multiple items (deep but narrow). The Neurobehavioral Cognitive Status Exam or NCSE (Kiernan, Mueller, Langston, & Van Dyke, 1987) and the Mini-Mental Status Exam or MMSE (Folstein, Folstein, & McHugh, 1975) have been recommended as broad but shallow screening instruments. In one study that evaluated the use of both of these instruments (Osato, Yang, & LaRue, 1993), it was found that in discriminating elderly inpatients with organic mental disorders from elderly inpatients with depressive disorders, the NCSE showed high sensitivity (100%) and low specificity (28%), whereas the MMSE showed high specificity (89%)

and low sensitivity (46%). Because the purpose of screening is to identify subjects for further evaluation, the NCSE with its greater sensitivity may be preferable in this population. Cross validation and application to an outpatient population is necessary before confident clinical recommendations can be made.

Other studies of screening tests exist. For example, Galasko et al. (1990) report that the MMSE demonstrated 67% sensitivity and 99% specificity in separating community-dwelling individuals with diagnoses of AD from community-dwelling individuals without AD. Hooijer, Dingreve, Jonker, and Lindeboom (1992) report similar sensitivity and specificity for the MMSE in their sample of 357 community-dwelling Dutch elderly, suggesting that the sensitivity and specificity rates for the MMSE in identifying dementia appear to be fairly stable across developed countries. Galasko et al. (1990) report that the MMSE is useful in identifying community-dwelling individuals in the early stages of AD. It is interesting to note that these same researchers reported that the items on the MMSE related to orientation to place and recall were as sensitive in identifying AD as the entire MMSE and that the addition of a verbal fluency test using letters as stimuli increased the sensitivity of identifying mild AD cases.

The most sensitive screening devices are those that tap a wide range of neuropsychological functions. These instruments, such as the Trailmaking test (Reitan & Wolfson, 1985), the Digit Symbol subtest of the WAIS-R, or the Kendrick Cognitive Test for the Elderly (Gibson & Kendrick, 1982), will help determine the presence of cognitive problems. If a more specific decision is pending, such as the differential determination of dementia versus depression, other approaches may be helpful. For example, by adding an incidental recall procedure to the Digit Symbol subtest, Hart, Kwentus, Wade, and Hamer (1987) found reasonable discrimination between depressed and demented individuals. Demented individuals tended to remember less than five of the symbols. The Kendrick measure has also been used for this specific discrimination. As noted earlier, McCue, Goldstein, and Shelly (1989) reported good discrimination using a short form of the LNNB. The LNNB's Memory and Pathognomonic scales were the best discriminators when used individually. It is interesting that the depressed patients with more severe symptomatology and less education were more likely to be misclassified as demented. The use of a screening test is insufficient by itself and should take place in the context of a general screening evaluation. Aspects of history and clinical presentation are also very important in this procedure.

SCREENING FOR COGNITIVE IMPAIRMENT

The first and most important stage in the assessment process is the information-gathering stage. Frequently, the diagnosis may hinge on information gathered as part of the history and initial interview. Furthermore, even the most sophisticated neuropsychological measure cannot be interpreted outside of the personal historical context. There are a number of historical factors that can influence performance on cognitive measures. For example, long-term employment involving exposure to neurotoxins can have a significant effect on scores from a memory test. The test performance of an individual who has completed a college education can be markedly different from the performance of an individual who has completed only the seventh grade. These examples point to the essential nature of the information-gathering stage of the assessment. Important historical information includes educational, occupational, academic, and social aspects.

The paramount principle in interpreting assessment results is whether the current level of performance represents a change from baseline level. Determining whether change has occurred may be problematic. Individuals with a progressive condition may be unaware of changes. Individuals functioning at higher levels and individuals with anxiety disorders may notice even slight changes in functioning. As a result of the differences in threshold for self-awareness, it is important to obtain information from another person who is familiar with the individual, typically a family member. However, significant others may be limited by an inability to conceptualize and identify areas of cognitive deficit and their own emotional acceptance of negative changes. A useful strategy is to seek out convergence across different sources of information.

The screening process begins with an identification of the presenting problem and the source of the complaint. It is very important that the clinician have an understanding of who is making the complaint and what the reasons may be for that complaint. In addition, as with any medical history, it is important to know the course of the problem.

The presenting problem is important in delineating the relevant issues. Many patients may identify their problems as being deficits in memory, but a more careful interview may indicate that skill deficits are present instead. For example, a frequent presenting complaint of older women with a dementing condition is that they have forgotten how to cook favorite recipes. A careful interview may uncover that, rather than impaired memory for the recipes, there may be deficits in the ability to connect the steps into a set of linked behaviors. Similarly, a complaint about deficits in memory may actually refer to deficits in word finding. Prior to beginning an evaluation or referring for specialized testing, the clinician should clarify the problem with a careful interview.

The identity of the person making the complaint is important. When the person making the complaint is the patient, there is likely to be some ability to discern impairment and evaluate oneself. In these cases, it is likely that the impairment is either subtle or in the beginning stages of decline. Standard screening instruments may be relatively insensitive to this form of presentation. Although specialized testing may uncover the subtle deficits, the clinician must make a decision regarding whether to refer to a specialist or monitor change over time. The anxious patient may benefit from the reassurance afforded by a comprehensive evaluation with negative results, but the cost of such an evaluation must be weighed against the benefit. If the clinician suspects that the beginning stages of a progressive condition are present, obtaining a baseline of cognitive function may be helpful in charting the course of the condition.

Even before obtaining a baseline, the interview can provide important information regarding the course of the condition. It is important to obtain corroboration whenever possible. A report of gradually increasing impairment may be indicative of dementia of the Alzheimer's type, whereas a report of abrupt decrement in cognitive function suggests vascular etiology or even a treatable medical condition.

The next stage in the assessment process involves some formal testing of cognitive function. Some of the most commonly used tests were described earlier in the section on neuropsychological instruments. In administering a test, the clinician attempts to obtain the optimal level of performance from the patient. Within that context, it is important to encourage the patient to try his or her hardest. It may also be necessary to make special effort to put the patient at ease with the assessment situation. An elderly individual may have concerns about the target comparisons for their test data. The clinician can reassure the patient that appropriate norms are being used and that appropriate comparisons with age peers will be made.

It is also important to obtain information regarding the emotional status of the patient. This goal can be partly accomplished in the clinical interview. Other methods include objective self-report instruments. Perhaps the most widely used of these instruments is the Geriatric Depression Scale (GDS; Yesavage, Brink, Rose, & Aday, 1983b). The GDS consists of 30 yes-or-no questions regarding symptoms of depression that are more relevant to the elderly. A somewhat less frequently used instrument, although still appropriate for the older patient, is the Zung Self-Report Depression Scale (Zung, 1965).

The clinician may wish to screen for cognitive impairment prior to making a decision to referral for a more extensive (and expensive) evaluation. The choice of screening measures should be guided by the availability of age-appropriate norms as well as by the sensitivity and specificity of the results. Erickson, Eimon, and Hebben (1992) published the results of surveying available norms for older individuals. Tables of the references are available from the first author (Erickson) and include information on mental status exams, neuropsychological batteries, and tests of intellectual abilities, memory, perceptual-motor skills, and executive functions. The information in the studies cited by Erickson et al. (1992) is somewhat dated in some instances, and the sample characteristics are less representative than would be optimal, but the information is incrementally better than relying on norms from younger subjects.

Once the interviewer has taken a history and determined that cognitive deficits may exist, the clinician may wish to administer a screening instrument. Frequently, the screening question is not just whether a person is cognitively impaired but whether a dementia of the Alzheimer's type is present. The most sensitive indicator is a test of delayed recall memory measure. Tests of naming functions, such as the Boston Naming Test, a test of executive functioning, such as the Wisconsin Card Sorting Test, and a test of constructional praxis, such as the Block Design subtest of the WAIS-R also may be helpful. The use of these tests is based on the knowledge that there is variability in clinical presentation of dementias, especially in the early stages, but there are certain skill areas that are more likely than others to show subtle impairment early in the disease.

Debring, van Gorp, Stuck, Mitrushina, and Beck (1994) report the results of an investigation comparing the relative sensitivity and specificity of various screening instruments in detecting early signs of dementia. These authors report that the use of a battery composed of the Rey Auditory Verbal Learning Test, the Digit Symbol subtest of the WAIS-R, Trails A and B, and the Rey-Osterreith Complex Figure is superior to the use of any of the procedures individually and superior to the use of the MMSE. This is a particularly important point because many clinicians routinely use the MMSE. The use of these procedures is a significant increment in time for administration. However, the increased sensitivity may warrant their use in selected cases. For example, Masur, Sliwinski, Lipton, Blau, and Crystal (1994) report on the capacity of a collection of procedures, namely, the Buschke Selective Reminding Test, the Fuld Object Memory Test, the Digit Symbol subtest of the WAIS-R, and a verbal fluency procedure, to predict which healthy older individuals will later develop dementia. As these authors point out, the ability to predict risk for dementia has benefits both for those at low risk, providing reassurance, and those individuals at high risk, allowing early interventions.

After screening for cognitive impairment, the decision to refer to a specialist is made. Not all clinical neuropsychologists are equally qualified to evaluate older adults. Naturally, if you can find a geriatric neuropsychologist or at least a neuropsychologist with extensive clinical experience with older patients, half the goal is accomplished. It is a good idea to ask about the experience of the specialist in this area, especially if a choice among potential specialists is possible.

Assessment is enhanced by clear referral questions. If there is difficulty in formulating the referral question, a short telephone consultation with the specialist is advised. For example, a referral question of "How will this person's level of memory impairment affect their ability to live independently" will elicit more useful information than a referral question of "Please evaluate memory." An evaluation aimed at diagnosis will often vary greatly from an evaluation in response to questions of competency or the capacity to live independently, even though the same test instruments may be used in both cases.

It is a good idea to acquire a consumer-oriented attitude toward referrals to specialists. Developing a relationship with a specialist such that he or she is familiar with the type of information you typically seek is beneficial to both professionals. Part of the relationship should include a reiterative information loop in which you provide feedback regarding the usefulness and accuracy of the specialist's recommendations.

Conclusions

Over the past 20 years, considerable attention has been focused on the cognitive changes associated with the aging process. The large amount of research conducted during this period has helped us to understand the qualitative and quantitative changes involved with normal aging and to distinguish these changes from the effects of degenerative diseases. Aging itself does not have a uniform, global effect on cognitive functioning. Instead, there is a more selective decline in functions that partly reflects neurocognitive slowing and partly reflects other, more poorly understood processes. Along with the increase in understanding of aging processes, there has been an increased realization of the need for age-appropriate norms for clinical neuropsychological assessment instruments. Although there is still more work that needs to be done in providing norms for the older subject, use of the current available norms can help both in the detection of cognitive impairment and in the differential diagnosis.

10

Psychological Manifestations of Physical Disease in the Elderly

Deborah W. Frazer
Martin L. Leicht
Matt Dane Baker

One of the most intriguing and challenging aspects of working with an elderly population is multidimensional assessment. Cognitive, psychosocial, familial, environmental, financial-legal, as well as medical factors grow increasingly salient with aging for determining intervention strategies. (See also Chapter 19, discussing interdisciplinary care.) Although medical conditions usually are the primary factor driving the patient's treatment, often there are associated psychological conditions. Yet practitioners are frequently ill-prepared to assess the psychological concomitants of medical illness. In part, our lack of knowledge is due to the lack of training opportunities in this area; in part, it is due to the lack of a well-researched knowledge base in the field.

The purpose of this chapter is to summarize recent findings about the relationships between selected medical and mental health conditions. In understanding these complex relationships, practitioners become more alert to the roles of both psyche and soma in the etiology and treatment of mental

217

health symptoms and therefore become more likely to both treat and refer patients appropriately. The specific medical conditions reviewed have been chosen based on prevalence, chronicity, and the existence of at least some research into related mental health problems.

Medical and mental health conditions interact in a number of ways. Mental health practitioners are trained to recognize and treat psychological reactions prompted by physical disorders and psychological conditions that render individuals vulnerable to physical disorders. Medical practitioners are trained to recognize and treat psychological symptoms that may arise in response to the treatment of physical complaints, such as drug reactions. Both types of practitioners are familiar with somatization disorders, in which psychological disorders manifest themselves as physical complaints. This chapter will focus on physical disorders that cause biologically based psychological symptoms as well as those that, when undetected, can appear as psychological symptoms.

The goals are to improve mental health practitioners' sensitivity to possible underlying medical conditions and to encourage mental health practitioners to adopt therapeutic strategies that are appropriate for selected medical conditions and their treatments. Thus, when there is strong indication that there may be a biological component to the depression or other mental disorder that accompanies a particular disease, consideration should be given to pharmacological agents and to psychotherapies that stress adaptation to and coping with the disease and its psychosocial ramifications.

A major difficulty of these complex interactions is that psychological symptoms are often nonspecific; that is, different patients might present signs of depression, anxiety, or cognitive impairment, all in relation to the same physical condition. With that caveat in mind, each section will begin with a brief description of the medical condition followed by reports of incidence and prevalence of mental health symptomatology, when known. Last, evidence will be reviewed on whether the mental health symptoms might be present prodromally and whether there is evidence for a biological basis for the associated mental health symptoms.

Parkinson's Disease

Parkinson's disease is a disease of the basal ganglia characterized by stiff and slow motor movements (rigidity and bradykinesia). The patient may have a resting hand tremor, which may occur on only one side. He or she may be unsteady when standing or walking and have difficulty initiating motor activity, such as walking. Other features include fatigue, a soft and monotonous voice, "masked facies" or rigid facial expression, constipation, decreased libido, and mental slowing (bradyphrenia). The course is chronic and progressive, with worsening of symptoms and associated disability typically occurring after 5 to 6 years. Most typical onset is in the fifth or sixth decade.

Many people may suffer from some or all of these Parkinsonian symptoms (known as *Parkinsonism*) without actually having Parkinson's disease; the symptoms may be due to a variety of causes, such as medication reactions or other neurodegenerative diseases.

Depression has long been recognized as a frequently associated feature of Parkinson's disease, although it was described in earlier decades as an understandable, reactive "demoralization" (Starkstein & Mayberg, 1993). Although many studies have suffered from ambiguous definitions of depression and questionable instrumentation, most report a high frequency of depression in Parkinson's disease. Mayeux and his colleagues (Mayeux, 1982, Mayeux et al., 1986; Mayeux, Stern, Rosen, & Leventhal, 1981) found depression in one quarter to one half of all Parkinson's patients. Starkstein, Preziosi, Bolduc, and Robinson (1990) report, with standardized questionnaires and criteria listed in the third edition of the *Diagnostic and Statistical Manual of Mental Disorders (DSM-III;* American Psychiatric Association, 1980) for depression, a 41% rate of depression among 105 consecutive outpatients being followed for Parkinson's disease. Half of the depressed patients met criteria for major depression and half for minor (dysthymic) depression. Among early-stage patients with unilateral symptoms, left hemisphere Parkinson's disease patients had significantly more frequent and severe depressions than those with right hemisphere Parkinson's disease. Among late-stage patients, depression was correlated only with age and activity in daily living impairment. Starkstein et al. (1990) suggest that, early in the disease, structural or biochemical changes, or both, in the left basal ganglia may be an etiological factor in the depression.

Can Parkinson's disease manifest as depression? Starkstein et al. (1990) found that of patients with both major depression and Parkinson's disease, 29% suffered a history of depression prior to the appearance of any motor symptoms. In contrast, only 5% of patients with minor depression and Parkinson's disease and 2% of patients with no depression and Parkinson's disease had prior histories of depression. Although this research does not directly address the issue of prodromal depression (i.e., depression as a first sign of Parkinson's disease), it does suggest that patients with major depression prior to Parkinson's onset are more vulnerable to a concomitant depression after onset.

To address the question of prodromal depression, Santamaria, Tolosa, and Valles (1986) studied 34 patients with recent-onset Parkinson's disease who were not being treated with dopaminergic agents. In 15 cases (44%), depression antedated motoric manifestations of Parkinson's disease. This group was also characterized by younger age at onset, a higher proportion of familial history of Parkinson's disease, and less severe motoric symptoms. Santamaria et al. (1986) propose the possibility of a specific subgroup of depression-associated Parkinson's disease, with chronically diminished brain serotonergic activity preceding Parkinsonian symptoms. Todes and Lee (1985) also reported premorbid predisposition to depressive illness in Parkinson's patients. Taken together, these studies suggest that for older patients being treated for depression, the mental health practitioner should be alert to early Parkinson's motor signs and if present, refer back to the primary physician for evaluation.

In addition to depression, cognitive impairment is frequently cited as a condition concomitant with Parkinson's disease. Cummings (1988) reviewed 27 studies representing 4,336 patients with Parkinson's disease for prevalence of overt dementia. He reported an overall prevalence rate of 39.9%, with a range from 30% in studies using nonstandardized interviews to 70% in studies using neuropsychological assessment techniques.

In the 20% to 40% of Parkinson's disease patients who develop frank dementia, approximately one half will be found to have the pathologic changes associated with Alzheimer's disease (i.e., neuritic plaques and neurofibrillary tangles) on autopsy (Katzman & Rowe, 1992). Impairments typically are manifested in memory, visuospatial skills, and set aptitude. Language function is usually spared. Cognitive impairments increase with age, akinesia, and duration of illness. The latter finding suggests that cognitive impairment is progressive, not prodromal, and would not usually be a presenting symptom of Parkinson's disease.

Anxiety has also been reported with Parkinson's disease (Schiffer, Kurlan, Rubin, & Boer, 1988; Stein, Heuser, Juncos, & Uhde, 1990). In a comparison of 16 depressed Parkinson's disease patients and 20 depressed multiple sclerosis patients, Schiffer et al. (1988) found significantly more comorbid anxiety disorders among the Parkinson's disease patients. Twelve of the 16 Parkinson's disease patients met the Schedule for Affective Disorders and Schizophrenia—Lifetime Version research diagnostic criteria for past or present generalized anxiety disorder or panic disorder. Only 2 of the 20 multiple sclerosis patients met these criteria. Stein et al. (1990) studied 24 Parkinson's disease patients without dementia. Nine (38%) of the 24 patients received a *DSM-III-R* (APA, 1987) diagnosis of current anxiety disorder. One had generalized anxiety disorder, three had panic disorder, one had panic disorder and social phobia, three had social phobia alone, and one had an anxiety disorder not otherwise specified.

Is there evidence for a biological basis for the depression seen in Parkinson's disease? In discussing psychological and biological factors in Parkinson's depression, Starkstein and Mayberg (1993) present evidence against a psychological explanation (depression often is seen before motor symptoms, and ADL impairments are not significantly correlated with depression until late stages of the disease). The authors go on to posit a biological mechanism related to frontal lobe or biogenic amine (dopamine) dysfunction, or both, although noting that further research is needed to explicate this mechanism. The high prevalence rate of depression in Parkinson's disease and the additional findings of Starkstein and Mayberg strongly suggest a biological basis. Therefore, pharmacological interventions and an adaptation-coping approach in psychotherapy would seem advisable.

Practitioners should also be alert to the possible side effects of the Parkinson's disease medications. The most commonly used pharmacological agents are the compounds containing levodopa, now often combined with carbidopa (e.g., Sinemet). Although the most common side effects are nausea, vomiting, anorexia, and dizziness, there is a risk of central nervous system effects, such as confusion, hallucinations, and nightmares. Newer medications, used as adjuncts to levodopa-carbidopa, may also increase the risk of confusion and hallucinations. These include bromocriptine (Parlodel), pergolide (Permax), and selegiline (Eldepryl) (Smith & Reynard, 1992).

Chronic Obstructive Pulmonary Disease

Chronic obstructive pulmonary disease (COPD) is a group of degenerative diseases of the airways. Prominent among these diseases are chronic bronchitis and emphysema. The central features are dyspnea (the patient's subjective sense of the inability to obtain enough air), cough, and sputum production. The preclinical course can be as long as 30 to 40 years followed by an active clinical phase of approximately 10 years.

Depressive symptomatology is the most prominent psychological feature associated with COPD, estimated to occur in one quarter to one half of COPD patients (Murrell, Himmelfarb, & Wright, 1983). Borson et al. (1986) and Kukull et al. (1986) estimate the prevalence of diagnosable major depression at 12% to 15% among COPD patients.

Although generalized anxiety and panic disorder are reported clinically, there have been no systematic studies of the prevalence of anxiety disorders in COPD (Borson & McDonald, 1989). It is known, however, that when metabolic demands are out of balance with respiratory response, the patient may experience hypoxia and dyspnea followed by a secondary, symptom-related anxiety. This secondary anxiety places further demands on the respiratory system, causing a feedback loop that exacerbates both respiratory and psychological symptomatology.

Can COPD present as depression or anxiety? There is no direct evidence of a prodromal or biologically based depression in COPD. It has been recognized for decades (Dudley, Martin, Masuda, Ripley, & Holmes, 1969), however, that COPD patients may deny or tolerate their respiratory symptoms for many years before seeking medical evaluation. During this preclinical course, the patient may be consciously or unconsciously restricting activity and socialization to minimize respiratory demands. Depression may occur in reaction to the loss of activity and social supports, or the depleted energy due to insufficient respiration may be interpreted as depression. Thus, the mental health practitioner should be alert to a profile with these features: a depressed or anxious (or both) client with a chronic cough, a history of recurrent respiratory infections, current or past history of smoking or exposure to environmental toxins, and decreased activity or socialization level. In these cases, the clinician should refer the patient to a physician for evaluation of pulmonary function.

Once the COPD has been diagnosed, the mental health issues should be an integral part of the treatment. The relationships of depression, anxiety, respiration, and activity levels are interactive. Therefore, mental health interventions can be key in maintaining the client's commitment to and compliance with treatment and rehabilitation programs, and the patient's adapting to losses in functional capacity, and maintaining positive relationships with caregivers.

As the disease progresses, the client may experience cognitive symptoms due to hypoxemia (oxygen deprivation) or hypercapnia (CO_2 retention). Deficits that have been reported (Block, 1983; Grant et al., 1987; McSweeny, Grant, Heaton, Adams, & Timms, 1985) include decreases in mental alertness, mental efficiency, complex problem solving, memory, and motor coordination and speed. Oxygen therapy substantially improves most of these cognitive symptoms. Theophylline, a commonly used bronchodilator, can cause cognitive impairment, anxiety, agitation, and insomnia. These symptoms are usually dose related and may reflect drug toxicity. Oral corticosteroids such as prednisone are also commonly used to treat COPD; they can cause a wide variety of mental disturbances ranging from anxiety, euphoria, and depression to psychosis. These symptoms may be severe enough to prompt discontinuing the drug, which requires careful medical supervision. Therefore, their presence should prompt referral to the treating physician for reevaluation of medication levels.

The use of inhaled bronchodilating agents is a common treatment for COPD patients. Some patients may overuse the inhalers in an attempt to avoid all sensation of dyspnea. Teaching breathing and relaxation techniques can help redirect the tendency to overuse the inhalers.

Sleep disturbance is a frequent complaint of COPD patients, which can further negatively affect affective and cognitive functioning. According to Borson and McDonald (1989), the well-managed COPD patient should not have to waken more than once per night for bronchodilator treatment. If a patient reports more severe sleep disturbance due to breathing difficulty, he or she should be encouraged to record and report these symptoms to the treating physician for a thorough evaluation.

Clearly in COPD, there is a complex interaction between the biological, psychological, and social factors of the disease and its management. Antidepressant medications appear to be efficacious in treating the minority of patients whose depressive syndromes meet criteria for major depression or minor depression with anxiety and some vegetative signs (Borson & McDonald, 1989). Commonly prescribed antianxiety medications (primarily benzodiazepines) can depress respiration and therefore should be used cautiously with COPD patients. Nonmedical therapies (e.g., relaxation training, breathing rehabilitation) that reduce biological symptoms are reported to be useful, as are individual and group therapies focused on adaptation to this difficult, progressive disease (Dudley, Glaser, Jorgenson, & Logan, 1980; Knapp & Mathe, 1985).

Cardiovascular Disease

As with COPD, the term *cardiovascular disease* actually refers to a group of disorders, including hypertension, coronary artery disease, valvular heart disease, arrhythmias and conduction disorders, heart failure, and the peripheral vascular diseases. In all of these disorders, due to either heart or vascular disease, the organism has difficulty sustaining a regular, sufficient blood supply throughout the body. Closely related are the cerebrovascular diseases, which affect the blood supply to the brain; these two types of vascular disease frequently coexist.

Cohen-Cole (1989) reports that patients with chronic heart disease experience significant depressive symptomatology at a rate of between 10% and 20% and major depression at a rate of about 5%. He further suggests that anxiety may be a prominent feature in cardiovascular disease because this disease is often more unpredictable and more life threatening than other chronic illnesses.

Most of the research on psychological factors in cardiovascular disease has focused on the relationship of depression and coronary artery disease (CAD). In a major meta-analysis of personality and disease, Friedman and Booth-Kewley (1987) found depression to be as major a risk factor for CAD as cigarette smoking. The predictive power of depression increased when the analysis was limited to prospective studies of myocardial infarction (MI). In a retrospective study, Lloyd and Cawley (1983) found that of 18 patients who were depressed after a first MI, 6 had been depressed prior to the MI. Therefore, there is evidence of a strong association between depression and

CAD and that depression may precede CAD; there is not, however, evidence of a specific prodromal period immediately prior to a coronary event. In contrast, geriatricians have learned to identify a sudden change in mental status as a potential prodromal or concurrent indicator (sometimes the only one) of MI in the elderly. This is particularly true for demented patients who may not be able to communicate other symptoms.

In addition to findings that depression is a risk factor for cardiovascular events, there is also a substantial literature that documents the negative effects of depression on outcome. Carney et al. (1988) followed 52 patients with known CAD over a 12-month follow-up period. Controlling for illness severity and other risk factors and using standardized measures of depression, the authors were able to show a twofold increase in the incidence of new cardiac events among the patients who were depressed at baseline. Depression was the best predictor of new cardiac events. Stern, Pascale, and Ackerman (1977) and Mayeux, Foster, and Williamson (1978) showed that depressed CAD patients fared more poorly with psychosocial rehabilitation relative to nondepressed patients. Rabins, Harvis, and Koven (1985) also found a twofold increase in mortality among CAD patients with major depression. Silverstone (1987) reported an increased risk of early death, reinfarction, or cardiac arrest associated with depression in the first 48 hours following a myocardial infarction.

Because of the apparent association of depression and cardiovascular disease, researchers have searched for a mechanism to explain the relationship. Early work on the relationship between psychological factors and cardiovascular disease focused on "Type A" personalities. Current work, summarized in Blascovich and Katkin (1993), focuses on the psychological mediators between environmental stressors and cardiovascular responses. The researchers represented in that volume are investigating various links and patterns among stress, individual cardiovascular reactivity, and last, cardiovascular disease. This work is very much still in progress but holds great promise for future understanding of the complex relationships between psychological and cardiovascular variables. It is also promising in that it will lead to appropriate therapeutic strategies with cardiovascular patients. The therapist may attempt to interrupt the stress-reactivity-disease process at either the psychological level (i.e., cognitive appraisal of stress) or at the physiological level (i.e., learned control of myocardial or vascular responses to perceived stress).

Whatever the preexisting psychophysiological vulnerabilities to cardiovascular disease, postevent reactions are common. Cohen-Cole (1989) notes the typical "homecoming" depression, when a post-MI patient is released from the hospital often unprepared for the fatigue, fears, and change of lifestyle that he or she faces. Education about MI (including sexual education), support, exercise, and smoking cessation groups all can be critical to full recovery. This type of counseling is often available in cardiac rehabilitation programs.

Last, cardioactive and antihypertensive medications are often psychoactive as well. In particular, Beta-blockers such as propanolol/Inderal, which has been shown to decrease mortality in CAD patients, can cause depression, mental confusion, or both (Hurst, 1986). To further complicate matters, antidepressant medications (especially the tricyclic antidepressants such as amitryptyline/Elavil, desipramine/Norpramin, and nortryptyline/Pamelor) can be especially complex to manage in a cardiac patient due to their potential cardiotoxicity. Therefore, it is particularly important when treating depression, anxiety, or both in a cardiovascular patient to have very close communication among patient, mental health practitioner, and physician.

In summary, there is evidence that preexisting depression may render individuals vulnerable to CAD, although there is no evidence of a specific prodromal period. Research on postevent depression has focused on psychological rather than biological bases, with the exception of medication reactions.

Cerebrovascular Disease

Closely related to the cardiovascular conditions are the cerebrovascular diseases. Whenever blood flow to the brain is reduced or interrupted, either due to heart disease or atherosclerotic changes in cerebral vessels, the patient will experience cognitive effects from the resulting anoxia. Usually, these effects are global and most evident in higher cortical functions (Rosenberg, 1980). When a patient complains of confusion, disorientation, and impaired memory, and particularly when these symptoms fluctuate, the clinician should always arrange for a dementia evaluation to differentiate reversible from irreversible conditions, vascular from neurodegenerative processes, and to rule out delirium.

A patient who reports repeated falls and who may or may not demonstrate cognitive deficits also should be thoroughly evaluated. Falls are extremely common among the elderly and can result from myriad causes, including musculoskeletal, sensory, and neurological disorders in addition to adverse drug reactions. If the etiology of the falls is unclear, the patient should be evaluated for underlying cardiac or cerebrovascular problems. Cardiac-related falls may be preceded by syncope (a brief loss of consciousness), although this may not be reported initially by the patient. Syncope represents an interruption in blood flow to the brain, due either to cardiac or cerebrovascular conditions. Cerebrovascular-related falls are often accompanied by dizziness, visual changes, syncope, asymmetric extremity weakness, or a combination of these.

By far, the most common cerebrovascular condition in the elderly is stroke. Caplan (1990) defines *stroke* as "a heterogeneous category of illness that describes brain injury, usually sudden, caused by vascular disease." He distinguishes between brain hemorrhage and brain ischemia and between permanent versus transient conditions (the latter primarily comprised of transient ischemic attacks). Power and Hachinski (1990) report that 85% of those suffering from stroke are over 65 years old and that stroke is the third leading cause of death in North America.

An impressive amount of research has been conducted on the relationship between stroke and depression. Lipsey and Parikh (1989) reported on a series of quantitative studies on poststroke depressive disorders. They demonstrated that clinical depression is a common consequence of stroke, occurring in 47% of the patients immediately following stroke (during hospitalization) and increasing to 60% of the patients at 6-month follow-up. None of the patients had been treated with antidepressants, reflecting the common attitude that poststroke depression is "normal." The authors further demonstrated the importance of the site of the lesion, with left anterior lesions showing significantly higher correlations with severity of depression. Using a placebo-controlled design, the authors went on to investigate the effectiveness of antidepressant therapy with poststroke patients and were able to show significant improvement with the use of nortriptyline/ Pamelor. Last, in two related studies, the same authors show the negative effects of untreated depression on poststroke cognitive and physical recovery.

Lipsey and Parikh's early work has been substantiated and extended by more recent studies. In a review of depression in poststroke patients admitted to acute units, general hospitals, and rehabilitation centers, Starkstein and Robinson (1993) reported prevalence rates ranging from 30% to 50%. Reporting findings from follow-up studies, these authors added that poststroke major depression appears to resolve after approximately 1 year, whereas poststroke minor depression lasts for over 2 years, on average. Lesion location is associated with duration of depression, with middle cerebral (cortical) artery areas associated with longer duration and subcortical, or cerebellar-brainstem, lesions associated with briefer durations of depression.

Using a prospective, longitudinal design with right hemisphere lesion patients, Starkstein and Robinson (1993) further investigated the relationship between lesion location and depression. They found that immediately poststroke, depression was more likely to occur in patients with right posterior lesion locations; however, at 6-month follow-up, depression was higher among patients with right anterior lesion locations. This suggests a dynamic relationship between location of insult and depression, with the length of time since stroke onset as a mediating variable.

In another series of studies, Starkstein and his colleagues (Starkstein, Robinson, Berthier, Parikh, & Price, 1988; Starkstein, Robinson, & Price,

1987) reported that subcortical stroke patients showed the same lateralization effects of depression: that strokes in the left anterior hemisphere (primarily the basal ganglia) were associated with more depression than either left posterior or right hemisphere strokes.

Looking at associated mental health symptoms, Starkstein et al. (1990) reported an association between poststroke depression and anxiety. Bolla-Wilson, Robinson, Starkstein, Boston, and Price (1989) reported an association between poststroke depression and cognitive impairment.

The work cited does suggest a biological component to poststroke depression, yet surprisingly few studies report on the use of antidepressants with this population. Starkstein and Robinson (1993) summarized these studies and concluded that both tricyclic antidepressants and electroconvulsive therapy can be useful in treating poststroke depression. The newer seratonergic agents will probably prove most appropriate because of fewer cardiac-related side effects. Both the patient and the family may be helped by understanding that the depression may be a direct effect of a brain lesion, particularly when the lesion is in the left anterior area.

Major strokes present obvious motor and cognitive symptoms and are not likely to appear prodromally as psychological symptoms. However, more subtle cognitive warning signs of cerebrovascular disease, such as brief confusional states, falls, dizziness, or fainting, may be reported to mental health practitioners and should be followed with a referral to the treating physician. Although depression does not seem to figure prodromally in stroke, it does seem to be frequently unrecognized or untreated poststroke. Furthermore, there is some evidence that certain risk factors for developing poststroke depression could be addressed preventively. Given the high toll among elders from cardiovascular and cerebrovascular conditions, mental health practitioners can also play an important medical prevention role through support for lifestyle modification. Structured programs for smoking cessation, healthy eating habits, and exercise all can be integrated into a more traditional psychotherapeutic approach.

Cancer

Cancer is the second leading cause of death in the United States (following heart disease). Fifty percent of all cancers occur in people over the age of 65 years (Cohen, 1990). Although all cancers have malignant growth of tissue in common, there is great variability in course, outcome, and associated psychological features according to site and type of lesion.

The diagnosis of cancer-related depression (the most commonly cited psychological feature) is complicated by the somatic features of the disease.

In addition, its treatment may be confounded with the vegetative signs of depression. Reported prevalence rates of major depression in cancer patients vary from 6% to 42%, with one study reporting a drop from 42% to 24% when somatic criteria were eliminated (Rodin, Craven, & Littlefield, 1993). Greenberg (1989) points out that clinical knowledge about the specific type of tumor, its course, and its treatment is necessary to diagnose depression in an individual case. Depressive signs such as anorexia, fatigue, and insomnia may be caused by radiation or chemotherapy or by intractable pain. If the fatigue is worse in the morning, however, depression may be the causal factor. If insomnia is not accompanied by pain, depression should be considered. Greenberg posits that anhedonia (inability to experience pleasure) is not common in cancer patients unless they are depressed.

A related, controversial issue is whether clinical depression or depressive personality features predispose a person to cancer or promote an existing cancer. Fox (1989) reviewed studies that link personality traits to cancer, especially tendencies toward self-blame, self-sacrifice, hopelessness, and despair. Three prospective studies were cited that investigated the relationship between the Minnesota Multiphasic Personality Inventory scale for depression and cancer. Although one of the latter studies (Shekelle et al., 1981) made a fairly strong case for predisposition to cancer among depressed males, from all the studies published to that point, Fox concluded that the evidence for this relationship is weak. The evidence is similarly mixed for a relationship between depression and mortality in cancer patients (Rodin et al., 1993). Much of this research is hampered by lack of standardized measures, variety of tumors studied, and variability of outcome measures.

Can cancer first appear as depression? There is long-standing and substantial evidence that this is the case in pancreatic cancer. Gilliam (1990) writes, "Depression is such a well-known presenting finding that unexplained depression in an elderly male without an antecedent history mandates a search for pancreatic cancer" (p. 643). Several studies have documented higher rates of early depression in pancreatic, as opposed to gastric or colon, cancer (Fras, Litin, & Pearson, 1967; Holland et al., 1986; Jacobsson & Ottosson, 1971). In a methodologically refined study, Joffe, Rubinow, Denicoff, Maher, and Sindelar (1986) were able to demonstrate that 50% of patients diagnosed with cancer of the pancreas fulfilled research diagnostic criteria for major depression during the year prior to diagnosis, whereas none of those with cancer of the stomach met the criteria. Several biological mechanisms have been postulated to explain the high prevalence, and tendency toward prodromal presentation, of depression in pancreatic cancer. To date, no single theory predominates.

In addition to prodromal depression in pancreatic cancer, there is some evidence of depression as a first or early symptom in lung cancer (Hughes, 1985) and head and neck cancer (Davies, Davies, & Delpo, 1986).

There is a large and complex literature on the psychological and psycho-pharmacological treatment of cancer-related disorders. As this is covered elsewhere in this volume (Chapter 15), the material will not be presented here.

Diabetes Mellitus

Diabetes is a complex disease with interrelated metabolic and vascular components. Metabolically, the diabetic patient suffers from hyperglycemia (high blood sugar) due to absent or diminished insulin secretion or ineffective insulin action. The vascular component consists of small vessel changes (leading to retinopathy and nephropathy) and large vessel changes (leading to cerebral vascular accidents, myocardial infarction, and peripheral vascular disease.) Neuropathy is also fairly common in the older diabetic population. Diabetes is typically divided into Type I (insulin-dependent diabetes mellitus or IDDM) and Type II (non-insulin-dependent diabetes mellitus or NIDDM).

Diabetic treatment consists of four interrelated components: diet; exercise; oral hypoglycemic agents such as glyburide-Micronase and glipizide-Glucatrol; and insulin. Management is complex (particularly when insulin is used), requiring carefully timed and regulated behaviors of eating, exercising, blood sugar monitoring, and medication administration. Emotional states can also affect blood sugar levels, with severe or intermittent stress upsetting a previously established balanced regimen. Recent evidence (Diabetes Control and Complications Trial Research Group, 1993) suggests that good control of blood sugar levels can reduce the vascular sequelae of diabetes in the insulin-dependent type.

NIDDM is the most prevalent form of the disease in older populations, with prevalence rates of 20% in persons aged 65 to 74 years (Davidson, 1990) and estimated rates at close to 40% in persons over age 80 years (Morley & Kaiser, 1990). Most research on diabetes mellitus has been done with IDDM patients, however, leaving the mechanisms and treatments for NIDDM less well understood.

Several researchers have investigated the role of emotions in diabetes mellitus. Using a Diagnostic Interview Schedule, Lustman, Griffith, Clouse, and Cryer (1986) estimated a lifetime prevalence of major depression among 114 insulin-dependent and non-insulin-dependent diabetics at 32.5% and point prevalence rates at 14%. There were no differences in rates of depression between the IDDM and NIDDM patients. Geringer, Perlmuter, Stern, and Nathan (1988) reported depression rates (based on a Zung Self-Rated Depression Scale) of 19% among NIDDM females. Five-year prevalence has been estimated at 17.7% (Robinson, Fuller, & Edmeades, 1988). Among diabetic patients applying for pancreatic transplants, Popkin, Callies, Lentz, Colon, and Sutherland (1988) found a point prevalence of major depression of 10.7% and a lifetime prevalence of 24%. Although it is difficult to draw a specific prevalence rate conclusion from these diverse studies, they do point to a generally high rate of major depression among diabetics. Lustman, Griffith, and Clouse (1988) conducted a follow-up study that indicated that 79% of the initially depressed diabetic patients suffered one or more relapses within a 5-year period. This is a significantly higher relapse rate than that of depressed medically well subjects who were also uncontrolled for treatment.

Can diabetes first appear as depression? Goldberg, Andres, and Bierman (1990) make the case that diabetes presents a different picture in the elderly than in younger patients. Whereas a younger patient will more often be diagnosed on the basis of hyperglycemia, an older patient is more likely to present degenerative changes in blood vessels and nerves that lead to athero-sclerotic complications, neuropathy, renal failure, and retinopathy. The onset is gradual and resembles age-related physiological changes. Zimmerman (1990) notes that NIDDM frequently is diagnosed in an asymptomatic patient during routine testing or as part of an evaluation for other medical problems.

Of most interest to the mental health clinician is the fact that the presenting symptoms may be fatigue and unexplained weight loss. Lustman et al. (1986) report loss of energy and difficulty concentrating to be common symptoms in diabetics with poor metabolic control. Perlmuter, Goldfinger, Shore, and Nathan (1990) summarize recent research on cognitive function in NIDDM, reporting that NIDDM is associated with poorer performance than age-matched controls on memory tasks among depressed diabetics. After control-ling for depression, NIDDM subjects still perform more poorly than controls on more complex tasks, such as serial learning, digit symbol, and problem solving.

Thus, the mental health clinician should be sensitive to the presentation of depression in an older patient with a family history of diabetes; personal history of gestational diabetes with weight loss, fatigue, and concentration difficulties; or both. Medical symptoms include blurred vision, frequent urination (polyuria), and unusual thirst (polydipsia), although these are more often present in IDDM than in NIDDM. Obesity is a factor in 80% of older patients with NIDDM. Mental health clinicians who are treating diabetic patients receiving medication should also be aware that acute anxiety accom-panied by dizziness, sweating, shakiness, and confusion or mental status changes may signal hypoglycemia (low blood sugar) secondary to treatment; referral for medication evaluation is warranted if such episodes occur, and especially if they are recurring at the same time each day.

Little has been published about the etiology of depression in diabetes. Lustman et al. (1986) posit that depression can either cause or be caused by poor glucose control. Psychiatric illness is associated with poor long-term glucose control. Popkin (1989) speculates that microvascular changes observed in the diabetic's retina and kidney also might be reflected in the central nervous system and thus provide an etiological pathway to explain the high prevalence of depression in diabetes. In addition, he cites research by Winokur, Maislin, Phillips, and Amsterdam (1988) on the relationship of glucose use among major depressives (nondiabetic), positing a possible biochemical relationship between diabetes and depression. These etiological theories, however, remain speculative.

The primary focus in the literature has been on depression as a reactive phenomenon in relation to diagnosis, lifestyle changes, control issues, and physical complications such as impotence and blindness. Because careful compliance with a difficult regimen can so dramatically affect outcome, it is particularly useful in this chronic disease for physical and mental health practitioners to work closely together to maximize the patient's ability and willingness to maintain metabolic control.

Other Endocrine and Metabolic Disorders

Diabetes mellitus illustrates the complexity of the neuroendocrine systems. Other examples that will be considered in this section include the disorders associated with thyroxine, cortisol, and calcium abnormalities. Each of these abnormalities has been shown to have affective or cognitive concomitants or both. In each case, the psychological disturbance may be the only evidence of disorder, and the disturbance is usually rapidly reversed with appropriate biological therapy. The frequency of these abnormalities increases with age, and the geriatric mental health practitioner should be especially alert to, and ready to refer for, endocrine-metabolic screening.

Geriatric mental health practitioners can find a detailed description of endocrine function in Gottlieb and Greenspan (1989). They describe the two primary neuroendocrine feedback loops: the hypothalamic-pituitary-adrenal axis (HPAA) and the hypothalamic-pituitary-thyroid axis (HPTA). In a simplified explanation, input to the brain influences the hypothalamus, which controls the secretion of pituitary hormones. The pituitary, in turn, controls the levels of cortisol and thyroid hormones from the adrenal and thyroid glands, respectively. Through a series of fast-acting and slow-acting feedback loops, the body attempts to keep circulating hormone levels in a delicate balance. Dysregulation of either the HPAA or HPTA can occur at any point within the web of feedback loops.

Hall, Gardner, and Popkin (1981) found that 46% of psychiatric inpatient subjects and 9% of their psychiatric outpatient subjects had physical disorders that directly contributed to the presentation of psychiatric disorders. In both their inpatient and outpatient samples, thyroid disorder was the most common endocrine abnormality, with 14% of the patients suffering from thyroid disease; 2% of the patients showed cortisol abnormalities, 2% had calcium dysfunction, and 9% showed abnormal glucose metabolism. Among 100 psychiatric inpatients with major depression, Gold, Herridge, and Hapworth (1987) found some degree of hypothyroidism in 15%. Thus, prevalence rates of endocrine abnormalities among younger psychiatric patients are substantial, particularly among those diagnosed with depression. Investigating elderly psychiatric patients, Tappy, Randin, Schwed, Wertheimer, and Lemarchand-Beraud (1987) found 4.5% had abnormal thyroid function tests—3.8% were hypothyroid and 0.6% were hyperthyroid. Among elderly people in the general population, the hyperthyroidism prevalence rate is 1% and hypothyroidism prevalence rate is 2% to 3% (Hall, MacLennan, & Lye, 1993).

THYROID DISORDERS

As is suggested by the prevalence studies mentioned, hypothyroidism frequently presents depressive signs and symptoms: sadness, disinterest, sleep disturbance, fatigue, psychomotor slowing, decreased appetite and libido, and poor concentration. Although constipation and psychomotor retardation may mimic the vegetative signs of depression, weight gain in the absence of increased food intake is unusual in depression and may provide a useful clue in distinguishing the disorders. Often, however, there are no additional physical signs of illness. Gregerman (1990) notes that two thirds of hypothyroid cases in the elderly present nothing more than debilitation and apathy. He states, "The most difficult step in diagnosis is the simple clinical appreciation of the possibility that the patient may be hypothyroid" (p. 726). Laboratory studies provide confirmation.

Gottlieb and Greenspan (1989) describe a grading system for hypothyroidism. Grade I, or overt hypothyroidism, is the most severe form, defined by abnormally low levels of circulating thyroid hormones (T3 and T4). In the intermediate form of hypothyroidism (Grade II), T4 may be in the normal range, but serum thyroid stimulating hormone (TSH) is elevated. In the least severe form (Grade III), serum levels of T3, T4, TSH, and the free T4 index are all within normal limits. However, on testing, the patient shows pituitary supersensitivity to exogenous administration of thyrotropin releasing hormone. Gottlieb and Greenspan maintain that the more severe the thyroid dysfunction (Grade I), the more direct the etiological pathway to depression. This depression may remit entirely with thyroid replacement alone. In contrast, depression associated with Grade III hypothyroidism probably requires administration of both thyroid replacement and antidepressant medications to relieve depressive symptoms.

Hyperthyroidism, which many associate with an almost maniclike state in younger patients, can have a different presentation in the elderly. Gregerman (1990) reports that "nervousness" (restlessness, irritability, and tremor) is almost universally reported by young patients but by less than 50% of the elderly. Younger patients typically report increased appetite, whereas only 10% of elderly patients report this; indeed, 30% of older patients report anorexia and weight loss. Elderly patients may be more likely than younger patients to report heart palpitations or a racing sensation.

The term *apathetic hyperthyroidism* describes a particular presentation seen mainly in the elderly. The essential features are depression, marked by disinterest and apathy; blunted or depressed affect or both; and slowed mentation.

Gottlieb and Greenspan (1989) note that hyperthyroidism in the elderly may be treated with antithyroid drugs, partial thyroidectomy or with radioactive iodine therapy. Achieving thyroid balance improves or eliminates psychiatric symptoms in most cases.

CORTISOL DISORDERS

Cortisol, which is produced by the adrenal glands, is involved in serotonin production and brain glucose metabolism. Indirectly, it is involved with electrolyte balance and blood pressure. Although disorders of the adrenal glands are relatively rare, Terry and Halter (1990) caution as follows:

> Many of the clinical problems seen in elderly people could be manifestations of adrenal disease. These range from hypertension and diabetes mellitus associated with overproduction of glucocorticoids to weight loss, fatigue, and hypotension that are manifestations of adrenal insufficiency. Thus it is important to keep adrenal disorders in mind when evaluating elderly patients who present with these problems. (p. 716)

The following is extracted from Gottlieb and Greenspan's (1989) discussion of cortisol abnormalities:

Hypocortisolism (Addison's disease) is a state of underproduction of the corticosteroids. Sixty percent to 90% of patients evidence psychiatric symptoms—primarily apathy, fatigue, sadness, negativism, irritability, poverty of thought content, and anorexia. Treatment with replacement corticosteroids generally reverses the psychopathological symptoms.

Hypercortisolism (Cushing's syndrome) is defined by high blood levels of cortisol, which could result from several different sources. Fifty percent to 90% of Cushing's syndrome patients evidence psychological manifestations, most of which precede any physical manifestation. There is no single psychological presentation of hypercortisolism. It can range from major depression with a high suicide risk (usually in Cushing's syndrome) to a hypomanic state (usually induced by exogenous administration of cortisol.) Either etiology can present with delirium, paranoid psychosis with hallucination, cognitive impairment, or a combination. Although psychological symptoms remit with cortisol rebalancing, remission may take 2 to 6 months.

CALCIUM DISORDERS

The regulation of serum calcium levels involves a complex interaction of the endocrine system (primarily parathyroid hormone) and calcitonin (a peptide produced by the thyroid gland), bone metabolism, intestine and kidney function, and vitamin D. Serum calcium regulation is essential for secretory cell function, including neuronal function. Therefore, dysregulation of serum calcium may manifest as psychological disturbance. Dysregulation can result from hyperparathyroidism or hypoparathyroidism, Paget's disease, excess Vitamin D intake, thiazide diuretic use, and malignancy. Malignancy may be a more common etiology of hypercalcemia in the elderly. There is an increasing frequency of disorders of calcium metabolism with advancing age (Raisz, 1990).

Hypercalcemia has been shown to be associated with psychological disturbance in about 50% of cases, with the type and degree of disturbance varying with disease intensity (Gottlieb & Greenspan, 1989). In mild cases, the patient may complain only of weakness or becoming easily fatigued (Lyles, 1990), whereas in moderate cases, anorexia, weakness, apathy, suicidal tendencies and mild cognitive impairment may mimic major depression. Severe cases, which may be associated with malignancy, can present with mental status changes, including acute psychosis and delirium. Short-term therapy, consisting of decreasing serum calcium levels (usually through hydration), can rapidly reverse psychological disturbances.

Hypocalcemia may also manifest as psychological disturbance in over 50% of cases, with the most prominent symptoms being severe depression, anxiety, fatigue, irritability, emotional lability, phobia, and social withdrawal. Cognitive impairment, dementia, and delirium are also common presentations. Most symptoms will remit rapidly with calcium ion replacement, although dementia of long standing may not show improvement (Gottlieb & Greenspan, 1989).

Conclusion

This chapter has attempted to look at a number of medical conditions in the elderly that are likely to have associated mental health conditions. The goal is to sensitize clinicians to the frequent comorbidity of medical and mental disorders, especially when the mental health symptoms are the initial or prominent presentation. In addition, it is important to recognize when psychotherapy should focus on adaptation and coping, support, or change. Perhaps more critically, mental health professionals need to recognize when psychological symptoms are the sole manifestation of an underlying illness, as in pancreatic cancer or hypothyroidism. In these cases, medical rather than psychosocial treatments are called for. To the extent that both medical and mental health professionals are aware of the complex interactions, interventions can be more specifically and appropriately focused.

Although the literature of the past decade has dramatically increased in the areas of health psychology, behavioral medicine, psychosomatic medicine, and geriatric psychiatry, the investigative work has just begun on the interface of medicine and mental health. Clearly needed are disease-specific studies that use sophisticated methodology to identify the prevalence, incidence, etiology, course, and treatment for mental health symptomatology within the framework of each of the common chronic diseases. In addition, studies are needed among the very old and frail who are frequently suffering from multiple chronic disease states and their attendant psychological symptoms. How best to even conceptualize, let alone identify and treat, these intricately comorbid conditions?

With health care cost and use issues coming to the fore, there will be added incentive to consider the psychological factors in medical disease that could be exacerbating cost and use problems. In addition to cost-effective care, quality care is far more probable when mental health and medical professionals are working closely together. In a close collaboration, each can contribute his or her expertise to difficult diagnostic problems, treatment planning, and monitoring of both somatic and nonsomatic treatments. Driven by both cost and quality considerations, we may hope to see the emergence of medical-mental health teams in the primary care of geriatric patients.

III

Psychological Disorders and Behavioral Problems

11

Dementia

James R. Youngjohn
Thomas H. Crook III

The unprecedented increases in the numbers of demented elderly persons stands to place enormous strains on an already overburdened health care system. Close to 2 million older U.S. citizens are now incapacitated by dementing disorders, and that number is expected to triple within the next 50 years. As President Clinton attempts to reform our nation's health delivery system, the provision of adequate care for demented older persons is expected to pose a significant challenge. Table 11.1 presents a list of some of the conditions that can cause the onset of dementia in older adults.

The specter of Alzheimer's and other dementing diseases represents one of the greatest fears of our rapidly expanding elderly population. Each of us is the unique product of the sum of our individual life experiences, and the loss of our memories can consequently be equated to the loss of our selves. Even worse, victims of progressive dementias can eventually be reduced to a vegetative state, whereby they are unable to recognize spouses or children, cannot maintain basic personal hygiene, or even utter comprehensible speech.

Table 11.1   Adult-Onset Degenerative Diseases Marked by Cognitive Impairments

---

Alzheimer's disease
Pick's disease
Creutzfeldt-Jakob disease
Kuru
Progressive multifocal leukoencephalopathy
Normal-pressure hydrocephalus
Huntington's chorea
Parkinson's disease
Progressive supranuclear palsy
Wilson's disease
Progressive myoclonic epilepsy

Consequently, the *fear* of dementia in healthy older persons may be a significant problem over and above the actual disorder.

Many older individuals correctly recognize increased frequencies of everyday memory failures. They realize that because they are unable to remember names after introductions, have problems misplacing objects, have difficulties retaining telephone numbers, or forget what they were supposed to buy at the grocery store, their memory is not what it used to be. Other times, family members or friends notice behavioral or cognitive changes, or both, in their loved ones. It is common for many of these persons to eventually appear in the clinic.

The Dementias and Related Conditions

AGE-ASSOCIATED MEMORY IMPAIRMENT

It is widely recognized that moderate declines in memory occur in the normal elderly (Fozard, 1985; Poon, 1985), who do not go on to develop dementia (Youngjohn & Crook, 1993b). These declines are characterized by failures in levels and rates of new learning and retrieval but not in the ability to retain information once it has been learned (Youngjohn & Crook, 1993a). Impaired retention has been shown to be relatively specific for dementia (Larrabee, Youngjohn, Sudilovsky, & Crook, 1993). Fortunately, sophisticated neuropsychological assessment procedures are now available that have been demonstrated to be highly accurate in discriminating normal age-associated memory decline from the malignant deterioration associated with early Alzheimer's disease and other dementias and thus allay unnecessary fears (Youngjohn, Larrabee, & Crook, 1992).

The need for a nosological category for those older persons that develop memory problems that are not associated with dementia has been addressed by a work group from the National Institute of Mental Health (Crook et al., 1986), who proposed criteria for age-associated memory impairment (AAMI). A slightly modified version of AAMI, age-related cognitive decline, has been included in the fourth edition of the American Psychiatric Association's (1994) *Diagnostic and Statistical Manual* (4th ed., revised; *DSM-IV*).

A number of age-related neurophysiologic and neurochemical changes have been postulated to be responsible for AAMI. These include limited atrophy of the hippocampus, a limbic structure that is integrally involved in new learning along with other brain structures (Golomb et al., 1993; Youngjohn & Crook, 1993a), neurotoxic effects of certain endogenous excitatory amino acids (McEntee & Crook, 1993), and diminishing activity of a number of neurotransmitters, including acetylcholine (McEntee & Crook, 1992), serotonin (McEntee & Crook, 1991), and the catecholamines (McEntee & Crook, 1990).

Although declining memory function may be a normal consequence of advancing age, few would argue that it is desirable. Consequently, an effective treatment of this condition would have considerable psychological, health, and sociological benefits (Crook, 1993). Preliminary investigations of a number of compounds have yielded some promising results. These include a phospholipid compound derived from bovine cortex, called BC-PS, that is felt to bolster the integrity of the neuronal membrane (Crook et al., 1991; Crook, Petri, Wells, & Massari, 1992), the serotonin receptor antagonist ondansetron (Crook & Lakin, 1991), and the angiotensin-converting enzyme inhibitor captopril (Sudilovsky et al., 1989). An additional agent, the adrenergic agonist guanfacine, may have some mood elevating characteristics but appears to have little effect on memory and learning in AAMI (McEntee et al., 1991).

ALZHEIMER'S DISEASE

Alzheimer's disease (AD) is the major cause of dementia in the elderly, making up about 55% of all cases of dementia (Mortimer, 1983). Indeed, it has been estimated that AD may affect almost half of the population of the United States aged 85 years and older (Evans, Funkenstein, & Albert, 1989). Clinically, AD remains essentially a diagnosis of exclusion, although behavioral, neuroradiologic, and biochemical markers are aggressively being sought (Crook & Miller, 1985).

Table 11.2 provides the diagnostic criteria developed by a work group convened by the National Institute of Neurological and Communicative Disorders and Stroke and the Alzheimer's Disease and Related Disorders

Table 11.2   Criteria for Clinical Diagnosis of Alzheimer's Disease

---

Criteria for clinical diagnosis of probable Alzheimer's include the following:

Dementia established by clinical examination and documented by Mini-Mental State Test (Folstein, Folstein, & McHugh, 1975) Blessed Dementia Scale (Blessed, Tomlinson, & Roth, 1968), or some similar examination and confirmed by neuropsychological testing

Deficits in two or more areas of cognition

Progressive worsening of memory and other cognitive functions

No disturbance of consciousness

Onset between the ages of 40 and 90 years, most often after age 65 years

Absence of systematic disorders or other brain disease that in and of themselves could account for progressive deficits in memory and cognition

Diagnosis of probable Alzheimer's disease is supported by the following:

Progressive deterioration of specific cognitive functions, such as language (aphasia), motor skills (apraxia), and perception (agnosia)

Impaired activities of daily living and altered patterns of behavior

Family history of similar disorders, particularly if confirmed neuropathologically

Laboratory results of normal lumbar puncture as evaluated by standard techniques; normal pattern or nonspecific changes in EEG, such as increased brain wave activity; and evidence of cerebral atrophy on computed tomography with progression documented by serial observation

Other clinical features consistent with diagnosis of probable Alzheimer's disease, after exclusion of causes of dementia other than Alzheimer's disease include the following:

Plateaus in the course of progression of the illness

Associated symptoms of depression; insomnia; incontinence; delusions; illusions; hallucinations; catastrophic verbal, emotional, or physical outbursts; sexual disorders; and weight loss

Other neurological abnormalities in some patients, especially seen in advanced disease, include motor signs such as increased muscle tone, myoclonus, or gait disorder

Seizures in advanced disease

CT normal for age

Association (McKhann et al., 1984). These criteria are now widely used in AD studies around the world.

Formal neuropsychological testing to establish the presence of pathologic cognitive impairment is an important step in making a differential diagnosis between the normal declines seen in AAMI and the malignant deterioration of AD. A variety of neuropsychometric approaches to the assessment of dementia in the elderly are presently available (Welsh, Butters, Hughes, Mohs, & Heyman, 1991; Youngjohn et al., 1992; Zec et al., 1992). Table 11.3 presents the Global Deterioration Scale (Reisberg, Ferris, de Leon, & Crook, 1982), a behavior rating system that can serve as a useful adjunct to neuropsychological testing for measuring cognitive and behavioral decline.

Before reaching a clinical diagnosis of probable AD, it is essential that all medical, neurological, and psychiatric factors that may be responsible for the symptoms be thoroughly investigated. Table 11.4 presents a partial list of

Table 11.2 Continued

Features that make diagnosis of probable Alzheimer's disease uncertain or unlikely include the following:

    Sudden, apoplectic onset

    Local neurological findings, such as hemiparesis, sensory loss, visual field deficits, and uncoordination early in the illness

    Seizures or gait disturbance at onset or very early in the course of illness

Clinical diagnosis of possible Alzheimer's disease:

    May be made on the basis of dementia syndrome in the absence of other neurological, psychiatric, or systemic disorders sufficient to cause dementia and in the presence of variations in onset, in presentation, or in clinical course

    May be made in the presence of second systemic or brain disorder sufficient to produce dementia, which is not considered to be the cause of dementia

    Should be used in research studies when single, gradually progressive severe cognitive deficit is identified in the absence of other identifiable cause

Criteria for diagnosis of definite Alzheimer's disease are these:

    Clinical criteria for probable Alzheimer's disease

    Histopathological evidence obtained from biopsy or at autopsy

Classification of Alzheimer's disease for research purposes should specify features that may differentiate subtypes of the disorder, such as these:

    Familial occurrence

    Onset before age 65

    Presence of trisomy-21

    Coexistence of other relevant conditions, such as Parkinson's disease

SOURCE: National Institute of Neurological and Communicative Disorders and Stroke and the Alzheimer's Disease and Related Disorders Association, as reported by McKhann et al. (1984).

these conditions, many of which are potentially reversible. Once a positive diagnosis for AD is made, the patient, family, and clinician can expect a progressive course. There can be marked variations in the rate and slope of decline. Some persons will experience plateaus where the progression will appear to slow or stop that can last up to several years. Others will have precipitous and relentless declines from one month to the next. The rapidly progressive variant of AD appears to be more likely when onset occurs early in life (Bondareff, 1983).

Etiology

The cause of AD remains obscure. There does appear to be a genetic component to AD, with the risk of developing the disorder in first degree relatives of AD victims being six times greater than the healthy elderly population (Mayeux, Sano, Chenn, Tatemichi, & Stern, 1991). Both autosomal dominant and polygenic models of transmission have been postulated (Farrer, O'Sullivan, Cupples, Growdon, & Myers, 1989; Heston, 1976; Heston

Table 11.3   Global Deterioration Scale

Stage	Clinical Phase	Clinical Characteristics
1. No cognitive decline	Normal	No subjective complaints of memory deficit. No memory deficit evident on clinical interview.
2. Very mild cognitive decline	Forgetfulness	Subjective complaints of memory deficit, most frequently in following areas: (a) forgetting where one has placed familiar objects and (b) forgetting names one formerly knew well. No objective evidence of memory deficit on clinical interview. No objective deficits in employment or social situations. Appropriate concern with respect to symptomatology.
3. Mild cognitive decline	Early confusional	Earliest clear-cut deficits appear, with manifestations in more than one of the following areas: (a) patient may get lost when traveling to an unfamiliar location, (b) coworkers become aware of patient's relatively poor performance, (c) word-finding and name-finding deficits become evident to intimates, (d) patient may read a passage of a book and retain relatively little material, (e) patient may demonstrate decreased facility in remembering names on introduction to new people, (f) patient lose or misplace an object of value, and (g) concentration deficit may be evident on clinical testing. Objective evidence of memory deficit is obtained only with an intensive interview conducted by a trained geriatric psychiatrist or neuropsychologist. Decreased patient performance is apparent in demanding employment and social settings. Denial begins to become manifest in the patient. Mild to moderate anxiety accompanies symptoms.
4. Moderate cognitive decline	Late confusional	Clear-cut deficit is apparent on careful interview. Deficit manifests in the following areas: (a) decreased knowledge of current and recent events, (b) difficulty remembering one's personal history, (c) concentration deficit elicited on serial subtractions, (d) decreased ability to travel, handle finances, and so on.

Table 11.3   Global Deterioration Scale

Stage	Clinical Phase	Clinical Characteristics
		Frequently, no deficit is apparent in the following areas: (a) orientation to time and person, (b) recognition of familiar persons and faces, and (c) ability to travel to familiar locations.
		The patient is unable to perform complex tasks. Denial is the dominant defense mechanism.
		Flattening of affect and withdrawal from challenging situations occur.
5. Moderately severe cognitive decline	Early dementia	Patient can no longer survive without some assistance.
		Patients are unable during interview to recall a major relevant aspect of their current lives (e.g., their addresses or telephone numbers of many years, the names of close members of their families (such as grandchildren), or the names of the high schools or colleges from which they graduated.
		Frequently, some disorientation to time (date, day of week, season, etc.) or to place is present.
		An educated person may have difficulty counting back from 40 by 4s or from 20 by 2s. Persons at this stage retain knowledge of many major facts regarding themselves and others. They invariably know their own names and generally know their spouse's and children's names.
		They require no assistance with toileting or eating but may have some difficulty in choosing the proper clothing to wear and may occasionally clothe themselves improperly (e.g., putting shoes on the wrong feet, etc.)
6. Severe cognitive decline	Middle dementia	They may occasionally forget the name of the spouse on whom they are entirely dependent for survival.
		They will be largely unaware of all recent events and experiences in their lives.
		They may retain some knowledge of their past lives but this is very sketchy.
		They are generally unaware of their surroundings, the year, the season, and so on.

(continued)

Table 11.3   Global Deterioration Scale

Stage	Clinical Phase	Clinical Characteristics
		They may have difficulty in counting from 10, both backward and, sometimes, forward. They will require some assistance with activities of daily living (e.g., may become incontinent, will require travel assistance but occasionally will display ability to travel to familiar locations).
		Diurnal rhythms are frequently disturbed.
		They almost always recall their own names.
		They frequently continue to be able to distinguish familiar from unfamiliar persons in their environment.
		Personality and emotional changes occur; these are quite variable and include (a) delusional behavior (e.g., patients may accuse their spouses of being impostors, may talk to imaginary figures in the environment or to their own reflection in the mirror); (b) obsessive symptoms (e.g., person may continually repeat simple cleaning activities); (c) anxiety symptoms such as agitation may be present, and even previously nonexistent violet behavior may occur; and (d) cognitive abulia (e.g., loss of willpower because one cannot carry a thought long enough to determine a purposeful course of action).
7. Very severe cognitive decline	Late dementia	All verbal abilities are lost. Frequently, there is no speech at all—only grunting.
		They are incontinent of urine and require assistance in toileting and feeding.
		They lose basic psychomotor skills (e.g., ability to walk). The brain appears to no longer be able to tell the body what to do.
		Generalized and cortical neurological signs and symptoms are frequently present.

& Mastri, 1977). The prevalence of an autosomal dominant pattern of AD transmission may have been obscured by the fact that in earlier generations, people may have died before the symptoms of the disease were apparent (Folstein & Breitner, 1981). Recent molecular genetics studies have identified AD loci on chromosomes 14, 19, and 21 (Clark & Goate, 1993). These recent discoveries may soon lead to a genetic test for the predisposition to develop AD. Consequently, it is important for clinicians to bear in mind the importance

Table 11.4   Causes of Dementias Mimicking Alzheimer's Disease

Degenerative diseases
Space-occupying lesions
Trauma
Infection
Vascular disorders
Epileptic disorders
Metabolic disorders
Endocrine disorders
Toxic reactions
Anoxia
Vitamin deficiencies

of questions of family members of AD patients concerning genetics and to provide straightforward information on both absolute and relative risks.

Pathology

The microscopic changes characteristic of AD were first described by Alois Alzheimer in 1907. These consist of senile plaques and neurofibrillary tangles distributed throughout the cortex and other structures, particularly the amygdala and the hippocampus. *Senile plaques* are globes of amyloid protein that are surrounded by degenerated cellular fragments. The frequency of cortical senile plaques is positively associated with severity of dementia (Blessed, Tomlinson, & Roth, 1968). *Neurofibrillary tangles* are accumulations of pairs of neuronal filaments wrapped around each other in helical fashion. The density of neurofibrillary tangles is also positively associated with dementia severity (Farmer, Peck, & Terry, 1976). A third histopathologic marker includes cellular degeneration in the hippocampus resulting in the formation of intracellular pockets, or *vacuoles,* filled with fluid and granular materials. Macroscopic brain changes are also sometimes seen in AD, including enlarged ventricles and cortical atrophy, but because of the frequency of these findings in the normal elderly, they are not considered pathognomonic for AD.

Numerous neurochemical abnormalities have been demonstrated in victims of AD. Perhaps the most notable is a significant decrease in acetylcholine levels (Davies & Maloney, 1976; Perry, Perry, Blessed, & Tomlinson, 1977). Acetylcholine is a neurotransmitter that is integrally involved in learning and memory (Drachman & Leavitt, 1974). Neuronal degeneration in the nucleus basalis of Meynert and adjacent areas of the basal forebrain have been shown to be responsible for much of the acetylcholine deficits that have been demonstrated throughout the cortex, hippocampus, and amygdala (Whitehouse et al., 1982).

Other neurotransmitter systems have also been shown to be affected by AD. These include the noradrenergic system (Bondareff, Mountjoy, & Roth, 1982), the serotonergic system (Gottfries, Roos, & Winblad, 1976), and the dopaminergic system (Gottfries, Gottfries, & Roos, 1969). Several neuropeptides, which serve both endocrine and neurotransmitter functions, have been demonstrated to be depleted in AD, including somatostatin and substance P (Davies, Katz, & Crystal, 1982). Newly emerging techniques, such as positron emission tomography, have revealed decreased cerebral metabolism in various brain locations (Ferris et al., 1980; Ingevar, 1983). It needs to be pointed out that like the changes in gross brain anatomy, many of the neurochemical changes (including the cholinergic deficit) also occur in the normal elderly (Gottfries, 1985). Often, there is a continuum of decline from young normals to elderly normals to dementia victims.

Treatment

In a landmark decision in March of 1993, the U.S. Food and Drug Administration's (FDA) central nervous system drug advisory committee recommended to approve tetrahydroaminoacridine (or tacrine, trade name Cognex) for the treatment of cognitive impairment in AD. This is the first FDA approval of a drug for treating AD in 20 years. Tacrine is a centrally acting anticholinesterase agent that is usually given in combination with high doses of lecithin. It has a longer duration of action and fewer side effects than physostigmine (another anticholinesterase compound). The primary adverse effects include dose-related hepatotoxicity, which has been observed in up to 40% of treated patients, as well as effects related to cholinergic excess.

Initial public enthusiasm was generated by a controlled study in 1986 (Summers, Majovski, & Marsh, 1986) demonstrating very encouraging results in AD patients. However, subsequent studies have either found no therapeutic effects relative to placebo controls (Chatellier & Lacomblez, 1990; Gauthier, Bouchard, & Lamontagne 1990) or only modest improvements (Eagger, Levy, & Sanakian, 1991). The most likely place for tacrine in therapy will be in selected patients meeting certain criteria. Because other neurotransmitter deficiencies have been detected in AD, tacrine will probably play only a partial role in palliative therapy.

Noradrenergic innervation to the cerebral cortex is diminished in patients with AD, with up to an 80% loss of neurons in the locus coeruleus (Bondareff et al., 1982). The norepinephrine agonist clonidine has not shown a consistent therapeutic effect in AD (Mohr, Schlegel, & Fabbgrini, 1989). Guanfacine, a norepinephrine agonist with a more selective central action than clonidine, is presently under investigation. Ondansetron is a serotonin antagonist that has been proposed for treatment of AD. Animal studies have revealed some positive effects on learning (Barnes, Costall, & Coughlan, 1990).

Nimodipine is a calcium channel antagonist currently marketed with FDA approval for the treatment of cerebrovascular disease. It has been suggested that neuronal calcium homeostasis is altered during aging and that this can result in toxic endogenous calcium levels. It has shown some promise in a multicenter placebo-controlled trial where it appeared to prevent further deterioration in AD (Tollefson, 1990).

Another promising agent is piracetam, a gamma-aminobutyric acid derivative. Because it was considered relatively unique in its effects relative to other psychotropics, it was designated a *nootropic* (noos = mind, tropic = toward). It has shown some efficacy in improving memory functions in healthy volunteers (Dimond & Brouwers, 1976). Oxiracetam is a related compound that is felt to have potential in improving memory performance (Pepeu & Spignoli, 1990). Its efficacy in initial trials with AD has been disappointing, however.

Angiotensin-converting enzyme (ACE) has been demonstrated to be elevated in AD (Arregul, Perry, Rossor, & Tomlinson, 1982). Captopril, an ACE inhibitor used in the treatment of hypertension, has had some promising results in improving cognitive function in hypertensive patients (Sudilovsky et al., 1989). A related compound, SQ-29852, is at least 100 times more potent than captopril and has been shown to antagonize scopolamine-induced cognitive impairment in animals (Costall et al., 1989).

VASCULAR DEMENTIA

In previous decades, a majority of dementia victims were felt to suffer from "hardening of the arteries." As noted earlier, it is now known that most cases of dementia are caused by AD, which is not a vascular disorder. However, there does exist a form of generalized cognitive impairment in some patients that is due to multiple small strokes. This is different from the circumscribed aphasic, amnesic, or other syndromes associated with single major strokes. The term *multi-infarct dementia* was coined by Hachinski, Lassen, and Marshall (1974). This term has been dropped in favor of *vascular dementia* in the *DSM-IV*.

Vascular dementia can be caused by generalized cerebrovascular disease and is often associated with essential hypertension, diabetes, or sources of cerebral emboli, such as valvular disease of the heart. Vascular dementia may account for 10% to 15% of all cases of dementia in the elderly, and up to 25% of patients diagnosed with probable AD also have vascular pathology associated with vascular dementia (Tomlinson, Blessed, & Roth, 1970).

Unlike AD, which has an insidious onset and gradual course, the onset of vascular dementia is typically abrupt and the course is stepwise and fluctuating, with rapid changes. Table 11.5 presents the *DSM-IV* diagnostic criteria

Table 11.5   Diagnostic Criteria for Vascular Dementia

A. The development of multiple cognitive deficits manifested by both
   1. Memory impairment (impaired ability to learn new information or to recall previously learned information) and
   2. One (or more) of the following cognitive disturbances:
      a. Aphasia (language disturbance)
      b. Apraxia (impaired ability to carry out motor activities despite intact motor function)
      c. Agnosia (failure to recognize or identify objects despite intact sensory function)
      d. Disturbance in executive functioning (i.e., planning, organizing, sequencing, abstracting).
B. The cognitive deficits in criteria A1 and A2 each cause significant impairment in social or occupational functioning and represent a significant decline from a previous level of functioning.
C. Focal neurological signs and symptoms (e.g., exaggeration of deep tendon reflexes, extensor plantar response, pseudobulbar palsy, gait abnormalities, weakness of an extremity) or laboratory evidence indicative of cerebrovascular disease (e.g., multiple infarctions involving the cortex and underlying white matter) are present that are judged to be etiologically related to the disturbance.
D. The deficits do not occur exclusively during the course of a delirium.

SOURCE: American Psychiatric Association (1994). *Diagnostic and Statistical Manual of Mental Disorders,* p. 146 (4th ed., revised).

Table 11.6   Hachinski Ischemia Scale

Feature	Score, if present
Abrupt onset	2
Stepwise deterioration	1
Somatic complaints	1
Emotional incontinence	1
History of hypertension	1
History of stroke	2
Focal neurological symptoms	2
Focal neurological signs	2
Total ischemia score[a]	

a. A score of 6 or more in a demented patient is indicative of vascular dementia.

for vascular dementia, and Table 11.6 displays the Hachinski Ischemia Scale, on which a score of 6 or more in a demented patient is considered indicative of vascular dementia (Blass & Barclay, 1985).

Treatment

The age of onset is typically much younger than for AD. It has also been suggested that the median survival from time of diagnosis is only 2 to 3 years

(Blass & Barclay, 1985). Consequently, effective treatment should be initiated as early as possible. Current treatments are designed to address the cause of the cerebrovascular pathology. These include aspirin and other agents that reduce platelet aggregation and clotting, anticoagulants, such as coumadin and heparin, and antihypertensives. Investigators are presently examining the effectiveness of nimodipine, a calcium antagonist that dilates cerebral vessels and increases cerebral blood flow, in treating vascular dementia.

There are known risk factors associated with vascular dementia, many of which can be controlled. With early and effective treatment, it is hoped that we will see declines in the incidence and prevalence of this disorder in the coming years.

PARKINSON'S DISEASE

Parkinson's disease (PD) is a prevalent movement disorder, affecting more than a quarter of a million elderly persons in the United States (Lieberman, 1974). The primary symptoms include rigidity, bradykinesia, and gait disorder. Although the etiology of PD is still obscure, the disease is characterized by degeneration of neurons in the mesencephalon, particularly in the substantia nigra, with a consequent depletion of available dopamine in the basal ganglia. The advent of L-Dopa therapy, the immediate precursor to dopamine, is considered one of the greatest therapeutic advances in modern neurology. L-Dopa is an effective treatment for the movement disorder components of the disease. It does not appear to alter the course of PD, however, nor does it ameliorate the associated dementia (Pillon et al., 1989).

James Parkinson's original description stated that the "senses and intellect remain uninjured" (Parkinson, 1817). Although some controversy remains regarding the exact nature of the cognitive decline in PD, there is an emerging consensus that dementia occurs in 30% to 50% of PD patients (Boller, 1980; Youngjohn, Beck, Jogerst, & Caine, 1992). Because of the relative frequencies of occurrence of senile plaques and neurofibrillary tangles, some argue that there is a link between the dementias of PD and AD (Boller, Mizutani, & Roessmann, 1980). Others point to distinct differences in neuropsychological profiles of PD and AD and have suggested that PD can result in a subcortical dementia that is characterized by deficits in speed of processing and executive functions, rather than the disorders of memory, language, and praxis seen in cortical dementia (Brown & Marsden, 1988; Cummings & Benson, 1988).

A confounding factor is the high co-occurrence of depression in PD, with estimates ranging from 39% (Mayeux, Stern, Cote, & Williams, 1984) to 90% (Mindham, 1970). It has been suggested that depression may have resulted in an overestimation of the rates of dementia in PD (Raskin, Borod, & Tweedy, 1990). Given the high rates of co-occurrence of depression and PD, some investigators believe that depression is a direct effect of the neuropathological changes in PD (Agid et al., 1986; Mayeux, 1989). Others suggest that depression is an understandable emotional reaction to the disabling aspects of the disease and is unrelated to organic processes (Bieliauskas, Klawans, & Glantz, 1986). Whatever the cause, depression has been shown to contribute to the cognitive impairments of many PD patients (Youngjohn et al., 1992). Consequently, antidepressant medications, including the tricyclics, MAO inhibitors, and serotonin antagonists, may be of benefit from both emotional and cognitive standpoints. Even so, it has been demonstrated that some of the cognitive impairments of PD remain, even when the level of depression is statistically controlled (Youngjohn et al., 1992).

NORMAL-PRESSURE HYDROCEPHALUS

Some nonprogressive meningeal and ependymal diseases can result in a hydrocephalic state, with characteristic enlargement of the cerebral ventricles. However, the cerebrospinal fluid (CSF) pressure can normalize such that CSF production equilibrates with absorption. Normal-pressure hydrocephalus (NPH) may follow subarachnoid hemorrhage from ruptured aneurysm, head trauma, viral or septic meningitis, or asymptomatic fibrosing meningitis of unknown etiology (Adams & Victor, 1981).

NPH is associated with a classic triad of symptoms, including a slowly progressive gait disorder termed *apraxia of gait,* sphincteric incontinence, and dementia. The mental changes usually appear first and can range from mild forgetfulness and cognitive slowing to a global dementia that is indistinguishable from AD. Urinary incontinence is more common than rectal incontinence. Gait is characteristically broad-based, shuffling, and stiff-legged and falls are frequent (Lishman, 1987).

Treatment involves placement of a ventricular shunt. Gratifying successes have been obtained, particularly in those patients displaying the complete triad and who, on intracranial pressure monitoring, have either elevated mean pressures or marked spontaneous pressure waves (Jeffreys & Wood, 1978). There can also be complications, however, including subdural hematomas and occlusion of the catheter. Shunting in cases of uncomplicated dementia with evidence of cortical atrophy in addition to enlarged ventricles is not indicated.

PICK'S DISEASE

Pick's disease is a rare degenerative dementia that is characterized by circumscribed, but marked, atrophy of the frontal lobes and the tips of the temporal lobes of the brain. Onset peaks between the 50s and 60s, and women are affected twice as often as men. An autosomal dominant genetic etiology has been proposed (Sjogren, Sjogren, & Lindgren, 1952), but most cases appear to arise sporadically.

Pick's disease is pathologically differentiated from AD by a lack of deterioration seen in other parts of the brain as well as a conspicuous absence of senile plaques and neurofibrillary tangles. The affected neurons are swollen and oval in shape and have irregularly shaped inclusions ("Pick bodies") that displace the nucleus toward the periphery (Lishman, 1987).

Clinically, these patients tend to display the sorts of changes in personality and behavior that are associated with frontal lobe dysfunction. These changes include decreases in initiative and drive, episodes of tactless, insensitive behavior, inappropriate facetiousness and euphoria, explosive temper, disinhibition and poor impulse control, and impaired insight. Memory impairment and dysphasic disturbances are seen, but apraxias and agnosias are less common than in AD (Lishman, 1987). Given the rarity of the disorder, no studies of treatment strategies have been reported. Cholinergic replacement has been suggested because of cell loss in the nucleus basalis of Meynert (Price et al., 1982), but cholinergic deficits have not been confirmed in Pick's.

PSEUDODEMENTIA

Pseudodementia refers to the presence of apparent cognitive deterioration in the absence of primary organic etiology. Many symptoms of depression can mimic subtle cognitive impairment, including slowed mental processing, distractibility and inattention, psychomotor retardation, social withdrawal, and a tendency to respond to mental status assessment items with "I don't know." This problem may be pronounced in the elderly, who have particularly high incidence rates of depression (Cheah & Beard, 1980).

When elderly patients themselves complain of impaired memory, they are frequently more likely to be suffering from depression than actual dementia (Bolla, Lindgren, Bonaccorsy, & Bleecker, 1991). This counterintuitive indication is felt to be the result of a combination of the self-denigration and negative thoughts typical of depression counterposed with the lack of awareness and poor insight commonly seen in dementia syndromes (McGlynn & Schacter, 1989). In contrast to the patient's self-report, when complaints that an older person's memory is poor emanate from the patient's relatives, the probability of an organic dementia is greatly increased (McGlone et al., 1990).

Depressive pseudodementia is suggested when onset is acute rather than insidious and is associated with personal loss or emotional distress. Because depression is highly treatable, many of these patients can make gratifying recoveries. Unfortunately, because depression frequently coexists with actual dementia (approximately 25% of probable AD patients also have depressed mood), the recoveries can be short-lived. Many patients originally diagnosed with depressive pseudodementia go on to develop frank dementia (Reifler, 1992). Consequently, Reifler (1986) has suggested that the term be abandoned in favor of *cognitive affective disorder, Types I & II.* In Type I, the cognitive impairment resolves with treatment for the affective disorder. In Type II, treatment usually ameliorates the depressed mood, but the dementia remains.

Conclusion

The dementing disorders of late life clearly represent major challenges to the individual clinician and to the scientific and medical communities in general. However, the magnitude of these problems has now been recognized. During the past several years, genuine progress has been made in describing the clinical symptomatologies and courses of these disorders and in discovering their structural and neurochemical bases. Dramatic progress is being made in discovering the genetic underpinnings of some of these disorders. Clear progress is also being made toward developing effective treatment. It is hoped that these tragic and disabling conditions will one day be eliminated from the human condition.

12

Schizophrenia and Delusional Disorder

Joanne Marengo
Jerry F. Westermeyer

This chapter presents current clinical and research findings on the etiology, course, and treatment of schizophrenia and delusional disorder in middle and later adulthood. Schizophrenia is observed during middle and later adulthood in (a) individuals who first develop symptoms during their young adult years and whose illness has extended into later life (i.e., early-onset schizophrenia) and (b) individuals who first develop symptoms during middle or later adulthood—after age 45 years (i.e., late-onset schizophrenia). Delusional disorder most frequently appears for the first time in middle or late adult life. To date, early-onset schizophrenia has received the most extensive clinical and research attention. Knowledge of late-onset schizophrenia and delusional disorder has increased in recent years, however, and clinical reports have provided an improved understanding of these disorders.

Schizophrenia

HISTORICAL BACKGROUND

Schizophrenia was first described clinically in the early 19th century by Pinel in France and by Haslem in England (Gottesman, 1991). In 1852, Benedict Morel labeled the disorder *dementia praecox* (i.e., "early loss of mind"), reflecting the observation that the symptoms of schizophrenia often develop early in life, during late adolescence or young adulthood.

Kraepelin's (1919) classification subsequently distinguished schizophrenia from other mental illnesses by emphasizing the illness's course and outcome. Kraepelin believed that affective (mood) disorders (i.e., depressive and bipolar illnesses) tended to have episodic or improving illness courses, whereas schizophrenia or dementia praecox tended to show a deteriorating illness course and poor outcome over time. E. Bleuler (1908/1950), who coined the modern term *schizophrenia* (i.e., "splitting of the mind"), also attempted to distinguish schizophrenia from other disorders by describing the loss of contact with reality and specific cognitive-integrative difficulties characteristic of the disorder. Although the term schizophrenia is at times used incorrectly to refer to notions of a "split personality," the disorder as described by Bleuler and Kraepelin involved a primary psychosis and major disruptions in the accurate perception of reality.

Today, it is recognized that the onset of schizophrenia is not confined to adolescence or young adulthood and schizophrenia does not result inevitably in a deteriorating course of illness. Late-onset forms of the disorder are recognized, and the course and outcome of schizophrenia appear heterogeneous. Schizophrenia continues to be identified by the presence of multiple and diverse psychotic (i.e., delusions and hallucinations) and negative (i.e., affective flattening, poverty of speech, and avolition) symptoms, and current investigators attempt to categorize these symptoms in various ways to improve the specificity and outcome of treatment (Kane et al., 1993).

EARLY-ONSET SCHIZOPHRENIA

Early-onset schizophrenia is the most commonly observed and studied form of schizophrenia. Its onset typically occurs between the late teens and mid-30s, and its course and outcome are variable.

Description and Diagnosis

The future diagnosis of schizophrenia may be based on physiological or biological markers, but such markers have not been isolated to date. Currently,

Schizophrenia and Delusional Disorder

Table 12.1 Diagnostic Criteria for Schizophrenia

A. *Characteristic symptoms:* Two (or more) of the following, each present for a significant portion of time during a 1-month period (or less, if successfully treated):[a]
   Delusions
   Hallucinations
   Disorganized speech (e.g., frequent derailment or incoherence)
   Grossly disorganized or catatonic behavior
   Negative symptoms (i.e., affective flattening, alogia, or avolition)
B. *Social-occupational dysfunction:* For a significant portion of the time since the onset of the disturbance, one or more major areas of functioning such as work, interpersonal relations, or self-care are markedly below the level achieved prior to the onset (or when the onset is in childhood or adolescence, failure to achieve expected level of interpersonal, academic, or occupational achievement).
C. *Duration:* Continuous signs of the disturbance persist for at least 6 months. This 6-month period must include at least 1 month of symptoms (or less, if successfully treated) that meet Criterion A (i.e., active-phase symptoms) and may include periods of prodromal or residual symptoms. During these prodromal or residual periods, the signs of the disturbance may be manifested by only negative symptoms or two or more symptoms listed in Criterion A present in an attenuated form (e.g., odd beliefs, unusual perceptual experiences).
D. *Schizoaffective and mood disorder exclusion:* Schizoaffective disorder and mood disorder with psychotic features have been ruled out because either (a) no major depressive, manic, or mixed episodes have occurred concurrently with the active-phase symptoms or (b) if mood episodes have occurred during active-phase symptoms, their total duration has been brief relative to the duration of the active and residual periods.
E. *Substance-general medical condition exclusion:* The disturbance is not due to the direct physiological effects of a substance (e.g., a drug of abuse, a medication) or a general medical condition.
F. *Relationship to a pervasive development disorder:* If there is a history of autistic disorder or another pervasive developmental disorder, the additional diagnosis of schizophrenia is made only if prominent delusions or hallucinations are also present for at least a month (or less, if successfully treated).

SOURCE: Adapted from American Psychiatric Association (1994). Used with permission.
a. Only one Criterion A symptom is required if delusions are bizarre or hallucinations consist of a voice keeping up a running commentary on the person's behavior or thoughts or two or more voices conversing with each other.

a diagnosis of schizophrenia is based on its observable signs and symptoms as presented in Table 12.1 (American Psychiatric Association [APA], 1994). There is no single defining symptom for schizophrenia. The essential features of the disorder are characterized as a syndrome that includes (a) the presence of characteristic psychotic and negative symptoms during an active phase of illness, (b) an observed decline in social-occupational functioning to a point below the level achieved prior to illness, and (c) an illness duration of at least 6 months (APA, 1994).

The symptoms of early-onset schizophrenia are most often conceptualized in terms of a disturbance in three primary domains: (a) a domain of psychosis, defined by hallucinations and delusions; (b) a cognitive domain, defined by disorganized speech or thinking and impaired attention; and (c) a negative symptom or deficit domain, defined by flat affect, poverty of speech, low social drive, a curbing of interests, and a diminished sense of purpose (Kane et al., 1993). Early-onset patients differ from each other in terms of the number, nature, and severity of these symptoms, and the heterogeneity of schizophrenia's symptoms is not well understood.

For example, in one individual, a normal perception may take on special significance and a bizarre delusional system may quickly develop. For another, thoughts that are experienced as alien to the individual may seem to have been placed in his or her mind by an external source. Still other individuals report that they are being made to carry out the actions or impulses of some external agent, or they may experience disturbing changes in the way their bodies feel, as if parts of their bodies seem too large or too small. For others, bodily sensations can become so depersonalized that they experience their body as though it were a machine (Davison & Neale, 1986). Here is an example:

> Ms. Y, a 24-year-old single woman, started thinking that her clock radio was talking to her. It didn't say anything in particular, but the comments were directed specifically at her. Later, she started hearing the sounds of birds' wings flying closer to her. She said that it sounded like a gigantic bird and the flapping of the wings would get louder and louder and then she would see the shadow of the bird hovering over her as if it were about to attack her. Ms. Y said it was so frightening that she had the feeling she had to either hurt herself or somebody else to get rid of the frightening feeling.

Differential Diagnosis

A diagnosis of early-onset schizophrenia is made only when it is established that the disturbance is not due to the direct physiological effects of a substance (e.g., a drug of abuse or medication) and is not due to a general medical condition. A wide variety of general medical conditions can present psychotic symptoms. Substance-induced psychotic disorder, substance-induced delirium, and substance-induced persisting dementia are distinguished from schizophrenia by the fact that a substance (e.g., a drug of abuse, a medication, or exposure to a toxin) is judged to be etiologically related to the delusions or hallucinations. In particular, substance-related disorders, such as those due to sustained amphetamine or cocaine use or phencyclidine use, may demonstrate symptoms similar to those of schizophrenia (APA, 1994). Other neurological and organic mental syndromes usually will involve observable brain lesions and more often exhibit signs of persistent disorientation and memory impairment than is found in schizophrenia. Symptoms resulting from other disorders, such as mental retardation, epilepsy, encephalitis, metabolic and systemic diseases (e.g., AIDS, multiple sclerosis), or Huntington's disease also may mimic schizophrenia and should be ruled out (Gottesman, 1991).

The diagnosis of schizophrenia is not made if psychosis results from a mood disorder, schizoaffective disorder (i.e., a disturbance in which, at some time, there is either a major depressive or manic syndrome concurrent with symptoms of schizophrenia), delusional disorder, obsessive-compulsive disorder, or personality disorder. Such differential diagnoses are difficult but important to make due to differences in long-term treatment and outcome.

Epidemiology

The lifetime risk for early-onset schizophrenia in the general population is about 1% (Gottesman & Shields, 1982) and is fairly uniform across cultures (Lin & Kleinman, 1988). Currently, it is estimated that there are about 2.5 to 3 million individuals with schizophrenia in the United States and about 100,000 new cases of schizophrenia diagnosed each year in the United States.

Compared with the 1% lifetime risk for schizophrenia in the general population, children with one parent with a diagnosis of schizophrenia have an elevated lifetime risk of 12%, and children with two parents with the diagnosis have the exceptionally high risk of 35% to 46%. However, 85% to 90% of individuals who receive a diagnosis of schizophrenia do not have a parent with the diagnosis.

The gender prevalence of early-onset schizophrenia remains controversial, although recent research suggests that schizophrenia as defined here is diagnosed more frequently in men. It also is generally agreed that the age of schizophrenia onset is earlier in men (20–25 years old) than in women (24–28 years old).

Etiology

The precise etiology of early-onset schizophrenia is not known. Some investigators embrace a *diathesis-stress* model of vulnerability to schizophrenia. This model assumes a biochemical or neurodevelopmental vulnerability to schizophrenia that is triggered ultimately by developmental, physiological, or environmental stressors (Weinberger, 1987; Zubin & Spring, 1977). Clinicians and researchers also postulate that genetic factors play a role in the etiology of early-onset schizophrenia based on the results of twin, adoption, and cross-fostering studies (Gottesman, 1991). As noted, first-degree relatives of an individual with early-onset schizophrenia have about a tenfold increase in risk for schizophrenia compared to the general population. Current literature also suggests an increased aggregation of schizotypal and paranoid personality disorders in families of individuals with schizophrenia (Kane et al., 1993).

As evidence of neuroanatomical and neurophysiological abnormalities in schizophrenia has accumulated, so too have theories regarding the brain regions or systems that may be implicated in this disorder. In addition to generalized neuropathology, a number of focal neuroanatomical regions have been implicated in schizophrenia, including the left hemisphere, right hemisphere, frontal lobes, basal ganglia, and temporal lobes (Blanchard & Neale, 1994). Neurotransmitter abnormalities also are being explored to explain the pathogenesis of schizophrenia (Carlsson, 1988; Weinberger, 1987). Other current theories of etiology emphasize factors such as viruses, obstetric complications, and hormonal changes. Indeed, there may be different etiologies within groups of individuals with schizophrenia, perhaps accounting for its symptom heterogeneity. However, more questions than answers mark this area of investigation, and findings related to the neurological, physiological, or psychological bases of the disorder remain inconclusive.

Premorbid History

Despite theories that emphasize social withdrawal and disruptions in infant attachment in the premorbid history of individuals with early-onset schizophrenia, no specific pattern of early disturbance in social relations has been identified across studies. As children, men diagnosed with early-onset schizophrenia have been characterized by teachers as negative, egocentric, and antisocial, whereas women who eventually received a diagnosis of schizophrenia have been described in childhood as emotionally unstable, introverted, and passive (Wallace, 1984). However, these deviant premorbid social patterns have been found in children at risk for other clinical disorders and therefore are no longer considered exclusively prognostic of schizophrenia (Wallace, 1984).

Course and Outcome of Early-Onset Schizophrenia

Although about 20% of individuals with early-onset schizophrenia show symptom remissions or recovery from the illness, research demonstrates that the prognosis for schizophrenia is poorer than a variety of other psychiatric disorders (McGlashan, 1988; Tsuang, Woolson, & Fleming, 1979; Westermeyer & Harrow, 1988). About 15% of individuals with schizophrenia will require continuous hospitalization. However, the majority of individuals demonstrate courses between recovery and the poorest outcomes (Bleuler, 1978; Ciompi, 1980; Marengo, 1994; Marengo, Harrow, Sands, & Galloway, 1991). Poorer premorbid adjustment, earlier age at onset, and a gradual onset of the illness are associated with a more chronic course of illness and longer intervals between episode remissions (Kane et al., 1993; Westermeyer &

Harrow, 1984). M. Bleuler (1978) observed that symptom worsening occurred primarily during the first 5 to 10 years after illness onset followed by an illness plateau or gradual symptom improvement. Long-term follow-up studies have suggested that the psychotic symptoms that are primary signs of early-onset schizophrenia ameliorate over time in some patients (Bleuler, 1978; Ciompi, 1980). Many patients move into middle and later adulthood with ongoing or episodic psychotic and negative symptoms, however.

Individuals with early-onset schizophrenia also have a higher early death rate than the general population. Schizophrenia is a life-shortening disease with most early deaths due to suicide (Allebeck, 1989; Westermeyer, Harrow, & Marengo, 1991). About 10% of individuals with early-onset schizophrenia commit suicide, usually as a nonpsychotic reaction to the illness among severely impaired men in young adulthood (Drake, Gates, & Whitaker, 1985; Westermeyer et al., 1991). Suicide occurs most often within the first few years after illness onset.

Many patients with early-onset schizophrenia who survive to middle and older adulthood and who experience ongoing symptoms also remain seriously impaired in terms of work and interpersonal relationships (Westermeyer, 1993). The capacities and needs of these individuals appear to vary in accord with the unique natural history of their disorder and the effects of previous treatment. Meeks et al. (1990) showed that of 111 chronically mentally ill persons over the age of 60 years, 74% demonstrated ongoing psychiatric symptoms and deficits in daily functioning and social contacts. However, the first cohorts of people with schizophrenia whose illness developed after effective treatment became available (around 1949) have come of age only recently. The outcome of this disorder therefore continues to change as a function of new developments in psychopharmacology, improved individual and community interventions, and ongoing clinical research (Katz, Curlik, & Nemetz, 1988).

Treatment

During the last part of the 19th century and the first half of the 20th century, it was believed that the severely mentally ill should be removed from the stresses of society. These individuals resided for years in asylums and state mental hospitals that usually were located in rural areas. A process known as "deinstitutionalization," in which the chronically mentally ill were discharged from long-term institutions into the community, was begun in the 1950s. In part, deinstitutionalization was motivated by the criticism that long-term institutionalization fostered dependency and increased social disability. Less restrictive community placements were seen as providing a normalization process in which individuals cared for themselves and increased their independence and self-esteem. The resident population of state mental hospitals fell from 559,000 in 1955 to 110,000 in 1985 as a result of deinstitutionalization (National Institute of Mental Health, 1985).

Today, community treatment includes services provided by community mental health centers, private day hospitals, halfway houses, work rehabilitation programs, and outreach programs (Bond, Miller, Krumwied, & Ward, 1988; Bond, Witheridge, Setze, & Dincin, 1985; Stein & Test, 1982; Test & Stein, 1980). Consistent with the heterogeneity of the disorder, treatment takes many forms and can include hospitalization, psychopharmacological intervention, family treatment, and psychosocial rehabilitation. Meeks et al.'s (1990) study of chronically mentally ill persons over age 60 years indicated that two thirds of these patients were living in the community and relied heavily on family contacts, although most appeared to have lost contact with outpatient mental health services. Other patients lived primarily in nursing homes (23.4%) or psychiatric hospitals (7.2%).

Medication

The therapeutic effectiveness of neuroleptics (i.e., antipsychotic medications) in diminishing the positive psychotic symptoms of schizophrenia has been established (Davis, Schaffer, Killian, Kinard, & Clem, 1980; May, Tuma, & Dixon, 1981). However, antipsychotic medications may cause adverse effects in a notable proportion of patients with schizophrenia. Extrapyramidal syndromes, such as akathisia (a compulsion to be in motion), acute dystonia, and Parkinsonism, may occur acutely in 35% to 60% of patients receiving neuroleptics. A number of individuals with early-onset schizophrenia (20% to 35%) also may develop tardive dyskinesia as a later adverse effect of neuroleptic use resulting in notable morbidity. Optimal therapy with antipsychotic agents includes patient education, careful selection of the pharmacologic agent, and an appropriate dosing regimen (Kane et al., 1993).

A new generation of antipsychotic medications has been introduced that differs from classic neuroleptics in site of action, side effect profiles, and clinical effects. In particular, clozapine has shown good therapeutic potential for treatment-resistant, chronic schizophrenia (Kane, Honingfeld, Singer, Meltzer, & the Clozaril Group, 1989). However, a potentially life-threatening blood infection results in 1% to 2% of clozapine users, and these individuals therefore must be closely monitored. Newer agents also have been studied, and one, risperidone, has been released for clinical use (Kane et al., 1993).

Compliance with medication treatment remains problematic. A positive therapeutic alliance, patient and family education, and optimizing the medical regimen for the individual provide a foundation for increased compliance and fewer adverse effects (Corrigan, Liberman, & Engel, 1990).

Individual, Family, and Social Therapy

Individuals with schizophrenia may respond well to supportive psychotherapy techniques. In this context, acutely psychotic patients do not respond positively to confrontive or intrusive interventions. A number of studies also have tested the efficacy of cognitive approaches to schizophrenic symptoms (Alford & Correia, 1994). In particular, a series of recent experimental studies has explored the efficacy of cognitive-behavioral interventions in modifying delusional beliefs (Chadwick & Lowe, 1990; Chadwick, Lowe, Horne, & Higson, 1994; Lowe & Chadwick, 1990). Highly structured interventions that pose a challenge to patients' delusional beliefs or allow patients to test such beliefs are employed. Preliminary studies have provided some evidence that treated patients can effectively regulate their delusional thinking.

With regard to family therapy, research suggests that individuals with schizophrenia who live in families high in expressed emotion (i.e., high in the frequency or severity of critical or hostile comments and marked overinvolvement on the part of relatives) demonstrate significantly higher rates of psychotic relapse (Falloon et al., 1985). Family therapies therefore tend to focus on reducing levels of expressed emotion, modeling family problem solving, and educating individuals and their families about the illness (Hogarty et al., 1991).

Social skills training also is undertaken in a number of treatment programs. The goal of social skills training is to develop the social competence of individuals with schizophrenia by enhancing both verbal and nonverbal social behavior and by developing more accurate social perceptions and judgments. Such training focuses on specific behaviors and uses instruction, coaching, modeling, behavioral rehearsal, feedback, and homework as primary modes of intervention (Wallace & Liberman, 1985).

Employing a variety of interventions and supports appears most beneficial in treating individuals with schizophrenia. Controlled studies demonstrate that medications augmented with family and psychosocial skill training produce better outcomes than medications alone (Hogarty et al., 1991). First-episode patients may respond to treatment within a few months of psychopharmacological intervention. The average time of response to treatment may be as long as 1 year, however, and is highly dependent on illness history and characteristics (Kane et al., 1993).

LATE-ONSET SCHIZOPHRENIA

Although rare, schizophrenia also may emerge for the first time in middle or later adulthood (Bridge & Wyatt, 1980a, 1980b; Cabins, Packer, & Thomas,

1984; Roth, 1987; Volavka & Cancro, 1986). In the United States, differences in the symptom presentation of early-onset and late-onset schizophrenia and generalized beliefs that late-life mental illnesses reflected purely organic syndromes resulted in excluding a diagnosis of schizophrenia when symptoms first appeared after age 45 years (APA, 1980). European investigators continued to mount evidence that schizophrenia could first emerge later in life (Miller & Cohen, 1987), however, and the diagnosis of schizophrenia in late life was eventually restored (APA, 1987).

Description and Diagnosis

A diagnosis of late-onset schizophrenia is based on symptom criteria identical to early-onset forms of the disorder (see Table 12.1). As in early-onset schizophrenia, a diagnosis of late-onset schizophrenia requires continuous signs of the disturbance to be present for at least 6 months. The onset of symptoms, including prodromal symptoms, must occur for the first time after age 45 years to receive the "late-onset" designation.

Although phenomenological similarities tend to outweigh differences between early-onset and late-onset schizophrenia, studies suggest that only about one third of patients with late-onset schizophrenia display the full array of positive psychotic symptoms characteristic of early-onset forms (Howard, Castle, Wessely, & Murray, 1993; Post, 1989). Most notably, late-onset patients less often demonstrate disorganized speech and thinking (i.e., loose associations or incoherence) and inappropriate affect (Jeste, Harris, Pearlson et al., 1988). They also demonstrate fewer negative symptoms than early-onset patients (Yassa & Suranyi-Cadotte, 1993). However, individuals with late-onset schizophrenia tend to more frequently exhibit visual, tactile, and olfactory hallucinations (Pearlson et al., 1989), persecutory delusions (with and without hallucinations), organized delusions, third-person running commentaries on their thoughts or actions, and accusatory or abusive auditory hallucinations than early-onset patients (Howard et al., 1993).

Because the content of delusions and hallucinations in late-onset schizophrenia often is persecutory in nature, the clinical picture of late-onset schizophrenia most resembles the paranoid subtype of schizophrenia (Post, 1966; Rabins et al., 1984; Volavka, 1985). A mixture of bizarre, persecutory delusions and auditory hallucinations in a relatively well-preserved personality is a hallmark of late-onset schizophrenia. Grandiose, erotic, jealous, and somatic delusions also can characterize the disturbance.

In accord with diagnostic criteria, patients with late-onset schizophrenia must show a marked deterioration in personal or social adjustment prior to the diagnosis. As symptoms emerge, these individuals also may demonstrate significant distress, panic, or aggression in response to threatening voices or perceived persecutors. An example is described by Post (1989):

A woman had entered a sexually unsatisfactory marriage for the first time at age 40 years. Her husband died with a paranoid illness in a psychiatric facility when she was 70 years old. For the next 6 years, she lived on her own, having only superficial contacts with other people, who described her as standoffish, snobbish, and eccentric. Eventually, the patient began to create disturbances in the building, alleging that a searchlight was being directed into her apartment, which was also at times entered by a man with a flashlight. She was watched by two men from an opposite apartment. For some time, she had been frightened by an object like a balloon with a large syringe attached, which also followed her about in the sky when she went out of her home. All symptoms disappeared after hospital admission but recurred soon after discharge, with the addition that she now believed that the persecutions were instigated because she had seen something that she ought not to have seen. (p. 2027)

Yassa (1991) provides a second example:

Mrs. B., an 82-year-old widow, was brought to the hospital by her children. Two years prior to her admission, the children noted the onset of strange behaviors in their mother. She would stare at them and inform them she was getting pregnant from their husbands. They also noted that she would stand in the corridors of her apartment immobile, refusing to eat because she heard Jesus ordering her not to eat. When examined in the hospital, she was found lying on her bed with her legs open and informed personnel that she was delivering babies. When asked to show them, she said that they were taken immediately for adoption. (p. 246)

Differential Diagnosis

Many conditions arising in later life, and particularly disturbances arising in individuals over 60 years old, can present persecutory delusions and hallucinations. In the spectrum of psychiatric conditions, late-onset bipolar disorders, delusional disorder, and dementia may present acute psychotic symptoms (Yassa, 1991).

A differential diagnosis of schizophrenia from bipolar disorder may be difficult. During acute stages of both illnesses, patients may show disorganized behavior, thought disturbances, and agitated or excitable states. Assessing the duration, intensity, and periodicity of affective symptoms prior to psychosis is essential to differentiating mood disorders from schizophrenia syndromes (Jeste, Manley, & Harris, 1991).

A number of potentially reversible medical and surgical illnesses also produce clinical pictures that resemble schizophrenia. Disorders that are associated with secondary psychosis in the elderly include certain endocrinopathies, hyperthyroidism and hypothyroidism, Addison's disease, Cushing's disease, many neurological disorders (e.g., Parkinson's and Alzheimer's diseases, multi-infarct dementia, neurosyphilis, etc.) and vitamin deficiencies

(Jeste et al., 1991). Because late-onset schizophrenia also is associated with deterioration in functional status and may produce uneven performance on cognitive testing, the disturbance can mimic dementia. Hence, whenever an older patient presents psychotic symptoms, organic pathologies must be ruled out (Jeste et al., 1991). Modern imaging methods have been of much help in identifying those conditions where structural abnormalities coexist with the onset of psychosis (Miller, Benson, Cummings, & Neshkes, 1986; Miller & Lesser, 1988).

Late-onset schizophrenia also must be distinguished from chronic forms of early-onset schizophrenia. Distinctions between early-onset and late-onset schizophrenia are made on the basis of history (i.e., age at onset of prodromal and active symptoms of schizophrenia). Some patients with an apparently late onset of psychosis may have been experiencing a more benign form of early-onset schizophrenia that did not require treatment until after age 45 years (Jeste et al., 1991). To reiterate, for a diagnosis of late-onset schizophrenia, all symptoms, including prodromal symptoms must first occur after age 45. Prodromal symptoms reflect a clear deterioration in previous levels of functioning and include marked social isolation, peculiar behavior, vague or digressive speech, and significant deteriorations in personal hygiene (Jeste et al., 1991).

Last, individuals with late-onset schizophrenia must be distinguished from senile recluses and nonpsychotic individuals who show eccentric behavior, secretiveness, and isolation. About 4% of the elderly demonstrate eccentricities or prefer an isolated existence (Post, 1989). Senile recluses are more extreme. They may lock themselves away in their homes, bar access to others, and emerge rarely. When on account of the concern of neighbors their homes are entered, recluses often are found in surroundings of severe neglect. Recluses tend to be educated, rarely come into health care contact, and are not psychotic (Post, 1989).

Epidemiology

Late-onset schizophrenia is a rare disorder, and its prevalence in the community is estimated to be between 0.1% and 0.6% of the population (Castle & Murray, 1993; Kay, Beamish, & Roth, 1964). Only 3% to 10% of first psychiatric admissions in individuals over age 60 are for late-onset schizophrenia (Gurland, 1991; Leuchter & Spar, 1985; Yassa, 1991), and the disorder represents between 10% and 33% of all forms of schizophrenia in elderly patients (Goodman & Siegel, 1986; Harris & Jeste, 1988). Among patients with late-onset schizophrenia, it has been reported that most (about 58%) experience a first onset of psychosis between 40 and 50 years old, 30% between ages 50 and 60 years old, and 12% after age 60 (Harris & Jeste, 1988).

Gender differences in late-onset schizophrenia have been widely reported. Clinical studies indicate that women are more prone to develop late-onset schizophrenia than men (Craig & Bregman, 1988; Grahame, 1984; Marneros & Deister, 1984). The female-male ratio for late-onset schizophrenia currently ranges from 2:1 to 12:1 across various studies (Kay & Roth, 1961; Rabins et al., 1984). The later the onset of schizophrenia (e.g., onset after age 60), the more marked is the preponderance of females receiving the diagnosis (Castle & Murray, 1993).

Etiology

The familial linkage of late-onset schizophrenia appears weaker than that of early-onset forms of the disorder. The risk for developing schizophrenia in siblings and children of late-onset schizophrenia patients (3.4%) is intermediate between that of early-onset schizophrenia (10%) and the general population (1%) (Katz et al., 1988; Post, 1989).

Premorbid History

Late-onset schizophrenia patients are more likely than early-onset patients to have better prognostic profiles and show better premorbid occupational functioning and higher marriage rates (Castle & Murray, 1993; Howard et al., 1993; Post, 1966). Investigators have noted, however, that many late-onset schizophrenia patients may demonstrate premorbid schizoid or paranoid personality traits or social isolation throughout life (Yassa & Suranyi-Cadotte, 1993).

Course and Outcome of Late-Onset Schizophrenia

Almost no longitudinal data exist on the course of late-onset schizophrenia. Although clinical observation indicates that late-onset patients may show a less severe illness course than early-onset patients, clinical follow-up studies also indicate that late-onset schizophrenia may be a chronic condition. Patients with this diagnosis do respond well to neuroleptics (Pearlson et al., 1989; Roth, 1987). Existent studies indicate that about 50% to 60% of late-onset patients demonstrate symptom remission with neuroleptic treatment, and about 20% require continuous protected care (Yassa, 1991). Spontaneous symptom remissions are uncommon in late-onset schizophrenia, and discontinuation of neuroleptic medication (frequently because of noncompliance) tends to be followed by symptom exacerbation. Prognostically, the presence of depression, assaultive behavior (Craig & Bregman, 1988), and auditory hallucinations have been associated with a more positive outcome among late-onset patients, whereas organic complications, sensory deficits, and visual hallucinations tend to be associated with less satisfactory outcomes (Holden, 1987).

Treatment

Patients with late-onset schizophrenia are often quite responsive to neuroleptic medications in lower doses (Jeste, Haris, Pearlson et al., 1988; Jeste, Lacro, Gilbert, Kline, & Kline, 1993). Tsuang, Lu, Stotsky, and Cole (1971) reported significant decreases in anxiety, excitement, irritability, hostility, suspiciousness, hallucinations, mannerisms, and other forms of manifest psychosis in older adults treated with neuroleptics. Available data suggest that all the commonly prescribed neuroleptic medications are equally efficacious in late-onset patients. Therefore, selection of an antipsychotic for use in this population usually is based on (a) the side effect profile of the medication, (b) the potential adverse consequences of adding a specific antipsychotic to a preexisting medication regimen and an assessment of concomitant physical illness, and (c) the patient's previous therapeutic response to a specific neuroleptic (Gierl, Dysken, Davis, & Lesser, 1987; Jeste et al., 1993). Neuroleptics carry a high risk of side effects such as tardive dyskinesia in middle-aged and elderly patients. Jeste et al. (1993) have reported a 26% cumulative incidence of tardive dyskinesia among schizophrenia patients over age 45 years treated with neuroleptics and followed for 1 year. These authors also report that as neuroleptics were withdrawn in late-onset patients, a significant increase in psychotic relapse followed. To date, the mechanisms by which aging increases the liability to develop tardive dyskinesia remain unclear (Jeste & Wyatt, 1987).

Many individuals with late-onset schizophrenia live in the community rather than in institutions. Rates of need for protected care in older patients remain high, however (Cohen, 1987; Meeks et al., 1990). Therapists who have worked with patients with schizophrenia have laid out a number of helpful approaches to improving the quality of life of these patients. Supportive psychotherapies have been viewed as particularly helpful in promoting therapeutic alliances that facilitate medication compliance and enhance the individual's sense of reality and of self. A friendly, tolerant, and sympathetic attitude is of paramount importance (Roth, 1987). For some patients, attention to psychodynamics has been advocated to provide meaning to individual symptoms. Such interventions may serve to enhance or stabilize the individual's social and interpersonal situation (Cohen, 1987).

Delusional Disorder

Delusional disorder is more circumscribed in its symptoms in comparison to schizophrenia and is characterized primarily by nonbizarre delusions (i.e., delusions of persecution, jealousy, love, grandiosity, or physical defect and disease). The disorder can erupt at any point in the life cycle but usually appears for the first time in middle or late adult life (Jeste et al., 1991).

Table 12.2   Diagnostic Criteria for Delusional Disorder

A. Nonbizarre delusions (i.e., involving situations that occur in real life, such as being followed, poisoned, infected, loved at a distance, deceived by spouse or lover, or having a disease) of at least 1 month's duration.

B. Criterion A for Schizophrenia has never been met.[a]

C. Apart from the effects of the delusion(s) or its ramifications, functioning is not markedly impaired and behavior is not obviously odd or bizarre.

D. If mood episodes have occurred concurrently with delusions, their total duration has been brief relative to the duration of the delusional periods.

E. The disturbance is not due to the direct physiological effects of a substance (e.g., a drug of abuse, a medication) or a general medical condition.

SOURCE: Adapted from American Psychiatric Association (1994) Used with permission.
a. Tactile and olfactory hallucinations may be present in delusional disorder if they are related to the delusional theme.

Although paranoid syndromes in the older adult can be transient, occurring in conjunction with other neuropsychiatric, toxic, and metabolic conditions, delusional disorder also can be a primary psychiatric disorder in adults.

Description and Diagnosis

The diagnostic criteria for delusional disorder are presented in Table 12.2. Paranoid signs include delusions of persecution and suspiciousness, interpersonal sensitivity, sullenness, jealousy, guardedness, and litigiousness (Heston, 1987). In the erotomanic type of delusional disorder, the individual may come to believe that a person, usually of higher status, is in love with them, or, in the somatic type, the individual may become convinced that he or she has some physical defect, disorder, or disease (APA, 1994). A diagnosis of delusional disorder requires the presence of nonbizarre delusions (i.e., delusions involving situations that occur in real life) for at least 1 month. Unlike schizophrenia, auditory or visual hallucinations, if present, are not prominent, and associated behaviors are not obviously odd.

In older adults, delusional ideas are usually limited in their content. That is, they may involve only one or two themes and often concern the individual's relationships with neighbors or, less commonly, relatives. The delusional content is usually persecutory or jealous but can involve erotic, grandiose, or somatic themes. Because delusional disorder incorporates the least pervasive and least disruptive symptoms in the psychotic spectrum, it is reportedly the least likely psychotic disorder to come to professional attention (Katz et al., 1988). Post (1989) provides an example:

> At the age of 65, a widow began to complain to her children who lived at some distance that she heard neighbors saying she was responsible for the loss of a

pension book and that she was dirty. In the hospital, all symptoms ceased without any specific treatment. They recommenced on return home but did not lead to any overt problems until 11 years later when she had to be seen again because she had started to shout back at her neighbors. The patient was slightly deaf but there had been no decline in her cognitive scores. She believed that people were talking to her from downstairs and were threatening to steal her clothing and calling her names (p. 2027).

Differential Diagnosis

A diagnosis of late-life delusional disorder can be made after organic causes for the symptom picture have been investigated and ruled out (Jeste et al., 1991). A delirium, a dementia, and other psychotic disorders that are due to a general medical condition may present symptoms that suggest delusional disorder (APA, 1994). The relative absence of cognitive impairment in delusional disorder can be helpful in the differential diagnosis of delusional disorder and dementia.

Delusions also may accompany an affective disorder. Therefore, for a diagnosis of delusional disorder to be made, it must be established that delusions preceded the onset of any affective syndrome (Jeste et al., 1991).

Epidemiology

Christenson and Blazer (1984) reported that 4% of 997 individuals over age 60 years, in a random community sample, evidenced generalized persecutory ideation, although half of these symptoms occurred in individuals with cognitive impairment. *Diagnostic and Statistical Manual of Mental Disorders* (4th ed., revised) studies (APA, 1994) estimate the population prevalence of delusional disorder at 0.3% with a lifetime risk of .5% to .1%.

Within patient samples, a recent study of the incidence of paranoid or delusional disorder by Heston (1987) indicated that although only about 2% of patients satisfied diagnostic criteria for delusional disorder, another 13% had paranoid ideation. Post's (1966) experience with a series of 93 consecutive inpatients with late-onset functional psychoses suggested that among late-onset psychotic patients, approximately one fourth receive the diagnosis of delusional disorder.

The average age of onset for delusional disorder appears to be earlier for men (40-49 years old) than for women (60-69 years old) in most (Jeste et al., 1991) but not all studies (Heston, 1987).

Etiology

Some studies have found an increased incidence of schizophrenia in families of patients with delusional disorder (Jeste et al., 1991), and several theories for the development of delusional symptoms in middle or later life have been advanced. It has been hypothesized that individuals may be first exposed to a causal agent in later adulthood or older age. It also has been proposed that some individuals may carry a long-term predisposition that is unmasked by one or more secondary factors common to middle and later adulthood.

Associations between sensory impairment and late-life paranoid states also have been investigated (Pearlson & Rabins, 1988). Some data suggest that deafness is three times more frequent in middle and older adult individuals with delusional (paranoid) disorder (30%) than in age-matched controls or individuals with affective disorder (11%). These hearing impairments, which affect receptive communication in social situations (i.e., social deafness), are of the conductive type associated with middle ear disease rather than the type induced by aging processes (Gurland, 1991). By its nature and by report, the deafness seems to begin many years before the onset of paranoid symptoms and predisposes individuals to delusional disorder without the presence of typical premorbid personalities (Eastwood, Corbin, Reed, Nobbs, & Kedward, 1985). Jeste, Harris, Pearlson et al. (1988) and Moore (1981), however, have reported that neither deafness nor partial blindness were common in individuals with delusional disorder in their samples of patients.

There does not appear to be a significant relationship between the evolution of delusional disorder and chronic somatic disease. Recent work has used computed tomography scanning to demonstrate organic lesions in a group of patients with symptoms of late-onset delusional disorders (Miller et al., 1986). Cerebral organicity is an important risk factor for paranoid symptoms and, if left untreated, contributes to a poorer prognosis (Flint, Rifat, & Eastwood, 1991).

Premorbid History

Only 10% to 30% of patients exhibiting delusional disorder are characterized by their relatives or friends as having been "normal" before the onset of their illness. More often, these individuals have been described with premorbid schizoid, avoidant, or paranoid personalities (APA, 1987; Post, 1989). Most studies have shown that an abnormal personality and an unfavorable social milieu are a long prelude to the emergence of frank paranoid symptoms in later life (Christenson & Blazer, 1984; Gurland, 1991; Kay, Cooper, Garside, & Roth, 1976; Post, 1966). These studies have variously characterized the premorbid personalities of individuals subsequently diagnosed with delusional disorder as quarrelsome-aggressive-hostile, egocentric-obstinate-domineering, suspicious-jealous-persecuted, or shy-sensitive-withdrawn. As in many late-onset psychotic disorders, work records often are good. If difficulties existed, they commonly are found in the area of social or interpersonal relationships (Kay et al., 1976).

Course and Outcome of Delusional Disorder

Data on the course and outcome of individuals with delusional disorder have not accumulated. Clinical observations suggest that the illness course is diverse, with a chronic course in some individuals and remissions and relapses in others.

Treatment

In the survey of community elderly by Christenson and Blazer (1984), only half of the individuals exhibiting pervasive persecutory delusions perceived the need for help and very few had had psychiatric contact. These individuals' lack of friends and other social contacts tend to militate against their coming to the notice of psychiatric services (Castle & Murray, 1993).

Neuroleptic medications are often efficacious, especially in agitated delusional patients. However, one common problem in the treatment of patients with delusional disorder is noncompliance. Raskind and colleagues (1979) have suggested that long-acting neuroleptics are preferable to oral, daily medication for these patients due to problems with compliance.

Psychotherapy may be an important modality of treatment for some patients with delusional disorder. A somewhat distant, medical-type approach has been advocated as most acceptable and least threatening to these patients, however (Christison, Christison, & Blazer, 1989; Jeste et al., 1991).

Conclusion

The past three decades have seen an increase in life course analyses that examine health and disturbance in individuals across the life span. Such studies are particularly pertinent to improving our understanding of the evolution of symptoms and the effectiveness of treatments for psychotic illnesses. Recent advances in brain imaging techniques, genetics, and psychopharmacology also may serve to accelerate early recognition and improved intervention in individuals with schizophrenia and delusional disorder.

Controversy remains particularly strong with regard to the relationship between early-onset and late-onset schizophrenia. Whether these are actually two forms of the same disorder or two different disorders is unknown. Differences do exist between these disorders in relationship to descriptive demographics, prevalence, course, and outcome. Some investigators believe that late-onset patients have a better prognosis and are more amenable to treatment than early-onset patients. However, definitive studies have not been conducted.

Delusional disorder is quite different from early-onset and late-onset schizophrenia in defining symptoms, the prevalence of the disorder, and premorbid history. Given the nonbizarre nature of its symptoms, its later age of symptom onset, and frequent physiological concomitants, delusional disorder may demonstrate a better prognosis than schizophrenia. Future systematic research is required to address this issue.

Improved treatments, more widespread educational and social support for patients and their families, and targeted psychopharmacology have been introduced for schizophrenia. At this juncture, a new generation of antipsychotic medications offers specific but cautious hope for improved treatment response. Although continuing psychopharmacological and genetic studies may provide increased preventive and treatment directions in the future, current services provided to individuals with schizophrenia and delusional disorder are directed toward broad-based psychological, social, and community support.

13

Mood Disorders in Older Adults

Rachel Wolfe
Jannay Morrow
Barbara L. Fredrickson

Depressive disorders are among the most common mental health problems experienced in old age. Despite this fact, popular stereotypes, and personal challenges often associated with aging, mood disorders are actually less common in older than younger persons (Weissman et al., 1988b). And although there is substantial overlap in the symptomatology, course, treatment, and outcome of mood disorders in older and younger persons, there are subtle yet salient differences that are pertinent to accurate diagnosis and successful treatment of elders. Our goal is to assist in these endeavors, and to this end, we overview issues of classification, epidemiology, and assessment as well as briefly discuss pharmacological and psychological treatments.

AUTHORS' NOTE: Our descriptions of diagnostic categories are based on *DSM-IV* (APA, 1994); however, most of the research described herein used *DSM-III-R* (APA, 1987) classifications. Because the two methods of classifying mood disorders are not markedly different, the meanings of the categories and research findings we describe should not be affected. Specific divergences between the two editions are presented concisely in Appendix D of *DSM-IV*.

Along the way, we highlight those research and clinical findings that are most pertinent to professionals dealing with elders who may have mood disorders.

Classification

Mood disorders are divided into two broad categories: depressive disorders and bipolar disorders. The most common depressive disorders (DDs) are major depressive disorder and dysthymic disorder. Central features of major depressive disorder (MDD) are persistent depressed mood and diminished interest or pleasure in most activities (anhedonia). The current *Diagnostic and Statistical Manual of Mental Disorders* (*DSM-IV;* American Psychiatric Association [APA], 1994) specifies additional diagnostic criteria, including symptoms that cause significant disruption in important areas of functioning (e.g., interpersonal, occupational) and are continuous for at least 2 weeks. Other core symptoms include sleep disturbance; weight or appetite disturbance; psychomotor changes; fatigue, feelings of worthlessness or guilt; difficulty in thinking, concentrating, and decision making; and suicidal ideation.

Dysthymia (DY) is a chronic, more moderate depressive disorder in which persistent depressed mood and other symptoms of depression (e.g., sleep disturbance, poor self-esteem, and hopelessness) must have occurred on most days for at least 2 years.

Bipolar disorders (BPDs) typically consist of intermittent episodes of depression and mania or hypomania. The critical feature of a manic or hypomanic episode is a period of persistent elevated, expansive, or irritable mood. Other criteria include decreased need for sleep, racing thoughts, distractibility, rapid speech or pressure to speak, increased activity, and excessive involvement in pleasurable, potentially risky behaviors. Mania and hypomania are distinguished primarily by degree of impairment and duration, with manic episodes lasting longer (a minimum of 1 week vs. 4 days) and causing markedly impaired social or occupational functioning. Because the symptom patterns, course, and treatment of bipolar disorders do not differ greatly between older and younger persons, and bipolar disorders, particularly ones of late onset, are considered somewhat rare in old age, we will not discuss bipolar disorders in great detail.

Once a mood disorder is diagnosed, the current episode may be further specified according to its severity (e.g., mild, moderate, and severe) and specific symptom features (e.g., psychotic, atypical, mixed). If episodes recur, the course of the disorder is characterized (e.g., seasonal patterning, rapid cycling).

Exclusionary criteria also apply. For example, the symptoms cannot result from an organic cause or other psychiatric condition. The *DSM-IV* provides a thorough description of mood disorders (APA, 1994).

Prevalence

As with all psychiatric conditions, prevalence estimates for mood disorders in the elderly differ according to sampling, evaluation, and classification methods. In general, mood disorders are less prevalent in old age than in any other period of adulthood (APA, 1994). Estimates of elderly community dwellers who meet MDD diagnostic criteria (1% to 6%) or DY (less than 2%) are quite low (Blazer, Hughes, & George, 1987; Weissman et al., 1988b; LaRue, 1992). One multisite community survey showed that the 1-year prevalence of MDD is roughly 1% for people aged 65 years and older, as compared to 4.5% for ages 18 to 29 years and 5.3% for ages 30 to 44 years (Weissman, Bruce, Leaf, Florio, & Holzer, 1991). For all DDs and subclinical levels of depressive symptoms and possibly BPDs, incidence peaks between the ages of 18 and 44 years, then declines with age (Blazer, 1989a; Leaf et al., 1988). Furthermore, initial onset of mood disorders appears to be rare in old age (Lewinsohn, Duncan, Stanton, & Hautzinger, 1986).

One might expect older adults to have a higher lifetime prevalence of DDs because the passage of time allows more possibilities for at least one episode, yet they have lower lifetime prevalence rates than younger persons do. Moreover, the lifetime rates of DDs decrease in old age: 9% for adults under age 55 years, 6% for adults aged from 55 to 64 years, 2% for adults aged 65 to 74 years, and .6% for adults aged 75 and older (George, Blazer, Winfield-Laird, Leaf, & Fischbach, 1988; Regier et al., 1988; Spaner, Bland, & Newman, 1994; Weissman et al., 1991). The reasons for these differences are unknown. They may reflect cohort effects, earlier mortality for those with mood disorders, differences among older and younger persons' recollections of episodes, or other factors (Blazer, 1989a; Weissman et al., 1988b).

In contrast to the low rates of DDs in old age, many studies report high prevalence rates (20% to 30% on average) of depressive symptoms; however, there is disparity in estimates (2% to 44%) that may be caused in part by failure to consider the gender of respondents (Blazer, Burchett, Service, & George, 1991; Blazer, Hughes, & George, 1987; Leaf et al., 1988). For example, self-reports of dysphoria and other symptoms decline with age until age 65; they then increase again for women but stay the same or decline for men (Leaf et al., 1988; Smith & Weissman, 1992). Most studies find that throughout adulthood, the 1-year and lifetime prevalence rates of DDs and depressive symptoms are two to three times greater for women than men (Blazer et al., 1991; Weissman et al., 1988b). Thus, depressive symptoms may cause problems for elders, particularly women; however, the disparity in estimates makes it difficult to unequivocally determine the extent or effects of depressive symptomatology in old age.

In contrast to community dwellers, rates of DDs are high for institutionalized and hospitalized elders. Elders living in nursing homes and congregate housing show 1-year rates of 6% to 25% for MDD and 16% to 30% for dysthymia or less severe but marked depressive symptoms (Ames, 1993; Parmelee, Katz, & Lawton, 1989, 1992; Phillips & Henderson, 1991). Hospitalized elders report rates of 6% to 40% for MDD and 13% to 26% for adjustment disorder with depressed mood or dysphoria (Koenig, Meador, Cohen, & Blazer, 1988; Rapp, Parisi, & Walsh, 1988). Even though depression rates are higher in hospitalized than community-dwelling elderly, one still finds lower levels of MDD in older (13%) versus younger inpatients (22%) (Koenig et al., 1991).

Although bipolar disorders in older adults have not been studied extensively, initial onset after age 65 is low, with prevalence rate as low as .2% (Addonizio & Alexopoulos, 1993; Shulman, 1993). For those elders with BPDs, the average age of onset is in the late 40s or 50s, and in community dwellers, prevalence rates of BPDs are lower for older than younger adults—.4% versus 1.4% (Stone, 1989; Weissman et al., 1988b). Though rare, BPDs may cause more problems for elders than for their younger counterparts, and the prognosis for elders with BPDs may be worse than for those with DDs. Recent findings suggest these poorer outcomes may be due to more extensive neurological and cognitive deficits (Shulman, Tohen, Satlin, Mallya, Kalunian, 1992). Some researchers suggest that the prevalence of BPDs are underestimated in older adults because of misdiagnosis and other factors (Davis, Segal, & Spring, 1983; Young & Klerman, 1992). In general, more needs to be known about BPDs in elders.

For readers who want more epidemiological information, comprehensive information on MDD, BPDs, and dysthymia are presented by Blazer, Hughes, and George (1987), Smith and Weissman (1992), and Weissman et al. (1988a, 1988b). Detailed epidemiological information about other mood disorders in elders is scant (e.g., atypical depression, adjustment disorder with depression), however, in part due to their low prevalence rates (George et al., 1988; Regier et al., 1988).

Lower prevalence should not be equated with lesser import; mood disorders can become a critical problem in old age. They account for a substantial proportion of psychiatric admissions among elders—particularly, acute care (Wattis, 1990). The seriousness of mood disorders in older persons may be exacerbated by life events, physical health problems, and health care atmosphere. Because primary care physicians, whom elders are most likely to visit, do not always diagnose or treat their older patients' mood disorders, their condition may worsen and can lead to hospitalization (Kirmayer, Robbins, Dworkind, & Yaffe, 1993). Concurrent physical illnesses and medication side effects also can mask or worsen symptoms of depression. Thus, although the rates of mood disorders are relatively low in older adults, it is important to recognize the potential pernicious effects mood disorders, particularly if misdiagnosed or mistreated, and depressive symptoms can have for elders.

Risk Factors

Factors that contribute to mood disorders often are discussed in terms of a diathesis-stress perspective: Predispositional factors interact with stressors to produce a clinical syndrome. In this model, biological, psychological, and situational factors are important in the etiology, maintenance, and course of mood disorders and although these factors have been amply studied, most of this research has focused on younger samples. Keep in mind that risk factors for depression in younger persons (e.g., bereavement, poor body image, social isolation, etc.) may not be associated with depression in elders, even if these factors are more prevalent in old age (Musetti et al., 1989).

PSYCHOSOCIAL STRESSORS

Stress and Coping

Most work on younger samples shows depression is associated with increased stressors and negative life events, but the relationship is complex with many plausible causal and mediating factors, including coping strategies, social support, and preexisting pathology. In older adults, the relationship between stressors and depressive symptoms is similar, though somewhat weaker, particularly when social support is available or physical health is relatively uncompromised (Phifer & Murrell, 1986). Research on older adults suggests that over 40% of depressed patients and over 60% of depressed community dwellers experienced at least one major negative life event in the previous year. This rate was two to three times greater than in the nondepressed groups. Acute and chronic stressors, poor health, death or serious illness of a loved one, relocation, and caring for a sick relative were associated with increased risk of depression (Murphy, 1982).

Very few studies have assessed the relationship between bipolar disorders and stressors. A review of the literature suggests that negative life events (e.g., dissolution of marriage, bereavement, losses, illness) are risks for episodes of mania and depression; however, research has not focused on elderly samples and considered depressive and bipolar disorders separately.

The stress and depression literature has received criticism concerning conceptual and methodological flaws and weak explanatory-predictive power of the findings. Related to that, problems stem from haphazard selection and exclusion variables, which produce an incomplete picture of the relationship between stress and depression. With these and other weaknesses in mind, we highlight only the stressors that have been amply researched in the elderly. We also discuss stressors that traditionally have been discussed as risks for depression in elders but where research has not borne out these perspectives. Because of space limitations, our discussion is brief, focusing on bereavement, loss, and caregiving. Later, we consider medical illnesses, which can be viewed as physical or psychosocial risk factors or both.

Bereavement

Deaths of loved ones occur more frequently in old age. Because normal grief and DDs share symptoms, the *DSM* makes a temporal distinction between the two, allowing for a diagnosis of DD when symptoms persist longer than 1 year. Although the course and effect of bereavement is similar in old and young adults (Fasey, 1990), older adults may have unique problems due to their own health problems or diminished financial and social resources (Osterweis, 1985). By and large, however, most older individuals cope well with bereavement—often better than younger people do (Parkes, 1992). Although bereavement is a risk factor for DD, for most bereaved persons, old and young alike, the symptoms of depression pass within a few months (Fasey, 1990).

Loss

Beyond the loss of loved ones, other losses, such as the inability to maintain life roles, are implicated as risks for depressive symptoms, particularly among older adults. Loss of ability to work or remain physically active may bring on feelings of inadequacy. In a society that values youthfulness, aging and loss of perceived physical ability or beauty can take tolls on self-worth (Rodeheaver & Stohs, 1991). Cognitive-behavioral theories see role loss in terms of reductions in reinforcements—for example, those previously obtained through jobs or social interactions, participation in hobbies or sports, or the accomplishment of physical tasks—and decreased reinforcement is associated with depression (Heiby, 1983; Teri & Lewinsohn, 1986).

Yet the precise relationships between role loss, aging, and depression remain unclear. For example, depression related to retirement may have more to do with physical health and income loss than with social factors; poor physical health often leads to retirement, so increased depression after retirement may be a result of medical illness rather than retirement per se (Pahkala, 1990). In fact, retirement does not usually precipitate depression (George, 1980).

Contrary to popular belief, changes in social contact, even diminished social contact, do not necessarily increase the risk of depression in elders (Carstensen, 1993). The reasons for the social changes may offer more insight into the relationship between social isolation and depression. If isolation is due to physical illness or increased caretaking responsibilities, those may be the proximate risks of depression (Schulz & Williamson, 1991). Also, it is the quality of social relations and whether friends and loved ones present more support than demands, that predicts depression (Gallo, 1990; Hannappel, Calsyn, & Allen, 1993).

Caregiving

Individuals who provide assistance with another's basic daily functioning must cope with the added practical and emotional demands of this role. Caregiving is associated with increased stress and feelings of anger, anxiety, guilt, and depression (Gallagher, Rose, Rivera, Lovett, & Thompson, 1989; see also Chapter 6, this volume). Caring for a loved one with dementia is particularly demanding. Even when controlling for previous episodes and family prevalence of DDs, 30% of older dementia caregivers experienced MDD, DY, and other DDs as compared to 1% of matched controls (Dura, Stukenberg, & Kiecolt-Glaser, 1990). An increased risk of DDs for dementia carers has emerged in other studies (Coppel, Burton, Becker, & Fiore, 1985; Gallagher et al., 1989; Lichtenberg & Barth, 1990). Caregiving in general is stressful; caring for others who are mentally or physically impaired also is a risk for depression (Hannappel et al., 1993; Tennstedt, Cafferata, & Sullivan, 1992; Thompson, Bundek, & Sobolew-Shubin, 1990). Last, the stage of caregiving is important. Caring for patients with more severe symptoms, in the later stages of dementia, or who have been recently placed in a nursing home is associated with higher risk among older caregivers (Lichtenberg & Barth, 1990).

DEMOGRAPHIC CHARACTERISTICS

Gender

In samples of all ages, there are no gender differences in BPDs. However, the higher overall rates of most depressive disorders in women versus men, particularly of MDD and DY, are well established (APA, 1994; Leon, Klerman, & Wickramaratne, 1993; Regier et al., 1988). Some studies have found similar gender differences among elders (e.g., Weissman et al., 1991). The New Haven Epidemiologic Catchment Area Program found marked gender differences only in self-reports of depressive symptoms (women report more)—not for DDs per se (Leaf et al., 1988). In general, there is some evidence that gender discrepancies diminish with age, though they may not disappear altogether.

Although considerable research has investigated why gender is related to depression in younger persons, the specific mechanisms remain unclear (see Nolen-Hoeksema, 1987), and even less is known about elders. In all age groups, economic status may be an important mediating factor, such that lower income is associated with increased risk for depression for both men and women (Hirschfeld & Cross, 1982). Women who work outside the home earn less than men; hence, they are put at greater economic disadvantage after retirement. Also, women who do not hold paid jobs often have little economic means after their husbands die.

Other mediators relate to stress and coping. For example, due to differences in life expectancy and social roles, women are more likely to be widows or caretakers; both roles may be risks for depression (Rodeheaver & Datan, 1988). Women's more ruminative and passive coping styles may place them at greater risk of depression. This association between coping styles and depressive symptoms has been supported in younger adults (Nolen-Hoeksema, 1991) and has received some support in elders coping with losses and other stressors (Neundorfer, 1991a, 1991b; Williamson & Schulz, 1992b). Little systematic research has focused on elders and the relationships between gender, coping styles, and DDs, however.

Socioeconomic Status (SES) and Race

At all ages, there is an increased risk of mood disorders in lower socioeconomic strata. The association between poverty and mood disorders may be explained in part by the uneven distribution of medical illnesses and psychosocial stressors among the social strata. In elders, when medical illness or other stressors are considered, the relationship between SES and risk of mood disorders typically is reduced significantly, if not extinguished (Blazer et al., 1991; Weissman et al., 1991).

Race is not a consistent predictor of late-life mood disorders, and when race emerges as a predictor, mood disorders often are better predicted by related risk factors—for example, illness, other psychiatric conditions, or negative events (Butler, Lewis, & Sunderland, 1991). Thus, although race and SES are often considered risk factors for mood disorders, stressors such as medical illness or caregiving may prove more important in predicting mood disorders in elders.

Physical Disability and Medical Illness

Disabled and ill persons of all ages are at greater risk for depressive symptoms (Turner & Noh, 1988; Wells, Golding, & Burnam, 1988). Depression may be a psychological reaction to the limitations, discomfort, and demands imposed by physical illness (Koenig & Blazer, 1992b). Also, medical illness and disability may function as stressors leading to or worsening depressive symptoms or they may trigger depressive episodes.

In studies of community-dwelling elders, those in poorer initial health or who later become physically ill are more likely to become depressed than are those in better health (Kennedy et al., 1989; Phifer & Murrell, 1986). Busse (1975) found that 60% to 85% of depressed elders could identify a specific physical ailment that precipitated their depression. Yet even though physical disability or illness is a risk factor for mood disorders in older adults (Koenig et al., 1991; Turner & Noh, 1988; Williamson & Schulz, 1992b) and mood disorders and illnesses have a high comorbidity rate in elders (20% to 70%) (LaRue, Dessonville, & Jarvik, 1985), the majority of physically ill older individuals do not develop mood disorders (Fisher, Zeiss, & Carstensen, 1993). Thus, the relationship between physical disability or illness and depression is not one of simple cause and effect. In fact, mastery skills, coping styles, and social support can mediate the relationship between failing health and depressive symptoms (Morris, Robinson, Raphael, & Bishop, 1991; Turner & Noh, 1988). Still, medical illness must be considered when diagnosing elders, and in the section on differential diagnosis, we discuss more possible relationships between illness and mood disorders.

Family History

Mood disorders, particularly bipolar disorders, run in families. This is true for all age groups. Even though the association between family history and mood disorders may be slightly weaker for older adults than younger adults, particularly when the first episode occurs in late life (APA, 1994; Blazer, 1989a; Shulman et al., 1992), the assessment section will suggest how family history will aid diagnosis.

Assessment

A thorough diagnostic interview is the best assessment tool for determining whether an older client has a mood disorder. In the interview, clinicians should determine the onset, duration, pervasiveness, and severity of presenting symptoms and evaluate the client's family history, health status, and medical history—including past and present prescriptions and over-the-counter medications. Physical evaluations should be sure to focus on neurological systems, and a number of laboratory tests can be helpful (see following section).

Practitioners should be aware that detecting mood disorders in older clients may be difficult for at least four related reasons. First, older adults may be reluctant to discuss or admit their psychological symptoms. For example, depression may be misdiagnosed as physical illness or dementia because patients may not admit to or attend to psychological symptoms of depression and instead, complain of somatic problems or confusion and indecisiveness. Second, clinicians inexperienced with older clients may not probe deeply or delicately enough to obtain useful diagnostic information. Third, older adults and clinicians may hold ageist biases. For example, they may believe that psychiatric problems, and depression in particular, are a normal part of aging. These beliefs may lead to erroneous views of depression as inevitable and untreatable (Katona, 1994). Fourth, most assessment and treatment research is based on younger samples. As such, generalizations to older adults may be premature.

In the section to follow, we review features the clinician should be alert to when assessing mood disorders in older adults.

IMPORTANT FEATURES OF MDD
AND DY IN OLDER ADULTS

Symptom manifestations of depressive disorders in older adults are generally similar to those exhibited in younger persons, and the same diagnostic criteria are applied to both populations (Blazer, Bachar, & Manton, 1986; Dessonville, Gallagher, Thompson, Finnel, & Lewinsohn, 1982; Oxman, Barrett, Barrett, & Gerber, 1990). Although there are few marked differences between younger and older adults in presentation of symptoms of dysthymia or MDD regardless of subtype, evidence suggests there are subtle, but possibly important, differences in how mood disorders, particularly MDD, present in older adults (Blazer, Bachar, & Hughes, 1987; Kaszniak & Allender, 1985). For example, depressed older adults may present more memory complaints, more self-reproach, less guilt, and less suicidal ideation (Blumenthal, 1975; Kaszniak, 1987; Mussetti et al., 1989). Thus, when assessing older clients, it is important to apply *DSM* criteria knowledgeably, with an eye for clinical features that may be particularly informative in this population. We highlight such features in the following discussion.

The hallmark feature of MDD is persistent depressed mood, and this may be the feature that clinicians look for most when assessing for DD. Yet dysphoria, especially sadness, may be less prominent or more difficult to recognize in depressed elders. In a comparison of younger and older depressed inpatients, older inpatients reported milder mood symptoms; this was particularly true of those who had late-onset MDD (Kongstvedt & Sime, 1992). To obtain an accurate diagnosis, then, clinicians must be sensitive to symptoms beyond sadness (Epstein, 1976; Katon, 1984; Salzman & Shader, 1978).

Because depressed elders are more likely to report negative moods other than sadness, questions targeting feelings of agitation, irritability, anxiety, and anger are useful (Avery & Silverman, 1984; Brown, Sweeney, Loutsch, Kocsis, & Reich, 1984). In addition, anhedonia may be more typical in depressed elders (Blumenthal, 1975; Mussetti et al., 1989). The interview, then, should target changes in the client's ability to experience pleasure, frequency of engaging in pleasurable activities, and level and intensity of pleasure experienced (Teri & Gallagher, 1991; Zeiss & Lewinsohn, 1986). Though relevant, these questions should probe beyond changes that are due to illness or disability limitations.

Diagnosis of DD is complicated further because somatic complaints often overshadow or mask mood symptoms (Katon, 1984). In comparisons of symptom patterns in older and younger depressives, older persons show more weight loss; more disturbances in sleep, sexual activity, and appetite; more motor retardation; and more lethargy and fatigue (Blumenthal, 1975; Brown et al., 1984; Kongstvedt & Sime, 1992; LaRue, 1992; Mussetti et al., 1989). Moreover, when depressed elders discuss feeling sad, down, or helpless, they may talk about those feelings as responses to somatic problems such as fatigue or disturbances of sleep or appetite (Fogel, 1991; Kaszniak & Allender, 1985). Coupled with the tendency to seek help from physicians, this symptom picture may prematurely lead diagnosis away from DDs. Finally, healthy elders often show changes in weight, sleep, appetite, and energy levels, thus differentiating normal aging from depressive symptoms can be challenging.

Careful inquiry into the nature of a client's physical symptoms can unveil their meaning. Affirmative answers to the following kinds of questions may indicate a mood disorder: Do the mood and somatic symptoms represent a recent change from previous functioning? Do they occur together with or ebb and flow with other symptoms of depression (e.g., pessimism, anhedonia, hopelessness, self-reproach, rumination, delusions) or both? Are there problems with early morning awakening and falling back to sleep? Is there a loss of interest in sex? Is an appropriate sexual partner available? Are you fatigued even when you haven't been active? Are you fatigued even when you've had enough sleep? Of course, clinicians should not overlook the fact that somatic complaints may represent true medical conditions. Thus, a complete physical should be conducted to rule out organic diseases.

IMPORTANT FEATURES OF MANIA AND
BIPOLAR DISORDERS IN OLDER ADULTS

The general symptom displays of bipolar disorders do not differ greatly between older and younger persons (Shulman, 1993; Young & Klerman,

1992); thus, assessment procedures will be similar. As with unipolar disorders, awareness of nuances in symptom presentation in older adults will aid diagnosis. For example, elders with BPDs may present more atypical features; a mixture of mania and dysphoria (Broadhead & Jacoby, 1990; Spar, Ford, & Liston, 1979); or be more irritable, argumentative, or hostile-angry and these symptoms may overshadow elevated mood (Georgotas & McCue, 1988; Koenig & Blazer, 1992b). Consequently, BPDs may be mistaken for agitated depression or psychotic conditions. To distinguish between these disorders, one must carefully examine the depression-mania cycles, thought patterns, behaviors, and overall symptom pattern. Agitated depressives will not evince manic episodes—they will show more depressive and pessimistic thoughts, memories, and delusions, whereas those with BPD typically will show mood-congruent thoughts and delusions, which shift from depressive to grandiose themes. Compared to younger clients, elders with BPDs may show more paranoid delusions, longer episodes of mania or depression, or more rapid cycling (Spar & LaRue, 1990; Young & Klerman, 1992). Elders with BPDs show more cognitive deficits and neurological damage than do their young counterparts or elders with unipolar disorders, and late onset is associated with greater cognitive and neurological deficits (Berrios & Bakshi, 1991; Broadhead & Jacoby, 1990; Shulman et al., 1992).

Last, because BPDs run in families and late onset is rare, the interview should elicit an accurate family and personal history of previous depressive and manic episodes (APA, 1994).

DIFFERENTIAL DIAGNOSIS

Physical Illness

As we have noted, physical illnesses are common in late life, and the relationships between illnesses and mood disorders are varied and complex. As such, practitioners must be skilled at differentiating mood disorders from physical illnesses because without proper diagnosis, a treatable condition may go unaddressed or a nonexistent condition may be treated unnecessarily, sometimes with potentially noxious medications. Furthermore, conditions that can be remedied only in the early stages might progress unchecked, placing the patient at risk.

Here we briefly recap and extend our discussion of some of the associations between illness and depression that are prevalent in old age. First, illness or disability may be a risk factor for depression (Morris, Robinson, & Raphael, 1990). Second, symptom manifestations of mood disorders and physical illness can be similar, so in some cases, only one disorder exists but the problem is obscured. In fact, studies find that when depressed elders present many somatic complaints to a primary physician, existing DDs can be overlooked (Kirmayer, Robbins, Dworkind, & Yaffe, 1993). Third, illnesses can produce conditions—organic or otherwise—that can cause, worsen, or imitate depression. Examples include neurological disorders, such as dementias, Parkinson's disease, brain tumors, head trauma, or aneurisms; metabolic disorders, such as hypothyroidism, diabetes, anemia, or Addison's, Cushing's, and Wilson's diseases; cardiovascular conditions, such as congestive heart failure, myocardial infarction, hypertension, and stroke; pneumonia; rheumatoid arthritis; and neoplasms. Fourth, medications used to treat illnesses can produce similar difficulties. Some antihypertensives (e.g., alphamethyldopa, clonidine, guanethidine, propanonol, and reserpine) are prone to producing depressionlike side effects. Similarly troublesome medications include hormones, corticosteroids, digitalis, antianxiety drugs, antimicrobials, analgesics, and antiparkinson's drugs (Janicak, Davis, Preskorn, & Ayd, 1993; Lehmann, 1982; Rapp et al., 1988; Spar & LaRue, 1990). Fifth, the demands of a depressive disorder can produce stressors that may aggravate existing medical problems. Sixth, depression can lead to self-medication or health-related behaviors that contribute to physical symptoms. For instance, depressed people may abuse alcohol, over-the-counter medications, or both or starve themselves. And finally, depression and illness can stem from independent causes and simply occur together.

It is important to remember that the relationship between physical illness and depression is often multifaceted, such that numerous mechanisms work together. Stroke is one example. Depressive reactions are common following stroke, occurring in approximately 30% of stroke patients (Ebrahim, Barer, & Nouri, 1987; Malec, Richardson, Sinaki, & O'Brien, 1990). Although the precise mechanisms remain unknown, recent analyses suggest that poststroke depressive reactions are related to organic changes and psychological factors, including stress reactions, coping, and social support (Koenig & Studenski, 1988; Morris et al., 1991 Swartzman & Teasell, 1993).

The multiple associations between illness and depression underscore the importance of obtaining a thorough medical history. Questions should target past and present medical problems and medication use, including alcohol and over-the-counter drugs (Dessonville et al., 1982). Medical examinations also can be critical for accurate diagnosis of mood disorders. These examinations should include a laboratory workup (LaRue, 1992). Tests for metabolic or electrolyte imbalances, vitamin deficiencies, and thyroid problems should be done to rule out fatigue and lethargy caused by illness or related complications. Complete urine and blood analyses are also recommended to rule out alcohol abuse, anemia, and infections (Osgood, 1992). Chaisson-Stewart (1985) presents a more complete description of the appropriate laboratory tests used to screen for physical illness. Again, a family history is diagnostically useful in uncovering the risk for mood disorders. Even poststroke depression is more common and longer lasting in elders with a family history of mood disorders (Morris et al., 1990).

Dementia

Symptoms of depression can resemble the early symptoms of organic brain disorders, and one of the most important diagnostic tasks may be to distinguish DDs from dementia. This distinction is crucial because depression is treatable, even when comorbid with dementia, whereas many dementias are not. Symptom overlap occurs across behavioral, cognitive, and affective areas of functioning: Either disorder may involve problems in memory, concentration, comprehension, and goal setting; emotional lability or excessive emotional responses; sadness; sleep disruption; agitation; behavioral inhibition; and apathy (Feinberg & Goodman, 1984; LaRue, 1992). Furthermore, some depressed elders (approximately 15%) show cognitive deficits that are comparable to those seen in dementias (Rabins, 1983). When depression is the diagnosis, this combination of depressive symptoms and cognitive deficits is referred to as *pseudodementia* or *dementia syndrome of depression* (DSD; APA, 1994). Cognitive skills in DSD patients usually return with successful treatment of the depression, and presently, this is the only way to confirm DSD (LaRue, 1992). Yet the long-term prognosis for DSD patients is unclear, and many DSD patients later exhibit irreversible dementia (LaRue, 1992; Strub & Black, 1988).

Research and clinical observation suggest that certain symptom patterns can help distinguish depressed persons, even those with DSD, from those suffering from dementia of the Alzheimer's type (DAT) and other dementias. Compared to those with DAT, depressed elders show fewer problems with everyday activities (e.g., finding their way home, knowing how to complete tasks, following instructions) and report more symptoms of anxiety, insomnia, and loss of interest in sex (Reynolds et al., 1988). Depressed persons also are more likely to experience early morning awakening and rapid mood changes (Reynolds et al., 1986).

Compared to the cognitive deficits seen in most dementias, the losses associated with depression appear to have a rapid onset and progression, and the patient often seeks help soon after the deficits emerge (LaRue, 1992; Strub & Black, 1988). Depressed persons show more problems with social skills, and family members and friends are more likely to be aware of the cognitive losses (LaRue, 1992; Wells, 1980). Compared to those with dementia, depressed persons voice more complaints about forgetfulness, and yet they display better memory performance on formal testing, underestimate their cognitive performance more, and, like younger depressed individuals, tend to have more negative memories and perceptions (Mohs, Rosen, Greenwald, & Davis, 1983; Weingartner & Silberman, 1982).

Depressed persons commit errors of omission, whereas those suffering from dementia make more random, confabulatory, and confusional errors. Those with dementia also have more difficulty with recent memory, acquiring and using knowledge, and making calculations. In dementia, cognitive deficits are worse at night and cognitive performance is more consistently and pervasively impaired (Spar & LaRue, 1990). In depressed persons, cognitive deficits tend to be more variable: Their performance goes up and down with their mood states and other depressive symptoms. Depressed patients may expend little effort when answering questions or completing test items. These behaviors may be marked by preemptive giving up or quickly saying, "I don't know," to questions (Spar & LaRue, 1990). By contrast, DAT sufferers are more vague, evasive, and perseverative and may suffer from greater speech disturbances (Mohs et al., 1983; Spar & LaRue, 1990). Table 13.1 summarizes features that may help distinguish depression from dementia.

Obtaining a family and patient history is important in determining the proper diagnosis. For example, if a patient has had a previous episode of depression, a family history of depression, or both, depression with DSD may be more likely than dementia per se. Although dementia and mood disorders are often distinguishable, it is important to highlight that they can coexist. Roughly 30% of DAT patients meet MDD diagnostic criteria, and a greater percentage suffer from depressive symptoms (Burns, 1991; Feinberg & Goodman, 1984; Reifler, Larson, Teri, & Poulsen, 1986). Depression may result from the realization that one is experiencing diminished cognitive functioning or from the frustration and stress caused by these losses (Reifler, Larson, & Hanley, 1982).

Some useful tests for examining cognitive functioning include the Mini-Mental State Examination (Folstein, 1983) and the Brief Cognitive Rating Scale (Reisberg, 1983). Chapter 9 (this volume), Crook, Ferris, and Bartus (1983), Kane and Kane (1984), and LaRue (1992) describe numerous tests and provide information concerning their reliability and validity.

Delirium

Symptoms of delirium are common in elders, particularly in the hospitalized old. Proper diagnosis is critical because complete recovery is possible when treated early, but untreated, the underlying condition can cause permanent damage or death (Rabins & Folstein, 1982). Overlapping symptoms shared by delirium and depression include dysphoria, delusions, irritability, trouble with decision making and concentration, sleep cycle disruptions, and inactivity (Lipowski, 1980).

Drug intoxication, malnutrition, acute stress, and head trauma can cause delirium, and it is common after surgery (Lipowski, 1983). Many medical

Table 13.1 Features to Help Distinguish Persons With Depression and Dementia

	Depression	*Dementia*
Clinical course	Onset clear, rapid progression	Onset unclear, slow progression
	Others are aware of deficits	Others are unaware of deficits, deficits hidden
	History of other psychological problems	No history of psychological problems
	Little change in cognitive skills at night	Diminished cognitive skills at night
	Recent external stressors	
Clinical behavior	Detailed complaints of losses	Few or vague complaints of losses
	Give up on cognitive tasks	Make efforts to succeed at cognitive tasks
	Point out failures and struggles	
	Distress over symptoms or performance	Diminish or ignore failure
	More affective symptoms	Little distress over symptoms
	Fewer problems with everyday behaviors	Fewer affective symptoms or blunted emotions
	Social skills deficits	Problems with everyday activities
	Early morning wakening	Social skills often unchanged
	Good verbal fluency	No early morning wakening
		Poor verbal fluency
Performance on cognitive tests	Give up	Keep trying
	"I don't know"	Errors are often near misses
	Commit errors of omission	Errors in orientation
	Memory loss is inconsistent	Memory loss for recent events is worse than for remote
	Good vocabulary performance	
	Performance variable across tasks	Poor responses on vocabulary
	Negative cognitions and memories	Performance consistently impaired across tasks

SOURCE: Based on Cummings (1989), LaRue (1992), Reynolds et al. (1986), Reynolds et al. (1988), Spar and LaRue (1990), and Strub and Black (1988).

conditions associated with depression are associated also with delirium (e.g., heart failure, cardiovascular problems, and cancer). A key distinguishing feature of delirium is sudden symptom onset, particularly delusions. Also, the delusions tend to be more changeable, situation related, and paranoid, whereas in mood disorders, they tend to be longer lasting and mood congruent, with a focus on interpersonal themes or worthlessness (Lipowski, 1980).

ASSESSMENT INSTRUMENTS

Structured Interviews

Structured interviews afford numerous advantages when assessing older clients. The format can help clinicians systematically probe beyond superficial symptoms, they do not depend on reading and comprehension skills, and they require less concentration and motivation on the part of the respondent. Compared to self-ratings and unstructured techniques, structured interviews are less likely to be undermined by respondents' memory lapses and are more reliable, even in the presence of cognitive impairments (O'Connor, Pollitt, Roth, Brook, & Reiss, 1990). We briefly discuss two interview-based assessments: the Schedule for Affective Disorders and Schizophrenia (SADS) and the Hamilton Rating Scale for Depression (HAM-D).

SADS (Endicott & Spitzer, 1978), a semistructured interview, is a commonly used means of screening for depression in elders (Dessonville et al., 1982). The client describes the features, history, and course of the problem, and the severity, duration, and pervasiveness of each symptom is rated on a 7-point scale. SADS taps various depressive symptom clusters, including dysphoria, reduced behavior, and self-deprecation, and it measures delusions, hallucinations, and substance use. Gallagher (1986) suggests that SADS is a preferred assessment tool because it standardizes diagnosis, fits well with *DSM* diagnostic criteria, and has good reliability and validity with older adults in distinguishing depressed versus nondepressed persons (Dessonville et al., 1982). The interviewer must undergo extensive training, however, and the interview is lengthy (Gallagher, 1986).

The HAM-D (Hamilton, 1960) can be administered in an interview format (in about 30 minutes). It distinguishes different levels of depression, is sensitive to treatment changes, and may be best suited to measure depression with melancholia (Yesavage, Brink, Rose, & Aday, 1983b). The interview measures 17 areas of functioning that are related to depression (e.g., sadness, sleep disturbance, guilt) on 5-point or 3-point severity scales. The HAM-D has been used with older adults, although its relative emphasis on somatic symptoms may undermine its sensitivity and specificity for screening depression in this age group (Yesavage et al., 1983; Zung, 1983). Other drawbacks are that it does not tap all of the relevant symptoms of depression or closely match *DSM* diagnostic criteria and training is intensive (Gallagher, 1986).

Self-Report Inventories

Combined with the history and interview, self-report inventories help to assess the severity, intensity, and longevity of depressive symptoms and measure treatment changes. Alone, most are not valid or reliable for diagnosis. The most commonly used scales with elders are the Beck Depression Inventory (Beck, Ward, Mendelson, Mock, & Erbaugh, 1961) and the Zung Self-Rating Depression Scale (Zung, 1967, 1983). A newer scale, the Geriatric Depression Rating Scale, was designed specifically with the elderly in mind. However, it has not been used or tested as extensively. The format, uses, strengths, and weaknesses of each scale are presented in Table 13.2.

Table 13.2   Self-Report Measures of Depression

Scale	Use	Format	Strengths	Weaknesses
Zung Self-Rating Depression Scale	Measures frequency of depressive symptoms; used for screening and assessing treatment effectiveness	Indicates frequency of occurrence	Brief, easy to administer, correlates well with clinician ratings	May have too many somatic items; validity and reliability with those over 70 years old is questionable
Beck Depression Inventory	Measures severity of depressive symptoms; used for screening and assessing treatment effectiveness	Self-rating: select from four choices of intensity for each symptom	Brief, low misclassification rate for elderly even when physical illness or cognitive deficits are present	Potential problems when chronic medical problems exist
Geriatric Depression Rating Scale	Presence or absence of various symptoms; can provide a severity rating; used for screening and assessing treatment effectiveness	Brief and simple yes-no format	Low misclassification rate even when physical illnesses and cognitive deficits are present; designed specifically for use with the elderly	Relatively new scale with few tests concerning validity and reliability

Management

Whether for financial, practical, or attitudinal reasons, community-dwelling older adults relatively rarely seek mental health care (George et al., 1988). Hence, older adults commonly are not treated for their psychiatric problems. When they do seek treatment, they often turn to their general practitioner and present somatic complaints. Thus, treatment often follows a medical model even when a psychological approach can help. Even hospitalized older patients receive inpatient psychiatric care less frequently than younger ones do (George et al., 1988).

Only recently have treatment studies rigorously focused on elders. The current evidence, though somewhat scant, suggests that successful treatment of mood disorders in older adults follows the same general principles, indications, and applications as in younger adults. Treatments differ to the degree that the situations, disorders, and concomitant problems of the populations differ. As we have seen, there are subtle differences among age groups in the presentation and preponderance of certain symptoms. Although problems such as medical illness, disability, cognitive deficits, or life stressors may be experienced by old and young persons, their frequency, severity, or characteristics may differ, and these differences may need to be addressed in treatment. This section overviews the interventions for elders that have been studied and highlights evidence regarding treatment efficacy and issues of particular interest to clinicians treating older clients.

SOMATIC INTERVENTIONS FOR DEPRESSIVE DISORDERS

Overview of Pharmacotherapy

Many safe and effective antidepressant medications are available at relatively low cost. Most research on antidepressants has targeted younger samples, but several studies demonstrate their general effectiveness in physically healthy elders (Reynolds, 1992), with response rates comparable in younger and older adults—50% to 80% (Gerson, Plotkin, Jarvik, 1988; Rockwell, Lam, Zisook, 1988). The use of antidepressants with frail elders has received less empirical attention, but recent evidence suggests their safety and efficacy, particularly the selective serotonin reuptake inhibitors such as fluoxetine, sertraline, and paroxetine (Evans & Lye, 1992; Hale, 1993). Given the newness of this area of study, some experts caution against the use of antidepressant treatment in high risk patients such as physically ill elders and the oldest-old (Katz, 1993; Koenig & Breitner, 1990). In deciding whether pharmacotherapy should be part of a treatment plan, clinicians need to consider the type of depression being treated, possible drug side effects, and concurrent medical conditions, psychopathology, or medications that may cause side effects (see also Chapter 22).

Type of Depression

In assessing whether someone is a good candidate for pharmacotherapy and when selecting the medication, clinicians should determine whether the depression is attributable to an identifiable factor, has specific features, or both. Depressive symptoms that seem to arise from life events (sometimes given the *DSM* diagnosis of "adjustment disorder with depressed mood") are generally less responsive to pharmacotherapy alone (Janicak et al., 1993).

Antidepressants seem to be most effective for those who are severely impaired or who have chronic or recurring major depression (Elkin et al., 1989; Janicak et al., 1993). Specific somatic approaches may be best suited for patients with specific features, such as melancholia, delusions, psychosis, or atypical patterns; agitated depression; cognitive deficits; medical illnesses; or multiple psychiatric problems.

Somatic Therapy for Bipolar Disorders

Lithium is the primary treatment of BPDs, with an effectiveness reaching 80% in younger adults (Janicak et al., 1993). Studies of lithium treatment in older persons suggests that lithium is effective, but its level of effectiveness and optimal usage in elders is less clear (Foster, 1992; Mirchandani & Young, 1993; Young & Klerman, 1992).

Side effects of lithium can be quite serious. Common side effects include delirium, tremors, muscle weakness, drowsiness, renal problems, arythmias, and gastrointestinal problems. Lithium may also cause hypothyroid disorders and heart conduction defects (Janicak et al., 1993). Dehydration from heat, exercise, alcohol, or medication can cause lithium intoxication. Individuals with kidney dysfunction, hypertension, heart or thyroid disease, or low salt intake usually should not take lithium (Wolfe & Hope, 1993). Older patients respond more slowly to lithium than do younger ones, so acute manic episodes may require supplemental somatic treatments to increase effectiveness or decrease side effects (Foster, 1992; Mirchandani & Young, 1993). In general, clinicians are advised to watch closely for possible drug interactions with lithium because of potentially serious complications (Janicak et al., 1993).

Electroconvulsive Therapy

Electroconvulsive therapy (ECT) has undergone a resurgence of popularity due to improvements in method since the 1960s. Often, ECT is administered with antidepressant medication. Still, there are lingering questions as to the effectiveness and safety of ECT, and given the prevalence of medical illness and relative frailty of older people, further research must address the advantages and disadvantages of using ECT in this population.

ECT is poorly studied in older adults; there are few controlled, prospective studies with comparison groups. Retrospective studies of elders have demonstrated ECT effectiveness to be comparable to antidepressants in the immediate alleviation of depressive episodes (Price & McAllister, 1989; Wesner & Winokur, 1989). Reviews of ECT treatment in depressives over age 60 years suggest that ECT has a high response rate—70% to 90%—but many patients experience complications—30% to 40% (Burke, Rubin, Zorumski, & Wetzel,

1987). In older adults, advantages of ECT over antidepressant medication are thought to include its rapid effects and fewer cardiovascular problems. ECT is used in treating both manic and depressive symptoms (see following section).

Adverse effects from seizures involved in ECT may be serious, particularly for older patients. These include hypoxia, arrythmias, delirium, transient hypertension and cardiovascular effects, and memory disturbances (Burke et al., 1987; Figiel, Krishnan, & Doraiswamy, 1990; Weiner, 1984). In addition, ECT is thought to be associated with increased frequency of subsequent depressive episodes; thus, although effective in the short run, the risk of future depressive episodes may increase (Wesner & Winokur, 1989). Older patients with heart or lung dysfunctions are at higher risk for serious adverse effects, and side effects of ECT increase with age among older adults, particularly cardiorespiratory problems, confusion, and falls (Burke et al., 1987). Cognitive and neurological deficits after ECT have been found to be more common in older than younger adults, especially among those patients with a previous history of ECT (Pettinati & Bonner, 1984).

ECT may be most useful in patients with medical conditions that contraindicate the use of antidepressants (e.g., Parkinson's disease, stroke), at high risk for suicide, whose depressions have been resistant to antidepressants, diagnosed with MDD with melancholia, whose physical or mental condition is rapidly deteriorating, or who previously have shown a good response to ECT (Janicak et al., 1993).

There are few well-conducted studies on the effectiveness of ECT for BPDs in elders, and the majority do not examine efficacy separately for bipolar and unipolar disorders. Some argue that ECT is effective for acute manic states and for patients with high risk of drug or medical complications, such as the physically ill and elderly (Burke, Rutherford, Zorumski, & Reich, 1985; Janicak et al., 1993). When ECT is used with lithium, it may prevent the early relapse often seen with ECT alone (Abou-Saleh & Coppen, 1988).

Given the scarcity of sound research and the potential for adverse side effects, clinicians should be cautious when considering the use of ECT in the elderly and should recognize the limitations of the information concerning the risks and benefits of ECT.

PSYCHOLOGICAL INTERVENTIONS

Psychological interventions warrant serious consideration because of their effectiveness and circumvention of drug side effects. Moreover, most evidence suggests that psychotherapy is equally effective as pharmacotherapy, and it is possible that psychological treatments provide better protection from future episodes of depression (Elkin et al., 1989; Hollon, De Rubeis, & Seligman, 1992; Robinson, Berman, & Neimeyer, 1990). Though many kinds of nonsomatic treatments exist, only a few have undergone systematic evaluation with depressed older adults.

Individual Psychotherapy

Outcome studies with depressed older adults have shown that behavioral, cognitive, and brief psychodynamic therapy effectively treat MDD (Jarvik, Mintz, Steuer, & Gerner, 1982; Thompson, Gallagher, & Breckenridge, 1987; Gallagher-Thompson, Hanley-Peterson, & Thompson, 1990). In general, there were no differences in effectiveness among the three types of treatments in these studies, and all were superior to a waiting-list control group. Each treatment consisted of 16 to 20 sessions, and outcomes were largely maintained at a 2-year follow-up. Similar nonspecific treatment effects also have been found with younger patients and are thought to be related to reassurance and social support, increased self-efficacy, skills enhancement, and belief in therapy (Burns & Nolen-Hoeksema, 1991; Elkin et al., 1989; Orlinsky & Howard, 1987; Zeiss, Lewinsohn, & Muñoz, 1979). Also, some treatments thought to be distinct actually have important overlapping features, which may help explain the similar outcomes. Also, it may be important to match therapy to a client's particular needs and skills. Failure to consider what aspects of therapy may best address specific symptoms and problems may obscure differential treatment effects.

Behavior therapy (BT) aims to increase the frequency of behaviors that alleviate depressive symptoms by increasing reinforcement opportunities (e.g., engaging in pleasant activities, mastery-oriented activities), and decreasing behaviors that increase or maintain depressive symptoms (e.g., overdependence, passivity). Thus, this model places great emphasis on social input and diminished reinforcement in the onset and maintenance of depression (Clarke & Lewinsohn, 1989; Lewinsohn, 1974). These factors sometimes differ across the lifespan; for example, old people may receive less social input because of their relative social isolation or physical limitations (Carstensen, 1993; Zeiss & Lewinsohn, 1986). Extensions of traditional behavioral models add self-regulation as an important aspect of depression, and the individual, like the environment, is a source of reinforcers and punishers (Heiby, 1983; Rehm, Kaslow, & Rabin, 1987).

In general, the goals of behavior therapy for depression are to increase the frequency of positive experiences and reinforcers in the person's daily life, pinpoint obstacles to reinforcement, and find substitute activities and new reinforcers when these obstacles cannot be overcome. Another goal is to increase social involvement and rewards as well as self-rewards through social skills and mastery training. Behavior therapy may use relaxation training, behavior diaries, activity schedules, and guided assignments. Lewinsohn and colleagues have developed successful behavioral strategies for depressed elders (Clarke & Lewinsohn, 1989; Zeiss & Lewinsohn, 1986).

The cognitive model emphasizes the role of negative thinking in development and maintenance of depression. Thus, *cognitive therapy* (CT) attempts to change patients' negative thinking (e.g., helplessness and hopelessness) and cognitive distortions (e.g., catastrophizing and overgeneralizing) (Beck, Rush, Shaw, & Emery, 1979; Dryden & Ellis, 1988; Teasdale & Barnard, 1993). Rather than focusing on events and behaviors per se, CT focuses on how they are interpreted because the more a person evaluates situations in negative ways, the greater the risk of depression. The basic aim is to train clients to identify and to change their automatic negative thoughts, misconceptions, or irrational thoughts. Often, CT provides coping and social skills training.

Cognitive and behavioral therapies have been effective in treating young and old individuals with a variety of psychiatric problems (Carstensen, 1988; Smyer, Zarit, & Qualls, 1990; Teasdale & Barnard, 1993). In practice, cognitive and behavioral techniques are often combined. Behavioral and cognitive-behavioral therapies have been found to be at least as effective as pharmacological treatments in alleviating major depressive disorder (Blackburn, Eunson, & Bishop, 1986; Elkin et al., 1989; Evans, Hollon, DeRubeis et al., 1992). Compared to other psychological approaches, CT and BT are generally of shorter duration, more problem focused and goal oriented, less interpretive, more directive and didactic, and more likely to use written materials (DeRubeis & Beck, 1988; Dryden & Ellis, 1988). These features make CT and BT adaptable to older patients suffering from memory problems or other cognitive deficits.

Psychodynamic therapy (PT) relies on the patient-therapist relationship, often using transference manipulations so that the patient's relationships are relived with the therapist. Briefer forms of psychodynamic therapy, such as the one used by Gallagher-Thompson et al. (1990), tend not to centrally focus on transference. Instead, brief PT often focuses on issues such as unresolved grief, self integration, or existential concerns. When dealing with problems of aging, many dynamic therapists believe that events in adulthood have more bearing on current problems than childhood experiences do (Smyer et al., 1990). PT is a diverse category, lacking the unity of cognitive or behavioral therapy.

The studies conducted by Thompson et al. (1987) demonstrate the effectiveness of their form of brief PT in alleviating depression, yet given the nonspecific treatment effects in these studies and the lack of unity within PT, it is difficult to generalize these findings. Also, PT possibly contains components that overlap with cognitive and behavioral treatments. In general, future work should concentrate on determining the important components of the different therapies and the circumstances under which treatment efficacy may be optimized by using specific strategies.

One recent study demonstrated the potential benefits of a specificity approach (Gallagher-Thompson & Steffen, 1994). Depressed caregivers received 20 sessions of cognitive-behavioral therapy (CBT) or brief PT. Both treatments showed equivalent response rates, roughly 70%; however, different treatments worked for different patients. CBT was more effective for those who had been providing longer-term caregiving, whereas PT benefited only those who had been caregiving for a brief time. Because caregiving is more stressful as it progresses, CBT's focus on problem solving, mastery, and coping may have been the key to its effectiveness. CBT may provide better skills for dealing with chronic or severe stressors.

Group Therapy

Group psychotherapy (GT) usually is based on therapeutic models that have been used individually and considered by many experts to be very well-suited for treating mental health problems in older adults. It provides a social environment and economical treatment. GT may decrease isolation and hopelessness by allowing social interaction and comparison. GT typically attempts to facilitate change by focusing on interactions in the group, whether targeting reinforcement, cognition, or relationship issues. Although there are few well-conducted studies of the effectiveness of GT for depressed elders, outcome studies suggest that response rates parallel those for individual approaches (Dhooper, Green, Huff, & Austin-Murphy, 1993; Gallagher, 1979; Leung & Orrell, 1993; Singer, Tracz, & Dworkin, 1991; Wolk & Goldfarb, 1967).

Combination Therapy

Many clinicians treat their depressed patients conjointly with pharmacotherapy and psychotherapy. Two recent meta-analyses (subjects aged 17 to 81 years) suggest that combination therapy, psychotherapy, and pharmacotherapy all are equally effective treatments (Manning, Markowitz, & Frances, 1992; Robinson et al., 1990). So, combination and monotherapy both work, yet the lack of response rate differences may reflect, in part, the failure to match therapy to the specific histories, symptom patterns, and characteristics of the clients. Each therapy may address different symptomatology, and in some cases, combination therapy may provide better long-term outcomes (DiMascio et al., 1979; Janicak et al., 1993). Drugs may be better suited for rapidly treating melancholia and somatic symptoms, including psychomotor, sleep, and appetite disturbances, whereas psychotherapy may affect symptoms such as depressed mood, anhedonia, guilt, and hopelessness. Moreover, psychotherapy can provide skills that help clients cope with future problems (DiMascio et al., 1979).

Matching the Patient to the Treatment

Once a diagnosis is made, the appropriate treatment depends on factors relating to the client, care provider, and community and social resources. Most clinicians suggest a good match between client and treatment modality, as well as between client and clinician, can maximize the potential for treatment effectiveness.

On the client level, physical health must be considered. For frail individuals or those with specific medical conditions, the side effects of certain somatic treatments may be too risky. Because the site of treatment must be accessible, a person's functional capacity factors into treatment choice. Considerations may include proximity to the patient's home and handicap access.

Matching specific types of symptoms or personal characteristics may improve and better maintain treatment outcomes (McKnight et al., 1984). For instance, if cognitive distortions (e.g., perceiving success as failure) are primary, CT may be most beneficial. Skill deficits, role losses, and diminished reinforcement may be addressed best by BT. Also, a patient's intellectual and emotional styles are important. For taciturn individuals or those with limited verbal skills, psychodynamic or cognitive therapy may be inappropriate because they heavily rely on verbal communication. Goal-oriented individuals or those who need more structure in a therapeutic setting, experience more stressors, or have poor coping skills may prefer cognitive or behavioral therapy.

The success of psychotherapy also depends on the patient-therapist match. The client must trust and feel comfortable with the clinician. Clinicians must be sensitive to and able to assess the special problems of older adults, and they must overcome their ageist beliefs and fears of aging if they are going to properly diagnosis and effectively treat older clients (Fry, 1986).

SUICIDE

For this cohort, suicide rates are higher among people over 65 years of age than for any other group in the U.S., with males over age 85 years showing the highest rates (National Center for Health Statistics, 1985). Some experts believe that suicide rates among elders are underestimated because they are easily confused with medical complications (e.g., Blazer, 1986). Because older adults are more likely to have chronic medical conditions, they have more opportunities to underdose or overdose on medication or disguise suicide as a medical accident.

Risk Factors for Suicide in Older Adults

Although suicide is more common in old age, some studies find that older adults report less suicidal ideation and make fewer unsuccessful suicide attempts. Yet they have a higher rate of completed suicides than younger adults do (Blazer et al., 1986). Limited evidence suggests that the biggest risk factors for suicide in older adults are physical illness and MDD, but other psychiatric conditions, history of alcohol or drug abuse, institutionalization, recent significant loss, and history of suicide attempts also are major risk factors (Koenig & Blazer, 1992b; Lapierre, Pronovost, Dube, & Delisle, 1992; Lyness, Conwell, & Nelson, 1992).

Detecting Suicidality

Detection of suicidal ideation is often the responsibility of a physician. As many as 75% of older suicide victims visit a physician shortly before their deaths (Murphy, 1988). Elders are less likely than younger persons to talk about their suicide intentions (Jervis & Boldt, 1980). Although intention to commit suicide may not be spoken of directly, the clinician should pay attention to and try to elicit both verbal and behavioral clues. Verbal clues could include comments such as, "People would be better off without me," or "There's no point in going on" (Osgood, 1985). Behavioral clues include giving away possessions, buying a gun, going to a doctor without any apparent physical ailment, and stockpiling pills. The clinician should also watch for potentially self-destructive behaviors such as refusing medications, not eating, or abusing alcohol or drugs (Osgood, 1985; Richardson, Lowenstein, & Weissberg, 1989).

A preliminary step in evaluating suicidality is to look for these signs of depression: changes in sleep, appetite, weight, and energy; crying episodes; hopelessness or helplessness; and social isolation. If these symptoms or other risk factors are apparent, such as painful, chronic, or debilitating illnesses, or even if the clinician simply is worried about the possibility of suicide, the clinician should ask about suicidal feelings and thoughts in a straightforward, systematic manner. Clinicians may fear that talking in a direct manner about suicide will encourage it; however, mental health practitioners have found that suicidal patients are often relieved to discuss their thoughts (Osgood, 1985, 1991). Direct questions should be asked, such as "Do you ever think that life isn't worth living?" or "Do you ever feel useless or that life is meaningless?" Evaluation of suicidal ideation should include questions about the thoughts, plans, intent, means, and availability of means. Examples of these sorts of questions are, "When you feel that your life isn't worth living, what goes through your mind?" (thoughts); "Have you ever thought of a plan to end your life?" (plans); "Were you serious about going through with it?" (intent); "What were you going to use to kill yourself?" (means); and "Do you possess or have access to the weapon (or drug, etc.)?" (availability) (Strasburger & Welpton, 1991).

Preventing Suicide

Once suicidality has been assessed, a suicide prevention strategy should be enacted. This may combine monitoring the patient's environment (e.g., removing potential suicide weapons), psychotherapy or pharmacotherapy, enlisting family members to increase social support, or treating associated substance abuse and medical conditions. Mental health care providers dealing with a suicidal patient usually take one or more preventive steps, including (a) making a contract with the patient, (b) informing family members of the risk, (c) voluntary hospitalization, or (d) involuntary hospitalization. Another important preventive step is treating associated substance abuse and medical conditions, which potentially reduces impulsive suicide (Osgood, 1991).

A verbal or written contract lowers the risk of impulsive suicide. In a verbal contract, the patient usually promises not to commit suicide and to call the clinician every time she or he has suicidal impulses. A written contract, which provides better protection for the clinician and possibly the client, typically includes steps to take when suicidal impulses arise and the phone numbers of whom to call. A sample contract is shown in Appendix 13.1.

Confidentiality must be broken in a psychotherapeutic or medical relationship if the patient is a danger to himself or herself. Family members can also monitor the patient's environment, removing guns or other weapons from the house or making sure the patient is not left alone. If risk is imminent or family members are not available, the clinician may suggest voluntary hospitalization.

If involuntary hospitalization is required, a number of steps must be taken, and these steps may depend on the patient's state of residence. Usually, the clinician or a family member of the patient must petition the local magistrate, who will then issue an order to police if probable cause is determined. The police then take custody of the patient and take him or her to a hospital for a clinical evaluation.

Prevention of suicide can begin before danger is imminent. Knowledge of suicide risk factors among older adults helps to target effective preventive strategies. Mood disorders and substance abuse are treatable risk factors, and early intervention may prevent suicidality. The involvement of friends and family members can help encourage an older person to seek treatment, provide social support, and alleviate loss-related suffering (Liptzin, 1991).

Protecting Against Malpractice Suits

The primary risk of liability regarding suicide is failure to recognize suicidality. Being aware of this possibility and taking necessary actions are essential; failure to do so may be considered a breach of the standard of care and could result in a "wrongful death" lawsuit (Strasburger & Welpton, 1991). Risk factors for suicide should be carefully assessed by obtaining a psychosocial, medical, and psychiatric history. Risks inherent in the treatment itself also need to be considered. These may include (but are not confined to) potential overdose, drug side effects, confusion following ECT, or failure to appropriately medicate patients (Blank, 1987). Failure to hospitalize and unwarranted hospitalization are also potential breaches.

The more careful, thorough, and well-documented the evaluation of the patient, the lower the potential for lawsuits in the event of suicide. Clinicians should keep careful notes of all pertinent information, including patient and family contacts, diagnostic information, treatment plans, and documentation of the clinician's treatment decision-making process (Strasburger & Welpton, 1991). Also important is explaining the uncertainty of any treatment to the patient and, if appropriate, the patient's family. Informed consent must be obtained before starting any treatment program. Severe depression may interfere with a person's ability to give informed consent. Exceptions to the requirement for informed consent are emergencies and the patient's voluntary waiver of the right to be informed.

If suicide does occur, maintaining an alliance with the victim's family may decrease risk of a lawsuit. Helping the family to deal with their loss by acknowledging regret, attending the funeral, and referring family members to psychotherapy can be important steps (Strasburger & Welpton, 1991).

Summary

The empirical evidence from recent epidemiological studies confirms that mood disorders are less common among older adults than other age groups. Nonetheless, mood disorders can present numerous serious problems for elders. This is particularly true if they are misdiagnosed or mistreated. Higher suicide rates among older adults also suggest that when mood disorders do occur in old age, they can be severe. Clinicians must be careful not to attribute symptoms to depression when the real problem may be physical illness or

302 PSYCHOLOGICAL DISORDERS

other age-related difficulties, yet they must also be careful not to dismiss depression as a normal part of aging. Accurate assessment of mood disorders in old age can be difficult due to a variety of confounding factors, but a well-founded understanding of the typical symptom manifestations, a thorough assessment, the use of age-calibrated diagnostic tools, and a complete medical, psychiatric, and family history can minimize these difficulties.

Many therapies are available for depression, but outcome studies with older adults are scarce. Psychotherapy appears to be effective for this age group, but it has not been extensively compared to pharmacotherapy or combination therapy. Moreover, physiological changes associated with aging can alter the timing and effectiveness of medications. Close monitoring of the patient and alertness to drug interactions are important.

Last, the clinician must be aware of the risk of suicide and the difficulties associated with detecting suicidality in elders. A straightforward discussion is the first step, and this may need to be followed by a series of preventive measures. A contract, particularly a written one, can help prevent impulsive suicide. Also, family and friends can be enlisted to help monitor the patient and possibly to participate directly in treatment.

Appendix 13.1
A Sample Antisuicide Contract

I, _____(patient's name), as part of my treatment program, agree to the following terms:

1. One of my major treatment goals is to live a long life with more pleasure and less unhappiness.
2. I understand that becoming suicidal stands in the way of achieving this goal, and I would like to overcome this tendency. Therefore, I agree to learn better ways to deal with my distress.
3. Because I understand that learning to deal with my distress will take time, I agree, in the meantime, not to kill myself between today and _____(proposed date).
4. If at any time I feel unable to resist suicidal impulses, I agree to call

   _____(name & number) or (phone number).

   If this person is unavailable, I agree to call

   _____(name & number)

   or

   to go directly to _____(hospital or agency & address).
5. My therapist, _____(name), agrees to work with me during therapy sessions to help me learn constructive alternatives to suicide and self-injurious behavior and to be available as much as is reasonable for crises.
6. I agree to abide by this agreement until it expires or until my therapist and I explicitly renegotiate it. I understand that it is renewable at or near _____ (date).

_____   _____
Signature   Date

_____   _____
Therapist's signature   Date

SOURCE: Adapted from Fremouw, de Perczel, and Ellis (1990). Copyright © 1990. All rights reserved. Reprinted by permission of Allyn & Bacon.

14

Anxiety Disorders

Jane E. Fisher
James P. Noll

In this chapter, we will examine the status of information on the assessment and treatment of anxiety disorders in older adults. Based on recent studies of the efficacy of interventions for anxiety disorders, there is considerable reason for optimism regarding the treatment of anxiety in the elderly. Although only a few empirical studies have examined the efficacy of psychological treatments of anxiety in the elderly, the data that are available are encouraging and suggest that interventions are as effective for the elderly as they are for younger adults.

Before reviewing assessment and treatment information, we will briefly review epidemiologic research on anxiety disorders in the elderly and discuss age-associated physiological and psychological changes that affect the course of anxiety in old age. When examining anxiety in the aged, it is important to consider the variable courses the disorder may have across the life span. Anxiety may develop for the first time in old age or it may have emerged earlier in life and continued into old age. If the onset occurred before old age,

AUTHORS' NOTE: Preparation of this chapter was supported in part by Grant R29 AG11241 from the National Institute on Aging.

consideration of the effects of aging on symptomatology becomes relevant. These age-associated influences have not been examined extensively by researchers, but where relevant data are available, they will be reviewed.

Epidemiology

Findings from epidemiologic studies of anxiety provide a varied picture of its prevalence among older adults. The study of anxiety in the aged and indeed, psychopathology and aging in general, is complicated by factors such as cohort effects, differential mortality, age-related differences in willingness to report symptoms, and selection biases associated with age. When considering lifetime prevalence rates, one would expect to find increasing prevalence of all disorders with age. In contrast, recent epidemiologic surveys have consistently found declining prevalence at later ages (Kessler et al., 1994; Robins & Regier, 1991) and highest prevalence rates in more recent cohorts. Although these studies are cross-sectional and therefore do not permit the determination of the influence of the methodological features mentioned, they do suggest the intriguing possibility that living into old age decreases an individual's vulnerability to developing anxiety. Longitudinal studies are needed to investigate the natural history of anxiety across the lifespan.

Although findings from epidemiologic studies have resulted in very different interpretations of the prevalence of anxiety in old age (e.g., see Fisher, Zeiss, & Carstensen, 1993; Hersen & Van Hasselt, 1992, for review), evidence suggests that anxiety is a serious problem for a significant number of older adults. A community survey in Kentucky found that 17% of elderly men and 21.5% of elderly women reported symptoms of anxiety severe enough to warrant intervention (Himmelfarb & Murrell, 1984). In contrast, Myers et al. (1984) reported on data obtained through the multisite epidemiologic catchment area (ECA). Prevalence rates over a 6-month period for simple phobias averaged 3.3% for males and 7.0% for females over age 65 years. The prevalence rates for agoraphobia averaged 1.6% for males and 3.0% for females over the age of 65 years. The prevalence rates for obsessive-compulsive disorder averaged 1.3% for males and 1.0% for females. No males met the diagnostic criteria for panic disorder. The prevalence rate for panic disorder in women over age 65 years averaged 0.2%. When compared with other age groups, the prevalence rates for all anxiety disorders within the ECA study were found to be lowest for the 65-plus group. The finding of cohort-associated decreases in anxiety disorder prevalence reported by Myers et al. (1984) is consistent with those recently reported by Kessler et al. (1994).

Another community survey (Wisocki, 1988) examining the prevalence of worrying in older adults ranging in age from 60 to 90 years found that 14%

of the elderly reported significant levels of worrying. This sample was obtained through senior centers and meal sites and therefore may not be representative of the general population of older adults; however, the findings are consistent with the rates found in several other studies (Blazer, George, & Hughes, 1991; Kessler et al., 1994; Myers et al., 1984).

The differences in prevalence rates reported in these studies may be due to the criteria used to identify affected individuals. As Gurian and Miner (1991, p. 31) report, anxiety tends to be a very common symptom among the elderly but an "uncommon syndrome." Studies using strict formal diagnostic criteria (e.g., *Diagnostic and Statistical Manual of Mental Disorders [DSM-IV];* American Psychiatric Association, 1994) to assign individuals to diagnostic classes may eliminate elderly individuals who present an atypical symptom picture. These individuals may experience anxiety symptoms severe enough to warrant intervention. At present we do not have enough information about the manifestation of anxiety in old age to allow us to draw firm conclusions about age-associated differences in symptomatology.

In general, the symptomatology of specific anxiety disorders does not appear to differ across adulthood. For example, a recent study found that elderly individuals with late-onset panic disorder did not experience significantly different symptoms during a panic attack when compared with adults with panic disorder whose onset occurred in early to middle adulthood (Raj, Corvea, & Dagon, 1993). Elderly individuals who developed panic disorder before age 60 tended to report higher rates of social phobia than late-onset panic patients. These early-onset patients also reported experiencing more compulsive symptoms and more headaches. Rates of depression were also higher for elderly individuals who began experiencing panic prior to age 60 years. Elderly individuals who first experienced panic in old age reported more shortness of breath, chest pains, and pressure during panic attacks than did early-onset elderly patients.

In considering generalized anxiety disorder (GAD), it appears that approximately 50% of elderly individuals (> 65 years) report they first began experiencing severe anxiety within the previous 5 years (Blazer et al., 1991). The remaining elderly individuals with GAD tended to report experiencing anxiety for a much greater duration.

Age-associated differences in health status and medication usage are arguably the most significant factors contributing to differences in the etiology of anxiety in old age. These factors will be reviewed in the discussion to follow.

Etiology of Anxiety

BIOLOGICAL FACTORS

Anxiety symptoms in older adults have been consistently found to be associated with medical illness (Heidrich, 1993; Himmelfarb & Murrell,

1984; Raj et al., 1993). The causal relationship between medical illness and anxiety is unclear, however. Anxiety and physical disorder may occur simultaneously, or one may precipitate the other. To date, the majority of studies of anxiety in old age have been cross-sectional, making it impossible to determine the causal relationship between the two factors. Still, their consistent covariation cannot be ignored. A recent study of elderly individuals with late-onset panic found that 54% experienced an acute medical stressor (e.g., surgery, diagnosis of cancer) shortly before the occurrence of their first panic attack (Raj et al., 1993). Although the sample of patients in this study was quite small ($n = 11$), the results point to the role of health-related stressors in the onset of panic. In these subjects, it is unclear whether the underlying physical illness contributed to the development of panic, the stress associated with physical illness increased the subjects' vulnerability to panic, or a combination of these was the causal factor.

In evaluating symptoms of anxiety in the medically ill, Wise and Rieck (1993) describe four diagnostic considerations that the clinician must make. These include (a) ruling out other psychiatric disorders that may be associated with anxiety, such as depression or delirium; (b) determination of whether the anxiety symptoms are secondary to the medical illness or are a medication side effect; (c) determination of the chronology of the medical illness and the anxiety symptoms; and (d) consideration of the anxiety symptoms as a normal response to the stress associated with being medically ill.

Evidence from several sources indicates that depression and anxiety share several characteristics in both their symptomatology and underlying neurochemistry. Given that the prevalence of depression in the medically ill is significantly higher than that of the general population (Rodin & Voshart, 1986), the differential diagnosis of anxiety and depression should be carefully considered.

Delirium also occurs frequently in medically ill patients (Lipowski, 1990) and is often accompanied by intense anxiety. Anxiety associated with delirium may be distinguished from an anxiety disorder by the features of disorganized thinking, thought disturbances (e.g., hallucinations and delusions), memory dysfunctions, disorientation, difficulties in attention and concentration, and a disturbance (e.g., reversal) of the sleep-wake cycle (Wise & Rieck, 1993).

CHRONIC ILLNESS AND ANXIETY

The high prevalence of chronic illness in older adults and the increased debility associated with acute illness increase the likelihood that anxiety may be secondary to a medical illness or a side effect of a medication.

Physical disorders that have been found to be accompanied by anxiety include metabolic conditions (e.g., hypoglycemia, anemia), endocrine conditions (e.g., hyperthyroidism, hypothyroidism, hyperadrenalism), cardiovascular conditions (e.g., ischemia, angina, congestive heart failure, myocardial infarction, dysrhythmia), neurological conditions (e.g., akathesia, postconcussion syndrome, seizure disorder), respiratory conditions (e.g., asthma, chronic obstructive pulmonary disease, pneumonia), excessive caffeine consumption, and withdrawal from alcohol and anxiolytics (Hersen, Van Hasselt, & Goreczny, 1993; Wise & Rieck, 1993).

Panic disorder has been associated particularly with mitral valve prolapse (Raj et al., 1993), Parkinson's disease (Raj et al., 1993; Stein, Heuser, Juncos, & Uhde, 1990) and chronic obstructive pulmonary disease (COPD; Karajgi, Rifkin, & Doddi, 1990; Raj et al., 1993; Yellowlees, Alpers, & Bowden, 1987). Studies of older adults with COPD have reported prevalence rates of panic disorder ranging from 8% (Karajgi et al., 1990) to 24% (Yellowlees et al., 1987). These findings suggest that COPD may be an etiologic factor for panic disorder in older adults. Vertigo has also been found to be associated with panic disorder in older adults (Raj et al., 1993). It is possible, however, that the dizziness associated with a panic attack was misdiagnosed as vertigo in these patients (Raj et al., 1993). Raj et al. note that because the vestibular system has been implicated in panic disorder, it is possible that the natural age-associated deterioration of this system causes severe dizziness, vertigo, and panic in older adults.

Phobias have been found to occur at higher prevalence rates in individuals with diabetes mellitus (Popkin, Callies, Lentz, Colon, & Sutherland, 1988), Parkinson's disease (Stein et al., 1990), and primary biliary cirrhosis when compared with the general population (Tarter, Hays, & Carra, 1988). The mechanisms underlying the development of phobic symptoms in these medical disorders have not been empirically established. Within diabetes mellitus, a classical conditioning model has been proposed wherein chronic autonomic instability and hypoglycemic syndromes are paired with environmental cues to produce phobic avoidance (Sheehan & Sheehan, 1982).

Within Parkinson's disease, the higher prevalence of social phobias has been explained by a dopaminergic dysregulation hypothesis. Dopaminergic deficits are purported to result in introversion and fear, leading to phobic avoidance of social situations (Stein et al., 1990).

Generalized anxiety disorder was found to occur at an extremely high rate (65%) in individuals with Graves disease (Trzepacz, McCue, Klein, & Levey, 1988) and in 10% of individuals with COPD (Anderson, Noyes, & Crowe, 1984) compared with a prevalence rate of 5.1% in the general population (Kessler et al., 1994).

DEMENTIA AND ANXIETY

The relationship between anxiety and dementia has not been adequately addressed by researchers. Several problems contribute to the difficulty in studying anxiety in those suffering from dementing disorders. First, there are no measures designed to assess anxiety in a cognitively impaired population. Most studies that have addressed anxiety in an elderly cognitively impaired population have inferred its presence from the high levels of agitation exhibited in this group. In the early stages of a progressive degenerative dementia such as Alzheimer's disease, assessment of emotional distress can be gathered through self-report (Teri & Keller, 1987), although this may be problematic (Nussbaum & Sauer, 1993). As verbal abilities are lost, it becomes necessary to infer such states from direct observation of patient behavior.

The development of anxiety in dementia patients seems highly likely given the challenges they confront in navigating through an increasingly confusing environment. Behavioral evidence of anxiety in dementia patients has been found in reports of caregivers (e.g., Fisher, Goy, Swingen, & Szymanski, 1994; Swearer, Drachman, O'Donnell, & Mitchell, 1988). Swearer et al. found that 63% of caregivers of dementia patients residing in the community surveyed reported that the patient exhibited one or more symptoms of anxiety, including general fearfulness, a fear of specific objects or events, restlessness, pacing, and appearing to worry over insignificant matters. Similarly, in a study of 42 dementia patients, nurses described all Alzheimer's disease patients residing in a nursing home who engaged in physically assaultive behaviors as appearing distressed when they were exhibiting aggressive behaviors toward others (Fisher et al., 1994). The physically aggressive behaviors were consistently described as being associated with an effort to escape from a stimulus (e.g., a nurse's request) or were associated with high levels of environmental stimulation.

Whereas the relationship between behavioral disturbances and factors such as cognitive impairment and functional status have been examined in dementia patients, the relationship between behavioral disturbances and emotional states such as anxiety has been ignored. Given that certain serious behavior problems, such as assaultive behavior, tend to occur when demands are placed on dementia patients to perform a task (e.g., during dressing and bathing) (Bridges-Parlet, Knopman, & Thompson, 1994), it would be informative to evaluate the extent to which anxiety contributes to the behavioral disturbance. A seemingly benign act on the part of the caregiver may appear quite threatening to the dementia patient whose cognitive abilities and coping resources are severely limited. Behavior problems, such as assaultive behavior, may function as efforts to escape from threatening situations. This relationship is supported by the finding that caregivers report that behavioral symptoms of anxiety tend to be significantly associated with angry outbursts (Swearer et al., 1988). Systematic observation of environmental stimuli associated with behavioral disturbances in dementia patients is needed. Attention should also be directed toward the development of methods for assessing emotional functioning in nonverbal patients.

MEDICATION

The elderly population's large consumption of prescription and nonprescription medications is an important factor in understanding anxiety in older adults. In particular, anticholinergic compounds, including antiparkinsonism medications, antidepressant medication, and antipsychotic medications, have been found to produce anxiety symptoms (Sifton, 1988).

PSYCHOLOGICAL FACTORS

Cognitive-behavioral theories of anxiety, in contrast to psychodynamically oriented theories, have been the most fruitful in informing the development of effective treatment strategies and will therefore be emphasized here. A brief discussion of psychodynamic approaches will be presented.

Psychodynamic theories. As with other theoretical approaches, anxiety in old age has not received much attention from psychodynamically oriented theorists. Freudian theorists have emphasized the role of anxiety-producing intrapsychic forces that threaten to escape conscious control (Verwoerdt, 1980). In old age, anxiety may also be associated with the anticipation of the loss of external resources and the subsequent helplessness or dependency. This anxiety, known as *secondary or depletion anxiety* (Verwoerdt, 1980), differs from anxiety that is the result of an overpowering influx of stimuli or anxiety that is the response to unacceptable impulses that occur across the life span. A review of the major databases (Medline, PsycLit) produced no empirical studies of this theory of anxiety in old age. Furthermore, there is little evidence that psychodynamically oriented theories have resulted in effective treatment methods for anxiety.

Cognitive-behavioral theories. Learning theorists have presented several explanations for the development of anxiety. *Two-stage theory* (Dollard & Miller, 1950) was the first learning theory to gain prominence. This theory posits that anxiety develops through a two-stage process. In the first stage, an individual experiences the pairing of a neutral stimulus with an aversive stimulus. Through respondent conditioning, the formerly neutral stimulus acquires anxiety-producing properties. Phobic avoidance of this now anxiety-arousing stimulus develops as the person seeks to avoid contact with it. The avoidance results in relief from anxiety and consequently, through negative reinforcement, becomes habitual. The idea that the avoidance of an aversive stimulus is reinforcing has been important for the development of exposure therapies. Although this theory is intuitively appealing, its explanatory power has been limited based on empirical tests. It has been found, for example, that fear continues after avoidance responses have stopped (Riccio & Sylvestri, 1973) and that some fears have been found to be acquired through modeling, with no direct pairing of the neutral and aversive stimulus experienced by the anxious individual (Rachman, 1977).

Cognitive theories of anxiety developed in an effort to redress the limitations of the two-factor theory. These theories focus on the role of cognitive events in the development and maintenance of anxiety. They assume that the expectancy of harm mediates anxiety responses, that these expectancies are learned, and that the intensity of anxiety is a function of the perception of the likelihood of danger.

Barlow (1988), in describing a cognitive model of panic, suggests that the physiological symptoms that accompany panic attacks become conditioned stimuli for future panic attacks. When these physiological symptoms occur, even in ordinary situations such as during physical exercise, the individual begins to anticipate a panic attack. The anticipatory anxiety associated with the causal attribution for the physical sensations intensifies the physiological response, and in spiraling fashion, the anxious cognitive and physiological reactions increase until an attack occurs. Cognitive therapy methods for reducing anxiety follow directly from this model.

Assessment

Anxiety in the elderly has several associated factors that must be considered during assessment (Hersen & Van Hasselt, 1992; Hersen et al., 1993). First, studies on anxiety in the elderly have rarely made the distinction between anxiety as a *syndrome* and anxiety as a *sign or symptom* (e.g., Barrios, 1988). Although the distinction between anxiety as a sign, symptom, or syndrome may initially sound trivial in the clinical treatment of anxiety in the elderly, this distinction ultimately determines the way in which clinicians conceptualize, assess, and treat anxiety (e.g., Mash, 1985). This distinction may be especially germane if the anxiety in the elderly is a function of physiological or biochemical factors (Hersen et al., 1993; Hussian, 1986). As mentioned earlier, several physiological or biochemical maladies can produce or simulate signs or symptoms of anxiety. Moreover, comorbidity of disease states may complicate the diagnostic picture. If anxiety signs or symptoms are present in the elderly, it may be difficult to determine whether the anxiety is a function of a known physical or biochemical abnormality or if the anxiety is an initial symptom of some unknown physical or biochemical abnormality (Hersen &

Van Hasselt, 1992). Second, as described in the previous section on epidemiology, the clinical picture of anxiety in the elderly may be dramatically different from that seen in a younger population. If the young and elderly do present different clinical pictures related to anxiety, then that may indicate a plausible reason for the widely varying estimates of the prevalence of anxiety in the elderly. Likewise, studies on the assessment of anxiety in the elderly may be unreliable due to an invalid nosological scheme for classifying anxiety disorders in the elderly (Hersen & Van Hasselt, 1992). Third, most scales that measure anxiety do not have published norms for the elderly (Hersen & Van Hasselt, 1992; Hussian, 1981; Sheikh, 1991). The lack of appropriate norms for the elderly or the inappropriate use of norms based on young subjects for the elderly may produce a high number of false positive or negative diagnoses (Hussian, 1981). Even when norms are provided by self-report measures of anxiety, the norms often aggregate the elderly into one class, ignoring research that indicates that anxiety may have different prevalence rates between the young old, middle old, and very old (Hersen & Van Hasselt, 1992; Shamoian, 1991). With these limitations considered, self-report, psychophysiological, and behavioral assessment measures will be reviewed in the next section.

SELF-REPORT MEASURES

As indicated in the previous section, many self-report measures of anxiety do not have norms for the elderly (Hersen & Van Hasselt, 1992; Hussian, 1981; Sheikh, 1991). In reviews of the most commonly used self-report indices for the assessment of anxiety, Sheikh (1991) and Hersen and Van Hasselt (1992) indicated that only a few commonly employed self-report measures for anxiety contain norms for the elderly. These scales are the Anxiety Status Inventory (ASI; Zung, 1971), Self-Rating Anxiety Scale (SAS; Zung, 1971), State-Trait Anxiety Inventory (STAI; Speilberger, Gorsuch, Lushene, Vagg, & Jacobs, 1983), and Hopkins Symptom Checklist (SCL-90; see Magni & DeLeo, 1984; Oxman, Barrett, Barrett, & Gerber, 1987). The STAI has been shown to have high internal consistency and predictive validity and adequate concurrent validity (Spielberger et al., 1983). The published norms aggregate the "elderly" into a 50-year-old to 69-year-old age bracket. Thus, the use of the STAI for the assessment of self-reported anxiety in individuals over 70 may be limited (Hersen & Van Hasselt, 1992; Sheikh, 1991). The ASI and SAS have been shown to have adequate reliability and predictive validity and may be adequate as a screening device for anxiety in the elderly (Hersen & Van Hasselt, 1992; Sheikh, 1991). Although the revised version of the SCL-90 (SCL-90-R) has been shown to have high internal consistency, test-retest reliability, and discriminant validity, geriatric norms are being developed and more research may be required (Hersen & Van Hasselt, 1992; Sheikh, 1991).

Another potential limitation of the currently available self-report measures involves their content validity. The domain of stimuli and conditions under which older adults may experience anxiety may differ from younger adults. Until empirical research examines whether such differences exist, the content validity of the available measures remains in question.

A recent study (Beck, Stanley, & Zebb, 1995) provides support for the use of the Penn State Worry Questionnaire (PSWQ; Meyer, Miller, Metzger, & Borkovec, 1990) with older adults. This study evaluated the psychometric properties of the PSWQ with data gathered from a sample of elderly individuals with generalized anxiety disorder and a normal control sample of elderly subjects. The PSWQ appeared internally consistent based on Cronbach's alphas of 0.887 and 0.803 for clinical and control samples, respectively. Factor analyses revealed a two-factor structure reflecting factors of worry and nonworry for both populations. The authors note that the factor structure of the PSWQ has been found to be unidimensional in younger samples. Evidence for the concurrent validity of the PSWQ was apparent in the significant correlations between the PSWQ and the STAI. Although these findings suggest that the PSWQ may be appropriate for use with older adults, further evidence of the discriminant validity of this measure is needed before conclusions regarding construct validity can be drawn. In interpreting the findings from this study, the contribution of method variance should be considered, given the findings of high correlations between the PSWQ and other self-report measures, including the Beck Depression Inventory and STAI, and the low correlations between the PSWQ and clinician-rated worry severity.

PSYCHOPHYSIOLOGICAL MEASURES

Research on the physiological assessment of anxiety has often assumed a uniform and massive activation of arousal (Bernstein, Borkovec, & Coles, 1986). However, the idea of a uniform pattern of arousal has been supplanted by a complex pattern of arousal elicited by specific stimuli (e.g., Lacey, 1967). Because anxiety is no longer viewed as resulting from a uniform arousal process, the physiological measurement of anxiety becomes more difficult because of low (but largely untested) reliability (Bernstein et al., 1986; Nietzel, Bernstein, & Russell, 1988). Moreover, a recent review found no studies specifically examining psychophysiological correlates of anxiety in the elderly (Hersen et al., 1993). There is some preliminary evidence, however, suggesting that the elderly may exhibit more reliable and consistent changes in blood pressure in response to stressors compared to the young (Ditto, Miller, & Maurice, 1987; Hersen et al., 1993; Robbins, Elias, & Schultz, 1990). Hersen et al. (1993) interpreted these results to indicate that blood pressure becomes more reactive with age due to baroreceptor sensitivity decreases. Furthermore, despite increased coping skills and decreased stressor exposure with age, anxiety is experienced, in part, due to increased cardio-vascular or physiological responding (Hersen et al., 1993). This interpretation also may partially explain the finding of the somatic presentation of anxiety in the elderly (Patterson, 1988; Wise & Rieck, 1993). If this is the case, then research on psychophysiological correlates of anxiety in the elderly is war-ranted, despite reluctance from clinicians to use physiological measurement technology (Nietzel et al., 1988).

BEHAVIORAL MEASURES

In a recent review of the assessment of anxiety in the elderly, Hersen et al. (1993) noted that most assessments of anxiety were conducted with self-report measures rather than through direct observation. Behavioral assessments of anxiety in the elderly have been conducted primarily in the context of treatment studies (Hersen et al., 1993). No studies have directly addressed the behavioral assessment of anxiety in the elderly. Moreover, the behavioral assessment of anxiety in the elderly will require systematization similar to that conducted with the behavioral assessment of anxiety in the young (Hersen et al., 1993). For example, behavioral avoidance tests, in which an individual is asked to approach a feared stimulus, have been modified for use with children (Bernstein et al., 1986; Nietzel et al., 1988). A large amount of research has revealed that behavioral avoidance tests with young individuals may be affected by social cues, the demands of the assessment situation, the communication of positive or negative consequences, and method variance (Nietzel et al., 1988). Future research may reveal whether similar factors affect the assessment of behavioral avoidance in the face of feared stimuli in the elderly.

Treatment

BEHAVIORAL TREATMENT

Many researchers have noted that successful behavioral treatments exist for the general population suffering from anxiety symptoms and disorders but that there is a paucity of research examining behavioral treatment efficacy for the elderly population (e.g., Hersen & Van Hasselt, 1992; Patterson, 1988). It may be that because the elderly often present anxiety in the form of bodily concerns (Patterson, 1988; Wise & Rieck, 1993) or because of comorbid medical disorders (Hersen et al., 1993), researchers may avoid the complex clinical picture of anxious elderly individuals, preferring the "pure" clinical picture of anxiety observed in younger subjects (Markovitz, 1993). In addition, perhaps due to the presentation of bodily concerns, pharmacotherapy has been the most commonly used treatment approach for reducing anxiety in elderly individuals (Patterson, 1988). Although anxiolytic medications have shown some benefit in anxiety reduction in the elderly (such as benzodiazepines) (Crook, 1985), serious side effects exist, such as hepatoxicity, drowsiness, gait disturbances, muscle weakness and incoordination, blurred vision, and depressed affect (Hersen & Van Hasselt, 1992; Salzman, 1990a). Moreover, because elderly individuals may be taking a variety of prescription and over-the-counter medications, the probability that drug interactions will occur is high, thereby increasing the potential for side effects (Hersen & Van Hasselt, 1992).

In light of the moderate efficacy of anxiolytic medications in the reduction of anxiety in elderly individuals and the potential for serious side effects, Hersen and Van Hasselt (1992, p. 628) asserted that behavioral treatments for anxiety in the elderly are "highly preferable and safer" relative to the administration of anxiolytic medications. Some studies of the behavioral treatment of anxiety in the elderly have demonstrated the efficacy of these methods (see Table 14.1). The behavioral treatment of anxiety in the elderly is in an incipient phase, however, and much more research is required before definitive statements concerning treatment efficacy can be made (Hersen & Van Hasselt, 1992). Although the behavioral treatment of anxiety in younger populations has been demonstrated (e.g., Barlow, 1988), the extrapolation of efficacious behavioral treatments to the elderly population is currently unclear because of the potential differential clinical picture of anxiety in the elderly.

Whereas Barlow's treatment package for anxiety (e.g., Barlow, 1988; Barlow & Craske, 1989; Craske, Barlow, & O'Leary, 1992) has proven to be effective for younger adults (Barlow, 1988), only a few recent preliminary studies support its efficacy with an elderly population (Stanley, Beck, Barron, & Wagner, 1994; Stanley, Beck, DeWitt, Deagle, & Zebb, 1994). Although the reader is referred to Barlow's treatment manuals (Barlow & Craske, 1989; Craske et al., 1992), the primary treatment components will be briefly discussed. For generalized anxiety disorder, Craske et al. (1992) suggested progressive muscle relaxation, cognitive therapy, problem-solving therapy, time management, goal setting, and exposure (the production of sensations associated with panic). For panic disorder with or without agoraphobia,

text continued on p. 320

Table 14.1 Behavioral Treatments for Anxiety in the Elderly

Author	Focus	Treatment	Outcome	Comments
Case Studies				
Garfinkel (1979)	A 75-year-old woman with complaints of chest tightness, choking, breathing difficulties, and increased anxiety in presence of strangers	Progressive muscle relaxation, visual imagery, anxiety hierarchy with systematic desensitization, and imaginal desensitization with in vivo exposure	Symptom-free after 5 months of treatment	Subject was resistant to baseline phase of systematic desensitization. As a result, social reinforcement was given during "talking time."
Rowan, Holburn, Walker, and Siddiqui (1984)	A 67-year-old woman with obsessive-compulsive disorder	In vivo exposure, modeling, fading, response prevention, social reinforcement and role playing	Improvement in Fear Questionnaire and Maudsley Obsessive Compulsive Inventory scores and results maintained at 6-month, 12-month, and 18-month follow-ups	The results may have been confounded because the subject was taking clomipramine and flurazepam (Hersen & Van Hasselt, 1992).
Thyer (1981)	A 70-year-old woman with dog phobia, agoraphobia, insomnia, and nightmares	Seven (7) sessions of in vivo exposure	Symptom free, walking dogs, and taking walks in neighborhood	Informal follow-up suggested results maintained
Haley (1983)	An 87-year-old "moderately demented" woman with anxiety in absence of family members	Relaxation training, reinforced with ice cream or wine for increase in time from calling out to family members, message board to indicate when family members would be back	Subject able to spend 50 minutes alone by end of treatment	

Reference	Subject	Treatment	Outcome
Garrison (1978)	A 65-year-old resident of a long-term facility experiencing agoraphobia	Stress management, including relaxation training, systematic desensitization, and meditation	Able to walk one mile from home at end of study; sustained results at 6-month and 12-month follow-ups

Single-Case Experimental Designs

Reference	Subject	Treatment	Outcome	
Junjinger and Ditto (1984)	A 65-year-old woman with obsessive-compulsive disorder, including checking behavior and obsessions concerning hurting others	A. Baseline for 6 days where nursing staff recorded checking behavior B1. Exposure with response prevention (10 sessions over 13 days) B2. B1 with verbal exposure involving exaggerated descriptions of injury with resulting consequences B3. B2 with staff probing subject if she had hurt anybody on a daily basis	Checking behavior near zero after B3 and results maintained at 7-month follow-up	
Woods and Britton (1985)	A 64-year-old woman with agoraphobia, fear of elevators, and fear of heights	Multiple baseline across settings (apartment and elevators), variant of systematic desensitization, social reinforcement	Fear ratings decreased over 5 to 6 months, family members indicated subject was leaving house more frequently	Fear of heights treated successfully after treatment
Turner, Hersen, Bellack, and Wells (1979)	A 66-year-old woman with compulsive behavior, including checking and contamination fears	ABABACA design with response prevention and flooding	Decreases to near zero in anxiety ratings and urges to check and wash after 7th phase; Beck Depression Inventory scores decreased	Moderate increase in anxiety ratings at follow-up

(continued)

Table 14.1 Continued

Author	Focus	Treatment	Outcome	Comments
Group Studies DeBerry (1982b)	Ten (10) anxious elderly women (69-84 years old)	Progressive relaxation and pseudorelaxation groups; both groups received a 10-week baseline with either relaxation or pseudorelaxation; relaxation group also received 10 weeks of home practice	Relaxation group improved more on anxiety measures, self-reported muscle tension, headaches, time to fall asleep, and midnight awakenings	Small number of subjects may limit generality
DeBerry (1982a)	Thirty-six (36) elderly women (65-75 years old) with anxiety, fatigue, insomnia, somatic concerns, and sadness	Subjects were randomly assigned to three groups: A—relaxation-meditation; B—relaxation-meditation with home practice; C—pseudotreatment control. All groups received 1-week baseline followed by 10 weekly 30-minute sessions	Groups A and B showed greater reductions in state anxiety compared to Group C. Group B showed the greatest reductions in anxiety ratings. No differences appeared between groups on Zung Depression measure	
DeBerry, Davis, and Reinhard (1989)	Fourteen (14) male and 18 female elderly subjects (65-75 years old) with anxiety, fatigue, tension, insomnia, somatic concerns, and sadness	Groups consisted of A—relaxation-meditation, B—cognitive restructuring, and C—pseudotreatment control	Significant differences appeared in state anxiety only for Group A	Attendance rates differed between groups

Study	Subjects	Treatment	Results	Comments
King and Barrowclough (1991)	Two (2) male and eight (8) female elderly subjects (66-78 years old) with panic, agoraphobia, or GAD	Treatment consisted of cognitive restructuring and a behavioral task (e.g., controlled breathing)	Ninety percent (90%) of subjects reported reductions in anxiety at 3-month to 6-month follow-up; 83% showed maintained improvement at follow-up on the Beck Anxiety Index, whereas 75% showed maintained improvement at follow-up on the Beck Depression Index	There was no control group. Subjects were on a variety of medications for the duration of the study
Scogin et al. (1992)	Fourteen (14) male and 55 female elderly subjects (mean age, 68 years old) with subjective anxiety or tension	Groups consisted of A—progressive muscle relaxation, B—imaginal relaxation, and C—control group	State anxiety was reduced after training but not at follow-up. No significant changes occurred in trait anxiety. No differences were found between progressive and imaginal relaxation.	

Barlow and Craske (1989) suggested breathing control exercises, progressive muscle relaxation, cognitive therapy, and exposure.

Barlow's treatment for anxiety involves exposure to a feared stimulus or situation. Research has shown, however, that the elderly may exhibit cognitive performance decrements under high arousal (Eisdorfer, 1968; Eisdorfer, Nowlin, & Wilkie, 1970; McCarthy, Katz, & Foa, 1991; Whitbourne, 1976). In the presence of high autonomic arousal and anxiety, cognitive performance may be impaired in that response rates may be decreased or that errors of omission may increase (Eisdorfer, 1968; McCarthy et al., 1991). In Barlow's treatment package, exposure may lead to high autonomic arousal and anxiety in the elderly, which in turn may lead to cognitive performance impairment and reduced learning ability. Thus, it may be beneficial to monitor the anxiety levels of the elderly during exposure. Exposure to exceedingly high levels of anxiety may have a detrimental effect on therapeutic outcome. Moreover, it may be beneficial to first teach anxiety management techniques, such as progressive muscle relaxation and breathing control exercises, before the introduction of exposure-based treatment to provide the elderly with skills to moderate anxiety during exposure (McCarthy et al., 1991).

In addition, some elderly persons may have difficulty with progressive muscle relaxation due to physical limitations such as arthritis (Scogin, Rickard, Keith, Wilson, & McElreath, 1992; Zeiss & Lewinsohn, 1986). Relaxation may also be limited with subjects with COPD due to difficulties in breathing (Scogin et al., 1992; Zeiss & Lewinsohn, 1986). In these cases, imaginal rather than progressive muscle relaxation training may be beneficial (Scogin et al., 1992).

SUPPORTIVE PSYCHOTHERAPY

Two recent studies (Stanley, Beck, Barron, & Wagner, 1994; Stanley, Beck, DeWitt, Deagle, & Zebb, 1994) have examined the efficacy of a nondirective supportive psychotherapy conducted in a group format for older adults with generalized anxiety disorder. The supportive psychotherapy focused on a 14-session group discussion of anxiety symptoms and experiences. Therapists encouraged participants to discuss their experiences and provide support for each other. Although participants were allowed to discuss strategies for coping with their anxiety, no specific skills were taught, and the therapist avoided providing differential reinforcement for any particular coping strategy.

The effectiveness of the supportive psychotherapy was compared with cognitive-behavior therapy (CBT), which was also conducted in a group format. The CBT included three components: progressive deep muscle relaxation, cognitive restructuring, and graduated exposure to anxiety-producing situations. Results indicated that both CBT and supportive psychotherapy were effective in reducing symptoms of GAD. CBT appeared to have produced a greater reduction in specific fears. Stanley, Beck, DeWitt, et al. (1994) note that further research with larger samples and long-term follow-up is necessary to adequately evaluate the differential effects of these interventions.

PSYCHOPHARMACOLOGICAL TREATMENT

Pharmacological agents are frequently used in the treatment of anxiety (Patterson, 1988). This is in large part due to the fact that recent cohorts of older adults are inclined to report anxiety symptoms to medical doctors. Furthermore, there is evidence that pharmacological intervention rather than psychotherapy is more frequently prescribed for older adults than for younger adults or children (Cohen & Eisdorfer, 1985).

Special considerations are required for the general use of pharmacological agents with the elderly experiencing anxiety (Markovitz, 1993; also see Chapter 22, this volume). First, medication absorption may be variable in the elderly due to elevations in levels of gastric acid. Second, the duration of time a medication is present in an elderly person's system may be reduced because the individual may have more difficulty metabolizing medications. Moreover, due to decreased liver blood flow, smaller amounts of medication may be entering the elderly person's system (thus, the half-life of the medication may be affected). Third, coexisting medical disorders may affect anxiolytic action with the elderly. Moreover, the medication used to treat the medical illness may interact with anxiolytic medication.

The benzodiazepines are the most commonly prescribed drugs in the treatment of anxiety (Markovitz, 1993; Stoudemire & Moran, 1993; Swartz et al., 1991) and have been prescribed for up to 50% of the elderly experiencing anxiety (Salzman, 1991b). However, there are several side effects and considerations in the use of benzodiazepines as an anxiolytic agent for the elderly. First, as indicated, the elderly may have decreased liver blood flow that may lead to decreased benzodiazepine metabolism and elimination. As a result, benzodiazepine metabolites may accumulate (Markovitz, 1993; Stoudemire & Moran, 1993). Thus, benzodiazepines that are conjugated (i.e., lorazepam, temazepam, and oxazepam) and more easily metabolized have been recommended for use with the elderly (Markovitz, 1993; Stoudemire & Moran, 1993). Second, high-potency benzodiazepines may produce an exaggerated response in the elderly and, therefore, low-potency benzodiazepines are recommended (Markovitz, 1993). Third, there are several side effects that may affect the elderly, such as memory disturbances, disorientation, drowsiness, and gait disturbances that may lead to falls (Markovitz, 1993; Stoudemire & Moran, 1993).

Buspirone is a relatively new anxiolytic medication that appears promising for reducing anxiety in the elderly (Levine, Napoliello, & Domantay, 1989).

Buspirone may be especially useful for elderly with GAD (Stoudemire & Moran, 1993). Buspirone does not have the sedating effects, memory disturbance effects, and accumulating effects of the benzodiazepines (Stoudemire & Moran, 1993). Moreover, there is preliminary evidence that buspirone may be effective in reducing agitation in the demented elderly (Colenda, 1988). Given that very serious forms of agitation, such as physical assault, tend to occur during caregiving when demands are placed on a dementia patient, Buspirone may provide a means of reducing the anxiety associated with such situations without the negative side effects of other anxiolytic agents.

Beta-blockers may also be effective in reducing anxiety in the elderly, especially for the reduction of physical symptoms such as tremulousness, perspiration, and tachycardia (Markovitz, 1993). Like Buspirone, beta-blockers may be effective for the elderly experiencing GAD, although beta-blockers generally do not reduce marked fear or panic (Markovitz, 1993; Stoudemire & Moran, 1993). In addition, beta-blockers may be contraindicated for individuals with asthma, chronic obstructive pulmonary disease, and heart disease (Stoudemire & Moran, 1993). Beta-blockers may also have side effects such as insomnia, nightmares, and nocturnal hallucinations (Stoudemire & Moran, 1993).

Despite the appeal for the use of neuroleptics in the treatment of anxiety, this class of medication is not generally recommended for use with the elderly (Markovitz, 1993). Neuroleptics are primarily avoided because of the potential for tardive dyskinesia. Other classes of anxiolytic drugs are recommended because of their efficacy and superior safety (Markovitz, 1993; Stoudemire & Moran, 1993). Neuroleptics have been used to treat anxiety and agitation associated with dementia, psychotic symptoms, delirium, or combinations of these.

Tricyclic antidepressants have been used in the effective treatment of anxiety (Markovitz, 1993). The selection of the appropriate antidepressant is primarily based on relative side effects (see Stoudemire & Moran, 1993, for a comparison of side effects). Similar to neuroleptics, the use of antidepressants has been limited due to the frequency of associated side effects, such as sedation, anticholinergic effects, and orthostatic effects (Stoudemire & Moran, 1993). A new serotonin specific re-uptake inhibitor (SSRI), fluoxetine, has been introduced, however, that does not have the associated side effects, although the efficacy on reducing anxiety in the elderly has not been empirically established (Stoudemire & Moran, 1993). Fluoxetine was approved by the FDA in 1994. Information regarding the efficacy of SSRIs for treating anxiety in the elderly is not yet available.

Conclusions

The research reviewed in this chapter indicates that although anxiety occurs at significant rates in the elderly, the treatment of anxiety appears to be as effective as it is for younger adults. When unique considerations in assessment and treatment are necessary, they involve factors associated with medical conditions. Despite these medical complications, aging seems to have a beneficial effect on the symptomatology of anxiety. This benefit is evident in the very low prevalence and incidence rates of most anxiety disorders in old age.

Although old age naturally presents the challenges of physical and emotional losses that may seem overwhelming to the young, the ability to competently cope with these losses is indeed probably the most remarkable aspect of the relationship between aging and anxiety. Perhaps through the study of the means by which the majority of older adults rise to the challenges associated with aging, researchers will better inform the treatment of anxiety across the lifespan.

15

Alcoholism in the Older Population

Joseph G. Liberto
David W. Oslin
Paul E. Ruskin

Demographic trends and addiction profile studies increasingly make clear that alcohol use among older U.S. citizens will be a major health concern over the next several decades. Census estimates predict that the number of Americans aged 65 and over will grow from 30 million to 52 million by the year 2020 (Spencer, 1989).

The Epidemiologic Catchment Area (ECA) study (Myers, Goldman, Hingson, Scotch, & Mangione, 1984) reported that alcohol abuse and dependence is the most common psychiatric disorder among men. Among younger women, it is one of the five most common disorders. When the findings from the ECA study are coupled with the census estimates, the potential magnitude of the problem of future alcohol abuse and dependence among older U.S. citizens is staggering.

In this chapter, we review the literature on the epidemiology, physical consequences, and treatment of alcohol use and abuse among elderly persons. We also present recommendations for diagnosis and treatment of alcohol disorders. In this light, we discuss the limitations of the current research and directions for future research.

Epidemiology

STUDY LIMITATIONS

Characterization of the older alcohol user is the first step in understanding and treating older alcoholics. This task is complicated both by the lack of a clear definition of alcoholism in the older population and by the questionable reliability of published data. No standard definition of alcoholism among older persons exists, and thus, criteria used to define alcoholism in younger populations are often applied to the elderly. In addition, whereas the fourth edition of the *Diagnostic and Statistical Manual of Mental Disorders (DSM-IV;* American Psychiatric Association, 1994) defines alcohol abuse and dependence as maladaptive patterns of alcohol use leading to significant impairment in social, occupational, or physical functioning, researchers often define alcoholism differently, making comparisons between studies difficult.

Alcohol use has also been measured using instruments such as the Diagnostic Interview Schedule (Robins, Helzer, Croughan, & Ratcliff, 1981), Mental Status Schedule (Spitzer et al., 1964), Structured Clinical Interview (Spitzer, Williams, Gibbons, & First, 1987), Michigan Alcohol Screening Test (Seltzer, 1971), SMAST (Pokorny, Miller, & Kaplan, 1972), Michigan Alcohol Screening Test, Geriatric Version (MAST-G; Blow et al., 1992) and CAGE (a mnemonic referring to four questions asked of patients regarding alcohol use) (Ewing, 1984). In addition, several nonstandardized surveys, scales, and structured interviews emphasize what individual authors view as the most important diagnostic parameters of alcoholism. Most of these instruments rely on young men as a reference group and do not account for issues such as retirement, death of peers, changes in physical limitations, and lost income, which can be prominent issues in the elderly.

Given this lack of a clear definition of alcohol abuse, it is not surprising that most authors appraise the severity of alcohol use by measuring the quantity and frequency of alcohol consumed over a defined time period. Yet quantity and frequency data give no indication of how alcohol is affecting patients dynamically, socially, or physiologically. The clinical interview is important in recognizing and understanding how alcohol use affects an individual. Family members and friends are also invaluable sources of information regarding someone's use of alcohol.

The second problem in the characterization of the older alcohol user involves the reliability of the data. All the studies reviewed here used self-reporting as the major method of obtaining data on the pattern of alcohol use. Self-reporting, however, probably underestimates alcohol use and abuse, given that denial plays such a prominent role in the pathology of alcoholism. Also, the ability to remember past events or report past average consumption may deteriorate with age and with longstanding use or abuse of alcohol (Graham, 1986). Nevertheless, even with the problems that exist, several clinically useful findings consistently emerge from epidemiologic studies.

PREVALENCE

Community-Based Cross-Sectional Studies

Community sample studies using a cross-sectional design have provided data important in defining the extent and nature of alcohol use in the older population. These studies typically report the percentages of abstainers, heavy drinkers, and daily drinkers. Abstention and daily drinking are the most clearly defined patterns of alcohol use. As shown in Table 15.1, in the studies reviewed, abstention ranges from 31% to 58% and daily drinking ranges from 10% to 22% in samples of older patients (Barnes, 1979; Calahan & Cisin, 1968; Douglass, Schuster, & McClelland, 1988; Fillmore, 1987; Goodwin et al., 1987; Herd, 1990; Knupfer, Fink, Clark, & Goffman, 1963; Knupfer & Room, 1964; Molgaard, Nakamura, Stanford, Peddecord, & Morton, 1990; Mulford, 1964; Myers, Goldman, Hingson, Scotch, & Mangione, 1981; Rathbone-McCuan, Lohn, Levenson, & Hsu, 1976; Schoenborn & Cohen, 1986; Siassi, Crocetti, & Spiro, 1973; Smart & Adlaf, 1988; Sulsky, Jacques, Otradovec, Hartz, & Russell, 1990; Wechsler, Demone, & Gottlieb, 1978; Werch, 1989).

Many of the studies reviewed used *heavy drinking* to identify alcohol abusers and can be divided into three groups based on the definition of heavy drinking. The first group, consisting of four studies, used a minimum consumption of 5 to 7 drinks per week. The percentage of elderly heavy drinkers was higher in these studies, with a range of 11% to 25% (Siassi et al., 1973; Smart & Adlaf, 1988; Sulsky et al., 1990; Werch, 1989). The second group consisted of three studies that had a higher threshold for heavy drinking and defined it as a minimum of 12 to 21 drinks per week (Goodwin et al., 1987; Molgard et al., 1990; Schoenborn & Cohen, 1986). This more stringent definition yielded lower rates (7% to 8%) of heavy drinkers in the older population. The third group of six studies used a quantity-frequency measure that incorporated levels of drinking similar to those reported in the second group (Barnes, 1979; Calahan & Cisin, 1968; Knupfer et al., 1963; Knupfer & Room, 1964; Wechsler et al., 1978). In these studies, heavy drinkers

Table 15.1 Characteristics and Findings Related to Alcohol Use of Selected Cross-sectional Studies of Community Samples of Older Persons

Authors	Study Year	Age Range of the Sample in Years	Sample Size	Percentage of Abstainers			Percentage of Daily Drinkers
				Male	Female	Total	
Knupfer, Fink, Clark, & Goffman	1960	≥60	104	38	39	38	
Knupfer & Room	1962	≥60	280	32	48	41	
Mulford	1963	≥55	1,501[a]			41	
Calahan & Cisin	1964-1965	≥60	624	35	56	49[b]	
Fillmore	1964	≥60	251	34			
Siassi, Crocetti, & Spiro	1968	≥60	59	46	77	58[b]	
Wechsler, Demone, & Gottlieb	1975	≥65	158	22	37	32[b]	
Barnes	1975	≥60	237	24	36	31	
Rathbone-McCuan, Lohn, Levenson, & Hsu	1976	≥55	220	40	21	33	
Smart & Adlaf[c]	1976-1977	≥60	617			43	10
Myers, Goldman, Hingson, Scotch, & Mangione	1977	≥	928			53	22
Fillmore	1979	≥60	142	42			
Goodwin et al.	1981	≥65	270	43[b]	59[b]	52[b]	
Smart & Adlaf[c]	1982-1984	≥60	400			35	14
Schoenborn & Cohen	1983	65 to 74	NR[f]			57[b]	
Herd	1984	≥60	145[d]	60			
Herd	1984	≥	187[e]	41			
Douglass, Schuster, & McClelland	1985	≥60	207			42	17
Werch	1987	≥60	30			37[b]	
Molgaard, Nakamura, Stanford, Peddecord, & Morton	1990	≥65	955			43[b]	
Sulsky, Jacques, Otradovec, Hartz, & Russell	1990	≥60	57				

a. The sample size reflects all ages, not just those aged 65 years and older.
b. Data were calculated from the published information, not reported directly.
c. This study was done in Canada.
d. African Americans only.
e. European Americans only.
f. Not reported.

represented 3% to 9% of the samples studied. As expected, studies that used more stringent criteria for heavy drinking found smaller proportions of heavy drinkers than studies that used less stringent criteria.

These cross-sectional studies reported quantity and frequency measures and failed to give clinical information about alcohol abuse and dependence. Alcohol abuse, as defined clinically, has been studied in only a few community samples; a rate of 2.2% was found among all elderly persons in general and a rate of 9.6% in a sample of older men (Bailey, Haberman, & Alksne, 1964).

The ECA study, an important and extensive epidemiologic study, reported psychiatric diagnoses in a random community cohort in five communities: New Haven, Connecticut; Baltimore, Maryland; Durham, North Carolina; Los Angeles, California; and Saint Louis, Missouri. Using the Diagnostic Interview Schedule to determine prevalence rates for psychiatric diagnoses as defined by the third edition of the *Diagnostic and Statistical Manual of Mental Disorders (DSM-III)*, the study found the 1-month and 1-year prevalence rates of alcohol abuse and dependence to be 1.9% and 3.1% for elderly men and 0.4% and 0.46% for elderly women, respectively (Helzer, Burnam, & McEvoy 1991; Myers et al., 1984).

These prevalence rates are considerably lower than the drinking rates shown in Table 15.1. The fact that the *DSM-III* definition of alcohol abuse or dependence is more rigorous than the broader concept of heavy drinking may account for the difference between the ECA data and other studies. In the ECA data, only 49% of the heavy or problem drinkers were considered to be dependent on or abusing alcohol (Helzer et al., 1991; Myers et al., 1984).

Several articles have addressed both cultural and demographic differences among elderly alcohol users. As is clear from Table 15.1 and other reports, numerous studies have shown that the prevalence of alcohol use and alcohol-related problems in elderly persons is much lower for women than for men (Calahan & Cisin, 1968; Douglass et al., 1988; Goodwin et al., 1987; Harford & Mills, 1978; Helzer et al., 1991; Sulsky et al., 1990; Wechsler, 1978). Conclusions are less clear from the few studies addressing differences among various ethnic groups. Two studies reported little to no difference in alcohol use between elderly African Americans and Caucasian Americans or among African Americans, Hispanics, and Caucasian Americans (Borgatta, Montgomery, & Borgatta, 1982; Molgaard et al., 1990). In a sample of African American and Caucasian American men, Herd (1990) classified 60% of the African American men over age 60 as abstainers compared to 41% of the Caucasian American men in this age group; higher rates of drinking were found for Caucasian American men. These differences in patterns of drinking between races remained relatively constant even after controlling for income. The ECA data also demonstrate differences in the 1-month diagnosis of alcohol abuse and dependence between African Americans (0.82% among males, 0.34% among females) and Caucasian Americans (1.74% among males and 0.42% among females) (Helzer et al., 1991).

Income has been examined as a potential risk factor for alcohol abuse among elderly persons. In several studies, lower-income elderly consumed less alcohol and had higher abstention rates than higher-income elderly (Borgatta et al., 1982; Douglass et al., 1988; Dunham, 1981; Glynn, Bouchard, LoCastro, & Laird, 1985). Borgatta et al. (1982) found the relationship between greater frequency of drinking and increased income to be strongest among subjects aged 65 years and older. The ECA data, however, revealed that for elderly employed men, the higher the current income, the lower the 1-year prevalence for alcoholism (Helzer, 1991). Thus, the percentage of those drinking alcohol may increase with income, whereas alcohol abuse or dependence may decrease, especially among men.

Few studies have looked at the effects of marital status and employment on alcohol use among elderly persons, and findings from these studies have been inconclusive. Dunham (Glynn et al., 1985), in a population of low-income elderly persons in Florida, found a much higher rate of abstention in married subjects compared with divorced, widowed, or never married subjects. However, Barnes (1979), in a community study in New York State, and Sulsky et al. (1990), in a study of noninstitutionalized elderly persons, reported no significant differences in abstention rates between married and nonmarried elderly groups.

Sulsky et al. (1990) noted no significant differences in abstention rates between people who were employed or unemployed. In contrast, Barnes (1979) found that among those aged 60 years and older, unemployed subjects were less likely to be abstainers but were only half as likely as employed subjects to drink heavily.

Hospitalized and Outpatient Populations

Several investigators have examined point prevalence rates of alcoholism in elderly hospital-based samples (Curtis, Millman, Joseph, Charles, & Bajwa, 1986; Gaitz & Baer, 1971; McCusker, Cherubin, & Zimberg, 1971; Simon, Epstein, & Reynolds, 1968). As shown in Table 15.2, the point prevalence of alcohol problems has been found to be markedly higher in hospital populations than in community populations (Buchsbaum, Buchanan, Lawton, & Schnoll, 1991; Curtis et al., 1986; Gaitz & Baer, 1971; Iber, 1990; Magruder-Habib, Saltz, & Barron, 1986; McCusker et al., 1971; Puryear, Lovitt, & Miller, 1991; Simon et al., 1968). The prevalence rates for hospital populations range from 20% to 50%, with even higher rates for men. Reports have also suggested high rates of alcoholism in elderly patients in outpatient

Table 15.2 Characteristics and Findings Related to Alcohol Use From Selected Studies of Hospital and Outpatient Samples of Older Persons

Authors	Study Year	Ages of Sample in Years	Sample Size	Percentage with "Alcoholism"			Definition of Alcoholism
				Male	Female	Total	
Hospital Studies							
Simon, Epstein, & Reynolds	1959	≥60	534			23	Clinician's diagnosis
Gaitz & Baer	1971	≥60	100			44	*DSM-III* guidelines
McCusker, Cherubin, & Zimberg	1971	50 to 69	36	63	35	50[a]	6-point rating scale
Curtis, Millman, Joseph, Charles, & Bajwa	1986	≥50	117	29[a]	5[a]	20[a]	*DSM-III*, abuse and dependence
Outpatient Studies							
Magruder-Habib, Saltz, & Barron	1986	>65	59			10.2	Veterans Alcohol Screening Test
Puryear, Lovitt, & Miller	1986	≥65	118			12	*DSM-III-R*, abuse and dependence
Iber	1988	≥60	311			6	More than 50 grams per day of alcohol
Buchsbaum, Buchanan, Lawton, & Schnoll	1989	≥60	105			5	*DSM-III*, abuse and dependence

a. Data were calculated from information given in the article, not reported directly.

settings (Buchsbaum et al., 1991; Iber, 1990; Magruder-Habib et al., 1986; Puryear et al., 1991). In a recent study by Buchsbaum et al. (1991), 105 people between the ages of 60 and 80 years who sought care in an urban primary care medicine clinic were interviewed about alcohol consumption. Both the lifetime and point prevalence of alcohol abuse and dependence were determined using *DSM-III* criteria. The lifetime prevalence was found to be 22%, whereas the point prevalence was 5%. The high prevalence of alcohol-related problems in hospital and outpatient populations underscores the need for thorough screening and treatment of older patients.

To review, cross-sectional studies yielded the following conclusions:

Elderly men drink larger amounts of alcohol and drink more often than elderly women.

No definitive relationship exists between race and alcohol use. Studies, however, have suggested higher rates of light drinking among Caucasian Americans than nonwhites and little difference in heavy drinking between these groups.

Lower income elderly persons consume less alcohol than higher income populations. Hospitalized and outpatient populations have much higher prevalence rates of alcoholism than community-based samples.

ALCOHOL USE AS A FUNCTION OF AGE

Cross-Sectional Studies

Most cross-sectional studies have shown considerably lower rates of alcohol use and higher abstention rates in elderly populations than in younger populations (Barnes, 1979; Cahalan & Cisin, 1968; Curtis, Geller, Stokes, Levine, & Moore, 1989; Fillmore, 1987; Helzer et al., 1991; Herd, 1990; Knupfer et al., 1963; Knupfer & Room, 1964; Mulford, 1964; Schoenborn & Cohen, 1986; Smart & Adlaf, 1988; Wechsler et al., 1978). Smart and Adlaf (1988) found that elderly subjects were less likely to drink five or more drinks in one sitting than younger subjects. Glynn et al. (1985) showed that not only did the rates of heavy drinking decline with age but problems associated with drinking also decreased in older groups. The ECA data (Helzer et al., 1991) support these findings by showing a decrease with age in the 1-month, 1-year, and lifetime prevalence rates of alcohol abuse or dependence.

In addition, several studies have suggested that rates of abstention rise and rates of heavy consumption decrease for persons aged over 75 to 80 years, compared to those 60 to 75 years old (Douglass et al., 1988; Goodwin et al., 1987; Molgaard et al., 1990; Rathbone-McCuan et al., 1976; Schoenborn & Cohen, 1986; Sulsky et al., 1990). Harford and Mills (1978), however, reported that the average number of days per month that subjects drank increased with age. This pattern of more frequent light drinking is supported by the findings of Smart and Adlaf (1988), who noted an increase in daily drinking among elderly persons compared with younger age groups.

Several difficulties arise in interpreting these findings. Perhaps the biggest problem is the failure to account for generational changes. Thus, data may reflect social development or cohort effects. Comparing populations of the same birth cohort presumably helps overcome the bias introduced by generational changes. Mulford (1964) reported no difference in abstention rates between a sample of elderly persons (63 to 72 years old) studied in 1963 and a younger sample (46 to 55 years old) from the same birth cohort studied in 1946. In contrast, Fillmore (1987) reported an increase in the abstention rate from 26% to 43% in a study comparing people 50 to 59 years old in 1964 with people 65 to 75 years old in 1979. A decrease in heavy drinking from 19% to 6% was also found, as well as a decrease in alcohol-related problems from 2% to 1%.

Two studies examined drinking practices among elderly people based on self-reported current and past alcohol use. Knupfer et al. (1963) found that most of the elderly stated that their alcohol use was slightly less at the time of the study than in previous years. Molgaard et al. (1990) questioned respondents about their alcohol use before and after the age of 40 years. They found that elderly patients reported no major changes in abstinence or severe drinking between early-life alcohol use and late-life use. The ECA study (Helzer et al., 1991) determined remission rates by comparing 1-year prevalence rates of alcohol abuse or dependence with lifetime rates of abuse or dependence. Remission rates of 77% in elderly men and 69% in elderly women were reported, suggesting that many patients with alcohol use disorders earlier in their life do not continue to abusively drink when they become older.

Although these studies, aimed at minimizing generational bias, suggest that drinking remains stable or decreases with age, the results are difficult to interpret because they fail to follow a set population in a longitudinal manner. Thus, bias may be introduced by biographical differences, social status, and personal and social development.

Longitudinal Studies

Natural history studies, examples of which are shown in Table 15.3, provide the most definitive way to determine the effects of aging on drinking patterns (Adams, Garry, Rhyne, Hunt, & Goodwin, 1990; Fillmore, 1987; Glynn, Bouchard, LoCastro, & Hermos, 1986; Stall, 1986; Temple & Leino, 1989). Like the cross-sectional studies, most longitudinal studies show that men consistently drink more frequently and in greater quantities than women (Adams et al., 1990; Fillmore, 1987; Gordon & Kannel, 1983; Temple & Leino, 1989). In addition, most of the longitudinal studies have shown an increase in abstention rates with age (Fillmore, 1986; Stall, 1986; Temple & Leino, 1989).

The Framingham Study (Gordon & Kannel, 1983), in which 3,096 people were interviewed between 1950 and 1954 and then again 20 years later, provided the first extensive look at alcohol use in a longitudinal study. The principal finding was that the average consumption of alcohol increased slightly but significantly in the elderly population due to a rise in consumption that was especially high for women.

More recent studies, however, have not shown a rise in consumption as an individual ages. Fillmore (1987), for example, studied two different samples from the general population, one group in 1967 and 1974 and the other in 1969 and 1974. Among subjects who were 50 years and older at the time of the first interview, 63% to 74% of those who were drinking almost daily continued that pattern over the next 5 to 7 years. In contrast, only 5% to 21%

Table 15.3 Characteristics and Findings Related to Alcohol Use From Selected Longitudinal Studies of Older Persons

Authors	Year of First Interview	Follow-Up Period in Years	Age at First Interview	Sample Size at Follow-Up	Percentage of Completion	Mean Consumption (Number of Drinks)	
						First Interview	Follow-Up
Stall	1964	19	30 to 69	85	35		
Temple & Leino	1964	20	50	32	71	44/month	44/month
Temple & Leino	1967	20	50	39	68	59/month	51/month
Fillmore	1967	7	50 to 60	85	74		
Fillmore	1967	7	60	76	74		
Fillmore	1969	5	50	167	74		
Glynn, Bouchard, LoCastro, & Hermos	1973	9	50 to 59	523[b]	87[a]	418/year	
Glynn, Bouchard, LoCastro, & Hermos	1973	9	60	170[b]	74[a]	361/year	342/year
Adams, Garry, Rhyne, Hunt, & Goodwin	1980	7	60	124[b]	61	21 g/day	20 g/day
Adams, Garry, Rhyne, Hunt, & Goodwin	1980	7	60	146[c]	61	16 g/day	17 g/day

a. Data were collected from information given in the article not reported directly.
b. Men only
c. Women only

of heavy drinkers, those who drank more than five drinks per occasion, continued to drink heavily over the same time period.

Temple and Leino (1989) examined two samples from the general population of San Francisco residents in the mid-1960s and in 1985. Overall, the best predictor of alcohol consumption at the later age was the consumption rate at the initial interview. Persons in older age groups at the initial interview tended to reduce their consumption over the 20-year follow-up period, but the reduction was not statistically significant.

Stall (1986), in 1986, further attempted to explore changes in drinking patterns with age. In this study, 85 male respondents in a general household survey in San Francisco (ages 30 to 69 years in 1964) were reinterviewed 19 years later. Respondents reported overall stability in the frequency and quantity of drinking, with 60% of respondents reporting the same frequency of use and 64% reporting the same quantity of drinking. However, 79% of the moderate to heavy drinkers decreased their quantity of alcohol use over time.

Glynn et al. (1986) reported data on 1,570 men enrolled in the Normative Aging Study from 1973 to 1982. At both times, older men had a much lower mean alcohol consumption and many fewer alcohol-related problems than younger men. No longitudinal declines in alcohol consumption were found for any age group, however. Most men (53.5%) remained consistent in their consumption of alcohol. Those who changed their drinking habits were more likely to decrease alcohol consumption. Over the duration of the study, no change was found in the number of subjects identified with alcohol-related problems.

Most recently, Adams et al. (1990) reported the results of a study of 3-day diet records collected between 1980 and 1987 for 270 healthy, independent residents of Albuquerque aged 60 years and older. For subjects of both sexes who reported any alcohol use, a decline of about 2% per year was found. The most significant declines were among heavy drinkers, those who consumed 30 grams or more of alcohol per day. There was little tendency for heavy drinkers to stop drinking over the course of the study, however. Most participants remained in the same drinking class; for example, 90% of the nondrinkers remained abstinent after 7 years.

The most consistent findings in recent longitudinal studies are summarized as follows:

> Abstainers tend to remain abstinent, and alcohol consumption by light drinkers tends to remain stable with age.
> The alcohol consumption of heavy drinkers decreases over time.
> Men drink more often and in greater quantities than women.

Age of Onset

Droller (1964) reported different patterns of lifetime alcohol use in the elderly alcoholic population. Some patients started drinking excessively in their 20s or 30s and continued that pattern into their older years. Others, however, had their first alcohol-related problem at an older age. Recent reports suggest that the age at which alcohol-related problems first occur may have practical relevance for the disease course and ultimate treatment outcome of alcohol abuse and dependence.

Several authors have examined the age at which alcohol problems began. Studies looking at clinical populations have reported significant proportions of late-onset alcoholism among older alcoholics. Atkinson, Tolson, and Turner (1990) investigated 132 male veterans 60 years of age or older who had been admitted to a geriatric outpatient treatment program over a 5-year time period. *Age of onset* was determined as the earliest age at which one of several alcohol-related problems developed. Of the 132 cases, 38% were in the early-onset group (onset before age 41), 47% were in the midlife-onset group (onset between ages 41 and 59), and 15% had a late onset (onset after age 59). Schuckit and Miller (1975) reported that 11 of 20 alcoholics (55%) on a Veterans Affairs medical ward experienced the onset of drinking problems at 40 years or older. Three studies have examined patients in psychiatric populations and have found prevalence rates of late-onset alcoholism to be between 11% and 30% (Gaitz & Baer, 1971; Hubbard, Santos, & Santos, 1979; Simon et al., 1968). Studies examining patients in alcohol treatment programs have reported late-onset alcoholism prevalence rates between 11% and 61% (Adams & Waskel, 1991; Atkinson et al., 1990; Atkinson, Turner, Kofoed, & Tolson, 1985; Bahr, 1969; Hurt, Finlayson, Morse, & Davis, 1988; Schonfeld & Dupree, 1991; Wiens, Mensutik, Miller, & Schmitz, 1982).

Brennan and Moos (1991) reported on 1,884 men and women between the ages of 55 to 65 years who had recent contact with one of two large medical centers. Classification of problem drinking was based on responses to a 17-item Drinking Problem Index developed for elderly persons. Late-onset problem drinking was defined as having developed alcohol-related problems within the preceding 2 years rather than after a specified age. Because their definition of late onset is more in keeping with definitions of recent onset, it is possible that some early onset individuals would be defined as late-onset individuals by other authors. Nevertheless, all patients in this study identified as late onset had their first alcohol-related problem after the age of 53 years. Of those respondents classified as problem drinkers, 32% were characterized as late-onset alcoholics.

Only one study (Hurt et al., 1988) has explored age of onset based on the *DSM-III* diagnostic criteria of alcohol abuse and dependence. Hurt and associates reviewed the charts of 216 patients over the age of 65 years who were admitted to an inpatient alcohol treatment program with a *DSM-III* diagnosis of alcoholism. Patients were defined as early-onset alcoholics if they developed alcohol abuse or dependence prior to age 60. In this group of patients, early-onset alcoholism was present in 59% of the men and 51% of the women. Late-onset alcoholism was present in 39% of the men and 46% of the women.

There are few demographic differences between early-onset and late-onset drinkers with regard to age, marital status, employment, living situation, and education (Atkinson et al., 1985; Hurt et al., 1988; Schonfeld & Dupree, 1991). Significant gender differences reported by Hurt and associates and Brennan and Moos (1991) suggest that one third of late-onset problem drinkers were female compared to one quarter of the early-onset problem drinkers. Thus, for women, the incidence of late-life alcoholism may be higher than early-life alcoholism, but this will need further clarification.

Other studies report clinical differences that may affect the natural course and treatment outcome of the illness. When compared to late-onset alcoholics, early-onset alcoholics report alcohol use more frequently and in greater quantities (Brennan & Moos, 1991; Koewler, 1982; Mulford & Fitzgerald, 1992). Early-onset alcoholics are more likely to have been in alcohol treatment programs and to have used self-help groups (Atkinson et al., 1990; Hurt et al., 1988). Medical morbidity and mortality appear more severe in the early-onset group with early-onset patients having higher rates of physical symptoms, falling, delirium tremens, diabetes, cirrhosis, and fatty liver disease (Brennan & Moos, 1991; Hurt et al., 1988; Koewler, 1982; Schonfeld & Dupree, 1991).

Schonfeld and Dupree (1991) reviewed the records of 170 elderly alcoholics (aged 60 years and older) admitted to a day treatment program over a 10-year period. Subjects were categorized as having an early onset of alcohol-related problems if they were in alcohol treatment or reported problems before age 50. Of the 170 subjects, 58% were in the late-onset group, 28% in the early-onset group, and 14% were judged unable to classify. An assessment battery that included the Gerontology Alcohol Project Drinking Profile and the Social Support Network Inventory were then administered to a subsample of 46 subjects (two groups of 23 matched early-onset and late-onset patients). Subjects in the early-onset group were found to be intoxicated more frequently and to experience physical withdrawal symptoms more often than the late-onset subjects. Supporting the findings of Atkinson et al. (1990), early-onset patients experienced more severe emotional problems and were more likely to drop out of treatment, and the late-onset group was more stable emotionally and socially. It is interesting that collateral ratings from family members rated the late-onset subjects as having more severe drinking problems than the early-onset group.

Studies that examined age of onset of alcohol-related problems suggested the following conclusions:

About one third to one half of elderly alcohol abusers experience the onset of drinking late in life.

Early-onset drinkers have greater medical morbidity than late onset drinkers.

Although men have higher rates of alcoholism in all age groups, women comprise a greater percentage of late-onset alcoholics than early-onset alcoholics.

Comorbidity

PSYCHIATRIC ASPECTS

Alcohol research has demonstrated greater psychiatric comorbidity in alcoholic populations than in general populations. Weiss and Rosenberg

(1984), for example, found that 23% of 84 alcoholics met *DSM-III* criteria for an anxiety disorder, and Behar, Winokur, and Berg (1985) described an increase in affective disorders among recovering alcoholics. Although data suggest that these findings are also true for elderly alcoholics, relatively few studies have examined the specific types of psychiatric comorbidity in older populations.

Finlayson, Hurt, Davis, and Morse (1988), in a study of 216 alcoholics aged 65 years and older who were admitted to an alcoholism inpatient treatment program, concluded that many patients warranted dual diagnoses. Based on retrospective chart reviews and *DSM-III* criteria, the most common comorbid psychiatric diagnoses were tobacco dependence (67%), organic brain syndrome (25%), atypical organic brain syndrome (19%), affective disorder (12%), drug dependence (9%), and drug abuse (5%). It is interesting that less than 1% of the sample was diagnosed as having an anxiety disorder. It is likely that anxiety disorders are underrepresented because of the difficulty in retrospectively teasing apart symptoms of anxiety from symptoms of alcohol abuse.

Studies looking at samples with primary psychiatric diagnoses have reported findings of an association between affective disorders and alcohol abuse in the elderly. Speer and Bates (1992), for example, reviewed medical records of 128 patients aged 55 years and older admitted to an intensive residential psychiatric treatment program. Of those patients with comorbid substance use disorders, the most frequent configuration involved the three diagnoses of major depression, alcoholism, and personality disorder. In addition, Cook, Winokur, Garvey, and Beach (1991) found a past history of alcoholism to be a major risk factor for chronicity of depression assessed at a 4-year follow-up in a prospective study of 58 depressed psychiatric inpatients over age 55 years.

Community sample studies also suggest an association between affective disorders and alcoholism in the elderly, but the results are inconclusive. Blazer and Williams (1980) classified 4.5% of 997 persons over age 64 years surveyed as having alcohol abuse. Approximately one half of those with alcohol abuse had comorbid depression or dysphoria. In addition, Jinks and Raschko (1990) conducted a community survey of 1,668 persons over the age of 60 years. They reported that 9.6% of the sample had alcohol abuse and that approximately two thirds of the alcohol abusers had comorbid psychiatric illness. Psychiatric diagnoses included depression (2.7%), bipolar disorder (0.7%), dementia (1.9%), schizophrenia (0.5%), and anxiety disorder (0.2%). Palinkas, Wingard, and Barrett-Connor (1990), however, found no association between depression scores and alcohol consumption in a study of 1,617 community-residing elderly people.

Because high suicide rates are associated with both aging (Koenig & Blazer, 1992a) and alcohol use (Klatsky & Armstrong, 1993), it would seem likely that the older alcoholic would be at particular risk for suicide. However, Klatsky and Armstrong found only a weak association between alcohol use and suicide among people over age 50 years. The association was much stronger below age 50 years. Furthermore, Conwell et al. (1990) found that on autopsy, elderly people who had committed suicide were much less likely than middle-aged suicides to have alcohol in the blood. Of those aged 50 to 55 years, 36.5% had alcohol in the blood, compared to only 5.8% above age 74 years.

Cognitive changes associated with alcoholism deserve special attention because some authors question the existence of alcoholic dementia and speculate that cognitive changes seen in alcoholics represent a spectrum of Wernicke's-Korsakoff's syndrome (Tarter & Edwards, 1985). In a study by Goodwin et al. (1987) of a cohort of 270 elderly men and women, no relationships were found between average or total past alcohol consumption and performance on various cognitive tests. In fact, those who had been drinking recently performed better on the mental status exam, Halstead Category Test, and Wechsler Visual Memory Exam than recent abstainers. It should be noted that most of these patients were moderate consumers of alcohol, and all were healthy.

Grant, Adams, and Reed (1984) studied neuropsychologic changes in 204 patients who were either alcoholics who had been abstinent for several years (mean abstinence of 3.7 years), recently detoxified alcoholics, or nonalcoholics. Subjects who had obvious neurological or medical illnesses were excluded from the study. Among those over age 40 years, the alcoholics who had been abstinent for several years were indistinguishable from the nonalcoholic subjects in cognitive test performance.

In healthy elderly alcohol-using populations, therefore, no significant cognitive decline has been found. On the other hand, reviews by Ron (1977) and Tarter and Ryan (1983) concluded that long-term chronic alcoholics exhibit cognitive deficits in the areas of visuospatial, memory, and perceptual-motor function. Differences between these findings could be explained by the fact that the healthy population samples studied by Goodwin et al. (1987) and by Grant et al. (1984) excluded more severe chronic alcoholics and patients with a diagnosis of dementia who would have been more likely to show significant cognitive deficits. A second explanation may be that alcoholic dementia is secondary to nutritional deficits, and healthier populations may be less nutritionally deprived and thus less susceptible to the cognitive effects of chronic alcohol use.

In our experience, many patients who have a diagnosis of dementia have a past history of alcohol abuse suggesting that alcohol abuse is at least a cofactor in the development of dementia. The recognition and treatment of Wernicke's-Korsakoff's syndrome (Victor, 1993) is important because this is a potentially preventable complication of alcohol use that leads to cognitive impairment. Wernicke's—Korsakoff's syndrome is clinically characterized by cognitive deficits (especially antegrade memory deficits), gait apraxia, and nystagmus. The pathophysiology of Wernicke's-Korsakoff's syndrome involves the lack of the vitamin thiamine. Giving alcoholic patients thiamine supplementation early in treatment can potentially prevent the dementing process (Victor, 1993).

MEDICAL ASPECTS

The physical effects of alcohol on elderly persons make alcohol use much more of a general health concern than in a younger population. It takes less alcohol to produce harmful results in older individuals. As the body ages, there is a reduction in lean body mass and a reduction in the ratio of body water to total body mass, which results in higher blood alcohol concentrations for a given amount of alcohol (Morse, 1988). Higher blood alcohol concentrations coupled with increased breakdown of the blood-brain barrier and aging body systems that are less equipped to repair damage result in greater medical morbidity. An increased morbidity in the elderly heavy drinker is represented by an increased risk for major illness, poorer physical functional status, impaired ability to perform activities of daily living, and increased use of medical services (Colsher & Wallace, 1990). Data also strongly suggest higher total and cardiovascular mortality rates for heavy drinkers (Shaper, 1990).

Alcohol has also been shown to affect nutritional status (Sherlock, 1984). In a study by Jacques, Sulsky, Hartz, and Russell (1989), noninstitutionalized elderly subjects between the ages of 60 and 100 years who lived in the greater Boston area were interviewed twice; a record of their diet for the preceding 3 days was made at each interview. Perhaps because of the modest level of alcohol use by these subjects, no association was found between nutrient deficiencies and alcohol use. High-density lipoprotein (HDL) cholesterol demonstrated a strong positive relationship with alcohol intake, whereas low-density lipoprotein (LDL) cholesterol remained unchanged. Liver function stayed in the normal range, but aspartate aminotransferase and alanine aminotransferase were higher with increased alcohol intake.

Goodwin et al. (1987) reported similar findings in 270 healthy men and women over 65 years old. No association was detected between past or present alcohol intake and vitamin status, liver function, renal function, or immunologic function. A strong correlation emerged, however, between the amount of alcohol consumed and red blood cell mean corpuscular volume and HDL cholesterol. Although neither of these studies included debilitated elderly alcoholics, they do show the effects of alcohol on healthy elderly persons.

One of the most comprehensive analyses of the medical effects of alcoholism in the elderly population was done by Hurt et al. (1988). They retrospectively reviewed 216 patients aged 65 years and older who had been admitted to an inpatient alcoholism treatment program at the Mayo Clinic from 1972 through 1983. Prevalence rates of medical diagnoses were then compared with the National Interview Survey data. The most common problem observed was alcoholic liver disease. In addition, chronic obstructive pulmonary disease, peptic ulcer disease, and psoriasis were found much more frequently among elderly alcoholics than in the elderly population in general. Rates of hypertension and diabetes mellitus were not significantly different. Other authors (Tobias, Lippman, Pary, Oropilla, & Embrey, 1989) have noted that alcohol may influence or cause disorders such as myopathy, cerebrovascular disease, gastritis, diarrhea, pancreatitis, cardiomyopathy, sleep disorders, and both intentional and unintentional injuries. One author has suggested that health problems related to alcohol abuse may be the best way to identify elderly alcohol users (Graham, 1986). Obtaining a clinical history of substance use is critical in all patients and may be helpful in explaining an otherwise perplexing set of clinical signs and symptoms.

Detoxification

Managing alcohol withdrawal in elderly patients has not been well studied. Some reports in the literature suggest that elderly alcoholics are more likely than younger patients to have comorbid physical and cognitive disorders that complicate the course of the withdrawal (Hurt et al., 1988). Higher rates of mortality from delerium tremens has also been reported in older patients when compared to younger patients (Feuerlein & Reiser, 1986). Brower, Mudd, Blow, Young, and Hill (1994) recently reported results of a retrospective chart review comparing clinical aspects of inpatient alcohol detoxifications in 48 older alcoholics (aged 60 years and above) and 35 younger alcoholic patients (aged 21 to 35 years). In their sample, older alcoholics had been problem drinkers for 19.2 years compared with 10.5 years in younger alcoholics. Past history, however, did not reveal a difference in the previous number of hospitalizations for alcohol dependence. Older alcohlics were more likely to have cardiac disease and hypertension and macrocytosis. Overall, when compared to younger alcoholics, elderly alcoholics exhibited more withdrawal symptoms over a longer period of time. The older group was more likely to have cognitive impairment (50% versus 8%), weakness (48% versus 8%), and high blood pressure (88% versus 69%) and less likely to suffer from headaches (4% versus 33%). Withdrawal symptoms of hallucinations, seizures, tremors, and anxiety were not statistically significant between the two groups.

Treatment

Few works to date have examined the effects of different treatments on the elderly alcoholic. As with the epidemiological studies, problems with study design impede the progress of research in this area. No clear definition of alcoholism or of outcome exists, and outcome is difficult to measure. Most agree that a positive outcome would be abstinence or at least a reduction in alcohol use.

Alcohol use, however, is difficult to measure. Although the blood alcohol level can be attained and breath analysis and urine testing can be done, negative results cannot be interpreted as a lack of alcohol use because alcohol is eliminated relatively quickly from the body (Polich, Armor, & Braiker, 1981). Self-reports and collateral reports suffer from inaccuracies. Some authors use compliance with outpatient alcohol treatment to measure outcome, although it is unclear whether engagement in outpatient care makes a difference in a patient's ability to remain sober.

One alternative in measuring outcome that has not been well explored in the elderly population is to define positive outcome in terms of improvement in psychosocial function as measured by any of several parameters, such as those measured by a quality of life scale. Perhaps a combination of several of the outcome measures noted would prove to be most valid.

Not many treatment outcome studies for elderly alcoholics have been reported. Janik and Dunham (1983) pooled data from 550 treatment programs in a variety of settings supported by the National Institute on Alcohol Abuse and Alcoholism. They found few treatment outcome differences between younger populations and populations aged 60 years or older. In general, treatment was provided using groups in which patients of different ages interacted together in group settings.

In a follow-up study of 16 patients 60 years and older who completed a traditional 28-day behavioral treatment program, Carstensen, Rychtarik, and Prue (1985) found that 2 to 4 years later, eight patients were abstinent during the 6-month period before the time of the interview, two reported significantly modifying their drinking behavior, and six continued to drink abusively. Other studies have also demonstrated that the elderly are more responsive to treatment compared to younger alcoholics (Atkinson, Tolson, & Turner, 1993; Koewler, 1982; Mulford & Fitzgerald, 1992). Kofoed, Tolson, Atkinson, Toth, and Turner (1987) compared outpatient treatment compliance in two cohorts of patients 54 years of age and older; one cohort received traditional mixed-age group therapy and the other received treatment in groups where all members were at least 54 years of age. The 1-year treatment completion rate increased fourfold for patients treated in the elder-specific groups. An equal number of relapses occurred in the two groups, but the relapses in the elder-specific group occurred over a much greater time period.

In the only prospective randomized trial to date, Kashner et al. (1992) examined the utility of age-specific treatment of older alcoholics. This study randomized 137 veterans into either a program for older-age alcoholics or a mixed-age traditional treatment program. Patients in the older-age program incurred fewer medical costs and were 2.1 times more likely to report abstinence at 1-year follow-up. The key feature of the older-age program is that all the activities, including group therapy, are limited to patients over 60 or 65 years old. This potentially serves the goals of increasing peer socialization, expanding shrinking social networks, and placing patients with common goals and life experiences together.

Clinical Considerations

The data reported in this chapter highlight areas of special need in assessing and treating the older alcoholic. It is clear that alcoholism is underrecognized in elderly clinical populations (Curtis et al., 1989; Zimberg, 1987). Curtis and colleagues, for example, found that physicians caring for patients on a medical ward were less likely to diagnose alcoholism in older patients than in younger patients. Only 37% of patients over the age of 60 who had screened positive for alcoholism using the CAGE and Short Michigan Alcohol Screening Test were diagnosed as alcoholic compared with 60% of those under age 60.

Several factors contribute to failures in diagnosis of alcoholism in older populations. First, diagnostic criteria appropriate for identifying alcohol-related problems in younger populations do not always apply to the older population. Warning signals such as marital difficulties, problems with work, and DUI (driving under the influence) charges may not present themselves because the elderly are more likely to live alone, more likely to be unemployed, and less likely to drive (Miller & Rollnick, 1991). Second, symptoms of increased isolation, confusion, and other cognitive and affective changes related to alcohol use are often interpreted as normal processes of aging and thus ignored. Third, countertransference issues coupled with feelings of not wanting to take away an older person's "last pleasure" may set the stage for observer denial and powerful enabling activity by relatives, friends, and clinicians.

Because of the difficulties diagnosing alcoholism in older persons, clinicians need to be aware of several issues when assessing elderly patients. Direct inquiry regarding the frequency and quantity of alcohol use may be useful. It is important to remember, however, that total use may be underestimated due to denial and memory loss and that even small amounts of alcohol use may have significant biopsychosocial consequences. Obtaining collateral histories from family and friends is often very helpful. Recently, GMAST—a geriatric version of the Michigan Alcohol Screening Test—was developed and validated for the elderly (Blow et al., 1992). This instrument, found in the appendix at the end of the chapter, can be used by clinicians as a screening instrument for alcoholism in the elderly. Older patients endorsing five or more responses on the 18-item GMAST are considered as having a probable alcoholism diagnosis.

In addition, several medical and behavioral presentations should alert clinicians of possible alcohol-related problems in the elderly. The most common presentation can be remembered by the mnemonic *SIMPLE:*

S—Seizures

I—Injuries or falls

M—Malnutrition and muscle wasting

P—Poor hygiene and self-neglect

L—Liver function abnormalities

E—Emotional and cognitive changes, including lability, confusion, memory changes, and unusual behavior.

Such clues should serve as red flags and should indicate the need to take a thorough addiction history from older patients (Bartels & Liberto, 1995).

Once the diagnosis of alcoholism has been made, it is important to note that the older alcoholic often presents different treatment needs. Because there are few data on the comparative efficacy of different treatment models with older adults, the authors suggest practical considerations through the following case vignette.

Mr. L is a 67-year-old widowed male who came to his primary care physician's office accompanied by his daughter after having fallen the previous day. He stated that he had tripped and used his hands to brace his fall, but he was otherwise unable to describe the incident. Physical examination and X-ray studies revealed minor bruising and a sprained right wrist but no other major medical consequences.

Mr. L's daughter described a general and gradual deterioration of Mr. L's function over the past few years. She noted that her father had several problems with his balance as well as "periods where he doesn't seem to remember anything." She reported increased social isolation and timed the initial onset of his symptoms to his retirement 2 years ago. She tended to minimize all these observations, however, by stating, "I guess its not good to get old."

Mr. L's physician explored the patient's addiction history. Mr. L noted that he had always drunk "socially." He acknowledged that he had been drinking a "little more" recently, but he was clear that he didn't feel his alcohol use was a problem. The patient's daughter generally confirmed the patient's drinking history but qualified her answers by stating that she wasn't with him all the time. Furthermore, she did remember a few occasions when he had drunk larger quantities but stated,

"He seemed to enjoy it and he was handling it OK." Both the patient and daughter denied past addiction treatment history, use of self-help groups, legal difficulty, or use of illicit drugs.

The physician administered the GMAST and the patient endorsed seven items indicating probable alcoholism. Even after being confronted with this information, Mr. L downplayed the consequences of his alcohol use. Laboratory studies were drawn, brain imaging and an EEG were ordered, and the patient was scheduled for a follow-up visit.

At follow-up, it was found that Mr. L had elevated liver function tests consistent with a pattern of alcoholic liver disease. Studies to assess other medical reasons for Mr. L's mental status changes were essentially normal. Mr. L's daughter began to voice stronger concerns about Mr. L's recent behavior and cognitive decline. She further noted that the family had become more vigilant about Mr. L's alcohol consumption and stated that he was drinking larger quantities and more frequently than he originally admitted. With the help of his physician and at his daughter's and the family's insistence, Mr. L reluctantly agreed to an evaluation by an addiction specialist.

Mr. L exemplifies some of the difficulties we experience with elderly problem drinkers, especially those who are identified in later life. Despite increased medical comorbidity, cognitive decline, and growing concerns of family, Mr. L doesn't see himself as an alcoholic. Mr. L's family at first also rationalizes Mr. L's alcohol use and associated symptoms as normal processes of aging. It is not until the physician and the family "force" Mr. L into treatment that the patient reluctantly agrees to examine his alcohol use.

In patients such as Mr. L, we feel that early treatment efforts to break down denial are paramount. It is our experience that failure to do so usually results in patients leaving treatment when the factors that coerce them into treatment are no longer present. Because social networks are sometimes intact, especially in the late-onset alcoholic, we make every effort to engage family and significant others in participating in the patient's treatment plan. On the other hand, it is our belief that the initial treatment focus often needs to be different in early-onset patients when compared to late-onset patients. Early-onset patients tend to suffer a much more chronic and debilitating natural course as evidenced by more legal, medical, and financial problems related to their alcohol use. Issues of denial are not as paramount because early-onset patients, having dealt with a lifetime of trouble related to their addiction, can often accept to some degree that they have problems with alcohol use. Addressing these biopsychosocial concerns is perhaps the most important intervention in engaging early-onset patients in treatment. In addition, treatment intervention for early-onset patients usually needs to center on providing external psychosocial support because social networks are commonly fragmented.

As in the case of Mr. L, assessment starts with a thorough history being taken and physical and laboratory examinations to rule out other medical causes for the patient's symptoms. Once the diagnosis of alcohol abuse or dependence is made, the type of early treatment intervention needs to be decided. Although not specific to older alcoholics, the American Society of Addiction Medicine (ASAM) has established criteria for placing patients in various levels of treatment based on the severity of withdrawal potential, medical complications, emotional stability, and relapse potential (ASAM, 1992). Patients with high relapse or withdrawal potential and patients with severe medical or psychiatric comorbidity require inpatient hospitalization. Inpatient hospitalization helps break the cycle of addiction by temporarily removing patients from the environment in which they are using alcohol. In addition, inpatient hospitalization provides the opportunity to begin detoxification from alcohol under controlled conditions while attending to issues of medical and psychiatric comorbidity. We believe that older patients, especially those with diagnosed cardiovascular disease, require inpatient or very closely monitored outpatient detoxification because of their increased risk for medical complications during withdrawal (Feuerlein & Reiser, 1986; Hurt et al., 1988). We give patients thiamine, hydrate them as necessary, and regularly monitor vital signs and objective symptoms of withdrawal. Intermediate or long-acting benzodiazepines (i.e., chlordiazepoxide, oxazapam, and lorazepam) are used as cross-tolerant detoxification agents. The use of oxazepam or lorazepam is warrented in patients with severe liver disease because these benzodiazepines are not hydroxylated by the liver and thus will not accumulate (ASAM, 1992). The benzodiazepine dosage is decreased daily over the course of the detoxification.

In addition to detoxification and management of comorbid medical or psychiatric conditions, the inpatient program provides an opportunity for early engagement of patients in addiction treatment. Establishing contact with significant others who are concerned about the patient is very important because involved family members have been shown to be positively correlated with good treatment outcome in general addiction research studies (ASAM, 1992). Furthermore, educational groups and group therapy can provide patients with the basic tools to develop recovery skills that will be necessary if treatment is to be successful.

Patients with less withdrawal or relapse potential and with less severe psychiatric and medical comorbidity can be managed in outpatient settings. Structured outpatient treatment generally includes supportive group psychotherapy and encouragement to attend regular self-help group meetings such as Alcoholics Anonymous (AA) or Alcoholics Victorious. Although the benefit of peer-specific activities, including group therapy, has not been definitively proven, we believe that when available, these activities provide advantages not available in mixed-age treatment settings. Elder-specific groups are typically found in more specialized settings, such as at university medical centers or Veterans Administration medical centers. Recently, many AA groups have been formed that predominately or solely consist of elder members. Furthermore, we find that individual therapy aimed at processing the patient's late-life losses is often needed. Outpatient rehabilitation, in addition to focusing on active addiction issues, usually needs to address issues of leisure time management. Social services, especially financial support, are also often needed to stabilize the patient in early recovery. Supervised living arrangements, such as halfway houses, group homes, and living with relatives, should also be considered.

The use of medications to support abstinence may be of benefit but is not well studied. The general principles used in treating younger patients should be applied to older drinkers. Benzodiazepines are important in the treatment of alcohol detoxification but have no clinical place in maintaining long-term abstinence because of their abuse potential and the potential of fostering an alcohol relapse. Disulfiram may benefit some well-motivated patients, but cardiac and hepatic disease limits the use of this agent in the alcoholic elderly. Other agents such as lithium, antidepressants, and naltrexone have an as yet unproven efficacy, and at this time, their use should be limited to research trials. It is important that comorbid medical and psychiatric disorders be identified and properly treated and may necessitate the need for referral or consultation to a psychiatrist with expertise in these areas.

Discussion

A better understanding of alcoholism in older people is necessary to effectively identify people with alcohol-related problems and to address the social and medical consequences of alcohol use in a growing elderly population. Most studies reported to date focus on the epidemiology of the disease in the form of community-based cross-sectional studies aimed at identifying the extent and nature of alcohol use. Recent studies with a longitudinal design provide additional insight into the natural history of alcohol use in the elderly population.

Table 15.4 contrasts the major findings from cross-sectional and longitudinal research studies. The most consistent finding is that alcohol-related problems, as well as quantity and frequency of alcohol consumption, are significantly more prevalent in elderly men than in elderly women. In addition, cross-sectional studies clearly show decreased alcohol use and decreased alcohol-related problems in the older population compared to the younger population. Longitudinal studies show similar declines in alcohol-related problems and consumption among those who drink more often and in greater quantities. Unlike cross-sectional studies, however, longitudinal studies do not show these declines in subjects who are lighter drinkers.

Table 15.4   Comparison and Findings of Cross-Sectional and Longitudinal Studies of
Elderly Alcohol Users, by Major Variables

	Cross-Sectional Studies: Older Versus Younger Populations	*Longitudinal Studies*
Quantity of alcohol used	Less use in the older population	Recent studies show overall stability or slight decrease with age
Prevalence of abstainers	Higher in the older population	Higher with increasing age
Prevalence of heavy drinking	Lower in the older population	Lower with increasing age
Prevalence of alcohol abuse and dependence	Abuse is lower in the older population, but dependence remains stable	Not sufficiently studied
Gender differences in alcohol use	Men drink more frequently and in greater quantities than women	Men drink more frequently and in greater quantities than women
Patterns of drinking	Not sufficiently studied	Light drinking remains stable with age; heavy drinking decreases

NOTE: Cross-sectional studies compare older and younger populations; longitudinal studies compare the same group of subjects at two points in time.

The difference in findings between cross-sectional studies and longitudinal studies may be secondary to a cohort effect in the cross-sectional data. Another possibility is that the longitudinal studies conducted to date have been of insufficient duration to pick up changes in drinking patterns for lighter and intermittent drinkers. Further research will be needed to determine the natural history of alcohol use in lighter drinkers.

Research is beginning to address other aspects of alcohol use, including medical consequences, psychiatric comorbidity, and treatment. Unfortunately, the majority of our understanding of these processes for the older alcohol user is inferred from studies of younger populations. Elderly alcohol users, however, have unique features that differentiate them from younger subjects, such as a higher incidence of medical comorbidity and elder-specific psychosocial stressors. As highlighted by the case vignette, elderly patients often present medical problems to primary care physicians that are related to alcohol intake. The medical and psychiatric aspects of elderly alcoholism have been incorporated into the development of the MAST-G and the mnemonic "SIMPLE," which are valuable screening tools for the identification of elderly alcoholics. These unique features, in addition to the age of onset of alcohol-related problems, may have relevance to both the course of the disease and the outcome of treatment.

It seems reasonable, and at least one study suggests, that special elder-specific substance abuse programs are more beneficial for the older alcoholic

(Kashner et al., 1992). Substance abuse day treatment programs, providing structure to the isolated elderly alcoholic, may also prove effective. The benefits of disulfiram treatment, self-help groups, individual therapy, and family intervention need to be studied more fully with elderly alcoholics. Care providers need to be aware that older alcoholics do respond to treatment and may in fact respond better to treatment than younger patients. Therefore, proper identification of the problem and referral for treatment is critical.

Many unanswered questions about elderly alcohol users remain that need further elaboration to yield more treatment options and better outcomes. As described earlier, several limitations in study design make comparisons of data between studies difficult. Greater consensus on diagnostic criteria for alcoholism is needed in the research community, with clearer relationships between quantity and frequency of alcohol use and clinical definitions of abuse and dependence. Measures of alcohol use and of outcome that incorporate a combination of factors, such as self-reports, collateral reports, blood alcohol levels, random breath analyses, random urine testing, and psychosocial assessments, are desirable. And last, longer study lengths and more frequent follow-up periods are required in longitudinal studies, including prospective treatment outcome studies, to better our understanding of concepts such as binge use, relapse, and remission of alcohol abuse and dependence.

Abstract

Alcohol abuse and dependence in elderly persons is of growing social concern. Research in this area has focused on the epidemiology of the disease. The most consistent findings of cross-sectional and longitudinal studies are that the quantity and frequency of alcohol consumption is higher in elderly men than in elderly women, as is the prevalence of alcohol-related problems. Most studies show a decrease with age in consumption and alcohol-related problems among heavy drinkers. Longitudinal studies show no changes in consumption among light drinkers. Elderly persons with lower incomes consume less alcohol than those with higher incomes. Hospitalized and outpatient populations have more problem drinkers, and the elderly alcoholic is at greater risk for medical and psychiatric comorbidity. About one third to one half of elderly alcoholics experience the onset of problem drinking in middle or late life, and these individuals may present different needs than the lifelong problem drinker. Identification and treatment of the older-age alcoholic is critical to reducing medical and psychiatric comorbidity as well as psychosocial declines.

16

Urinary Incontinence

Kathryn Larsen Burgio
Julie L. Locher

Urinary incontinence is the involuntary loss of urine. It is a common condition affecting approximately 30% of older adults living in the community (Diokno, Brock, Brown, & Herzog, 1986) and over half of those who reside in nursing homes (Ouslander, Kane, & Abrass, 1982). Mild incontinence may be managed with only minor accommodations of lifestyle, but moderate or severe incontinence has more serious implications. It predisposes patients to other health problems (e.g., skin breakdown, urinary tract infections) and has negative consequences on the emotional and social well-being of its sufferers (Wyman, Harkins, & Fantl, 1990). It can adversely affect daily activities and interpersonal relationships, limit social activities, and contribute to both depression and anxiety in some individuals. Still, there is considerable variability in how individuals respond to incontinence, with some studies reporting little effect on measures of self-esteem and psychological well-being (Breakwell & Walker, 1988; Simons, 1985). Incontinence is a significant source of dependence among the elderly and a widely cited factor in nursing home admissions (Johnson & Werner, 1982). The costs of incontinence are enormous, accounting for more than 10 billion dollars per year in the United States (Hu, 1990).

Urinary incontinence is a multifaceted condition for which a variety of treatments have been developed, ranging from surgical to medical and behavioral. Although most cases of incontinence can be significantly improved or cured with the treatments available today, fewer than half of individuals with this problem are evaluated or treated (Burgio, Ives, Locher, Arena, & Kuller, 1994; Consensus Conference, 1989).

Even as treatments for incontinence are improved and made more available, barriers to treatment exist in the attitudes held by patients and health care providers. Because incontinence is socially unacceptable and can be embarrassing, many incontinent persons ignore or conceal the problem and avoid seeking help. Many of those who do seek help are encouraged to accept incontinence as a natural and inevitable consequence of advancing age or of childbearing. As a result, incontinence is often regarded as untreatable and patients are managed less than optimally. One study of U.S. nursing homes found that incontinence was mentioned infrequently in physicians' notes and that less than 5% of patients received a diagnostic evaluation (Ouslander et al., 1982). In another study of three nursing homes, incontinence was included in the medical problem list of less than 5% of the incontinent residents (Ribeiro & Smith, 1985).

Urinary incontinence affects individuals of every age, but it is most prevalent among the elderly. As a result, incontinence is commonly and mistakenly attributed to age. In fact, older adults are more likely to have conditions that predispose them to incontinence or contribute to the causes of incontinence. Many of these conditions may be controlled or avoided if properly identified. Urinary incontinence is not a normal aspect of aging nor is it irreversible. Elderly patients should be managed with the same effort afforded to younger patients with incontinence and with special attention to age-related deficits, such as impaired mobility, diminished vision, or deficits in mental status. Incontinence is a problem with many possible causes, each of which needs to be explored. Only through careful assessment can specific deficits be identified and rational treatment implemented.

This chapter describes behavioral approaches to the assessment and treatment of urinary incontinence with special attention to common causes of incontinence in the elderly. Behavioral interventions are especially relevant for the elderly for several reasons. Among the most compelling reasons for using behavioral treatment procedures is their effectiveness. Given proper training and adequate time, the great majority of appropriately selected patients experience significant improvement or cure. A second reason for using behavioral treatment with the elderly is the increased risk of surgery in these patients and the number of those with medical conditions that preclude surgery. Third is the fact that behavioral treatments avoid the side effects of medications for incontinence. The most widely used medications for incontinence often produce side effects such as mucous membrane dryness, constipation, confusion, drowsiness, urinary retention, blurry vision, or exacerbation of glaucoma, any of which can produce significant discomfort and lead to discontinuation of the drug.

Last, the 1988 National Institute of Health Consensus Conference on Urinary Incontinence in Adults concluded that "in general, the least invasive procedure should be tried first" and that "for many types of incontinence, behavioral treatments meet this criterion" (Concensus Conference, 1989, p. 2689). Behavioral procedures are efficient, low risk, and without documented side effects, making them an attractive treatment option for many older adults.

It should not be inferred from this that behavioral treatment will be the best solution for everyone. Sometimes, surgery or medication will be the best option. Management of incontinence should be based on the same principles as management of any medical disorder: All incontinent patients should first be evaluated, and the decision to intervene behaviorally should be reached concurrently by the physician and behavioral therapist.

Physiology of Urinary Incontinence

Normal micturition and urinary continence involve a complex set of physiological responses, described in depth by Bradley, Timm, and Scott (1974). As the bladder fills, stretch receptors in the bladder wall signal the sacral spinal cord. At a critical threshold volume, a spinal cord reflex (the micturition reflex) stimulates the bladder to empty. This is accomplished by rhythmic contractions of the detrusor muscle, a smooth muscle that surrounds the bladder, and relaxation of the external urinary sphincter, a striated muscle that surrounds the urethra. The micturition reflex stimulates bladder emptying in infants and spinal cord–transected patients. Voluntary control over urination is accomplished through inhibition of the micturition reflex via neural circuits from the cerebral cortex. Continence requires that the individual anticipate the threshold for bladder emptying and avoid incontinence by voiding before the threshold is reached or more commonly, by perceiving bladder distention and inhibiting reflex contractions until an appropriate setting for urination is reached. One must also be able to occlude the urethra to prevent incontinence during uninhibited bladder contraction or sudden pressure rises associated with physical activities such as coughing or sneezing. Also important to the maintenance of continence is the ability to voluntarily empty the bladder. Failure to emit these physiological responses at the appropriate times results in one of the following common types of incontinence: (a) *stress incontinence,* in which the outlet does not stay closed tightly during transient pressure rises;

(b) *urge incontinence,* in which bladder contractions are not inhibited; and (c) *overflow incontinence,* in which urine is lost from a chronically full bladder because the bladder does not empty properly. A fourth type of incontinence— *functional incontinence*—can occur in individuals who have normal physiological responses but cannot toilet appropriately because of functional deficits, such as cognitive or mobility impairment.

Types and Causes of Incontinence

In up to one third of cases, urinary incontinence is a transient difficulty related to urinary tract infection or an acute illness that produces confusion or immobilizes the patient (Isaacs & Walkey, 1964; Yarnell & St. Legar, 1979). Transient incontinence is resolved with appropriate treatment of the precipitating condition. Persistent incontinence, or established incontinence, can be classified as stress incontinence, urge incontinence, overflow incontinence, or functional incontinence according to the primary mechanism of urine loss.

STRESS INCONTINENCE

Stress urinary incontinence is the involuntary loss of urine that occurs following a sudden rise in intra-abdominal pressure produced by physical activities such as coughing, sneezing, jogging, or lifting. Incontinence results when a corresponding rise in bladder pressure exceeds urethral resistance in the absence of detrusor contraction. The cause for the leakage is inadequacy of the bladder outlet, in which the urethra is unable to stay closed tightly during the transient pressure increases. Stress incontinence occurs so commonly in women that mild incontinence is accepted as normal by many women, and a surprising number are not inconvenienced enough to seek treatment. One study of the prevalence of stress incontinence in young, nulliparous women reported that 51% experienced stress incontinence, although only 16% had daily leakage (Wolin, 1969). In men, stress incontinence is uncommon and is usually a result of urologic surgery, such as prostatectomy. One commonly accepted etiologic factor of female stress incontinence is perinatal damage to the supporting tissues of the pelvic floor. The precise mechanism of urine loss is a topic of debate. Anatomical explanations emphasize the loss of the vesicourethral angle due to overstretched or damaged pelvic floor tissues. A normal angle between the bladder floor and urethra provides transmission of pressure to the urethra and bladder simultaneously during physical activities. Thus, urethral pressure is increased at the same time as the transient rise in bladder pressure and prevents leakage. When the position of the urethra is altered by loss of urethral support, sudden increases in abdominal pressure are transmitted to the bladder leaving urethral pressure unaltered and leading to incontinence. Surgery for stress incontinence reestablishes control by restoring the urethra to its proper position in the pelvis where pressure from a cough is transmitted equally to the bladder and urethra. Surgical approaches are known to be effective in properly selected patients, but study patients have been predominantly younger women and little attention has been paid to effectiveness in elderly patients. Furthermore, the presence of other medical conditions can preclude surgery in some elderly patients.

Functional explanations of stress incontinence attribute urinary leakage to a lack of awareness or voluntary control of pelvic muscles (Kegel 1948, 1956) or a failure of the striated muscle of the distal urethral sphincter to contract during transient rises in intra-abdominal pressure. The usual method for improving weak muscles is physiotherapy. Behavioral methods for training patients to exercise and use pelvic muscles are described in detail later in this chapter.

Stress incontinence is commonly associated with atrophic vaginitis in postmenopausal women and may be treated with topical or oral estrogen. Studies of estrogen therapy have reported beneficial effects on urinary control (Faber & Heidenreich, 1977; Judge, 1969; Walter, Wolf, Barlebo, & Jensen, 1978). Long-term estrogen therapy carries a risk of endometrial cancer, which can be reduced or eliminated by administering the estrogen in low, cyclic doses with progestin (Harman & Robinson, 1982).

URGE INCONTINENCE

Urge incontinence is the accidental loss of urine associated with a sudden desire to void. Urine is lost when the detrusor muscle surrounding the bladder spasms, forcing urine through the urethra. Normally, detrusor contraction is inhibited until a toilet can be reached. The category of urge incontinence encompasses a group of disorders including bladder instability, detrusor hyperreflexia, spastic bladder, neurogenic bladder, or uninhibited bladder. This inability to inhibit detrusor contraction can be caused by neurological disorders or injuries that impair central nervous system control, such as cerebrovascular accident, brain tumor, dementia, Parkinson's disease, multiple sclerosis, or spinal cord injury. Bladder dysfunction can also be produced by local inflammation or irritation of the bladder or urethra resulting from conditions such as urinary tract infection, fecal impaction, benign prostatic hypertrophy, uterine prolapse, or bladder carcinoma. It has also been asserted that bladder instability can result from poor bladder habits, such as frequent voiding. Repeated low-volume voiding prevents the bladder from accommodating normal urine volumes and is purported to decrease bladder capacity, resulting in increased urinary frequency, urgency, and urge incontinence

(Frewen, 1978, 1980). Often, urge incontinence is characterized by large-volume urine loss, which can lead to embarrassment and serious restriction of activities even if such incontinent episodes are infrequent. The primary interventions for urge incontinence are medications and behavioral procedures.

Several pharmacologic agents have proven effective in reducing urge incontinence. Two drugs—oxybutynin chloride and imipramine—have been tested in a small number of elderly patients, with 60% to 70% showing improvement (Castleden, George, Renwick, & Asher, 1981; Moisey, Stephenson, & Brendler, 1980). The major disadvantage of this class of drugs is their side effects. In the study of oxybutynin chloride, 55% of the patients reported side effects, primarily dry mouth, and 20% discontinued the drug as a result. Imipramine is well known to behavioral therapists because it is frequently used as an antidepressant. Its major side effects in the elderly are mucous membrane dryness, confusion, drowsiness, or urinary retention. The behavioral procedures, which are described later in the chapter, have the advantage that they avoid these side effects.

OVERFLOW INCONTINENCE

Overflow incontinence is the leakage of urine when pressure in a chronically full bladder exceeds urethral resistance. This may be due to an atonic (acontractile) bladder or to a functional or mechanical obstruction of the bladder outlet. Atonic bladder commonly results from spinal cord trauma or diabetes mellitus. In the elderly, outlet obstruction can be due to fecal impaction (Willington, 1980). An estimated 55.6% of constipated nursing home residents are incontinent, compared to approximately 42% of those who are not constipated (Van Nostrand, Zappolo, Hing et al., 1979). Other sources of obstruction are benign prostatic hypertrophy, carcinoma of the prostate, and bladder-sphincter dyssynergia, in which the sphincter contracts simultaneously with bladder contractions. Treatment of overflow incontinence almost always requires surgery to remove the obstruction or catheters to keep the bladder empty. Medications to reduce urethral pressure have been shown to be effective for some patients. Behavioral treatment is rarely appropriate for treatment of overflow incontinence.

FUNCTIONAL INCONTINENCE

Functional incontinence is the loss of urine resulting from an inability or unwillingness to use the toilet appropriately. Whether or not an individual has bladder or sphincter deficits, functional incontinence can be precipitated by limitations that prevent the individual from reaching the toilet in time. Factors that contribute to functional incontinence may include deficits of mobility, mental status, motivation, or environmental barriers. Arthritic pain, muscle weakness, disorders of balance, joint abnormalities, fractures, and fatigue are examples of physical conditions that limit mobility and normal toilet use. Ouslander et al. (1982) studied 299 elderly nursing home patients with frequent incontinence and reported that only 15% were ambulatory. The other 85% suffered severe impairments of mobility, which caused them to be wheelchair bound or bed bound. They described the predicament of many patients who appreciate the sensation of bladder fullness but are unable to postpone urination until staff assistance is available. In a recent study by Yu et al. (1990), 80% of their incontinent patients had one or more neurologic disorders including "organic brain syndrome" and senile dementia. Eighty-eight percent showed at least a mild cognitive disorder. Ninety-two percent of the population needed assistance using the toilet or a bedpan, and as a group, they displayed severe deficits in all activities of daily living. Limitations in activities of daily living, particularly in mobility, ability to transfer to the toilet, and to dress independently, were found by Resnick and colleagues to be more important than cognitive deficits in determining incontinence (Resnick, Baumann, Scott, Laurino, & Yalla, 1988). In fact, even patients with severe dementia were likely to be continent if the abilities to transfer and dress were preserved. Continence in patients with mobility impairment depends on their abilities to acquire toileting skills, the availability of caregivers to assist toileting on a regular schedule, or the promptness with which caregivers can respond to the expressed desire to void.

In patients with significant cognitive impairment, incontinence may be related to memory deficits, confusion, depression, or fears that interfere with appropriate voiding. Ouslander et al. (1982), using the Short Portable Mental Status Questionnaire (Pfeiffer, 1976), showed that most elderly, incontinent nursing home patients have some degree of cognitive impairment and that the severity of this impairment was related to the degree of incontinence. Similarly, incontinence is occasionally a manipulative behavior for the purpose of eliciting attention or the result of indifference to the social consequences of wetting. It is not unusual in institutional or home settings for incontinence to elicit more attention than dryness. Under these circumstances, treatment may involve the rearrangement of environmental contingencies so that positive behavior (e.g., toileting and dryness) elicits attention and incontinence elicits negative or neutral consequences (e.g., disapproval).

Environmental factors, such as lack of privacy, uncomfortable toilet facilities, poor lighting, and physical barriers, can also contribute to functional incontinence. Factors involved in functional incontinence are crucial variables in nursing home patients whose lack of bladder control is often secondary to the disabilities that necessitated institutional care. Intervention for functional incontinence aims to restore regular toileting by removing environmental barriers, by providing prompts and physical assistance for toileting, and by introducing contingencies that encourage normal voiding habits.

Assessment

The purpose of behavioral assessment is to characterize incontinence and to identify the mechanism of urine loss. Knowledge of an underlying disease is often useful but not always sufficient to identify the mechanism or to treat incontinence. Urine loss will occur when intravesical (bladder) pressure exceeds urethral resistance, regardless of the presence or the nature of an underlying disease. Furthermore, the cause of urinary incontinence in the older adult is often multifactored and may be amenable to change by more than one means. Behavioral assessment should be accompanied by medical screening, including history taking and physical examination, to detect conditions that may not be apparent otherwise and to exclude conditions that are inappropriate for behavioral intervention. Examination of urine to detect urinary tract infection is an indispensable component of the routine medical evaluation. Postvoid catheterization for residual urine will detect overflow incontinence, which usually requires medical or surgical intervention. Physical examination will reveal the presence of fecal impaction, benign prostatic hypertrophy, atrophic vaginitis, and other conditions that are reversible causes of incontinence.

THE HISTORY

Behavioral evaluation of incontinence begins with an interview of the patient or a caregiver, if the patient is unable to participate. Using carefully selected questions, the interviewer can elicit information that in many cases will provide a clear picture of the behavioral mechanisms (or correlates) of the incontinence and help formulate a preliminary diagnosis. Care should be taken to identify the circumstances (or antecedents) of incontinence, to obtain a description of typical incontinent episodes, and to ascertain the effects of wetting. Patients with urge incontinence usually give a clear description of accidents that occur in the presence of a strong urge to void and an inability to reach the toilet in time. Typical antecedents of urge incontinence are the sounds of running water, thoughts about going to the bathroom, the sight of a toilet, or cold weather. A common report is the occurrence of accidents as one returns home and unlocks the door of the house. This difficulty, termed *key in the door syndrome,* is partially the result of classical conditioning in which arriving home has been repeatedly paired with bladder emptying.

Patients with stress incontinence are usually able to identify specific physical activities that precipitate incontinence. Common among these are coughing, sneezing, lifting, bending, or stooping. One must be alert to identify cases in which the physical activity is subtle. Patients occasionally report the absence of physical activity when in fact they are walking, turning, or standing up from a sitting position. Incontinence can occur with slight jarring movements (as when climbing stairs) or with changes in position of which the patient may be unaware.

BLADDER DIARY

Bladder diaries are used to document voiding habits and patterns of incontinence on a daily basis. Diaries serve two purposes. First, they provide a picture of the patient's behavior that, together with the interview, can be used to identify preventable causes of incontinence and formulate an accurate diagnosis and treatment plan. Second, they function as a vehicle for evaluating progress and testing the effectiveness of treatment. Self-recording eliminates an important source of error by circumventing the patient's verbal report. It is difficult for patients to judge the frequency or patterns of incontinence retrospectively, especially if the patterns are irregular. Keeping a diary for a period of 2 weeks will often reveal patterns of variability that the patient finds difficult to communicate. Patients are sometimes surprised at the actual number of accidents, once they are required to record them. We have seen patients who profess improvement, whereas their diaries showed no change in the volume or frequency of accidents. Thus, we emphasize the importance of bladder diaries for preventing any tendencies patients may have to report positively on their progress for the purpose of pleasing the doctor. A variety of diary forms have been developed for documentation of bladder habits, some of which are complex. If patients or caregivers are expected to keep meaningful records, a simple bladder form is crucial. A form that we have used to document the most necessary information is presented in Table 16.1 (Whitehead, Burgio, & Engel, 1984). Space is provided to record the time of voiding, the time of incontinent episodes, whether the accident was large or small based on whether the outer clothing was wet, and last, the reason for or circumstances of incontinence, which is helpful in identifying the antecedents of incontinence.

OBSERVATION OF MOBILITY AND TOILETING SKILLS

The ability to reach and use the toilet appropriately is a basic skill for the maintenance of continence. Direct observation of one or more toileting

Table 16.1   Bladder Diary

Name _____ Date _____

Instructions:
  1. In the first column, mark the time every time you void.
  2. In the second or third column, mark every time you accidentally leak urine.
  3. In the fourth column, enter the event that caused the accident or the circumstances
     of the accident.

Urinated in the Toilet	Small Accident	Large Accident	Reason for the Accident

Number of pads used today _____   Number of accidents today _____

Comments: _____
_____
_____
_____
_____

episodes is the best method of determining these skills. The time needed to reach the toilet, to undress, and to position appropriately for voiding is measured (Burgio, Burgio, McCormick, & Engel, 1991). If any of these cannot be performed independently, note is taken of the required assistance and its availability in the patient's natural environment. The type of clothing worn is also of interest, particularly if it might be modified to facilitate undressing. In physically handicapped patients, behavioral observation can help determine skill deficits, such as inadequate transfer skills, that might be overcome with training. During direct observation, it will also become clear whether the patient knows where the bathroom is and whether he or she has an understanding of its appropriate use. A relevant example of the latter is from our experience with a patient who, when guided to the toilet and instructed to void, tore toilet paper from the roll, placed it in the toilet, and flushed. Over weeks of observation, he was not observed to use the toilet but voided consistently in a diaper.

MENTAL STATUS EVALUATION

Appropriate voiding habits and continence can be seriously disrupted by depression or cognitive deficits, such as confusion, disorientation, and memory impairment. Although these deficits may surface in other areas of assessment, it is often useful to evaluate them using standardized tests. The Mini-Mental State Examination (Folstein, Folstein, & McHugh, 1975) is a brief test of mental status that includes assessment of orientation, alertness, memory, attention, and judgment. However, because it was designed for rapid and easy assessment of acutely ill patients, it does not fully evaluate the range of cognition, and when indicated, it should be supplemented by more elaborate neuropsychological instruments. Depression may be evaluated using a structured device, such as the Center for Epidemiological Study's CES-D Scale (Radloff, 1977) or the Geriatric Depression Scale (Yesavage et al., 1983a).

URODYNAMIC TESTING

Physiological measurements of bladder pressure and sphincter activity are routine methods for assessing bladder or sphincter dysfunction. The *cystometrogram* is a test that measures bladder pressure during rapid bladder filling and is a standard procedure in urology clinics. It is often complemented by measurement of intraurethral pressures (urethral pressure profile) or measurement of pelvic floor activity (sphincter electromyography [EMG] or manometry). The cystometrogram is very useful in evaluating bladder physiology and, with modification, provides an extremely useful behavioral evaluation of incontinence. When a behavioral analysis is made of bladder and sphincter physiology, incontinence is characterized as a behavioral deficit. Central to this approach is the acceptance of physiological responses as behavior. In a behavioral analysis, incontinence occurs when an individual (a) fails to voluntarily inhibit reflex bladder contractions or (b) fails to adequately contract the striated (voluntary) sphincter muscles of the pelvic floor to obstruct bladder emptying. Both bladder inhibition and sphincter contraction are acquired physiological responses that preserve continence. Because bladder function is responsive to environmental conditions, the patient should be tested in surroundings that preserve privacy and permit relaxation. The patient should be made as comfortable as possible in an unusual situation. During bladder filling, emphasis should be placed on the evaluation of bladder sensation because sensation provides critical information about bladder function and cues voluntary inhibition of bladder contractions. It is important to determine not only the sensory threshold for bladder filling but also the amount of time between the onset of sensation and the threshold for uninhibited bladder contractions in urge-incontinent patients. This is the amount of time the patient has to reach a toilet or to implement bladder inhibition before incontinence occurs. Filling the bladder slowly improves the accuracy of this assessment. Once the patient reports bladder sensation, the response to this sensation can be observed; specifically, one should note carefully the ability to voluntarily inhibit bladder contractions and the use of periurethral muscles to occlude the urethra. The inhibition of bladder contractions cannot be observed directly but must be inferred from the threshold for uninhibited contractions. However, one can increase the reliability of assessment by encouraging the patient to try to prevent urine loss throughout bladder filling. It should be noted that this need for patient cooperation greatly limits the usefulness of cystometrograms in the assessment of urge incontinence in patients with cognitive impairment or under conditions where there is reason to suspect that the patient will be uncooperative.

Voluntary contractions of the periurethral muscles can be measured in a variety of ways, one of which is the use of an air-filled balloon at the external anal sphincter. Because the innervation of the external urethral sphincter is similar to that of the external anal sphincter, this balloon provides an index of urethral sphincter activity. To minimize the effects of motivational state, the patient is specifically instructed to contract the sphincter muscles and to hold the contractions for a specified period of time. The test should also include a measure of intra-abdominal pressure, such as rectal pressure. The purpose of this measure is to distinguish increases in bladder pressure that are attributable to increases in intra-abdominal pressure as well as to detect inappropriate responses to the desire to void. Many incontinent patients respond to the sensation of urgency by tensing abdominal muscles in an effort to prevent incontinence (Burgio, Whitehead, & Engel, 1985). This response increases bladder pressure and thus contributes to the likelihood of an accident.

Some investigators report that careful history and physical examination provide an accurate diagnosis of urinary tract dysfunction (Hinman, 1979). Hilton and Stanton (1981) developed a clinical algorithm for categorizing incontinent women and compared its outcome to the results of urodynamic assessment. They concluded that the algorithm provided 83% accuracy in diagnosis. Other investigators have noted significant disparities between clinical and urodynamic investigations (Katz & Blaivas, 1983). Certainly, urodynamic procedures occasionally detect urinary tract abnormalities that go unnoticed during clinical examination, and the discrepancy warrants alteration of the treatment plan. However, other discrepancies (e.g., normal urodynamic findings in patients with urge incontinence) may not necessitate changing the intervention indicated by the clinical interview (Hilton & Stanton, 1981). In addition, the validity of urodynamic testing needs to be evaluated. Because the procedure of bladder filling is accelerated, it may produce instability in patients who otherwise have stable patterns. Abnormal patterns have been documented in patients who do not experience incontinence (Brocklehurst & Dillane, 1966), and we have seen stable patterns in patients who clearly describe urge incontinence outside the clinic setting. Clinicians are becoming increasingly aware that the test situation lacks certain components that stimulate bladder instability. It is for this reason that supine cystometry is usually complemented by provocative maneuvers, such as standing or coughing, which in many cases will reveal instability otherwise masked by the quiet, supine position. But there remain many antecedents of incontinence aside from bladder filling (e.g., running water, cold weather, laughing) that are usually absent from the test situation.

Urodynamic testing in patients with cognitive impairment poses a significant problem because it relies on the active cooperation and understanding of the patient. First, it is necessary that patients understand that they should make every effort to inhibit urine loss and second, they must be motivated to do so. If either criterion is not met, the mechanism of an uninhibited detrusor contraction may be uninterpretable.

The contribution of a dysfunctional urinary tract in determining incontinence in the nursing home population is controversial. Researchers have reported the percentage of nursing home residents with normal bladder function to be as low as 1% (Resnick et al., 1988) and as high as 41% (Resnick, Yalla, & Laurino, 1989). Moreover, it is questionable whether a finding of bladder instability is predictive of incontinence. Resnick et al. (1988) have suggested that abnormal bladder function may be incidental to normal aging and not strongly predictive of incontinence in these patients. One setting in which urodynamic monitoring is clearly required is during intervention using biofeedback techniques, in which patients learn to alter physiological responses.

Intervention

The choice of behavioral intervention depends on the results of the behavioral evaluation of the patient's deficits. Generally, elderly patients will fall into one of two categories: those who are capable of learning self-management procedures and those who require ongoing intervention from a caregiver. Usually but not necessarily, the former will be community dwelling and the latter will be institutionalized. Community-dwelling patients usually have demonstrable bladder or sphincter dysfunction but are otherwise functional in terms of self-care, often have little or no cognitive impairment, and usually are capable of independent living. They can be managed in an outpatient setting where the patient receives training in self-management skills in the clinic, and prescribed practice is implemented at home. In contrast, institutionalized patients are often characterized by functional dependence and significant cognitive or mobility impairment and will require assistance in the management of incontinence. Many of these will be unaware of or indifferent to their incontinence. Management requires family or institutional staff to implement treatment procedures that involve the control of environmental factors.

STRESS INCONTINENCE

Stress incontinence occurs because the urethra does not stay closed tightly during transient rises in abdominal pressure caused by physical exertion. Behavior therapy for stress incontinence consists of teaching skills to prevent urine loss through voluntary contraction of periurethral muscles. The goal is to increase intraurethral pressure for a short period of time during the activity that causes leakage (coughing, sneezing, lifting, or other physical exertion). The training improves not only the strength of pelvic muscles but voluntary control over the muscles as well.

Pelvic muscle training had been done in several ways. Originally, gynecologist Arnold Kegel used a biofeedback device, the perineometer, for this purpose (Kegel, 1948, 1956). The pneumatic chamber was placed in the vagina and when pelvic muscles contracted, the increased pressure exerted on the perineometer chamber was registered on a handheld pressure gauge. This method provided immediate visual feedback of muscle contraction and was used to identify the proper muscles and to guide and coordinate pelvic muscle exercise.

Historically, it has been more common to teach pelvic muscle contraction through brief instructions to lift the pelvic floor or interrupt the urinary stream. Verbal or written instructions are not widely effective, however, probably because patients do not correctly identify the pelvic muscles. More useful is the technique in which the examiner provides immediate verbal feedback of several attempted muscle contractions based on vaginal or anal palpation. Perhaps the best technique is to actually measure pelvic muscle activity and provide immediate feedback of muscle activity using biofeedback training. *Biofeedback* is a form of behavioral training that attempts to reverse incontinence by altering physiological responses of the bladder and the pelvic floor muscles that mediate incontinence. The targets of the intervention are the striated muscles of the pelvic floor or abdominal wall and the smooth detrusor muscle that mediates bladder emptying. Physiological change is possible through the use of operant conditioning in which suitably motivated patients can learn by observing the results of their attempts to voluntarily control bladder and sphincter responses. Intraurethral resistance can be increased by training patients to contract periurethral muscles. There is evidence in the literature that biofeedback increases the efficacy of training and improves treatment outcome (Burgio, Robinson, & Engel, 1986; Shepherd, Montgomery, & Anderson, 1983). Measurement of external anal sphincter activity or vaginal muscle activity using manometry or electromyography can be used to teach pelvic muscle contraction and relaxation.

The most common error in pelvic muscle training involves the voluntary contraction of other muscles, most typically abdominal or gluteal muscles. Abdominal contraction that presents itself as a bearing down response is particularly problematic because it increases intravesical rather than intraurethral pressure. During training, abdominal muscle activity should be measured using a rectal balloon (intra-abdominal pressure) or surface electrodes (abdominal electromyogram). The patient can then be given simultaneous biofeedback of abdominal and pelvic muscles, allowing him or her to learn through operant conditioning (trial and error learning) how to contract the pelvic muscles selectively while keeping abdominal muscles relaxed. Without this selective control, pelvic muscle contraction can be uncoordinated, counterproductive, and clinically ineffective.

Once the pelvic muscles are located and brought under selective control, it is crucial to begin an individualized program of home practice in which the patient increases strength and control through daily exercises. A sample of patient instructions is presented in Table 16.2.

Although the optimal number of exercises has not been agreed on, 45 to 50 exercises per day has yielded good results in several studies. The exercises should be divided among two or more sessions per day. Such distribution across the day helps to avoid problems with muscle fatigue and encourages

Table 16.2   Pelvic Muscle Exercises

Do 45 pelvic muscle exercises *every* day
   15 at a time, three times a day
   Do 15 lying down in the morning
   Do 15 standing up in the afternoon
   Do 15 sitting in the evening
For each exercise
   Squeeze for _____ seconds
   Relax for _____ seconds
Remember to relax all the muscles in your abdomen when you do these exercises and continue
   to breathe normally.
Once a day, practice slowing or stopping the stream of urine when you void.

---

awareness and use of muscles. To build muscle strength, it is important that pelvic muscle contractions be sustained for up to 10 seconds with a least equal periods of rest between contractions. Most patients are not capable of 10-second contractions at first, in which case one can begin with the level of ability demonstrated by the patient (even if it is 1 second) and increase gradually.

In addition to building strength, it is important to instruct patients to contract their muscles voluntarily to prevent urine loss during coughing, lifting, or whatever activities are known to produce incontinence. Exercise alone can increase resting tone, but active, maximal contraction is usually needed to prevent incontinence through a transient rise in intraurethral pressure. Improvement in continence is gradual, usually evident by the 4th week of training and may continue up to 6 months.

A typical account of pelvic muscle exercise failure is the woman who tries the exercises for a few days, then finding them ineffective, she gives up. The challenge of behavioral treatment is to establish and sustain patient compliance for an adequate period of time until results are achieved. Once the patient can prevent accidents by using these skills and can experience a sense of renewed control over bodily function, the positive effects of treatment reinforce the patient's efforts, and the behavior is more likely to be sustained.

Research on pelvic muscle training and exercise indicate that 27% to 73% of patients are cured and 38% to 100% improved. Two studies are worthy of particular note because they are randomized clinical trials. The first, conducted by Wells and colleagues, compared pelvic muscle exercise to phenylpropanolamine in older women (Wells, Brink, Diokno, Wolfe, & Gillis, 1991). Phenylpropanolamine is a medication that tightens the sphincter and increases pressure in the urethra. Although the site of action of the two treatments is different (one affects striated muscle, the other smooth muscle), they produced similar results as measured by patients' subjective reports of improvement (77% vs. 84%) as well as by diary.

The second study was a randomized trial comparing groups treated with pelvic muscle exercise to an untreated control group (Burns, Pranikoff, Nochajski, Desotelle, & Harwood, 1990). Pelvic muscle training without biofeedback produced an average 54% reduction of incontinence compared to an average 6% reduction in the control group. Teaching pelvic muscle exercise using vaginal EMG biofeedback resulted in a mean 61% improvement, which was not significantly better than treating without biofeedback.

As noted, however, this finding is inconsistent with two smaller yet controlled studies that have demonstrated an advantage for patients treated with biofeedback (Burgio et al., 1986; Shepherd et al., 1983). Although the best methods for teaching the exercises and the optimal exercise regimen have not been established, many studies demonstrate convergently that pelvic muscle training and exercise is a highly effective conservative intervention for stress incontinence.

URGE INCONTINENCE

The underlying problem in urge incontinence is that the muscle of the bladder wall spasms involuntarily and forces urine out through the urethra. Behavioral approaches to urge incontinence focus on reducing incontinence through temporal voiding schedules or by teaching patients how to inhibit detrusor spasm voluntarily.

Bladder Training and Voiding Schedules

Voiding schedules are the primary components of procedures such as habit training and bladder retraining. In habit training, a fixed or flexible voiding schedule is adopted that avoids incontinence by having the patient empty the bladder regularly and before it reaches a volume that triggers urgency and incontinence (Clay, 1980; Sogbein & Awad 1982). The voiding schedule can be adjusted to the needs and habits of the patient (Clay, 1978). The goal is to avoid incontinence by emptying the bladder regularly, but the intention is not to change bladder function or capacity.

Bladder retraining is different in that the aim is to restore a normal pattern of voiding and normal bladder function. Bladder training encourages the patient to adopt an expanded voiding interval. By gradually increasing the intervals between voidings, it attempts to correct the bad habit of frequent voiding, improve the ability to suppress bladder instability, and eventually diminish urgency. Frewen (1978, 1980) provided the rationale for this approach. He suggested that urinary frequency is a precursor and a precipitant of bladder instability and that urgency is not only a symptom of detrusor

Table 16.3   Bladder Training Instructions

Review the bladder diary and determine the longest interval of time between daytime voids that
   is comfortable for the patient. This is the beginning voiding interval.
Give these instructions to the patient:
   Void first thing in the morning.
   Void every time the voiding interval passes during the day.
   Void just before bed.
   If you have an urge, suppress the urge and wait until your interval has passed before voiding.
   If your time has passed and you don't have an urge, go anyway.
When the patient feels comfortable on the schedule for 3 consecutive days, increase the
   interval (usually by 30 minutes).
Increase the voiding interval gradually until a normal frequency is reached (every 3 to 4 hours).

---

instability but also an initiating factor because it increases frequency of urination, which contributes to decreased bladder capacity. The Frewen bladder drill program requires patients to resist the sensation of urgency, to postpone voiding, and to urinate by the clock rather than in response to an urge. The goal is to increase bladder capacity gradually over several days or weeks. Frewen advocated admission to a hospital for 7 to 10 days for a combination of bladder drill, supportive therapy, anticholinergic medication, and sedatives. He reported an 82% to 86% cure rate (i.e., absence of abnormal symptoms and normal cystometrogram) in women aged 15 years to 77 years (Frewen, 1978, 1979, 1982). Jarvis tested the inpatient bladder drill without adjunctive medication in the treatment of women aged 17 years to 79 years with urge incontinence, obtaining cure rates of 61% to 90% (Jarvis, 1981, 1982; Jarvis & Miller, 1980). Others reported 44% to 52% of patients cured, with an additional 25% to 34% showing improvement with bladder drill. There is a single randomized clinical trial of bladder training that was conducted with older women (Fantl et al., 1991) resulting in an average 57% reduction in the frequency of incontinent episodes. Bladder training, like habit training, has the advantage that there are no documented side effects and the procedures are easy to implement. An example of bladder training instructions is presented in Table 16.3.

Bladder Biofeedback

In the interventions described earlier, toileting habits are the primary targets of behavioral change. Learning to suppress detrusor contraction can also be accomplished through bladder pressure biofeedback. The earliest reported use of a biofeedback procedure for urge incontinence was by Wilson (1948). He reported that 10 of 23 elderly patients with precipitancy or incontinence were improved or made completely continent and 5 others were somewhat improved following a diagnostic cystometrogram. During cystometrograms, bladder pressure readings were available to his patients and may have provided a mechanism for feedback that allowed them to acquire better control. Wilson referred to his method as *inhibitory reeducative training,* but he clearly described a form of intervention that would now be termed *biofeedback.* Willington (1980) has also described a method of biofeedback in which a patient's catheter is attached to a vertical tube in which the fluid level is visible to the patient. The fluid level remains low as long as the bladder remains relaxed but rises noticeably when bladder contractions occur. Cardozo and her colleagues published a bladder pressure biofeedback procedure for treating urge incontinence (Cardozo, Abrams, Stanton, & Feneley, 1978; Cardozo, Stanton, Hafner, & Allan, 1978). This method provides both auditory and visual feedback of bladder pressure during repeated bladder filling. Twenty-seven women, aged 18 to 64 years, with bladder instability were treated in four to eight 1-hour sessions at weekly intervals. Improvement was seen in 81% of the women; of these, 41% were judged to be cured. Through this method, patients are given visual or auditory feedback of bladder pressure during repeated bladder filling. They practice suppressing detrusor contraction whenever they experience urgency to void or observe a rise in bladder pressure. Most often this technique is used in combination with pelvic muscle biofeedback.

Pelvic Muscle Training

Pelvic muscles also play a critical role in the control of detrusor function. Using the same training techniques described for stress incontinence, patients can learn to contract their pelvic muscles strongly and repeatedly in response to urgency. Pelvic muscle training can be performed simultaneously with bladder pressure biofeedback (bladder-sphincter biofeedback). In 1979, investigators at the National Institute on Aging developed a procedure that provides simultaneous feedback of bladder pressure, sphincter activity, and intra-abdominal pressure using the instrumentation shown in Figure 16.1 (Burgio, Whitehead, & Engel, 1985). The third component, intra-abdominal pressure, was added because many patients exhibit a tendency to tense abdominal muscles while trying to prevent incontinence. This behavior is counterproductive because it increases bladder pressure and consequently increases the probability of urine loss. Simultaneous feedback of the three pressures provides a mechanism for operant conditioning of bladder, sphincter, and abdominal muscle responses. Specifically, patients acquire selective responses: bladder inhibition (relaxation) or active contraction of pelvic floor muscles coupled with abdominal relaxation. This allows patients to observe bladder pressure and coordinate pelvic muscle contractions with any rise in

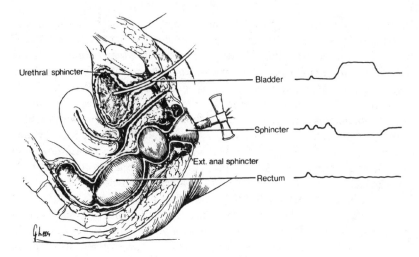

Figure 16.1. Diagram of Female Pelvic Anatomy Showing Devices Used for Bladder and Sphincter Biofeedback

bladder pressure. As shown in Figures 16.2 and 16.3, strong contractions of the pelvic muscles can suppress detrusor contractions. In addition, increasing intraurethral pressure helps to prevent urine loss caused by detrusor contraction until the contraction subsides.

Urge Strategies

Patients with urge incontinence typically display a maladaptive response to the sensation of urgency. When they sense the urge to void, they rush to the toilet, often leaking along the way. This behavior is counterproductive because it produces increased intra-abdominal pressure on the bladder, often increasing the sensation of fullness; it can stimulate detrusor contraction; and it may interfere with the ability to concentrate on detrusor inhibition. Furthermore, the closer one comes to the toilet, the greater are the cues that trigger urination.

Through a lifelong process of classical conditioning in which voiding is repeatedly paired with the visual cues of the bathroom, the cues eventually become cues for voiding and the thought or sight of the bathroom can elicit detrusor contraction. For people with urge incontinence, it can be the bathroom itself that enhances urgency and elicits detrusor instability. For a person with urge incontinence, the worst time to head for the bathroom is when they already have a strong desire to void. The best time is before they have an urge or after they have successfully reduced or eliminated an urge to void (see

Abdominal Pressure

Anal Sphincter

Bladder

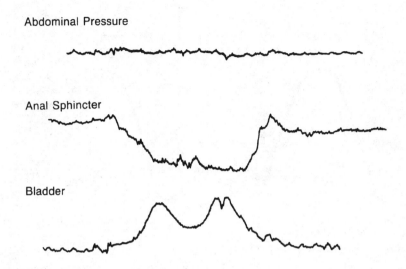

Figure 16.2. Bladder Contraction Accompanied by Reflex Sphincter Relaxation
SOURCE: Burgio (1992, p. 215). Used with permission.

Abdominal Pressure

Anal Sphincter

Bladder

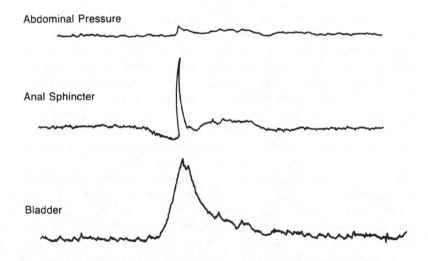

Figure 16.3. Sphincter Contraction Accompanied by Bladder Inhibition
SOURCE: Burgio (1992, p. 215). Used with permission.

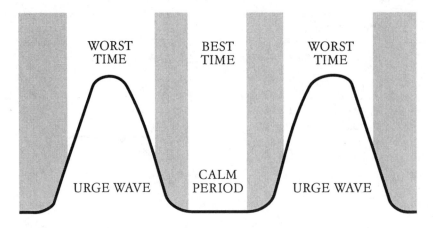

Figure 16.4 When to Void
SOURCE: Burgio, Pearce, and Lucco (1989, p. 80).

Figure 16.4). Behavioral training offers a new response pattern, outlined in Table 16.4, for coping with the feeling of bladder urgency. Instead of rushing, patients are encouraged to remain still and relaxed, repeatedly contract pelvic muscles to inhibit detrusor spasm, practice suppressing urgency, wait for the urge to subside, and then to walk calmly to the toilet.

Instructions to this effect often seem counterintuitive, but most patients can be successfully convinced to try a new strategy based on the failure of their current habits. It is important for patient and therapist to recognize that the urge strategy involves practice and skill and to accept that initial attempts may fail. However, the first successful attempt often brings with it a rush of insight that confirms the direction of the therapy and reinforces compliance with the new strategy. To avoid early failure, the therapist should be certain that the patient has properly identified pelvic muscles and has completed a week or more of daily exercise. Familiarity with pelvic muscle contraction will increase the patient's ability to use the muscles under the stressful circumstances of the new urge strategy.

The behavioral training program consisting of the biofeedback procedure combined with urge strategies was tested in an outpatient clinic. After a 2-hour voiding schedule failed to resolve incontinence in 18 elderly patients with urge incontinence, the biofeedback procedure was implemented. Patients achieved 39% to 100% reductions of incontinence following an average of four training sessions (Burgio et al., 1985). Included in the sample were four men with bladder instability secondary to cerebrovascular accident who achieved total continence by the 6-month follow-up. Other studies have produced similar results with mean improvements ranging from 75% to 85% (Baigis-Smith, Smith, Rose, & Newman, 1989; Burgio, Stutzman, & Engel,

Table 16.4   The Urge Strategy in Six Steps

1. Stop what you are doing and stay put. Sit down when possible, or stand quietly. Remain very still. When you are still, it is easier to control your urge.
2. Squeeze your pelvic floor muscles quickly several times. Do not relax fully in between.
3. Relax the rest of your body. Take a few deep breaths to help you relax and let go of your tension.
4. Concentrate on suppressing the urge feeling.
5. Wait until the urge subsides.
6. Walk to the bathroom at a normal pace. Do not rush. Continue squeezing your pelvic floor muscles quickly while you walk.

SOURCE: Burgio, Pearce, and Lucco (1989, p. 81).

1989; Burton, Pearce, Burgio, Engel, & Whitehead, 1988; McDowell, Burgio, Dombrowski, Locher, & Rodriguez, 1992). Together, these studies demonstrate that biofeedback-assisted training is a practical and effective approach to treating geriatric urge incontinence.

Clearly, the behavioral approaches to urge incontinence can and should be combined. For example, patients who have learned to contract pelvic muscles and inhibit detrusor contraction will be ultimately prepared to postpone urination in a bladder retraining program.

FUNCTIONAL INCONTINENCE

The therapeutic approach is completely different for patients with dementia, physical immobility, or both, producing functional incontinence. The goal with this group of patients is not to improve bladder function but to prevent wetness by reestablishing appropriate toileting. Whether patients live at home or in an institutional setting, they are dependent on caregivers in their daily living and for implementation of behavioral treatment. The major challenge of treating this group of patients is gaining and maintaining the compliance of the caregiver in providing treatment. Older adults with functional incontinence may or may not have any urinary tract dysfunction requiring other forms of treatment. What they require in the way of behavior therapy is a program of prompted voiding (Burgio, Engel, McCormick, Hawkins, & Sheve, 1988; Schnelle et al., 1983). Prompted voiding is a well-developed method that increases the availability of toileting assistance, provides regularly scheduled reminders (prompts) to use the bathroom, and provides encouragement through reinforcement for appropriate toileting and periods of dryness. There are several variations of the prompted voiding procedure. An example of specific instructions for caregivers and institutional staff is presented in Table 16.5.

Table 16.5   Instructions for Prompted Voiding

Begin with a 2-hour daytime voiding schedule.
Approach the patient at the scheduled time.
Wait 5 seconds to give him or her an opportunity to self-initiate toileting.
Prompt the patient, "It's time to use the bathroom."
  If the patient agrees or does not respond, assist to the bathroom.
  If the patient responds negatively, urge but don't force to use the bathroom.
In the bathroom, check pad or undergarments.
  Give verbal praise for dryness.
  Give corrective feedback for wetness, "Your pad is wet. It is important that you try to hold it
    and let us know if you need help."
Assist the patient with toileting as needed.
  Give praise for appropriate voiding.
Inform the patient about when you will return, and remind him or her to call for assistance,
  if needed.
Praise all instances of self-initiated or independent toileting.
Adjust the schedule up or down, as needed. Do not exceed a 4-hour interval.

SOURCE: Adapted from Burgio, Engel, McCormick, Hawkins, and Sheve (1988).

Research on the use of prompted voiding has produced a wide range of outcomes (Burgio et al., 1988; Burgio et al., 1990; Hu et al., 1989; Schnelle et al., 1983; Schnelle et al., 1989). Much of the variability is attributable to differences in patient populations. In studies of nursing home residents, reductions are in the 10% to 20% range. When an effort is made to select likely responders, better results are obtained (Schnelle et al., 1989). Because prompted voiding is an environmental treatment administered by staff or caregivers, gains are lost when the program is stopped. Therefore, it has become clear that for this therapy to be effective over the long term, it will be necessary to further develop and implement supervisory systems for staff management and quality control (Burgio & Burgio, 1989; Burgio et al., 1990).

Conclusion

Although it is clear that more extensive research is needed, enough data exist to justify the application of behavioral methods in clinical practice. Behavioral procedures alone or in conjunction with medical approaches are known to be effective in the treatment of the major types of incontinence. Currently, biofeedback procedures and other behavioral techniques are not readily available to the vast majority of elderly people. Continence clinics are well established in some countries but are less common in the United States. This may be because the concept is relatively new, and much has yet to be learned about the relative effectiveness of various procedures and patient selection. What is needed now is a transfer of technology from the research setting into clinical practice, especially into nursing practice. Outpatient services, including biofeedback, could be administered by professional nurses trained in these techniques, provided that patients are medically screened and consultative services with behaviorally trained professionals are available. Appropriate settings include the offices of family physicians, geriatricians, or gynecologists. Clinics might also be established at health maintenance organizations or hospitals, where nurses are available to perform the catheterization and biofeedback procedures. Behavioral programs to treat incontinence in institutionalized elderly persons will also benefit from interdisciplinary collaboration. Despite the fact that many nurses in these settings have little or no formal training in behavioral principles, they play a critical role in the successful management of incontinent patients. Treatment of institutionalized patients usually requires environmental control, which includes ongoing staff intervention under nursing supervision. Behavioral procedures are useful, provided they are used appropriately by adequately trained staff. Carefully implemented programs that take into account the physical and mental limitations of nursing home patients can improve continence skills and preserve the dignity of patients. Involvement of behavioral specialists as consultants or in teaching roles will promote the appropriate and systematic application of behavioral techniques. Behavioral specialists can enhance their effectiveness in these roles by developing a knowledge of bladder physiology and by obtaining appropriate clinical training in the behavioral treatment of incontinence. Attitudes toward incontinence and behavioral treatment may be modified eventually when these services are more common and known to be effective. Continence programs established within existing health care systems may not only make current and new interventions available to more elderly patients but will be evidence to both patients and professionals that incontinence is treatable and not a hopeless consequence of the aging process.

17

Wandering and Aggression

Jiska Cohen-Mansfield
Perla Werner
William J. Culpepper II
Michele A. Wolfson
Eric Bickel

Wandering and aggressive behaviors are some of the most disturbing behavioral phenomena associated with cognitive decline in elderly persons because they impose risks to the elderly person and, at times, to those around them. When an elderly person hits another person or when he or she wanders and gets lost, the problem cannot be ignored and warrants immediate action. Indeed, these behaviors frequently result in nursing home admission, the use of medication, and other interventions. Although several researchers have investigated wandering or pacing and aggression in elderly persons, their etiology, correlates, and management strategies are still understudied. The aim of this chapter is to summarize recent literature concerning pacing or

AUTHORS' NOTE: The authors acknowledge support from NIA grants AG08675 and AG11502. The authors would like to thank Dr. Steve Lipson for his comments on a previous version of the manuscript.

wandering and aggressive behaviors in elderly persons. It focuses on the prevalence of these behaviors, their assessment, and the different interventions described to treat or accommodate these very disruptive behaviors.

Wandering and aggression will be discussed separately, and for each, the following questions will be addressed:

The dimension of the problem: How is the behavior defined? What is the scope of the problem in terms of prevalence and effect? How is the behavior assessed?

Understanding the problem: Who is most likely to manifest the behavior? Under what situational conditions is the behavior likely to occur? What are the possible causes of the behavior?

Treatment: What types of interventions have been tried? What other approaches may be appropriate based on the current understanding of the problem?

Wandering and Pacing

THE DIMENSION OF THE PROBLEM

Wandering and pacing are ambulatory behaviors. Usually, wandering is aimless and not goal directed; pacing may be repetitive, as in pacing back and forth along a corridor, and may be goal oriented or purposeful. It is yet unclear what descriptors of the behavior are essential for proper characterization. Several methods for classifying have been suggested and are summarized in Table 17.1. These demonstrate different emphases in describing the behavior, such as the reason for the behavior—for example, caused by medication, intent to escape, or need for stimulation (Hussian, 1987); the description of the actual travel route taken (Martino-Salzman, Blasch, Morris, & McNeal, 1991); effect on others—for example, trespassing, level of supervision, and intent (i.e., purposeful or goal directed vs. aimless). Although some of these classifications were published several years ago, no studies have been found that demonstrate their reliability, validity, or effectiveness. From a clinical point of view, however, the awareness of these dimensions is important for addressing the needs of wanderers and their caregivers.

Pacing and wandering pose significant problems for elderly persons and their caregivers. For the wanderers themselves, there is a risk of getting lost and being unable to find their way back, occasionally having fatal results (Burnside, 1980); in addition, there is a correlation between falls and wandering (Buchner & Larson, 1987; Cohen-Mansfield, Werner, Marx, & Freedman, 1991). For family caregivers, wandering disrupts their activities because the wanderer has to be monitored, and if their relative is a night wanderer, this

Table 17.1   Summary of Nomenclatures Developed to Describe Pacing and Wandering Behavior.

Source	Nomenclature	Clarification
Butler & Barnett (1991)	Purposeful wanderer	Walking with apparent intent and caregiver knows persons' whereabouts
	Escapist	Purposeful intent on going elsewhere, frequently from institution to home
	Aimless wanderer	Confused, purposeless walk
	Critical wanderer	Confused wanderer who leaves the premises without caregiver's knowledge
Hussian (1987)	Akathisias	Neuroleptic induced
	Exit seekers	Attempting to leave the unit or facility
	Self-stimulators	Turning door knobs and pacing continuously
	Modelers	"Shadowing" or following other pacers
Martino-Salzman et al. (1991)	Direct travel	Moving from one location to another without diversion
	Random travel	Moving in a roundabout, haphazard manner to many locations or areas
	Pacing	Repetitive walking back and forth in a limited area
	Lapping	Repetitive walking, circling large areas
Milke (1988)	Absconding	Leaving an activity, unit, or facility
	Locomotive restlessness	Walking with no obvious purpose or destination
	Group walking	Aimless locomotion as part of a group
	Motoric restlessness	Fiddling with objects, small repetitive muscle movements
	Navigational difficulty	Errors in way finding, visual scanning of the environment
	Searching	Actively looking for objects or persons
	Trespassing	Uninvited entry into another's room
Snyder et al. (1978)	Goal-directed: searching	Searching for something that is often unobtainable
	Goal-directed: industrious	Drive to do things or remain busy
	Non-goal-directed behavior	Aimlessly wandering, drawn from one stimulus to another

results in frequent awakenings. Oftentimes, this burden becomes insurmountable and results in institutionalization (Moak, 1990). In the institution, the elderly person who wanders requires much supervision, environmental modification, or both to secure the environment. In addition, attention needs to be given to other persons who may be disturbed by the wanderer entering their rooms and invading their privacy.

PREVALENCE

Several studies have reported the prevalence of pacing or wandering behavior in the elderly, with prevalence rates ranging from 3% (Reisberg et al., 1987) to 59% (Rabins, Mace, & Lucas, 1982). Teri, Larson, and Reifler (1988) found that 26% of 127 outpatients suffering from dementia of the Alzheimer's type were described as wandering; Cohen-Mansfield, Werner, Marx, and Freedman (1991) found that 39% out of 402 nursing home residents studied either paced or wandered, including ambulation in a wheelchair, and of these, 76% wandered on a daily basis. Everitt, Fields, Soumerai, and Avorn (1991) found that 22% out of 346 nursing home residents paced or wandered and that 50% of these paced or wandered one or more times per day. Burns, Jacoby, and Levy (1990) found that 18.5% of 178 patients (including both community dwelling and institutionalized) with probable or possible Alzheimer's disease wandered. In a sample of 1,139 nursing home residents, a prevalence in pacing or wandering of 9.2% was found. However, only wandering into unsafe areas, other residents' rooms, or escaping restraints were included (Zimmer, Watson, & Treat, 1984).

As can be expected, rates vary by the populations used, the ways in which the information was obtained, and the definitions of the behavior. Additional studies reporting prevalence rates are summarized in Cohen-Mansfield, Werner, Marx, and Lipson (1993).

ASSESSMENT

Use of objective and reliable assessment is essential to accurate documentation of behavior; this is a prerequisite for studying causes, prevalence, and intervention for the behavior.

The assessment of wandering, like other assessments, depends greatly on the goal of assessment: Goals can include the determination of the frequency of the ambulatory behavior, the reason for the behavior, or the effect of the behavior.

The assessment of the frequency of ambulatory behaviors can be performed through several methods:

Informant Ratings. The frequency of pacing or wandering can be rated by informants by methods such as one item on the Cohen-Mansfield Agitation Inventory (CMAI; Cohen-Mansfield, Marx, & Rosenthal, 1989; Teri et al., 1988), two items on the Disruptive Behavior Rating Scales (Mungas, Weiler, Franzi, & Henry, 1989), an item on the Nursing Home Behavior Problem Scale (Ray, Taylor, Lichtenstein, & Meador, 1992), and one item on the Behavioral and Emotional Activities Manifested in Dementia (Sinha et al.,

1992). The Dementia Behavior Disturbance Scale (Baumgarten, Becker, & Gauthier, 1990) is another example of an informant rating scale. This scale, used with community-residing elderly, includes three items for the assessment of wandering: wanders in the house at night, gets lost outside, and wanders aimlessly outside or in the house during the day.

Direct Observation of the Behavior by Trained Observers. Such observations can be recorded via time-sampling methods and ratings on questionnaires such as the Agitation Behavior Mapping Instrument (Cohen-Mansfield, Werner, Marx, & Freedman, 1991) or the Wandering Observational Tool (Hoeffer, Rader, & Siemsen, 1987) or through use of videotapes (activated by an automatic detection system that detects electronic ankle tags on residents) that are then rated by trained observers (e.g., Martino-Salzman et al., 1991). The observer may use a stopwatch to record time in motion, or may use handheld computer or a bar-scanning method to facilitate data collection while observing (Bridges-Parlet, Knopman, & Thompson, 1994). One advantage of observation is that when a person is followed, the observer can ascertain the route or other environmental concomitants of wandering.

Technological Devices. These devices include (a) accelerometers, which measure movement, with instruments such as the Actigraph (Ambulatory Monitor, Inc.), Personal Activity Monitor (Individual Monitoring Systems), and Large Scale Integrated Activity Monitor (LaPorte et al., 1979) and (b) instruments that count the number of steps taken, such as a pedometer or the Stepsensor (Madson, 1991). Using mechanical or electronic devices may be less expensive than direct observation because a measuring device requires a one-time investment rather than the time costs for observation and coding.

Assessing the reason for the behavior will depend in part on the cognitive skills of the wanderer. For more cognitively intact persons, asking them about their behavior may be useful. For cognitively impaired individuals, interviewing a close relative to determine the wanderer's level and types of physical activity in the past may be useful. In addition, it is useful to observe the wanderer or to interview the caregiver about the elderly person's mood and other behaviors, as well as the route and destination of travel, or about the circumstances under which the behavior occurs. Some pacers indicate that they are searching for their home and therefore seem to need a more comforting environment, whereas others seem to be quite content during their wandering.

The effects of wandering and pacing can be measured by variables such as the number of times the person gets lost, the number of hours spent in locating the wanderer, the number of times the police have been asked to search for the individual, or the number of activations of an alarm system, if one is in place.

UNDERSTANDING THE PROBLEM

Several studies have reported that elderly persons who pace or wander are more cognitively impaired than residents who do not exhibit this behavior (Burns et al., 1990; Cohen-Mansfield, Werner, Marx, & Freedman, 1991; Cooper, Mungas, & Weiler, 1990; Dawson & Reid, 1987; Snyder, Rupprecht, Pyrek, Brekhus, & Moss, 1978; Teri et al., 1988). Persons who pace or wander are significantly more likely to experience delusions (Lachs, Becker, Siegal, Miller, & Tinetti, 1992) and have impaired language skills (Algase & Tsai, 1991). In comparison to other nursing home residents, they were found to have fewer physical diagnoses and better appetites, were more likely to have experienced life-threatening situations or stressful life events in the past, and were more likely to have been divorced or separated (Cohen-Mansfield, Werner, Marx, & Freedman, 1991; Monsour & Robb, 1982; Teri et al., 1988). Monsour and Robb (1982) found that wanderers had been more active than nonwanderers premorbidly.

Algase and Tsai (1991) found that there was a rhythmic component to pacing and wandering activity, with pacing and wandering occurring most frequently during the hours of 2 to 4 p.m. and 6 to 7 p.m. In contrast, Cohen-Mansfield, Werner, Marx, and Freedman (1991) found that residents who paced did so at high levels throughout the day and manifested less pacing during mealtimes. The physical environment has been reported to be related to this activity. For example, Cohen-Mansfield, Werner, Marx, and Freedman (1991) found that pacing and wandering occurred more frequently when there was adequate lighting and low noise levels and wandering tended to occur in corridors where there was sufficient space to ambulate.

Based on these findings, several explanations for the causes and the meaning of pacing and wandering seem to emerge:

Exercise. For some persons, wandering is a form of exercise. It provides stimulation for cognitively impaired persons who are rarely involved in exercise and receive little stimulation both because of their dementia and because of the limited sensory stimulation in the physical environment. Indeed, findings such as (a) better physical health among nursing home residents who pace and (b) that nursing home residents tended to pace or wander under optimal environmental conditions (unlike other agitated behaviors, which tended to occur when the person was experiencing discomfort) suggest that pacing may be beneficial for a person suffering from dementia. Sometimes, this exercise continues a lifelong pattern of exercise. For these persons, the pacing or wandering seems to play a beneficial role.

Discomfort. At times, wandering and pacing are a clear sign of discomfort on the part of the elderly person. Frequently, the person is upset about being in a nursing home and is searching for home. Clinically, it appears that some persons pace back and forth as an expression of discontent.

Replaying Past Roles. Some persons who wander are trying to perform past roles, such as going to work or going to shop, in inappropriate environments or at inappropriate times. Inappropriate timing is especially pronounced when the person has a disturbed sleep-wake rhythm and may, for example, want to go shopping during the middle of the night. Some individuals may be interpreting their environments as part of past experiences, such as being in life-threatening situations.

Physical Causes. In other cases, specific reasons for wandering, such as the use of neuroleptics, may apply. In this case, the person is suffering from *akathisia,* which is a compulsion to be in motion; it is frequently manifested by restlessness and pacing. Akathisia can be an extrapyramidal reaction to antipsychotic drugs. It occurs in about 25% of patients with tardive dyskinesia (Gelenberg & Katz, 1993; Mutch, 1992).

TREATMENT

Numerous articles provide anecdotal reports of intervention or management techniques that have been found to be effective for specific occurrences or institutions. The goal of the treatment depends on the meaning of the behavior and its effect, as discussed earlier. Interventions that have been used in the past have either been designed to accommodate or enhance the pacing and wandering behavior through environmental designs or to prevent or limit the behavior.

Caregiver training should precede any specific intervention. The goal is to train the caregiver to assess the reason for the behavior and to intervene accordingly. An important concept to convey when training caregivers is that some wandering or pacing may be adaptive in providing physical stimulation and exercise. It may provide continuation of an aspect of the person's premorbid lifestyle, particularly for those for whom physical activity played a key role (Monsour & Robb, 1982). As such, these types of behaviors should not be restricted or eliminated but should be accommodated.

The first step in assessment of the wandering behavior is to observe the person and try to ascertain the reasons for the behavior (i.e., does he or she appear calm or content, is he or she trying to get somewhere?). What are the travel patterns? Are the patterns consistent? Are there consistent antecedents to the pacing or wandering behavior? Is the environment safe enough to allow the person to pace or wander freely? (Butler & Barnett, 1991; Davidhizar &

Cosgray, 1990; Fopma-Loy, 1988; Heim, 1986; Hiatt, 1980; Hirst & Metcalf, 1989; Monsour & Robb, 1982).

Gaining insight into the person's premorbid lifestyle and coping strategies through relatives and records may enhance the staff's ability in interpreting the information gleaned through observation (Monsour & Robb, 1982). On the basis of this assessment, the intervention may focus on changing the environment to accommodate the behavior, on limiting the effects of the behavior, or on calming the older person.

When the safety or well-being of the resident or other residents is threatened, general techniques used with persons suffering from dementia are needed, such as the use of a calm and pleasant demeanor and nonverbal cues. For example, if a resident is headed toward the end of a corridor that is being mopped, the caregiver may fall into step with the resident, engage them in conversation, and redirect their path to a more appropriate area. This can be achieved by continuing to talk while walking to another area or by gently taking the person's arm and slowly maneuvering them away from the risky area.

Accommodating Pacing or Wandering

Interventions to accommodate pacing or wandering include the following:

Locked or Semilocked Doors. Locked or semilocked doors secure the environment to ensure the safety of the elderly person by preventing them from leaving the unit or facility where they can be properly monitored (Butler & Barnett, 1991; Coons, 1988; Cornbleth, 1977; Grossberg et al., 1990; Knopman & Sawyer-DeMaris, 1990; Rabins, 1991). Semilocked doors are doors with entry mechanisms that require cognitive skills beyond those of most persons who wander. Some persons become extremely agitated when making repeated attempts to exit via a locked door, however.

Stimulus Control. Stimulus control using visual cues has been used in both clinical and research settings. Visual cues such as visual barriers on doors—used to address the problems associated with exit-seeking behavior—have been the focus of several studies. Hussian and Brown (1987) evaluated the utility of several two-dimensional grid patterns placed on the floor directly in front of an exit door for eight male elderly residents of a public mental hospital who manifested exit-seeking behaviors. Three-strip, 4-strip, 6-strip, and 8-strip horizontal patterns and a 10-strip vertical pattern of beige tape on a brown floor were compared to baseline (no grid pattern) regarding the number of crossings (i.e., crossings to and touching the exit door knob). The 8-strip horizontal grid was more effective than the other patterns resulting in a 69%

decrease in exit door contacts. In an attempt to extend the latter findings, Chafetz (1990) failed to find any reduction in exiting attempts using an 8-strip horizontal pattern of black tape on a white floor placed directly in front of two glass exit doors. Chafetz attributed the lack of effectiveness to the glass doors, which enabled the residents to see outside, enticing them to the exit door and distracting their attention from the floor grids. In a similar study, Namazi, Rosner, and Calkins (1989) evaluated the effectiveness of several different types of visual barriers in reducing exit attempts. The visual barriers consisted of a horizontal grid pattern (same as described earlier), a diagonal grid pattern that extended from the lower third of the door to an equal distance on the floor in front of the door, a beige (same color as the door) or green patterned cloth placed over the middle portion of the door (hiding the door knob), or a plastic door knob cover. Nine residents of a dementia unit were assessed using each of the visual barriers. Results revealed that the beige and the green patterned cloth over the middle portion of the door eliminated all attempts to exit in all nine residents. The authors attributed this remarkable finding to the problems demented elderly people have with visual agnosia. In other words, the door knob may be the only feature that distinguishes the door from the wall; once that cue is removed, then the door is no longer perceived as an exit door and thus no attempts are made to leave. Reducing failed attempts to exit may prevent significant exacerbations in agitation, making caregiving easier and, more important, maintaining a more positive mood in the residents.

The concept of stimulus control of behavior purports that altering the stimulus properties of common objects in the environment tends to decrease their effectiveness in triggering agitated behaviors. Alternately, stimulus control can be used to enhance stimuli to promote appropriate behavior. Examples include visual barriers on doors used clinically to prevent nursing home residents from trespassing into other residents' rooms, using strips of cloth that are attached across residents' doorways with velcro. Nursing staff members found that the mere strip of cloth is sufficient to dissuade wanderers from entering other residents' rooms. Other visual cues include placing the nursing home resident's picture on his or her door or signs specifically prepared with large-print letters designating landmarks on the unit or the resident's name specifying his or her room (Bertram, 1989).

Identity Bracelets. Identity bracelets are bracelets worn by persons who wander so that their identity and address will be obvious if they get lost (Butler & Barnett, 1991; Gaffney, 1986). Some nursing care facilities use colored bracelets, aimed at helping staff members near exit doors to rapidly identify pacers.

Alarm Systems. Alarm systems are usually placed on exit doors and are activated by alarm bracelets or other devices worn by the elderly person. The alarm alerts the caregiver when the person leaves the house or the facility (Blackburn, 1988; Negley, Molla, & Obenchain, 1990). Other alarms can alert a caregiver when the person has gone beyond a prescribed distance from the home. Still others are activated whenever anyone exits the door and can be deactivated by using a code. When an alarm system is put in place, staff members have to be trained to respond to the alarm immediately. Similar to alarms on exit doors, some facilities post pictures of residents who are not allowed to leave without an escort.

Sheltered Outdoor Areas. Sheltered outdoor areas are enclosed areas that are safe for free walking. Many facilities have now developed such areas to provide older persons the option to walk outdoors with minimal restriction.

Preventing or Limiting Wandering

Interventions aimed at preventing or limiting the wandering behavior include the following:

Addressing the Psychological Need of the Older Person. When the elderly person seems to pace or wander because of discontent, the best approach is to address the reason for dissatisfaction. If the person is looking for his or her home, the environment may need to be modified to look or feel more like their home environment. Sometimes, a caregiver needs to accompany the wanderer outdoors and thus allow him or her to complete an agenda of walking (Rader, Doan, & Schwab, 1985). If the person is bored or looking for an activity he or she used to engage in, regularly planned activities may be appropriate, including arts and crafts, music, exercise, dance, and so on. At times, the older person needs to be comforted and needs to talk with a caregiver (Burnside, 1980; McGrowder-Lin & Bhatt, 1988; Rader, 1987; Rosswurm, Zimmerman, Schwartz-Fulton, & Norman, 1986; Sawyer & Mendlovitz, 1982). If a person frequently trespasses into other persons' rooms, then identification of what the resident is after can be used to provide those items in his or her own room. For example, Donat (1986b) described a resident who frequently trespassed into other residents' rooms causing them much distress. An observation revealed that when trespassing, the resident tended to look out the window and observe an area that could not be viewed from her room or spend time in front of a dresser with a mirror, rubbing her hand through her hair. Most of the trespassing was eliminated by a room change to one with the desired view and with a mirror.

Physical and Chemical Restraints. In the past, physical and chemical re-straints have been used that forcibly limit the behavior (Burnside, 1980;

Coons, 1988; Cornbleth, 1977; Heim, 1986; Rader, 1987; Rader et al., 1985; Sawyer & Mendlovitz, 1982; Snyder et al., 1978). Although effective in decreasing wandering behaviors, physical restraints deprive the older person of dignity and freedom in daily life. In addition, physical restraints have been associated with serious injuries (King & Mallet, 1991) and increased agitation (Werner, Cohen-Mansfield, Braun, & Marx, 1989). The immobility may also have physical consequences, such as urinary retention, muscle atrophy, and osteoporosis (Rosen & Giacomo, 1978). Similarly, psychotropic medication used to control wandering is associated with severe side effects (e.g., King & Mallet, 1991). In consequence, the Omnibus Budget Reconciliation Act (1987) mandated that medications and physical restraints not be used to treat wandering and pacing in nursing home residents.

White Noise. White noise at night was used by Young, Muir-Nash, and Ninos (1988). Two of eight patients experienced reduced nighttime wandering.

Differential Reinforcement. Differential reinforcement of other behavior was used by Fatis et al. (as described in Hussian, 1987) in a case study of an institutionalized 76-year-old female suffering from Alzheimer's disease. Results of a reversed design showed that wandering decreased and social interactions increased during intervention.

Aggressive Behaviors

THE DIMENSION OF THE PROBLEM

Aggressive behaviors present a unique challenge to caregivers. These behaviors may involve physical danger to the elderly person's caregiver, to other persons in the elderly person's proximity, and even to the elderly persons themselves. Moreover, aggressive behaviors may elicit negative reactions from persons in the aggressive person's environment leading to an exacerbation of the behavior. Aggressive behavior is frequently cited as the most common reason for institutionalization in geriatric psychiatry units (Moak, 1990; Petrie, Lawson, & Hollender, 1982) or for admission to a nursing home (Reisberg et al., 1987). Up to 20% of the caregivers of people with dementia report physical violence as a serious care problem (Rabins et al., 1982).

There is no consensus regarding the definition of aggressive behaviors. Different studies include diverse behaviors under the category of aggressive behaviors. An aggressive behavior, according to Ryden (1988), is a hostile action directed toward other persons or objects or toward oneself. Her definition includes physically aggressive behaviors, verbally aggressive behaviors, and sexually aggressive behaviors. Physical and verbal manifestations of aggression are also included in the categories described by other researchers (Everitt et al., 1991; Jackson et al., 1989; Marx, Cohen-Mansfield, & Werner, 1990; Rovner, Kafonek, Filipp, Lucas, & Folstein, 1986). Other studies include a broader definition involving behaviors such as refusing treatment and refusing to eat (Winger, Schirm, & Stewart, 1987), passive aggression (Rovner et al., 1986), and physical or verbal threats (Patel & Hope, 1992a). Aware of the diverse definitions of aggression available in the literature, Patel and Hope (1993), in a comprehensive review of aggressive behaviors, suggest the following definition: "Aggressive behavior is an overt act, involving the delivery of noxious stimuli to (but not necessarily aimed at) another object, organism or self, which is clearly not accidental" (p. 458). Although this definition does not answer all the questions as to which types of behaviors should be included (only physical, also verbal?), it provides a guide for working with aggressive elderly persons suffering from dementia.

Classification systems for subtypes of aggressive behaviors generally focus on the following dimensions: (a) the nature of activity, such as physical aggression, verbal aggression, and sexually aggressive behavior (Ryden, 1988); (b) the target of the behavior—that is, disturbing or endangering self versus others; (c) the degree of disruption—such as disturbing versus endangering (Winger et al., 1987; Zimmer et al., 1984); or (d) the environmental conditions under which the behavior occurs, such as nighttime, during intimate care, and so forth (Patel & Hope, 1993).

PREVALENCE

Several studies have examined the prevalence of aggressive behaviors in elderly persons, some of which are summarized in Cohen-Mansfield et al. (1993). Prevalence rates vary from 8% to 91% in institutional settings and from 1% to 47% in the community. This variety stems from several reasons:

Definition. As previously noted, different studies include different behaviors in their assessment. Therefore, any comparison should give a detailed list of the type of aggressive behaviors included.

Frequency Base. Different studies use different frequency scales to assess the behaviors. These differences may lead the reader to misleading conclusions regarding the prevalence rates reported in the different studies. For example, the prevalence rate of 49% for the 408 nursing home residents reported by Marx et al. (1990) may at first glance appear lower than the combination of aggressive behaviors reported by Burgio, Jones, Butler, and Engel (1988; i.e., 26% tantrum-like behaviors, 20% physical aggression, 9% self-injury, 4% property destruction, and 3% spitting). However, both studies are comparable because Burgio et al.'s includes categories of aggression that are not mutually exclusive (i.e., a resident could be physically aggressive, verbally abusive, and self-injurious).

Sources of the Information. Differences in the prevalence rates reported may also be the result of the sources of information used to collect the data. For example, whereas several of the studies rely on either formal or informal caregivers' reports (e.g., Everitt et al., 1991; Marx et al., 1990; Rovner et al., 1986), other studies are based on information extracted from incident reports (Malone, Thompson, & Goodwin, 1993), review of patients' charts (Haller, Binder, & McNeil, 1989), or on direct observations (Palmstierna & Wistedt, 1987). In addition, differences between studies may stem from differences in the composition of the population under study, the type of facility, and the reliability and validity of the assessment instrument used.

Despite the variability in prevalence rates, several findings emerge from the different studies. Rates of aggressive behaviors are higher in institutional settings than in the community. Verbally and physically aggressive behaviors are more prevalent than sexually aggressive behaviors and self-abusive behaviors. Verbal aggression is more prevalent than physical types of aggression (Marx et al., 1990; Patel & Hope, 1992b).

ASSESSMENT

The assessment of aggressive behaviors, like that of pacing and wandering, depends on the goal of assessment and may include assessment of its frequency, the reason for the behavior, or the effect of the behavior. Assessment of frequency of occurrence can be based on informant ratings by caregivers (family members in the community and formal caregivers in institutional settings) or on direct observation of the behaviors as they occur in their natural environment. Although several instruments were developed specifically for the assessment of aggressive behaviors, the majority of instruments assess a wider range of behavioral problems and have aggressive behaviors either as a subscale or as separate items of the global scale.

Informant Ratings

The Ryden Aggression Scale (Ryden, 1988) is a 25-item scale specifically developed for the assessment of aggressive behaviors in the community. It includes three subscales: physically aggressive behaviors (including 16 items, such as threatening gestures, pushing, throwing an object), verbally aggressive behaviors (including 4 items: hostile language, cursing, name-calling, and verbal threats), and sexual aggression (including 5 items: hugging, kissing, touching body parts, intercourse, and making obscene gestures). Another scale recently developed for assessing aggressive behaviors is the Rating Scale for Aggressive Behavior in the Elderly (Patel & Hope, 1992a, 1992b). This 23-item scale was developed for use in an inpatient psychogeriatric population; 19 items inquire about observable behavior, 3 items inquire about the consequences of aggressive behavior, and 1 item asks for a global judgment of overall aggressiveness. The scale was designed to be completed by nursing staff and contains items from three factors: verbal aggression, physical aggression, and antisocial behavior. The Social Dysfunction and Aggression Scale (SDAS; Wistedt et al., 1990) was also developed specifically to assess aggressive behaviors. Unlike the other instruments, however, the SDAS is based on physicians' ratings. Other assessment instruments tap other problem behaviors as well (e.g., CMAI; the Dementia Behavior Disturbance Scale, Baumgarten et al., 1990; the Nursing Home Behavior Problem Scale, Ray et al., 1992) and include between 1 to 11 items describing physical or verbal agitation or both. The most commonly used items are physical attacks, including hitting and kicking, physical or verbal threats or both, and destroying property. The Disruptive Behavior Rating Scales (Mungas et al., 1989) measure physically aggressive behaviors (hitting, kicking, biting, spitting, throwing things, and using weapons) and verbally aggressive behaviors (yelling or screaming, swearing, threatening physical harm, criticizing, and scolding). The majority of the assessment instruments use rating scales ranging from 3 to 7 points to assess frequency of occurrence, and many also include severity scales to assess the disruptiveness of the behaviors according to caregivers' perceptions.

Assessments Based on Direct Observations

Several instruments have been developed for the assessment of aggressive behaviors using direct systematic observations. Generally, these instruments are more time-consuming and costly, especially when used to examine physically aggressive behaviors, which tend to occur at low frequencies. These assessments do, however, allow the researcher-clinician to describe the behaviors as they occur in their natural environment. Some instruments are designed to have staff members as the observers (such as the Staff Observation Aggression Scale by Palmstierna & Wistedt [1987] and the Pittsburgh Agitation Scale by Rosen et al. [1994]) and may provide good diagnostic tools to understand the circumstances under which the observed behaviors occur and to develop appropriate interventions accordingly. Others, such as the Agitation Behavior Mapping Instrument (Cohen-Mansfield, Werner, & Marx, 1990), rely on trained observers.

Assessing the reason or intended function for aggression is like assessing the reasons for wandering or pacing. The level of function, including cognitive ability and performance of activities of daily living (ADLs), should be taken into account as well as examination of past habits of aggressive conduct and environmental antecedents and consequences to the aggressive behavior.

The effects of aggressive behaviors are usually assessed via informant ratings of levels of disruptiveness of the behaviors, but other measures, such as number of injuries caused by the behavior and cost of damage to persons and property, could also be used.

Several studies have also examined the perceptions of caregivers regarding the disruptiveness of aggressive behaviors. For example, nurses in both acute care settings and in nursing homes rated 4 physically aggressive behaviors of the 29-item Disruptive Behavior Inventory (strikes out at staff, physically abuses others, self-destructive behavior, and dangerous behavior) as the most disruptive (Sternberg, Whelihan, Fretwell, Biellecki, & Murray, 1989). Similarly, in a study of 346 patients in 12 intermediate care facilities in Massachusetts, nurses from 2 shifts reported that 59% of the physically abusive participants caused mild to moderate distress and another 32% caused severe distress; 73% of the verbally abusive participants caused mild to moderate distress and another 17% caused severe distress (Everitt et al., 1991). In another study, physically assaultive and verbally abusive residents were identified by 116 nursing home staff members of a 350-bed nursing home as some of the most difficult to manage (Hoffman, 1987). Given these results, it is not surprising that exposure to aggressive behaviors (physical or verbal) was found to be the highest predictor of job dissatisfaction in a study of health care staff members from a state geriatric long-term care hospital (Dougherty, Preston, Jones, & Payne, 1992).

UNDERSTANDING THE PROBLEM

Studies examining the correlates of aggressive behaviors have focused on the characteristics of elderly persons who manifest aggressive behaviors and described the environmental correlates of aggressive behaviors.

Characteristics of Elderly Persons Manifesting Aggressive Behaviors

Aggressive elderly persons tend to be more cognitively impaired than nonaggressive elderly persons (Fleishman, Rosin, Tomer, & Schwartz, 1987;

Marx et al., 1990; Meddaugh, 1987; Patel & Hope, 1992b; Ryden, 1988; Swearer, Drachman, O'Donnell, & Mitchell, 1988; Winger et al., 1987) and more functionally dependent on the help of others to perform their activities of daily living (Marx et al., 1990; Meddaugh, 1987). Males are more likely to be aggressive than females. This tendency holds true for nursing home residents (Jackson et al., 1989; Marx et al., 1990; Ryden & Bossenmaier, 1988) as well as for community-dwelling elderly persons (Ryden, 1988). Aggressive persons have longer lengths of stay than nonaggressive persons, as reported by Winger et al. (1987) for a Veterans Administration Medical Center and by Nilsson, Palmstierna, and Wistedt (1988) for two long-term psychogeriatric hospital units.

Some relationships among health indicators and aggression have been found. Marx et al. (1990), in a survey of 408 nursing home residents, found that aggressive residents were more incontinent of urine than nonaggressive residents. This relationship may be confounded with cognitive functioning (Werner et al., 1989), however, and there was no significant relationship with the number of medical diagnoses (Cohen-Mansfield, Marx, Werner, & Freedman, 1992). Similarly, Malone et al. (1993), in a study of aggressive incident reports in a 350-bed skilled nursing facility, found that the aggressive behavior of six residents with recurrent aggressive behavior was associated to urinary tract infections.

Conflicting findings have been reported in regard to the relationship between psychotic symptoms and aggression. In a study of 181 patients with probable Alzheimer's disease attending a research clinic, Deutsch, Bylsma, Rovner, Steele, and Folstein (1991) found the presence of delusions to be a significant correlate of physical aggression. In contrast, Swearer et al. (1988) did not find a correlation between the severity of hallucinations or delusions and assaultive behavior. These studies demonstrate that the relationship of aggression to medical and psychiatric conditions is yet inconclusive.

Especially interesting is the relationship between aggression and the aggressive premorbid personality in the elderly person. Caregivers of 58% of the participants in a community-based study perceived aggressive behavior as resulting from premorbid personality traits (Ware, Fairburn, & Hope, 1990); Ryden (1988) found a positive relationship between aggression prior to the onset of the dementing illness and the score on the Ryden Aggression Scale; and Hamel et al. (1990) found premorbid aggression to be a correlate of aggression in patients suffering from dementia. Marx et al. (1990) found a significant correlation between manifestation of aggressive behaviors in the nursing home and reports of having manifested these behaviors immediately prior to nursing home entry.

The quality of the relationships between elderly persons and their family members has also been found to be related to aggression. Hamel et al. (1990)

found aggressive behavior to be predicted by a more troubled premorbid relationship between caregiver and care receiver. Marx et al. (1990) found poor quality of social interactions (e.g., intimacy with staff and visitors) as one of the correlates of the manifestation of aggressive behaviors in nursing home residents. However, Marx et al.'s data were cross-sectional and did not establish whether the poor quality of social interaction preceded or followed the aggressive behavior.

Environmental Correlates

Several researchers found aggression associated to temporal factors, although no consistent results emerged. Cohen-Mansfield et al. (1992), in the earlier-mentioned observational study, found that aggressive behaviors were manifested significantly more often during the evening hours than during the daytime hours, a finding that supports the occurrence of "sundowning" in the nursing home. Similarly, Donat (1986a), based on a 3-month survey of incident reports in a 330-bed ICF, found that 61% of the incidents involving an aggressor occurred between 5 p.m. and 8 p.m.—that is, when staffing levels were lower and when activities were not available. Malone et al. (1993), in a study of incident reports of aggressive behavior in a 350-bed SNF, found that aggressive events occurred mostly during the evening (50%) and day shifts (47%). However, Patel and Hope (1992b) found that aggressive behaviors were not related to time of day. Colenda and Hamer (1991), in two exploratory surveys at a geropsychiatric state hospital, found that most aggressive events occurred during the day shift. Similarly, Meyer, Schalock, and Genaidy (1991) found aggressive episodes in hospitalized geriatric patients to be more frequent during the day shift, suggesting that aggressive behaviors are more frequent at times when personal care is provided. Indeed, in a study of 40 psychiatric inpatients (mean age = 81 years) observed over 6 weeks, most of the aggressive events observed occurred when staff members were helping with ADLs (Nilsson et al., 1988). Ryden (1988) and Ware et al. (1990), in their studies about aggression in the community, also found aggression associated with intimate care during ADL times. These findings may suggest that aggressive behaviors may occur in response to touch or invasion of personal space. Indeed, Marx, Werner, and Cohen-Mansfield (1989) found an increase in nursing home residents' aggressiveness when they were touched.

Ryden (1988), in a study on aggression in community-dwelling elderly, found a noisy atmosphere to be associated with aggression. However, Cohen-Mansfield, Werner, and Marx (1988, 1990), in an observational study of 24 highly agitated nursing home residents, failed to find an association between aggressive behaviors and the level of noise, quality of light, and the presence of music in the environment. In this study, aggressive behaviors occurred more frequently (a) in social situations; (b) at night when it was cold; (c) in environments where the resident was in close contact with another person, such as the bath; or (d) when in touching contact with another person, at lunch and during the evening.

Antecedents

Several studies described the characteristics that triggered aggressive behaviors and the reactions that these behaviors provoked. In their observational study of 24 nursing home residents, Cohen-Mansfield, Werner, and Marx (1991) found that only 26% of the aggressive behaviors observed were triggered by an observable event. When aggressive behaviors were triggered, they were more likely to be triggered by staff members than by others. Concurring findings in a geropsychiatric population reported that aggressive behaviors were most often triggered by unknown or not observable behaviors (Colenda & Hamer, 1991). Meyer et al. (1991), in a study of 78 geriatric patients in a psychiatric hospital, found that the most common antecedent to aggressive behavior was being asked to do something.

Objects of Aggressive Behavior

In Cohen-Mansfield et al.'s (1992) observational study, aggressive behaviors tended to be directed at staff members. Similar findings were reported by Patel and Hope (1992b) on the basis of a staff questionnaire, in which 63% of the patients rated as aggressive directed their aggression toward staff members. Analyzing the Physical Intervention Reporting Form, which is completed as part of hospital policy, Meyer et al. (1991) found that staff members were more likely to be the targets of aggressive behaviors compared to other patients (59.54% vs. 40%). Similarly, Colenda and Hamer (1991) reported that aggressive demented patients in a geropsychiatric state hospital were involved in more patient-staff aggressive events than patient-patient events. Among the patients who did not suffer from dementia, there were fewer aggressive events, and those were less likely to involve staff members. According to Bridges-Parlet et al.'s (1994) observational study of 20 physically aggressive nursing home residents, the majority of the physically aggressive behavior was directed toward staff, usually during bathing, toileting, grooming, dressing, or during redirection of the resident. However, in a study of incident reports in a skilled nursing facility, Malone et al. (1993) found that 62% of the victims of aggressive behavior were other nursing home residents and 37% were employees.

Consequences

Concerning the reactions to aggressive behaviors, Hamel et al. (1990), in a study of 213 community-dwelling patients suffering from dementia, found that the typical caregiver reaction was to retreat or to ignore such behavior. Similarly, in institutional settings, the most commonly observed reaction was to take no action (Cohen-Mansfield et al., 1992; Nilsson et al., 1988). Cohen-Mansfield, Werner, and Marx (1991) found that when there was a reaction to the aggressive act, staff members were more likely to react than visitors, volunteers, or other residents, and their reaction was usually corrective. Only 0.6% of staff members' reactions toward an aggressive event were disagreeable. In contrast, when other residents reacted, their reactions were unpleasant in 32% of those reactions (Cohen-Mansfield, Werner, & Marx, 1991). Nilsson et al. (1988) report that there was no reaction in 76% of the aggressive events; in 18% of the events, the staff talked to the patient; and in 6%, the patient was taken off physical restraints.

In terms of explaining aggressive behaviors, several possibilities emerge from the studies of correlates to these behaviors:

1. The neurological damage associated with severe dementia may cause disinhibition, especially among persons with a tendency toward antisocial or aggressive behaviors.
2. Aggressive behaviors are, at times, responses to real or perceived noxious stimuli, such as invasion of personal space, invasion of privacy, an uncomfortable environment (e.g., a cold environment or physical restraints; Cohen-Mansfield & Werner, 1993), or an infection. Sometimes, these behaviors may be a response to internal stimuli, as in hallucinations and delusions.
3. Aggressive behaviors seem to have an interactive component, which is either triggered or enabled by the presence of others. Aggressive behaviors may thus sometimes be the manifestation of an effort to interact in the presence of dementia and communication difficulties; it may be a response to an incomprehensible or misinterpreted request by staff, as in the performance of ADL.

Beyond these general principles, it is important to try to understand the meaning of the behavior for the aggressive person as well as the sequence of events leading to the aggressive act. One example is of a woman who constantly followed and disturbed a male resident because she mistook him to be her late husband. After continuous behavior on her part, the male resident, who could not comprehend her approaches, struck her. Another example is that of a Holocaust survivor resident who aggressively resisted going to the shower, which, in her mind, was equated with the gas chambers—which the Nazis referred to as showers when directing Holocaust victims to go to their deaths.

TREATMENT

The most important principle in treating the aggressive person is the effort to understand the meaning of the sequence that led to the aggressive behavior.

In these two examples, the treatment would follow from this understanding. The woman who mistook the other resident to be her husband probably needed to be separated geographically from that resident and to find other companionship. The Holocaust survivor should not receive showers. It would be helpful to find out how she bathed at home and try to simulate that sequence. Otherwise, alternative methods, such as sponge bathing, would need to be tried.

In a more general vein, caregivers need to look for stimuli that may bother the resident, such as a cold environment, or for an infection. Generally, privacy and dignity of the person need to be upheld to the maximal level possible. If it is necessary to get close to the resident, this may need to be done slowly and in several steps, which alerts the resident to the approaching caregiver rather than alarming him or her. Similarly, given the difficulty in communication, this process may need to be adapted to the person's needs by using nonverbal cues, a pleasant way of addressing the person, and allowing time for the communication to evolve. At times, flexibility is needed. If the resident is unable to understand a request, the caregiver may need to accommodate him or her, such as bringing the meal to the person rather than bringing the older person to the meal. Similarly, the scheduling of an event may not fit the older person's internal schedule (Knopman & Sawyer-DeMaris, 1990), and the caregiver may be the one who needs to be flexible. At times, more radical approaches may be used. If two residents are repeatedly observed engaging in aggressive behavior, separating them into different units may be necessary.

In the literature, three main types of interventions are described: behavioral interventions, educational interventions, and pharmacological interventions.

Behavioral Interventions

Several studies report positive results implementing behavioral interventions. Most studies are based on case studies or small samples, however, and standardized assessments of the behaviors before and after the interventions are lacking. Several of the studies use reinforcement. For instance, Mishara and Kastenbaum (1973) reported a decrease in the amount of self-injurious behaviors among elderly long-term mental hospital patients through a token economy program in which patients were reinforced for engaging in desirable behaviors. Tokens could be exchanged for items and privileges such as cigarettes or permission to leave the ward. In addition, staff members were trained to better understand the patients. Rosberger and MacLean (1983) described a case study of a 79-year-old female whose aggressive behaviors decreased following exposure to social reinforcement of appropriate behaviors by staff. In two studies, Vaccaro (1988a, 1988b) described the successful implementation of operant techniques with aggressive elderly persons in psychiatric facilities; however, it does not seem that the older persons suffered from dementia. In the first study, a 69-year-old Caucasian male in an adult ward in a developmental center was rewarded for nonaggressive behavior with food or drink (e.g. cookies, juice) and was placed in a barren room following aggressive episodes. Later, the tangible reinforcement was switched to social reinforcement, such as verbal praise. The second study used similar differential schedules with a group of six highly aggressive elderly persons (mean age = 70 years) residing in an adult ward of a developmental center.

In summary, most of the studies concerning behavioral approaches to aggression involved long-term residents of psychiatric facilities rather than persons manifesting aggressive behavior because of advanced dementia. The studies, though limited in scope and methods, may provide ideas for alternative approaches for clinicians. The tailoring of these interventions to persons suffering from advance dementia needs further investigation.

Educational Interventions

Several studies examined the effects of educating caregivers for the management of aggressive behaviors. Mentes and Ferraro (1989) developed an education program for nursing aides focusing on the identification of risk factors and the prevention of aggressive episodes. The program described by Mentes and Ferraro had three main objectives: (a) know the resident (i.e., identify potential factors that may place the resident at risk for aggression), (b) think about strategies to prevent the possibility of aggression, and (c) use protective interventions if a resident causes injury to self or others. The objectives of the program were provided to nursing aides in six weekly, 1-hour sessions that included talks and experiential learning, such as videotape vignettes and role playing. This program proved to be effective in decreasing the number of aggressive incidents. Feldt and Ryden (1992) described a care program designed to create therapeutic environments for residents manifesting aggressive behaviors. These environments are aimed at increasing the residents' feelings of safety and physical comfort; enabling them to experience a sense of control, thus providing optimal levels of stress; and providing them with pleasurable experiences. The practical results of such a program still await empirical confirmation. Feldt and Ryden (1992) described an educational program provided to nursing assistants caring for cognitively impaired aggressive residents. The content areas covered by the program included knowledge about cognitive functioning, precipitants of aggression, communication techniques, ways of preventing aggressive incidents, and management of personal feelings. A follow-up evaluation of the educational program's effect showed that nursing assistants saw their caregiving tasks as significantly more rewarding and less frustrating.

Pharmacological Interventions

The use of pharmacological interventions with elderly persons manifesting aggressive behaviors is quite common and includes different types of medications.

Anxiolytic drugs are usually used for a short-term treatment of aggressive behaviors. For instance, Fritz and Stewart (1990) described two case studies in which very low doses of lorazepam (.5 mg and 1 mg) were successfully prescribed before nursing care to decrease the aggressive behavior of two demented nursing home residents. Colenda (1988) described the use of buspirone to decrease the aggressive behavior of a 74-year-old woman manifesting frequent angry outbursts. However, these drugs, as well as other antianxiety agents, may have adverse effects, such as persistent lethargy, hypotension, and pseudoparkinsonism (Marin & Greenwald, 1989).

Antidepressants have also been used to control aggressive behaviors in elderly persons. Seven male patients at a Veterans Administration medical center were treated with trazodone for their aggressive behaviors (Pinner & Rich, 1988). Doses ranged between 150 mg and 400 mg per day. Three patients ceased manifesting aggressive behaviors 4 to 6 weeks after their pharmacological treatment. However, another three did not show any decrease in their aggressive behaviors. One patient was unable to complete the trial.

Antipsychotic drugs are the most commonly used agents to control severe and continued aggression (Maletta, 1992; Risse & Barnes, 1986). For example, the successful use of haloperidol for treating aggression was described by Herrera (1985) for an 84-year-old woman suffering from Alzheimer's disease. Although the use of antipsychotic drugs for managing aggressive behaviors may be effective, these agents should be prescribed carefully, given their adverse effects. To minimize these adverse effects, Yudofsky, Silver, and Hales (1990) suggested establishing a treatment plan using a standardized assessment instrument (the Overt Aggression Scale) to monitor the efficacy of the pharmacological intervention. Howell and Watts (1990) suggested the use of high potency neuroleptic agents (such as haloperidol) only when an acute pharmacological intervention is necessary. If long-term therapy is necessary, intermediate potency agents such as molindone are suggested, to reduce the risk of extrapyramidal side effects.

Carbamazepine (Tegretol) is the only anticonvulsant agent used effectively to treat aggressive behaviors. Marin and Greenwald (1989) described three case studies of aggressive nursing home residents whose aggression was controlled using 100 mg of carbamazepine.

Beta-blockers have also been used to control occasional aggressive behavior (Maletta, 1992). In the elderly population, several case studies have described decreases in aggressive behaviors after administration of propranolol (Petrie & Ban, 1981; Yudofsky, Williams, & Gorman, 1981).

Estrogen was reported as effective in decreasing aggressive physical behavior in two elderly men suffering from dementia (Kyomen, Nobel, & Wei, 1991).

As noted, the efficacy of different medications for aggression has been challenged (Billig, Cohen-Mansfield, & Lipson, 1991; Butler, Burgio, & Engel, 1987; Schneider, Pollock, & Lyness, 1990) and awaits further research. It is recognized that controlled double-blind studies are extremely difficult to conduct in this population and therefore research frequently lags behind clinical practice.

Conclusions and Future Goals

Wandering and aggression are major problems for elderly persons and their caregivers. Both behaviors are associated with late stages of dementia, and some of the same issues arise in their discussion. Definitional consensus is still needed for each, which limits reliable determination of prevalence rates. In both cases, assessment needs to address concomitants of the behaviors to identify probable causes of the behavior and to match interventions to the interpretation of the behavior. The research that has been done suggests that wandering or pacing and aggression have different etiologies and have different meanings for the elderly persons who manifest them. Accordingly, the appropriate treatments may vary substantially. Considerable additional research is needed to help caregivers elucidate the origin of both behaviors and the appropriate treatments.

From ethical, efficacy, and legal standpoints, restraints of any kind (physical or chemical) are neither an appropriate nor acceptable means for dealing with persons who pace or wander or those who are aggressive. Thus, the question is, how do we deal with these persons? The answer is neither easy nor simple. For wandering or pacing behaviors, caregivers need to be aware that the majority of these behaviors should not be restricted. In fact, they should be accommodated. In many instances, the pacing behavior is adaptive in that it provides exercise and physical stimulation that the resident may not get otherwise. Thus, regularly scheduled exercise (at appropriate levels of intensity) may help fulfill some of the need to pace. Similarly, regularly scheduled, chaperoned walks around the facility or trips to a protected garden may further fulfill needs by providing a temporary escape from the environment of the unit to the outdoors.

To better accommodate the resident's pacing or wandering, the environment can be optimized. This may entail making sure there is proper lighting, an appropriate floor surface without ridges or holes, removal of obstacles from corridors and other commonly used areas, and placement of orienting markers on the unit to help residents locate their rooms, the bathroom, water fountains, and so forth. If the person engages in trespassing or exit seeking, the use of an alarm may be appropriate.

Some aggressive behaviors may be triggered by discernible situations or stimuli. Trying to focus attention on the possible stimuli that trigger the behavior may help caregivers decrease the occurrence of aggressive episodes or trespassing behaviors.

Approaches should involve a change in attitude as well as in philosophy of care. In a setting in which caregivers have been educated to restrain patients and adhere to schedules, this may not be an easy task. Caregivers should be trained and educated to understand these behaviors. They should learn to address the causes of the behaviors by evaluating the individual needs of each elderly person. For both aggression and wandering, the first step is to observe the person and try to discern patterns and antecedents to the behavior as well as to determine whether the behaviors pose any danger to themselves or others. Obtaining information on the person's premorbid lifestyle may shed light on their current behavior.

More systematic research is needed in this area. As previously stated, most of the literature is based on case studies and clinical experience. Generally, case studies indicate strategies that can work, but they do not indicate the rate of efficacy of the treatments or the ways in which treatments could be matched to the persons' characteristics or specific behaviors. Studies attempting to understand and characterize the behaviors are needed. These will promote development of interventions matched to specific needs, thereby providing a better quality of life for elderly persons and, indirectly, the caregiver.

18

Sleep Disturbances

Richard R. Bootzin
Dana Epstein
Mindy Engle-Friedman
Marie-Anne Salvio

Sleep disturbances, such as difficulty in falling asleep, frequent or prolonged awakenings during the night, early morning awakenings, or the subjective experience of poor quality sleep, are common complaints among older adults. Next-day effects on mood, performance, fatigue, and motivation are also reported. In a national survey, the prevalence of "serious" insomnia (defined as considerable difficulty in falling asleep or staying asleep within the preceding 12 months) increased from 14% for the 18 years to 34 years age group to 25% for the 65 years to 79 years age group (Mellinger, Balter, & Uhlenhuth, 1985). The number of individuals with less severe insomnia also rose with increasing age. All told, 45% of those persons aged 65 to 79 years had some difficulty with insomnia in the preceding 12 months.

The disproportionate use of sleep medication in older adults corroborates the survey reports of sleep disturbances. Of those taking prescription medication for sleep, 69% were individuals aged 50 to 79 years (Mellinger, Balter,

& Uhlenhuth, 1985). The use of hypnotics may be even greater among the institutionalized elderly. A U.S. Public Health Service survey of prescribing patterns in skilled nursing facilities found that prescriptions for hypnotics had been written for 94% of the 98,505 patients studied (U.S. Public Health Service, 1976). Another study found that the proportion of residents receiving hypnotics in 23 nursing homes varied from 2.3% to 56.5% (Mogan, Gilleard, & Reive, 1982). Subsequent studies of the prescription of hypnotics in nursing homes revealed that few notations are made in patients' charts concerning either a diagnosis of sleep disturbance or the type of sleep problem (Cohen et al., 1983; Salvio, 1992). Furthermore, there was no relationship between the occurrence of sleep problems as rated by either the patients or nurses and the use of hypnotics (Cohen et al., 1983), and there was only rare documentation of the effects of the hypnotics on the patients' sleep (Salvio, 1992). Not only do older adults consume disproportionate amounts of sleep medication, but persons living in institutions may have such medications prescribed and continued with little regard for the nature of the sleep disorder or the effects of the medication on sleep.

Despite the reliance on sleep medication, the use of hypnotics is both ineffective and potentially dangerous for the chronic insomniac. Tolerance to hypnotics develops rapidly, so larger and larger doses are required to produce improved sleep. Continuous hypnotic use results in less deep sleep, less rapid eye movement (REM) sleep, and more light, fragmented sleep. In addition, there are often severe withdrawal effects from hypnotics. Individuals who have been on hypnotics for months, particularly benzodiazepines, are likely to experience severe rebound insomnia, which can last for as long as 3 to 4 weeks, when they discontinue taking hypnotics. The insomniac may conclude that the hypnotics are needed to avoid rebound effects. Consequently, hypnotics may lead to drug dependence. Hypnotics are not the treatment of choice for persistent insomnia (National Institutes of Health, 1983).

Causes of Sleep Disturbance

Sleep disturbances can result from developmental changes associated with aging as well as from a number of other factors.

THE EFFECTS OF AGING ON SLEEP

The most frequent sleep complaints of older adults are increased frequency and duration of nocturnal awakenings and complaints of light, disturbed sleep (Miles & Dement, 1980). These complaints parallel developmental changes in psycho-physiological sleep parameters that occur with advancing age (Bliwise, 1994).

The measure of sleep that has been generally accepted as most reliable and valid is *polysomnography* (Bootzin & Engle-Friedman, 1981). Polysomnography consists of the all-night recording of the electroencephalogram (EEG), the electrooculogram, and the electromyogram (EMG). Other physiological parameters, such as respiration, heart rate, and temperature, can be measured for special purposes.

One of the most consistent findings associated with aging, documented through polysomnography, is an increase in the frequency of awakenings, particularly during the latter half of the night (Agnew, Webb, & Williams, 1967; Reynolds et al., 1985; Webb, 1982; Williams, Karacan, & Hursch, 1974). Older adults also have more difficulty falling back to sleep than younger individuals. For example, Webb and Campbell (1980) found that individuals 50 to 60 years old took longer to fall asleep when awakened after the first 80 minutes of the night than subjects 21 to 23 years old. This increased difficulty in falling back to sleep later in the night may account for the increased frequency of early morning awakenings among the elderly.

As a consequence of increased time awake and difficulty falling back to sleep, older adults get less total sleep at night than younger adults (Williams et al., 1974). Because daytime naps increase in frequency with age (Zepelin, 1973), the total sleep of the elderly is about equivalent to that of younger individuals if the sleep distribution throughout the entire 24-hour day is considered (Webb & Swinburne, 1971; Zepelin, 1973). Sleep efficiency is so poor, however, that elders may stay in bed for many hours. In a study of nursing home patients, for example, residents spent an average of 15 hours in bed per day to get 8 hours of sleep (Ancoli-Israel, Parker, Sinaee, Fell, & Kripke, 1989).

A marked reduction in slow-wave sleep (stages 3 and 4) is also observed with aging (Coleman et al., 1981, Reynolds et al., 1985). One fourth of the population over the age of 60 years may have little or no stage 4 sleep. The reduction in the amount of slow-wave sleep is due primarily to the reduction in amplitude of the EEG waves so that they do not meet the criterion for scoring as slow-wave sleep (Agnew et al., 1967; Feinberg, Koresko, & Heller, 1967; Kales, 1975; Prinz, Obriest, & Wang, 1975; Webb & Dreblow, 1982). Thus, slow EEG-frequency sleep still occurs in the elderly, but there is a marked loss in EEG amplitude.

There are gender and age differences among elders, particularly related to sustaining sleep and the amount of slow-wave sleep obtained. Although there is an age-related decrease in the slow-wave sleep of the elderly, aging women appear to have more slow-wave sleep than men (Hoch, Reynolds, Kupfer, Berman, Houck, & Stack, 1987). For older women, a higher and more stable relationship exists between self-reported soundness of sleep and the polysomnographic variable of slow-wave sleep (Hoch et al., 1987).

When age was considered across three decades, "younger old" males (in their 60s and 70s) had more difficulty maintaining sleep than same-age women (Reynolds et al., 1985). A meta-analysis addressing gender differences in sleep behavior of older adults supports this finding (Rediehs, Reis, & Creason, 1990). "Older old" men (in their 80s), however, have been found to better maintain sleep than their female counterparts (Reynolds et al., 1991).

REM sleep occurs every 90 to 100 minutes and is the stage of sleep typically associated with dreaming. The largest proportion of REM sleep occurs in the latter half of the night because REM periods tend to increase in duration throughout the night. There are small decreases in REM sleep with aging (Coleman et al., 1981; Williams et al., 1974). Unlike younger individuals, older adults have REM periods that remain uniform or decrease in duration during the night (Reynolds et al., 1985). Increased REM early in the night's sleep is often associated with depression. In addition, shortened latency to REM sleep and lower amounts of REM have been found to be associated with intellectual decline (Feinberg et al., 1967).

Variability in a number of sleep parameters, including time in bed, total sleep time, sleep latency, number of awakenings, and time awake after sleep onset, increases with age (Williams et al., 1974). In addition, older adults are likely to have more deleterious effects from sleep loss on next-day performance and mood. Webb and Levy (1982) found that in comparison to people aged 18 to 22 years, those aged 40 to 49 years showed significantly poorer performance on auditory vigilance, addition, and mood scales following 2 nights of sleep deprivation.

It should be emphasized that although there are substantial changes in sleep associated with aging, these changes do not always result in a subjective complaint of sleep disturbance. Changes in slow-wave sleep and REM sleep, for example, may not influence judgments about the quality of sleep, whereas frequent awakenings will (Bonnet & Johnson, 1978).

The changes in sleep parameters observed in the older adult may be due to a degradation of the central nervous system. Changes in the brain, including decreases in neurons, metabolic rate, and blood flow, may affect both sleep and intellectual performance (Prinz, 1977). For example, there are striking sleep changes in persons with dementia, including frequent nocturnal awakenings and decreased REM sleep. These changes parallel but exceed in magnitude the changes of normal aging (Prinz et al., 1982).

PHYSICAL DISORDERS

In addition to developmental changes, there are many other causes of sleep disorders. As can be seen in Table 18.1, these include physical disorders, substances, circadian rhythm disorders, psychological factors, poor sleep environments, and poor sleep habits. Thus, the label *insomnia* encompasses

Table 18.1   Causes of Insomnia

Physical disorders	Periodic movements during sleep, restless legs, gastroesophageal reflux, sleep apnea, fibromyalgia, arthritis, chronic pain, cardiac problems
Substances	Caffeine, nicotine, alcohol, hypnotics, tranquilizers, other prescription medication, substances of abuse
Circadian rhythm problems	Shift work, jet lag, delayed sleep phase syndrome, advanced sleep phase syndrome
Psychological factors	Stress, psychopathology, nightmares, inactivity, reinforcement for insomnia
Poor sleep environment	Noise, ambient temperature, light, sleeping surface, bed partner
Poor sleep habits	Extended time in bed, naps, irregular schedule, bed as a cue for arousal

Source: Bootzin and Perlis (1992). Copyright 1992, Physicians Postgraduate Press. Used with permission.

many, more specific, disorders. More detailed information about the diagnosis of sleep disorders can be found in the *International Classification of Sleep Disorders: Diagnostic and Coding Manual* (American Sleep Disorders Association [ASDA], 1990).

Respiratory Disturbances

The most common physical disorders that affect sleep are sleep-related respiratory disturbances, including *sleep apnea* (a cessation of airflow for 10 seconds or longer) and *hypopnea* (50% or greater reduction of airflow for 10 seconds or longer). These may occur repeatedly throughout the night's sleep, producing frequent brief arousals during sleep and leading to excessive daytime sleepiness. Prevalence has been estimated to be 1% to 2% in middle-aged men. Three types of sleep apnea have been defined: (a) *obstructive*—cessation of airflow despite thoracic and abdominal respiratory effort, (b) *central*—cessation of airflow characterized by cessation of respiratory movements due to disordered central regulation of respiration, and (c) *mixed*—cessation of airflow without respiratory movement initially and then followed by respiratory effort.

Obstructive Sleep Apnea (OSA). Diagnosis may be made on the basis of the following: (a) complaint of excessive daytime sleepiness or insomnia, (b) frequent episodes of obstructed breathing during sleep, and (c) polysomnographic findings that include more than five apneic episodes per hour and one of the following: frequent arousals, bradycardia, or arterial oxygen desaturation (ASDA, 1990).

Obesity is most often associated with OSA, although not all patients are overweight. Respiratory pauses and sleep apneas increase with age. Respiratory disturbances have been found in both asymptomatic older persons (McGinty et al., 1982) and symptomatic older adults (Ancoli-Israel, Kripke, Mason, & Messing, 1981). Nocturnal respiration was found to become increasingly more irregular with increasing age.

The course of treatment is dependent on the severity of the condition and the prominent symptoms associated with it. Initial treatment may consist of dietary control of weight, avoiding the use of alcohol at bedtime, keeping the individual from sleeping on his or her back, and avoiding the use of sedative hypnotics, which as depressants, may exacerbate the respiratory problems and reduce the patient's ability to wake up and breathe.

Patients with evidence of oxygen desaturation below 85% respond positively to continuous positive air pressure, which is administered by means of a nasal mask. This results in an increase in lung volume and oxygen saturation, thereby decreasing apneas. There are also a number of surgical procedures, such as uvulopharyngopalatoplasty, which are intended to surgically widen air passageways, but they have had mixed success.

Central Sleep Apnea. Patients with central apnea have many fewer respiratory events at night than do patients with OSA. Unlike those who complain of daytime sleepiness associated with OSA, patients with pure central sleep apnea rarely complain of daytime sleepiness or hypersomnolence. Hypersomnolence becomes more apparent as the proportion of obstructive apnea increases.

Treatment for pure central apnea is primarily pharmacological. Respiratory stimulants have been found to be effective for central sleep apnea for a short time, but results have been variable with long-term use.

Muscular Disorders

Two muscular disorders—*periodic limb movement disorder* (PLM) and *restless legs syndrome* (RLS)—can also impair sleep, and the prevalence of both disorders increases with age.

PLM disorder is characterized by periodic episodes of repetitive and stereotypic limb movements during sleep. The most common sleep characteristics associated with PLMs are frequent arousals and complaints of nonrestorative sleep. Patients are often unaware of PLMs and present complaints of insomnia or excessive daytime sleepiness or seek help as a result of a bed partner's complaints of excessive nighttime movement.

RLS is a disorder characterized by irresistible leg movements, usually prior to sleep onset (ASDA, 1990) and often described as a creeping sensation. The most prominent characteristic of this disorder is the partial or complete relief of the sensation with leg motion and the return of the symptom with cessation of movement. Symptoms are often exacerbated soon after getting into bed and tend to cease long enough for the patient to fall asleep only to reappear later in the night. RLS may also occur at times during the day after prolonged periods of sitting. The severity of symptoms with RLS may wax and wane throughout a patient's lifetime. Remissions may last for years and symptoms reappear suddenly without warning. Symptoms are associated with a number of conditions, such as the last trimester of pregnancy, caffeine intake, fatigue, exceptionally warm environment, prolonged exposure to cold, anemia, and rheumatoid arthritis (ASDA, 1990).

Treatment for PLM and RLS is pharmacological. The most effective drugs to date are benzodiazepines, L-dopa, and opioids. The use of benzodiazepines should be considered carefully, especially in the elderly, because they may induce or exacerbate sleep apnea.

Other Physical Disorders

A number of other physical disorders experienced by the older adult can interfere with sleep. Older adults often suffer from painful conditions such as arthritis, low back pain, osteoporosis, fibromyalgia, and headaches as well as chronic illnesses associated with pain, including cancer; diabetes; and cardiovascular, gastrointestinal, and chronic obstructive pulmonary diseases. Diabetes may interfere with sleep through underregulation of blood sugar, resulting in glycosuria and nocturia, or through overregulation leading to hypoglycemia (Prinz & Raskind, 1978).

Bed rest is often recommended for the treatment of pain. However, for persons with insomnia, there are detrimental effects of prolonged time in bed, particularly sleep fragmentation and maladaptive conditioning to the bed and bedroom. Medical treatments may include analgesics and hypnotics. Opiates and nonopiates can affect sleep architecture detrimentally, whereas hypnotics' usefulness is time limited. Successful reduction of sleep difficulties has been reported from using stimulus control instructions, sleep restriction, and relaxation-based methods to treat insomnia accompanying chronic pain (back pain, cancer, and hemophilia; Cannici, Malcolm, & Peek, 1983; Morin, Kowatch, & O'Shanick, 1990; Morin, Kowatch, & Wade, 1989; Stam & Bultz, 1986; Varni, 1980).

Alzheimer's Disease. Disturbed sleep-wake patterns are a hallmark of Alzheimer's disease. Loss of slow-wave sleep and an increase in the amount and frequency of nighttime wakefulness have been reported at early stages of the disease with significant amounts of daytime sleep emerging with advanced severity (Vitiello, Bliwise, & Prinz, 1992). Controversy exists regarding whether there is a decrease in REM sleep (Bliwise, 1993). Decreased sleep efficiency, increased percentage of stage 1 sleep, and higher rate of arousals and awakenings have been confirmed by meta-analysis (Benca, Obermeyer, Thisted, & Gillin, 1992).

The aspect of sleep disturbance most likely to be brought to the attention of the clinician is what has been called *sundowning*. This describes late afternoon or early evening exacerbation of behavioral disruption and agitation. Sundowning is a complex and poorly defined syndrome. It has been suggested that it may be mediated by disruptions of the circadian system (Satlin, Volicer, Ross, Herz, & Campbell, 1992). Several treatment approaches have been suggested (Bliwise, 1993). The first step is to rule out underlying causes, such as toxins, infection, metabolic disorders, or medications. Pharmacological treatment includes hypnotics, which have minimal effect, and neuroleptics, which are overprescribed and have strong risks for side effects in older persons. Behavioral treatments are preferable and could be initiated on a unit policy basis for inpatients or individually for outpatients. Treatments might include regularly scheduled activities both in the day and during the usual nighttime awakenings, exposure to bright outdoor light, bright light therapy, and sleep restriction (Bliwise, 1993; Okawa et al., 1991; Satlin et al., 1992). In outpatient situations, the clinician should assess the caretakers because they may suffer sleep disturbances themselves and benefit from respite breaks.

SUBSTANCES

Both prescription and nonprescription substances can cause sleep disturbances. The use of drugs to induce or to suppress sleepiness may cause adverse effects with chronic use. Although alcohol and sedative-hypnotics are thought to induce a state of unconsciousness that resembles sleep, the resemblance to natural sleep is weak. Hypnotics produce disruptions in sleep architecture and increases in arousal thresholds. The use of stimulants to suppress sleep can produce persistent insomnia.

Hypnotics

The prescription of sedative-hypnotics is the most frequently used treatment for insomnia. Of the sedative-hypnotics, benzodiazepines are the most frequently prescribed, having almost completely replaced barbiturates (Morin & Kwentus, 1988). These drugs have definite effects on sleep architecture, including reduction in sleep latency, decrease in the number of nocturnal awakenings, increase in total sleep time, and decrease in amount of REM and delta sleep.

The use of sedative-hypnotics to induce sleep is effective for short-term use, with effects that last 2 to 4 weeks. With continued use, tolerance develops rapidly, and larger doses are required to achieve a soporific effect. As dosage is increased to offset tolerance, daytime carryover effects also increase and may include symptoms such as excessive sleepiness, poor motor coordination, visual-motor problems, and late afternoon restlessness (ASDA, 1990). Cessation of sedative-hypnotics results in withdrawal symptoms that may promote psychological dependence. Severe insomnia has been shown to be among the most frequent withdrawal symptoms. These symptoms promote psychological dependency because the individual becomes convinced that the hypnotics are the only thing preventing night after night of sleeplessness.

Besides their disruptive effects on sleep, hypnotics have a number of deleterious side effects. The pharmacological effects of hypnotics depend on dose, absorption rate, and serum half-life (Greenblatt, 1992; Nicholson, 1994). Hypnotics with long half-lives (such as flurazepam) are likely to produce drug hangovers and daytime sedation. Hypnotics with short half-lives (such as triazolam) may produce rebound insomnia the very same night the medication was taken and daytime anxiety. Withdrawal effects are usually stronger with the short half-life hypnotics. With the long half-life hypnotics, there is still medication in the blood stream for days after the insomniac stops taking the medication. Thus, the insomniac is going through a tapered withdrawal.

Recently, a new, nonbenzodiazepine hypnotic has been introduced in the United States—zolpidem. Zolpidem is an imidazopyridine that is related to benzodiazepines but so far has not been shown to have rebound or daytime residual effects (Nicholson, 1994). Zolpidem is a very short half-life medication and is primarily useful for sleep onset problems. However, zolpidem, like all hypnotics, is a central nervous system depressant and may exacerbate other health problems.

The elderly are particularly vulnerable to deleterious side effects because they are more likely to have disorders that can be aggravated by hypnotics, such as respiratory, hepatic, renal, or cardiac disorders (Institute of Medicine, 1979). In addition, the decreases in protein-binding ability, circulation time, and kidney and liver metabolism associated with aging lengthen the time drugs remain in the body, extending the period of potential toxicity (Albert, 1981). The elderly are also likely to have increased risk of toxic interactions from multiple drug use (Miles & Dement, 1980). This is exacerbated by the fact that older persons are more likely to substitute one drug for another, exchange drugs with friends, consult a number of physicians, and use drugs beyond their expiration dates (Hemminki & Heikkila, 1975).

The same side effects, multiple drug interactions, and disrupted sleep that are associated with hypnotics also apply to tranquilizers such as diazepam (Valium). Tricyclic antidepressants suppress REM sleep and can exacerbate periodic limb movements. The new generation of antidepressants—selective serotonin reuptake inhibitors—also produce increased physiological arousal during sleep, resulting in reduced delta activity and decreased sleep efficiency (Armitage, Trivedi, Rush, & Hoffmann, 1995).

The active ingredient in most over-the-counter sleep medication is an antihistamine. Because drowsiness is a side effect of antihistamines, over-the-counter medications have been promoted as facilitating the onset of sleep. However, polysomnographic investigations of these mediations have not found them to be more effective than placebos (e.g., Kales, Tan, Swearingen, & Kales, 1971). In addition to ineffectiveness, a number of hazards are associated with them. As depressants, they potentiate the effects of alcohol, hypnotics, and tranquilizers. They can also produce side effects of confusion, disorientation, and memory disturbance (Institute of Medicine, 1979).

Other substances that are available without a prescription that have been used to facilitate sleep include chamomile tea, valerian root, and tryptophan. None of these substances has been shown to be helpful for persistent insomnia. It should also be emphasized that because these substances are not regulated by the Food and Drug Administration, the consumer cannot be assured of purity. There is substantial current interest in the use of melatonin for sleep, particularly for the elderly, as well as for the regulation of the sleep-wake circadian rhythm. Although there are many promising research results (e.g., Haimov et al., 1995; Zhdanova, Wurtman, Lynch, Morabito, & Matheson, 1995), important questions about dose size and long-term effects have yet to be answered.

Alcohol

The problems associated with hypnotics and tranquilizers are true for alcohol as well. Like other depressants, alcohol is REM-sleep depriving. Continued use results in tolerance to the alcohol as a sleep-inducing agent, and sleep fragmentation becomes more prominent. Often, patients will become desperate and increase the amount of alcohol or add other sedatives in order to sleep. Patients will often report that they have no sleep disturbance as long as they continue to take the alcohol nightly. Withdrawal from heavy drinking produces a REM-rebound effect that is accompanied by restless sleep and nightmares. Alcohol also exacerbates sleep apnea.

An important additional danger is that alcohol potentiates the effects of hypnotics and other depressants. Thus, the combination of alcohol and hypnotics may intensify and prolong deleterious side effects (Institute of Medicine, 1979). It is likely, too, that alcohol will be less well tolerated by the older than the younger adult because toxic substances remain in the body for extended periods of time in the older adult.

Stimulants

Many drugs such as cocaine, amphetamines, and caffeine are used primarily for their sleep suppressing effects. Caffeine is contained in many foods and beverages, including coffee, tea, soft drinks, and chocolate. Other drugs, including analgesics (those that contain caffeine), bronchodilators, decongestants, and appetite suppressants, disturb sleep architecture as a side effect of long-term use. There is an increase in sleep latency, a decrease in total sleep time, and an increase in spontaneous awakenings (ASDA, 1990; Brown et al., 1995). As tolerance to the alerting and euphoric effects of these drugs increases, higher doses are necessary. Cessation of these drugs may be associated with withdrawal symptoms such as sleepiness, irritability, lassitude, and severe depression (ASDA, 1990).

Nicotine is also a central nervous system stimulant and produces lighter and more fragmented sleep. Complaints of insomnia, anxiety, or both may be due to excessive ingestion of caffeine, nicotine, or other stimulants. Because caffeine has a plasma half-life of approximately 6 hours, the older adult might continue to experience its effects long after it was ingested. Reducing or eliminating the intake of caffeine, particularly in the afternoon and evening, and quitting smoking can lead to substantial improvement in sleep.

CIRCADIAN RHYTHM PROBLEMS

Circadian rhythm disorders occur when individuals attempt to sleep at times that are inconsistent with their underlying biological clocks. In *delayed sleep phase syndrome* (DSPS), the sleep-wake circadian rhythm is delayed compared to when the individual attempts to sleep. Individuals with this problem report difficulty falling asleep at a desired bedtime but have normal sleep if they attempt to sleep a few hours later. DSPS individuals commonly identify themselves as "night people" and report being most alert during the late evening and night hours. This problem is often seen in adolescents and young adults. In contrast, in *advanced sleep phase syndrome,* sleep occurs at a time earlier than desired and the individual awakens earlier than desired. Normal aging in older adults is often associated with a phase advance.

Two common environmentally caused circadian rhythm problems are shift work and time zone changes. Because of family and social demands, night shift workers usually attempt to live their days off on a different schedule than their work days. A disrupted sleep-wake schedule often results in disturbed and shortened sleep, sleepiness on the job, reduced performance levels, and psychological distress due to disruptions in family and social life. Workers on rotating shift schedules have greater difficulty than those on permanent night shifts. The severity of the problem increases with age.

Many researchers recommend that rotating shift schedules should be designed to be consistent with a natural underlying tendency of humans to phase delay. That is, the direction of rotation should be progressively later and the duration of the shift should be long enough to allow for adaptation. European researchers, on the other hand, prefer a very rapidly rotating system of 2 days on each shift because that allows the circadian rhythm to remain constant (Akerstedt, 1985). A variety of methods for enhancing alertness and performance among shift workers have been suggested (Penn & Bootzin, 1990). The optimal timing of work breaks, social activity during breaks, bright light, and other sensory stimulation have the most potential for short-term alerting effects. Stress-coping techniques, sleep hygiene information, and family counseling have the most potential for addressing the long-term effects of shift work.

Disturbed sleep associated with rapid time zone change (jet lag) is due to a desynchrony between the endogenous sleep-wake rhythm and the light-dark cycle. Symptoms include an inability to sustain sleep and excessive sleepiness. For most people, these symptoms subside after a few days, depending on the number of time zones crossed. Frequent travelers, such as transatlantic airline crews, may experience more persistent difficulties. Westward travel is associated with disturbed sleep at the end of the sleep period, which coincides with habitual wakeup time, and eastward travel is associated with sleep onset insomnia. Due to the natural tendency to phase delay, westbound travel is easier to adjust to than traveling eastbound.

Recent results show that properly timed exposures to bright light (2,500–10,000 lux) for 2 to 3 days to a week can shift the phase of the sleep rhythm. As a means of comparison, typical indoor room light is less than 500 lux; a few minutes after dawn, sunlight produces about 2,500 lux; and at noon, sunlight is in the 100,000 lux range. The direction of the shift depends on the timing of the exposure to light. A phase advance is achieved by light exposure in the morning, whereas a phase delay is achieved by light exposure in the evening. In addition to the proper timing of bright light, it is also important to have periods of darkness during which no bright light is allowed.

Preliminary results indicate that bright light therapy may be effective for a number of circadian rhythm sleep disorders (Terman, 1994). Bright light treatment during night shift work resulted in increased duration of daytime sleep and improved alertness on the job. Bright light has also been shown to benefit jet lag sufferers and those with sleep phase disorders. Encouraging results have also been reported for the use of bright light with sleep maintenance insomniacs. Exposure to bright light in the evening has been found to delay wake-up time, increase total sleep (Lack & Wright, 1993), and increase sleep efficiency (Campbell, Dawson, & Anderson, 1993).

PSYCHOLOGICAL FACTORS

As a person ages, many important life events occur that may be difficult to adjust to and thus may affect sleep. For example, a spouse may die, the person may retire, living arrangements may change, or the individual may become aware of changes in his or her own physical and intellectual functioning. Individuals who ordinarily have little trouble sleeping often develop insomnia during periods of stress (Healey et al., 1981).

Retirement and Inactivity

Retirement and the lack of scheduled activities may inhibit the establishment of consistent sleep and wake times in older persons. Morgan (1987) suggests that after retirement, life may become less complex and demanding so that daytime napping surfaces by default. Older adults appear to return to the polyphasic alternation of sleep and wakefulness of infancy. Disruptions of circadian wake-sleep schedules have been found to be particularly common in institutionalized elderly (Wessler, Rubin, & Sollberger, 1976).

An active lifestyle and structured schedule may be an important facet of entraining circadian rhythms and improving sleep patterns after retirement. Elderly women engaged in a highly structured lifestyle with regular wake and meal times, scheduled activities, and an expectation to remain active as long as possible experienced shorter sleep latency, longer time spent asleep, greater sleep efficiency, and greater REM sleep compared to age-matched female controls (Hoch et al., 1987). Community-dwelling older adults who participated three times per week in a 9-month exercise program reported faster sleep onset and less difficulty falling back to sleep after nighttime awakening (Stevenson & Topp, 1990). Polysomnographic reports of older adults who participate in regular exercise revealed more continuous sleep, less wake time, and deeper sleep than sedentary subjects (Edinger et al., 1993). There were increases in slow-wave sleep and decreases in nighttime awakenings for older male participants in a 6-month exercise program (Vitiello et al., 1992).

Psychopathology

There is a large literature on the relationship between psychopathology and sleep disturbance (see Bootzin, Manber, Perlis, Salvio, & Wyatt, 1993). On self-reported personality inventories, insomniacs have been found to be more introverted, anxious, neurotic, and depressed than normal sleepers. Older insomniacs have been found to be less depressed and anxious than their younger counterparts (Roehrs, Zorick, Sicklesteel, Wittig, & Roth, 1983).

Sleep problems are one of the primary symptoms of a major depressive episode (American Psychiatric Association, 1994). It is estimated that approximately 90% of all individuals with depression will have at least a mild degree of sleep architecture abnormality (Reynolds, 1989). Sleep parameters are often predictive of other symptoms of depression, such as diminished pleasure seeking (anhedonia), depressed or unresponsive mood, and poor appetite (Giles, Roffwarg, Schlesser, & Rush, 1986).

Several sleep parameter abnormalities have been observed in depressed individuals, including the elderly depressed. The most common finding is a decreased REM latency. Also, the first few REM periods of the night are longer and more intense, with higher counts of phasic activity than later periods (Reynolds, 1989). It should be noted that shortened REM latency may not be specific to depression. Short REM latencies have been found in patients with narcolepsy, obsessive-compulsive disorder, schizophrenia, mania, anxiety disorder, alcoholism, Alzheimer's and Korsakoff's diseases, sleep apnea, and insomnia (Benca, 1994; Wehr & Sack, 1988). Thus, REM disturbances are involved in a broad range of psychopathology.

Difficulty initiating and maintaining sleep is also common in depression. Early morning awakenings are seen more frequently in older compared to younger depressives. Decreased amounts of slow-wave sleep have also been observed, with men showing a greater reduction than women (Reynolds et al., 1990).

When sleep variables of elderly depressed individuals are compared to their younger counterparts, the elderly show decreased sleep efficiency, decreased REM latency, decreased total sleep, increased intermittent wakefulness, and decreased slow-wave sleep (Gillin, Duncan, Murphy et al., 1981). The most salient difference in EEG sleep profiles between the elderly and younger cohorts with depression is that the former are more likely to demonstrate sleep maintenance difficulty, whereas the latter are more likely to have problems initiating sleep.

Sleep abnormalities may reflect a vulnerability for depression because they persist beyond the active phase of the depression and may be in evidence before the first episode of depression (Hauri, Chernik, Hawkins, & Mendels, 1974; Giles, Kupfer, & Roffwarg, 1990). In general, it appears that the sleep abnormalities found in depressed individuals point to some malfunction of either an REM sleep activation mechanism, a slow-wave activating and REM sleep inhibition system, some component of a circadian timing circuit, or some combination of the three (Bootzin et al., 1993).

It is commonly recommended that antidepressant medication be prescribed for patients whose insomnia is diagnosed as resulting from depression. It is difficult if not impossible, however, to determine whether depression (or anxiety) is directly causing insomnia because all that is observed is covariation (Bootzin & Nicassio, 1978). In cases in which psychological problems accompany sleep disturbance, separate therapeutic attention should be given to each. The therapist should not assume that improvement in one will automatically produce improvement in the other.

POOR SLEEP ENVIRONMENT

Among the many environmental factors that affect sleep are noise, temperature, room or bed sharing, institutionalization, and the need for vigilance during sleep. Sensitivity to environmental factors increases with age and is subject to great individual variability. There is no ideal room temperature or degree of mattress firmness. People can learn to sleep comfortably in a wide range of temperatures and on many different surfaces. Individuals may have developed strong preferences, however, so that sleep is disrupted if the sleep environment does not correspond to those preferences. This problem is frequently observed when people move to a new setting. The unfamiliarity of the setting and the lack of familiar personal belongings may cause a prolonged period of disrupted sleep.

Noise decreases both the amount of deep sleep and the continuity of sleep. There is an increase in body movements and sleep stage shifts. Even people who habitually sleep in noisy environments do not fully adapt to the noise. Studies show that a presentation of an auditory stimulus is often followed by very brief arousal (3-15 seconds). The fragmentation of sleep often leads to increased daytime sleepiness (Stepansky, Lamphere, Badia, Zorick, & Roth, 1984). Because the elderly are more easily awakened (Zepelin, McDonald, & Zammit, 1984) and have more difficulty falling back to sleep once awakened (Webb & Campbell, 1980), noisy environments are likely to be particularly troublesome. Unpredictable noise is especially disturbing (Sanchez & Bootzin, 1985). Thus, continuous white noise, such as from a fan, can be useful means of reducing the effects of the noise.

POOR SLEEP HABITS

There are many daily living activities that have been found to be "inconsistent with the maintenance of good quality sleep and full daytime alertness" (ASDA, 1990, p. 73). These include highly irregular sleep-wake schedules, extended time in bed, irregular naps, and engaging in activities at bedtime that are incompatible with falling asleep.

The relationship between biological rhythms and the sleep-wake cycle is the basis for the common recommendation to maintain a regular sleep schedule. Those who keep irregular schedules for long periods of time are at risk for developing sleep disturbances. Conversely, those with sleep disturbances frequently benefit from regularizing their sleep schedule.

The elderly are more likely to nap than young adults. The sleep-wake cycle of many elderly, especially those in nursing homes, resembles the polyphasic sleep-wake cycle of infancy. Three factors that may lead to daytime napping in the elderly are (a) attempts to compensate for lost sleep, (b) understimulation and weakening of social constraints, and (c) deterioration of the circadian sleep-wake rhythm (Morgan, 1987). In addition, napping may not interfere with nighttime sleep in the elderly to the same extent that it does in young adults (Feinberg et al., 1985; Morin & Gramling, 1989).

Insomniacs may engage in activities at bedtime that are incompatible with falling asleep (Bootzin & Nicassio, 1978). They may, for example, use their bedrooms for reading, talking on the telephone, watching television, snacking, listening to music, and probably most disturbing of all, worrying. The result is that the bed is no longer just a cue for sleeping; instead, it becomes a cue for physiological arousal.

Cognitive intrusions may be particularly disruptive. Worries and concerns are often accompanied by emotional upset, yet they may appear in the absence of excessive physiological arousal (Starker & Hasenfeld, 1976). The content of the insomniac's concerns may shift from the general pressures of current and future problems to persevering worries regarding the inability to fall asleep or to get enough sleep during the night. The bedroom, then, can become a cue for the anxiety and frustration associated with trying to fall asleep. Insomniacs often sleep well any place other than in their own beds. For example, they may sleep better in a sleep laboratory than they do at home (de la Pena, 1978). In contrast, people who have no difficulty falling asleep in their own beds often have difficulty doing so in strange surroundings.

Treatment of Sleep Disturbances

Many clinicians view the sleep difficulties of older persons as a normal developmental change, and the problem is often ignored or overlooked. Chronic sleep difficulty can affect the daily functioning and quality of life of older adults. Insomnia is a strong predictor of mortality and nursing home placement for community-dwelling elderly (Pollack, Perlick, Linser, Wenston, & Hsieh, 1990) and a salient factor in caretakers' decisions to place the elder in institutional care (Pollak & Perlick, 1987; Sanford, 1975).

During the past 20 years, a number of short-term nonpharmacological interventions for insomnia have been developed and evaluated (for reviews, see Bootzin & Perlis, 1992; Lacks & Morin, 1992; Lichstein & Riedel, 1994). Two separate meta-analyses have been published (Morin, Culbert, & Schwartz, 1994; Murtagh & Greenwood, 1995). There are many overlapping conclusions. Both meta-analyses concluded that psychological treatments have been found to improve the sleep of insomniacs over control conditions and improvements were maintained at 6-month follow-ups. Overall, treatment reduced average sleep onset latency from 64.3 to 36.6 minutes and reduced average time awake after sleep onset from 70.3 to 37.6 minutes (Morin et al., 1994). Polysomnographic measures were included in only about 15% of the studies reviewed. Consequently, the results of the meta-analyses were based on daily sleep diaries. The results from studies using polysomnography were similar in pattern, although with smaller effects, to those found from the larger group of studies (Morin et al., 1994).

The strongest treatment effects were seen in those who were not regular users of hypnotics and in clinically referred patients as compared to volunteers (Murtagh & Greenwood, 1995). It is often difficult to withdraw chronic insomniacs from hypnotics. Thus, it is generally a wise policy not to prescribe hypnotics for sleep problems to begin with. Older adults generally find behavioral therapies more acceptable than pharmacotherapy in the treatment of insomnia (Morin, Gaulier, Barry, & Kowatch, 1992).

Of particular interest to readers of this volume is the finding that neither age nor gender was related to outcome in either meta-analysis. Although only a small number of behavioral treatment outcome studies have focused on older adults, those that have indicate that geriatric insomnia is treatable with behavioral techniques.

A number of cognitive-behavioral treatments have been found to be effective for treating insomnia. These include sleep hygiene information, stimulus control instructions, sleep restriction, relaxation training, biofeedback, and cognitive therapy.

SLEEP HYGIENE INFORMATION

Sleep hygiene is basically an educational component of treatment. Insomniacs often engage in activities that interfere with the facilitation of good sleep and daytime functioning. Sleep hygiene usually consists of providing basic knowledge about sleep processes and functions, developmental changes in sleep, sleep-wake schedules, naps, the sleep environment, and activities and substances that interfere with sleep. In addition to the information described, emphasis is usually also placed on the individual variability of sleep need and on our capacity to function well on less than adequate sleep.

With regard to the latter point, there are only small performance deficits associated with 1 or 2 nights of sleep deprivation. Even studies of sleep deprivation with the elderly indicate that the effects on performance are small (e.g., Bonnet, 1984). The major effects of sleep deprivation are fatigue and irritability. Fatigue, however, follows a daily circadian rhythm even if the individual goes without sleep entirely (Kleitman, 1963). A person will be fatigued and have a low body temperature at times when she or he would ordinarily be asleep. On the other hand, the individual will be alert even after sleep deprivation at times when she or he is ordinarily awake. Thus, the day's performance is not as dependent on the previous night's sleep as many insomniacs expect.

Sleep hygiene has been tested both separately and as part of treatment packages (Edinger, Hoelscher, Marsh, Lipper, & Ionescou-Pioggia, 1990; Engle-Friedman, Bootzin, Hazlewood, & Tsao, 1992; Hoelscher & Edinger, 1988; Morin, Kowatch, Berry, & Walton, 1993). When sleep hygiene information is given as the only treatment, it has been found to be of modest efficacy (Morin et al., 1994). Nevertheless, all older adults should receive sleep hygiene information as part of a more comprehensive treatment. Hauri (1991) cautions against giving written lists of sleep hygiene rules and instead recommends targeting three or four rules pertinent to the patient's specific problem.

STIMULUS CONTROL INSTRUCTIONS

Stimulus control instructions consist of a set of instructions designed to help the insomniac establish a consistent sleep-wake rhythm, strengthen the bed and bedroom as cues for sleep, and weaken them as cues for activities that might interfere with sleep (Bootzin, 1972, 1977; Bootzin, Epstein, & Wood, 1991). Persons are taught to reassociate the bed and bedroom with rapidly falling asleep or back to sleep and to focus on internal cues of sleepiness rather than relying on clock time to signal bedtime.

Stimulus control instructions are one of the most effective, if not the most effective, nonpharmacological treatment of insomnia currently available (Lacks & Morin, 1992; Morin et al., 1994; Murtagh & Greenwood, 1995). It is the most frequently tested behavioral treatment for older adults and has demonstrated significant improvement in disturbed sleep parameters of the elderly (Davies, Lacks, Storandt, & Bertelson, 1986; Engle-Friedman et al., 1992; Morin & Azrin, 1987, 1988; Puder, Lacks, Bertelson, & Storandt, 1983).

The following six rules constitute the stimulus control instructions (Bootzin, Epstein, & Wood, 1991):

1. Lie down intending to go to sleep only when you are sleepy.
2. Do not use your bed for anything except sleep; that is, do not read, watch television, eat, or worry in bed. Sexual activity is the only exception to this rule. On such occasions, the instructions are to be followed afterward, when you intend to go to sleep.
3. If you find yourself unable to fall asleep, get up and go into another room. Stay up as long as you wish and then return to the bedroom to sleep. Although we do not want you to watch the clock, we want you to get out of bed if you do not fall asleep immediately. Remember, the goal is to associate your bed with falling asleep *quickly!* If you are in bed more than about 10 minutes without falling asleep and have not gotten up, you are not following this instruction.

4. If you still cannot fall asleep, repeat Step 3. Do this as often as necessary throughout the night.

5. Set your alarm and get up at the same time every morning irrespective of how much sleep you got during the night. This will help your body acquire a consistent sleep rhythm.

6. Do not nap during the day.

The focus of the instructions is primarily on sleep onset. For sleep maintenance problems, the instructions are to be followed after awakening, when the patient has difficulty falling back to sleep. Although these stimulus control instructions appear simple and straightforward, compliance is better if the instructions are discussed individually and a rationale is provided for each rule (Bootzin et al., 1991).

Two modifications of the rules have frequently been implemented for older insomniacs. For rules 3 and 4, those over 60 years of age are instructed to get out of bed after about 20 minutes instead of after 10 minutes. This recognizes that older individuals usually take longer to fall asleep than do younger individuals.

The goals of rule 6 are to keep insomniacs from disrupting their sleep patterns by irregular napping and to prevent them from losing the advantage of the sleep loss of the previous night for increasing the likelihood of faster sleep onset the following night. A nap that takes place 7 days a week at the same time would be permissible. For those elderly insomniacs who feel that they need to nap, a daily nap of 30 to 45 minutes or the use of 20 to 30 minutes of relaxation as a nap substitute is recommended.

Cognitive-behavioral treatments for insomnia, including stimulus control instructions, are primarily self-management treatments. The treatments are carried out by the patients at home. Consequently, compliance may be a problem. Most compliance problems can be solved by direct discussion with the patients. A common problem is the disturbance of the spouse's sleep when the insomniac gets out of bed. Discussion with the spouse is often helpful in ensuring full cooperation. During the winter in cold climates, some patients may be reluctant to leave the warmth of their beds. Suggestions for keeping warm robes near the beds and keeping an additional room warm throughout the night, along with encouragement to try to follow the instructions, are usually effective in promoting compliance.

SLEEP RESTRICTION THERAPY

Sleep restriction therapy (Spielman, Saskin, & Thorpy, 1987) is based on the observation that many insomniacs, especially older adults, spend too much time in bed attempting to sleep and therefore have poor sleep efficiency. The aim of sleep restriction therapy is to consolidate sleep through the restriction of the amount of time spent in bed. Sleep restriction therapy prescribes an individualized sleep-wake schedule that limits the person's amount of time in bed to his or her estimated average amount of nighttime sleep. Partial sleep deprivation is thereby induced, with the resultant consolidation of sleep. Daytime sleepiness may be experienced at the beginning of treatment, but as sleep becomes more consolidated (i.e., efficient), the sleep-wake schedule is altered by increasing the amount of time in bed.

Sleep restriction therapy has been tested against stimulus control instructions and relaxation therapy and has been included in several treatment packages. Significant reduction in time awake after sleep onset, increase in sleep efficiency and total sleep time, and less time in bed have been reported (Anderson et al., 1988; Edinger et al., 1990; Friedman, Bliwise, Yesavage, & Salom, 1991; Hoelsher & Edinger, 1988; Rubinstein et al., 1980).

Persons spending too much time in bed attempting to sleep can benefit by sleep restriction therapy. For example, a patient who spends 9 hours in bed but sleeps only 5 hours would be prescribed an initial time in bed of 5 hours. No matter how little a patient reports that he is sleeping, the prescribed sleep window is always at least 4.5 hours. Using the rules established by Glovinsky & Spielman (1991) for older adults, weekly 15 minute increases or decreases are made, contingent on sleep efficiency (sleep time ÷ time in bed × 100%). Sleep efficiency ≥ 85% warrants an increase of time in bed, whereas sleep efficiency ≤ 80% would result in a decrease. Changes in sleep scheduling focus on bedtime. Wakeup time remains consistent throughout and, it is hoped, after treatment.

In scheduling the amount of time in bed, a flexible approach by the therapist along with active participation by the patient has been suggested to ensure compliance (Friedman et al., 1991). Issues to consider during therapy include initial daytime sleepiness and tasks-activities to keep busy and stay awake during the afternoon and evening until the scheduled bedtime (Glovinsky & Spielman, 1991). Consolidation of sleep as evidenced by consistent sleep efficiency of equal to or greater than 85% on daily sleep diaries indicates treatment success.

RELAXATION TRAINING AND BIOFEEDBACK

A commonly recommended treatment for insomnia is some type of relaxation training. This includes a variety of procedures, such as progressive relaxation, autogenic training, transcendental meditation, yoga, hypnosis, and EMG biofeedback. As treatments for insomnia, all of these procedures are based on the same premise: if people can learn to be relaxed at bedtime, they will fall asleep faster. Because many insomniacs are aroused and anxious during the day, relaxation training may provide a double benefit—first, as a general coping skill to deal more effectively with the stresses of the day and second, as a means of helping to induce sleep (Bootzin & Nicassio, 1978). The different types of relaxation and meditation procedures have all been found to be about equally effective as treatments for insomnia in controlled studies.

Despite its wide evaluation as a treatment for insomnia in younger adults, relaxation training has had limited testing with older adults. Progressive relaxation (Engle-Friedman et al., 1992; Friedman et al., 1991) has been found to improve the sleep of older adults with insomnia. One common problem in using relaxation with the elderly is that the patient may experience arthritic pain as a result of tensing and releasing particular muscle groups. In such instances, the patients are instructed not to tense that muscle group but to just release the tension from whatever level of tension is already present (Engle-Friedman et al., 1992). Lichstein and Johnson (1993) recommend passive, simple relaxation procedures with an emphasis on individualizing the technique for the older adult. Regardless of the type of relaxation method employed, it is important to teach relaxation as a "portable" skill. The reliance on tapes may foster dependence on the machine and make it less likely that the insomniac will be able to use relaxation as a general coping skill for other life stressors.

EMG biofeedback is listed as a relaxation procedure because it might be characterized best as biofeedback-assisted relaxation. Patients are usually taught a relaxation procedure to practice at home when biofeedback is not available. A different type of biofeedback attempts to strengthen a 12 Hz to 14 Hz rhythm from the sensory-motor cortex and is called sensory-motor rhythm or SMR biofeedback. Both types of biofeedback have had about equal overall effectiveness; however, EMG biofeedback has been found to be most effective for anxious insomniacs with sleep onset problems, whereas SMR biofeedback has been found to be most effective for nonanxious insomniacs with sleep maintenance problems (Hauri, 1981; Hauri, Percy, Hellekson, Hartmann, & Russ, 1982).

COGNITIVE THERAPY

There are a number of cognitive symptoms that contribute to insomnia, such as worry, cognitive intrusions, and dysfunctional beliefs about sleep and its consequences. Among the cognitive interventions are paradoxical intention, cognitive restructuring, thought stopping, and articulatory suppression.

Paradoxical Intention. A cognitive intervention that has been frequently evaluated is paradoxical intention (PI). Many insomniacs exacerbate their problem by worrying about whether they will be able to fall asleep. To reduce the anticipatory anxiety associated with "trying" to fall asleep, insomniacs are instructed to get into bed and stay awake rather than try to fall asleep. Because this would presumably reduce the anxiety associated with trying to fall asleep, the insomniac should become more relaxed and fall asleep faster than they would otherwise. Paradoxical instructions tend to be most effective with patients who are resistant and reactant to therapeutic suggestions (Shoham, Bootzin, Rohrbaugh, & Urry, 1995). The rationale provided by the therapist for the paradoxical instruction may be a crucial component of its effectiveness. In a meta-analysis of the application of PI to a number of different problems, Shoham-Salomon and Rosenthal (1987) found that rationales that emphasize a positive benefit or the positive qualities of the person having the problem are more effective than rationales that are neutral or that emphasize negative aspects of the problem.

Cognitive Restructuring. Insomniacs often subscribe to a number of irrational beliefs about sleep. Older persons with insomnia have more faulty appraisal, unrealistic expectations, and misattributions regarding their sleep than older good sleepers (Morin, Stone, Trinkle, Mercer, & Remsberg, 1993). Examples of these beliefs would be that the individual must get at least 8 hours of sleep to feel refreshed and function well the next day or that if the individual goes for 1 or 2 nights without sleep, he or she will have a nervous breakdown or that the individual should avoid or cancel social, family, and work obligations after a poor night's sleep (Morin, 1993). Cognitive therapy directed at changing maladaptive attitudes and beliefs is called *cognitive restructuring.* Five types of dysfunctional cognitions are identified. These are (a) misconceptions about the causes of insomnia, (b) misattributions or amplifications of the consequences of poor sleep, (c) unrealistic sleep expectations, (d) diminished perceptions of control and predictability of sleep, and (e) faulty beliefs about sleep-promotion practices (Morin, 1993). Treatment involves providing accurate information and having the insomniac identify and rehearse alternative belief statements. These techniques have been effective as part of a multicomponent treatment in increasing sleep efficiency and reducing sleep latency, time awake after sleep onset, and early morning awakening (Morin, Kowatch, Berry, & Walton, 1993).

Thought Stopping and Articulatory Suppression. Most insomniacs complain of cognitive intrusions when trying to sleep. Two techniques that have been used to help insomniacs suppress cognitive intrusions are *thought stopping* and *articulatory suppression.* In thought stopping, the insomniac says, "Stop!" forcefully every time obsessive rumination occurs (Wolpe, 1973). This briefly disrupts the chain of thought, and repetitions decrease the frequency of subsequent cognitive intrusions. A related procedure is articulatory suppression (Levey, Aldaz, Watts, & Coyle, 1991). In this procedure, insomniacs are instructed to repeat a word such as *the* subvocally three to four times a second until sleep occurs. This treatment is based on cognitive research that indicates that articulatory suppression interferes with short-term memory. It has been effectively used in insomnia treatments to reduce cognitive intrusions that interfere with sleep.

Multicomponent cognitive treatments that combine PI, thought stopping, and the identification of irrational beliefs about sleep have been found to be as effective as noncognitive behavioral treatments for insomnia (Sanavio, Vidotto, Bettinardi, Rolletto, & Zorzi, 1990). A multicomponent treatment consisting of stimulus control instructions, sleep restriction, cognitive restructuring, and sleep education has been found to be effective for the sleep maintenance problems of older adults (Edinger et al., 1990; Morin, Kowatch et al., 1993). Epstein (1994) used this combination of interventions with 22 older insomniacs in a 6-week treatment program following a small group format. After treatment, there was significant improvement in time awake after sleep onset, sleep efficiency, and total sleep time. These gains were maintained at a 3-month follow-up.

Conclusion

In the past decade, there have been enormous advances in our understanding of the etiology and treatment of sleep disorders, including advances in the neurophysiology and pharmacology of sleep, the processes and mechanisms of circadian rhythms, the detrimental effects of disturbed sleep on cognition and performance, and continued documentation of the effectiveness of cognitive-behavioral treatments for sleep disorders through comparative outcome studies.

Evidence has been accumulating that persistent insomnia in the elderly can be effectively treated with short-term psychological therapies. Improvement in sleep has been shown to be substantial and equivalent to that found in younger insomniacs. In fact, improvement has occurred on some measures (such as awakenings) that are associated with developmental changes of aging and would be expected to be difficult to treat.

Although the results with older insomniacs are encouraging, there have been only a small number of treatment outcome studies focused primarily on the elderly. It is our hope that the promising results reported here will stimulate further research on the etiology and treatment of sleep disturbance in the elderly.

IV

Interfacing With Geriatrics

19

Interdisciplinary Health Care Teams: The Basic Unit of Geriatric Care

Antonette M. Zeiss
Ann M. Steffen

As a mental health practitioner in a university-based hospital, you often receive referrals for the evaluation and treatment of patients who attend a variety of specialty clinics at the medical center. Your most recent referral is to assess and treat Barbara J., a 69-year-old woman exhibiting symptoms of depression. The medical resident treating her severe rheumatoid arthritis in the hospital's rheumatology clinic had become alarmed and made the referral after Barbara J. began to cry during her most recent medical appointment.

Your clinical decisions regarding the assessment and treatment of Barbara J. will be influenced by your model of depression and how it is treated in older adults. Barbara's response to treatment, however, will also depend on your ability to work effectively with professionals from a variety of disciplines who are involved in her care. What difference in your work would there be if you were an official member of the interdisciplinary rheumatology team versus operating separately as a referral service? Few of us have received formal training in the advantages and tasks involved in working in interdisciplinary team settings. This chapter is designed to introduce both the conceptual and practical issues that are a part of interdisciplinary team work.

Why Teams?

Geriatric patients are characterized by two pervasive qualities: their problems are *complex* and *chronic* (Binstock & George, 1990; Birren & Schaie, 1990; Dornbrand, Hoole, & Pickard, 1992; Schneider & Rowe, 1990). Problem complexity has many dimensions, including the following: patients may have multiple problems, each exacerbating the others; problems may present differently in geriatric patients than in younger patients; geriatric patients are likely to present inconsistent information about their health concerns; current problems are influenced in complex ways by a lengthy history of medical problems, psychosocial problems, or both; and patients bring complex attitudes toward health care based on their past involvement with other health care providers (Hickey & Rakowski, 1981). Chronic health problems, such as cardiovascular complaints, arthritis, or pulmonary decline, are more typical of older individuals than younger ones (Federal Council on Aging, 1981). Although older patients can, of course, also present acute problems, the typical health care visit is more likely to be prompted by chronic concerns among elders (Woolf, Kamerow, Lawrence, Medalie, & Estes, 1990; Zawadski & Eng, 1988).

Older patients are also more heterogeneous than younger patients. Age typically brings decline as measured by average capacity in many biological functions (e.g., visual acuity, cardiac efficiency, speed of male erection, lung capacity); age also typically is characterized by increased variability (Fries & Crapo, 1981). Looking within a group of older adults, the range of capacities will be highly variable for any function, with some individuals displaying better function than the average younger person, whereas others display severe decline. There is also variability within individuals, with some functions remaining at high levels and others showing decline of varying degrees.

Because of these issues, the model of patient care that is the best fit for the management of such patients (i.e., those with chronic, complex problems that present in diverse ways and where stereotyped expectations about patients are inappropriate) is the interdisciplinary team model. This chapter will review basic aspects of interdisciplinary team theory, the natural history of team development, skills necessary for interdisciplinary teamwork, strategies for interdisciplinary team treatment planning, and models of effective interdisciplinary teams.

Table 19.1   Types of Health Care Teams

Type of Team	Defining Characteristics
Unidisciplinary team	Members are from a single discipline; all members have the same role
Intradisciplinary team	Members are from a single discipline but at different levels of training; roles and responsibilities are assigned by training level
Multidisciplinary team	Members are from different disciplines; team members have independent roles and meet to share information
Interdisciplinary team	Members are from different disciplines; team members have interdependent, collaborative roles and meet to plan treatment and evaluate patient response
Transdisciplinary team	Members are from different disciplines but team members have largely similar roles and responsibilities

Interdisciplinary Team Theory

To say that a group of health care providers is a "team" says very little because there are many different kinds of teams organized in different ways to perform different functions. A group that is a team shares a common workplace and set of patients, but teams differ among themselves in their membership composition, commitment to common goals, degree of collaboration in accomplishing team-related tasks, handling of leadership, and the kind of attention paid to team process. Theoretically, these factors could be combined in a large number of ways; in practice, the five kinds of teams shown in Table 19.1 are commonly identified (Takamura, 1985; Takamura, Bermost, & Stringfellow, 1979). Interdisciplinary teams will be described in some detail, along with briefer descriptions of the other kinds of health care team organization.

TYPES OF TEAMS

Unidisciplinary teams (from the Latin *uni,* or one) are made up of many providers from a single background, such as a group of public health nurses providing home care. All team members share the same professional skills and training, speak a common language of health care, and function in the same role within the group.

Intradisciplinary teams (from the Latin *intra,* or within) are also composed of professionals from one discipline but include team members from different levels of training and skill within the discipline. For example, a geriatric

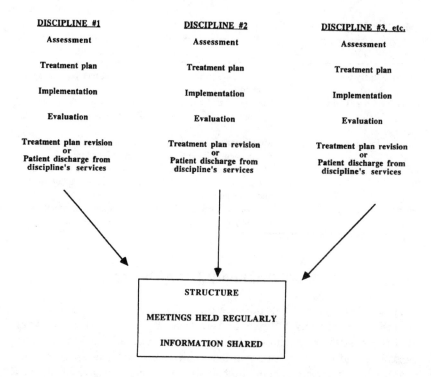

Figure 19.1. Organization of Multidisciplinary Team Care

mental health outpatient clinic team might be composed of a licensed psychologist, a postintern, prelicensing psychological assistant, a psychological technician, and two psychology practicum students.

The term *multidisciplinary team* is often used as if it were synonymous with *interdisciplinary team,* but the two are actually different in very important ways. A multidisciplinary team (from the Latin *multi,* or many) is composed of members from more than one discipline so that the team can offer a greater breadth of services to patients. However, in a multidisciplinary team, each discipline does its own assessment, generates its own treatment plan, implements the plan, evaluates progress, and refines the plan based on their own evaluation (see Figure 19.1). Team members share information with each other, typically at meetings attended by all team members. There is no attempt to generate or implement a common plan, although members may choose to use information obtained in the meeting to revise their own goals or intervention strategies. Multidisciplinary teams are hierarchically organized; there is a designated program "chief," who is usually the highest ranking professional (commonly an MD). The designated leader is responsible to oversee the

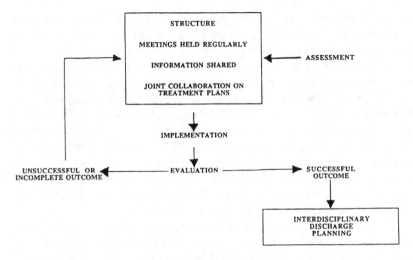

Figure 19.2. Organization of Interdisciplinary Team Care

program, lead meetings, resolve conflicts, allocate case load, and so forth. Other team members feel responsible only for the clinical work of their discipline and need not share a sense of responsibility for program function and team effectiveness.

Interdisciplinary teams (from the Latin *inter*, or among) also are composed of members from more than one discipline, making a breadth of resources available to patients. Interdisciplinary teams work much more collaboratively, however, as shown in Figure 19.2. Individual team members do their own assessment but generally have worked out overall assessment strategies so that patients are not asked redundant questions or submitted to repeated tests. Assessment information is shared with the team as a whole to generate an overall conceptualization of the relationships between biological, psychological, and social aspects of the case (the *biopsychosocial* model). This model is used to generate shared team goals for overall outcomes and to delineate how different disciplines will work together to create desired outcomes. Team members can then implement interventions, either individually or collaboratively as necessary, and evaluate progress. Those evaluations become new assessment data that are brought back to the team to revise the team's goals and strategies for reaching them. This process is repeated as often as necessary until goals are achieved and the patient can either be discharged or a maintenance plan can be put in place.

In an interdisciplinary team, the group as a whole takes responsibility for program effectiveness and team function. Leadership functions are shared among members with the expectation that everyone must be equally committed to both the clinical content of the program and to the process in which team members work together. All team members are assumed to be colleagues, and there is no hierarchical team organization. One member may be designated team coordinator, but this is understood to be an administrative role and does not imply that the team member has higher status, a stronger say in resolving conflict, or the ability to make unilateral decisions. Because interdisciplinary teamwork requires so much collaboration and consensus decision making, team members must have a high degree of interpersonal skill. The team also must make a commitment to spending time developing effective working strategies and to attending consistently to the process of working together as well as to the quality of the outcomes of their work. Communication skills, role development, leadership skills, conflict resolution skills, and skills for comprehensive conceptualization of cases are necessary for all team members.

In *transdisciplinary teams* (from the Latin *trans,* or beyond), disciplinary lines are blurred and team members share role functions to a high degree. For example, nurses, psychologists, social workers, and occupational therapists in an Adult Day Health Care program might all drive the van to bring in patients, run groups, see individual cases for supportive counseling, supervise lunchtime interactions, work with patients on increasing physical and cognitive activity, and so on. This model does not have wide application in geriatric settings because patients generally need the special skills of each discipline, obtained through extensive specialized training, not just generic skills that many disciplines might share.

ADVANTAGES OF INTERDISCIPLINARY TEAMS

The major reason to adopt a particular model of health care is that it provides the most cost-effective results. In cost-effectiveness analyses, effectiveness should be considered first: Does the approach reduce symptoms, increase quality of life, promote health, prevent future illness, and so forth? If more than one approach is effective, then it is meaningful to ask what the relative costs are of each approach and to select the program that provides the greatest effectiveness for the least cost. Well-functioning interdisciplinary teams provide cost-effective care by increasing the effectiveness of outcomes, thereby decreasing costs for continued treatment (e.g., Hendriksen, Lund, & Stromgard, 1984). There are four usual ways in which this occurs. First, interdisciplinary teams reduce duplication of services, compared to multidisciplinary teams, because team members carefully plan how to allocate resources and to cover necessary tasks; this may involve the collaboration of more than one discipline but precludes duplication. For example on a multidisciplinary team, both the social worker and the psychologist might begin individual psychotherapy for depression with a patient; this would not happen on an interdisciplinary team. Second, a related cost saving effect is that problems do not fall through the cracks when care is organized by an interdisciplinary team. It is not uncommon on units staffed by multidisciplinary teams for discharge to be planned and then delayed repeatedly as staff members discover that not all the necessary work has been done—for example, the home care coverage is arranged before the physical therapist has become aware of the need to see the patient and then home care plans have to be rearranged. A third advantage is that interdisciplinary teams can generate more creative interventions because the ideas and knowledge of a group can be brought to bear, and team members can stimulate each other's ideas. Last, interdisciplinary teams can reduce institutional costs because they increase staff morale and reduce staff turnover (Lichtenberg, Strzepek, & Zeiss, 1990; Sbordone & Sherman, 1983). As a result, more continuous care can be provided and the cost of recruiting and training replacement staff is reduced.

Although there is a need for more research to examine each of the elements of this argument in favor of the cost-effectiveness of teams, the evidence available does support the interdisciplinary team approach. For example, Zeiss and Okarma (1985) compared interdisciplinary team approaches to multidisciplinary care in an outpatient rheumatology clinic setting. Interdisciplinary team approaches were shown to improve patient outcomes on measures of quality of life (such as life satisfaction, self-rated pain, and depression) and measures of health care use (e.g., inpatient stays, the most costly care delivery modality). Other research showing the effectiveness, cost-effectiveness, or both of interdisciplinary teams is reviewed in Lichtenberg (1994).

Concern is sometimes expressed that interdisciplinary teams may be too costly because of the number of disciplines involved. Interdisciplinary teams have no specific complement of personnel, however; it is not necessary that every team have a physician, nurse, psychologist, social worker, pharmacist, occupational therapist, and so on. Teams need to include members of those professions who are essential to provide effective care for the identified patient population. Thus, a well-designed interdisciplinary team involves no more personnel than would normally staff a clinic or inpatient unit for that population. The staff members are simply organized differently than they would be if the unit had some other type of team (or no team framework at all).

DISADVANTAGES OF INTERDISCIPLINARY TEAMS
(AND WAYS TO DEAL WITH THEM)

Even though interdisciplinary teams can be effective, they are not necessarily the treatment of choice in all care settings. Settings where patients have simple, routine problems would probably benefit more from some other form of care because in-depth discussion of each case is unnecessary if everyone is going to receive essentially the same straightforward intervention. A clinic offering acute care to generally healthy adults, for example, is best staffed by nurses working with physicians; adding staff and meetings for the majority of the presenting concerns would serve no useful purpose. If a 40-year-old woman comes down with bronchitis, adding collaborative care from a social worker, pharmacist, psychologist, and other disciplines to a routine medical visit is unlikely to be cost-effective or satisfying to either the patient or the providers. It is rare, however, that elderly individuals have straightforward problems or benefit from routinized care. If an 80-year-old woman comes down with bronchitis, it may be essential to know that she is caregiver for a demented husband, what other medications she is taking, what her immune status is, and other issues pertinent to her physical and emotional well-being. Social work, pharmacy, psychology, psychiatry, or other team members may be essential in planning not only acute treatment for her bronchitis but also backup care for her demented husband.

The other potential drawback of interdisciplinary teams is that they are not organized to provide rapid response to crisis situations; they are organized to provide care for chronic, complex problems. If a patient calls with an acute problem on Tuesday morning and the next team meeting is not scheduled until the following Monday afternoon, there must be a way for individual team members, or a smaller set of team members, to make emergency decisions. Interdisciplinary teams can handle this by allocating such authority to team members with the understanding that the issues will be raised at the next team meeting so that the implications of the crisis can be factored into the team's overall plan and the treatment responsibilities of other team members.

Natural History of Team Development

Groups do not immediately become well-functioning interdisciplinary teams by deciding to make a commitment to that model of care. Much learning and development of the team must occur over a period of time that lasts at least several months and sometimes longer. The term *team building* is sometimes used to describe activities during this period, but it is a particularly inappropriate term because of the implications of the word *building,* which could imply that a solid structure, impervious to change, is being built. In fact, good teams learn to change continually and to respond fluidly to new demands, new patients, new staff, new health care policies, and so on, through a coordinated, collaborative process. Thus the term *team development* is preferable because it implies an ongoing, fluid process.

PROCESSES OF TEAM DEVELOPMENT

The sequence of experiences that groups go through in the process of developing cohesion and a high level of function has been described by many authors (e.g., Center for Interdisciplinary Education in Allied Health, 1980; Gersick, 1989; Scholtes, 1988) but most influentially by Tuckman (1965). He identified four processes that usually occur in sequence in the process of team development. He labeled these four processes *forming, storming, norming,* and *performing;* they will be described in more detail. It is important to note that these are processes, not stages. If these four processes are seen as four stages that all teams must go through, the opportunity to understand each team's unique pattern can be obscured. In addition, because these are fluid processes, it is not helpful to think of the team as being in only one stage at any given time. For example, a team may be still storming with regard to some issues, whereas it has already progressed to performing in other areas. Furthermore, teams can change by leaping forward or falling back in response to personnel changes, the development of new treatment options, stresses or positive events in team members' lives, or a variety of other events. Nonetheless, these processes can be examined to help in conceptualizing the changes and skills necessary for effective team functioning without falling into a rigid stage theory framework.

Forming

Teams may be formed when programs develop or expand or when programs are consolidated. A new team must deal with a number of issues, including what staff members are part of the team; what patients will be served; what resources are available, such as hospital beds or outpatient visit rooms; how the team treatment planning process will be organized; and so on. Early in the life of the team, these decisions about content matters take priority and little attention is paid to the process of working together. Team members typically feel a bit awkward with each other and are willing to develop team relationships but unsure of what that involves. Team members may have concerns about trust, wondering whether it is all right, for example, to express disagreement or concern about how the group is working together.

Storming

As the team continues to work together, process issues become unavoidable. It becomes clear that team members do not always agree about content issues—for instance, how the team treatment planning should be set up. Differences in personal style may need to be faced: One person may directly handle concerns in ways that others see as too brusque, or a team member may try so hard to be tactful that no one can tell what he or she is saying. Team members may make different assumptions about basic working structure; some may assume that starting the meeting at 10:00 a.m. means 10 on the dot, whereas others assume it means any time before 10:15. More substantive issues may arise, such as different beliefs about whether the first level intervention for depression should be antidepressant medication or psychotherapy. The group will have to find a way to voice disagreement that communicates a desire to stay engaged and work out the issues fairly in a collaborative process. If it cannot, the group will be likely to disband or fall back to multidisciplinary functioning where individuals can make autonomous decisions without the need for collaboration and consensus.

Norming

If the group can work on areas of disagreement constructively, a working strategy will evolve. This strategy can be thought of as the *ground rules* or norms that describe the way the group will work together and resolve conflict. Norms can be very specific (e.g., "starting at 10:00 a.m. means any time before 10:05") or more general (e.g., "When team members disagree, we will engage in a complex process to show our respect and trust for each other and remind each other that good people can disagree; then we will start to work on the substance of the issue"). If the norms developed are reasonable and effective, the group will set aside time to check on its progress (often referred to as *process time*) and to continue clarifying its norms. In addition, content decisions will be made and acted on, and the group will begin to feel cohesive.

If the norms are ineffective, the group will feel stuck, and rising frustration will throw the group back into storming. For example, if the team develops a norm that polite agreement will be voiced on most occasions when disagreement occurs, team meetings may seem peaceful at first, but team members who privately disagree are likely to implement their own ideas rather than the ideas ostensibly agreed on in the meeting. This leads to hard feelings and the belief that meetings waste time; the group will have to learn to express disagreement openly and honestly before effective norms can be established that really resolve issues arising from the storming process.

Performing

Over time, the group will develop a high level of effectiveness, called performing, in which the team becomes expert at using its process to make decisions and get work done. Ground rules will rarely need to be explicitly stated; the group might seem to be on automatic pilot, especially to outsiders who see a seamless performance with deceptively little effort needed to make complex decisions. The group will feel cohesive and morale will be high.

Team Evolution

Unfortunately, maintaining function in performing mode consistently over time is unlikely and not a realistic team goal. Key staff members leave, a needed new discipline is added to the team, the program is moved to a different building, or trainees rotate through at 4-month intervals. The group must be able to change accordingly, and it is most likely that the team will go back through the four processes of team development before settling into performing mode again. The new team and its resources and responsibilities must be examined in a forming phase. Old norms may no longer work (for example, if the team member whose role it was to draw out quieter team members has gone), so there will be a storming process as the implications of change for the day-to-day life of the team become clear. The team will develop new norms, which maintain as much of what worked before as possible but which also enthusiastically embrace the different skills and personal style of any new team members. If continual change is a reality—for example, if new trainees appear at frequent intervals—the team will develop metanorms for how to allow trainees to have some effect on the group without having to constantly redefine the group from scratch.

DILEMMAS OF TEAM WORK

One helpful way to think about the processes groups need to go through to become performing teams is summarized in Table 19.2. Groups must learn to deal effectively with three inevitable challenges: interdependence, complexity, and disagreement.

The first issue the team faces is *interdependence;* by definition, an interdisciplinary team seeks to share responsibility for patients by working collaboratively. That usually leads to turf battles early in the life of the team as each team member realizes that his or her skills overlap, often substantially, with the skills of other team members. In well-functioning teams, this will be a source of camaraderie and confidence, but early in the team's development, members can fight over who "should" be doing various activities. For example, teams might argue about whether social workers or psychologists should do family therapy, or whether pharmacy or nursing staff members should do home visits to check patients' medicine cabinets and prevent mistakes in the home drug regimen. In the storming process, these issues will be highlighted

Table 19.2 Dilemmas of Teamwork

Theme	Problem	Opportunity	Work To Be Done
Interdependence	Turf battles	Collaboration	Knowledge of and respect for diversity and shared abilities
Complexity	Endless assessment	Comprehensive care	Conceptualization, key issues, language of function
Disagreement	Destructive conflict	Integration of multiple perspectives	Communication skills

to develop team-specific agreements (norms) about how such tasks will be distributed or shared. The upcoming section on team role maps gives more detail on this process.

The second issue is *complexity*. By definition, interdisciplinary teams are established to deal with complexity, and case discussions, to be useful, must increase the complexity of the whole group's understanding of the interrelationships of each patient's biological, functional, social, and psychological problems. On a well-functioning team, this leads to a breadth of understanding that allows effective comprehensive care. Early in the life of the team, it can lead to information overload and frustration that cases are discussed seemingly without end. In the storming process, the team must develop strategies for integrating information and capturing the team's complex understanding of the patient in a written format that facilitates treatment planning and implementation. The section on team treatment planning to follow provides some examples of formats that teams can use for developing treatment plans that capture complexity and promote collaborative intervention.

The third issue is *disagreement*. Interdisciplinary teams rely on healthy conflict in which the different perspectives and knowledge of team members can be presented. It is illusory to believe that these different perspectives will always be complementary; sometimes, they are in direct contradiction. For example, the patient may have told one team member that he or she is sleeping better since starting a behavioral sleep hygiene program but told another team member that the sleep problems are unchanged. Teams that are having problems are likely to treat these differences as issues in which one team member is right and the other is wrong, leading to conflict destructive of team cohesion and effective patient care. In a functioning team, however, the team members will recognize that there is direct conflict and see it as an opportunity to learn something more about the patient and themselves. The patient may be trying to manipulate one team member to obtain pain medications. Or the patient may be more demented than the team realized and generating unreliable answers to questions. It is also possible that different team members have different interview styles that elicit different information from the patient, or team members may selectively attend to different kinds of information patients present. The important point to remember is that the ability to consider multiple possibilities and integrate multiple perspectives in handling conflict is the hallmark of a highly functioning team. A detailed analysis of strategies for learning to handle conflict effectively is beyond the scope of this chapter, but important sources giving such analyses are presented in the section on Resources at the end of the chapter.

Thus, interdisciplinary teams must develop the capacity not only to deal with the patient issues the program was originally designed to treat but also to deal with the interpersonal world of collaborative care. Skills that are necessary for all team members include knowledge and respect for other team members' abilities, the capacity to conceptualize cases holistically, the expertise to develop written team treatment plans that capture the clinical conceptualization, communication skills, leadership skills, conflict resolution skills, and the capability to anticipate and respond to change.

Role Definition on Interdisciplinary Teams

One of the activities that helps a team progress is the development of a shared understanding of the role of each team member. An example of such a role map is shown in Figure 19.3; this role map is adapted from one generated for a hospital-based home care team. This Department of Veterans Affairs program serves homebound older patients and their caregivers; all team members drive to each patient's home to assess needs and provide services. Team members shown in the diagram are a physician, four nurse practitioners, a social worker, an occupational therapist, a pharmacist, and a psychologist. Each discipline is represented by a circle, and each circle overlaps with others. Within each discipline's circle are listed the components of their role. Clinical responsibilities assumed only by that discipline appear in the part of the circle that does not overlap with others. In areas where two circles overlap, clinical responsibilities appear that either discipline might perform or that the two team members might perform as cotherapists. For example, either psychology or medical personnel might do cognitive screening.

There are also areas where three, or even more, circles overlap. In those intersections appear tasks that several team members might perform; for example, nursing, medicine, or pharmacy staff members might all educate patients about the effects and side effects of medications. The diagram has been simplified for clarity and does not include all the roles of any of the disciplines; a more complex version could be generated that did demonstrate the complete range of tasks performed.

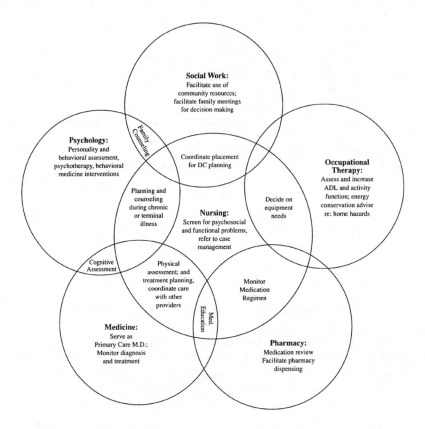

Figure 19.3. Geriatric Interdisciplinary Team Role Map

Generating and examining such a diagram provides several kinds of information. First, it can delineate all the clinical services that patients could receive from this team. Second, it clarifies for each discipline what they offer to the team and what the team will expect them to provide. Third, it clarifies areas that on a well-functioning team will be opportunities for conjoint efforts or, in a poorly functioning team, will be sources of conflict that can be termed *turf battles*. If pharmacy and nursing members each want to hold the unique right in this setting to educate the patient about medications, for example, the two disciplines are likely to be in conflict about this issue. If each sees the other as a collaborative resource instead, team work (and patient care) will be enhanced. Fourth, the diagram suggests what disciplines may have the most difficulty speaking each other's language. The roles of pharmacy and psychology members, for example, overlap very little in this setting. In a well-functioning team, members will see these as complementary functions and take pride in being able to provide a range of services well beyond the purview of any one discipline. In a poorly functioning team, members will complain about time taken to discuss issues outside their own scope of practice and compete for time to discuss the issues most closely connected to their own role.

To generate a role map that captures the realities of a specific program and the disciplines represented on its team takes some time but is usually well worth the effort. Each team member needs to specify his or her role and present it for team discussion; often, this results in adding tasks to the list that the team member did not specify but recognized when mentioned by other team members. This also begins to highlight the areas of overlap as team members recognize some of their own tasks on colleagues' lists. After all disciplines have presented their roles, someone on the team, or a small group, needs to organize the lists to capture graphically the areas of overlap and areas of unique function. This document can then become a tool to help in shaping norms and to help in the process of socializing new team members and reaching or returning to the performing level of team process.

Interdisciplinary Team Treatment Planning

Interdisciplinary teams generate treatment plans through two interlocking processes. First, the team must be able to conceptualize patients broadly, incorporating all the relevant information and the relationships between different problems. Thus, the team must go beyond simply listing patient concerns on a problem list to look at the relationships between problems. For example, a patient's depression may be triggered by loss of independence in activities of daily living (ADLs) and the depression may be the primary reason (because of the patient's apathy and hopelessness) for medication nonadherence. Psychology or psychiatry personnel could list depression on the problem list; occupational therapy staff members could list difficulties with ADLs; pharmacy members could list medication nonadherence. But the efforts of each discipline to deal with these problems will be enriched if the linkages between problems are understood. (This type of conceptualization will be demonstrated in more detail in the case study in the following section.)

Second, the team must have a structured format for guiding and capturing on paper the treatment planning process. That structure should, at minimum, specify what problems will be treated, what the goals of treatment are, what treatment strategies will be used, and what team members will be involved. It is helpful to indicate what team members will be involved by name as well as discipline to emphasize accountability. The plan may indicate time frames specifying what interventions should begin immediately, which ones will be implemented after progress is made on initial problems, and the expected time span to accomplish the goals. The plan could also include space to update the status of progress generally, such as noting if the treatment goals are accomplished

The plan should be available to all team members to guide their activities in implementing their own roles and it should be available at team meetings to guide discussion. To ensure continuous availability, teams can circulate copies to all members or keep charts in an easily accessible place. To guide team discussions, plans can be shown using overhead transparencies, circulated at the meeting, or a team member can review highlights of the plan before case discussion.

Interdisciplinary Team Concepts in Action: Team Response to a Patient With Rheumatoid Arthritis

To further clarify the use of the team treatment planning process, we return now to the case that opened the chapter, Barbara J., a woman referred to a mental health practitioner for the assessment and treatment of depression. Let's look at this case in more detail to see how an interdisciplinary perspective influences her treatment. This case also offers the opportunity to contrast how an interdisciplinary team would approach the planning and treatment processes differently from a multidisciplinary team.

Barbara J. is an African American woman in her late 60s. She has been married to her husband, Paul, for 40 years. They have been in the same two-story home for their entire marriage and enjoy gardening, visiting with family and friends, and participating in some church activities. Approximately 6 years ago, Barbara began to wake in the mornings feeling tired and sore all over her body. She started noticing joint stiffness in the mornings and after long periods of sitting still. Most affected were her hands and feet.

Over the past 5 years, Barbara has developed severe rheumatoid arthritis. Her joint stiffness and pain have become increasingly frequent, and outgrowths of the inflamed tissue have invaded and damaged the cartilage in her wrist and knee joints, making them look somewhat deformed. Barbara is currently on methotrexate and sees the rheumatologist monthly for blood tests. At the clinic, the medical residents rotate every 4 months, and Barbara feels frustrated when she has to retell information to a new doctor. She sometimes gets disgusted and angry with clinic staff and forgets the questions she has about her medications. On several occasions, Barbara lost track of her medication schedule, became overmedicated, and developed severe nausea and diarrhea.

Barbara has difficulty with buttons, zippers, and opening jars and, because of her swollen knees, is no longer able to kneel to do the gardening that she loves. She is afraid of falling when on uneven ground, so she does not walk around her yard as much as in the past. On days when she feels good, family and friends tend to forget that she has arthritis; then, on her "bad" days, they feel that she is exaggerating her discomfort. They encourage Barbara to "get up and forget her worries" and Barbara often complies, resulting in over doing it and having flare-ups on days following family get-togethers.

Barbara says that she sometimes feels depressed and useless. She used to baby-sit her infant granddaughter but can no longer keep up with a toddler. She has considered volunteering somewhere but can't make a regular commitment because she can't predict ahead of time how she will feel on any one day. Barbara likes to go to a weekly bible study and potluck at her church but tends to feel worse the day after, so she has stopped going. She reports that she is often "blue" and tearful and describes a poor appetite and waking at 4:00 a.m. several days a week.

During the 40 years of their marriage, Barbara and Paul have enjoyed physical intimacy and Barbara describes feeling sad that she does not desire sexual intercourse as much as she used to. She says that she often feels tired and is afraid that having intercourse would put too much physical stress on her joints. Barbara also admits to feeling self-conscious about the way she looks and has a hard time believing that her husband still finds her sexually attractive.

You can see from this case description that a competent professional in any one discipline cannot address the many issues involved in Barbara's physical and mental health. As is the case with many older adults, her treatment should involve the cooperation of a number of disciplines, including nursing, social work, medicine, psychiatry, pharmacy, occupational therapy, and psychology. The psychologist involved in the case would probably conduct a careful mood assessment, then contact the psychiatry consultation service to determine if Barbara's medication regimen is commonly associated with depression. Several key issues likely to be related to Barbara's negative mood would be examined: decreased participation in activities that are both meaningful and pleasurable for her, beliefs that she is no longer useful to others, responses to family when they encourage her to overdo, and fears of increased pain and disability. The psychologist may consider some neuropsychological assessment to evaluate Barbara's short-term memory, given that she has forgotten to take some doses of medication in the past. There are additional areas that could be targeted for change, such as her frustration and communication difficulties with clinic staff and sexual intimacy with her husband. Psychiatry and psychology personnel may discuss together the usefulness of prescribing antidepressant medications.

The other disciplines involved in her care would have their own concerns and areas of interest. The rheumatology medical resident assigned to Barbara would continue to evaluate the choice of medications with the goal of reducing pain and minimizing joint damage. The nursing staff members may want to further educate Barbara and her family about rheumatoid arthritis and the reasons for daily fluctuations in pain and discomfort. Occupational therapy staff members would work with Barbara on selecting assistive devices to aid her in difficult tasks (e.g., buttons, zippers, jar lids), create hand splints that would protect her wrist joints from further damage, and plan ways for her to continue important daily activities (e.g., design a tabletop garden for which she would not have to kneel). The social worker involved in the case would be aware that Barbara and Paul's two-story house is a problem because of Barbara's swollen knees and would discuss housing and long-term plans with them. Barbara's episodes of overdosing on methotrexate would be of concern to the pharmacist who may consider ways to reduce the likelihood of this recurring.

So far, it may appear that each professional could execute her or his own treatment plans without the input of the other disciplines (i.e., as a multidisciplinary team). On closer inspection, the evaluation and treatment goals in each area overlap in ways that create the potential for conflict as well as cooperation. For example, the psychologist's suggestions for increasing pleasant activities may appear to directly contradict what Barbara has been told by the occupational therapist and the rheumatology medical resident. In addition, the psychologist and social worker might be convinced that her medication overdose and seeming confusion during appointments are related to her anxiety about her illness, some recent decline in short-term memory that should be monitored, her response to the staffing patterns of the clinic, and a lack of support from her family. From a different perspective, the medical resident may believe that too much time is spent in team meetings discussing Barbara's emotional and psychosocial reactions to her illness. After all, the frequency of the flare-ups would decline significantly if she would just carefully follow her medication regimen and not engage in strenuous physical activity. These conflicts might be traced to several aspects of the team setting: poor patterns of communication during and outside of team meetings, a decision-making process that minimizes opportunities for discussion or dissent, and a lack of understanding and respect for each discipline's norms and perspectives for patient care.

In contrast to how a multidisciplinary team would approach the patient, the interdisciplinary team in this case would spend more time and attention coordinating Barbara's evaluation and care. Through regularly scheduled opportunities for education during team meetings, the interdisciplinary team members would develop a greater understanding of the competencies and perspectives of the other disciplines. This would result in the team's enhanced ability to identify shared treatment goals and the specific needs for collaboration necessitated by each patient.

What team response could be expected in Barbara's case? The following section describes an interdisciplinary effort focused on several interwoven goals and strategies. From the information provided in the case description plus some additional assessments, a treatment plan was developed that targeted Barbara's painful flare-ups, depression, frustration with clinic visits, and episodes of overmedicating herself. Table 19.3 shows that this plan included goals, specific intervention strategies, the disciplines working together to provide services, and the time frame for completing each intervention. The reader will also notice from Table 19.3 that the suggested interventions were closely linked to a jointly formed conceptualization of each problem.

After targeting Barbara's four main problems and agreeing on etiological models for each, the team identified goals that could be linked to time-specific interventions facilitated by team members. For example, increased knowledge about the link between overexertion and flare-ups, instruction in energy conservation strategies, and decreasing Barbara's use of stairs in her two-story house were all viewed as important components of the plan to decrease the incidence and severity of Barbara's flare-ups. The team viewed Barbara's depression to be heavily influenced by her progressively decreasing involvement in pleasurable activities due to chronic pain and decreased mobility. The team decided to encourage Barbara to participate in brief psychotherapy with the team psychologist with the further expectation that the psychologist and Barbara would work with the occupational therapist on selecting activities and environments that would match her interests and degree of physical disability. Antidepressant medications were not recommended by the psychiatrist because of the strong situational components tied to her recent depression (i.e., decreased involvement in pleasant activities, chronic pain) and Barbara's difficulty in managing her arthritis medications.

Although a number of the interventions could be accomplished in one or two clinic visits, several were ongoing (i.e., continued as long as Barbara participated in the rheumatology clinic). These focused on decreasing Barbara's frustration with clinic staff and anxiety at clinic appointments by assigning her to a specific long-term clinic staff member, a social worker in this case. This improved the team's overall knowledge of Barbara's current medical and psychosocial status and helped Barbara formulate specific questions for the medical resident.

As a result of the treatment plan, Barbara and her family became more knowledgeable about rheumatoid arthritis; this helped Barbara choose the appropriate level of activity for a particular day and also led to her family's increased acceptance of Barbara's judgment. With the encouragement of clinic staff, Barbara also participated in an arthritis self-help course being offered by the local chapter of the Arthritis Foundation. Together, these interventions helped her start a regular exercise program, learn to pace herself throughout the day, and prioritize activities. Barbara was also much more

Table 19.3   Treatment Plan for Barbara J.

Problem Area	Treatment Goal	Intervention	Disciplines Involved	Time Frame
Frequent flare-ups (believed by the team to be linked to the patient's overexertion in response to family requests)	Decrease overexertion; increase energy conservation	Patient and family education about the link between over-exertion & flare-ups	Nursing and occupational therapy	2 months
		Encourage patient to attend arthritis self-management classes	Nursing and psychology	1 month
		Assist patient and husband in making long-range plans about housing	Social work (supported by medicine)	6 months
		Assertion training	Psychology	2 months
Depression (linked to reduced pleasant activities and marital intimacy due to chronic illness)	Increase pleasant activities and the level of physical intimacy with husband	Brief psycho-therapy using the occupa-tional therapist as consultant on adapting activities	Psychology and occupational therapy	4 months
		Joint appoint-ment for patient and husband with medical and psychology personnel for problem solving regarding sexual activity	Medicine and psychology	2 months

willing to talk with the occupational therapist about other possible interventions (e.g., use of wrist splints at night to protect her wrist joints, use of assistive devices).

Table 19.3 Continued

Problem Area	Treatment Goal	Intervention	Disciplines Involved	Time Frame
Frustration with clinic staff and dissatisfaction with visits (due to poor communication skills, frequent change in medical residents, and increased anxiety on days of clinic visits)	Improve communication skills with clinic staff	Appoint one long-term staff member to meet with client at beginning of every visit and assist her in developing questions for other staff	Social work	Ongoing
	Maintain as much staff consistency as possible	Preclinic discussion of her case with the resident to ensure knowledge of the treatment plan	Entire team	Ongoing
Accidental over-medication (due to poor medication management)	Increase use of medication scheduling aids	Education in medication scheduling; offer reinforcement for appropriate medication use	Pharmacy and nursing	1 month

Barbara was initially surprised at the team's feedback that her feelings of depression were important and could be treated. She had expected someone in the clinic to tell her to "not be so emotional and just deal with it." After talking to the psychologist about the team's view of her depression, Barbara attended four individual sessions with the psychologist and learned to identify the activities that were most closely linked with feelings of happiness and satisfaction. In conjunction with her energy conservation strategies, she carefully planned ways to retain the daily activities most meaningful to her. She reported that, although still feeling sad at times, she generally felt less tearful and more energetic. In addition, her appetite and sleep schedule returned to a more normal basis for her. The team also arranged an appointment for Barbara and her husband to meet with her rheumatology medical resident and the psychologist. During this visit, Barbara and Paul were able to discuss their concerns about the effect of Barbara's pain and physical functioning on sexual activity. They agreed to try different body positions and touching that resulted in less pressure on her affected joints. Barbara also began to use a warm bath and pain medication just prior to making love and reported that this was helpful.

The social worker (who was a long-term member of the team) was Barbara's primary clinic contact. This meant that the social worker greeted Barbara as she waited for her appointment, reviewed how things were going for her, and assisted Barbara in writing down questions or concerns that she had. The team used this information in their preclinic review so that the resident seeing her at any one clinic appointment was familiar with the treatment plan and Barbara's status.

Barbara was also able to keep better track of her medications through the suggestions and encouragement of the pharmacist and the nurse. They helped her understand the differences between medications and set up a procedure for organizing her weekly medication regimen. There were no further instances of taking too much medication, and Barbara was better able to report to the rheumatology resident on whether different medications were having their intended effect.

Resources and Training Materials

Although the case of Barbara J. demonstrated an interdisciplinary team at work in a hospital setting, we believe that this type of case formulation and treatment is important when working with older adults in a variety of mental and physical health care settings. This chapter has introduced the concepts and practice of interdisciplinary teamwork with the expectation that more resources and experience will be needed for those wanting to apply this information to their own work groups. The next section of this chapter discusses additional written materials and training guides that may be useful.

The disciplines of industrial and organizational psychology, social psychology, and business management have traditionally devoted the most attention to studying group behavior, decision making and conflict resolution. More recently, however, a separate literature on interdisciplinary team functioning in health care settings has also developed. Some basic early work is covered in an annotated bibliography (Czirr & Rappaport, 1984); we will also touch on some early work but will emphasize more recent publications. Although it is beyond the scope of this chapter to review these literatures in depth, the following section outlines several articles and books that provide a context for understanding interdisciplinary team issues.

OUTCOMES AND DESCRIPTIONS
OF INTERDISCIPLINARY TEAMS

The literature on team functioning in geriatrics is dominated by articles describing and evaluating interdisciplinary programs (e.g., Rubenstein et al., 1984; Zimmer, Eggert, & Schiverton, 1990) and discussing barriers to effective team functioning (e.g., Chafetz, West, & Ebbs, 1988; Saltz, 1992). Qualls and Czirr (1988) discuss how models for professional functioning differ across disciplines and influence team participation and collaboration. Goldstein (1989) looks at team functioning from the perspective of physicians and offers practical advice for developing team approaches in geriatric health care settings. Drinka and Streim (1994) provide case examples of teams functioning ineffectively and suggest intervention strategies to help teams escape from "health care purgatory." In his book, *A Guide to Psychological Practice in Geriatric Long-Term Care,* Lichtenberg (1994) does an excellent job advocating for an interdisciplinary approach in long-term care settings. The chapter on creating effective interdisciplinary teams is particularly useful for those needing more information on models for training nursing assistants, organizational interventions in long-term care settings, and specific examples of team-development approaches (including the Department of Veteran's Affairs' Interdisciplinary Team Training Program). Lichtenberg (1994) also reviews the empirical literature on the relationship between team functioning and patient outcome, noting studies such as the work by Feiger and Schmitt (1979) that demonstrate a relationship between collegiality in interdisciplinary health teams and improved physical, social, and emotional functioning in patients.

TEAM TRAINING GUIDES

There are a variety of hands-on training manuals for those interested in practical advice and examples of team development exercises. Some of these guides target work groups in business, whereas others are specific to health care settings. We have found several to be particularly helpful and will present brief descriptions of what they have to offer. Although not specific to health care environments, *The Team-Building Sourcebook* (Phillips & Elledge, 1989) is a comprehensive resource for practicing team consultants and others who are involved in team development. This guide discusses the steps of the team development process and provides numerous examples and activities to be used in addressing the specific needs of a given team. A strength of this resource text is the inclusion of agendas and workshop suggestions for a variety of tasks given specific amounts of time for team development activities. For example, the "Implementation" section of the book outlines the possible contents of team development workshops lasting from 4 hours to 2 days. Eleven modules are presented with step-by-step instructions for conducting team development sessions, complete with handouts and materials to be used in flip charts.

The Team Handbook: How to Use Teams to Improve Quality (Scholtes, 1988) is another excellent team-training guide. Although it was also developed with business consulting in mind, the handbook is relevant for health care professionals. This work discusses quality improvement concepts, then shows how productive meetings and cooperative work groups are important components of increasing team efficacy. Scholtes addresses common problems in team settings (e.g., dominating or reluctant participants, feuding team members) and makes specific recommendations on how to work through these difficulties. The handbook also includes an entire chapter of team development activities and exercises, from handling introductions to helping team members make observations about group process.

A Guide to Team Development was developed by an interdisciplinary team (Angermeyer et al., 1980) at The University of Kentucky's Center for Interdisciplinary Education in Allied Health. This field manual was designed for faculty members who train students in team development. It identifies tasks and exercises focused on organizing team meetings, goal setting, decision making, generating an open and creative environment for team problem solving, and evaluating the team process.

If you specifically need an assessment tool for evaluating interdisciplinary training efforts, one possibility is *The Interdisciplinary Education Perception Scale* (IEPS) (Luecht, Madsen, Taugher, & Petterson, 1990). The IEPS is an attitude inventory that assesses perceptions of professionals and has four factors: beliefs about competence and autonomy, perceived need for cooperation, perceptions of actual cooperation among different disciplines, and understanding others' values.

COMMUNICATION TRAINING

There are occasions when a group has already accomplished many of the tasks needed to function as an interdisciplinary team, yet team members have difficulty resolving conflict or communicating clearly. We recommend two books that specifically address conflict resolution and communication skills. Gottman, Notarius, Gonso, and Markman's (1976) *A Couple's Guide to Communication* is a classic in the psychotherapy and counseling literature for very good reasons. Although it targets communication difficulties in married couples, this work provides the rationale and description of exercises that can improve communication in a variety of contexts and settings. The first five chapters in the book, covering skills such as listening, validation, constructively expressing grievances, negotiating agreements, and handling hidden agendas are especially helpful. We also highly recommend Fisher, Ury, and Patton's (1991) *Getting to YES: Negotiating Agreement Without Giving In,* a book based on work done by the Harvard Negotiation Project. *Getting to YES* addresses both the conceptual orientation and practical implications of principled negotiation, a method of negotiation that can be used in a wide variety of circumstances. In principled negotiation (also called *negotiation on the merits*), negotiators are encouraged to separate the people from the problem, focus on interests instead of positions, generate a variety of alternatives before making decisions, and base results on some objective standard. These authors also discuss handling several common dilemmas in negotiations, including negotiating with someone who is more powerful and working with others who continue to rely on positional bargaining or unprincipled tactics.

FACTORS THAT INFLUENCE TEAM FUNCTIONING

Interdisciplinary teams are based on nonhierarchical interactions, but team members come from a larger social structure that often emphasizes rank and status. We will briefly address work done in areas such as the behavior of low-ranking group members and cultural and gender differences as they influence the decision-making strategies of groups. Lichtenberg et al. (1990) discuss factors that limit the participation of psychiatric aides in treatment teams. They use a particular program, the Veteran's Administration's Interdisciplinary Team Training in Geriatrics Program (ITTG; now known as the Interdisciplinary Team Training Program or ITTP), as an example of how to bring about change.

Mechanic (1962) discussed the attributes of the social structure of an organization that led to greater power and influence by lower-ranking group members. When these concepts are applied to team members from traditionally lower-ranked disciplines (i.e., recreational therapists, nursing assistants, clerks), Mechanic's work has implications for team interventions. For example, teams can increase opportunities for these staff members to interact and have access to other professionals, which will increase their influence in teams and improve the quality of team decisions. The team can also develop ways to recognize explicitly that individuals from low-ranking disciplines often have important expert knowledge that is not readily available to others in the team.

On a related topic, Kirchmeyer and Cohen (1992) discuss the concept of constructive conflict and then empirically demonstrate how specific behaviors in multicultural groups may increase the participation of ethnic minorities. This approach is described in more detail by Tjosvold (1991) who presents some actions that can be taken by designated group leaders to encourage the active involvement of all team members. Kelley and Streeter (1992) review issues and research on gender in organizations, covering wide topics such as trends in work patterns and perceived gender differences in performance and job attitudes.

Helping With Interdisciplinary Team Development

It should be clear that all interdisciplinary teams, no matter how motivated and talented the members, will have difficulty from time to time. The material presented thus far is intended to provide (a) a theoretical background for how teams function, (b) an example of good interdisciplinary team treatment planning, and (c) information on resources where you can learn more about team functioning and essential skills for teamwork. It is also helpful to consider how you can try to have a positive effect as a team member or if you are helping with program development.

First, you will need to respect a fundamental tenet of interdisciplinary team development: By definition, no single person can make a group become an interdisciplinary team. If you are enthusiastic about interdisciplinary team ideas and want to see them put into action in your setting, you cannot mandate them to occur even if you have the institutional power to define program goals and organizational structure. Interdisciplinary teams ultimately depend on, and are the embodiment of, a powerful principle: People support what they help create. A group can become an interdisciplinary team only if the group members decide themselves that they want to take on the responsibilities of shared leadership and interdependent functioning. Your role can be one of bringing the concept to the table and trying to generate shared enthusiasm for it, but it cannot be mandated from above. If the group must function in a way mandated by authority, it is, by definition, not an interdisciplinary team.

If the group embraces the interdisciplinary concept, you can help create experiences that will move the group forward. It is usually essential early in the life of the team to generate a vision statement that articulates team members' understanding of program goals, including what patients are to be served, what resources are available to serve them, and the expected effect of the program. This can help the team negotiate the storming process by providing a grounding in a commonly held set of values.

When the team has a shared sense of purpose, other training experiences largely mirror the organization of this chapter. Team members need to learn about interdisciplinary concepts and to confirm their commitment to shared responsibility for the success of the team. They need to recognize how much there is to know, for example, about each others' professions, about sharing leadership, and about communication skills and conflict resolution. The group optimally will decide together on strategies for appropriate additional training. Team members can train each other, or it may be necessary to bring in a team consultant. It will be especially important to bring in a consultant if the team cannot successfully handle the storming process, either because the group avoids all conflict or because conflict escalates uncontrollably.

In the training process, it is particularly helpful to find a balance between content and process. During process time, team members can share personal reactions to the tensions and pleasures of interdisciplinary work and discuss experiences with communication styles in the group. During content training, it is very helpful to have the group develop its own unique role map. This also provides an opportunity for each discipline to educate the others about its skills, training experiences, licensure status, and model of health care. The group can also look at different approaches to team treatment planning and choose one that best fits the team's mission and style of working.

As a team member, you can suggest such strategies and contribute, along with other team members, to implementing the group's decisions. If you find that the group does not develop effectively or that you seem to make all the suggestions or guide all the training experiences, bringing in a team consultant would be a good idea. The more you try to carry a reluctant team, the less interdisciplinary it will be and the more you will become the de facto leader of a multidisciplinary team. In such cases, the most helpful thing you can do is to relinquish power and encourage other team members to join in the process of assessing the team's problems and generating solutions.

Summary

Interdisciplinary teams are a particularly appropriate way to organize health care for geriatric patients, who typically have complex, chronic problems. The interdisciplinary team provides care in which several disciplines coordinate assessment and treatment so that problems can be dealt with consistently and comprehensively. Interdisciplinary teams are characterized by a nonhierarchical organization in which responsibility for the effective functioning of the team is shared by all team members. This requires that team members be excellent representatives of and advocates for their disciplines. It also requires that team members have training in team theory, leadership skills, and communication skills, including conflict resolution skills. Interdisciplinary teams go through a process of development. Newly formed teams work out goals and basic models of function; this process usually highlights areas of disagreement among team members in strategies of care, personal interaction styles, or both. As groups work out these disagreements, they develop shared norms that define the team's working strategies. With experience, most interdisciplinary teams reach a high level of function and deliver cost-effective care along with supporting staff morale.

Interdisciplinary teams are committed to the idea that patients will be best served when their care is coordinated and provided by team members who learn from each other, rely on each other, and are willing to challenge each other when appropriate. Interdisciplinary teams require the wise and creative integration of diverse viewpoints and function best when team members value diversity, remain cohesive when viewpoints conflict, and negotiate agreement to which all team members are committed.

20

Common Medical Problems in Geriatric Patients

Eleanor S. Segal

It is estimated that 80% of elders have at least one chronic health condition. Arthritis leads the list, with 48% of noninstitutionalized persons over the age of 65 years having complaints that can be diagnosed as arthritis (Rundall, 1992). Hypertension (38%), hearing impairment (29%), heart disease (28%), cataracts (16%), deformity or orthopedic impairment (16%), chronic sinusitis (15%), diabetes mellitus (9%), visual impairment (8%), and tinnitus (7%) finish the list of the 10 most common conditions. In a similar listing of the 10 leading causes of death for persons 65 years of age and over (Rundall, 1992), heart disease, hypertension, and diabetes appear again, ranking 1, 3, and 5 respectively. Malignant neoplasms and chronic obstructive pulmonary disease (COPD) rank 2 and 4. This chapter contains the etiology, typical or atypical presentations, and treatment strategies for the more common diseases and disorders that are found in the elderly. Chapter 10 will discuss screening for the psychological manifestations of some physical diseases.

It is helpful to group common problems into categories for discussion, but it is important to remember that persons with multiple chronic illnesses are not merely the sum of their diseases but human beings who may have profoundly different reactions and coping styles to conditions that look exactly the same "on paper." An oxygen-dependent COPD patient may cheerfully wheel about on his or her special electric scooter volunteering to help children learn library computer skills or may remain in bed with visual impairment, osteoporosis, and osteoarthritis, chronically depressed and in great pain. The focus of this chapter on treatment strategies that will improve quality of life reflects the growing expectation of patients that care providers should be responsible for patient well-being beyond the mere prescription of pills and platitudes. Furthermore, many patients are anxious and willing to form health partnerships and participate in their treatment planning.

One way of categorizing common problems is to look at different body systems. Doing so results in the following list:

Diseases of bone and joint
    Arthritis (includes osteoarthritis, rheumatoid arthritis, polymyalgia rheumatica, and gout)
    Paget's disease of bone
    Osteoporosis
    Fractures and other injuries from falls
    Deformity and other orthopedic impairment, including chronic back syndromes
Vascular diseases
    Cardiovascular diseases (includes hypertension, ischemic heart disease, congestive heart failure, valvular heart disease, arrhythmias, and peripheral vascular disease)
    Cerebrovascular disease (includes stroke, transient ischemic attacks, and subdural-subarachnoid hemorrhage)
Neurological disorders
    Parkinson's disease and other causes of tremor and gait disorder
    Demyelinating diseases
    Seizure disorder
    Herpes zoster and postherpetic neuralgia
Diseases of the special senses
    Eye: causes of visual impairment, including cataracts, macular degeneration, and glaucoma (also diabetic retinopathy)
    Ear: tinnitus, hearing impairment
    Nose: chronic sinusitis; disorders of smell and taste
    Mouth: oral and dental conditions
Pulmonary diseases
    COPD
    Asthma and other restrictive lung diseases

Acute and chronic lung infections
Genital and urinary disorders
  Prostatitis and urinary tract infections
  Urinary and fecal incontinence
Neoplastic diseases (cancer; blood disorders, including lymphomas, leukemias, and immune deficiency syndromes)
Endocrine disorders (diabetes mellitus and thyroid disease)
Chronic pain and its management

Diseases of Bone and Joint

The most prevalent of the chronic diseases, *arthritis* is a catch-all term for a group of diseases, including degenerative joint disease (DJD), rheumatoid arthritis, polymyalgia rheumatica, and gout. Most elders, when they say they have arthritis, are really talking about joint pains that keep them from moving as freely or as comfortably as they wish.

Osteoarthritis, or DJD, often presents itself as pain and limitation of motion in a large weight-bearing joint such as the hip or knee. Patients complain of cracking or rubbing sounds (heard as crepitus in the joint) and difficulty climbing stairs. They find it hard to rise after sitting quietly for long periods of time but usually do not complain of sleep loss due to pain, although they may have morning stiffness. Characteristic Heberden's nodes, bony protuberances at each side of the distal interphalangeal joints of the fingers and toes, are not actually all that common. DJD can also occur in joints damaged by old injury or fracture. Treatment consists of encouraging mild but daily exercise, avoiding overuse or underuse, and judicious use of nonsteroidal anti-inflammatory agents or mild pain medication such as acetaminophen. (Nonsteroidals, although successful in treating acute inflammation, carry with them their own risk of precipitating gastrointestinal bleeding and occasional renal failure and are best reserved for intermittent use.) Although DJD has been thought of as a nonsystemic disease (contrasting it to rheumatoid arthritis), it can present some systemic symptoms such as fatigue. Treatment of severely damaged individual osteoarthritic joints now includes surgical joint replacement not only of hips and knees but even of smaller non-weight-bearing joints. Newer types of artificial joints even come with 20-year "guarantees" and have made a tremendous difference in patients' quality of life.

Polymyalgia rheumatica occurs most commonly in the fifth decade of life but can present in older persons, with weakness and aching of the arms and shoulder or hip girdle. It, plus giant cell arteritis (temporal artery arteritis), is considered important to diagnose (failure to treat with steroids can result in retinal artery thrombosis and blindness), and treatment with low-dose steroids is usually successful.

Rheumatoid arthritis often begins in younger patients (highest incidence of onset is in the third and fourth decades). Elderly patients are usually in later stages of the disease with more chronic disabilities, although it does occur de novo (Murphy, 1992). Although traditional teaching is that elderly patients with rheumatoid arthritis do not have acute pain and flare-ups, with hot, red, symmetrically swollen (fusiform swelling) smaller joints, there are many older rheumatoid arthritis patients who do have recurrent acute episodes. Chronic rheumatoid arthritis, definitely a systemic disease, is hallmarked with joint and synovial destruction, physical deformities of bones, and often eye (keratoconjunctivitis sicca, "dry eye"), mouth (Sjogren's syndrome), blood (chronic normocytic anemia), renal (chronic renal insufficiency), and even occasional pulmonary (rheumatoid lung) findings.

Patients have often been treated with high-dose corticosteroids and thus can have some or all of the iatrogenic consequences of steroid treatment, including Cushingoid or moon face, hypertension, osteoporosis, truncal obesity, thin striated skin, and risk of ulcer disease.

Treatment, again, is based on identifying symptoms and treating appropriately with exercise, medication (nonsteroidals; disease-modifying antirheumatic drugs, including gold, methotrexate, chloroquine; and pain relievers), and if necessary, corrective surgery. Use of adaptive devices and modified clothing fasteners allows the person with rheumatoid arthritis to continue independent living. Courses teaching adaptive skills and self-efficacy have shown that independent rheumatoid arthritis patients taking them have improved health outcomes (H. Holman & K. Lorig, personal communication, 1994).[1]

Gout, a disorder of production or excretion of uric acid, characterized by uric acid crystals in joints during an acute attack of joint inflammation, chronic recurrent arthritis, and joint destruction with possible renal failure, can manifest itself with acute pain, usually in a single joint. Subcutaneous nodules along the extensor tendons (*tophi*) are actually deposits of uric acid crystals. It is important to differentiate the diagnosis of gout and pseudogout (chondrocalcinosis, with calcium instead of urate crystals) because treatment can differ for each condition. Patients with high levels of uric acid in the blood because of lymphoma or leukemia are usually treated prophylactically before symptom development.

Paget's disease of bone (osteitis deformans) is a disease characterized by a state of increased cellular activity in affected bones, which can enhance an underlying disorder of the bone cells leading to a loss of control of their growth rate (Lane, 1994). It may be an incidental diagnosis because of blood work abnormalities, or the patient may present with severe back, hip, or head pain. X rays demonstrate "holes" in the bony architecture and a blood workup reveals serum alkaline phosphatase elevations, often five times normal levels. Patients for whom Paget's causes pain may be treated with calcitonin, bisphosphonates, and occasionally other agents approved by the U.S. Food and Drug Administration to treat other conditions (Lane, 1994) because Paget's patients sometimes become resistant to calcitonin. Sarcomas, malignant tumors, occur in less than 0.1% of pagetic patients but because they are rare in the elderly, 20% to 30% of sarcomas in older patients arise in patients with Paget's disease. It is important to have a high index of suspicion when a patient with Paget's suddenly has a dramatic change of pain status in the affected area and to evaluate an X-ray picture of bone loss with computerized tomography (CT) or magnetic resonance imaging (MRI) to allow rapid treatment of sarcoma to help avoid limb loss and improve prognosis (Lane, 1994).

Chronic back pain is widely prevalent and can be frustrating to treat in the elderly. Disc disease has recently been shown to respond no differently to surgery than to treatment with pain medications and judicious exercise unless the disc is completely ruptured with free fragments in the spinal canal. Other common causes of back and leg pain include muscle spasm and strain, vertebral facet syndromes, sacroileitis, and abnormal positioning of vertebrae (spondylolisthesis) or narrowing of the spinal canal (spinal stenosis). The use of MRI has made it far easier to diagnose bulging discs or varying degrees of spinal stenosis, but unfortunately, the degree of abnormality on the MRI is not well correlated with the degree of pain and disability the disc problem has caused in a particular patient (Ciocon, 1994).

Osteoporosis is one of the most common causes of disability due to fractures and injuries sustained from falls. It is estimated that postmenopausal women lose 2% to 5% of their bone mass a year for the first 10 years after menopause. When bone mass reaches a critically low level (osteopenia), there is a 75% to 80% risk of fracture due to decrease in structural strength (Karpman, 1987). It is possible that women have chronic deficits in calcium balance (a report came out that 9-year-old 4th grade girls drink Diet Coke instead of milk in an effort to remain slim; L. Mellon, personal communication, June 1988) that increase risk for more rapid development of postmenopausal osteoporosis and consequent fracture of the long bones, often hip or wrist, or compression fracture of the thoracic or cervical spine. It is estimated that a woman over the age of 50 has a 40% to 50% chance of developing osteoporosis during her lifetime. Postmenopausal hormone replacement therapy (HRT), with or without Vitamin D, fluoride, or calcium (Rowe, 1985), is presently felt to decrease risk of osteoporosis for women. Recently, weight training for postmenopausal women has been demonstrated to reverse bone loss in comparison to a control group that continued to lose bone at a rate of 2% (Nelson, 1994). Different ethnic groups have varying degrees of risk of osteoporosis, African Americans having less risk than European Americans, and osteoporosis and hip fracture also occur more in thin women who have lower levels of circulating estrogen and women who smoke. Screening measurements of populations at risk using bone densitometry have been considered to try to identify persons at extra risk because X rays do not show osteopenia until loss is greater than 40%. Repeat measurements need to be made because rate of loss is an important variable in treatment planning. Older men, of course, are also susceptible to bone loss from aging and at about age 80 years, are equally osteopenic and equally at risk for fracture as women.

Falls, with or without resulting fractures, are a cause for great concern. Once having fallen, the elderly patient often becomes fearful of falling, so much so that he or she curtails usual activities. A cycle is set in place where muscles less used become weaker and less likely to support the body of the person to whom they belong. Thus, a weak person becomes weaker and even more susceptible to falling. Encouraging new studies have shown that even extremely frail elderly patients can benefit from judicious weight training, and can improve muscle mass and strength in as little as 4 weeks (Tinetti, 1988). There are reports that weight training in the elderly can even help reverse osteopenia. Other interested researchers are looking at ways to improve balance and decrease the effects of loss of proprioception and vision that contribute to falls in the elderly. Nursing homes are exploring ways to eliminate demeaning restraints and to keep their patients safe from serious falls by such techniques as keeping beds low with wheels locked and using special cushions on chairs to keep patients who are truly unsafe ambulators seated but not confined with belts or vests.

A common cause of orthopedic impairment is cerebrovascular accident (CVA), or stroke (Rosenfield, 1991). Patients may sustain paralysis of arm and leg as well as aphasia and may recover some motor function, more often leg than arm, still with some residual weakness. It has been said that a patient who has a stroke enters the hospital not walking and not talking and leaves walking but not talking. (This, of course, is descriptive of a CVA in the dominant brain hemisphere.) This makes sense if one thinks of a drawing of a little man (homunculus) superimposed upside down on the left and right cerebral hemispheres of the brain and considers that deprivation of blood flow because of arterial blockage might have the least effect on the brain's control center that is most distal to the blockage (the feet of the homunculus) because there is more chance for collateral circulation to bring needed oxygen to that area.

Even though a patient may get some or most return of leg function, the arm may remain relatively immobile. The patient may be required to use special splints to prevent contracture and dependent swelling or aids such as a cane (held with the unaffected arm) to help ambulation. When speaking to patients, it is best to avoid the words *good arm* or *good leg*. Patients who have true paralysis of one leg can often be taught to move easily in a wheelchair, using the unaffected leg as a propellant. Walkers are best reserved for patients who have bilateral arm function and can be used as support for patients who are unstable based on either neurologic or musculoskeletal weakness.

Vascular Diseases

Vascular disease is a great cause of morbidity and mortality in the United States. It is estimated that one quarter of the adult population has hypertension, and half of them are unaware of it. Hypertension has been shown to increase risk for cardiovascular disease, especially congestive heart failure, stroke, and renal failure, and successful treatment of hypertension decreases these risks (Fries, 1980). Although older studies of hypertensives focused on diastolic blood pressure to predict risk (Kannel, 1987), more recently there is evidence that isolated systolic hypertension, seen mainly in the elderly who have less compliant arterial vasculature, is also strongly associated with risk of cardiac failure and stroke (Higgins et al., 1993). The U.S. government recently published its fifth list of guidelines for hypertension treatment (Joint National Committee, 1993), and although small doses of diuretics and beta-blockers are still listed as first-line therapies, many experts in the field of hypertension management believe that angiotensin-converting enzymes, calcium channel blockers, or both may still be the more effective first-line therapy, particularly in the elderly.

Ischemic heart disease, as a result of arteriosclerotic vascular disease, is the primary cause of death in U.S. adults. Interestingly enough, a study of the contribution of a statistically significant combination of three of the major risk factors (hypertension, high cholesterol, and smoking) for heart disease in adult men with no significant clinical cardiovascular disease begun in the 1970s (Stamler, 1993) could never demonstrate whether intervention given to the special care group above and beyond "usual [physician's] care" helped decrease heart attack rates, because heart disease started showing a decline at that time. This was probably a result of greater public awareness of the dangers of smoking and eating cholesterol-laden and saturated-fat-laden foods and may parallel the decline in the percentage of smokers in the United States from 35% to 40% to the current level of 19% (Gilpin, 1994).

Treatment of ischemic heart disease has also improved with the advent of calcium channel blockers and different preparations of coronary artery vaso-dilators (nitroglycerin in pills, pastes, and patches and in mononitrate and dinitrate forms) and, of course, improved diagnostic imaging techniques (two-dimensional and transesophageal echocardiography) and types of surgical intervention, such as coronary artery bypass grafts and percutaneous transluminal coronary angioplasty. Patients with newly diagnosed heart attacks can be treated with "clot-busting" drugs (tissue plasminogen activator, streptokinase), blood-thinning agents such as heparin or warfarin or even the old standby, aspirin, to prevent infarct extension or new blockage. Patients post-myocardial infarction (MI) are now encouraged to improve muscle strength and cardiovascular endurance, and post-heart-attack exercise programs with fit older persons working away on treadmills and stationary bicycles are a far cry from the scenes of the heart attack "victims" of the 1950s sitting quietly in their rooms fearfully awaiting the next possibly fatal event.

Concerns of the next decade focus on prevention and early detection because current diagnostic tests such as electrocardiograms (EKGs) and treadmill tests have proved to have disappointing predictive value. The often heard story of the patient who dropped dead after a normal EKG underscores the ominous amount of false negatives that occur with these screening tools. Women are at even greater risk, for they have been found to have less attention paid to and thus less accurate diagnosis of the etiology of their chest pains and less invasive treatment for their sometimes extensive coronary artery disease (Bell et al., 1993). Recent studies of HRT have shown that its major use may be in preventing excess coronary deaths in women, perhaps as many as 50% (R. Marcus, personal communication, December 1994). Estrogen has been shown to elevate levels of high-density lipoprotein (HDL) cholesterol, the so-called good cholesterol, and the inverse relationship between circulating blood levels of HDL cholesterol and the occurrence of myocardial infarction is being studied. Although the net effect is life saving, presumably from both the standpoint of preventing bone dissolution and death from hip fracture and the prevention of fatal coronary events, because HRT in older women with uteruses has been shown to increase the rate of death from endometrial cancer, it must never be undertaken without appropriate screening techniques in place, such as endometrial biopsy along with pelvic examinations and Pap smears.

Congestive heart failure (CHF) is often associated with ischemic or valvular heart disease, reflecting the inability of a weakened heart to pump blood efficiently to the body, which causes back pressure to fill the lungs, liver, and dependent parts of the body with fluid. Although rheumatic mitral valve disease is still a cause of CHF (the hallmark being cough and the frothy pink sputum of pulmonary edema), elderly patients more commonly have aortic valvular stenosis with severe constriction of the outflow track due to calcium deposits. Treatment is based on decreasing back pressure, improving pump strength and cardiac output, and (more controversially) valve replacement (porcine more commonly than artificial). In the young-old with severe cardio-myopathy, cardiac transplant has been offered, which is even more controversial based on cost and dollar resources for health care needs.

Another consequence of a damaged aortic valve is idiopathic hypertrophic subaortic stenosis in which the outflow track below the constricted valve becomes hypertrophic, increasing the chances of a sudden fatal arrhythmia. (This is one reason "drop attacks" need to be carefully investigated.) Other common serious arrhythmias include stage III heart block (atrioventricular dissociation with or without pauses), multiple-focus ventricular ectopy, and sick sinus syndrome with supersensitive carotid sinus, where even slight massage of the carotid sinus can cause temporary or permanent cardiac arrest. Prolonged conduction between atrium and ventricle is also common, and various supraventricular tachycardias and bundle branch blocks, although frequent, are considered less ominous. Atrial fibrillation, common with mitral valve disease and subsequent atrial dilatation, poses a special risk of clot formation and the dislodging of parts of the clot that pass through the aorta to the coronary arteries or to the cerebral arteries causing MI or stroke, respectively. Diagnosis can be made with either plain EKG or with special monitors (including the old standby Holter monitor, where continuous EKG recording can be made for a given period of time). Electrophysiologic cardiac studies, mappings of the entire conduction system of the heart, can be done to find the foci of potentially fatal arrhythmias. Treatment can include implantation of a cardiac pacemaker, surgery, or implantation of special miniature defibrillators that shock a heart back into function every time it stops.

Peripheral (arterial) vascular disease is a common cause of morbidity. Large-vessel disease can be treated with vasodilators or bypass surgery and needs to be diagnosed as soon as possible. Aortic aneurysms (the abdominal aortic aneurysm or *triple A* is more easily operated on than the thoracic aortic aneurysm) need to be suspected and diagnosed early before separation of the intimal layer causes development of a false lumen and major systemic blood loss. Small-vessel disease that can occur as a result of diabetes or smoking (Buergher's disease) is not amenable to vascular surgery and may result in loss of a limb secondary to ischemia. Prevention presumably includes tight control of diabetes and cessation of smoking. A recent study has shown that asking a patient to stop smoking during an office visit results in more patients stopping than saying nothing at all (Sawicki, 1993). The use of nicotine gum or patches has been found to be safer than having that patient continue to smoke, even in the person with vascular compromise, and may be able to improve the chance of the patient quitting.

Cerebrovascular disease, secondary to hypertension and arteriosclerotic vascular disease, is another major cause of morbidity and mortality. Ischemic strokes—mainly thrombotic (65%) and sometimes embolic (15%), the latter often based on atrial fibrillation—can result in loss of limb function, ability to speak, and ability to function in society. Hemorrhagic strokes, although a smaller percentage of strokes (15%), also result in brain tissue death. Although rehabilitation techniques have been honed to a fine art, prevention is considered the key to success in treatment. Ninety percent of patients have some degree of residual impairment poststroke (40% mild, 40% moderate, 10% requiring institutionalization; Brummel-Smith, 1992). Transient ischemic attacks are sometimes warning signals of impending stroke. They include temporary loss of limb function, confusion, loss of speech, and transient monocular blindness and are reversible: thus the use of the acronym RIND for *reversible ischemic neurologic deficit*. Prevention of thrombotic stroke with platelet antiaggregants such as aspirin or ticlopidine or embolic stroke with blood thinners such as warfarin has proved successful (American Heart Association, 1991).

Surgical intervention to decrease carotid artery blockage of greater than 70% (diagnosed by hearing a bruit followed by carotid echoscan or angiography) has recently been shown to have a positive health outcome (Strandness, 1993). In one large study of physicians, the use of aspirin as a prevention for recurrent myocardial infarction did show an increase in deaths from hemorrhagic stroke (Alper, Gibb, & Wexler, 1993), so it is possible that aspirin taken as a prevention for stroke and myocardial infarction (and more recently for colon cancer as well) may result in a slight increase in the number of hemorrhagic strokes and subarachnoid or subdural hemorrhage due to falls. It is important to remember that in all patients, especially in those taking aspirin, nonsteroidals, or blood thinners, an episode of confusion, disorientation, or somnolence several weeks after a seemingly minor fall could be a subdural hemorrhage that can be diagnosed by head CT scan and treated with surgical evacuation if necessary. Subarachnoid hemorrhages that can occur from arteriovenous malformations (AVMs) often manifest more dramatically, with severe headache and incapacitation, and are more difficult to treat. Newer radiologically guided techniques such as using an intraarterial catheter to inject a gluelike substance or coils to block arterial supply of the AVM are showing great promise for the successful treatment of previously considered inoperable AVMs (B. Lane, personal communication, June 1993).

Neurological Disorders

Neurological disorders, such as Parkinson's disease, characterized by tremor and rigidity of gait with or without mental status changes, are also common in the elderly. Thought to be a depletion of dopamine in the substantia nigra, treatment involving replacement of dopamine has been used for many years.

Recently, newer drugs are thought to be able to slow progression of the disease so that early diagnosis, often subtle and difficult, is imperative. Gait disorder can also be caused by stroke, either major or multiple minor (lacunar infarcts), and diagnosis and appropriate treatment with proper assistive ambulation devices is crucial to prevent falls and fractures. Other causes of tremor can be familial and benign (Katherine Hepburn was the most visible public person with such a tremor). Unfortunately, some familial benign intention tremors are believed to be relieved with alcohol ingestion so that persons with this disorder are known to self-medicate with alcohol, increasing their risk of alcoholism.

Amyotrophic lateral sclerosis (ALS) and multiple or systemic sclerosis (MS) are demyelinating diseases of the long tracts resulting in multiple neurologic deficits. MS can present very insidiously, with ocular muscle changes causing diplopia, weakness, and fatigue and urinary symptoms such as frequency and incontinence. It is a disease characterized by periodic remission and reexacerbation, and although medical treatment has been mainly symptomatic, recent advances in possible drug treatment have been reported (Nightingale, 1993). ALS can be generalized or bulbar. The patient with bulbar ALS, although able to physically function, is deprived of the ability to speak and ultimately to swallow and may become profoundly depressed. MS patients have been reported as having a euphoria that often prevents them from registering the tragedy of their disease, but this reported euphoria is found more often in the breach than in the observance.

Other central nervous system diseases, such as the congenitally acquired Huntington's disease, although usually presenting in the fifth decade, often claims its victims before age 65 due to dementia, inanition, and infection. Late-stage Alzheimer's disease, in which the ability to ambulate is lost long after the abilities to remain continent and to communicate and understand is an increasingly more common cause of neurological deficits. Dementia of the Alzheimer's type accounts for 60% of dementias and may affect as much as 45% of the old-old (over 85 years) population. Normal-pressure hydrocephalus, with its characteristic broad-based gait and urinary incontinence, should always be considered in a dementia workup because of its supposedly treatable nature.

Seizure disorder in the elderly may be a new diagnosis, reflecting brain damage from stroke, metastases, or alcohol abuse. Diagnosis should be made on the basis of symptoms, electroencephalogram findings, and occasionally head CT and treatment undertaken accordingly with careful monitoring of antiseizure medication that can cause obtundation and falls. Although state regulations about driving vary, the elderly person with a recently diagnosed seizure disorder should not drive.

Herpes zoster, or shingles, which involves inflammation of a particular nerve dermatome by the varicella virus, is listed here because the neurological consequences of the disease can be so severe. Although there is usually just sensory damage, damage of function has been observed when longer nerves are involved. The pain of postherpetic neuralgia is more debilitating and difficult to treat in the elderly. Early diagnosis of a painful vesicular rash that does not cross the midline is imperative, particularly in the ophthalmic branch of cranial nerve V, which can result in loss of eyesight if not treated, especially in immune-compromised patients. Rapid treatment with acyclovir, intravenously if necessary, is required, and the use of steroids to decrease occurrence of postherpetic neuralgia has been proposed (Wieman, 1992). Treatment of postherpetic neuralgia as any chronic pain condition, but adding topical capsaicin, has proven beneficial, possibly by its action in depleting substance P, an endogenous neuropeptide involved in pain impulse transmission (Gen-Derm Corporation, 1993).

Diseases of the Special Senses

Age-related senile macular degeneration is the most common cause of legal blindness (visual acuity 20/200 or worse) in the United States. It has a prevalence of 28% in the 75 years to 85 years age group (Kane, 1989). Diabetic retinopathy, glaucoma, and cataracts are the other common causes of blindness. Diabetic retinopathy can be prevented in some cases by tight control of blood sugar and frequent fluorescein angiography with laser obliteration of the proliferative retinopathic vessels that can destroy vision.

Cataracts, or opacification of the lens, occur as part of the aging process and may appear as blurred or cloudy vision that makes reading difficult. Surgery to remove the lens and implant an artificial lens gives perfect distance vision to people who may never have had it in their lives due to myopia and can be successfully undertaken in the very debilitated elderly patient.

Glaucoma, both closed and open angle, can be diagnosed by measuring ocular pressure as part of periodic screening but may manifest with either loss of central vision (central scotoma), with acute eye pain or with systemic symptoms such as abdominal pain and vomiting. Glaucoma needs to be included in the differential diagnosis of acute onset of abdominal pain in the older person. Treatment can include topical beta-blockers that act by decreasing production of aqueous humor, alpha antagonists that dilate scleral veins and improve outflow of aqueous, surgery (trabeculectomy) to prevent buildup of aqueous humor, or a combination of these. Untreated glaucoma causes blindness.

Tinnitus, defined as continual sounds in the ear (buzzing, humming, or ringing) affects almost 9% of the population over 65 years. It may be caused by tiny abnormalities of blood flow to the ear. Presbycusis, the loss of medium-pitched to high-pitched frequency discrimination that happens in the older age population, may make the perception of tinnitus worse by masking peripheral sounds. Differential diagnosis should rule out salicylate toxicity, and treatment mainly focuses on diversion of the patient by use of other masking sounds, such as a radio.

Hearing impairment in the elderly is often neurosensory as opposed to conductive loss and is less amenable to the use of hearing aids, which amplify sounds sometimes uncomfortably (*recruitment*). Currently, there are various types of assisted listening devices, including theater sound systems, telephone sound augmentation, and hearing aids. Profoundly deaf individuals can avail themselves of closed caption television programs and TTY for telephone typewritten communication. Deaf or hearing-impaired persons need to be able to ask for assistance, and those who communicate with them need to remember to look at them when speaking, speak clearly, although not particularly slowly and certainly not loudly, enunciate well, and be ready to give clarification when points don't seem to be understood.

Chronic sinusitis is the seventh most common chronic complaint of elderly persons and is characterized by so-called postnasal drip, cough, and headache. Most cases are not true infection but merely thickening of maxillary or frontal sinuses and, although not life threatening, are frustrating and annoying to the persons affected. More serious is the loss of smell that can occur after a viral illness, which results in loss of taste for food. Loss of the taste buds at the tip of the tongue (salty, sweet) can result in persons adding excess salt and sugar to their foods, harmful to people with salt-sensitive essential hypertension (50% of elderly hypertensives) and diabetes mellitus (Nelson & Franci, 1992).

Poor oral hygiene with chronic gingivitis and pockets of plaque formation can result in loss of permanent teeth. Older patients, who may have been subjected to old-style dentistry with removal of all their teeth, may suffer with plates that are ill fitting due to bone resorption and shrinkage of the jaw line. Chewing with dentures requires 60% more energy than chewing with natural teeth (or even gums), and at least one study has shown that 22% of elderly patients in a nursing home, when given a pureed diet because of absent teeth, lose weight (E. Brown, personal communication, March 1993). The solution is to pay careful attention to the dentition of older persons. Even in the nursing home, dementia patients can be reminded to brush their teeth or gums, giving them a feeling of self-pride that they are helping themselves and resulting in better oral hygiene.

Examination of the teeth, gums, tongue, mouth, and lips on a regular basis, with dental visits that include teeth cleaning and tartar and plaque removal, helps quick identification of oral tumors with resulting improvement in morbidity and mortality (Brangman, 1992).

Pulmonary Diseases

COPD, the fourth commonest cause of death in persons over 65 years, is felt to be a disease predominantly related to smoking behavior. It is important to realize that when the current cohort of elderly patients was in its prime, cigarette smoking was considered glamorous, sexy, and almost indispensable. The U.S. military in World War II passed out free cigarettes donated by cigarette companies to young soldiers, and many of these youths carried their smoking habit to old age (or to the grave).

Patients with COPD and obstructive bronchitis can progress to developing emphysema, the trapping of air in small airways of the lung, with resultant poor flow of air and poor exchange of oxygen. Patients with emphysema can be described as *pink puffers* or Type A COPD patients. They develop dyspnea early in their disease, coughing and wheezing are not prominent, and exhalation time is prolonged greater than 6 seconds. Such patients have just enough pO_2 to maintain a decent oxygen saturation if not stressed with exercise or cardiac failure (at 60% pO_2, one still maintains about 95% oxygen saturation, thus one is not "blue" or cyanotic) and a normal or moderately elevated level of CO_2. In contrast, *blue bloaters,* or Type B COPD patients, present with obstructive bronchitis: intermittent cough and wheezing and late appearance of dyspnea despite early development of hypoxia (low levels of oxygen pressure) and hypercapnea (high levels of carbon dioxide; Celli, 1985). Persons with COPD in early stages require from three to five medications to maintain daily activities, and during the late stages, 12 medications, often including oxygen, are the average (Celli, 1985). The disease has an incredible cost in time lost from work and early deaths. Recently, surgical removal of the most severely dilated lobes of emphysematous lung has been shown to help 82% of patients in whom all conservative measures have failed (Buist, 1990; Perry, 1993).

Asthma, a reversible restrictive airway disease, is another cause of major morbidity and mortality. Shockingly, asthma deaths have been rising in the early 1990s, as has the number of asthmatics, with African Americans having a disproportionate number of deaths. There is a concern that inappropriate or even prescribed use of beta-adrenergic inhalants may be contributing to these excessive deaths, and the use of inhaled parasympathomimetics or anti-inflammatory or anti-mast-cell agents on a regular basis to prevent acute attacks may become the treatments of choice. Other restrictive lung diseases that are environmental, such as silicosis, black lung disease, and asbestosis, are more common in the elderly than in younger patients because of the absence of environmental safety standards during most of their working years and lack of recognition by the medical community of dangers posed by certain elements or chemicals during that time. (Asbestos comes most quickly to mind.)

Acute lung infections can include viral or bacterial pneumonias (Legionnaire's disease is a relatively recent cause of morbidity) that result in chronic lung damage. Osler called pneumonia the "old man's friend," because it was often the precipitating cause of a quiet, pain-free death in elderly debilitated persons.

Tuberculosis (TB) is having a resurgence not only because of a population of immigrants from Mexico and Southeast Asian refugees who may be carriers but also because of the emergence of resistant strains of TB (multidrug resistant TB; mycobacterium avium intracellular) in part because of the presence of HIV, the cause of AIDS. Persons with HIV disease often develop Pneumocystis carinii pneumonia, and early diagnosis is crucial because drugs are available that can be used for prophylaxis and prevention in early disease (Roche Laboratories, 1994).

Genital and Urinary Disorders

Benign prostatic hypertrophy is a cause of urinary frequency and occasional urinary retention, although it is not associated with the development of prostatic cancer. Drug treatment has proved beneficial in some cases, although surgery (transurethral resection of the prostate) is sometimes needed to improve urinary outflow.

Many times, urinary incontinence in community-dwelling elders is unreported due to embarrassment or feelings of hopelessness. Common causes of involuntary loss of urine include *stress incontinence,* where the urethra does not stay shut during coughing or sneezing (or any raising of the intravesical pressure), causing dribbling of small amounts of urine, *urge incontinence,* where the feeling of needing to urinate is immediately followed by bladder muscle (detrusor) contraction and urethral relaxation, causing loss of larger amounts of urine, *overflow incontinence,* where a weak or paralyzed bladder fills up with urine and then mildly contracts so that urine leaks out (the "neuropathic" bladder of diabetes or MS), and the type of incontinence called DHIC (*detrusor hyperreflexia and impaired contractility*) where the unfortunate patient can "flood" without warning (Resnick, 1987). Two thirds of patients with incontinence can be helped with bladder retraining techniques, toileting schedules, drugs, or a combination of these. Even dementia patients who no longer have control of their sphincters (functional incontinence) can often be kept dry by establishing toileting regimes. It is no longer considered appropriate to catheterize incontinent elderly patients because of the almost certain development of urinary infections and ultimately, urosepsis.

Fecal and even urinary incontinence may be secondary to fecal impaction, where a hard mass of feces in the rectal ampulla causes diarrhea around it and flattens the urethra of the female patient causing leakage of urine. Elderly patients need to be aware of personal toileting patterns and act quickly when they change. Stool softeners and laxatives have the potential for abuse in the elderly, particularly because their early training often stressed the importance of a daily bowel movement and implicated constipation in all sorts of systemic and constitutional symptoms, such as headache and irritability.

Neoplastic Diseases

Many neoplastic diseases with relatively high 5-year survival rates are important to treat because this can allow elderly persons their normal life spans: Breast, colon, and lung cancer; chronic lymphocytic leukemia; multiple myeloma; and non-Hodgkin's lymphoma are often considered in this light. Prostate cancer appears in the necropsy findings of a substantial percent of males over the age of 80 years, whether there have been symptoms or not (Harman & Nankin, 1985). Prostate cancer has not been shown to benefit from early diagnosis so that the use of the blood test prostate-specific antigen as a screening tool for prostate cancer to improve health outcomes is still somewhat controversial (Stamey, 1983). It is still important to diagnose many neoplasms early because older people are quite amenable to the usual treatments, although their personal preferences must be taken into consideration when offering painful or unusually aggressive treatments. It is important that the elderly still get appropriate cancer screening tests: mammograms and Pap smears for women and stool hemoccults—although controversial in predictive value, they are cheap and easy—or visual colon examinations (the "gold standard," not practical for screening people without increased risk) or both for both men and women. It has been shown that women over the age of 70 years, for example, have a worse prognosis than younger women when they develop breast cancer (Korzeniowski, 1994), and indeed, all elderly patients with cancer do worse than their younger cohorts, with a median age for cancer diagnosis in the general population of 65.4 years, and a median age for death of 67.9 years (National Cancer Institute, 1978).

Elderly patients, although they often believe they are not at great risk, are not immune from HIV disease, either because they have one of the more common risk factors, such as unprotected sexual relations with a carrier or unprotected IV drug abuse or because of transfusions incurred during the time when HIV was in donated blood at blood banks but no screening tools were used that could detect it (1979-1985). Again, early diagnosis and aggressive treatment does have a positive effect on length and quality of life.

Endocrine Disorders

Diabetes mellitus, affecting 10 million Americans, and thyroid disease, affecting up to one third of older U.S. citizens, are the two most prevalent endocrine disorders. Diabetes of adult onset can be linked with hyperinsulinemia, obesity, and hypertension (syndrome X; Zavaroni, 1994) and is important to diagnose and control, either with diet, oral hypoglycemic agents, or insulin. Thyroid hypofunction is one of the more obscure causes of pseudodementia but can also result in syndrome of inappropriate antidiuretic hormone secretion, heart failure, and hypercholesterolemia. Thyroid hyperfunction can present very differently in the elderly than in the young (apathetic hyperthyroidism). Thyroid cancer is a thoroughly treatable condition if diagnosed early by palpation of the thyroid for nodules followed by appropriate ultrasound, biopsy, or both. Thyroid stimulating hormone and T4 blood tests reliably screen for most treatable thyroid disease.

Management of Chronic Pain

Older patients often complain of chronic pain, either secondary to arthritis or after an infection with herpes zoster. Chronic pain can lead to depression (indeed, some studies have shown that 20% or more of older people are clinically depressed; Norris, 1987) and can result in a vicious cycle of inactivity, muscle weakness, stiffness, more pain, and more depression. It is important to work closely with the elderly patient and consider the use of all modalities of pain control, including exercise, physical therapy, pain medication (either nonnarcotic, narcotic, or nonsteroidal) and augmentation of pain medication with small doses of antidepressants when indicated. Comments such as "At your age, what do you expect?" when the elderly person complains about loss of mobility or painful joints, are thankfully becoming rarer. Those of us who care for and about older persons recognize that they can have and deserve a good quality of life despite the presence of chronic illness.

Note

1. H. Holman and K. Lorig teach an effective course titled The Arthritis Self-Management Program at the Stanford University School of Medicine, Palo Alto, California.

21

Geriatric Rehabilitation

Laura Mosqueda

It is appropriate to take a rehabilitative approach to all aspects of clinical geriatrics. This is because rehabilitation and geriatrics share a basic goal—namely, to improve and maintain function (Williams, 1987). The greatest fears of older adults relate to loss of independence—for example, fear of being placed in a nursing home or of not being able to take care of personal needs such as bathing and toileting. If we help elders maintain function, then we also help them maintain independence and thus quality of life. To do this, however, we must move beyond the traditional medical model that targets diseases and incorporate psychosocial factors into a view of the whole person.

The biopsychosocial model (see Figure 21.1) helps us understand this ideal. The model addresses three major aspects of a person's life: physical condition, psychological state, and socioeconomic status. The intersection of these three areas, rather than any individual area, helps the clinician understand an individual's functional abilities. Application of the theory is often difficult but always worthwhile. It requires a team approach because no one health care provider has sufficient time or knowledge to be expert in all areas. Further-more, it takes communication among team members to ensure that coordina-

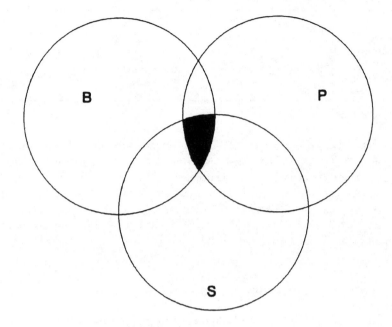

Figure 21.1. A Biopsychosocial Model of Human Functioning

NOTE: B = biological sphere, P = psychological sphere, S = socioeconomic sphere, and the intersection represents function.

tion of care occurs. The clinician must also incorporate the patient and family into the rehabilitative process. In fact, whenever possible, the patient should be the leader of the team so that his or her values are understood and his or her goals are addressed.

Definitions

IMPAIRMENT, DISABILITY, HANDICAP

The World Health Organization has defined several terms in an attempt to promote common usage (World Health Organization, 1980). An *impairment* is a disorder at the level of an organ system. For example, macular degeneration is a relatively common eye disorder among the elderly. The destruction of the macula (the part of the retina most important for color perception and

Table 21.1   Instrumental Activities of Daily Living (IADLs)

Shopping
Cooking
Housekeeping
Finances
Transportation
Medication Management

fine details) is an impairment. *Disability* refers to the loss of function an impairment may cause. The person with macular degeneration may be disabled if he or she is unable to drive because of the deterioration in vision. A person becomes *handicapped* if the disability prevents him or her from fulfilling social roles. Therefore, if society does not provide alternate means of transportation for this individual so he or she is unable to shop or get to appointments, he or she has been handicapped.

INSTRUMENTAL ACTIVITIES OF DAILY LIVING

Instrumental activities of daily living, or IADLs, are those functions that are necessary to remain independent in the community (see Table 21.1). They include tasks such as shopping, cooking, and housecleaning. If a person is unable to carry out any of these tasks then he or she must receive some outside help if living alone. The clinician must investigate the reason an elder may be having difficulty: Is it a physical problem or a cognitive problem (or both)? The answer will determine the appropriate next step. An elder who is not able to cook because he or she cannot lift a pot off the stove will require an entirely different approach than the elder who is not able to cook because he or she continually burns food, forgetting that the stove is on.

ACTIVITIES OF DAILY LIVING

The activities of daily living, or ADLs, are those functions that are necessary to remain independent in one's own home (see Table 21.2). *Mobility* refers to one's ability to move from one point to another. For some people, this refers to walking ability, for others it refers to wheelchair skills, and for others, it refers to a combination of both. Some people are independent with their mobility but have difficulty with transfers. For example, they are able to move from the bedroom to the kitchen but are unable to get out of bed without help. Elders with weak hip extensors may have great difficulty arising from the low couches in their living rooms.

Table 21.2   Activities of Daily Living (ADLs)

Mobility
Bathing and hygiene
Transfers
Toileting
Dressing
Feeding oneself

Toileting oneself can be a fairly complicated process for a disabled older adult. It involves dexterity and balance to manage one's clothing, range of motion to clean oneself, and strength to get safely on and off the toilet. Other bathroom activities, such as bathing and hygiene, involve similar physical skills.

As with the other ADLs, dressing is a task that requires both cognitive and physical abilities. Selecting appropriate clothing is difficult for some of the elderly with dementias. The act of dressing requires visuospatial skills (e.g., putting the left arm in the correct sleeve) as well as adequate balance, range of motion, strength, and flexibility.

The ability for elders to feed themselves is also considered an ADL. Many people who are unable to cook can remain independent with the help of food delivery services (such as Meals on Wheels) and the help of family members who bring them meals and stock their freezers.

The Roles of Team Members

PATIENTS, CAREGIVERS, OR BOTH

When a patient suffers a sudden, unexpected disabling condition, such as a stroke, there is a tendency for the physicians and family to encourage the patient to take on a "sick" role (Silverstone & Williams, 1984). The patient (and sometimes the family) is rarely asked about preferences for care and may not be consulted when important decisions are being considered, such as nursing home placement from the acute hospital. A rehabilitative approach encourages all members of the health care team to confer with the patient, family members, or both before making any nonemergent decisions regarding care (see Figure 21.2).

In addition to promoting patient autonomy, this approach also leads to greater cooperation between the patient and the health care team. Consider the following case example:

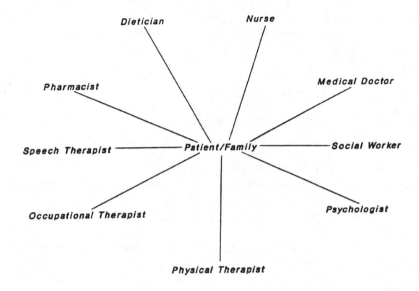

Figure 21.2. The Patient-Centered Approach to Rehabilitation

Mr. H is an 85-year-old man who had a left hemispheric stroke 6 weeks ago. His physical recovery has been quite good: He is able to ambulate with the use of a walker and has limited use of his right upper extremity. He has some difficulty in expressing himself but is able to make his needs known if given enough time. His family is very supportive of his efforts and wants to help him return to his own home. Much to everyone's surprise, he began to refuse to participate in physical or occupational therapy sessions.

When a family conference was held to inquire about this change, Mr. H explained that he was now walking and did not see the point of continuing these boring and sometimes painful exercises. When we asked about goals beyond walking, the team discovered that Mr. H wanted to resume his gardening activities, something he did not express when the rehabilitation program started. New goals relating to this activity were established by Mr. H and he was once again interested in pursuing his therapy sessions.

NURSES

Nurses play a crucial role in many settings. In an acute rehabilitation hospital, they reinforce what the patient is learning in therapies, tell the therapists how the patient is doing outside of the gym, and assist with the training of family members. Even in an acute medical setting, nurses may take a leading role in a rehabilitative approach by encouraging the elder to do as much as possible for himself or herself and by assisting with proper positioning to avoid secondary complications (e.g., pressure sores, contractures, shoulder subluxation).

Some nurses are involved in home visits and case management activities. They are in an excellent position to look for early evidence of functional decline and promote a safe environment.

Social Workers

Like nurses, social workers may be dealing with the elderly in inpatient or outpatient settings. In an acute setting, they assist in identifying community resources that may make the difference between independent living and nursing home placement. The case of a 72-year-old woman is illustrative:

> The woman has had a stroke and requires 3 weeks in a rehabilitation program to become independent with most of her ADLs. She wants to return to the home of her married daughter who has three small children. Her daughter and son-in-law would like for her to move back in but are concerned that the patient will require too much care, especially during the day when the daughter is also looking after the children.

The social worker may identify this issue early in the hospitalization and begin looking for adult day care centers in this person's community. When one is found, the patient may attend 3 days per week, thus relieving the daughter of a significant amount of caregiving responsibility. For this reason, the family may be able to take the patient back to their home.

PHYSICAL THERAPISTS, OCCUPATIONAL THERAPISTS, SPEECH PATHOLOGISTS

These disciplines are expert at the assessment and treatment of a variety of ADLs and IADLs. Physical therapists tend to concentrate on mobility-related issues, such as balance, gait, endurance, and ability to transfer. Occupational therapists are oriented to other ADLs such as bathing, grooming, and hygiene as well as higher-level activities (IADLs) such as driving and cooking. Speech pathologists assess cognitive function and communication skills. Swallowing ability may be evaluated by speech pathologists, occupational therapists, or (rarely) physical therapists.

It is critically important to involve these rehabilitation specialists when there is any question of an elder's functional status. If there are safety hazards in the home, a therapist may recommend adaptive equipment, such as grab bars in the bathroom. An older adult who is at risk of falling may benefit from an exercise program and a properly fitted walker. A patient with expressive aphasia may be able to use a communication board if given some training. These types of rehabilitative interventions help keep people in the community and help make them less dependent on caregivers.

PSYCHOLOGISTS

Psychological disorders such as depression and anxiety are particularly common in the disabled elderly (Kemp, 1993). Not only are these disorders distressing for the individual experiencing the symptoms, they also interfere with the individual's ability to participate in a rehabilitation program. Psychologists often help the patient and the team when the patient is "not motivated" to participate. They can also treat specific psychological disorders that may be impeding progress.

PHARMACOLOGISTS

Many elders are put on multiple medications and then experience multiple side effects. Pharmacologists assist with analyzing the necessity and appropriateness of the medication regimen. It is not uncommon to find that medications are impairing intellect, balance, or energy level.

PHYSICIANS

Physiatrists are physicians who specialize in physical medicine and rehabilitation. Most referrals to rehabilitative programs, however, come from internists and family physicians, who receive little training in the field of rehabilitative medicine. It is important for these physicians to make appropriate referrals to inpatient and outpatient programs. When in doubt, consultation may be sought from physiatrists or therapists.

Even if the physician is not directly involved in the rehabilitation program, he or she can assist by making sure that all illnesses are identified and treated in such a way that the patient's function is maximized. Some diseases, such as congestive heart failure, may present nothing more than a feeling of fatigue. Other common illnesses that are usually thought of as being minor, such as urinary tract infections, may cause very significant symptoms in the disabled elderly.

DIETITIANS

Malnutrition is a fairly common but underrecognized problem among the elderly, especially for those with chronic diseases. Nutritional experts, such as dietitians, may identify nutritional problems and make recommendations for treatment. This becomes particularly important for people with swallowing disorders or feeding tubes or both.

RECREATION THERAPISTS

Many acute inpatient rehabilitation programs have recreation therapists available for their elderly patients, as do some outpatient programs. These therapists can assist with reintegration into society by taking people on group outings into the community, such as a visit to a shopping mall. Many older adults are unable to pursue the same leisure activities they enjoyed before the onset of a disabling condition. The recreation therapist may help them explore new ways to participate in the same activity or explore new types of activities.

Rehabilitation Settings

INPATIENT SETTINGS

There are several Medicare criteria to justify a stay in an acute rehabilitation setting: The patient must be able to participate in a minimum of 3 hours of therapy per day, the patient must require at least two different types of therapy (e.g., occupational and physical therapy), and last, the patient must show evidence of significant progress. It is recognized that many older adults may have difficulty participating fully during the initial phase of the program. Some elders are on medications that interfere with physical or cognitive functioning or both and so must be detoxified to participate in the program. Others may exhibit an increase in confusion when moved to a new environment; after several days, patients' confusion often clears as they become familiar with the new surroundings.

The acute setting is typically used for those who have experienced a sudden decline in function, such as occurs with a stroke. Many disabled older adults who have been hospitalized for a reason unrelated to their disability also benefit from an acute rehabilitation program prior to going home. Consider the following case:

Mrs. H is a 92-year-old woman with severe osteoarthritis of her knees. Ten years ago, she had a stroke that resulted in limited movement of her right arm and leg.

She is able to ambulate short distances with the use of a front-wheeled walker and requires minimal help with dressing and bathing activities. Her daughter, with whom she lives, assists her with a daily exercise program to maximize her strength and range of motion. She recently had pneumonia, which necessitated 5 days of hospitalization. During the hospitalization, she has been at bed rest and has not been doing her daily exercises. Now that it is time for her to go home, she is unable to ambulate and needs significantly more help in her other ADLs.

A short stay in an acute rehabilitation setting, where she could receive physical therapy to help her with her gait and occupational therapy to work on bathing and dressing activities, may make the difference between returning home and going to a skilled nursing facility.

OUTPATIENT SETTINGS

Elders who are in need of only one or two types of therapy and who would benefit from one to three therapy sessions per week are appropriate candidates for outpatient services. It is important to make sure that the individual has access to transportation services to go between home and therapy. As with the inpatient programs, these programs are guided by setting goals and making progress. Because the patient comes to the therapist, specialized equipment such as mats and parallel bars are available.

HOME

When an elder would benefit from a rehabilitation program but has difficulty getting out of the house, in-home therapy is a good intervention. The therapist comes to the individual's home, typically once or twice a week, for evaluation and treatment. Although specialized equipment is not as available as it is in other settings, therapists have an opportunity to see how patients function in their own environments and thus make treatment recommendations based on realistic assessments. For example, a patient who is able to rise from a chair in the therapy gym may not be able to rise from his favorite living room chair, which is low and has deep cushions.

Home programs are also very helpful for caregivers. Caregivers may be taught how to help so that they promote their loved one's independence but do not hurt themselves in the process. Therapists who visit the home give advice regarding modifications or equipment that will promote safety and independence. Simple interventions such as removing throw rugs or adding grab bars may be recommended.

SUBACUTE AND SKILLED NURSING FACILITIES

People who are unable to withstand the intensity of acute inpatient rehabilitation and are not ready to move to a community living situation may benefit from a less rigorous rehabilitative program. Subacute rehabilitation programs, often located within skilled nursing facilities, provide this less intensive level of rehabilitation. Some patients may move directly to a more independent living situation from the subacute facility; others may gain enough strength and endurance to move to an acute rehabilitation program. And for others, it may provide the opportunity to maximize their functioning so they may be more independent in the skilled nursing setting.

Who Benefits From Rehabilitation?

Rehabilitation potential is a nebulous concept, yet we are continually trying to assess what people may benefit from a rehabilitation program (Mosqueda, 1993). As mentioned earlier in this chapter, all older adults benefit from a rehabilitative approach. Potential must be examined from the perspective of the biopsychosocial model, particularly when trying to identify the most appropriate rehabilitative setting.

Any older adults who are not functioning at their maximal levels may be helped by rehabilitation programs if the programs meet their personal goals and needs. When a patient is interested in pursuing therapy, a careful physical assessment will determine if there are illnesses that are not optimally treated and if there are specific physical limitations (e.g., poor cardiac output, which causes limited endurance).

If the rehabilitation program involves learning new information, the patient must have some memory capability. Many patients with a dementia (and, therefore, impaired memory) can participate successfully in rehabilitative programs if the team members are aware of the limitations and work within the patient's capabilities. Clinical experience teaches that most patients must be able to follow at least a two-step command to be in an acute inpatient rehabilitation program, whereas people with a lower cognitive status may do well in a home or subacute program.

Rehabilitation for Specific Diseases

STROKE

Strokes are a common cause of disability among the elderly (Bonita, 1992). Risk factors include atrial fibrillation, hypertension, diabetes, and a history

Table 21.3 Predictors of Poor Functional Outcome Following a Stroke

Coma
Bowel incontinence
Severe hemiplegia or hemiparesis
Severe cognitive impairment
Neglect syndrome

of prior stroke. The consequences of a stroke depend on the location of the stroke and the extent of damage and therefore range from death to complete (or almost complete) recovery. Many people have significant spontaneous recoveries of function in the first 6 months following a stroke (Lehmann et al., 1975). It is likely that rehabilitation during this time will enhance functional gains (Lind, 1982). A rehabilitation program also provides an opportunity for patients and families to adjust to the sudden onset of a new disability. Depression is very common following a stroke and often goes undiagnosed and therefore untreated for years (Clothier & Grotta, 1991). All members of the team should be alert to evidence of poststroke depression because it is a treatable illness.

It is known that some factors are predictive of limited functional recovery after a stroke (Dombovy, Sandok, & Basford, 1986; Granger, Hamilton, & Fieldler, 1992; Granger, Hamilton, Gresham, & Kramer, 1989); these are listed in Table 21.3. People who are initially comatose tend to have a poor prognosis. If 2 to 4 weeks have passed since the stroke and a patient still has severe weakness on the affected side, is incontinent of bowel, has a neglect syndrome, or has severe cognitive impairment, functional gains will probably be minimal.

Armed with this type of information, the clinician may make recommendations regarding the appropriateness of rehabilitation and the type of program that would be best, taking into account the patient's social as well as medical situation. Consider this case:

Mr. B is a 71-year-old widower who had a left hemispheric stroke 4 days ago. He now has moderate strength on his right side and has a moderate expressive and receptive aphasia; he knows when he has to go to the bathroom and has sphincter control but is sometimes incontinent because he cannot get to the bathroom by himself and is unable to communicate when he needs to go. His family (two adult children and a sister) is emotionally supportive but unable to provide practical support because they all live in different cities. Prior to the stroke, Mr. B was living independently in a second floor apartment; the building has no elevator. He has Medicare and a private supplemental insurance, but his monthly income is just enough to allow him to pay rent and pay for his basic necessities.

It is likely that Mr.B will benefit from an acute inpatient program: He will need occupational, physical, and speech therapies, nurses on all shifts will be involved in improving his continence as well as reinforcing lessons learned in therapies, the psychologist will assist in cognitive evaluation and look for evidence of disorders such as depression and anxiety, and the social worker will assist in contacting family members and arranging a family conference early in the patient's stay. Many of the therapeutic goals will be based on where Mr.B wants to live following hospitalization.

HIP FRACTURE

Hip fractures are a thought to be a common cause of morbidity and mortality in the elderly (Magaziner, Simonsick, Kashner, Hebel, & Kenzora, 1990). The incidence of hip fractures rises dramatically with age, and these fractures are typically caused by a fall (Rodriguez, Sattin, & Waxweiler, 1989). However it must be remembered that a healthy elder is not likely to fall so that hip fractures also may be a marker of underlying illnesses; it may be these illnesses that make some of the elderly prone to a high rate of morbidity and mortality following a fracture.

Treatment for a hip fracture will depend on the location and type of fracture as well as the functional status of the patient. If the person is seriously ill, surgery may be dangerous. Age alone is not a contraindication to surgical repair. If the person was not ambulatory prior to the fracture surgical repair may be unnecessary. However, surgical repair is often the best alternative. Postoperative instructions will vary according to the type of repair. A repair that allows for early ambulation, such as a prosthetic replacement, is ideal so that the patient does not also suffer from the devastating effects of bed rest and inactivity.

Adaptive Equipment

There is a great variety of low-technology adaptive equipment that can help maintain a person independently and safely in their own home (Sammons, 1994), but the equipment is best chosen by an experienced clinician in conjunction with the elder. For example, people who purchase wheelchairs or canes from the store do not usually know how to identify the proper fit and are usually unaware of the myriad types available. On the other hand, therapists who choose "the best" equipment for an elder may discover it in a closet 2 months later because it did not fit the older adult's needs or self-concept. Again, a case example is useful:

Mrs. Y is a 94-year-old woman who has some balance problems. A physical therapy assessment confirms that this woman is at risk of falling. A front-wheeled walker is recommended as the option that will provide her with the most stability, but the patient refuses, stating "I don't want to look like an old lady!" A compromise is eventually reached: The therapist does a home evaluation to point out safety hazards, and the patient agrees to have railings installed at her front stairs.

Bathroom equipment is often very helpful. Raised toilet seats may make getting on and off the toilet much easier. A tub transfer bench is a bench that straddles the lip of a bathtub, allowing the patient to sit down and swing his or her legs over the tub, thus eliminating the dangerous maneuver of stepping over the lip. Once in the tub, the patient has the option of sitting on the bench or standing. Shower hoses and long-handled scrub brushes assist people with poor balance, limited range of motion, or both.

There are many pieces of adaptive equipment for the kitchen that make cooking a safer and more enjoyable experience. People with upper extremities that are painful or weak may benefit from jar openers or devices that extend their reach. A variety of cutting boards and utensils are available for people who have limited use of one or both hands. Dressing equipment includes a gadget that helps people with poor dexterity button their clothes and a device that allows people to put on their shoes and socks without bending down.

Physical therapists are expert at assessment for devices related to mobility and transfers. For people with communication disorders, speech therapists can assess the appropriateness of equipment, such as communication boards that use pictures rather than words. Occupational therapists are the specialists most familiar with equipment related to the other ADLs and IADLs such as driving, cooking, and dressing.

Conclusion

Although there are traditional diagnoses associated with rehabilitation such as stroke and hip fracture, everyone who works with the elderly could and should take a rehabilitative approach with all elders. This approach will remind us to look at physical, psychological, and social functions so that we may help our patients achieve the highest possible quality of life based on their own definitions.

22

Geriatric Psychopharmacology

Jeanette Schneider

Psychotropic drugs are among the most widely prescribed drugs for the elderly. According to a 1983 study (Thompson, Moran, & Nies, 1983), these medications were the fifth most commonly prescribed of all medicines. Table 22.1 outlines the basic classes of psychotropic drugs as well as the conditions for which they are prescribed. Wise use of these drugs involves familiarity with their effects and side effects in elderly patients as well as an awareness that the human interaction between patient and physician is crucial to compliance and, ultimately, successful therapy.

This chapter reviews the general pharmacological factors to be considered in prescribing drugs for elderly patients and the use of psychotropic drugs for treating specific problems, including depression, anxiety, insomnia, psychosis, mood swings, agitation, and behavioral disturbance.

Table 22.1. Classes of Psychotropic Drugs

Class	Condition(s)
Anxiolytic	Anxiety disorders: Generalized anxiety disorder, post-traumatic-stress disorder, panic disorder, phobic disorder
	Agitation: Depression, acute mania, acute psychosis, dementia
	Insomnia: Concomitant psychiatric disorders
Antidepressants	Anxiety disorders: Panic disorder, phobic disorder, OCD
	Major depressive disorder, dysthymia
	Bipolar affective disorder, depressed schizoaffective disorder, depression with agitation-aggression (e.g. Trazodone)
	Chronic pain.
Neuroleptics	Acute and chronic psychosis (schizophrenia, schizoaffective disorder, schizophreniform disorder, brief reactive psychosis, bipolar affective disorder, major depression with psychotic features)
	Agitation-aggression (e.g., in dementia)
	Delirium
Lithium	Bipolar affective disorder, cyclothymia
	Schizoaffective disorder
	Major depressive disorder (e.g., tricyclic antidepressant augmentation)
	Aggression (intermittent explosive disorder, dementia, organic mood, anxiety and personality syndromes)
Anticonvulsants	Bipolar affective disorder
	Schizoaffective disorder
	Chronic pain
	Agitation-aggression: intermittent explosive disorder; dementia; organic mood, anxiety, and personality syndromes
Beta blockers	Performance anxiety
	Aggression (e.g., organic mental syndromes)
	Lithium-induced tremor
	Neuroleptic-induced akathesia
Disulfiram	Alcohol prophylaxis

Prescribing Drugs for Elderly Patients

Several factors must be considered in appropriate drug treatment of elderly individuals. First, age-related physiological alterations in organ function affect numerous aspects of drug metabolism and action. An awareness of these changes is essential in choosing and monitoring psychopharmacological drugs in elderly patients.

Second, diagnostic assessment and pharmacological treatment of psychiatric illness in the geriatric population are frequently complicated by comorbidity with physical illness(es), each of which may result in, or exacerbate, psychiatric symptoms (see Chapter 10, this volume). Psychiatric symptoms in elderly patients may be the manifestation of an underlying physical disorder. Knowledge of the patient's chronic illness and a comprehensive physical evaluation of current medical status is clearly mandatory in prescribing psychotropic drugs. Thorough knowledge of the individual's previous psychiatric history is similarly important. Current symptoms may represent exacerbations or relapses of a chronic psychiatric disorder or may be new in origin. This is an extremely important diagnostic differential; the onset of most psychiatric illness tends to appear earlier, in youth or young adulthood. The etiology of new, particularly sudden, onset of psychiatric symptoms in the elderly must be considered organic or drug related until proven otherwise.

Third, psychiatric symptoms in elderly patients may also be the result of medication. Table 22.2 illustrates various psychiatric symptoms that may be associated with medications used to treat physical disorders. Detailed medication assessment, including both prescribed and over-the-counter (OTC) medications, is thus essential. Addressing the issue of OTC medications is particularly important, as their use is often not acknowledged unless specifically questioned. Furthermore, currently available OTC medications now include drugs (e.g., ibuprofen and diphenhydramine) that can have particularly serious physiologic and psychiatric effects.

Fourth, the increased use of multiple medications, both prescribed and OTC, in the elderly can result in adverse drug reactions as well as iatrogenic psychiatric illness. It is well known that the risk of iatrogenic adverse physical or psychiatric consequences, or both, increases dramatically as the number of medications increases.

Fifth and last, not only are adverse side effects more common in the elderly, but the ultimate consequences of such adverse side effects are often more severe, given this population's increased frailty and diminished reserve capacity (e.g., orthostatic hypotension leads to falls, which may more often result in fractures).

Age-Related Changes in Drug Metabolism and Effects

Physiologic concomitant's of aging include pharmacokinetic and pharmacodynamic changes. An overview of this complex subject is provided in the following sections; the reader is referred to several excellent reviews for further study (Abernathy, 1992; Jenike, 1989; Norman, 1993; Young & Meyers, 1991).

Pharmacokinetic Changes

Pharmacokinetics refers to various aspects of drug metabolism, including absorption, distribution, metabolism (most psychotropic drugs are hepatically metabolized), and excretion (chiefly renal).

Table 22.2   Psychiatric Effects of Selected Drugs

Drug Class	Drug	Possible Effects
Analgesics-anti-inflammatories	Aspirin	Confusion, paranoia,
	Indomethacin	Delusions, emotional dissociation, hallucinations, hostile behavior, hypomania, paranoia
	Sulindac	Bizarre behavior, depression, illusions, paranoia
Anticonvulsants	Carbamazepine	Loose associations, psychosis
	Phenytoin	
	Primidone	
Antidepressants	Amitriptyline	Delusions, forgetfulness, illogical thoughts, paranoid delusions, sleep disturbances
	Amoxapine	Delusions, mania
	Imipramine	Forgetfullness, illogical thoughts, paranoid delusions, sleep disturbances
	Nortriptyline	Paranoid delusions
	Trazodone	Increased activity, paranoia, pressured speech
Antiparkinson agents	Amantadine	Agitation, illusions
	Bromocriptine	Delusions, paranoia
	Levodopa	Hallucinations, illusions, insomnia, psychotic symptoms
Benzodiazepines	Diazepam	Delusions
	Flurazepam	Depression
	Triazolam	Paranoia
Cardiac-cardiovascular	Digitoxin	Agitation, delusions, paranoia
	Digoxin	Delusions, depression, fatigue, incoherency, paranoia, social withdrawal
	Disopyramide	Agitation, depression, insomnia
	Methyldopa	Depression, inability to concentrate
	Mexiletine	Confusion, disorientation
	Nadolol	Guilt, insomnia, sadness
	Procainamide	Delusions, hallucinations
	Propranolol	Depression, decreased energy and sleep, paranoia, paranoid delusions, visual and perceptual disorders
	Thiazides	Depression
H-2 blockers	Cimetidine	Agitation, confusion, depression, insomnia, lethargy, manic symptoms
	Ranitidine	Depression
Steroids	Prednisolone	Hallucinations, paranoid delusions
	Prednisone	Depression, euphoria, hypomania

SOURCE: Lamy, P. P., Salzman, C., & Nevis-Olesen, J. (1992). "Drug Prescribing Patterns, Risks, and Compliance Guidelines," in Salzman (1992).

Absorption

Alterations in gastrointestinal (GI) function with aging include decreased GI mobility, delayed gastric emptying, reduced intestinal blood flow, and increased gastric pH. To date, there is little evidence that these age-related changes are of clinical significance (Norman, 1993; Plein & Plein, 1981).

Distribution

Unlike absorption, alterations in the tissue distribution of psychotropic drugs with age are extremely important in geriatric psychotropic drug use. With increasing age, there is a decrease in total body water and an increase in total body fat with reduced lean body mass (Greenblatt, Sellers, & Shader, 1982). Thus, the volume of distribution of lipid-soluble drugs (as are most active psychotropics) is enhanced, resulting in increased elimination half-lives.

Protein Binding

With the exception of lithium and the new antidepressant venlafaxine, all psychotropic drugs are highly protein bound, existing in an equilibrium between this bound fraction and a free, pharmacologically active fraction. Age-related alterations in the levels of binding proteins affect the proportion of unbound, active drug. Levels of the major drug-binding protein, albumin, decrease with age, thereby increasing the level of unbound drug in the elderly. This may be a factor in the increased sensitivity of the elderly to adverse side effects, although the plasma concentration of an unbound drug is not simply a reflection of the amount unbound but also on its clearance. Thus, the relationship between the function of unbound drug and drug toxicity is not as simple as might initially be considered.

Hepatic Metabolism

The liver is the primary site of psychotropic drug metabolism, producing both active and inactive metabolites that ultimately are eliminated via the kidneys. Many psychotropic drugs, including all neuroleptics and antidepressants (with the exception of trazodone), undergo an extensive "first pass effect," or extraction of the drug via the enterohepatic circulation prior to its reentry into the systemic circulation. Age-related decreases in hepatic blood flow impede partial extraction, resulting in increased drug entry into the systemic circulation and thus increased plasma drug concentrations.

The liver carries out a number of biochemical conversions, the specific processes being dependent on the given psychotropic drug. Age-related changes in any of these processes may have considerable significance in metabolic clearance of a drug, its metabolites, or both and the resulting therapeutic and adverse consequences. There is also considerable interindividual variation, with resultant diverse effects on drug clearance and thus the relationship of drug dose to plasma level. For instance, there is considerable individual variation in the rate of demethylation, as well as age-related changes. Oxidation (phase I) reactions may be slowed with increased age, slowing hepatic drug clearance. Phase II biotransformations, such as glucuronidation, appear to be relatively unaffected by age.

An ideal pharmacological agent in the elderly individual is one that possesses a relatively short half-life (preferably < 24 hours) and no active metabolites. Prolonged presence in the body of a drug, its active metabolite, or both places the individual at increased risk for toxic side effects.

Renal Excretion

Most, if not all, psychotropic drugs, including lithium, are eliminated via the kidney, either unchanged (e.g., lithium), as water-soluble active metabolites, or as inactive, often glucuronidated, metabolic end products. Several age-related changes in kidney function impede renal clearance of drugs, prolonging elimination half-lives and elevating plasma levels. These include decreased renal blood flow, decreased glomerular filtration rate (50% decline by age 70 years), and decreased creatinine clearance leading to an increase in elimination half-life.

For lithium and other renally excreted active drug metabolites, the reduction of creatinine clearance with increased age results in increased plasma concentrations at a fixed drug dose. This is an important consideration in determining appropriate drug dosage, particularly in those drugs with a low therapeutic index (e.g., lithium) or potentially serious adverse side effects (e.g., water-soluble active metabolites of cyclic antidepressants may have cardiac and anticholinergic side effects). A frequently used indicator of kidney function, serum creatinine, may not be sufficient for adequate assessment of renal status in the elderly, given the age-related decline in creatinine production and renal clearance.

PHARMACODYNAMIC CHANGES

Pharmacodynamic changes with age refer to alterations in central nervous system (CNS) receptor sensitivity or number, neurotransmitter levels, and enzyme activity that affect the response to, and effects of, psychotropic drugs. Discussion of this area is complicated by the diverse, and at times conflictual, literature in the field; for interested readers, a thoughtful review of neurotransmission and aging is available by Sunderland (1992).

Briefly, aging has multiple effects on the neurotransmitters dopamine (DA), norepinephrine (NE), serotonin (5HT), and acetylcholine (ACh). These neurotransmitters and their respective receptor populations are implicated in mood, behavior, and cognition. The activity of enzymes involved in the synthesis and catabolism of these neurotransmitters is age related. Tyrosine hydroxylase, DOPA decarboxylase (DA, NE), and choline acetyltransferase (ACh) show decreased activity (Goodnick & Gershon, 1984). In contrast, the activity of monoamine oxidase, involved in the catabolism of DA, NE, and 5HT, and acetylcholinesterase (ACh catabolism) increases with age (Gottfries et al., 1983; Oreland & Gottfries, 1986). Decreased levels of DA in the elderly may be a reflection of this altered metabolic activity. The levels of 5HT and ACh have been variously demonstrated as decreased or normal with age, whereas NE levels have been found normal or increased. Such alterations in neurotransmitter levels may alter the pharmacological effects of psychotropic agents.

Alterations in receptor number (e.g., decreased D2, 5HT1 receptors), sensitivity (e.g., noradrenergic beta receptors), or both have been reported to occur with age. Such modulatory changes in receptors have important consequences in the pharmacological action of psychotropic drugs.

In general, the elderly show increased sensitivity to both the therapeutic and toxic side effects of pharmacological agents. This is a reflection of the pharmacokinetic alterations mentioned previously as well as these pharmacodynamic changes.

Side Effects of Psychotropic Drugs

Unfortunately, the therapeutic benefits of psychotropic medications are not to be had without a price; unwanted and potentially adverse side effects occur with all of these drugs, the magnitude and severity of which must be weighed carefully against their efficacy in alleviating targeted symptoms (Arana & Hyman, 1991; Jenike, 1989; Salzman, 1992; Schatzberg & Cole, 1991; Settle, 1992; Young & Meyers, 1991). Indeed, choice of a psychotropic drug for a particular disorder is generally made based on consideration of side effect profile as well as pharmacokinetic and pharmacodynamic parameters. These selection criteria are predicated on the cumulative findings of many researchers that the therapeutic efficacy of drugs within a specific class (e.g., antidepressants) are all roughly equivalent. Such appears to be the case for antipsychotics (except clozapine) in the treatment of psychosis, antidepressants in depression (discussion to follow), anxiety with benzodiazepines, and so forth.

Common and particularly problematic side effects in the elderly are sedation, orthostatic hypotension, and anticholinergic and cardiac side effects. Sexual dysfunctions also occur.

SEDATION

Although the sedative properties of psychotropic drugs contribute to their efficacy in treating anxiety and agitation, they may be responsible for unwanted side effects, including confusion and falls. Numerous studies have demonstrated an association between the use of psychotropic drugs and increased risk of falls in the elderly (Ballinger & Ramsey, 1975; Davie, Blumenthal, & Robinson-Hawkins, 1981; MacDonald, 1985; Prudham & Evans, 1981; Ray, Griffin, Schattner, Baugh, & Melton, 1987). Ray et al. (1987) reported a dose-related increased risk of hip fracture with long half-life (> 24 hours) anxiolytic-hypnotics (e.g., flurazepam), tricyclic antidepressants (TCAs; e.g., imipramine, amitriptyline), and antipsychotics (e.g., haloperidol, thioridazine) but not with short half-life anxiolytic-hypnotics (e.g., diphenhydramine, hydroxyzine, choral hydrate). Unfortunately, short half-life benzodiazepines were not included in this study. Both the sedative and orthostatic hypotensive properties of psychotropic drugs were considered factors in this increased incidence of falls and resultant hip fractures. Notably, controversy has recently arisen regarding the role of psychotropic drugs, including benzodiazepines, in falls in this population. Greenspan, Myers, and Maitland (1994), studying risks for hip fracture in ambulatory elderly individuals, found no significant association with medications; positive risk factors included direction and force of fall, reduced femoral bone mineral density, and lower body mass index.

ORTHOSTATIC HYPOTENSION

Orthostatic hypotension, or a drop in blood pressure when the patient assumes an upright position, results from blockade of alpha-adrenergic receptors in the peripheral nervous system. In addition to falls, orthostatic hypotension has been implicated in the genesis of myocardial infarction and cerebrovascular accidents (Muller, Goodman, & Bellet, 1961; Thaysen et al., 1981).

ANTICHOLINERGIC SIDE EFFECTS

Anticholinergic side effects are common in "older generation" psychotropic drugs, such as TCAs and low-potency antipsychotics. These include both peripheral effects, such as dry mouth, constipation, urinary hesitation or retention, blurred vision, flushing, and decreased sweating, and central nervous system manifestations, including confusion, delirium, sedation, and agitation. Older individuals demonstrate increased sensitivity to these effects and may experience severe symptoms at therapeutic doses of the prescribed medication. Mild anticholinergic side effects may affect compliance; more severe manifestations of anticholinergic toxicity may compromise the ability to physiologically tolerate the medication.

Peripheral Side Effects

Dry mouth is ubiquitous and, at the least, an annoyance. It may be somewhat relieved with mouth washes, hard candies, or chewing gum. Constipation is also a common side effect that generally responds to the use of stool softeners, dietary fiber or bulk agents, and increased fluid intake. Ileus, essentially a paralysis of the bowel, is a reflection of anticholinergic toxicity and requires timely intervention, including discontinuation of offending medications and possibly, the addition of a cholinergic agonist.

Urinary hesitancy and retention are potentially limiting side effects most commonly seen in men with prostatic hypertrophy or in anticholinergic toxicity; retention may require emergency catheterization of the bladder. The cholinergic agonist bethanechol (Urecholine) has been used effectively in treatment of anticholinergic-induced urinary and bowel dysfunction (Arana & Hyman, 1991; Pollack & Rosenbaum, 1987; Settle, 1992) but introduces its own systemic effects.

Blurred vision may occur due to impaired accommodation of the lens. Medications with anticholinergic properties are contraindicated in the presence of closed or narrow angle glaucoma.

Central Nervous System Effects

The limited studies on cognitive and performance effects of anticholinergic medications have shown somewhat inconsistent findings (Settle, 1992). Assessment of the anticholinergic effects of antidepressant medications in depressed individuals is complicated by the cognitive difficulties so often associated with the illness. The risk of medication-induced cognitive dysfunction or delirium appears to increase with age, however, as well as preexisting cognitive impairment (Settle, 1992). The risk of anticholinergic delirium from TCAs has been shown to be a function of age, preexisting cognitive impairment, and dose or plasma drug level (Preskorn & Jorkovich, 1990). In the elderly, delirium may occur at a relatively low plasma level.

Anticholinergic delirium may present as an exclusively CNS phenomenon or may have concomitant peripheral signs (e.g., tachycardia, pupil dilatation, etc.), which may help in the diagnosis. As with any delirium, rapid intervention is essential, including discontinuation of the offending medication(s).

Careful clinical assessment, plasma drug level monitoring, or both may allow for future reinstitution of the same drug at reduced dose. The use of concomitant medications with additional anticholinergic effects must also be closely followed.

In general, the use of pyschotropic drugs with significant anticholinergic potential (e.g., low-potency antipsychotics, tertiary amine TCAs), alpha-1 adrenergic blockade, sedation (unless indicated), or a combination of these should be avoided.

CARDIAC SIDE EFFECTS

Cardiac side effects of psychotropic drugs range from nonspecific, clinically unimportant electrocardiogram (EKG) changes to alterations in cardiac rhythm or conduction.

The cardiac side effects of TCAs include prolongation of cardiac conduction, Type 1A quinidine-like antiarrhythmic effects, and orthostatic hypotension. The tricyclics are extremely toxic in overdose in all age groups, in part because they cause cardiac arrthymias at high plasma levels. Although these agents have demonstrated therapeutic benefit in the treatment of depression in elderly individuals with cardiac disease (Glassman et al., 1985; Jefferson, 1992; Salzman, Schneider, & Lebowitz, 1993) and other concomitant medical illness, they carry the risk of severe, even fatal, side effects, particularly in individuals with underlying cardiac disease.

Other classes of psychotropic drugs with potential cardiac side effects include the mood-stabilizing agents carbamazepine and lithium. Carbamazepine is structurally similar to the antidepressant imipramine, and can also prolong cardiac conduction. At therapeutic levels, lithium may produce nonspecific EKG changes (e.g., T-wave flattening or inversion) that are generally benign. In patients with preexisting cardiac disease, lithium may cause SA node dysfunction and tachycardia.

The low-potency antipsychotics thiordazine and mesoridazine and the high-potency neuroleptic pimozide can prolong cardiac conduction and may thus promote heart block or prolong the QTc interval, thereby increasing the risk of *torsade de pointes* ventricular tachycardia (Arana & Hyman, 1991). The use of high-potency antipsychotics is thus recommended in the setting of preexisting cardiac disease, particularly in the elderly.

SEXUAL DYSFUNCTION

Contrary to commonly held opinion, libido and sexual activity continue well into old age. Unfortunately, the result of this bias is that adverse effects of medications on sexual function are likely to be overlooked in older patients. Difficulties in all aspects of sexual function, including decreased libido, impaired arousal or erectile dysfunction, anorgasmia, and delayed or retrograde ejaculation, have been reported with a wide variety of psychotropic drugs (Segraves, 1992).

At the risk of oversimplifying an extremely complex neurophysiological process, sexual function involves multiple neurotransmitters (e.g., epinephrine, 5HT, and ACh) in sophisticated integrated neuronal pathways. Erection and ejaculation are a function of alpha-adrenergic stimulation. Orgasm is related to the inhibition of 5HT transmission.

Many of the TCAs and monoamine oxidase inhibitors (MAOIs), as well as lithium carbonate, have been reported to result in decreased libido (Harrison et al., 1986). This appears to be associated with the selective serotonin reuptake inhibitors (SSRIs) as well. One study (Walker et al., 1993) showed an improvement in libido and overall sexual functioning (as well as depression) after discontinuation of fluoxetine and treatment with buproprion.

Assessment of pharmacologically induced loss of libido is complicated by that commonly seen in depression. It is thus important to ascertain the status of sexual desire (and function) prior to pharmacological intervention. Neostigmine (7.5–15 mg 30 minutes prior to intercourse) has been recommended for increasing libido (Kraupl-Taylor, 1972); its use must be considered carefully in the elderly.

Erectile dysfunction is a problem common to most antipsychotics, the TCAs, and lithium carbonate. Anti-psychotic-induced impotence is felt to be hormonally medicated by drug-induced hyperprolactinemia. Notably, the novel antipsychotic clozapine (see later discussion) is *not* associated with elevated prolactin levels. The mechanism of TCA-induced erectile dysfunction is not clearly known but is postulated to be secondary to alpha-adrenergic blockade.

Anorgasmia is associated with several antidepressants, including SSRIs, MAOIs, and TCAs. It appears to be chiefly related to serotonergic stimulation. In all currently available SSRIs (fluoxetine, sertraline, paroxetine, and fluvoxamine), anorgasmia is a frequent problem (Herman et al., 1990; Grimsldy & Jann, 1992; Reimherr et al., 1990).

Both yohimbine (Jacobsen, 1992) and cyproheptadine (McCormicks & Brotman, 1990) have been used to alleviate sexual dysfunction induced by fluoxetine. But although efficacious in the treatment of sexual dysfunction, the serotonergic antagonist cyproheptadine acted against the salutary mood effects of fluoxetine (Feder, 1991a). Thus, its use may be limited. Anorgasmia and ejaculatory dysfunction secondary to several tricyclics (e.g., imipramine) have been successfully resolved with the cholinergic agent bethanechol (Gross, 1982). Use of this agent must be considered in the context of the individual's overall medical status. More recently, Walker et al. (1993) demonstrated an improvement in libido as well as orgasmic function after switching depressed patients from fluoxetine to buproprion. Similar results were previously reported with substitution of buproprion for numerous TCAs (Gardner & Johnson, 1985).

Trazodone, a serotonergic reuptake inhibitor whose primary metabolite (m-CPP) is a serotonergic antagonist, has been reported to reduce libido and arousal (Sullivan, 1988) An important, though fortunately rare, side effect of this drug is priapism, which can result in impotence if untreated.

Literature to date suggests that buproprion has minimal adverse effects on sexual function (Gardner & Johnson, 1985) and, at least from this standpoint, provides a reasonable alternative for individuals experiencing antidepressant-related sexual dysfunction. Particularly in the elderly, this drug has the advantage of minimal anticholinergic and alpha-1 adrenergic blocking activity (i.e., minimal orthostatic hypotension), as well as low cardiac side effects.

Drug Interactions

Drug interactions include both the additive effects of drugs with similar side effects (e.g., increased confusion produced by two drugs with anticholinergic side effects) as well as the indirect effect of one drug on another's pharmacokinetic or pharmacodynamic properties.

Several drug interactions involving psychotropic drugs and other commonly prescribed medications are shown in Table 22.3. Examples include cardiovascular drugs, collectively the most commonly prescribed drugs, which can interact with antidepressants and low-potency neuroleptics possessing alpha-1 adrenergic blocking activity to produce additive increases in orthostatic hypotension. Antacids slow the absorption of many drugs, including TCAs and neuroleptics, lowering their effective dose. Inhibition of hepatic metabolism (e.g., by cimetidine, SSRI antidepressants) increases the blood levels of numerous drugs, including several with severe potential toxicity, such as Coumadin, tricyclic antidepressants, terfemadine, and astemizole. Ibuprofen and other nonsteroidal antiinflammatory agents slow renal clearance, thus impeding the elimination of active drugs such as lithium. Given its low therapeutic index, even a small increase in lithium may result in toxic side effects. Combination of SSRI antidepressants with MAOIs may result in the potentially fatal serotonin syndrome, a serious—indeed potentially fatal—consequence of increased 5HT levels.

These represent only a small number of the adverse drug reactions possible in combining psychotropic drugs with other psychotropic or nonpsychotropic drugs. Knowledge of potential interactions is essential in preventing further,

Table 22.3 Drug Interactions

Drug	Effect
Amphetamines	Decreased metabolism (increased levels) of antipsychotics, antidepressants, anticonvulsants
Antacids	Decreased absorption of tricyclic antidepressants (TCAs), benzodiazepines (BZDPEs), antipsychotics
Antiarrhythmic RX-TCAs	± Arrhythmogenic
Anticoagulants (Coumedin)	Increased prothrombin time with antipsychotics
	Increased bleeding with TCAs, trazodone
Anticonvulsants (Phenytoin, Carbamazepine, Phenobarbital) Valproic Acid	Increased metabolism of TCAs, BZDPEs, antipsychotics
Antidepressants-antipsychotics	Possible increase in levels of both
Antihypertensives-antipsychotics Antidepressants (TCAs, MAOIs)	Increased vulnerability to orthostatic hypotension
Anti-inflammatory agents	
ASA	Lithium (Li) level unaltered
NSAIDS	Increased Li level
Caffeine	Decreased antipsychotic effect (excretion)
	Decreased Li level
Cimetidine	Decreased metabolism of TCAs, BZDPEs, antipsychotics
Digoxin	Increased digoxin level with trazodone
Disulfiram	Decreased metabolism (increased levels) of TCAs, BZDPEs
Diuretics	
Proximal loop (e.g., thiazides)	Decreased Li excretion, increased Li level
Osmotic	No Li excretion, Li level unaltered
Alcohol	Increased sedation
Selective serotonin reuptake inhibitors	
	Decreased metabolism of TCAs, BZDPEs, terfenadine, astemizide
	Serotonergic syndrome with MAOIs
	May increase Li levels
Li	Increased neurotoxicity: antipsychotics, carbamazepine, ± tremor, myoclonus with TCAs

iatrogenically induced, morbidity. An excellent, well-referenced compendium of adverse psychotropic drug interactions can be found in Salzman's (1992) book.

Pharmacological Treatment of Depression

Relatively few controlled studies on pharmacological intervention in the elderly have been done (Hale, 1993). Such studies in the old-old, those over 80 years, or those older individuals with medical illness are even more scarce.

Thus, the elderly are treated pharmacologically mostly by extrapolation from data obtained from younger individuals. There are several excellent comprehensive reviews of antidepressant drug use in the elderly (Alexopoulos, 1992; Hale, 1993; Jenike, 1989; Young & Meyers, 1991).

DRUG-RESPONSIVE DEPRESSION

The etiology of depression in late life is often quite complex. It may be a primary psychiatric disorder, most often with a long history of mood disorder, or an intrinsic manifestation of medical illness. It's often part of multifaceted psychosocial and functional impairments. It may be due to the medications to treat such physical illness. Depression may also be the result of the many losses (personal, social, occupational, etc.) so prevalent in this population.

Treatment of depression must thus reflect the multifaceted nature of its etiology. It requires comprehensive medical evaluation and treatment as well as psychosocial assessment and intervention and is often responsive to psychotherapeutic engagement, pharmacological treatment, or a combination of the two.

The vegetative symptoms of depression (i.e., disturbance of sleep, appetite, and energy as well as motor slowing or agitation) are, at least initially, the most responsive to antidepressant medications. Improvement in these symptoms with a particular drug often heralds subsequent amelioration of affect. Severe depression with psychotic symptoms warrants use of both antidepressant and antipsychotic medications (or electroconvulsive therapy). Depression without prominent vegetative symptoms that has shown little or no response to nonpharmacological treatment stratagems should be challenged with antidepressant drug treatment.

SELECTION OF AN ANTIDEPRESSANT

The general categories of antidepressant drugs include the tricyclics, the SSRIs, a miscellaneous group of new drugs with differing structures (which currently includes trazodone, buproprion, venlafaxine, and nefazodone), the MAOIs, and the psychostimulants. Although the TCAs have long been the mainstay of depression therapy, the favorable side effect profile of the SSRIs has led to their increasing popularity. They are typically substantially more expensive than the TCAs and there is no evidence that they are more effective.

Selection of an antidepressant drug (as with other psychotropics) is predominantly a function of its side effect profile and consideration of medical contraindications to the use of a particular agent. History of a previous positive response to a particular agent often warrants its reinitiation, although a drug with a similar pharmacodynamic effect or neurotransmitter selectivity but with fewer potential side effects may be preferable. Drug cost may be a particularly important issue with the elderly; unfortunately, the least expensive drugs (TCAs, MAOIs) often also have the most potentially problematic side effects.

The selection of antidepressants for patients with cardiovascular disease bears special consideration. The cardiac side effects of TCAs include prolongation of cardiac conduction, quinidine-like antiarrhythmic effects, and orthostatic hypotension. In patients with preexisting conduction deficits, treatment with TCAs can result in progression of the block (e.g., left bundle branch block to complete heart block; Roose et al., 1987). Screening for cardiac conduction defects with EKG should be done before tricyclics are initiated; TCAs are contraindicated in patients with high degrees of AV block.

The antiarrhythmic properties of the tricyclics were once considered beneficial in the treatment of depressed individuals with preexisting arrhythmias and in suppression of ventricular ectopy, but recently, concern has been expressed about their safety in patients with ischemic heart disease. Studies of antiarrhythmic drugs with properties similar to the TCAs have shown increased mortality (Cardiac Arrhythmia Suppression Trial Investigators, 1989, 1992; Glassman, Roose, & Bigger, 1993; Morganroth & Goin, 1991). Although not established definitely, the mechanism of this increased mortality is postulated to result from antiarrhythmic action on ischemic myocardium. Pending further investigation, it seems prudent to use the TCAs with extreme caution, if at all, in individuals with ischemic heart disease, ventricular arrhythmias, or both.

New generation antidepressants (e.g., SSRIs, trazodone, buproprion) have been purported to exhibit few, if any, cardiac side effects and thus may be reasonable alternatives to the TCAs for cardiac patients. In a study of buproprion in depressed patients with serious heart disease (Roose et al., 1991), no deleterious effects on cardiac function were noted. However, buproprion's efficacy in severely depressed patients was questionable. Its efficacy in older depressed individuals remains to be clearly established.

The SSRIs appear to be relatively free of the effects on cardiac conduction seen with the TCAs. Fluoxetine-induced bradycardia has been described (Ellison, Milotsky, & Ely, 1990, Feder, 1991b); one report has questioned the precipitation of atrial fibrillation by fluoxetine (Buff, Brenner, Kirtane, & Gilboa, 1991). To date, the effects of SSRIs on patients with cardiac disease, ventricular arrhythmias, or both have not been systematically studied (Hale, 1993). Their efficacy and safety in severely depressed elderly individuals with cardiac disease remains to be demonstrated.

Glassman et al. (1993) suggest the following treatment stratagems in depressed patients with cardiovascular disease:

Mild to moderate depression with ischemic heart disease: Initial trial of SSRI or buproprion, then consider TCA if no response.

Severe depression with ischemic heart disease: Initiate TCA, weighing cardiac versus psychiatric morbidity and mortality and known efficacy of TCAs.

Mild to severe depression with severe ischemic heart disease: Consider SSRI, buproprion, ECT.

APPROACH TO ANTIDEPRESSANT DRUG TREATMENT

As with all psychotropic drugs, "start low and go slow" is the order of the day with the elderly. As with the young, successful pharmacological intervention is dependent on treatment at an adequate dose and blood level (whether measured or not) for an adequate period of time. In general, the elderly require a longer time period (6-12 weeks) for a significant response to antidepressant medication. Thus, any antidepressant trial in the elderly must extend to at least this interval.

Drug level monitoring is not routinely performed for antidepressants with the exception of nortriptyline, whose dose-response curve demonstrates a curvilinear relationship, with optimum response in the range of 50 mg/ml to 150 mg/ml (Gardner & Johnson, 1985). Therapeutic drug monitoring is also important in the following situations:

Compliance. Noncompliance with prescribed medication is a particularly common issue with the elderly and an important factor in lack of therapeutic response. Drug level measurement provides a reasonable tool for assessing compliance.

Lack of Efficacy at Usual Therapeutic Doses. Individual variation in drug metabolic rates is considerable. Provided that compliance is not an issue, drug level measurements can provide information about the possibility of accelerated drug metabolism and resultant lowered drug level.

Drug Toxicity. Measurement of drug level, as an indicator of metabolic rate or accumulation, may be helpful in an individual experiencing an unexpected degree of side effects or manifesting symptoms and signs of drug toxicity.

MAINTENANCE THERAPY IN DEPRESSION

In most individuals, mood disorders are chronic and recurrent. Treatment must therefore be aimed at both initial resolution of symptoms and prevention of relapse. Relapse prevention is unfortunately not straightforward. Relapse rates of as much as 20% to 30% have been reported in depressed patients within 4 to 6 months of recovery, even with continued medication. Higher relapse rates (up to 70%) have been seen in patients where antidepressant medication has been discontinued after resolution of the episode. Previous maintenance stratagems have generally employed antidepressant doses approximately 50% lower than the therapeutic dose used in successful symptom resolution. However, 3-year and 5-year outcome studies of maintenance therapies in recurrent depression in younger individuals have demonstrated significant prophylactic effects of the antidepressant (imipramine) maintained at the acute therapeutic dose (Frank, Kupfer, Perel et al., 1991; Kupfer et al., 1992).

The prognosis in elderly depressed individuals in general seems less favorable than in the younger population. It appears that the rate of relapse increases with age (Zis & Goodwin, 1979). Fortunately, some studies indicate that continued medication does reduce relapse in geriatric patients. In one study of elderly depressed patients treated with nortriptyline or phenelzine at acute therapeutic doses for 4 to 8 months after resolution of depressive symptoms, over 70% remained aysmptomatic; it is interesting to note that all patients who relapsed had been chronically depressed for a period exceeding 2 years (Cole, 1985; Georgotas, McCue, Cooper, Nagachandran, & Chang, 1988).

Few guidelines about the duration of treatment for the optimum outcome are available. Recommendations for treatment currently suggest a 6-month maintenance regimen following remission of a first episode of major depression, and 12 or more months (possibly indefinite) maintenance following a second (or more) depressive episode. Maintenance is best determined on an individual basis, however, governed by the history and severity of depressive episodes, their effects on functional capabilities, and potential consequences of further illness tempered by the tolerability and risks of ongoing antidepressant medication.

The risk of suicide is highest for the elderly than for any other age group; this consequence must always be considered in treatment planning, both acute and ongoing, for depression in this population.

ANTIDEPRESSANT DRUGS

TCAs

The tricyclics are postulated to act acutely via inhibition of NE reuptake, 5HT reuptake, or both. The extent of NE versus 5HT reuptake blockade varies among the different drugs; tertiary amine derivatives are more serotonergic than the more noradrenergic secondary amine derivatives. The time course of this blockade is inconsistent with the clinical response, which occurs over several weeks. More chronic effects of these drugs, which may underlie their efficacy, include down regulation of alpha and beta adrenergic as well as serotonergic receptors.

Side Effects. The available TCAs and their major side effects are displayed in Table 22.4. The secondary amine tricyclics possess less anticholinergic activity, less alpha-1 adrenergic blockade, less sedation, and generally less cardiotoxicity than the tertiary amine derivatives, such as amitriptyline. They are thus favored for use in the elderly, who are particularly vulnerable to these adverse effects

Of the secondary amines, desipramine and nortriptyline are the best choices for general use; the other secondary amines have properties that limit their use. Desipramine possesses the least anticholinergic activity of the tricyclics and in general, though not uniformly in the elderly, produces little sedation. Nortriptyline may be preferred in individuals with autonomic dysfunction because it appears to possess the least potential of the tricyclics for orthostatic hypotension (Roose et al., 1981). Both nortriptyline and desipramine also possess comparatively low antihistaminergic activity, responsible in part for the sedation and weight gain often seen with tricyclic therapy.

Most tricyclics can lower the seizure threshold, but this is not generally significant except in patients with a preexisting seizure disorder or in drug overdose (Jick, Jick, Knauss, & Dean, 1992). Maprotiline does exhibit an increased risk of seizures at elevated doses (> 225 mg/day) as does clomipramine, a tertiary amine derivative often used in the treatment of obsessive-compulsive disorder (> 250 mg/day; Schatzberg & Cole, 1991).

The secondary tricyclic amoxapine, a metabolite of the antipsychotic loxapine, is unique among the tricyclics in that one of its hydroxymetabolites possesses antidopaminergic (i.e., antipsychotic) activity and can cause extrapyramidal side effects, including akathesia, dystonias, dyskinesias, and parkinsonian symptoms (Blazer, 1993). Protriptyline is one of the most stimulating of the TCAs but has strong anticholinergic and cardiovascular side effects as well as a long elimination half-life, which can prolong adverse effects should they occur.

The TCAs have cardiotoxic potential, particularly in individuals with preexisting conduction deficits. Pretreatment EKGs are essential in geriatric patients, as are periodic EKGs throughout drug treatment. Use of tricyclics is absolutely contraindicated (without pacemaker) in individuals with left bundle branch block, bifascicular block, and second degree or third degree AV block on the EKG. Close monitoring with interval EKGs is also warranted in patients with ventricular arrhythmias, right bundle branch block, first AV

Table 22.4   Relative Side Effects of Cyclic Antidepressants in the Elderly Patient

Drug Type	Sedation	Hypotension	Anticholinergic Side Effects	Altered Cardiac Rate and Rhythm
Tricyclic antidepressants—tertiary amines				
Imipramine	Mild	Moderate	Moderate to strong	Moderate
Doxepin	Moderate to strong	Moderate	Strong	Moderate
Amitriptyline	Strong	Moderate	Very strong	Strong
Trimipramine	Strong	Moderate	Strong	Strong
Clomipramine	Moderate to strong	Moderate to strong	Strong	? Moderate to strong
Tricyclic antidepressants—secondary amines				
Desipramine	Mild	Mild to moderate	Mild	Mild
Nortriptyline	Mild	Mild	Moderate	Mild
Amoxapine	Mild	Moderate	Moderate	Moderate
Protriptyline	Mild	Moderate	Strong	Moderate
Maprotiline	Moderate to strong	Moderate	Moderate	Mild
Monoamine oxidase inhibitors (MAOIs)				
Phenelzine	–/–	Moderate to strong	Very mild	Very mild
Tranylcyromine	–/–	Moderate to strong	Very mild	Very mild
Selegine	–/–	Mild	Very mild	Very mild
Psychostimulants				
Dextroamphetamine	—	Mild to moderate[a]	—	Mild to moderate
Methylphenidate	—	Mild to moderate[a]	—	Mild to moderate
Pemoline	—	Mild to moderate[a]	—	Mild to moderate
Selective serotonin reuptake inhibitors (SSRIs)				
Fluoxetine	+/–	Mild	Very mild	Reports of episodic bradycardia
Sertraline	+/–	Mild	Very mild	None to date
Paroxetine	+/–	Mild	Very mild	None to date
Fluvoxamine	+/–	Mild	Very mild	None to date
Azolopyridines				
Trazodone	Moderate	Moderate to strong	Very mild (except dry mouth)	Moderate to strong
Aminoketones				
Buproprion	+/–	—	Very mild	—
Phenylethylamines				
Venlafaxine	Very mild	Very mild	Very mild	Very mild

SOURCE: Adapted from Salzman (1992).
a. Hypertension: mild to moderate

block, or prolonged QT interval. QT interval prolongation on the EKG is associated with increased risk of serious ventricular arrhythmias (Moss, 1986). A corrected QT interval longer than 0.44 milliseconds is also an absolute contraindication to TCA therapy because there is an increased risk of sudden death from ventricular tachyarrhythmias.

Studies of the effects of imipramine and nortriptyline on left ventricular function have shown no changes in the ejection fraction, even in patients with preexisting left ventricular dysfunction and reduced ejection fractions (Glassman et al., 1983; Roose et al., 1986). Thus, the tricyclics appear to be comparatively safe in patients with impaired ventricular function who do not have serious conduction deficits.

Dosage. The TCAs are metabolized in the liver and cleared by the kidneys. Reduced hepatic function and renal clearance in the elderly necessitates careful dose adjustment for appropriate therapeutic levels. Reduction in renal clearance may result in the accumulation of hydroxymetabolites, which may contribute to TCA cardiotoxicity (Young, 1991).

Therapeutic drugs levels for desipramine and nortriptyline appear to be equivalent for the elderly and young adults (Cutter & Narang, 1987). Nortriptyline is unique among the tricyclics in demonstrating a curvilinear dose response curve (therapeutic window) of 50 to 150 mg/ml (Schatzberg & Cole, 1991). Studies of desipramine in geriatric patients indicate a minimum effective therapeutic level of 125 mg/ml. The range of therapeutic plasma levels for desipramine is 125 to 300 mg/ml (Schatzberg & Cole, 1991).

Generally, the starting dose of a TCA should be reduced to one third to one half the suggested standard adult dose. Adjustments in dose should be made slowly, as clinically indicated, increasing by 25% to 50% every 3 to 5 days until a therapeutic blood level is reached, a clinical response is evident, or side effects become limiting. An average starting dose of desipramine or nortriptyline in the elderly is 10 to 25 mg.

SSRIs

The SSRIs include fluoxetine (Prozac), sertraline (Zoloft), paroxetine (Paxil), and fluvoxamine (Luvox). All act via specific blockades of presynaptic 5HT autoreceptors and have little comparative effect on adrenergic neurotransmission. Although their effectiveness in treating severely depressed or medically ill (or both) geriatric patients remains to be clearly established, numerous studies demonstrate comparable efficacy to tricyclics and more favorable side effect profiles (Cohn et al., 1990; Dunner et al., 1992; Feighner, Boyer, Meredith, Charles, & Hendrickson, 1988; Houillin & Douge, 1989). The SSRIs are promising alternatives in individuals thought vulnerable to the adverse side effects of the TCAs. Notably, fluoxetine and the most recently released SSRI fluvoxamine (Luvox) have also demonstrated efficacy in the treatment of obsessive-compulsive disorder (Freeman, Trimble, Deubin et al., 1994; Tollefson, Rampey, Potvin et al., 1994).

Side Effects. The SSRIs frequently produce GI disturbance (nausea, vomiting, diarrhea) and headache, which are generally, but not always, self-limited. Symptoms can be minimized by taking the medication with food.

The SSRIs have comparatively little anticholinergic activity and produce little orthostatic hypotension. In general, they appear to have minimal cardiotoxicity. Fluoxetine, however, has been reported to cause sinus bradycardia (Feder, 1991b). Further investigation is warranted, particularly in older individuals with cardiac disease.

Sexual dysfunction, especially anorgasmia, is relatively common and may necessitate a switch to another drug such as buproprion.

Extrapyramidal side effects, generally associated with neuroleptics, have been reported with fluoxetine (Bouchard, Pourcher, & Vincent, 1989; Lipinski, Mayalla, Zimmerman, & Pope, 1989). Unlike the side effects with TCAs (with the exception of amoxaphine), extrapyramidal side effects generally associated with neuroleptics have infrequently been reported with fluoxetine (Roose et al., 1981). Most common among these is akathisia, a motor restlessness or inability to sit still, which can produce great subjective distress (note that with antipsychotics, this is the side effect most commonly associated with noncompliance).

Concerns about the apparent increase in suicidal ideation with fluoxetine led to the suggestion of a possible association between akathisia and the development of suicidal ideation (Rothschild & Locke, 1991; Teicher, Gold, & Cole, 1990). However, an FDA-sponsored investigation of possible increased suicidal ideation with fluoxetine (Fava & Rosenbaum, 1991) found no difference in incidence of suicidal ideation between fluoxetine and other antidepressants. The role of drug-induced akathisia in precipitating suicidal thoughts with any antidepressant merits further investigation.

Dosage. The SSRIs are distinguished by their pharmacokinetic differences; these are the primary determinants in choosing among them (Preskorn, 1993). The half-life of fluoxetine in healthy adults (T 1/2 2-4 days) is considerably longer than that of either paroxetine or sertraline (T 1/2 24 hours) or fluvoxamine (16 hours). Fluoxetine is converted to an active metabolite, norfluoxetine, whose half-life is extended (7-15 days). Accumulation of fluoxetine and norfluoxetine thus occurs and may result in increased side effects and drug interactions not well tolerated by the elderly. Neither sertraline, paroxetine, or fluvoxamine have significantly active metabolites.

All available SSRIs exhibit some degree of hepatic enzyme inhibition, thereby affecting the metabolism of hepatically metabolized drugs, including their own. Paroxetine is the most potent inhibitor followed by norfluoxetine and fluoxetine. Least potent inhibitors are sertraline and fluvoxamine. Thus for example, concomitant administration of fluoxetine and a TCA or a neuroleptic, both of which are hepatically metabolized, results in an increased level of the latter drug (Aranow et al., 1989; Ciraulo & Shader, 1990). Furthermore, fluoxetine, paroxetine, and fluvoxamine inhibit their own metabolism and thus display nonlinear kinetics; higher doses produce disproportionately elevated plasma drug levels. Sertraline demonstrates linear pharmacokinetics over its usual dose range; alterations in dose give predictable, proportionate drug levels. Clinically, this is significant in terms of dose adjustment; it is particularly important to adjust changes in fluoxetine, paroxetine, or fluvoxamine dose in small increments to avoid disproportionate changes that might result in adverse effects.

The SSRIs have flat dose response curves; that is, above a minimum effective dose (estimated as the dose at which 80% inhibition of 5HT reuptake occurs), there is no further increase in antidepressant response. Thus, increasing the dose beyond this minimum has no therapeutic benefit and may increase the incidence or severity of adverse side effects.

In the elderly, therapeutic dose ranges have yet to be clearly delineated. Initial doses of the SSRIs should be low; estimated ranges are as follows:

Fluoxetine, 5 to 20 mg per day

Sertraline, 12.5 to 150 mg per day

Paroxetine, 10 to 40 mg per day

Fluvoxamine, 50 to 150 mg per day (dose recommendation for obsessive-compulsive disorder)

Serious adverse consequences of the combination of an SSRI and irreversible MAOIs currently available are described in the section on MAOIs (see later discussion).

OTHER NEW ANTIDEPRESSANTS

Trazodone (Desyrel) is a triazolopyridine derivative, structurally quite different from other antidepressants. It inhibits 5HT reuptake, and its primary metabolite (m-chlorophenylpiperazine) may act as a serotonergic agonist. This metabolite may be responsible for trazadone's anxiolytic activity, which appears distinct from its sedative properties (Bressler & Katz, 1993). Indeed, trazodone was originally developed as an antianxiety agent and has been used effectively to reduce agitation and aggression in dementia patients.

In several controlled studies with geriatric patients, trazodone has been found to have comparable efficacy to other antidepressants such as imipramine and buproprion (Gerner, Estabrook, Steur, & Jarvik, 1980; Kane, Cole, Sarantakes, Howard, & Borenstein, 1983). However, some inconsistency in its antidepressant effects has been noted (Alexopoulos, 1992; Salzman, 1993).

Trazodone has proven effective in low doses (e.g., 25-100 mg at bedtime) for insomnia and may be particularly useful in combination with more activating antidepressants, such as SSRIs or buproprion, for this purpose.

Side Effects. Major side effects of trazodone are hypotension and sedation. Either of these can be sufficiently problematic in the elderly to limit the dose or warrant discontinuation of the medication. Trazodone has minimal anticholinergic side effects and a benign cardiac side effect profile compared with the tricyclics. However, it has been associated with arrhythmias (e.g., ventricular tachycardia) in patients with and without preexisting cardiac disease (Aranson & Hafez, 1986).

Trazodone has little adverse effect on sexual function. Indeed, increased libido has been reported in both women and men. Priapism is a potential adverse effect of trazodone seen rarely in young men and even less frequently in older men. Patients must be made aware of this potential problem; although spontaneous detumescence does occur, prolonged erections (e.g., greater than 1 hour) require timely medical intervention to prevent permanent damage. Intravavernosal administration of alpha-adrenergic agonist (e.g., epinephrine, norepinephrine) are effective acute treatments. Other side effects of trazodone include nausea and headaches.

Few drug interactions have been reported with trazodone. Combined use of trazodone and digoxin has been reported to increase digoxin levels, however (Rauch & Jenike, 1984). The digoxin level should be carefully monitored, especially when trazodone is initiated in patients on established therapeutic digoxin regimens.

Dosage. Trazodone is rapidly absorbed after oral administration and has a short half-life (approximately 5-9 hours). Multiple daily dosing is therefore recommended, although daytime sedation may be troublesome. Effective doses in young adults range between 200 to 600 mg per day; the elderly generally are treated at lower doses (e.g., 25-200 mg per day), but doses equivalent to those in younger individuals may be necessary. Therapeutic plasma drug levels are not well established for trazodone (Preskorn, 1993). Clinical response and adverse side effects are the primary guidelines in prescribing trazodone as is the case with virtually all antidepressants (nortriptyline possibly being the only exception).

The initial dose of trazodone in the elderly is 25 mg per day. CNS-compromised individuals, such as patients with dementia, may exhibit increased sensitivity, requiring even lower doses (e.g., 10 mg per day), which can be given in the liquid form. The dose should be increased gradually as tolerated and preferably given with food to a maximum of 150 to 200 mg daily.

Buproprion

Buproprion (Wellbutrin), a phenylethylamine, is a novel unicyclic antidepressant structurally related to amphetamine and to the sympathomimetic diethylproprion. Its exact mechanism of antidepressant reaction is unclear, although it is thought to be primarily related to the neurotransmitter dopamine. Buproprion has negligible activity in NE or 5HT reuptake inhibition and does not affect monoamine oxidase activity. Chronically, buproprion does not down regulate beta adrenergic receptors, as do the TCAs and MAOIs, but does result in decreased catecholamine turnover.

Few studies of buproprion use in geriatric patients have been done to date. However, several reports provide evidence for its efficacy in this population (Branconnier, Cole, & Ghazvimian, 1983; Kane et al., 1983).

Side Effects. Buproprion's side effect profile offers several advantages in the treatment of geriatric depression. Anticholinergic side effects and adverse cardiovascular side effects, including orthostatic hypotension and cardiac conduction deficits, are minimal. Agitation, GI disturbance (nausea, vomiting, constipation), and headache are common. Insomnia may occur, although sedation has been seen in several geriatric patients (J. Schneider, unpublished observations).

Sexual dysfunction is uncommon with buproprion and it has been shown to be an effective alternative for patients who experience sexual difficulties such as anorgasmia with fluoxetine (Walker et al., 1993).

There has been considerable concern regarding the incidence of seizures with buproprion. As with other antidepressants, buproprion should be used with consideration of factors predisposing to an increased risk of seizures— for instance, preexisting or family history of seizure disorders (or both), other neurological or medical conditions, and concurrent medications that lower the seizure threshold. In clinical trials prior to its release, at doses < 450 mg per day, seizures occurred with an incidence of 0.3%, roughly equivalent to estimates for TCAs. A dose-dependent increase in incidence was seen at higher doses (2.3% and 2.8% incidence at 600 mg per day and > 600 mg per day, respectively; Davidson, 1989). A subsequent multicenter study (Johnston et al., 1991) has shown that, at recommended doses (300-450 mg per day), buproprion was associated with a 0.36% seizure incidence. Current recommendations for use of buproprion limit doses to 450 mg per day, with each dose not exceeding 150 mg.

Buproprion has been associated with a number of neuropsychiatric side effects, including psychosis (Golden, James, Sherer et al., 1985), confusion, catatonia, and delirium (Dager & Heritch, 1990). Buproprion appears to act like other antidepressants in its ability to precipitate mania (Fogelson, Bystritsky, & Pasnau, 1992). Ataxia, myoclonus, and dystonia, as well as, paradoxically, parkinsonian symptoms (Szuba & Leuchter, 1992) have also been reported.

As an indirect dopamine agonist, buproprion has been used to improve neurological as well as mood symptoms in Parkinson's disease patients (Goetz, Tanner, & Kawans, 1984) and may be a useful alternative to amantadine or anticholinergic antiparkinsonian agents in treating Parkinson's disease. A limitation may be the increased frequency of adverse side effects seen in patients taking both buproprion and Sinemet or L-dopa.

Dosage. Buproprion is readily absorbed, reaching a maximum plasma level within 1 to 3 hours, coincident with maximal GI side effects. Its half-life, and those of its three biologically active metabolites, are 8 to 10 hours and roughly 24 hours respectively. Given their long half-lives, these three metabolites may accumulate with repeated administration. The drug is not known to induce or inhibit the metabolism of other drugs.

Buproprion is given in multiple doses with no single dose > 150 mg. It should be taken with food and the last dose given early to avoid sleep disturbance. Therapeutic blood levels are not well established; Preskorn (1993) describes relatively consistent levels of 20 to 75 mg/ml for maximum antidepressant response in several studies (Goodnick & Sandoval, 1992). The effects of aging on buproprion metabolism are not well known. The recommended dose in young adults is 300 to 400 mg per day; generally, doses for older individuals range one third to one half less, but equivalent doses may be necessary.

Venlafaxine

Venlafaxine (Effexor) is a novel drug whose chemical structure is unrelated to other antidepressants (Montgomery, 1993). Both venlafaxine and its active metabolite (o-desmethylvenlafaxine, or ODV) inhibit the reuptake of both NE and 5HT. As with the TCAs and SSRIs, it is a comparatively weak inhibitor of dopamine reuptake. Several placebo-controlled trials of venlafaxine (Kahn, Fabre, & Rudolph, 1991; Mendels, Johnston, Mattes, & Reisenberg, 1993; Schweizer, Weise, Clary, Fox, & Rickels, 1991) have demonstrated its efficacy in treating depression, as well as in maintenance. Although these studies included older individuals (65 years old or greater), to date no studies with exclusively geriatric patients have been done with venlafaxine.

Venlafaxine has a very favorable side effect profile, with essentially no anticholinergic, antihistaminergic (sedation, weight gain), or alpha-1 adrenergic blockade activity (orthostatic hypotension) and no quinidine-like effects on cardiac conduction (as seen with the TCAs). In animal models, it has been shown to cause rapid adrenergic downregulation, postulated to account for its rapid onset of action, a feature hoped to be applicable in humans as well.

Side Effects. Prominent side effects are similar to the SSRIs and include nausea, somnolence, headache, sweating, and nervousness. Most are self-limited, resolving within 1 to 2 weeks. Dose-dependent sustained increases in blood pressure occur in some patients. Mean elevations of approximately 2 to 5 mm Hg diastolic blood pressure (DBP) have been seen in 7% or more of patients at doses of 201 to 300 mg per day, and in 13% at doses greater that 300 mg per day (10-15 mm DBP increases are seen in a small percentage of patients). This may be limiting in individuals with hypertension, and regular blood pressure checks are important, especially in these individuals. There is no evidence to date that hypertensive patients are at increased risk for venlafaxine-caused elevations in blood pressure.

Dosage. The elimination half-lives of venlafaxine and ODV in young and healthy adults are 5 and 11 hours, respectively. Unlike virtually all psychotropic drugs with the exception of lithium, venlafaxine and ODV are not highly protein bound (27%-30%). Thus, the potential for drug interactions with drugs that are highly bound is comparatively low. But as with tricyclics and SSRIs, care must be taken in appropriate concomitant use of venlafaxine and irreversible MAOIs.

Dose-response studies in placebo-controlled clinical trials indicate that the minimum effective dose is 75 mg per day, with a range of doses from 75 to 375 mg per day, given either twice or three times daily.

The optimum dose or plasma level of venlafaxine have not been definitively established. The currently recommended dosage range for young healthy adults is 75 to 225 mg per day in moderately depressed patients and as high as 350 mg per day in those with severe depression. Starting doses of 75 mg per day are recommended, with increments of 75 mg every 4 days as needed. In geriatric patients, lower starting doses (i.e., 25-50 mg per day) are preferred.

Nefazodone

Nefazodone (Serzone) is an extremely interesting new antidepressant that has been shown in placebo-controlled trials to be effective in moderate and severe depression (Feighner, Pambakian, Fowler, Boyer, & D'Amillo, 1989; Mendels et al., 1995). It lacks the anticholinergic, antihistaminergic, and alpha 1-adrenergic blockade activity of TCAs as well as most SSRI-related side effects, including GI disturbance, sexual dysfunction, anxiety, restlessness, and extrapyramidal symptoms. A double-blind, placebo-controlled comparison of imipramine and nefazodone in the treatment of major depression demonstrated similar therapeutic efficacy (nefazodone doses at 100-500 mg per day) but considerably fewer adverse side effects with nefazodone (Fontaine et al., 1994).

Nefazodone's dual mechanism of action involves presynaptic 5HT reuptake blockade (as with the SSRIs and TCAs) and postsynaptic 5HT2 receptor antagonism. Effects on two of the multiple 5HT receptors (Zifa & Fillion, 1992), one presynaptic and the other postsynaptic, may allow for synergistic therapeutic action as well as minimization of side effects. Furthermore, nefazodone, as a 5HT2 receptor antagonist, may be effective in reducing anxiety symptoms often associated with depression (Katz et al., 1993).

Development of other serotonergic drugs with receptor subtype-specific actions will, it is hoped, allow for a more focalized approach to desirable therapeutic effects (Dubovsky, 1994; Stahl, 1992; Sussman, 1994).

MAOIs

The MAOIs inhibit the intracellular catabolism of biogenic amines, including the DA, NE, and 5HT. As with the tricyclics, chronic administration of these agents results in downregulation of noradrenergic and serotonergic receptors (Leonard, 1993). Two forms of monoamine oxidase exist: Type A (MAO-A) is specific for NE and 5HT and is localized in the CNS, sympathetic terminals, liver, and gut. Type B (MAO-B), specific for dopamine and phenylethylamine, is found chiefly in the CNS and platelets.

The MAOIs may be particularly useful in atypical depression characterized by hyperphagia (increased appetite), hypersomnia, and anergia. The frequent adverse side effects, as well as potentially serious drug and dietary interactions (e.g., hypertensive crises resulting from MAOIs and OTC sympathomimetic-containing drugs—many cold medicines), have limited their use in the geriatric population. However, new, reversible, and specific agents (RIMAs) undergoing extensive testing and clinical trials in Europe may provide excellent alternatives with low side effect and good safety profiles.

Currently, three MAOIs are available in the United States for the treatment of depression: the hydrazine derivatives isocarboxazid (Marplan) and phenelzine (Nardil) and the nonhydrazine derivative tranylcypromine (Parnate). All are irreversible, nonspecific MAO-A and MAO-B inhibitors. A fourth MAOI, selegiline (Deprenyl or Eldepryl), is MAO-B specific at low doses (< 10 mg per day) and is used in the treatment of Parkinson's disease (Parkinson Study Group, 1989). At higher doses, it becomes nonspecific and necessitates the same dietary and medication restrictions as the other nonselective agents. Selegiline's efficacy in the treatment of depression, generally at higher doses (60 mg daily), may show promise for geriatric patients, especially as it appears to have fewer side effects (Sunderland et al., 1994).

Side Effects. Orthostatic hypotension is the most common and often most problematic side effect of MAOIs in the elderly. This effect may not become evident for several weeks after initiation of the MAOI; thus, frequent blood pressure checks for orthostatic changes are important. Approaches to counteract this problem in younger individuals (e.g., increased salt intake to maintain blood volume, use of a mineralcorticoid such as Florinef), may not be feasible in a medically ill, depressed older individual.

Weight gain, sexual dysfunction (especially anorgasmia), and insomnia are common. Anticholinergic side effects are generally very mild. No adverse effects on cardiac conduction have been noted (Young & Myers, 1991).

The most serious potential hazards of MAOI therapy are those related to drug interactions. A hyperadrenergic or hypertensive crisis may be precipitated by ingestion of a pressor-amine-containing substance, such as tyramine-containing foodstuff, sympathomimetic-containing OTC cold remedy, or other sympathomimetic drug (e.g., L-Dopa, TCAs). Hypertension, severe headache, neuromuscular irritability, diaphoresis, mydriasis, as well as cardiac arrhythmias and cerebrovascular consequences may result. Thus, extreme care must be used in eliciting a full drug history, including OTC medications. Furthermore, compliance to a somewhat restricted diet (Table 22.5) must be ensured; this may be a major limitation in the use of the currently available nonspecific MAOIs. Similar interactions between MAOIs and sympathomimetic drugs also warrant careful attention when prescribing additional drugs or when switching from MAOI to another class of antidepressant. For example, when switching from an irreversible MAOI such as phenelzine to a tricyclic, a washout period of at least 2 weeks is required before initiation of the tricyclic to allow for restoration of MAO activity. On the other hand, an MAOI may be added concomitantly with, or after initiation of, a tricyclic without adverse consequences. Indeed, an MAOI, TCA, and stimulant combination has been successfully used in the treatment of refractory depression (Feighner, Herbstein, & Damlouji, 1985).

Another potentially serious interaction is that between MAOIs and serotonergic agents (e.g., the SSRIs, clomipramine, meperidone [Demerol]), resulting in excess central 5HT and a clinical syndrome of hyperpyrexia (the serotonin syndrome), hyperreflexia and myoclonus, delirium, ataxia, seizures, and coma (Feighner, Boyer, Tyler, & Neborsky, 1990). Thus, combinations

Table 22.5   Dietary Recommendations During Use of Monoamine Oxidase Inhibitors

Dietary Suggestions	*Foods to Avoid*
Foods containing tyramine (an amino acid) should be avoided because use of such foods may cause high blood pressure.	Beer and red wine
Patients on MAOI medication should be aware that aged, overripe, and fermented foods contain greater amounts of tyramine.	Cheese (except cottage and cream cheeses) Smoked or pickled fish, dry sausage (summer sausage, salami, pepperoni), brewer's yeast.
Avoid food that is aged for flavor, is spoiled, or has been improperly refrigerated. See Foods to Avoid.	Fava beans (Italian green beans)
When eating at restaurants, be aware that many ethnic foods have ingredients that are high in tyramine.	

SOURCE: Pharmacy Service Patient Education, Department of Veterans Affairs Medical Center, Palo Alto, CA, 1993.
NOTE: Due to food-drug interaction, abnormally high blood pressures may result from ingestion of the listed foods to avoid.

of MAOI and highly serotonergic agents (e.g., SSRIs) are contraindicated. In switching from an SSRI to an MAOI, a period of time adequate to clear a serotonergic agent must be given prior to initiation of the MAOI. The long half-life of fluoxetine and its metabolite norfluoxetine thus necessitates a 5- to 8-week washout period (perhaps longer in the elderly). Discontinuation of a standard MAOI must be followed by a period of at least 2 weeks prior to initiation of an SSRI agent.

Dosage. Typical initial regimens for phenelzine in the elderly are 7.5 to 15 mg per day, adjusted slowly to maximum doses of 45 to 60 mg per day. Tranylcypromine is preferred by some (Jenike, 1989) for older individuals because it has fewer side effects than phenelzine and requires less time for recovery of enzyme activity after discontinuation. Others warn against its use in the elderly because it has been associated with acute hypertensive crisis and fatal subarachnoid or intracranial hemorrhage. The usual starting dose is 10 mg per day; the maximum dose is 30 to 40 mg per day.

Psychostimulants

Prior to the advent of the tricyclics and MAOIs, the psychostimulants were used extensively for the treatment of depression. Currently, these drugs—dextroamphetamine, methylphenidate, and magnesium pemoline—are FDA approved only for the treatment of narcolepsy, attention deficit hyperactivity disorder in children, and obesity. However, there has been a resurgence in their use for mood disorders, particularly in medically ill elderly (Woods, Tesar, Murray, & Cassem, 1986). Pemoline has several properties that may be particularly desirable in the elderly. It has relatively mild stimulant activity and the least sympathomimetic activity of these agents. Of low abuse potential, it is not a controlled substance. Liver function must be monitored routinely, however, as elevation of hepatic enzymes can occur.

The psychostimulants act via stimulation of release of dopamine, NE, and 5HT. They also inhibit dopamine and noradrenaline reuptake and are weak inhibitors of monoamine oxidase. In general, the amphetamines appear to be less effective than standard antidepressants, such as TCAs, for primary depression (Chiarello & Cole, 1987; Satel & Nelson, 1989) but have great promise in the treatment of depression refractory to other agents, such as the tricyclics or the MAOIs, and also in geriatric patients with medical illness, especially those who manifest apathy, anergia, abulia, anorexia, lack of motivation, or social withdrawal (Chiarello & Cole, 1987; Feighner et al., 1972; Kaplitz, 1975; Katon & Raskind, 1980; Kaufman, Cassem, Murray, & MacDonald, 1984; Lazarus, Winemiller, & Lingarn, 1992; Massand, Pickett, & Murray, 1991; Satel & Nelson, 1989).

Two characteristics of the psychostimulants make them excellent alternatives to other antidepressants in certain situations. The first is *rapid response*. Usually, a rapid response is seen within days, not weeks as with most antidepressants. The rapidity of response may be of critical importance, for example, in individuals whose neuropsychiatric status has precluded appropriate and timely rehabilitation efforts, which may ultimately result in a less favorable outcome. Second is the *favorable side effects profile*. The psychostimulants are generally well tolerated, even in patients with severe medical illnesses or cardiac disease that precludes the use of standard antidepressants.

Some heterogeneity in responsiveness and the need for chronic treatment with stimulants has been noted (Chiarello & Cole, 1987; Little, 1993; Silberman, Reus, Jimerson, Lynott, & Post, 1981). Several studies indicate the differential effects, and presumably underlying mechanistic differences, of dextroamphetamine and methylphenidate (Little, 1993; Silberman et al., 1981). Thus, an individual may be responsive to one but not the other of these agents; an unsuccessful therapeutic trial of one agent does not predict the efficacy of the other, and a second trial of the alternative agent is warranted.

Rapid response without subsequent long-term need for the stimulant occurs in some patients; in others, chronic treatment is required to avert relapse. This is probably a reflection of the neurochemical complexity inherent in depression, perhaps most particularly in the context of medical illness.

Side Effects. The chief side effects of these sympathomimetic amines are central. They include anorexia and insomnia as well as changes in arousal, tremor, confusion (especially in cognitively impaired individuals), and paranoid delusions. Anorexia is, perhaps somewhat paradoxically, often alleviated rather than exacerbated in elderly depressed or apathetic patients responsive to stimulants. Exacerbation of preexisting anxiety is the only consistently described adverse side effect and is thus a relative contraindication. Sinus tachycardia, changes (usually upward) in blood pressure, nausea, and arrhythmias (e.g., atrial fibrillation) have all been noted.

In most studies, the incidence of side effects precluding use of these agents is low; in one series of 129 patients, discontinuation of medication was reported due to adverse side effects in 8% (Pickett, Massand, & Murray, 1990). In most cases, the stimulant could be discontinued within several days of improvement without significant relapse.

Dosage. Both methylphenidate and dextroamphetamine require multiple daily doses because of their short elimination half-lives—1 to 2 hours for methylphenidate with effects persisting for 3 to 4 hours and 8 to 12 hours for dextroamphetamine. The last dose should be given in late afternoon to avoid difficulties with insomnia. Pemoline, with a longer half-life of 12 to 13 hours, can be given as a single daily dose.

All the psychostimulants are, to some extent, hepatically metabolized. In patients with renal disease, methlyphenidate, which is fully metabolized hepatically, is the preferred drug. Because they undergo hepatic metabolism, the psychostimulants can compete with other hepatically metabolized drugs, thus increasing the plasma levels of the latter. Examples include TCAs, SSRIs, antipsychotics, and anticonvulsants.

Doses of dextroamphetamine in the elderly range from 2.5 to 60 mg per day, generally in divided doses. An average effective dose is 7.5 to 10 mg, but there is considerable variation. Methylphenidate is also given in divided doses, varying from 2.5 to 60 mg per day with an average dose of 15 to 20 mg per day. Pemoline, given once daily in the morning, has a daily dose range of 37.5 to 112.5 mg; the average dose is 75 mg per day.

Low dose methylphenidate (1.25-5 mg per day) has been used effectively in the treatment of two old-old medically ill patients (Gurian & Rosowsky, 1990), one aged 91 years, the other, 104 years. In both cases, the methylphenidate was prescribed on an ongoing basis. After 9 months of treatment, no adverse side effects were reported, and no indications of a decline in efficacy or tolerance were seen.

Monitoring of vital signs is particularly important in elderly patients, given the stimulants' sympathomimetic effects. Often, an initial test dose (e.g., 2.5-5.0 mg) of dextroamphetamine is given, and vital signs monitored 45 to 60 minutes thereafter. Appreciable changes (e.g., changes in BP > 20 mm Hg, changes in heart rate > 20 beats per minute) warrant caution in further use and consideration of alternatives.

The duration of treatment is empirical and assessed in each individual clinical situation. In some patients, brief treatment for several days, followed by discontinuation of the drug, is effective, with no subsequent treatment necessary. In others, prolonged treatment over months and even years is most beneficial. In the elderly, the development of tolerance is comparatively infrequent; the dose of stimulant remains at its original effective dose indefinitely. Certainly, at some time after symptom improvement or resolution, gradual discontinuation and a trial without the medication is desirable.

Discontinuation of amphetamines and methylphenidate should be gradual so as to avoid distressing withdrawal phenomena such as fatigue or dysphoria.

Treatment of Anxiety

Anxiety in the elderly is often multidetermined, the consequence of medical illness, psychiatric disorder, psychosocial factors, or some combination of these. The new onset or exacerbation of anxiety in an elderly patient, especially if sudden, must be considered organic (physical illness, medication) until proven otherwise.

Treatment of anxiety should reflect its etiology, duration, severity, and the degree to which it impairs functioning and compromises the individual's quality of life. In anxiety secondary to medical illness or medication, treatment of the underlying disorder(s) or adjustment of medications is paramount. Remaining anxiety symptoms can be approached similarly to those in "primary" anxiety.

Nonpharmacological approaches to alleviating anxiety are essential, with or without concomitant psychopharmacological treatment. Psychosocial intervention, such as assistance with finances, relocation, support in meaningful reinvolvement, and decreasing isolation, may do much toward alleviating anxiety (as well as any comorbid depression).

Indications for psychopharmacological treatment, outlined quite well by Weiss (1994), include severe and persistent symptoms that affect the individual's quality of life. Somatic intervention may be necessary for somatic complaints, if only for psychological reasons. Previous response to particular medications may serve as a helpful guideline in the selection of therapeutic agents. Several excellent discussions of the treatment of anxiety have recently been published and are excellent resources when considering pharmacological treatment of anxiety in the elderly (Jenike, 1989; Markovitz, 1993; Salzman, 1992; Stoudemire & Moran, 1993; Weiss, 1994; Wise & Rieck, 1993).

Several classes of psychotropic medications are currently used in the treatment of anxiety, including the benzodiazepines, azapirones (e.g., buspirone), antidepressants (TCAs, SSRIs), beta-adrenergic blockers, neuroleptics, and more recently, mood stabilization agents such as valproate.

BENZODIAZEPINES

The benzodiazepines, especially the hypnotic benzodiazepines, are the most commonly prescribed drugs in the treatment of anxiety. They have been used successfully as anxiolytics in a variety of medical disorders as well as primary agents in the treatment of generalized anxiety disorder, depression and panic disorder (alprazolam or clonazepam), or as adjunctive anxiolytics in numerous psychiatric disorders. They can effectively reduce acute anxiety in exacerbations of psychiatric disorders such as mania and organic syndromes. Benzodiazepines have the advantages of comparatively rapid onset of therapeutic action, demonstrated anxiolytic efficacy in multiple settings, and wide therapeutic indexes in overdose (compared with older anxiolytics such as barbiturates).

Side Effects

The benzodiazepines have been associated with several adverse side effects to which the elderly may be particularly vulnerable and the consequences severe. These include excessive sedation, psychomotor slowing and ataxia, cognitive impairment (including anterograde amnesia and possibly long-term memory deficits), confusion, disorientation, and behavioral disinhibition (Ayd, 1994; Salzman, 1992; Scharf, Fletcher, & Graham, 1988; Weiss, 1994; Wengel, Burke, Ranno, & Roccaforte, 1993). Given these risks, benzodiazepines should generally be avoided in patients with cognitive impairment (delirium, dementia).

Benzodiazepines, including both long and short half-life drugs, have been implicated as risk factors for falls and hip fractures in the elderly (Grisso et al., 1991; Ray, Griffen, & Downdy, 1989). As noted previously, however, Greenspan et al. (1994) have cast some doubt on this association, reporting that it is the duration and force of the fall rather than the benzodiazepine that are the significant risk factors for fractures.

Benzodiazepines can result in physiological dependence, especially with continued use. Withdrawal syndromes may, though not always, develop after benzodiazepine withdrawal, especially if abruptly discontinued.

With careful use of low doses, benzodiazepines do not cause serious respiratory compromise and may be used, with appropriate caution, in individuals with chronic obstructive lung disease (COPD) or emphysema. Indeed, anxiety is common in acute exacerbations of these disorders, and judicious use of low-dose lorazepam or oxazepam may be an important step in overall treatment. Benzodiazepines may worsen sleep apnea and in general, should be avoided in these disorders. Note, however, that clonazepam, a long-acting benzodiazepine, has been used to successfully treat nocturnal myoclonus associated with central sleep apnea (Guilleminault, Crowe, Quera-Salva, Miles, & Partinen, 1988).

Long-Term Versus Short-Term Use

According to the American Psychiatric Association's task force on benzodiazepine dependence, toxicity, and abuse (American Psychiatric Association, 1990; Salzman, 1991a) most people taking benzodiazepines on a long-term basis are older individuals with medical illness, often suffering from depression as well as anxiety, and are frequently seen by physicians. Many take benzodiazepines for years at the original dose without apparent difficulty or apparent development of tolerance. Most take these drugs as needed for sleep or occasional symptom relief.

Concerns about the efficacy of benzodiazepines in long-term use, dependence, tolerance, and adverse side effects have resulted in considerable controversy about their use over extended periods (File, 1985; Rickels et al., 1986). Taylor (1988) has decried the universal condemnation of the benzodiazepines, noting that for many individuals with chronic disabling anxiety, the therapeutic benefit may well justify the potential risks.

Currently, short-term use (4 months or less) is recommended for benzodiazepines (Woods, Katz, & Winger, 1987). Definitive diagnosis, clearly defined symptoms and treatment objectives, carefully monitored benzodiazepine use, and periodic evaluation of the need for continued use are all important. Thus, decisions about longer-term use of these agents may be particularly difficult because the balance between successful abatement of seriously distressing or disabling symptoms of anxiety and not inconsequential side effects is often tenuous.

Selection of Benzodiazepines

The choice of an individual benzodiazepine requires careful consideration in regards to the elderly because the pharmacological properties of these drugs are distinct and exhibit age-associated alterations that may have significant clinical effects. Time to onset of action is also variable, as is the degree of sedation (Wise & Rieck, 1993). Benzodiazepines with shorter elimination half-lives are generally less problematic in the elderly because they lack the tendency for potentially toxic accumulation, although the half-life of those drugs that are metabolized by oxidation may be prolonged.

Particularly attractive benzodiazepines for older individuals are those metabolized by conjugation (glucuronidation) to renally excreted inactive metabolites. In contrast to hepatic oxidation, conjugation appears to be unaffected by age and results in little or no change in T1/2 compared with younger individuals. These benzodiazepines include lorazepam (Ativan), oxazepam (Serax), and temazepam (Restoril). Average daily doses for the elderly (see Table 22.6) are lorazepam, 0.5 to 4 mg; oxazepam, 10 to 30 mg; and temazepam, 15 to 30 mg. Divided doses may be preferred, to avoid excess sedation, although this may decrease compliance.

Longer-acting benzodiazepines may be employed with care in treatment of the elderly. Low doses given once a day, or better yet every other day or every third day, are preferable to minimize excessive drug accumulation and toxicity.

The potency of a benzodiazepine may also be an important consideration in choosing a specific agent because high-potency drugs (alprazolam, lorazepam, clonazepam) may be associated with more severe discontinuation symptoms when abruptly discontinued than those with lower potency. Thus, for an elderly individual at risk for benzodiazepine toxicity due to extreme age, concomitant medical illness, or other medication, a short half-life, low-potency agent such as oxazepam (Serax) might be the preferred choice (Salzman, 1990).

The high-potency, short half-life benzodiazepines (e.g., alprazolam, triazolam) may be particularly problematic in terms of toxic side effects, such as cognitive impairment, physiological dependence, and severe withdrawal syndromes. Both alprazolam (Xanax) and triazolam (Halcion) have been associated with severe psychiatric side effects, including behavioral disturbances, confusion, amnesia, and intense perceptual disturbances. Alprazolam may have particular therapeutic objectives that warrant its use in some cases of panic disorder and depression; the potential for serious adverse side effects with triazolam warrant use of an alternative benzodiazepine hypnotic, such as temazepam (Restoril).

Drug Interactions

The benzodiazepines act in additive fashion with CNS depressants to increase sedation, perhaps to excess, and worsen cognitive and psychomotor function. Drugs that induce hepatic metabolic activity (e.g., anticonvulsants) may enhance benzodiazepine metabolism and thus lower plasma levels. In contrast, drugs that inhibit hepatic metabolism (e.g., cimetidine, omeprazole, erythromycin, fluoxetine, paroxetine) result in elevated benzodiazepine levels.

Withdrawal Symptoms

Withdrawal symptoms following discontinuation (especially if abrupt) of benzodiazepines are common, particularly after continued use for several

Table 22.6 Comparison of Benzodiazepine Anxiolytics

Drug	Half-Life (in hours)	Active Half-Life Metabolites	Doses Recommended for the Elderly (in milligrams per day)	Route of Administration	Onset of Effect (after oral dose)
Short acting					
Oxazepam (Serax)	5 to 15	None	10 to 30	Oral	Intermedieate to slow
Lorazepam (Ativan)	10 to 20	None	0.5 to 4.0	Oral,im,[a] iv[b]	Intermediate
Alprazolam (Xanax)	6 to 15	3 to 7	0.125 to 0.5	Oral	Rapid
Temazepam (Restoril)	12 to 24	None	15 to 30	Oral	Intermediate
Triazolam (Halcion)	2 to 5	None	0.25 to 0.5	Oral	Intermediate
Long acting					
Chlordiazepoxide HCl (Librium)	8 to 28	36 to 200	5 to 30	Oral, im, iv	Rapid
Diazepam (Valium)	26 to 53	36 to 200	2 to 10	Oral, im, iv	Rapid
Prazepam (Centrax)	30 to 200	36 to 200	10 to 5	Oral	Intermediate to slow
Clorazepate dipotassium (Tranxene)	30 to 200	36 to 200	7.5 to 15	Oral	Rapid
Quazepam (Doral)	40	72	7.5 to 15	Oral	Rapid
Clonazepam (Klonopin)	18 to 50	Yes	0.25 to 1.0	Oral	Intermediate

SOURCE: Adapted from Jenike (1989).
a. im = intramuscular
b. iv = intravenous

months, and may be most severe with the short-acting benzodiazepines. Discontinuation of these drugs is thus best done via slow, gradual taper to minimize symptoms, including rebound anxiety, insomnia, restlessness, GI upset, and so on. Alprazolam may result not only in a particularly difficult discontinuation syndrome but also in considerable interdose rebound anxiety. The first problem can be approached by switching to another benzodiazepine, such as lorazepam, with subsequent taper of this agent. Decreasing the interdose interval can be helpful in the latter. With its somewhat unusual antidepressant and antipanic properties, supplementation of alprazolam with a low dose of another long-acting benzodiazepine might be helpful for those whose depression or panic symptoms are compounded by alprazolam's interdose anxiety.

AZAPIRONES

Buspirone (Buspar) is an azapirone anxiolytic agent distinct from the benzodiazepines in its structure, mechanism of action, and side effects. Acting as a partial serotonergic agonist, controlled studies have demonstrated its efficacy in treating anxiety, or anxiety and comorbid depression, in the elderly (Napoliello, 1986; Robinson, Napoliello, & Schenk, 1988).

A recent review of buspirone summarizes its use in a variety of clinical situations (Gelenberg, 1994). A trial of buspirone for relief of anxiety symptoms may be especially important in medically ill elderly where benzodiazepine-related sedation and drug interactions can be particularly problematic. It has been used in a number of anxiety disorders; it appears to be more effective in generalized anxiety than episodic panic disorders. Its efficacy in phobic disorders and posttraumatic stress disorder is being investigated. It has also been used to augment SSRIs or chlomipramine in the treatment of obsessive-compulsive disorder. As noted earlier, buspirone has been used to treat depression, either independently or in augmentation of other antidepressants. Buspirone has also been used in the treatment of agitation in dementia (see discussion to follow).

Several characteristics make buspirone especially attractive in the geriatric patient: It is nonsedating and has no deleterious effects on psychomotor or cognitive function. In contrast to the benzodiazepines, buspirone does not potentiate the effects of alcohol or other CNS depressants. It does not appear to produce physiological dependence or withdrawal symptoms on abrupt discontinuation. Furthermore, it lacks potential for respiratory depression and thus may be useful in individuals with sleep apnea or other respiratory compromise (e.g., COPD), which as noted previously, is often associated with significant anxiety. Buspar's metabolism appears relatively unaffected by age or hepatic dysfunction; drug interactions appear to be minimal.

Table 22.7 Nonbenzodiazepine Anxiolytics and Hypnotics

Type	Representative Drugs	Dose (in milligrams)	Side Effects
Antihistamines	Diphenhydramine	25 once daily	Anticholinergic
	Hydroxyzine	25 once daily	
Neuroleptics			
High potency	Haloperidol	0.5 twice daily	Extrapyramidal dystonia
	Thiothixene	1 twice daily	Akathesia
	Fluphenazine	1 twice daily	Tardive dyskinesia
Low potency	Chlorpromazine	10 twice daily	Anticholinergic
	Thioridazine	10 twice daily	Orthostatic hypotension
			Sedation
			Tardive dyskinesia
Beta-blockers	Propranolol	40 four times daily	Bronchial constriction
	Atenolol	50 to 100 once daily	Sinus bradycardia
Sertonergic	Buspirone	5 to 15 three times daily	Nausea
			Dizziness
			"Spacey" feelings
	Chloral hydrate	250-500 at bedtime	Gastric irritation
			Induced liver enzymes
Imidazopyridine	Zolpidem tartrate	5 to 10 at bedtime	Headache
			Drowsiness
			Dizziness
			Nausea

SOURCE: Adapted from Jenike (1989).

A relative drawback to buspirone is its slow onset of action (generally, 2-3 weeks). This may be trying for anxious individuals who seek rapid relief. There is evidence that buspirone is not as effective in patients previously treated with benzodiazepines. Possible factors in this may be related to its slow onset and lack of sedation or muscle relaxtion.

Side Effects

Side effects are generally transient and include dizziness, nausea, headache, nervousness, and excitement. Initial increased anxiety due to the drug may result in poor compliance and failure to complete an adequate therapeutic trial.

Dosage

Buspirone has a short half-life and is best prescribed in divided doses. Geriatric doses are roughly equivalent to those for younger patients (20-30 mg per day; see Table 22.7). Antidepressant activity has been reported at higher doses (40-60 mg; Rickels et al., 1991).

ANTIDEPRESSANTS

TCAs, MAOIs, and SSRIs have all been successfully employed in resolving anxiety, especially that associated with depression. They are effective in primary anxiety disorders, including panic disorder, obsessive-compulsive disorder, and PTSD, and in generalized anxiety disorder (Kahn et al., 1986). Trazodone in low dose (e.g., 25-100 mg at bedtime) may be helpful in inducing sleep in the anxious and/or depressed insomniac.

ANTIHISTAMINES

Hydroxyzine (Atarax) and diphenhydramine (Benadryl) are H1-histamine antagonists that have often been used for treatment of anxiety and insomnia. Their antihistaminergic and anticholinergic properties can result in excess sedation, however, as well as confusion, disorientation, and other cognitive impairment. Their use for the elderly should therefore be limited to low dose, short-term therapy.

Doses in the elderly average 10 to 75 mg at bedtime for Benadryl and 25 to 100 mg per day (divided doses) for hydroxyzine (see Table 22.7).

BETA ADRENERGIC BLOCKERS

Beta adrenergic blockers such as propranolol have been used in the treatment of generalized anxiety, performance anxiety, and agitation in dementia patients as well as to treat the side effects of psychotropic drugs, such as lithium-induced tremor and neuroleptic-induced akathesia (see discussion to follow; Jenike, 1989).

These agents have been used effectively in the treatment of anxiety in geriatric patients, chiefly by blocking its somatic peripheral autonomic effects (e.g., diaphoresis, tachycardia, palpitations, urinary frequency, etc.; Ouslander, 1981). In medically ill elderly, the use of beta blockers requires special consideration. Their use is contraindicated in patients with sinus bradycardia or severe heart disease and congestive heart failure. Nonselective Beta 1 and Beta 2 blockers (e.g., propranolol, pindolol, timolol) are also contraindicated in asthma, COPD, and diabetes mellitus. Cardioselective Beta 1 blockers (e.g., atenolol, metoprolol) can be used in these patients. CNS side effects (e.g., insomnia, nightmares, hallucinations) are reduced by employing less lipophilic beta blockers (e.g., atenolol).

The beta blockers also have demonstrated efficacy in alleviating agitation and aggressive behavior in dementia and other organic mental syndromes, as will be discussed later. Typical geriatric doses of propranolol for treatment of anxiety are 5 to 10 mg one to four times a day (see Table 22.7). Treatment of agitation associated with dementia may require higher doses (see discussion to follow).

NEUROLEPTICS

Neuroleptics, described in more detail in the section on antipsychotic drugs, are indicated in the treatment of acute exacerbations of psychotic disorders as well as ongoing maintenance of chronic psychotic illness. High-potency neuroleptics are also indicated in the treatment of delirium and have been advocated in the treatment of agitation and aggression in patients with dementia. These drugs have many potentially severe and irreversible side effects (e.g., drug-induced Parkinsonism, akathesia, tardive dykinesia or dystonia) which contraindicate their use in treatment of milder forms of anxiety.

Treatment of Insomnia

Management of sleep disorders includes nonpharmacological interventions as well as medications. Both of these are discussed in an excellent fashion by Jenike (1989).

Nonpharmacological approaches to the treatment of insomnia center on improving sleep hygiene. This involves behavioral modifications such as regular exercise, evening fluid restriction to reduce nocturia, circumscribed use of bedroom for sleep only, avoidance of stimulant beverages (e.g., caffeine, nicotine), and avoidance of daytime napping. Education about normal, age-related decreased sleep duration and increased awakenings is important as is optimal stabilization of anxiety-provoking medical illness (e.g., COPD).

Pharmacological management includes the benzodiazepine sedative hypnotics, trazodone or selected antidepressants, antihistamines, chloral hydrate, and zolpidem, a new nonbenzodiazepine hypnotic.

Benzodiazepine hypnotics are selected according to the same criteria as are anxiolytic benzodiazepines. Thus, short-term use of a short-acting benzodiazepine with no active metabolites is preferred. *Temazepam* (Restoril) meets these criteria and is thus the agent of choice within this drug class. The average dose in the elderly population is 15 to 30 mg at bedtime. *Triazolam* (Halcion) is a short-acting, high-potency benzodiazepine hypnotic noted for its adverse side effects. These include nightmares, disinhibition, and perceptual disturbances and a comparatively high incidence of severe discontinuation symptoms. Triazolam should be used with caution in the elderly.

Trazodone in low doses (25-100 mg at bedtime) has been used effectively in facilitating sleep. Orthostatic hypotension is the most common limiting problem, especially in the elderly. Low doses of other antidepressants may be employed, but generally, these agents are limited to insomnia associated with depression.

Antihistamines (e.g., diphenhydramine) may be useful for insomnia, but long-term use should be avoided, given their tendency for excess sedation and anticholinergic side effects.

Chloral hydrate is a safe and inexpensive hypnotic also indicated for the short-term treatment of insomnia. Its rate of onset is rapid, and it has a short half-life (8 hours). It appears to produce little dependence. Its side effects include gastric irritation and induction of hepatic microsomal enzymes occurs which may decrease the blood levels of other similarly metabolized drugs (e.g., coumadin).

Zolpidem (Ambien) is a recently released hypnotic agent with rapid onset and short duration of action (Hoehns & Perry, 1993). Unlike the benzodiazepines, zolpidem has little or no effects on muscle tension, motor performance, or cognitive function. Furthermore, at therapeutic doses (5-10 mg at bedtime; see Table 22.7) there is no disruption of sleep stages (Nicholson & Pascoe, 1986), and no tolerance or dependence has been noted after 5 weeks of chronic treatment with 10 mg per day (Scharf, Roth, Vogel, & Walsh, 1994). No rebound insomnia has been observed on discontinuation of this drug. Zolpidem's short half-life (2-3 hours), minimal effects on motor performance, and generally benign effects on discontinuation certainly make it an attractive choice for geriatric patients beleaguered by insomnia. It's efficacy in treating insomnia in the elderly population has been investigated (Scharf, Mayleben, Kaffeman, Krall, & Ochs, 1991; Shaw, Carson, & Coquelin, 1992); a dose of 10 mg per day was found to be effective in geriatric psychiatric inpatients, with minimal side effects (File, 1985).

Zolpidem has been associated with the appearance of psychotic symptoms (Cavallero, Covelli, & Smeraldi, 1993; Iruela, Ibanaz-Rojo, & Baca, 1993). Thus, further evaluation of the drug's side effect profile is warranted as its use increases in the United States.

Antipsychotics

Antipsychotic medications are indicated in the treatment of acute or chronic psychosis resulting either from functional psychiatric disorder (e.g., schizophrenic spectrum, mood disorder, etc.) or organic etiology (e.g., medical illness, medication, traumatic head injury, delirium, dementia). These drugs include the older agents, often referred to collectively as *neuroleptics,* and the newer atypical agents clozaril and risperidone.

INDICATIONS FOR ANTIPSYCHOTIC DRUGS

Schizophrenia and schizoaffective disorders require long-term antipsychotic treatment, generally at lower maintenance doses than those required in acute psychotic decompensations. Although schizophrenia is predominantly an illness beginning in the second or third decades, schizophrenic elderly individuals may manifest the residual type of the disease, with little if any active psychotic content but with other "negative symptom" stigmata of the illness (e.g., blunted affect) and of chronic neuroleptic treatment (especially tardive dyskinesia). In general, low maintenance doses of neuroleptic are required. Other older individuals continue to experience active psychotic symptoms necessitating higher doses.

Delusional disorder, generally with onset in middle to late life and characterized by a so-called nonbizarre delusion, appears to be less responsive to conventional antipsychotic treatment. Pimozide (Orap) may be of benefit in this disorder.

Mood disorders with psychotic features, including major depression and acute mania, may be best treated in the elderly by electroconvulsive therapy (ECT; Blazer, 1993; Mukherjee, Sackheim, & Schnur, 1994). Alternatively, pharmacological intervention involves the use of antipsychotics in combination with antidepressants (for major depression with psychotic features) and mood stabilizing agents such as lithium, valproate, and carbamazepine (for mania or bipolar disorder).

Dementia, regardless of etiology, often results in disturbed behavior, such as agitation, screaming, wandering, assaultiveness, and psychotic symptoms (e.g., hallucinations, paranoid ideation, and misidentification syndromes; Rubin, Drevets, & Burke, 1988; Wragg & Jeste, 1989). Nonpharmacological (e.g., enviromental) management of these symptoms is important and may alone be sufficient. Many individuals with both cognitive and sensory (visual and auditory) impairment develop paranoid ideation, especially persecutory. Appropriate correction of sensory deficits, if possible, may be the only required intervention in these situations.

As with other psychiatric symptomatology, the appearance of disordered thought or psychotic thought content, especially if new or sudden in onset, warrants thorough investigation for underlying organic etiologies.

The use of antipsychotic medications in the elderly must be carefully weighed against the gravity of the clinical situation. The relatively high incidence of potentially irreversible and often disabling movement disorders, particularly in those individuals with affective disorders, prompts consideration of alternative treatments.

As with other psychotropic drugs, age-related changes in drug distribution, hepatic metabolism, renal function, and CNS sensitivity result in altered pharmacokinetic and pharmacodynamic parameters that must be carefully considered in neuroleptic use in the elderly. Drug interactions with other highly protein-bound drugs (competitive displacement) and microsomal enzyme inhibitors (e.g., fluoxetine) result in altered blood levels of unbound, active drug and may require dose modulation.

DRUG SELECTION

All of the conventional antipsychotics are of equivalent efficacy in the treatment of psychosis. Furthermore, their potency is directly correlated with their binding affinity to the dopamine D2 receptor. This has thus been argued as the central mechanism of therapeutic action of antipsychotic drugs. However, the advent of the atypical antipsychotics—clozapine and, more recently, risperidone—with comparatively weak D2 receptor affinity indicates a more intricate mechanism with interplay of several neurotransmitters, including dopamine and 5HT (Meltzer, 1993).

As with antidepressants, the choice of a specific antipsychotic medication is chiefly dependent on its side effect profile. The standard antipsychotic drugs have varying anticholinergic, sedative, and alpha-1 adrenergic blockade activities (see Table 22.8), which serve as important determinants in drug choice. The high-potency neuroleptics (e.g., haloperidol, fluphenazine) have little of these properties but a higher incidence of extrapyramidal side effects, including acute extrapyramidal reactions, neuroleptic-induced parkinsonism, and akathesia. The low-potency neuroleptics (e.g., thioridazine, chlorpromazine) have fewer extrapyramidal side effects but considerable anticholinergic, antihistaminergic, and alpha-1 adrenergic blockade activity. These agents, particularly thioridazine, are also known to have effects on cardiac conduction and should be avoided in patients with conduction abnormalities.

In general, use of the higher potency neuroleptics is recommended in the elderly, especially those with medical illness, cognitive impairment, or both, which increases their vulnerability to anticholinergic, hypotensive, and sedative side effects. Thus, for example, anticholinergic side effects of low-potency drugs may cause increased confusion, disorientation, and delirium in demented individuals. The tradeoff, however, is that the elderly are more vulnerable to extrapyramidal side effects associated with many of the high-potency drugs, particularly drug-induced parkinsonism and akathisia.

Table 22.8 Side Effects of Antipsychotics

Generic Name	Trade Name	Sedative	Anticholinergic	Hypotensive	Extrapyramidal[a]	Dose (in milligrams)
Low potency						
Chlorpromazine	Thorazine	High	High	High	Low	100
Thioridazine	Mellaril	High	High	High	Low	100
Intermediate potency						
Perphenazine	Trilafon	Moderate	Moderate	Moderate	Moderate	10
Loxipane succinate	Loxitane	Moderate	Moderate	Moderate	Moderate	15
Molindone HCI	Moban	Moderate	Moderate	Low	Moderate	10
High potency						
Haloperidol	Haldol	Low	Low	Low	High	2
Thiothixene	Navane	Low	Low	Low	High	5
Trifluoperazine HCI	Stelazine	Moderate	Low	Low	Moderate	5
Risperidone	—	Low	Low	Moderate	Low to moderate	0.6
Clozapine	Clozaril	High	Mild	Moderate to high	Very low	—

SOURCE: Adapted from Jenike (1989).

a. Extrapyramidal side effects include acute dystonias, neuroleptic-induced parkinsonism, akathisia, akinesia, tardive dyskinesia, and tardive dystonia.

MOVEMENT DISORDERS ASSOCIATED
WITH ANTIPSYCHOTIC DRUGS

Neuroleptic-induced parkinsonism, with shuffling gait, bradykinesia, muscular rigidity, stooped posture, tremor, drooling, and masklike facies, may be quite problematic, particularly in terms of gait instability and resultant falls. Treatment options include anticholinergic agents such as benzotropine mesylate (Cogentin), trihexylphenidyl (Artane), and diphenydramine (Benadryl). In the elderly, alternatives to these anticholinergic agents are preferable; the dopamine agonist amantadine (Symmetrel) is often used in treating neuroleptic-induced parkinsonism (with doses of 100-300 mg per day).

Akathisia, a syndrome of inner restlessness and inability to sit still, is a distressing problem that often leads to noncompliance with neuroleptic regimens. Antipsychotic-induced akathisia often results in agitation, restlessness, and disruptive behavior in individuals whose disordered behavior the neuroleptic is designed to treat. Unfortunately, this may be viewed inappropriately as psychotic symptomatology and addressed by increasing the neuroleptic dose, further exacerbating the situation. Treatment strategies include lowering the antipsychotic dose, use of anticholinergic agents or dopamine agonists (e.g., amantadine), or a combination of the two. The beta adrenergic blocker propranolol has shown considerable efficacy in reducing this distressing side effect (Lipinski, Zubenko, Cohen, & Barreira, 1984). Low doses (30-100 mg per day) are generally effective. Caution regarding the use of beta adrenergic antagonists applies here as well (e.g., contraindicated in sinus bradycardia, CHF, asthma).

Acute dystonias, extrapyramidal reactions occurring more often with high-potency drugs, are common in young males but quite rare in the elderly. Treatment generally consists of intramuscular administration of an anticholinergic agent (for the elderly, 1 mg Cogentin or 25 mg Benadryl are usually sufficient).

Meige's syndrome, an idiopathic syndrome occurring in late life that consists of involuntary movements of the neck, jaw, and face as well as blepharospasm (blinking, eyelid spasms) has also been associated with long-term neuroleptic use (Ananth, Edelmuth, & Dargan, 1988). Differential diagnosis includes acute dystonias and tardive dyskinesia. Of the three, only acute dystonias respond to anticholinergic medication; this can be used as a diagnostic tool. Meige's syndrome, like tardive dyskinesia, may be quite disabling. Reduction or withdrawal of neuroleptic, if possible, may lead to symptom resolution.

Tardive dyskinesia and tardive dystonia are abnormal involuntary movement disorders resulting from the use of neuroleptics. All standard neuroleptics (clozapine is not included) can result in these abnormal movement disorders.

Tardive dyskinesia characteristically involves stereotyped, repetitive, rhythmic movements most often of mouth, cheek, and tongue muscles but also of the hands, feet, and trunk. *Chorea,* nonrhythmic and flowing movements of one more part of the body, and *athetosis,* slow, writhing, snakelike movements, are frequent manifestations. It is important to note that spontaneous dyskinesias occur in roughly 5% of geriatric patients. Another important differential, particularly in older patients, is loose, ill-fitting dentures that require adaptive movements to keep in place.

Tardive dystonia is a sustained movement, or contraction of muscle groups, resulting in, for example, facial grimacing and blepharospasm, torsion of the neck (torticollis), opisthotonos, and sustained contractions of extremities.

In the general population, risk factors for the development of tardive movement disorders include increased duration of antipsychotic use, increasing age, female gender, and presence of mood disorder. From several studies of geriatric patients treated for the first time with neuroleptics (Crane & Smects, 1974; Lieberman, Kane, Woerner, & Weinhold, 1989; Saltz, Kane, Woerner, & Lieberman, 1989; Yassa, Natase, Dupont, & Thibeau, 1992), it appears that the incidence of tardive dyskinesia is high in the elderly and may develop relatively quickly after the initiation of neuroleptic treatment. Thus, the geriatric population is at particular risk in the use of antipsychotics. The prevalence of tardive dyskinesia in all age groups is approximately 15%, excluding spontaneous dyskinesias. Yassa et al. (1992), studying geriatric patients with diagnoses of major depression, primary degenerative dementia, delusional disorder, and alcoholic dementia who received neuroleptic for the first time, reported a 35% incidence of tardive dyskinesia (this includes patients with spontaneous dyskinesias, roughly 5%). There was also a disproportionate incidence in those patients with major depression—60% of these patients had tardive dyskinesia. Most developed the movement disorder within the first 2 years of neuroleptic treatment. It is interesting that in the elderly population studied, no gender differences in the incidence of tardive dyskinesia were noted. Furthermore, no statistically significant differences were observed in younger (65-75 years) and older (75-85 years) geriatric patients.

Approaches to the treatment of tardive dyskinesia and tardive dystonia include reduction or discontinuation of the neuroleptic drug. In this situation, a resultant withdrawal dyskinesia often appears but generally remits over time. In geriatric patients, remission of symptoms after neuroleptic withdrawal is less common (33-50%; Young & Meyers, 1991). There are also a number of pharmacological interventions (Ouslander, 1981), including 1200 to 1400 IU per day of vitamin E (Egan et al., 1992; Shriqui, Bradwejn, Annable, & Jones, 1992), dopamine-depleting agents resperine and tetrabenazine (Jeste, Lohr, Clark, & Wyatt, 1988), anticholinergic medications sometimes useful for tardive dystonia (Burke et al., 1982), the partial serotonergic agonist buspirone (Moss, Neppe, & Drevets, 1993), calcium channel blockers (Dubovsky, 1986), the MAOI L-deprenyl, gamma-aminobutyric acid agonists (Jeste & Wyatt, 1982), and subsitution of the atypical antipsychotic clozapine (Lieberman et al., 1991; Meltzer & Luchins, 1984).

NEUROLEPTIC MALIGNANT SYNDROME

Neuroleptic malignant syndrome (NMS) is a fortunately rare but potentially fatal reaction to antipsychotic medication characterized by extrapyramidal dysfunction (i.e., extreme muscular rigidity, tremor), hyperthermia, and autonomic instability. Leukocytosis, elevated creatinine phosphokinase (CPK) levels, and myoglobinuria are generally present. With an incidence of 0.5% to 1% of patients taking neuroleptic medication, it occurs predominantly in young and middle-aged people (20-40 years old) but has been seen in older patients.

Treatment of NMS is primarily supportive. The offending neuroleptic must be discontinued immediately. Benzodiazepines and amantadine may be useful for milder symptoms. Dantrolene, bromocriptine, or both can be used for more severe symtoms, including rigidity, elevated white blood count, increased CPK, and myoglobinuria. If continued neuroleptic treatment is required after resolution of symptoms, the use of a neuroleptic from an alternative chemical class is recommended. In some cases, patients have tolerated reinstitution of the NMS-causing neuroleptic, especially when doses are very gradually increased; others have redeveloped the symptoms of NMS. High-potency neuroleptics may have increased prediliction for causing NMS. Rechallenging with a lower-potency drug may be advantageous if this drug's anticholinergic, hypotensive, and sedative effects can be tolerated.

OTHER SIDE EFFECTS

Antipsychotics have a panoply of other side effects in diverse systems, which will be briefly summarized here:

Opthalmologic Side Effects. The most significant side effect concerns the use of elevated doses (> 800 mg per day) of thioridazine (Mellaril), which can result in pigmentary retinopathy and loss of vision. Other neuroleptics cause a reversible pigmentation of lens and cornea that is usually benign.

Thermoregulation. Neuroleptics interfere with homeostatic temperature regulation mechanisms; patients are thus poikilothermic and very sensitive to temperature extremes.

Dermatologic Side Effects. Neuroleptics are associated with increased photosensitivty; sun screen protection is thus particularly important.

Hematologic Side Effects. In general, hematologic side effects are quite uncommon. Agranulocytosis occurs rarely (< 0.01%) with standard antipsychotics, mostly with low-potency agents, such as chlorpromazine. It tends to occur within the first 2 months of treatment. Sore throat, fever, or flulike symptoms early in the course of neuroleptic treatment should prompt evaluation of the white blood cell count. Agranulocytosis is a serious and more frequent problem with clozapine (incidence 1-2%), necessitating weekly cell counts.

Seizures. Antipsychotics, particularly of low potency, are associated with reduction of the seizure threshold and increased seizure risk, especially in the elderly, those with a preexisting seizure disorder, or predisposing CNS pathology. Practically speaking, the standard antipsychotics very rarely promote seizures, even in predisposed patients. Clozapine, however, is associated with a dose-related increase in seizure incidence (1-2%) at doses lower than 300 mg per day and 3% to 5% at 600 to 900 mg per day. Prophylactic anticonvulsant treatment (e.g., valproate) is indicated at the higher clozapine doses.

Endocrine Side Effects. Hyperprolactinemia is the most common endocrinologic effect of the standard antipsychotics. In females, this can result in amenorrhea and galactorrhea. In men, erectile failure may result. Clozapine has little or no effect on prolactin levels.

ATYPICAL ANTIPSYCHOTICS

Clozapine

Clozapine is an atypical antipsychotic currently indicated for the treatment of schizophrenia refractory to conventional neuroleptics and for those unable to tolerate their adverse side effects (in particular, extrapyramidal symptoms). Its pharmacodynamic profile is quite distinct from that of standard antipsycotics in its relatively weak dopamine D2 receptor blockade; its more robust dopamine D4, serotonin 5HT1c, 5HT2, 5HT3, and histamine H1 receptor blockade; and its preference for limbic rather than striatal areas. These differences presumably underlie clozapine's efficacy and mild extrapyramidal profile.

Clozapine has several significant advantages over standard antipsychotics besides its low extrapyramidal side effect profile (little or no production of tardive dyskinesia), including efficacy in improving both positive and negative symptoms as well as thought organization and little effect on prolactin levels. However, its use in the elderly may be limited by its strong anticholinergic, hypotensive, and sedative profile. Also, its relative proclivity toward agranulocytosis and seizure activity greatly limits its use.

Low-dose clozapine has been used with some success in the treatment of psychosis, tremor, and other motor symptoms in Parkinson's disease (Aravelo & Gershanik, 1993; Bernardi & Del Zompo, 1990; Friedman & Lannson, 1989, 1990; Wolk & Douglas, 1992).

Very few studies of clozapine use in the geriatric population have been done other than those with Parkinson's disease. However, a report of its successful use in an 82-year-old woman with psychosis and tardive dyskinesia without limiting side effects has been published (Bajulaize & Addonizio, 1992).

Risperidone

Risperidone (Risperdal) is a recently released antipsychotic with selective serotonin 5HT2 and dopamine D2 receptor antagonism. Analagous to clozapine, it appears to be useful in the treatment of both positive and negative symptoms of schizophrenia, with minimal extrapyramidal side effects at lower doses. Two of three placebo-controlled double-blind studies to date (Chouinard et al., 1993; Marder & Meibach, 1994) compared fixed doses of risperidone (2, 6, 10, 16 mg per day) with haloperidol (20 mg per day). Results indicated improvement in both positive and negative symptoms with dystonia and parkinsonian side effects equivalent to placebo at an optimum dose of 6 mg per day. No studies of its efficacy or safety in the geriatric population have been reported. Risperidone has the advantage of minimal hematologic side effects; no blood count monitoring is required. Anticholinergic side effects are minimal. Thus, this drug may be better tolerated in the elderly.

Drugs for Mood Stabilization

Mood stabilization agents are indicated in the treatment of psychiatric disorders that exhibit cyclic disturbance of mood with symptoms varying in intensity from mania to severe depression. Mood syndromes arising from physical illness, medication, or both may also require mood stabilizing medication in addition to treatment of the underlying disorder. They have also been used in disorders with mood lability and episodic outbursts of anger or aggression (e.g., intermittent explosive disorder and post-traumatic stress disorder).

In the elderly, mania is a heterogenerous syndrome with a multiplicity of possible underlying etiologies (Young & Klerman, 1992). Seen in 5% to 10% of the elderly undergoing treatment for mood disorders (Yassa, Naiv, &

Iskander, 1988), its onset in late life is comparatively rare and predominantly associated with underlying organic, especially neurological, disorders (Snowden, 1991; Tohen, Shulman, & Satlin, 1994). In new onset mania, the absence of past individual or family psychiatric histories of manic episodes or bipolar illness should strongly suggest an underlying organic etiology.

Differential diagnoses of mania in the geriatric population include idiopathic psychiatric disorders (e.g., bipolar disorder, schizoaffective disorder, schizophrenia, delusional disorder) as well as mood syndromes secondary to myriad neurological disorders, delirium, dementia (Stone, 1989), systemic illnesses, and pharmacological agents.

In any secondary, or organic, mania, treatment of the underlying disorder or discontinuation of mania-producing medication may ultimately result in resolution of psychiatric symptoms. Initial treatment, however, as in the manic decompensation of idiopathic psychiatric illness, may of necessity be behavioral (i.e., reduction of agitation or irritability, chiefly via sedation, using benzodiazepines, antipsychotics, or both). Treatment of mania resulting from irreversible CNS pathology (e.g., cerebrovascular accident) is similar to that of primary psychiatric illnesses, including acute benzodiazepine or antipsychotic (preferably high potency) medication or both as well as initiation and continuation of mood stabilizing agent(s).

The pharmacotherapy of mania in the elderly has recently been reviewed (Liptzin, 1992; Mirchandani & Young, 1993; Zajecka, 1993). Mood stabilizing drugs include lithium salts (Lithobid, Eskalith CR) and the anticonvulsants carbamazepine (Tegretol), valproic acid or valproate (Depakene, Depakote), and clonazepam (Klonopin). The calcium channel blocker verapamil has also been used with some success in the treatment of mania (Dubovsky, Franks, Allen, & Murphy, 1986).

Lithium

Since its inception in the 1970s, lithium has been the drug of choice in the treatment of acute manic episodes and in long-term prophylaxis (Keck & McElroy, 1993). Estimates of lithium's efficacy in the treatment of acute mania and subsequent prophylaxis range from 50% to 80%. Post (1993) and Goodwin and Jamison (1990) have noted that roughly 50% of bipolar patients are poorly responsive to, fail prophylaxis with, or are intolerant to lithium.

Age-associated physiological changes in the elderly result in pharmacokinetic changes that reduce the dose of lithium required for a given plasma level as compared with younger persons (Hardy, Shulman, Mackenzie, Kutcher, & Silverberg, 1987), often by 30% to 60%. Increased time to reach steady-state concentrations (reflecting increased half-life) dictates that the dose of lithium be changed over a longer time interval.

Lithium has a narrow therapeutic index: That is, drug toxicity may occur at doses close to those needed for therapeutic effect. This is particularly so in the elderly, who often manifest increased sensitivity to lithium's adverse side effects at levels lower than the standard therapeutic range for younger individuals. The potential for toxicity is further enhanced in the elderly by the high frequency of comorbid physical illness, the use of multiple medications, or both. In older individuals, a complete physical and neurological examination; laboratory evaluation, including renal and thyroid function; and an EKG are requisite for the initiation of lithium treatment. Ongoing assessment of renal function is essential.

Side Effects. The side effects of lithium include renal, GI, and thyroid disturbances; headache; weight gain; acne; exacerbation of psoriasis; and alopecia. Cardiovascular effects and neurotoxicity also occur.

Nephrogenic diabetes insipidus with polyuria and polydipsia is a frequent side effect and can often be treated successfully with a thiazide diuretic. Addition of a diuretic to an established lithium regimen generally requires a reduction in lithium dose and a careful watch on lithium levels. Renal interstitial nephritis, glomerular sclerosis, and tubular atrophy have all been seen in patients who have undergone long-term treatment with lithium. However, the ultimate consequences of these pathological changes on kidney function remain unclear. Comparison of 24-hour creatinine clearance values in the course of lithium treatment with that prior to initiation of lithium is helpful in assessing alterations in kidney function.

GI side effects (nausea, diarrhea, and vomiting) are often seen early in lithium treatment. They may be ameliorated by lowering the dose or by the use of a slow-release preparation, which decreases peak lithium levels and associated side effects.

Thyroid disturbance occurs because lithium inhibits the release of both thyroid hormones: triiodothyronine and thyroxine. This often results in a diffuse goiter and hypothyroidism. When this occurs, thyroid hormone replacement or choice of a different drug for mood stabilization, such as carbamazepine or valproate, are treatment alternatives.

Adverse cardiovascular side effects are more likely to occur in patients with preexisting disease. A pretreatment EKG is therefore essential in older individuals. Lithium may cause sinus node pacemaker dysfunction and bradycardia and may aggravate conduction deficits. T-wave flattening and inversion on the EKG is common and benign.

Neuropsychiatric effects include lethargy, tremor, ataxia, extrapyramidal symptoms, confusion, and disorientation. Patients with preexisting cognitive deficits are particularly susceptible to further impairment with lithium. Delirium as well as cerebellar dysfunction may result from lithium toxicity and persist weeks after its discontinuation (DePaulo, Folstein, & Correa, 1982; Schon, 1984). A fine resting tremor commonly occurs, which is often amenable to treatment with low-dose propranolol (10 mg once a day to 10 mg three times a day). Lithium may also produce extrapyramidal parkinsonian symptoms (Jefferson, 1983) or worsen those of preexisting Parkinson's disease. Neurotoxicity may be potentiated by concurrent use of neuroleptics or other mood stabilizers.

Drug Interactions. Possible drug interactions, including OTC agents, are an important consideration in prescribing medications for patients taking lithium. Nonsteroidal antiinflammatory agents, with the exception of sulindac, reduce lithium clearance and, without appropriate dose adjustment, can result in lithium toxicity. Lithium's interaction with several other drugs (e.g., digoxin, verapamil, methyldopa, erythromycin) have been reported; however these, interactions may be idiosyncratic rather than generalized phenomena (Goodwin & Jamison, 1990).

Dosage. The starting dose of lithium carbonate in geriatric patients is 75 to 300 mg per day. Subsequent dose adjustments must reflect the prolonged half-life (approximately 30 hours in healthy elderly individuals) and time to reach steady-state blood levels in this population.

Therapeutic lithium levels in geriatric patients have not been fully established. In contrast to the therapeutic range (0.6-1.2 m Eq/L) in younger individuals, many older patients show therapeutic response at lower lithium levels (0.4-0.6 m Eq/L). Others require doses of lithium within the standard therapeutic range.

Lithium is available in different formulations with differing half-lives, including standard and slow-release forms of lithium carbonate and liquid lithium citrate. Slow-release preparations may be advantageous for individuals experiencing adverse effects of regular preparations; the slow-release medications have a lower peak plasma level, which may produce fewer side effects. Alterations in dosage of medications with prolonged half-lives must also be made at greater time intervals so as to approach steady state. Lithium levels should be drawn after each dose adjustment; blood for lithium level determinations must be drawn 10 to 12 hours after the last lithium dose.

Anticonvulsants

Bipolar disorder with rapid cycling (alteration of mood between depression, mania, and euthymia), mixed or dysphoric mania, and secondary mania are relatively refractory to lithium; however, these disorders do appear to be more responsive to the anticonvulsants currently used in mood stabilization:

carbamazepine and valproate. The efficacy of these two drugs in acute mania and long-term prophylaxis have been reported in multiple studies and reviews (Bowden et al., 1994; Chou, 1991; Fawcett & Kravitz, 1985; Kahn, Stevenson, & Douglas, 1988; McElroy, Keck, Pope, & Hudson, 1989; Pope, McElroy, Keck, & Hudson, 1991; Prien & Gelenberg, 1989; Schatt, Fawcett, & Zajecka, 1993). These agents may be used alone or in combination with each other. No controlled studies have been performed exclusively with geriatric patients; however, several reports of their efficacy in geriatric patients have been reported (Kellner & Noher, 1991; McFarland, Miller, & Straumfjord, 1990). Controlled studies in these patients are awaited.

Carbamazepine (CBZ, Tegretol). CBZ is somewhat unpredictability absorbed and reaches peak plasma levels 2 to 6 hours after administration. Its half-life in younger patients is 12 to 15 hours; steady state is reached in 2 to 4 days.

CBZ is highly protein bound and thus competes with other similarly bound drugs for protein-binding sites; this may result in increased levels of free drugs.

CBZ is hepatically metabolized via the P450 microsmal enzyme system, which it induces, thus increasing its own metabolism. This induction often is evident after 2 to 3 months of chronic treatment, necessitating a dose increase at that time to maintain drug concentration at a particular level.

Therapeutic plasma levels are not well defined for mania; in general, the therapeutic anticonvulsant levels (4-12 mg/ml) are used. In the geriatric population, lower levels (e.g., 4-8 mg/ml) may be effective therapeutically and minimize the side effects more frequent at higher doses. Clinical presentation should be the predominant factor in determining the optimum CBZ dose.

Most adverse side effects of CBZ occur at the beginning of treatment, at times of rapid dose increase, or at peak serum levels. Common side effects include sedation, lethargy, tremor, ataxia, blurred vision, and nausea. Transient elevations in liver enzymes are common early in treatment but rarely problematic except in the setting of preexisting hepatic disease. Twofold elevations of liver function tests warrant careful evaluation and possible discontinuation of the drug. Transient leukopenia and thrombocytopenia are also common in the first months of treatment. The possibility of serious blood dyscrasias, including agranulocytosis or aplastic anemia, though rare (roughly 1 in 125,000), requires complete blood count checks every 2 to 3 weeks for the first 2 to 3 months of treatment and subsequently, every 3 to 6 months. White blood cell counts of $\leq$ 3,000 warrant more frequent monitoring and possible discontinuation as indicated.

CBZ is structurally similar to the TCA imipramine, and has quinidine-like Type 1A antiarrhythmic activity. It can potentially cause disturbances in cardiac conduction and thus must be used with appropriate caution in individuals with AV conduction abnormalities (i.e., AV block) or arrhythmias.

A macular rash occurs with 10% to 15% incidence. Rarely, Stevens-Johnson syndrome has been reported and necessitates withdrawal of the drug.

Hyponatremia may occur with carbamazepine secondary to syndrome of inappropriate antidiuretic hormone secretion. Carbamazepine interacts with several drugs, resulting in altered serum levels. Cimetidine, erythromycin, fluoxetine, and calcium channel blockers inhibit CBZ metabolism, thus increasing its serum level. Phenytoin and phenobarbital induce hepatic metabolism, reducing CBZ levels. CBZ itself, via induction, reduces the level of several drugs, including warfarin, divalproex sodium, and TCAs.

Initial doses of CBZ in the elderly should be 100 mg per day and increased slowly, as tolerated and as clinically indicated, to approximately 400 to 800 mg per day.

Valproate (Depakane, Depakote). Valproate is absorbed over 1 to 3 hours, depending on the formulation of the drug—rapid release, enteric-coated, capsule, or tablet. Like CBZ, it is highly protein bound; its level may increase due to competitive displacement by other protein-bound drugs. Valproate blood levels may not be clinically very useful because there is a nonlinear relationship between dose and blood level, especially at higher doses. Determination of dose should thus be based on clinical presentation and side effects. Valproate is hepatically metabolized but does not induce the P450 microsmal system, as does CBZ. Thus, steady-state plasma levels are generally relatively constant at a given dose.

Side effects of divalproex sodium most commonly include sedation as well as GI disturbance, tremor, ataxia, lethargy, weight gain, and alopecia. Transient elevations in hepatic enzymes occur in nearly half of patients at the start of treatment. Liver function tests at 2 to 3 week intervals in the first 3 months of treatment, and subsequently every 3 to 6 months, are probably appropriate. Serious hepatotoxicity can occur, albeit rarely. Fatal hepatotoxicity has occurred only in young children. Debate about monitoring liver function tests centers on the rarity versus the severity of the potential problem.

Valproate has relatively few drug interactions in comparison with CBZ. Other highly protein-bound drugs, such as aspirin, CBZ, phenytoin, and phenobarbital, taken together with valproate may result in altered serum levels of one drug or the other. Valproate does inhibit CBZ metabolism and competes with CBZ for protein binding. When used in combination, initial increased levels of both might be expected and warrant dose reduction of both. Subsequent induction of hepatic metabolism by CBZ affects the metabolism of both drugs; thus, drug levels must be frequently monitored. The therapeutic range for valproate in the treatment of geriatric mania is not established. The standard anticonvulsant range is 50 to 120 mg/ml. In geriatric patients, an initial low dose of the enteric-coated formulation is often recommended to minimize side effects. Doses of 125 mg per day at the start can be gradually increased as tolerated to reach a serum level between 50 to 150 mg/ml.

Pharmacotherapy of Agitation and Behavioral Disturbance

Of the triad of cognitive impairment, personality changes, and behavioral manifestations that occur in dementia, behavior is frequently the most problematic and often the primary determinant in placement outside the home.

Agitation, irritability, and aggression are the most common behavioral manifestations in the dementias and other neuropsychiatric illnesses (Chandler & Chandler, 1988; Reisberg et al., 1987). Screaming, head banging, pacing, wandering, uncooperativeness, perseverative activitites such as opening and shutting drawers, kicking or swinging extremeties, agitation, and overt aggression toward others often require psychopharmacological intervention. Yudofsky, Silver, and Hales (1990) have proposed diagnostic criteria for "organic aggressive syndrome" to describe individuals with CNS pathology who manifest aggressive behavior. These authors have developed the Overt Aggression Scale (Yudofsky, Silver, Jackson, Endicott, & Williams, 1986) as a means of quantifying verbal as well as physical aggression against self, others, or objects. Use of this scale has proved beneficial in documenting aggressive behaviors and their response to pharmacological treatment.

As with other psychiatric symptoms in the elderly that are new, sudden in onset, or are significant deviations from baseline status, it is essential to rule out reversible organic or environmental etiologies. Treatment of the causative physical disorder or appropriate modification of the setting in which the person resides may alleviate behavioral difficulties without the need for psychopharmacological intervention. The risk-benefit ratio in the use of pharmacological agents for agitation or other problematic behavior must also be carefully weighed in the elderly, given their increased sensitivity to, and vulnerability for adverse consequences of, psychotropic medications.

Several different classes of medications have been used in the treatment of agitation and other behavioral disturbances (Kunik, Yudofsky, Silver, & Hales, 1994). They include neuroleptics; benzodiazepines; serotonergic agents (e.g., trazodone, buspirone); mood stabilization agents, including lithium, carbamazepine, and valproate; and also beta adrenergic blockers, such as propranolol.

NEUROLEPTICS

Neuroleptics have in the past been the mainstay of pharmacological treatment for agitation, regardless of etiology.

Low doses of high-potency neuroleptics (especially haloperidol) are indicated in the management of agitation in delirium (Wise & Rundell, 1988). Intravenous haloperidol, given intermittently or as a continuous drip, has been used extensively in seriously ill delirious patients (Adams, 1988; Fernandez, Holmes, Adams, & Kavanaugh, 1988; Tesar, Murray, & Cassem, 1985), often in combination with low doses of lorazepam. Wise and Rundell (1988) have outlined guidelines for the use of haloperidol in delirium. Starting doses in the elderly vary, depending on the level of agitation, from 0.5 to 5 mg orally or 0.25 to 2.5 mg intravenously. If agitation continues 30 minutes after the first dose, a second dose, double that of the first, is given. After three doses, low-dose (0.5-1.0 mg) intravenous lorazepam is administered, either simultaneously or alternatively with the haloperidol, every 30 minutes until the patient is calm. The total dose over the initial 24-hour period is repeated over the next 24 hours and is then, one hopes, gradually tapered with a 50% reduction in dose every 24 hours. Notably, doses of intravenous haloperidol are equivalent to half of the oral dose. Also, haloperidol administered intravenously has fewer extrapyramidal side effects than if given orally.

Droperidol, used as an anesthetic, may be an excellent alternative to haloperidol in the treatment of agitation secondary to delirium (Szuba, Bergman, Baxter, & Guze, 1992). It has several advantages when compared with haloperidol, including higher potency, more rapid onset of action, and shorter half-life. It also has a low incidence of extrapyramidal side effects.

In the past, neuroleptics, along with benzodiazepines, have been the first-line agents in the treatment of agitation and aggression in elderly individuals with dementia. Unfortunately, these patients have often received medication more for chemical restraint than for therapeutic benefit, "treating" the staff rather than the patient. In one comparison study (Cohen-Mansfield, 1986), agitated individuals were given more medication—and incurred more falls—than their nonagitated counterparts. Reviews of the use of neuroleptics in treating agitation and aggression (Devanand, Sackheim, & Mayeux, 1988; Schneider, Pollock, & Lyness, 1990) indicate only moderate efficacy for these problems. Furthermore, both the short-term side effects (e.g., anticholinergic side effects, akathisia) and long-term consequences (e.g., tardive dyskinesia) of these drugs warrants limitation of their use to agitation secondary to psychotic ideation or acute and extreme agitation requiring rapid sedation. Treatment of hallucinations or other psychotic ideation in the demented individual is *not* warranted unless it has produced agitation that cannot be assuaged with nonpharmacological maneuvers.

In general, low-potency neuroleptics should be avoided in elderly individuals, especially those with cognitive impairment, given the likelihood of amplified cognitive dysfunction, confusion, or delirium secondary to their anticholinergic side effects. Hypotension and excess sedation may also be problematic with these drugs.

BENZODIAZEPINES

Benzodiazepines, especially lorazepam (Ativan) and oxazepam (Serax), have been used in the treatment of acute agitation and aggression (Coccaro et al., 1990; Yudofsky et al., 1990). Lorazepam has the advantage of parenteral (intramuscular or intravenous) administration. Small doses (0.5-2 mg, maximum 4-6 mg per day) are given intermittently over a short period. Following resolution, the drug is gradually tapered; reemergence of agitation or aggression may then warrant consideration of other agents in ongoing treatment.

Benzodiazepine treatment for the elderly, especially those with dementia or other CNS pathology, may be limited due to paradoxical disinhibition (Gardos, 1980; Shader & Greenblatt, 1982). Sedation due to these drugs may also be problematic in the elderly.

SEROTONERGIC AGENTS

Dementia, particularly of the Alzheimer's type, involves not only the loss of cholinergic neurons but those of multiple neurotransmitters, including 5HT. This neurotransmitter has been implicated in the modulation of inpulsivity and aggression. Thus, several serotonergic agents (e.g., buspirone, trazodone) have been employed in the treatment of agitation and aggression in dementia.

BUSPIRONE

An anxiolytic agent with partial 5HT 1A receptor agonist activity, described in a previous section, buspirone has been described in several controlled reports and studies to be effective in reducing agitation in patients with dementia (Colenda, 1981; Sakayue, Camp, & Ford, 1993). Doses of 30 to 35 mg per day appear to be optimum, although higher (e.g., 40-60 mg per day) or lower (5 mg per day) may be effective. Adverse side effects of buspirone include agitation and nervousness. Though generally transient, their occurrence would obviously limit buspirone's utility in already agitated individuals.

Trazodone

Trazodone has been shown in numerous case reports to be effective in treating agitation and aggression in demented patients (Simpson & Foster, 1986; Pinner & Rich, 1988). The required dose is variable, ranging from 25 mg per day to near maximum recommended doses of 500 mg per day. Gradual titration of the dose over the progressive course of the disease is useful as chronic prophylaxis for recurrent agitation or aggressive episodes (J. Schneider, unpublished observations).

Common side effects of trazodone include orthostatic hypotension and sedation, either of which may be limiting. Trazodone lacks anticholinergic activity that might lead to further cognitive compromise, confusion, or delirium in cognitively impaired individuals.

LITHIUM

Lithium's effectiveness in reducing agitation in patients with dementia is equivocal, although it has been reported useful in agitated mentally retarded individuals. Its low therapeutic index and potential CNS toxicity, especially in the elderly with dementia, limit its practical application in this population.

ANTICONVULSANTS

The anticonvulsants carbamazepine (Tegretol) and valproic acid or valproate (Depakene, Depakote) have been used in mood stabilization of individuals with bipolar mood disorder. Carbamazepine is effective in treating impulsive or violent behavior, such as intermittent explosive disorder (Denicoff, Meglathery, Post, & Tandeciarz, 1994; Gupta, Fish, & Yerevanian, 1987; Mattes, 1984), and has been shown to reduce impulsivity in borderline personality disorder (Cowdry & Gardner, 1988). Several studies have indicated carbamazepine's usefulness in dementia-related agitation (Gleason & Schneider, 1992; Schneider & Sobin, 1992). Doses ranged from 100 to 1,000 mg per day; blood levels varied from 1.5 to 12 mg/ml. Side effects included transient leukopenia, sedation, and ataxia. The possibility of agranulocytosis or aplastic anemia, although rare (estimates of agranulocytosis are 1 in 125,000 cases), necessitates frequent blood monitoring.

Although less well studied to date, valproate is believed to have similar effects to carbamazepine in treating impulsive or violent behavior (Denicoff et al., 1994).

BETA ADRENERGIC BLOCKERS

Propranolol has been successfully employed in the treatment of agitation, aggression, and explosive rage in elderly patients with psychosis or dementia

(Weiler, Mungas, & Bernick, 1988) as well as organic mental syndromes where agitation is prominent (Greendyke, Kanter, Schuster, Verstreake, & Wooton, 1986; Petrie & Ban, 1981; Yudofsky, Williams, & Gorman, 1981). Doses of propranolol varied from 60 to 520 mg per day.

A protocol for the use of propranolol has been developed by Yudofsky et al. (1990). Patients with bronchial asthma, COPD, CHF, insulin dependent diabetes, persistent angina, significant peripheral vascular disease, or hypothyroidism are excluded from use of this agent. The initial dose of propranolol is low (20 mg per day) and raised by 20 mg per day every 3 days in patients without hypotension or sinus bradycardia. Patients without cardiovascular or cardiopulmonary disease can be initiated on propranolol at 20 mg three times daily. The dose of propranolol is subsequently increased by 60 mg per day every 3 days, unless pulse and blood pressure are low and limiting (e.g., systolic BP < 90, pulse < 50). The dose should be increased to 12 mg/kg as tolerated and held at that dose for at least 8 weeks before assessing response. Note that there is often a latency period of 4 to 8 weeks after reaching a therapeutic dose before the onset of therapeutic effect. The possibility of drug interactions warrants careful monitoring of concurrent medications. Propranolol, for example, can increase the level of neuroleptic being used. Beta blockers such as pindolol and nadolol have also been used in successful treatment of aggression (Greendyke & Kanter, 1986; Polakoff, Forgi, & Ratey, 1986).

APPENDIX 22.1

Psychotropic Drugs—Geriatric Dosages

Generic Name	Trade Name	Approximate Daily Dosage Range[a] (in milligrams)
Antidepressants		
Tricyclic antidepressants		
Amitriptyline	Elavil, Endep, Amitril	10 to 75
Amoxapine	Asendin	10 to 300
Clomipramine	Anafranil	10 to 250
Desipramine	Norpramin, Pertofrane	10 to 75
Doxepin	Adapin, Sinequan, Curetin	10 to 75
Imipramine	Tofranil, Janimine, SK to Pramine, Presamine, Imavate	10 to 75
Maprotiline	Ludiomil	10 to 75
Nortriptyline	Pamelor, Aventyl	10 to 50
Protriptyline	Vivactil	5 to 20
Trimipramine	Surmontil	10 to 75
Monoamine oxidase inhibitors		
Isocarboxazid	Marplan	10 to 30
Phenelzine	Nardil	15 to 60
Selegiline	L-Deprenyl, Eldepryl	5 to 60
Tranyclypromine	Parnate	10 to 30
Psychostimulants		
d-Amphetamine	Dexedrine	2.5 to 60
Methylphenidate	Ritalin	2.5 to 60
Pemoline	Cylert	37.5 to 112.5
Selective serotonin reuptake inhibitors		
Fluoxetine	Prozac	5 to 80
Paroxetine	Paxil	10 to 40
Sertraline	Zoloft	25 to 200
Fluvoxamine	Luvox	50 to 150
Atypical antidepressants		
Bupropion	Wellbutrin	75 to 450
Venlafaxine	Effexor	25 to 200
Trazodone	Desyrel	25 to 200
Nefazodone	Serzone	150 to 400
Antianxiety Agents		
Benzodiazepines		
Alprazolam	Xanax	0.25 to 2
Chlorodiazepoxide	Librium, A-poxide, Clipoxide, SK Lygen	10 to 40
Clonazepam	Klonopin	0.25 to 2
Clorazepate	Tranxene	7.5 to 30
Diazepam	Valium	2 to 20
Halazepam	Paxipam	10 to 40
Lorazepam	Ativan	0.5 to 2
Oxazepam	Serax	10 to 45

Generic Name	Trade Name	Approximate Daily Dosage Range[a] (in milligrams)
Prazepam	Centrax, Verstran	10 to 15
Nonbenzodiazepine anxiolytics		
Hydroxyzine	Atarax, Vistoril	25 to 100
Buspirone	Buspar	5 to 80
Zolpidem	Ambien	5 to 20
Benzodiazepine hypnotics		
Estazolam	Pro-Som	0.5 to 2
Flurazepam	Dalmane	15 to 30
Quazepam	Doral	7.5 to 15
Temazepam	Restoril	15 to 30
Triazolam	Halcion	0.125 to 0.25
Antipsychotics		
Acetophenazine	Tindal	10 to 100
Carphenazine	Proketazine	12.5 to 100
Chlorpromazine	Thorazine	10 to 200
Chlorprothixene	Taractan	10 to 100
Clozapine	Clozaril	25 to 450
Fluphenazine	Prolixin, Permitil	0.25 to 4
Haloperidol	Haldol	0.25 to 4
Loxapine	Loxitane, Daxolin	10 to 100
Mesoridazine	Serentil	10 to 200
Molindone	Moban, Lidone	5 to 100
Perphenazine	Trilafon	2 to 32
Pimozide	Orap	0.25 to 4
Piperacetazine	Quide	10 to 80
Prochlorperazine	Compazine	5 to 20
Risperidone	Risperidal	2 to 20
Thiroidazine	Mellaril	10 to 200
Thiothixene	Navane	1 to 15
Trifluoperazine	Stelazine	1 to 15
Triflupromazine	Vesprin	10 to 75
Mood Stabilizers		
Carbamazepine	Tegretol	50 to 1200
Lithium	Cibalith-S, Eskalith, Eskalith CR, Lithane, Lithobid	75 to 1500
Valproic Acid	Depakene, Depakote	125 to 1800
Verapamil	Calan, Isoptin, Verelan	120 to 480
Antiparkinsonian Agents		
Amantadine	Symmetrel	50 to 150
Benztropinemesylate	Cogentin	0.5 to 2
Biperiden	Akineton	1 to 4
Diphenhydramine	Benadryl	10 to 50
Procyclidine	Kemadrin	1 to 5
Trihexyphenidyl	Artane	1 to 4
Behavioral Disorders		
Buspirone	Buspar	5 to 80
Carbamazepine	Tegretol	50 to 1200

Generic Name	Trade Name	Approximate Daily Dosage Range[a] (in milligrams)
Haloperidol	Haldol	0.25 to 4
Lithium	Cibalith, Eskalith, Eskalith CR, Lithane, Lithobid	75 to 900
Propranolol[b]	Inderal	10 to 100
Trazodone	Desyrel	25 to 200
Valproic Acid	Depakane, Depakote	125 to 1800

SOURCE: Adapted from Salzman (1992).
a. Upper doses are not clearly established for the elderly; highest dosages are not recommended for usual treatment.
b. Alternative B-adrenergic blockers may be used in equivalent doses.

References

Abel, E. K. (1991). *Who cares for the elderly: Public policy and experiences of adult daughters.* Philadelphia: Temple University Press.

Abernathy, D. R. (1992). Psychotropic drugs and the aging process: Pharmacokinetics and pharmacodynamics. In C. Salzman (Ed.), *Clinical geriatric psychopharmacology* (2nd ed., pp. 61-76). Baltimore: Williams & Wilkins.

Abernethy, V. (1984). Compassion, control, and decisions about competency. *American Journal of Psychiatry, 141,* 53-60.

Abou-Saleh, M. T., & Coppen, A. J. (1988). Continuation therapy with antidepressants after electroconvulsive therapy. *Convulsive-Therapy, 4,* 263-268.

Abramson, L. Y., Seligman, M. E. P., & Teasdale, J. Y. (1978). Learned helplessness in humans: Critique and reformulation. *Journal of Abnormal Psychology, 87,* 49-74.

Adams, F. (1988). Emergency intravenous sedation of the delirious medically ill patient. *Journal of Clinical Psychiatry, 49,* 22-26.

Adams, P., Davies, G. T., & Sweetname, P. (1970). Osteoporosis and the effect of aging on bone mass in elderly men and women. *Quarterly Journal of Medicine, 39,* 601-615.

Adams, R. D., & Victor, M. (1981). *Principles of neurology* (2nd ed.). New York: McGraw-Hill.

Adams, R. D., & Victor, M. (1993). *Principles of neurology* (5th ed.). New York: McGraw-Hill.

Adams, S. L., & Waskel, S. A. (1991). Late onset of alcoholism among older midwestern men in treatment. *Psychological Reports, 68,* 432-434.

Adams, W. L., Garry, P. J., Rhyne, R., Hunt, W. C., & Goodwin, J. S. (1990). Alcohol intake in the healthy elderly, changes with age in a cross-sectional and longitudinal study. *Journal of the American Geriatrics Society, 38,* 211-216.

Addonizio, G., & Alexopoulos, G. S. (1993). Affective disorders in the elderly. *International Journal of Geriatric Psychiatry, 8,* 41-47.

Agid, Y., Ruberg, M., Dubois, B., Pillon, B., Cusiman, G., Raisman, R., Cash, R., Lhermitte, F., & Javoy-Agid, F. (1986). Parkinson's disease and dementia. *Clinical Neuropharmacology, 9,* 22-36.

Agnew, H., Webb, W., & Williams, R. L. (1967). Sleep patterns in late and middle-aged males: An EEG study. *Electroencephalography and Clinical Neurophysiology, 23,* 168-171.

Akerstedt, T. (1985). Adjustment of physiological circadian rhythms and the sleep-wake cycle to shift work. In S. Folkard & T. H. Monk (Eds.), *Hours of work: Temporal factors in work scheduling* (pp. 199-210). New York: John Wiley.

Albert, M. S. (1981). Geriatric neuropsychology. *Journal of Consulting and Clinical Psychology, 49,* 835-850.

Albert, M. S. (1988). General issues in geriatric neuropsychology. In M. S. Albert & M. B. Moss (Eds.), *Geriatric neuropsychology* (pp. 3-10). New York: Guilford.

Albert, M. S. (1994). Brief assessments of cognitive function in the elderly. In M. P. Lawton & J. A. Teresi (Eds.), *Annual review of gerontology and geriatrics: Focus on assessment techniques* (pp. 93-106). New York: Springer.

Albert, M. S., & Heaton, R. K. (1988). Intelligence testing. In M. S. Albert & M. B. Moss (Eds.), *Geriatric neuropsychology* (pp. 13-32). New York: Guilford.

Albert, M. S., & Kaplan, E. (1980). Organic implications of neuropsychological deficits in the elderly. In L. W. Poon & J. L. Fozard (Eds.), *New directions in memory and aging* (pp. 403-432). Hillsdale, NJ: Lawrence Erlbaum.

Albert, M. S., & Moss, M. B. (1988). *Geriatric neuropsychology.* New York: Guilford.

Alberts, G. (1991). *Development of a measure of therapist trustworthiness.* Unpublished doctoral dissertation. West Virginia University, Morgantown.

Alberts, G., & Edelstein, B. (1992). *Identifying and measuring therapist behaviors associated with client-perceived trustworthiness.* Paper presented at meeting of the Association for Advancement of Behavior Therapy, Boston, MA.

Alexander, M. P. (1988). Clinical determination of mental competence: A theory and a retrospective study. *Archives of Neurology, 45,* 23-26.

Alexopoulos, G. S. (1992). Treatment of depression. In C. Salzman (Ed.), *Clinical geriatric psychopharmacology* (2nd ed., pp. 137-174). Baltimore: Williams & Wilkins.

Alexopoulos, G. S., Young, R. C., Meyers, B. S., Abrams, R. C., & Shamoian, C. A. (1988). Late-onset depression. *Psychiatric Clinics of North America, 11,* 101-115.

Alford, B. A., & Correia, C. J. (1994). Cognitive therapy of schizophrenia: Theory and empirical status. *Behavior Therapy, 25,* 17-33.

Algase, D., & Tsai, J. (1991). Wandering as a rhythm. *The Gerontologist 31,* 140.

Allebeck, P. (1989). Schizophrenia: A life-shortening disease. *Schizophrenia Bulletin, 15,* 81-90.

Allegrante, J. P., MacKenzie, C. R., Robbins, L., & Cornell, C. N. (1991). Hip fracture in older persons: Does self-efficacy-based intervention have a role in rehabilitation? *Arthritis Care and Research, 4*(1), 39-47.

Alper, P., Gibb, R. P., & Wexler, D. (1993). Improving access to primary care (letter). *JAMA, 269,* 1943-1944.

Altman, W. M., & Parmelee, P. A. (1992). Discrimination based on age: The special case of the institutionalized aged. In D. K. Kagehiro & W. S. Laufer (Eds.), *Handbook of psychology and law* (pp. 408-421). New York: Springer-Verlag.

Altman, W. M., Parmelee, P. A., & Smyer, M. A. (1992). Autonomy, competence, and informed consent in long term care: Legal and psychological perspectives. *Villanova Law Review, 37,* 1671-1704.

American Association of Retired Persons. (no date). *Applied research on health and ethnicity: American Indian and Alaska Native elderly.* Washington, DC: Author, Minority Affairs Special Activities Department.

American Bar Association. (1989). *Guardianship: An agenda for reform—Recommendations of the National Guardianship Symposium and Policy of the American Bar Association.* Washington, DC: Author, Commissions on the Mentally Disabled and on Legal Problems of the Elderly.

American Bar Association. (1990). *Guardianship of the elderly: A primer for attorneys.* Washington, DC: Author, Commission on Legal Problems of the Elderly and Young Lawyers Division, Committee on the Delivery of Legal Services to the Elderly.

American Dietetic Association. (1987). Position of the American Dietetic Association: Nutrition, aging, and the continuum of health care. *Journal of the American Dietetic Association, 87,* 344-346.

American Heart Association. (1990). *Risk Factor Prediction Kit.* Dallas, TX: Author.

American Heart Association. (1991). *1992 Heart and stroke facts.* Chicago: Author.

American Psychiatric Association. (1980). *Diagnostic and statistical manual of mental disorders* (3rd ed.). Washington, DC: Author.

American Psychiatric Association. (1987). *Diagnostic and statistical manual of mental disorders* (3rd ed., rev.). Washington, DC: Author.

American Psychiatric Association. (1994). *Diagnostic and statistical manual of mental disorders* (4th ed.). Washington, DC: Author.

American Psychiatric Association. (1989). *Treatments of psychiatric disorders* (Vol. 2). Washington, DC: Author.

American Sleep Disorders Association. (1990). *The international classification of sleep disorders: Diagnostic and coding manual.* Rochester, MN: Author.

American Society of Addiction Medicine. (1992). *American Society of Addiction Medicine patient placement criteria.* Washington, DC: Author.

Ames, D. (1993). Depressive disorders among elderly people in long-term institutional care. *Australian and New Zealand Journal of Psychiatry, 27,* 379-391.

Ananth, J., Edelmuth, E., & Dargan, B. (1988). Meige's syndrome associated with neuroleptic treatment. *American Journal of Psychiatry, 145,* 513-515.

Ancoli-Israel, S., & Kripke, D. F. (1991). Prevalent sleep problems in the aged. *Biofeedback and Self Regulation, 16,* 349-359.

Ancoli-Israel, S., Kripke, D. F., Mason, W., & Messing, S. (1981). Sleep apnea and nocturnal myoclonus in a senior population. *Sleep, 4,* 349-358.

Ancoli-Israel, S., Parker, L., Sinaee, R., Fell, R. L., & Kripke, D. F. (1989). Sleep fragmentation in patients from a nursing home. *Journal of Gerontology, 44,* M18-M21.

Anderer, S. J. (1990). *Determining competency in guardianship proceedings.* Washington, DC: American Bar Association, Division of Public Services.

Anderson, D. J., Noyes, R., & Crowe, R. R. (1984). A comparison of panic disorder and generalized anxiety disorder. *American Journal of Psychiatry, 141,* 572-575.

Anderson, K. M., Wilson, P. W., Odell, P. M., & Kannel, W. B. (1991). An updated coronary risk profile: A statement for health professionals. *Circulation, 83,* 356-362.

Anderson, M. W., Zendall, S. M., Rosa, D. P., Rubinstein, M. L., Herrera, C. O., Simons, O., Caruso, L., & Spielman, A. J. (1988). Comparison of sleep restriction therapy and stimulus control in older insomniacs. *Sleep Research, 17,* 141.

Andres, R., Elahm, D., Tobin, J. D., Muller, D. C., & Brant, L. (1985). Impact of age on weight goals. *Annals of Internal Medicine, 103,* 1030-1033.

Angermeyer, K., Clark, D., Connelly, T., Ellenor, G., Marion, R., Mitchell, C., & Walsh, T. (1980). *A guide to team development.* Lexington: University of Kentucky, College of Allied Health Professions.

Annas, G. J. (1991). The health care proxy and the living will. *New England Journal of Medicine, 324,* 1210-1213.

Anthony, J. C., & Aboraya, A. (1992). The epidemiology of selected mental disorders in later life. In J. E. Birren, R. B. Sloane, & G. D. Cohen (Eds.), *Handbook of mental health and aging* (2nd ed., pp. 27-73). New York: Academic Press.

Anthony, J. C., LeResche, L., Niaz, U., Von Korff, M. R., & Folstein, M. F. (1982). Limits of the Mini-Mental State as a screening test for dementia and delirium among hospital clients. *Psychological Medicine, 12,* 397-408.

Anthony-Bergstone, C., Zarit, S., & Gatz, M. (1988). Symptoms of psychological distress among caregivers of dementia patients. *Psychology and Aging, 3,* 245-248.

Antonucci, T. C., & Akiyama, H. (1991). Convoys of social support: Generational issues. *Marriage and Family Review, 16,* 103-123.

Antonucci, T. C., & Jackson, J. (1987). Social support, interpersonal efficacy, and health: A life course perspective. In L. L. Carstensen & B. A. Edelstein (Eds.), *Handbook of clinical gerontology* (pp. 291-311). New York: Pergamon.

Appelbaum, P. S., & Grisso, T. (1988). Assessing patients' capacity to consent to treatment. *New England Journal of Medicine, 319,* 1635-1638.

Appelbaum, P. S., & Roth, L. H. (1981). Clinical issues in the assessment of competency. *American Journal of Psychiatry, 138,* 1462-1467.

Appelgate, W. W., Blass, J. P., & Williams, T. F. (1990). Instruments for the functional assessment of older patients. *New England Journal of Medicine, 322,* 1207-1214.

Arana, G. W., & Hyman, S. E. (1991). *Handbook of psychiatric drug therapy* (2nd ed.). Boston: Little, Brown.

Aranow, R. B., Hudson, J. I., Pope, H. G., Jr., Grady T. A., Laage, T. A., Bell, I. R., & Cole, J. O. (1989). Elevated antidepressant plasma blood levels after addition of fluoxetine. *American Journal of Psychiatry, 146,* 911-913.

Aranson, M. D., & Hafez, H. (1986). A case of trazodone-induced ventricular tachycardia. *Journal of Clinical Psychiatry, 47,* 388-389.

Aravelo, G. J., & Gershanik, O. S. (1993). Modulatory effect of clozapine on levodopa response in Parkinson's disease: A preliminary study. *Movement Disorders, 8,* 349-354.

Ardila, A., & Rosselli, M. (1989). Neuropsychological characteristics of normal aging. *Developmental Neuropsychology, 5,* 307-320.

Areen, J. (1987). The legal status of consent obtained from families of adult patients to withhold or withdraw treatment. *Journal of the American Medical Association, 258,* 229-235.

Armitage, R., Trivedi, M., Rush, A. J., & Hoffmann, R. (1995). The effects of fluoxetine on period-analyzed sleep EEG in depression. *Sleep Research, 24,* 381.

Arregul, A., Perry, E. K., Rossor, M., & Tomlinson, B. E. (1982). Angiotensin converting enzyme in Alzheimer's disease: Increased activity in caudate nucleus and cortical areas. *Journal of Neurochemistry, 38,* 1490-1492.

Atkins, P. W. (1984). *The second law.* New York: Scientific American Books.

Atkinson, R. M. (Ed.). (1984). *Substance abuse and use in late life alcohol and drug abuse in old age.* Washington, DC: American Psychiatric Press.

Atkinson, R. M., Tolson, R. L., & Turner, J. A. (1990). Late versus early onset problem drinking in older men. *Alcoholism: Clinical and Experimental Research, 14,* 574-579.

Atkinson, R. M., Tolson, R. L., & Turner, J. A. (1993). Factors affecting outpatient treatment compliance of older male problem drinkers. *Journal of Studies on Alcohol, 54,* 102-106.

Atkinson, R. M., Turner, J. A., Kofoed, L. L., & Tolson, R. L. (1985). Early versus late onset alcoholism in older persons: Preliminary findings. *Alcoholism: Clinical and Experimental Research, 9,* 513-515.

Avery, D., & Silverman, J. (1984). Psychomotor retardation and agitation in depression: Relationship to age, sex, and response to treatment. *Journal of Affective Disorders, 7,* 67-76.

Avorn, J. (1990). The elderly and drug policy: Coming of age. *Health Affairs, 9,* 6-19.

Axelrod, B. N., Jiron, C. C., & Henry, R. R. (1993). Performance of adults aged 20-90 on the Abbreviated Wisconsin Card Sorting Test. *The Clinical Neuropsychologist, 7,* 205-209.

Ayd, F. J. (1994). Prescribing anxiolytics and hypnotics for the elderly. *Psychiatric Annals, 24,* 91-97.

Babcock, R. L., & Salthouse, T. A. (1990). Effects of increased processing demands on age differences in working memory. *Psychology and Aging, 5*, 421-428.

Babin, R. W., & Harker, L. A. (1982). The vestibular system in the elderly. *Otolaryngolic Clinics of North America, 15*, 387-393.

Bachman, D. L., Wolf, P. A., Linn, R., Knoefel, J. E., Cobb, J., Balanger, A., White, L. R., & Agostino, R. B. (1993). Incidence of dementia and probable Alzheimer's disease in a general population: The Framingham study. *Neurology, 43*, 515-519.

Baer, D. J. (1973). The control of developmental processes: Why wait? In J. R. Nesselroade & H. W. Reese (Eds.), *Life-span developmental psychology: Methodological issues* (pp. 187-193). New York: Academic Press.

Bahr, H. M. (1969). Lifetime affiliation patterns of early and late-onset heavy drinkers on skid row. *Quarterly Journal of Studies on Alcohol, 30*, 645-656.

Baigis-Smith, J., Smith, D. J., Rose, M., & Newman, D. K. (1989). Managing urinary incontinence in community-residing elderly persons. *The Gerontologist, 29*, 229-233.

Bailey, M. B., Haberman, P. W., & Alksne, H. (1964). The epidemiology of alcoholism in an urban residential area. *Quarterly Journal of Studies on Alcohol, 26*, 19-40.

Bajulaize, R., & Addonizio, G. (1992). Clozapine in the treatment of psychosis in an 82-year old woman with tardive dyskinesia. *Journal of Clinical Psychopharmacology, 12*, 364-365.

Bak, J. S., & Greene, R. L. (1980). Changes in neuropsychological functioning in an aging population. *Journal of Consulting and Clinical Psychology, 48*, 395-399.

Baker, F. M. (1989). Screening tests for cognitive impairment. *Hospital and Community Psychiatry, 40*, 339-340.

Baker, F. M., Kamikawa, L. M., Espino, D. S., & Manson, S. M. (1990). Rehabilitation in ethnic minority elderly. In S. J. Brody & L. G. Paulson (Eds.), *Aging and rehabilitation: Vol. 2. The state of practice*. New York: Springer.

Balin, A. K., & Pratt, L. A. (1989). Physiological consequences of human skin aging. *Cutis, 43*, 431-436.

Ballinger, B. R., & Ramsey, A. C. (1975). Accidents and drug treatment in a psychiatric hospital. *British Journal of Psychiatry, 126*, 426-430.

Baltes, M. M. (1982). Environmental factors in dependence among nursing home residents: A social ecology analysis. In T. A. Wills (Ed.), Basic processes in helping relationships (pp. 405-425). New York: Academic Press.

Baltes, M. M. (1988). The etiology and maintenance of dependency in the elderly: Three phases of operant research. *Behavior Therapy, 19*, 301-319.

Baltes, M. M. (1995). Dependency in old age: Gains and losses. *Current Directions in Psychological Science, 4*, 14-19.

Baltes, M. M., & Barton, E. M. (1979). Behavioral analysis of aging: A review of the operant model and research. *International Journal of Behavioral Development, 2*, 297-320.

Baltes, M. M., Horgas, A. L., Klingenspor, B., Freund, A., & Carstensen, L. L. (1996). Geschlechtsunterschiede in der Berliner Altersstudie in den bereichen gesundheit, soziale integration, persönlichkeit und selbst [Gender differences in the Berlin Aging Study in the domains of health, social integration, self, and personality]. In K. U. Mayer & P. B. Baltes (Eds.), *The Berlin aging study*. Berlin: Akademie Verlag.

Baltes, M. M., & Lascomb, S. L. (1975). Creating a healthy institutional environment for the elderly via behavior management: The nurse as change agent. *International Journal of Nursing Studies, 12*, 5-12.

Baltes, M. M., Neumann, E. M., & Zank, S. (1994). Maintenance and rehabilitation of independence in old age: An intervention program for staff. *Psychology and Aging, 9*, 179-188.

Baltes, M. M., & Reisenzein, R. (1986). The social word in long-term care institutions: Psychological control toward dependency. In M. M. Baltes & P. B. Baltes (Eds.), *The psychology of control and aging* (pp. 315-343). Hillsdale, NJ: Lawrence Erlbaum.

Baltes, M. M., Reisenzein, R., & Kindermann, T. (1985, July). *Dependence in institutionalized children: An age-comparative analysis.* Poster presented at the 8th Biennial Meeting of the International Society for the Study of Behavioral Development, Tours, France.

Baltes, M. M., & Silverberg, S. B. (1994). The dynamics between dependency and autonomy: Illustrations across the life span. In D. L. Featherman, R. M. Lerner, & M. Perlmutter (Eds.), *Life-span development and behavior* (Vol. 12, pp. 41-90). Hillsdale, NJ: Lawrence Erlbaum.

Baltes, M. M., & Skinner, E. A. (1983). Cognitive performance deficits and hospitalization: Learned helplessness, instrumental passivity, or what? Comments on Raps, Peterson, Jonas, and Seligman. *Journal of Personality and Social Psychology, 45,* 1013-1016.

Baltes, M. M., & Wahl, H. W. (1987). Dependence in aging. In L. L. Carstensen & B. A. Edelstein (Eds.), *Handbook of clinical gerontology* (pp. 204-221). New York: Pergamon.

Baltes, M. M., & Wahl, H. W. (1992). The dependency-support script in institutions: Generalization to community settings. *Psychology and Aging, 7,* 409-418.

Baltes, M. M., Wahl, H. W., & Reichert, M. (1991). Successful aging in long term care institutions? *Annual Review of Gerontology and Geriatrics, 11,* 311-337.

Baltes, M. M., & Zerbe, M. (1976a). Independence training in nursing home residents. *The Gerontologist, 16,* 428-432.

Baltes, M. M., & Zerbe, M. (1976b). Re-establishing self-feeding in a nursing home resident. *Nursing Research, 25,* 24-26.

Baltes, P. B. (1987). Theoretical propositions of life-span developmental psychology: On the dynamics between growth and decline. *Developmental Psychology, 23,* 1013-1016.

Baltes, P. B., & Baltes, M. M. (1990). Selective optimization with compensation. In P. B. Baltes & M. M. Baltes (Eds.), *Successful aging: Perspectives from the behavioral sciences* (pp. 1-34). New York: Cambridge University Press.

Baltes, P. B., & Lindenberger, U. (1988). On the range of cognitive plasticity in old age as a function of experience: 15 years of intervention research. *Behavior Therapy, 19*(3), 283-300.

Baltes, P. B., Reese, H. W., & Lipsitt, L. P. (1980). Life-span developmental psychology. *Annual Review of Psychology, 31,* 65-110.

Baltes, P. B., Smith, J., & Staudinger, U. M. (1992). Wisdom and successful aging. In T. Sonderegger (Ed.), *Nebraska symposium on motivation* (Vol. 39, pp. 123-167). Lincoln: University of Nebraska Press.

Barlow, D. H. (1988). *Anxiety and its disorders.* New York: Guilford.

Barlow, D. H., & Craske, M. G. (1989). *Mastery of your anxiety and panic.* Albany, NY: Graywind.

Barnes, G. (1979). Alcohol use among older persons: Findings from a western New York state general population survey. *Journal of the American Geriatrics Society, 27,* 244-250.

Barnes, J. M., Costall, B., & Coughlan, J. (1990). The effects of ondansetron, a $5\text{-}HT_3$ receptor antagonist on cognition in rodents and primates. *Pharmacology, Biochemistry, and Behavior, 35,* 955-962.

Barrios, B. A. (1988). On the changing nature of behavioral assessment. In A. S. Bellack & M. Hersen (Eds.), *Behavioral assessment: A practical handbook* (3rd ed., pp. 3-41). New York: Pergamon.

Bartels, S., & Liberto, J. G. (1995). Dual diagnosis in the elderly: Double jeapardy: Chronic mental illness and substance use disorders. In A. Lehman & L. Dixon (Eds.), *Substance disorders among persons with chronic mental illnesses.* Chur, Switzerland: Harwood.

Bartoshuk, L. M. (1989). Taste: Robust across the age span? *Annals of the New York Academy of Science, 561,* 65-75.

Bartram, H. P., & Wynder, E. L. (1989). Physical activity and colon cancer risk? Physiologic considerations. *American Journal of Gastroenterology, 84,* 109-112.

Barusch, A. S., & Spaid, W. M. (1989). Gender differences in caregiving: Why do wives report greater burden? *The Gerontologist, 29,* 667-676.

Bassey, E. J., Morgan, K., Dallosso, H. M., & Ebrahim, S. B. J. (1989). Flexibility of the shoulder joint measured as range of abduction in a large representative sample of men and women over 65 years of age. *European Journal of Applied Physiology, 58,* 353-360.

Baum, D., & Gallagher, D. (1985-86). Case studies of psychotherapy with depressed caregivers. *The Clinical Gerontologist, 4,* 19-29.

Baumgarten, M., Becker, R., & Gauthier, S. (1990). Validity and reliability of the Dementia Behavior Disturbance Scale. *Journal of the American Geriatrics Society, 38*(3), 221-226.

Baxter Institute. (1993). *Health habits in the U.S.* Washington, DC: Author.

Bayles, K. A., & Kaszniak, A. W. (1987). *Communication and cognition in normal aging and dementia.* Boston: College-Hill.

Baylor, A. M., & Spirduso, W. W. (1988). Systematic aerobic exercise and components of reaction time in older women. *Journal of Gerontology: Psychological Sciences, 43,* P121-P126.

Beaty, W. W., & Goodkin, D. E. (1990). Screening for cognitive impairment in multiple sclerosis: An evaluation of the Mini-Mental State Examination. *Archives of Neurology, 47,* 297-301.

Bebbington, A. C. (1988). The expectation of life without disability in England and Wales. *Social Science and Medicine, 27,* 321-326.

Beck, A. T. (1972). *Depression: Causes and treatment.* Philadelphia: University of Pennsylvania Press.

Beck, A. T., Rush, J., Shaw, B., & Emery, G. (1979). *Cognitive therapy of depression.* New York: Guilford.

Beck, A., Ward, C., Mendelson, M., Mock, J., & Erbaugh, J. (1961). An inventory for measuring depression. *Archives of General Psychiatry, 4,* 53-58.

Beck, J. C. (1987). Right to refuse antipsychotic medication: Psychiatric assessment and legal decision making, *Mental and Physical Disability Law Reporter, 11,* 368-372.

Beck, J. G., Stanley, M. A., & Zebb, B. J. (1995). Psychometric properties of the Penn State Worry Questionnaire in older adults. *Journal of Clinical Geropsychology, 1,* 33-42.

Beers, M., Avorn, J., Soumerai, S. B., Everitt, D. E., Sherman, D. S., & Salem, S. (1988). Psychoactive medication use in intermediate-care facility residents. *Journal of the American Medical Association, 260,* 3016-3020.

Behar, D., Winokur, G., & Berg, C. J. (1985). Depression in the abstinent alcoholic. *American Journal of Psychiatry, 141,* 1105-1107.

Bell, B., Wolf, E., & Bernholtz, C. D. (1972). Depth perception as a function of age. *Aging and Human Development, 3,* 77-81.

Bell, D., Kasschau, P., & Zellman, G. (1976). *Delivering services to elderly members of minority groups: A critical review of the literature.* Santa Monica, CA: RAND.

Bell, M. R., Holmes, D. R., Berger, P. B., Garrett, K. N., Bailey, K. R., & Gesh, B. J. (1993). Changing in-hospital mortality of women undergoing PCTA. *JAMA, 269,* 2091.

Belloc, N., & Breslow, L. (1972). Relationship of physical health study and health practices. *Preventive Medicine, 1,* 409-421.

Benca, R. M. (1994). Mood disorders. In M. H. Kryger, T. Roth, & W. C. Dement (Eds.), *Principles and practice of sleep medicine* (2nd ed., pp. 899-913). Philadelphia: W. B. Saunders.

Benca, R. M., Obermeyer, W. H., Thisted, R. A., & Gillin, J. C. (1992). Sleep and psychiatric disorders: A meta-analysis. *Archives of General Psychiatry, 49,* 651-668.

Bengtson, V. (1979). Ethnicity and aging: Problems and issues in current social science inquiry. In D. E. Gelfand & A. J. Kutzik (Eds.), *Ethnicity and aging: Theory, research, and policy.* New York: Springer.

Benton, A. L., Eslinger, P. J., & Damasio, A. R. (1981). Normative observations on neuropsychological performances in old age. *Journal of Clinical Neuropsychology, 3,* 33-42.

Benton, A., & Tranel, D. (1993). Visuoperceptual, visuospatial, and visuoconstructive disorders. In K. M. Heilman & E. Valenstein (Eds.), *Clinical neuropsychology* (3rd ed.). New York: Oxford University Press.

Berger, R. M. (1982). *Gay and gray.* Urbanna: University of Illinois Press.

Berger, R. M. (1992). Research on older gay men: What we know, what we need to know. In N. J. Woodman (Eds.), *Lesbian and gay lifestyles: A guide for counseling and education* (pp. 217-234). New York: Irvington.

Berger, R. M., & Kelly, J. J. (1986). Working with homosexuals of the older population. *Social Casework: The Journal of Contemporary Social Work, 4,* 203-210.

Bergman, M. (1971). Hearing and aging. *Audiology, 10,* 164-171.

Bergman, M., Blumenfeld, V. G., Cascardo, D., Dash, B., Levitt, H., & Margulies, M. K. (1976). Age-related decrement in hearing for speech: Sampling and longitudinal studies. *Journal of Gerontology, 31,* 533-538.

Berkman, L. F., & Syme, L. (1979). Social networks, host resistance, and mortality: A nine-year follow-up study of Alameda county residents. *American Journal of Epidemiology, 109,* 186-204.

Bernardi, F., & Del Zompo, M. (1990). Clozapine in idiopathic Parkinson's disease. *Neurology, 40,* 1151.

Bernier, J. J., Vidon, N., & Mignon, M. (1973). The value of a cooperative multicenter study for establishing a table of normal values for gastric acid secretion and as a function of sex, age, and weight. *Biologie et Gastro-Enterologie (Paris), 6,* 287-296.

Bernstein, D. A., Borkovec, T. D., & Coles, M. G. H. (1986). Assessment of anxiety. In A. R. Ciminero, K. S. Calhoun, & H. E. Adams (Eds.), *Handbook of behavioral assessment* (2nd ed., pp. 353-403). New York: John Wiley.

Bernstein, L., Ross, R., Lobo, X., Hanisch, R., & Henderson, B. E. (1987). The effect of moderate physical activity on menstrual cycle pattern in adolescence: Implications for breast cancer prevention. *British Journal of Cancer, 55,* 681-685.

Berrios, G. E., & Bakshi, N. (1991). Manic and depressive symptoms in the elderly: Their relationships to treatment outcome, cognition and motor symptoms. *Psychopathology, 24,* 31-38.

Bertram, M. (1989). The use of landmarks. *Journal of Gerontological Nursing, 15*(2), 6-8.

Bess, F. H., Lichtenstein, M. J., Logan, S. A., Burger, M. C., et. al. (1989). Hearing impairment as a determinant of function in the elderly. *Journal of the American Geriatrics Society, 37,* 123-128.

Bickel, H. (1989). Wahrscheinlichkeit und Dauer einer stationèren Pflege im Alter [Probability and duration of care for the elderly in nursing homes]. *Das Üffentliche Gesundheitswesen, 51,* 661-673.

Bieliauskas, L. A., Klawans, H. L., & Glantz, R. H. (1986). Depression and cognitive changes in Parkinson's disease: A review. *Advances in Neurology, 45,* 437-438.

Billig, N., Cohen-Mansfield, J., & Lipson, S. (1991). Pharmacological treatment of agitation in a nursing home: One possible role of sub-typing. *Journal of the American Geriatrics Society, 39*(10), 1002-1005.

Binstock, R. H., & George, L. K. (1990). *Handbook of aging and the social sciences.* San Diego: Academic Press.

Birren, J. E., & Schaie, K. W. (Eds.). (1990). *Handbook of the psychology of aging* (3rd ed.). San Diego: Academic Press.

Blackburn, I. M., Eunson, K. M., & Bishop, S. (1986). A two-year naturalistic follow-up of depressed patients treated with cognitive therapy, pharmacotherapy, and a combination of both. *Journal of Affective Disorders, 10,* 67-75.

Blackburn, P. (1988). Freedom to wander. *Nursing Times, 84*(49), 54-55.

Blackford, R. C., & LaRue, A. (1989). Criteria for diagnosing age-associated memory impairment: Proposed improvements in the field. *Developmental Neuropsychology, 5,* 295-306.

Blair, S., Kohl, H. W., Paffenbarger, R. S., Jr., Clark, D. G., Cooper, K. H., & Gibbons, L. W. (1989). Physical fitness and all-cause mortality: A prospective study of healthy men and women. *Journal of the American Medical Association, 262,* 2395-2401.

Blanchard, J. J., & Neale, J. M. (1994). The neuropsychological signature of schizophrenia: Generalized or differential deficit? *American Journal of Psychiatry, 151*, 40-48.

Blank, K. (1987). Depressive illness in the elderly: Legal and ethical issues. In R. Rosner & H. I. Schwartz (Eds.), *Geriatric psychiatry and the law* (pp. 167-187). New York: Plenum.

Blascovich, J., & Katkin, E. S. (Eds.). (1993). *Cardiovascular reactivity to psychological stress and disease.* Washington, DC: American Psychological Association.

Blass, J. P., & Barclay, L. L. (1985). New developments in the diagnosis of dementia. *Drug Development Research, 5*, 39-58.

Blazer, D. (1986). Depression. *Generations, 10*, 21-23.

Blazer, D. (1989a). The epidemiology of depression in late life. *Journal of Geriatric Psychiatry, 22*, 35-52.

Blazer, D. (1989b). The epidemiology of psychiatric disorders in late life. In E. W. Busse & D. G. Blazer (Eds.), *Geriatric Psychiatry* (pp. 235-260). Washington, DC: American Psychiatric Press.

Blazer, D. (1993). *Depression in late life* (2nd ed.). St. Louis, MO: Mosby Year Book.

Blazer, D., Bachar, J. R., & Hughes, D. C. (1987). Major depression with melancholia: A comparison of middle-aged and elderly adults. *Journal of the American Geriatric Society, 35*, 927-932.

Blazer, D., Bachar, J., & Manton, K. (1986). Suicide in late life: Review and commentary. *Journal of the American Geriatrics Society, 34*, 519-525.

Blazer, D., George, L., & Hughes, D. (1991). The epidemiology of anxiety: An age comparison. In C. Salzman & B. D. Lebowitz (Eds.), *Anxiety in the elderly.* New York: Springer.

Blazer, D., George, L., Landerman, R., Pennybacker, M., Melville, M. L., Woodbury, M., Manton, K. G., Jordan, K., & Locke, B. (1985). Psychiatric disorders: A rural/urban comparison. *Archives of General Psychiatry, 149*, 574-583.

Blazer, D., & Williams, C. D. (1980). Epidemiology of dysphoria and depression in an elderly population. *American Journal of Psychiatry, 137*, 439-444.

Blazer, D. G. (1982a). *Depression in late life.* St. Louis, MO: C. V. Mosby.

Blazer, D. G. (1982b). Social support and mortality in an elderly community population. *American Journal of Epidemiology, 115*, 684-694.

Blazer, D. G., Burchett, B., Service, C., & George, L. K. (1991). The association of age and depression among the elderly: An epidemiologic exploration. *Journal of Gerontology, 46*, 210-215.

Blazer, D. G., Hughes, D. C., & George, L. K. (1987). The epidemiology of depression in an elderly community population. *The Gerontologist, 27*, 281-287.

Bleeker, M. L., Bolla-Wilson, K., Kawas, C., & Agnew, J. (1988). Age-specific norms for the Mini-Mental State Exam. *Neurology, 38*, 1565-1568.

Blessed, G., Tomlinson, B. E., & Roth, M. (1968). The association between quantitative measures of dementia and of senile change in the cerebral grey matter of elderly subjects. *British Journal of Psychiatry, 114*, 797-811.

Bleuler, E. (1908/1950). *Dementia praecox or the group of schizophrenias* (J. Zinkin, Trans.). New York: International Universities Press.

Bleuler, M. (1978). *The schizophrenic disorders: Long-term patient and family studies.* New Haven, CT: Yale University Press.

Blieszner, R. (1993). Socialist-feminist perspective on widowhood. *Journal of Aging Studies, 7*, 171-182.

Bliwise, D. L. (1993). Sleep in normal aging and dementia. *Sleep, 16*, 40-81.

Bliwise, D. L. (1994). Normal aging. In M. H. Kryger, T. Roth, & W. C. Dement (Eds.), *Principles and practice of sleep medicine* (2nd ed., pp. 26-39). Philadelphia: W. B. Saunders.

Block, A. J. (1983). Neuropsychological aspects of oxygen therapy. *Respiratory Care, 28*, 885-888.

Blow, F. C., Brower, K. J., Schulenberg, J. E., Demo-Dananberg, L. M., Young, K. J., & Beresford, T. P. (1992). The Michigan Alcoholism Screening Test: Geriatric Version (MAST-G): A new elderly-specific screening instrument. *Alcoholism: Clinical Experimental Research, 16,* 172.

Blumenthal, J. A., Emery, G. F., Madden, D. J., George, L. K., Coleman, R. E., Riddle, M. W., McKee, D. C., Reasoner, J., & Williams, R. S. (1989). Cardiovascular and behavioral effects of aerobic exercise training in healthy older men and women. *Journal of Gerontology: Medical Sciences, 44,* M147-M157.

Blumenthal, M. D. (1975). Measuring depressive symptomatology in the general population. *Archives of General Psychiatry, 32,* 971-978.

Bolla, K. I., Lindgren, K. N., Bonaccorsy, C., & Bleecker, M. L. (1990). Predictors of verbal fluency (FAS) in the healthy elderly. *Journal of Clinical Psychology, 46,* 623-628.

Bolla, K. I., Lindgren, K. N., Bonaccorsy, C., & Bleecker, M. L. (1991). Memory complaints in older adults. *Archives of Neurology, 48,* 61-64.

Bolla-Wilson, K., Robinson, R. G., Starkstein, S. E., Boston, J., & Price, T. R. (1989). Lateralization of dementia of depression in stroke patients. *American Journal of Psychiatry, 146,* 627-634.

Boller, F. (1980). Mental status of patients with Parkinson's disease. *Journal of Clinical Neuropsychology, 2,* 157-172.

Boller, F., Mizutani, T., & Roessmann, V. (1980). Parkinson's disease, dementia and Alzheimer's disease: Clinicopathological correlations. *Annals of Neurology, 1,* 329-335.

Bond, G. R., Miller, L. D., Krumwied, M. H. A., & Ward, R. S. (1988). Assertive case management in three CMHCs: A controlled study. *Hospital and Community Psychiatry, 39,* 411-418.

Bond, G. R., Witheridge, T. F. Setze, P. J., & Dincin, J. (1985). Preventing rehospitalization of clients in a psychosocial rehabilitation program. *Hospital and Community Psychiatry, 36,* 993-995.

Bondareff, W. (1983). Age and Alzheimer's disease. *Lancet, 1,* 1447.

Bondareff, W., Mountjoy, C. Q., & Roth, M. (1982). Loss of neurons or origin of the adrenergic projection to cerebral cortex (nucleus locus ceruleus) in senile dementia. *Neurology, 32,* 164-168.

Bonita, R. (1992). Epidemiology of stroke. *Lancet, 339,* 342-344.

Bonnet, M. H. (1984). The restoration of performance following sleep deprivation in geriatric normal and insomniac subjects. *Sleep Research, 13,* 188.

Bonnet, M. H., & Johnson, L. C. (1978). Relationship of arousal threshold to sleep stage distribution and subjective estimates of depth and quality of sleep. *Sleep, 1,* 161-168.

Bootzin, R. R. (1972). Stimulus control treatment for insomnia. In *Proceedings of the 80th Annual Convention of the American Psychological Association* (pp. 395-396). Washington, DC: American Psychiatric Association.

Bootzin, R. R. (1977). Effects of self-control procedures for insomnia. In R. B. Stuart (Ed.), *Behavioral self-management: Strategies and outcomes* (pp. 176-195). New York: Brunner/Mazel.

Bootzin, R. R., & Engle-Friedman, M. (1981). The assessment of insomnia. *Behavioral Assessment, 3,* 107-126.

Bootzin, R. R., Epstein, D., & Wood, J. M. (1991). Stimulus control instructions. In P. Hauri (Ed.), *Case studies in insomnia* (pp. 19-28). New York: Plenum.

Bootzin, R. R., Manber, R., Perlis, M. L., Salvio, M., & Wyatt, J. K. (1993). Sleep disorders. In P. B. Sutker & H. E. Adams (Eds.), *Comprehensive handbook of psychopathology* (2nd ed., pp. 531-561). New York: Plenum.

Bootzin, R. R., & Nicassio, P. (1978). Behavioral treatments for insomnia. In M. Hersen, R. M. Eisler, & P. M. Miller (Eds.), *Progress in behavior modification* (Vol. 6). New York: Academic Press.

Bootzin, R. R., & Perlis, M. L. (1992). Nonphamacologic treatments of insomnia. *Journal of Clinical Psychiatry, 53*(Suppl. 6), 37-41.

Borchelt, M., Horgas, A. L., & Steinhagen-Thiessen, E. (1993, November). *The bidirectional relationship between polypharmacy and functional health in late life.* Paper presented at the 46th Annual Scientific Meeting of the Gerontological Society of America.

Borgatta, E. F., Montgomery, R. J. V., & Borgatta, M. L. (1982). Alcohol use and abuse, life crisis events, and the elderly. *Residential Aging, 4,* 378-405.

Bornstein, R. A., & Kelly, M. (1991). Risk factors for stroke and neuropsychological performance. In R. A. Bornstein & G. G. Brown (Eds.), *Neurobehavioral aspects of cerebrovascular disease* (pp. 182-201). New York: Oxford University Press.

Bornstein, R. F. (1993). *The dependent personality.* New York: Guilford.

Borson, S., Barnes, R. A., Kukull, W. A., Okimoto, J. T., Veith, R. C., Inui, T. S., Carter, W., & Raskind, M. A. (1986). Symptomatic depression in elderly medical outpatients. *Journal of American Geriatrics Society, 34,* 341-347.

Borson, S., & McDonald, G. J. (1989). Depression and chronic obstructive pulmonary disease. In R. G. Robinson & P. V. Rabins (Eds.), *Depression and coexisting disease* (pp. 40-60). New York: Igaku-Shoin.

Bortz, W. (1982). Disuse and aging. *Journal of the American Medical Association, 248,* 1203-1207.

Bortz, W. (1984). The disuse syndrome. *Western Journal of Medicine, 141,* 67-74.

Bortz, W. (1985). Physical exercise as an evolutionary force. *Journal of Human Evolution, 14,* 145-156.

Bortz, W. (1986). Aging as entropy. *Experimental Gerontology, 21,* 321-328.

Bortz, W. (1987). Redefining human aging. *Journal of the American Geriatrics Society, 37,* 1092-1096.

Bortz, W. (1990). The trajectory of dying: Functional status in the last year of life. *Journal of the American Geriatrics Society, 38,* 146-150.

Bortz, W. M. (1993). The physics of frailty. *Journal of the American Geriatrics Society, 41,* 1004-1008.

Boswell, T. D., & Curtis, J. R. (1983). *The Cuban-American experience: Culture, images, and perspectives.* Totowa, NJ: Rowman & Allanheld.

Botwinick, J. (1977). Intellectual abilities. In J. Birren & K. W. Schaie (Eds.), *Handbook of the psychology of aging.* New York: Van Nostrand Reinhold.

Bouchard, R. H., Pourcher, E., & Vincent, P. (1989). Fluoxetine and extrapyramidal side effects. *American Journal of Psychiatry, 146,* 1352-1353.

Bowden, C. L., Bragger, A. M., Swann, A. C., Calabrese, J. R., Janicak, P. G., Petty, F., Dilsaner, S. C., Davis, J. M., Rush, A. J., Small, J. G., Garza-Trevino, E. S., Goodnick, P. J., & Morris, D. D. (1994). Efficacy of divalproex vs. lithium and placebo in the treatment of mania. *JAMA, 271,* 918-924.

Bowman, B. B., & Rosenberg, I. H. (1983). Digestive function and aging. *Human Nutrition: Clinical Nutrition, 37C,* 75-89.

Bozzola, F. G., Gorelick, P. B., & Freels, S. (1992). Personality changes in Alzheimer's disease. *Archives of Neurology, 49,* 297-300.

Brabbins, C. J., Dewey, M. E., Copeland, J. R. M., Davidson, I. A., & McWilliam, C. (1993). Insomnia in the elderly: Prevalence, gender differences and relationships with morbidity and mortality. *International Journal of Geriatric Psychiatry, 8,* 473-480.

Bradley, W., Timm, G. W., & Scott, F. B. (1974). Innervation of the detrusor muscle and urethra. In *Symposium on Neurogenic Bladder, Urologic Clinics of North America* (Vol. 1, pp. 3-27). Philadelphia: W. B. Saunders.

Branch, L. G., Horowitz, A., & Carr, C. (1989). The implications for everyday life of incident self-reported visual decline among people over age 65 living in the community. *The Gerontologist, 29,* 359-365.

Branch, L. G., Katz, S., Kniepman, K., & Papsidero, J. A. (1984). A prospective study of functional status among community elders. *American Journal of Public Health, 74,* 266-268.

Branconnier, R. J., Cole, J. O., & Ghazvimian, S. (1983). Clinical pharmacology of buproprion and imipramine in elderly depressives. *Journal of Clinical Psychiatry, 44*(5, Sec. 2), 130-133.

Brandt, J., Spencer, M., & Folstein, M. (1988). The telephone interview for cognitive status. *Neuropsychiatry, Neuropsychology, and Behavioral Neurology, 1,* 111-117.

Brangman, S. (1992). The mouth. In R. Ham (Ed.), *Primary care geriatrics* (2nd ed., pp. 498-504). St. Louis, MO: Mosby Year Book.

Brauer, P. M., Slavin, J. L., & Marlett, J. A. (1981). Apparent digestibility of neutral detergent fiber in elderly and young adults. *American Journal of Clinical Nutrition, 34,* 1061-1070.

Breakwell, S. L., & Walker, S. N. (1988). Differences in physical health, social interaction, and personal adjustment between continent and incontinent homebound aged women. *Journal of Community Health, 5,* 19.

Brennan, P. L., & Moos, R. H. (1991). Functioning, life context, and help-seeking among late-onset problem drinkers: Comparisons with nonproblem and early-onset problem drinkers. *British Journal of Addiction, 86,* 1139-1150.

Brenner, M. H., Curbow, B., Javitt, J. C., Legro, M. W., & Sommer, A. (1993). Vision change and quality of life in the elderly: Response to cataract surgery and treatment of other chronic ocular conditions. *Archives of Ophthalmology, 3,* 680-685.

Breslow, L., & Somers, A. (1977). The lifetime health monitoring program: Practical approaches to preventive medicine. *New England Journal of Medicine, 296,* 601-609.

Bressler, R., & Katz, M. (1993). Drug therapy for geriatric depression. *Drugs and Aging, 3,* 195-219.

Bridge, T. P., & Wyatt, R. J. (1980a). Paraphrenia: Paranoid states of late life: 1. European research. *Journal of the American Geriatric Society, 28,* 193-200.

Bridge, T. P., & Wyatt, R. J. (1980b). Paraphrenia: Paranoid states of late life: 2. American research. *Journal of the American Geriatrics Society, 28,* 201-205.

Bridges-Parlet, S., Knopman, D., & Thompson, T. (1994). A descriptive study of physically aggressive behavior in dementia by direct observation. *Journal of the American Geriatric Society, 42,* 192-197.

Broadhead, J., & Jacoby, R. (1990). Mania in old age: A first prospective study. *International Journal of Geriatric Psychiatry, 5,* 215-222.

Brock, D. B., Guralnik, J. M., & Brody, J. A. (1990). Demography and epidemiology of aging in the United States. In E. L. Schneider & J. W. Rowe (Eds.), *The handbook of the biology of aging* (3rd ed., pp. 3-23). New York: Academic Press.

Brocklehurst, J. C. (1978). The large bowel. In J. C. Brocklehurst (Ed.), *Textbook of geriatric medicine and gerontology.* New York: Churchill Livingstone.

Brocklehurst, J. C., & Dillane, J. B. (1966). Studies of the female bladder in old age: 1. Cystometrograms in non-incontinent women. *Gerontologia Clinica, 8,* 306-319.

Brody, E. (1981). Women in the middle and family help to older people. *The Gerontologist, 21(5),* 471-480.

Brody, E., Hoffman, C., Kleban, M. H., & Schoonover, C. B. (1989). Caregiving daughters and their local siblings: Perceptions, strains, and interactions. *The Gerontologist, 29,* 529-538.

Brody, H. (1955). Organization of cerebral cortex: 3. A study of aging in the human cerebral cortex. *Journal of Comparative Neurology, 102,* 511-556.

Brooks, G. A., & Fahey, T. D. (1984). *Exercise physiology: Human bioenergetics and its applications.* New York: John Wiley.

Brouwer, W. H., Waterink, W., Van-Wolffelaar, P. C., & Rothengatter, T. (1991). Divided attention in experienced young and older drivers: Lane tracking and visual analysis in a dynamic driving simulator [Special Issue: Safety and mobility of elderly drivers: Part 1]. *Human Factors, 33,* 573-582.

Broverman, I. K., Broverman, D. M., Clarkson, F. E., Rosenkrantz, P. S., & Vogel, S. R. (1970). Sex-role stereotypes and clinical judgments of mental health. *Journal of Consulting and Clinical Psychology, 34,* 1-7.

Brower, K. J., Mudd, S., Blow, F. C., Young, J. P., & Hill, E. M. (1994). Severity and treatment of alcohol withdrawal in elderly versus young patients. *Alcoholism Clinical and Experimental Research, 18,* 196-201.

Brown, D. R. (1992). Physical activity, aging, and psychological well-being: An overview of the research. *Canadian Journal of Sport Sciences, 17,* 185-193.

Brown, M. M., & Hachinski, V. (1989). Vascular dementia. *Current Opinion in Neurology and Neurosurgery, 2,* 78-84.

Brown, R., Sweeney, J., Loutsch, E., Kocsis, J., & Reich, T. (1984). Involutional melancholia revisited. *American Journal of Psychiatry, 141,* 24-28.

Brown, R. G., & Marsden, C. D. (1988). "Subcortical dementia": The neuropsychological evidence. *Neuroscience, 25,* 363-387.

Brown, S. L., Salive, M. E., Pahor, M., Foley, D. J., Corti, C., Langlois, J. A., Wallace, R. B., & Harris, T. B. (1995). Occult caffeine as a source of sleep problems in an older population. *Journal of the American Geriatric Society, 43,* 860-864.

Browning, M. A. (1990). Depression. In M. O. Hogstel (Ed.), *Geropsychiatric nursing* (pp. 130-176). St. Louis, MO: C. V. Mosby.

Brummel-Smith, K. (1992). Stroke. In R. Ham (Ed.), *Primary care geriatrics* (2nd ed., pp. 633-642). St. Louis, MO: Mosby Year Book.

Bruner, A., & Norris, T. (1971). Age related changes in caloric nystagmus. *Acta Otolaryngolica,* Suppl., 282.

Brust, J. C. M. (1989). Cerebral infarction. In L. P. Rowland (Ed.), *Merritt's textbook of neurology* (8th ed., pp. 206-214). Philadelphia: Lea & Febiger.

Buchner, D. M., & Larson, E. B. (1987). Falls and fractures in patients with Alzheimer-type dementia. *JAMA, 257*(11), 1492-1495.

Buchsbaum, D. G., Buchanan, R. G., Lawton, M. J., & Schnoll, S. H. (1991). Alcohol consumption patterns in a primary care population. *Alcohol and Alcoholism, 26,* 215-220.

Buff, D. D., Brenner, R., Kirtane, S. S., & Gilboa, R. (1991). Dysrrhythmia associated with fluoxetine treatment in an elderly patient with cardiac disease. *Journal of Clinical Psychiatry, 52,* 174-176.

Buist, A. S. (1990). Reflections on the rise in asthma morbidity and mortality. *JAMA, 264,* 1719-1720.

Burgio, K. L. (1992). Biofeedback therapy. In J. T. Benson (ed.), *Female pelvic floor disorders: Investigation and management.* New York: Norton.

Burgio, K. L., & Burgio, L. D. (1989). Institutional staff training and management: A review of the literature and a model for geriatric long-term care facilities. *International Journal on Aging and Human Development, 30*(4), 287-302.

Burgio, K., Burgio, L. D., McCormick, K. A., & Engel, B. T. (1991). Assessing toileting skills and habits in an adult day care center. *Journal of Gerontological Nursing, 17,* 32-35.

Burgio, K. L., & Engel, B. T. (1990). Biofeedback-assisted behavioral training for elderly men and women. *Journal of the American Geriatrics Society, 38,* 338-340.

Burgio, K. L., Ives, D. G., Locher, J. L., Arena, V. C., & Kuller, L. H. (1994). Treatment seeking for urinary incontinence in older adults. *Journal of the American Geriatrics Society, 42,* 208-212.

Burgio, K. L., Pearce, K. L., & Lucco, A. J. (1989). *Staying dry: A practical guide to bladder control.* Baltimore: Johns Hopkins University Press.

Burgio, K. L., Robinson, J. C., & Engel, B. T. (1986). The role of biofeedback in Kegel exercise training for stress urinary incontinence. *American Journal of Obstetrics and Gynecology, 157,* 58-64.

Burgio, K. L., Stutzman, R. E., & Engel, B. T. (1989). Behavioral training for post-prostatectomy urinary incontinence. *Journal of Urology, 141,* 303-306.

Burgio, K. L., Whitehead, W. E., & Engel, B. T. (1985). Urinary incontinence in the elderly: Bladder-sphincter biofeedback and toileting skills training. *Annals of Internal Medicine, 104,* 507-515.

Burgio, L., Engel, B., Hawkins, A., McCormick, K., Sheve, A., & Jones, L. (1990). A staff management system for maintaining improvements in continence with elderly nursing home residents. *Journal of Applied Behavior Analysis, 23*(1), 111-118.

Burgio, L., Engel, B. T., McCormick, K., Hawkins A., & Sheve A. (1988). Behavioral treatment for urinary incontinence in elderly inpatients: Initial attempts to modify prompting and toileting procedures. *Behavior Therapy, 19,* 345-357.

Burgio, L. D., Burgio, K. L., Engel, B. T., & Tice, L. M. (1986). Increasing distance and independence of ambulation in elderly nursing home residents. *Journal of Applied Behavioral Analysis, 19,* 357-366.

Burgio, L. F., Jones, L. T., Butler, F., & Engel, B. T. (1988). Behavior problems in an urban nursing home. *Journal of Gerontological Nursing, 14*(1), 31-34.

Burke, L. B., Jolson, H. M., Goetsch, R. A., & Ahronheim, J. C. (1992). In J. W. Rowe & J. C. Ahronheim (Eds.), *Annual Review of Gerontology and Geriatrics: Vol. 12. Focus on medications and the elderly* (pp. 1-28). New York: Springer.

Burke, R. E., Fahn, S., Jankovic, J., Marsden, C., Lang, A., Gollomp, S., & Ilson, J. (1982). Tardive dystonia: Late-onset and persistent dystonia caused by antipsychotic drugs. *Neurology, 32,* 1335-1346.

Burke, W. J., Rubin, E. H., Zorumski, C. F., & Wetzel, R. D. (1987). The safety of ECT in geriatric psychiatry. *Journal of the American Geriatrics Society, 35,* 516-521.

Burke, W. J., Rutherford, J. L., Zorumski, C. F., & Reich, T. (1985). Electroconvulsive therapy and the elderly. *Comprehensive Psychiatry, 26,* 80-86.

Burns, A. (1991). Affective symptoms in Alzheimer's disease. *International Journal of Geriatric Psychiatry, 6,* 371-376.

Burns, A., Jacoby, R., & Levy, R. (1990). Behavioral abnormalities and psychiatric symptoms in Alzheimer's disease: Preliminary findings. *International Psychogeriatrics, 2*(1), 25-36.

Burns, B. S., & Taube, C. A. (1990). Mental health services in general medical care and in nursing homes. In B. S. Fogel, A. Furino, & G. L. Gottlieb (Eds.), *Mental health policy for older Americans: Protecting minds at risk* (pp. 63-84). Washington, DC: American Psychiatric Press.

Burns, D., & Nolen-Hoeksema, S. (1991). Coping styles, homework assignments and the effectiveness of cognitive-behavioral therapy. *Journal of Consulting and Clinical Psychology, 59,* 305-311.

Burns, P. A., Pranikoff, K., Nochajski, T., Desotelle, P., & Harwood, M. K. (1990). Treatment of stress incontinence with pelvic floor exercises and biofeedback. *Journal of the American Geriatrics Society, 38,* 341-344.

Burns, P. A., Pranikoff, K., Nochajski, T. H., Hadley, E. C., Levy, K. J., & Ory, M. G. (1993). A comparison of effectiveness of biofeedback and pelvic muscle exercise treatment of stress incontinence in older community-dwelling women. *Journal of Gerontology: Medical Sciences, 38,* M167-M174.

Burnside, I. M. (1980). Wandering behavior. In I. M. Burnside (Ed.), *Psychosocial nursing care of the aged* (2nd ed.). New York: McGraw-Hill.

Burton, J. R., Pearce, K. L., Burgio, K. L., Engel, B. T., & Whitehead, W. E. (1988). Behavioral training for urinary incontinence in elderly ambulatory patients. *Journal of the American Geriatrics Society, 36,* 693-698.

Burton, L. M. (1992). Black grandparents rearing children of drug-addicted parents: Stressors, outcomes, and social service needs. *The Gerontologist, 32*(6), 744-751.

Busse, E. W. (1975). Aging and psychiatric diseases of late life. In M. F. Reiser (Ed.), *American handbook of psychiatry* (Vol. 4, pp. 67-89). New York: Basic Books.

Butler, F. R., Burgio, L. D., & Engel, B. T. (1987). Neuroleptics and behavior: A comparative study. *Journal of Gerontological Nursing, 13*(6), 15-19.

Butler, J. P., & Barnett, C. A. (1991). Window of wandering. *Geriatric Nursing, 12*(5), 226-227.

Butler, R. N. (1969). Ageism: Another form of bigotry. *The Gerontologist, 9*, 243-246.

Butler, R. N. (1989). Sexual problems in the elderly: The use and abuse of medications. A Geriatrics panel discussion. *Geriatrics, 44*, 61-71.

Butler, R. N., & Lewis, M. I. (1993). *Love and sex after 60*. New York: Ballantine.

Butler, R. N., Lewis, M., & Sunderland, T. (1991). *Aging and mental health: Positive psychosocial and biomedical approaches*. New York: Merrill.

Cain, W. S., Reid, F., & Stevens, J. C. (1990). Missing ingredients: Aging and the discrimination of flavor. *Journal of Nutrition in the Elderly, 9*, 3-15.

Cain, W. S., & Stevens, J. C. (1989). Uniformity of olfactory loss in aging. *Annals of the New York Academy of Science, 561*, 29-38.

Caine, E. D. (1993). Should age-associated cognitive decline be included in DSM-IV? *The Journal of Neuropsychiatry and Clinical Neurosciences, 5*, 1-5.

Calahan, D., & Cisin, I. H. (1968). American drinking practices: Summary of findings from a national probability sample. *Quarterly Journal on Studies of Alcohol, 29*, 130-151.

Callahan, C. M. (1992). Psychiatric symptoms in elderly patients due to medications. In J. W. Rowe & J. C. Ahronheim (Eds.), *Annual review of gerontology and geriatrics* (Vol. 12, pp. 41-75). New York: Springer.

Campbell, A., Converse, P. E., & Rodgers, W. L. (1976). *The quality of American life*. New York: Russell Sage.

Campbell, S. S., Dawson, D., & Anderson, M. W. (1993). Alleviation of sleep maintenance insomnia with time exposure to bright light. *Journal of the American Geriatrics Society, 41*, 829-836.

Candy, S. E., Troll, L. W., & Levy, S. O. (1981). A developmental exploration of friendship functions in women. *Psychology of Women Quarterly, 5*, 456-472.

Cannell, C. F., & Kahn, R. L. (1968-1969). Interviewing. In G. Lindzey & E. Aronson (Eds.), *The handbook of social psychology* (2nd ed., Vol. 2, pp. 526-595). Reading, MA: Addison-Wesley.

Cannici, J., Malcolm, R., & Peek, L. (1983). Treatment of insomnia in cancer patients using muscle relaxation training. *Journal of Behavior Therapy and Experimental Psychiatry, 14*, 251-256.

Caplan, L. (1990). Cerebrovascular disease. In W. Abrams & R. Berkow (Eds.), *The Merck manual of geriatrics* (pp. 948-973). Rahway, NJ: Merck.

Cardiac Arrhythmia Suppression Trial Investigators. (1989). Preliminary report: Effect of encainide and flecainide on mortality in a randomized trial of arrhythmia suppression after myocardial infarction. *New England Journal of Medicine, 321*, 406-412.

Cardiac Arrhythmia Suppression Trial Investigators. (1992). Effect of the antiarrhythmic agent moricizine on survival after myocardial infarction. *New England Journal of Medicine, 327*, 227-233.

Cardozo, L. D., Abrams, P. D., Stanton, S. L., & Feneley, R. C. L. (1978). Idiopathic bladder instability treated by biofeedback. *British Journal of Urology, 50*, 27-30.

Cardozo, L. D., Stanton, S. L., Hafner, J., & Allan, V. (1978). Biofeedback in the treatment of detrusor instability. *British Journal of Urology, 50*, 250-254.

Carlsson, A. (1988). The current status of the dopamine hypothesis of schizophrenia. *Neuropsychopharmacology, 1*, 179-186.

Carney, R. M., Rich, M. W., Freedland, K. E., Saini, J., Tevelde, A., Simeone, C., & Clark, K. (1988). Major depressive disorder predicts cardiac events in patients with coronary artery disease. *Psychosomatic Medicine, 50*, 627-633.

Carrillo, C. (1990). Application of refugee laws to Central Americans in the United States. In W. H. Holtzman & T. H. Bornemann (Eds.), *Mental health of immigrants and refugees*. Austin, TX: Hogg Foundation.

Carstensen, L. L. (1988). The emerging field of behavioral gerontology. *Behavior Therapy, 19*, 259-281.

Carstensen, L. L. (1991). Selectivity theory: Social activity in life-span context. In K. W. Schaie & M. P. Lawton (Eds.), *Annual review of gerontology and geriatrics* (Vol. 11, pp. 195-221). New York: Springer.

Carstensen, L. L. (1993). Motivation for social contact across the lifespan: A theory of socioemotional selectivity. *Nebraska symposium on motivation*. Lincoln: University of Nebraska Press.

Carstensen, L. L., Gottman, J. M., & Levenson, R. W. (1995). Emotional behavior in long-term marriage. *Psychology and Aging, 10*, 1-10.

Carstensen, L. L., & Pasupathi, M. (1993). Women of a certain age. In S. Matteo (Ed.), *Critical issues facing women in the 90s* (pp. 66-78). Boston: Northeastern University Press.

Carstensen, L. L., Rychtarik, R. G., & Prue, D. M. (1985). Behavioral treatment of the geriatric alcohol abuser: A long term follow-up study. *Addictive Behaviors, 10*, 307-311.

Carter, J. H. (1982). Predicting visual responses to increasing age. *Journal of the American Optometric Association, 53*, 31-36.

Castle, D. J., & Murray, R. M. (1993). The epidemiology of late-onset schizophrenia. *Schizophrenia Bulletin, 19*, 691-700.

Castleden, C. M., George, C. F., Renwick, A. C., & Asher, M. J. (1981). Imipramine—a possible alternative to current therapy for urinary incontinence in the elderly. *Journal of Urology, 125*, 318-320.

Cauley, J. A., Seeley, D. G., Ensrud, K., Ettinger, B., Black, D., & Cummings, S. R. (1995). Estrogen replacement therapy and fractures in older women. *Annals of Internal Medicine, 122*, 9-16.

Cavallero, R., Covelli, M., & Smeraldi, E. (1993). Psychotic reactions to zolpidem. *Lancet, 342*, 374-375.

Cavanaugh, J. C. (1989). The importance of awareness in memory aging. In L. W. Poon, D. C. Rubin, & B. A. Wilson (Eds.), *Everyday cognition in adulthood and late life* (pp. 416-436). Cambridge, UK: Cambridge University Press.

Cavanaugh, J. C., & Poon, L. W. (1989). Metamemorial predictors of memory performance in young and older adults. *Psychology and Aging, 4*, 365-368.

Celli, B. (1985). Chronic obstructive pulmonary disease [Special issue]. *American Family Practice Annual*, 49-60.

Cerella, J. (1990). Aging and information-processing rate. In J. E. Birren & K. W. Schaie (Eds.), *Handbook of the psychology of aging* (pp. 201-221). San Diego: Academic Press.

Cerella, J., Poon, L. W., & Williams, D. M. (1980). Age and the complexity hypothesis. In L. W. Poon (Ed.), *Aging in the 1980s* (pp. 332-340). Washington, DC: American Psychological Association.

Cerhan, J. U. (1990). The Hmong in the United States: An overview for mental health professionals. *Journal of Counseling and Development, 69*, 88-92.

Chadwick, P. D. J., & Lowe, C. F. (1990). Measurement and modification of delusional beliefs. *Journal of Consulting and Clinical Psychology, 58*, 225-232.

Chadwick, P. D. J., Lowe, C. F., Horne, P. J., & Higson, P. J. (1994). Modifying delusions: The role of empirical testing. *Behavior Therapy, 25*, 35-49.

Chafetz, P. K. (1990). Two-dimensional grid is ineffective against demented patients' exiting through glass doors. *Psychology and Aging, 5*(1), 146-147.

Chafetz, P., West, H., Ebbs, E. (1988). Overcoming obstacles to cooperation in interdisciplinary long term care teams. *Journal of Gerontological Social Work, 11*, 131-140.

Chaisson-Stewart, G. M. (1985). *Depression in the elderly: An interdisciplinary approach*. New York: John Wiley.

Chandler, J. D., & Chandler, J. E. (1988). The prevalence of neuropsychiatric disorders in a nursing home population. *Journal of Geriatric and Psychiatric Neurology, 1,* 71-76.

Chaplin, J. (1988). *Feminist counseling in action.* London: Sage.

Chatellier L., & Lacomblez, L. (1990). Tacrine (THA) and lecithin in senile dementia of the Alzheimer type: A multicentre trial. *British Medical Journal, 300,* 495-499.

Chauhan, J. (1989). Relationships between sour and salt taste perception and selected subject attributes. *Journal of the American Dietetic Association, 89,* 652-658.

Cheah, K. C., & Beard, O. W. (1980). Psychiatric findings in the population of a geriatric evaluation unit: Implications. *Journal of the American Geriatrics Society, 28,* 153-156.

Chen, H.-C., Ashton-Miller, J. A., Alexander, N. B., & Schultz, A. B. (1991). Stepping over obstacles: Gait patterns of healthy young and old adults. *Journal of Gerontology: Medical Sciences, 46,* M196-M203.

Chiarello, R. J., & Cole, J. O. (1987). The use of psychostimulants in general psychiatry: A recommendation. *Archives of General Psychiatry, 44,* 286-295.

Chodzko-Zajko, W. J. (1991). Physical fitness, cognitive performance, and aging. *Medicine and Science in Sports and Exercise, 23,* 868-872.

Chodzko-Zajko, W. J., Schuler, P., Solomon, J., Heinl, B., & Ellis, N. R. (1992). The influence of physical fitness on automatic and effortful memory changes in aging. *International Journal of Aging and Human Development, 35,* 265-285.

Chou, J. C. (1991). Recent advances in treatment of acute mania. *Journal of Clinical Psychopharmacology, 11,* 3-21.

Chouinard, G., Jones, B., Remington, G., Bloom, D., Addington, D., MacEwan, G. W., Labelle, A., Beauclair, L., & Arnott, W. (1993). A Canadian multicenter placebo-controlled study of fixed doses of risperidone and haloperidol in the treatment of chronic schizophrenic patients. *Journal of Clinical Psychopharmacology, 13,* 24-40.

Chrischilles, E. A., Foley, D. J., Wallace, R. B., Lemke, J. H., Semla, T. P., Hanlon, J. T., Glynn, R. J., Ostfeld, A. M., & Guralnik, J. M. (1992). Use of medications by persons 65 and over: Data from the established populations for epidemiologic studies of the elderly. *Journal of Gerontology: Medical Sciences, 47,* M137-M144.

Christ, D. M., McKinnon, L. T., Thompson, R. I., Atterbom, H. I., & Egan, P. A. (1989). Physical exercise increases natural cellular-mediated tumor cytotoxicity in elderly women. *Gerontology, 35,* 66-71.

Christensen, H., Hadzi-Pavlovic, D., & Jacomb, P. (1991). The psychometric differentiation of dementia from normal aging: A meta-analysis. *Psychological Assessment: A Journal of Consulting and Clinical Psychology, 3,* 147-155.

Christenson, R., & Blazer, D. (1984). Epidemiology of persecutory ideation in an elderly population in the community. *American Journal of Psychiatry, 141,* 1088-1091.

Christian, E., Dluhy, N., & O'Neill, R. (1989). Sounds of silence: Coping with hearing loss and loneliness. *Journal of Gerontological Nursing, 15*(11), 4-9.

Christison, C., Christison, G., & Blazer, D. G. (1989). Late-life schizophrenia and paranoid disorders. In E. W. Busse & D. G. Blazer (Eds.), *Geriatric psychiatry* (pp. 403-414). Washington, DC: American Psychiatric Press.

Cicerelli, V. (1989). Feelings of attachment to siblings and well-being in later life. *Psychology and Aging, 4,* 211-216.

Ciocon, J. O. (1994). Caudal epidural blocks for elderly patients with lumbar canal stenosis. *Journal of the American Geriatric Society, 42*(6), 593-596.

Ciompi, L. (1980). The natural history of schizophrenia in the long term. *British Journal of Psychiatry, 136,* 413-420.

Ciraulo, D. A., & Shader, R. I. (1990). Fluoxetine drug-interactions: 1. Antidepressants and antipsychotics. *Journal of Clinical Psychopharmacology, 10,* 48-50.

Ciurlia-Guy, E., Cashman, M., & Lewsen, B. (1993). Identifying hearing loss and hearing handicap among chronic care elderly people. *The Gerontologist, 33,* 644-649.

Clark, R. F., & Goate, A. M. (1993). Molecular genetics of Alzheimer's disease. *Archives of Neurology, 50,* 1164-1167.

Clarke, G., & Lewinsohn, P. M. (1989). The Coping With Depression Course: A group psychoeducational intervention for unipolar depression [Special Issue: Depression: Treatment and theory]. *Behaviour Change, 6,* 54-69.

Clay, E. C. (1978). Incontinence of urine: A regime for retraining. *Nursing Mirror, 146,* 23-24.

Clay, E. C. (1980). Promoting urine control in older adults: Habit retraining. *Geriatric Nursing, 1,* 252-254.

Clothier, J., & Grotta, J. (1991). Recognition and management of post stroke depression in the elderly. *Clinical Geriatric Medicine, 7,* 493-506.

Coccaro, E. F., Kramer, E., Zemishlany, Z., Thorne, A., Rice, M. C., Giordani, I. B., Kamalamma, D., Bhupendra, M. P., Torres, J., Nora, R., Neufeld, R., Mohs, R. C., & Davis, K. L. (1990). Pharmacologic treatment of noncognitive behavioral disturbances in elderly demented patients. *American Journal of Psychiatry, 147,* 1640-1645.

Cohen, D., & Eisdorfer, D. (1985). Major psychiatric and behavioral disorders in the aged. In R. Andres, E. Bierman, & W. Hazzard (Eds.), *Principles of geriatric medicine.* New York: McGraw-Hill.

Cohen, D., Eisdorfer, C., Prinz, P., Breen, A., Davis, M., & Gadsby, A. (1983). Sleep disturbances in the institutionalized aged. *Journal of the American Geriatrics Society, 31,* 79-82.

Cohen, G. (1990). Psychopathology and mental health in the mature and elderly adult. In J. E. Birren & K. W. Schaie (Eds.), *Handbook of the psychology of aging* (2nd ed. pp. 359-371). New York: Van Nostrand Reinhold.

Cohen, G. D. (1987). Psychotherapeutic approaches to schizophrenia in later life. In N. E. Miller & G. D. Cohen (Eds.), *Schizophrenia and aging* (pp. 287-298). New York: Guilford.

Cohen, H. J. (1990). Oncology and aging: General principles of cancer in the elderly. In W. R. Hazzard, R. Andres, E. L. Bierman, & J. P. Blass (Eds.), *Principles of geriatric medicine and gerontology* (2nd ed., pp. 72-84). New York: McGraw-Hill.

Cohen, L. M., McCue, J. D., & Green, G. M. (1993). Do clinical and formal assessments of the capacity of patients in the intensive care unit to make decisions agree? *Archives of Internal Medicine, 153,* 2481-2485.

Cohen-Cole, S. A. (1989). Depression in heart disease. In R. G. Robinson & P. V. Rabins (Eds.), *Depression in coexisting disease* (pp. 27-39). New York: Igaku-Shoin.

Cohen-Mansfield, J. (1986). Agitated behaviors in the elderly: 2. Preliminary results in the cognitively deteriorated. *Journal of the American Geriatric Society, 34,* 722-727.

Cohen-Mansfield, J., Marx, M. S., & Rosenthal, A. S. (1989). A description of agitation in a nursing home. *Journal of Gerontology: Medical Sciences, 44*(3), M77-M84.

Cohen-Mansfield, J., Marx, M. S., Werner, P., & Freedman, L. (1992). Temporal patterns of agitated nursing home residents. *International Psychogeriatrics, 4*(2), 221-240.

Cohen-Mansfield, J., & Werner, P. (1995, January/February). Environmental influences on agitation: An integrative summary of an observational study. *American Journal of Alzheimer's Disease and Related Disease & Research,* pp. 32-39.

Cohen-Mansfield, J., Werner, P., & Marx, M. S. (1988). *Should agitated nursing home residents be exposed to music or television? 12 case studies* (Monographs of the Research Institute of the Hebrew Home of Greater Washington No. 53). Rockville, MD: Research Institute of the Hebrew Home of Greater Washington.

Cohen-Mansfield, J., Werner, P., & Marx, M. S. (1989). An observational study of agitation in agitated nursing home residents. *International Psychogeriatrics, 1*(2), 153-165.

Cohen-Mansfield, J., Werner, P., & Marx, M. S. (1990). *Relationship between agitation and physical environment in a nursing home: An observational study* (Monographs of the Research

Institute of the Hebrew Home of Greater Washington No. 45). Rockville, MD: Research Institute of the Hebrew Home of Greater Washington.

Cohen-Mansfield, J., Werner, P., & Marx, M. S. (1991). The social environment of the agitated nursing home resident. *International Journal of Geriatric Psychiatry, 7,* 789-798.

Cohen-Mansfield, J., Werner, P., Marx, M. S., & Freedman, L. (1991). Two studies of pacing in the nursing home. *Journal of Gerontology: Medical Sciences, 46*(3), M77-M83.

Cohen-Mansfield, J., Werner, P., Marx, M. S., & Lipson, S. (1993). Assessment and management of behavior problems in the nursing home setting. In L. Z. Rubenstein & D. Wieland (Eds.), *Improving care in the nursing home: Comprehensive reviews of clinical research* (pp. 275-313). Newbury Park, CA: Sage.

Cohn, C. K., Shrivastava, R, Mendels, J., Cohn, J. B., Fabre, F. L., Claghorn, J. L., Dessain, E. C., Itil, T. M., & Lautin, A. (1990). Double-blind multicenter comparison of sertraline and amiltriptyline in elderly depressed patients. *Journal of Clinical Psychiatry, 51*(Suppl. B), 28-33.

Cohn, M. D., Horgas, A. L., & Marsiske, M. (1990). Behavior management training for nurse aides: Is it effective? *Journal of Gerontological Nursing, 16,* 1-5.

Cohn, M. D., Smyer, M. A., & Horgas, A. L. (1994). *The ABCs of behavior change: Skills for working with behavior problems in nursing homes.* State College, PA: Venture.

Cole, M. G. (1985). The course of elderly depressed outpatients. *Canadian Journal of Psychiatry, 30,* 217-220.

Coleman, R. M., Miles, L. E., Guilleminault, C. C., Zarcone, V. P., van den Hoed, J., & Dement, W. C. (1981). Sleep wake disorders in the elderly: A polysomnographic analysis. *Journal of the American Geriatrics Society, 29,* 289-296.

Colenda, C. C. (1981). Buspirone in treatment of agitated demented patients (letter). *Lancet, 1,* 1169.

Colenda, C. C. (1988). Buspirone in treatment of agitated dementia patients. *Lancet, 2,* 510.

Colenda, C. C., & Hamer, R. M. (1991). Antecedents and interventions for aggressive behavior of patients at a geropsychiatric state hospital. *Hospital and Community Psychiatry, 42*(3), 287-292.

Colling, J., Ouslander, J., Hadley, B. J., Eisch, J., & Campbell, E. (1992). The effects of patterned urge-response toileting (PURT) on urinary incontinence among nursing home residents. *Journal of the American Geriatrics Society, 40,* 135-141.

Colsher, P. L., & Wallace, R. B. (1990). Elderly men with histories of heavy drinking: Correlates and consequences. *Journal of Studies of Alcohol, 51,* 528-535.

Comas-Diaz, L. C. (1989). Culturally-relevant issues and treatment implications for Hispanics. In D. R. Kaslow & E. P. Salett (Eds.), *Crossing cultures in mental health.* Washington, DC: Sietar International.

Commonwealth Fund. (1987). *Old, alone, and poor: Technical analyses.* Baltimore, MD: Author, Commission on Elderly People Living Alone.

Cone, J. D. (1981). Psychometric considerations. In M. Hersen & A. S. Bellack (Eds.), *Behavioral assessment: A practical handbook* (2nd ed., pp. 38-61). New York: Pergamon.

Cone, J. D. (1988). Psychometric considerations and the multiple models of behavioral assessment. In A. S. Bellack & M. Hersen (Eds.), *Behavioral assessment: A practical handbook* (3rd ed., pp. 42-66). New York: Pergamon.

Connidis, I. A., & Davies, L. (1992). Confidants and companions: Choices in later life. *Journal of Gerontology, 47,* 115-122.

Consensus Conference. (1989). Urinary incontinence in adults. *JAMA, 261,* 2685-2690.

Conwell, Y., Rotenberg, M., & Caine, E. D. (1990). Completed suicide at age 50 and over. *Journal of the American Geriatrics Society, 38,* 640-644.

Cook, B., Winokur, G., Garvey, M., & Beach, V. (1991). Depression and previous alcoholism in the elderly. *British Journal of Psychiatry, 158,* 72-75.

Cooney, T. M., Schaie, K. W., & Willis, S. L. (1988). The relationship between prior functioning on cognitive and personality dimensions and subject attrition in longitudinal research. *Journal of Gerontology: Psychological Sciences, 43,* P12-P17.

Coons, D. H. (1988). Wandering. *American Journal of Alzheimer's Care and Related Disorders & Research, 3*(1), 31-36.

Cooper, J. K., Mungas, D., & Weiler, P. G. (1990). Relation of cognitive status and abnormal behaviors in Alzheimer's disease. *Journal of the American Gerontological Society, 38*(8), 867-870.

Copeland, J. R., Kelleher, M. J., Kellett, J. M., Gourlay, A. J., Gurland, B. J., Fleiss, J. L., & Sharpe, L. (1976). A semistructured clinical interview for the assessment of diagnosis and mental state in the elderly: The Geriatric Mental State Schedule: 1. Development and reliability. *Psychological Medicine, 6,* 439-449.

Coppel, D. B., Burton, D., Becker, J., & Fiore, J. (1985). Relationships of cognitions associated with coping reactions to depression in spousal caregivers of Alzheimer's disease patients. *Cognitive Therapy and Research, 9,* 253-266.

Cormier, W. H., & Cormier, L. S. (1991). *Interviewing strategies for helpers* (2nd ed.). Pacific Grove, CA: Brooks/Cole.

Cornbleth, T. (1977). Effects of a protected hospital ward area on wandering and nonwandering geriatric patients. *Journal of Gerontology, 32*(5), 573-577.

Cornelius, S. W., & Caspi, A. (1987). Everyday problem-solving in adulthood and old age. *Psychology and Aging, 2,* 144-153.

Corrigan, P. W., Liberman, R. P., & Engel, J. D. (1990). From noncompliance to collaboration in the treatment of schizophrenia. *Hospital and Community Psychiatry, 41,* 1203-1211.

Costall, B., Coughlan, J., Horovitz, Z. P., Kelly, M. E., Naylor, R. J., & Tomkins, D. M. (1989). The effects of ACE inhibitors captopril and SQ29,852 in rodent tests of cognition. *Pharmacology, Biochemistry, and Behavior, 33,* 573-579.

Costello, R. B., & Moser-Veillon, P. B. (1992). A review of magnesium intake in the elderly. A cause for concern? *Magnesium Research, 5,* 61-67.

Cowdry, R., & Gardner, D. (1988). Pharmacotherapy of borderline personality disorder: Alprazolam, carbamazepine, trifluoperazine, and tranylcypromine. *Archives of General Psychiatry, 45,* 111-119.

Craig, T. J., & Bregman, Z. (1988). Late onset schizophrenia-like illnesses. *Journal of the American Geriatrics Society, 36,* 104-107.

Craik, F. I. M. (1992). Human memory. In F. I. M. Craik & T. A. Salthouse (Eds.), *The handbook of aging and cognition* (pp. 51-110). Hillsdale, NJ: Lawrence Erlbaum.

Craik, F. I. M., & Rabinowitz, J. C. (1984). Age differences in the acquisition and use of verbal information. In H. Bouma & D. G. Bouwhuis (Eds.), *Attention and performance X* (pp. 471-499). Hillsdale, NJ: Lawrence Erlbaum.

Craik, F. I. M., & Tulving, E. (1975). Depth of processing and the retention of words in episodic memory. *Journal of Experimental Psychology: General, 1,* 268-294.

Crane, G. E., & Smects, R. A. (1974). Tardive Dyskenisia and drug therapy in geriatric patients. *Archives of General Psychiatry, 30,* 341-343.

Craske, M. G., Barlow, D. H., & O'Leary, T. (1992). *Mastery of your anxiety and worry.* Albany, NY: Graywind.

Craven, R., & Bruno, P. (1986). Teach the elderly to prevent falls. *Journal of Gerontological Nursing, 12*(8), 27-33.

Croft, L. H. (1982). *Sexuality in later life: A counseling guide for physicians.* Boston: John Wright.

Cronin-Golomb, A. (1991). Abstract thought in aging and age-related neurological disease. In F. Boller & J. Grafman (Eds.), *Handbook of neuropsychology* (Vol. 4, pp. 279-309). New York: Elsevier.

Crook, T. (1985). Diagnosis and treatment of mixed anxiety-depression in the elderly. *Internal Medicine for the Specialist, 6,* 154-176.

Crook, T., Ferris, S., & Bartus R. (Eds.). (1983). *Assessment in geriatric psychopathology.* New Canaan, CT: Mark Powley.

Crook, T., & Lakin, M. (1991). Effects of ondansetron in age-associated memory impairment. In G. Racagni (Ed.), *Biological psychiatry* (Vol. 2). New York: Elsevier.

Crook, T., & Miller, N. (1985). The challenge of Alzheimer's disease. *American Psychologist, 40,* 1245-1250.

Crook, T., Petrie, W., Wells, C., & Massari, D. C. (1992). Effects of phosphatidylserine in Alzheimer's disease. *Psychopharmacology Bulletin, 28,* 61-66.

Crook, T. H. (1993). Diagnosis and treatment of memory loss in older patients who are not demented. In R. Levy, R. Howard, & A. Burns (Eds.), *Treatment and care in old age psychiatry* (pp. 95-111). Hampshire, UK: Wrightson.

Crook, T. H., Bartus, R. T., Ferris, S. H., Whitehouse, P., Cohen, G. D., & Gershon, S. (1986). Age-associated memory impairment: Proposed diagnostic criteria and measures of clinical change: Report of a National Institute of Mental Health workgroup. *Developmental Neuropsychology, 2,* 261-276.

Crook, T. H., & Larrabee, G. J. (1988). Interrelationships among every day memory tests: Stability of factor structure with age. *Neuropsychology, 2,* 1-12.

Crook, T. H., Tinklenberg, J., Yesavage, J., Petrie, W., Nunzi, M. G., & Massari, D. C. (1991). Effects of phosphatidylserine in age-associated memory impairment. *Neurology, 41,* 644-649.

Crook, T. H., Youngjohn, J. R., Larrabee, G. J., & Salama, M. (1992). Aging and everyday memory: A cross-cultural study. *Neuropsychology, 6,* 123-136.

Crose, R., & Drake, L. K. (1993). Older women's sexuality. *The Clinical Gerontologist, 12,* 51-56.

Cuellar, J. (1988). Impact of culture on health care of ethnic elders: A state-of-the-art report, Native American elders. In L. A. Llorens (Ed.), *Health care for ethnic elders: The cultural context* (Working Paper Series, 7, pp. 29-30). Palo Alto, CA: Stanford Geriatric Education Center.

Cullum, C. M., Heaton, R. K., & Nemiroff, B. (1988). Neuropsychology of late-life psychoses. *Psychiatric Clinics of North America, 11,* 47-59.

Cummings, J. L. (1988). Intellectual impairment in Parkinson's disease: Clinical, pathologic, and biochemical correlates. *Journal of Geriatric Psychiatry and Neurology, 1,* 24-36.

Cummings, J. L. (1989). Dementia and depression: An evolving enigma. *Journal of Neuropsychiatry, 1,* 236-242.

Cummings, J. L., & Benson, D. F. (1988). Psychological dysfunction accompanying subcortical dementias. *Annual Review of Medicine, 39,* 53-61.

Cunningham, D. A., Nancekievill, E. A., Paterson, D. H., Donner, A. P., & Rechnitzer, P. A. (1985). Ventilation threshold and aging. *Journal of Gerontology, 40,* 703-707.

Curtis, J. L., Millman, E. J., Joseph, M., Charles, J., & Bajwa, W. (1986). Prevalence rates for alcoholism, associated depression and dementia on the Harlem Hospital medicine and surgery services. *Advances in Alcohol and Substance Abuse, 6,* 45-65.

Curtis, J. R., Geller, G., Stokes, E. J., Levine, D. M., & Moore, R. D. (1989). Characteristics, diagnosis, and treatment of alcoholism in elderly patients. *Journal of the American Geriatrics Society, 37,* 310-316.

Cutler, W., Garcia, C. R., & McCoy, N. (1987). Perimenopausal sexuality. *Archives of Sexual Behavior, 16,* 225-234.

Cutter, N. R., & Narang, P. K. (1987). Implications of dosing tricyclic antidepressants and benzodiazepines in geriatrics. *Psychiatric Clinics of North America, 7,* 845-861.

Czaja, S. J., Weber, R. A., & Nair, S. N. (1993). A human factors analysis of ADL activities: A capability-demand approach [Special Issue]. *Journal of Gerontology, 48,* 44-48.

Czirr, R., & Rappaport, M. (1984). Toolkit for teams: Annotated bibliography on interdisciplinary health teams. *The Clinical Gerontologist, 2,* 47-54.

Dager, S. R., & Heritch, A. J. (1990). A case of buproprion-associated deliruim. *Journal of Clinical Psychiatry, 51,* 307-308.

Dalsky, G. P. (1988). Weight-bearing exercise, training, and lumbar bone mineral content in post-menopausal women. *Annals of Internal Medicine, 108,* 824-828.

Danzinger, R. S., Tobin, J. D., Becker, L. C., Lakatta, E. E., & Fleg, J. L. (1990). The age-associated decline in glomerular filtration in healthy normotensive volunteers: Lack of relationship to cardiovascular performance. *Journal of the American Geriatrics Society, 38,* 1127-1132.

Dargent, P., & Breart, G. (1993). Epidemiology and risk factors of osteoporosis. *Current Opinion in Rheumatology, 5,* 339-345.

Davidhizar, R., & Cosgray, R. (1990). Helping the wanderer. *Geriatric Nursing, 11*(6), 280-281.

Davidson, J. (1989). Seizures and buproprion: A reveiw. *Journal of Clinical Psychiatry, 50,* 256-261.

Davidson, M. B. (1982). The effect of aging on carbohydrate metabolism: A comprehensive review and a practical approach to the clinical problem. In S. G. Korenman (Ed.), *Endocrine aspects of aging.* New York: Elsevier.

Davidson, M. B. (1990). Carbohydrate metabolism and diabetes mellitus. In W. Abrams & R. Berkow (Eds.), *The Merck manual of geriatrics* (pp. 789-815). Rahway, NJ: Merck.

Davie, J. W, Blumenthal, M. D., & Robinson-Hawkins, S. (1981). A model of risk of falling for psychogeriatric patients. *Archives of General Psychiatry, 38,* 462-467.

Davies, A. D. M., Davies, C., & Delpo, M. C. (1986). Depression and anxiety in patients undergoing diagnostic investigations for head and neck cancers. *British Journal of Psychiatry, 149,* 491-493.

Davies, H., Priddy, M., & Tinklenberg, J. (1986). Support groups for male caregivers of Alzheimer's patients. *The Clinical Gerontologist, 5*(3/4), 385-395.

Davies, P., Katz, D. A., & Crystal, H. A. (1982). Choline acetyltransferase, somatostatin, and substance P in selected cases of Alzheimer's disease. In. S. Corkin, K. L. Davis, J. H. Growdon, E. Usdin, & R. J. Wurtman (Eds.), *Aging: Vol. 19. Alzheimer's disease: A report of progress in research* (pp. 9-14). New York: Raven.

Davies, P., & Maloney, A. J. F. (1976). Selective loss of central cholinergic neurons in Alzheimer's disease. *Lancet, 2,* 1403.

Davies, R., Lacks, P., Storandt, M., & Bertelson, A. D. (1986). Countercontrol treatment of sleep-maintenance insomnia in relation to age. *Psychology and Aging, 1,* 233-238.

Davis, D., Grant, P., & Rowland, D. (1992). Alone and poor: The plight of elderly women. In L. Glasse & J. Hendricks (Eds.), *Gender and aging* (pp. 79-90). New York: Baywood.

Davis, G. W., & Fuller, W. (1991). Common folk remedies used by Black elders: Their source and use. In N. Hikoyeda & M. Gruzden (Eds.), *Traditional and non-traditional medication use among ethnic elders* (Working Paper Series, 10). Palo Alto, CA: Stanford Geriatric Education Center.

Davis, J. M., Schaffer, C. B., Killian, G. A., Kinard, C., & Clan, C. (1980). Important issues in the drug treatment of schizophrenia. *Schizophrenia Bulletin, 6,* 70-87.

Davis, J. M., Segal, N. L., & Spring, G. K. (1983). Biological and genetic aspects of depression in the elderly. In D. Breslau & M. R. Haug (Eds.), *Depression and aging* (pp. 273-306). New York: Springer.

Davis, J. P., & Bernstein, P. A. (1992). Age-related changes in explicit and implicit memory. In L. W. Squire & N. Butters (Eds.), *Neuropsychology of memory* (2nd ed., pp. 249-261). New York: Guilford.

Davis, M. A., Murphy, S. P., & Neuhaus, J. M. (1988). Living arrangements and eating behaviors of older adults in the United States. *Journal of Gerontology: Social Sciences, 43,* S96-S98.

Davis, M. A., Randall, E., Forthofer, R. N., Lee, E. S., & Margen, S. (1985). Living arrangements and dietary patterns of older adults in the United States. *Journal of Gerontology, 40,* 434-442.

Davison, G. C., & Neale, J. M. (1986). *Abnormal Psychology.* New York: John Wiley.

Dawson, P., & Reid, D. W. (1987). Behavioral dimension of patients at risk of wandering. *The Gerontologist, 27*(1), 104-107.

de la Pena, A. (1978). Toward a psychophysiologic conception of insomnia. In R. L. Williams & I. Karacan (Eds.), *Sleep disorders: Diagnosis and treatment.* New York: John Wiley.

Dean, C. (1995). *Vitamin E, free radicals, running performance and longevity.* Manuscript submitted for publication.

DeBerry, S. (1982a). The effects of meditation-relaxation on anxiety and depression in a geriatric population. *Psychotherapy: Therapy, Research, and Practice, 19,* 512-521.

DeBerry, S. (1982b). An evaluation of progressive muscle relaxation of stress related symptoms in a geriatric population. *International Journal of Aging and Human Development, 14,* 255-269.

DeBerry, S., Davis, S., & Reinhard, K. E. (1989). A comparison of meditation-relaxation and cognitive behavioral techniques for reducing anxiety and depression in a geriatric population. *Journal of Geriatric Psychiatry, 22,* 231-247.

Debring, C. E., van Gorp, W. G., Stuck, A. E., Mitrushina, M., & Beck, J. (1994). Early detection of cognitive decline in cognitively higher functioning older adults: Sensitivity and specificity of a neuropsychological screening battery. *Neuropsychology, 8,* 31-37.

DeGraaf, C., Polet, P., & VanStaveren, W. A. (1994). Sensory perception and pleasantness of food flavors in elderly subjects. *Journal of Gerontology: Psychological Sciences, 49,* P93-P99.

Dehn, M., & Bruce, R. (1972). Longitudinal variations in maximal oxygen intake with age and activity. *Journal of Applied Physiology, 33,* 805-807.

Dement, W. C. (1986). *Some must watch while some must sleep.* New York: Norton.

Denicoff, K. D., Meglathery, S. B., Post, R. M., & Tandeciarz, S. (1994). Efficacy of car-bamazepine compared with other agents: A clinical practice survey. *Journal of Clinical Psychiatry, 55,* 70-76.

Dennerstein, L., & Burrows, G. D. (1982). Hormone replacement therapy and sexuality in women. *Clinics in Endocrinology and Metabolism, 11,* 599-623.

DePaulo, J. R., Folstein, M. R., & Correa, E. I. (1982). The course of delirium due to lithium intoxication. *Journal of Clinical Psychiatry, 43,* 447-449.

Depner, C. E., & Ingersoll-Dayton, B. (1988). Supportive relationships in later life. *Psychology and Aging, 3,* 348-357.

DeRubeis, R. J., & Beck, A. T. (1988). Cognitive therapy. In K. S. Dobson (Ed.), *Handbook of cognitive-behavioral therapies* (pp. 273-306). New York: Guilford.

Dessonville, C., Gallagher, D., Thompson, L. W., Finnel, K., & Lewinsohn, P. M. (1982). Relation of age and health status to depressive symptoms in older adults. *Essence, 5,* 99-118.

Deutsch, L. H., Bylsma, D. O., Rovner, B. W., Steele, C., & Folstein, M. F. (1991). Psychosis and physical aggression in probable Alzheimer's disease. *American Journal of Psychiatry, 148*(9), 1159-1163.

Devanand, D. P., Sackheim, H. A., & Mayeux, R. (1988). Psychosis, behavioral disturbance, and the use of neuroleptics in dementia. *Comprehensive Psychiatry, 29,* 387-401.

Devaney, K. O., & Johnson, H. A. (1980). Neuron loss in the aging visual cortex in man. *Journal of Gerontology, 35,* 836-841.

DeVries, H. (1970). Physiologic effects of an exercise training program in men age 52-88. *Journal of Gerontology, 25,* 325-335.

Dhooper, S. S., Green, S. M., Huff, M., & Austin-Murphy, J. (1993). Efficacy of a group approach to reducing depression in nursing home elderly residents. *Journal of Gerontological Social Work, 20,* 87-100.

Diabetes Control and Complications Trial Research Group. (1993). The effect of intensive treatment of diabetes on the development and progression of long-term complications in insulin-dependent diabetes mellitus. *The New England Journal of Medicine, 329,* 977-986.

DiMascio, A., Weissman, M., Prusoff, B., Neu, C., Zwilling, M., & Klerman, G. L. (1979). Differential symptom reduction by drugs and psychotherapy in acute depression. *Archives of General Psychiatry, 36,* 1450.

Dimond, S. J., & Brouwers, E. Y. M. (1976). Increase in the power of human memory in normal man through the use of drugs. *Psychopharmacology, 49,* 307-309.

Diokno, A. C., Brock, B. M., Brown, M. B., & Herzog, A. R. (1986). Prevalence of urinary incontinence and other urological symptoms in the noninstitutionalized elderly. *Journal of Urology, 136,* 1022-1025.

Ditto, B., Miller, S., & Maurice, S. (1987). Age differences in the consistency of cardiovascular response patterns in healthy women. *Biological Psychology, 25,* 23-31.

Dixon, R. A. (1989). Questionnaire research on metamemory and aging: Issues of structure and function. In L. W. Poon, D. C. Rubin, & B. A. Wilson (Eds.), *Everyday cognition in adulthood and late life* (pp. 394-415). Cambridge, UK: Cambridge University Press.

DiZio, P., & Lackner, J. R. (1990). Age differences in oculomotor responses to step changes in body velocity and visual surround velocity. *Journal of Gerontology: Medical Sciences, 45,* M89-M94.

Dobbs, A. R., & Rule, B. G. (1987). Prospective memory and self-reports of memory abilities in older adults. *Canadian Journal of Psychology, 41,* 209-222.

Dollard, J., & Miller., N. E. (1950). *Personality and psychotherapy.* New York: McGraw-Hill.

Dombovy, M., Sandok, B., & Basford, J. (1986). Rehabilitation for stroke: A review. *Stroke, 17,* 363-369.

Donat, D. C. (1986a). Altercations among institutionalized psychogeriatric patients. *The Gerontologist, 26*(3), 227-228.

Donat, D. C. (1986b). Modifying wandering behavior: A case study. *The Clinical Gerontologist, 6,* 41-42.

Dornbrand, L., Hoole, A. J., & Pickard, C. G. (1992). *Manual of clinical problems in adult ambulatory care.* Boston: Little, Brown.

Doty, R. L. (1989). Influence of age and age-related diseases on olfactory function. *Annals of the New York Academy of Science, 561,* 76-86.

Doty, R. L., Shaman, P., Applebaum, S. L., Giberson, R., Sikosorski, L., & Rosenberg, L. (1984). Smell identification ability: Changes with age. *Science, 226,* 1441-1443.

Dougherty, L. M., Preston, D. G., Jones, S. S., & Payne, H. C. (1992). Effects of exposure to aggressive behavior on job satisfaction of health care staff. *Journal of Applied Gerontology, 11*(2), 160-171.

Douglass, R. L., Schuster, E. O., & McClelland, S. C. (1988). Drinking patterns and abstinence among the elderly. *International Journal of the Addictions, 23,* 399-415.

Downton, J. H., & Andrews, K. (1990). Postural disturbance and psychological symptoms amongst elderly people living at home. *International Journal of Geriatric Psychiatry, 5,* 93-98.

Drachman, D. A., & Leavitt, J. L. (1974). Human memory and the cholinergic system: A relationship to aging. *Archives of Neurology, 30,* 113-121.

Drake, R. E., Gates, C., & Whitaker, A. (1985). Suicide among schizophrenics: A review. *Comprehensive Psychiatry, 26,* 90-100.

Dressel, P. L. (1988). Gender, race, and class: Beyond the feminization of poverty in later life. *The Gerontologist, 28,* 177-180.

Dreyfuss, F., Dasber, H., & Assael, M. I. (1969). The relationship of myocardial infarction to depressive illness. *Psychotherapy and Psychosomatics, 17,* 73-81.

Drinka, T. J., Smith, J., & Drinka, P. J. (1987). Correlates of depression and burden for informal caregivers of patients in a geriatric referral clinic. *Journal of the American Geriatrics Society, 35,* 522-525.

Drinka, T. J. K., & Streim, J. E. (1994). Case studies from purgatory: Maladaptive behavior within geriatric health care teams. *The Gerontologist, 34,* 541-547.

Droller, H. (1964). Some aspects of alcoholism in the elderly. *Lancet, 2,* 137-139.

Dryden, W., & Ellis, A. (1988). Rational-emotive therapy. In Dobson (Ed.), *Handbook of cognitive-behavioral therapies* (pp. 214-272). New York: Guilford.

Dubovsky, S. L. (1986). Calcium antagonists: A new class of psychotropic drugs? *Psychiatric Annals, 16,* 724-728.

Dubovsky, S. L. (1994). Rationales for new serotonergic agents. *Journal of Clinical Psychiatry,* *55*(2 Suppl.), 34-44.

Dubovsky, S. L., Franks, R. D., Allen, S., & Murphy, J. (1986). Calcium antagonists in mania: A double blind placebo controlled study of verapamil. *Psychiatry Research, 18,* 309-320.

Dudley, D. L., Glaser, E. M., Jorgenson, B. N., & Logan, D. L. (1980). Psychosocial concomitants to rehabilitation in COPD: 1. Psychosocial and psychological considerations. *Chest, 77,* 413-420.

Dudley, D. L., Martin, C. J., Masuda, M., Ripley, H. S., & Holmes, T. H. (1969). *Psychophysiology of respiration in health and disease.* New York: Appleton-Century-Crofts.

Dunham, R. G. (1981). Aging and changing patterns of alcohol use. *Journal of Psychoactive Drugs, 13,* 143-151.

Dunner, D. L., Cohn, J. B., Walshe, T., III, Cohn, C. K., Feighner, J. P., Fieve, R. R., Halikas, J. P., Hartford, J. T., Hearst, E. D., Settle, E. C., Menolascino, F. J., & Muller, D. J. (1992). Two combined, multicenter double-blind studies of paraxotine and doxepin in geriatric patients with major depression. *Journal of Clinical Psychiatry, 53*(2 Suppl.), 57-60.

Dupree, L. W., & Patterson, R. L. (1985). Assessing deficits and supports in the elderly. In M. Hersen & S. M. Turner (Eds.), *Diagnostic Interviewing* (pp. 337-359). New York: Plenum.

Dura, J. R., Stukenberg, K. W., & Kiecolt-Glaser, J. K. (1990). Chronic stress and depressive episodes in older adults. *Journal of Abnormal Psychology, 99,* 284-290.

Dwyer, J., & Coward, R. T. (Eds.). (1992). *Gender, families, and elder care.* Newbury Park, CA: Sage.

Eagger, S. A., Levy, R., & Sanakian, B. J. (1991). Tacrine in Alzheimer's disease. *Lancet, 337,* 989-992.

Eastell, R., Yergey, A. L., Vieira, N. E., Cedel, S. L., Kumar, R., & Riggs, B. L. (1991). Interrelationship among vitamin D metabolism, true calcium absorption, parathyroid function, and age in women: Evidence of an age-related intestinal resistance to 1,25-dihydroxyvitamin D action. *Journal of Bone Mineral Research, 6,* 125-132.

Eastwood, M. R., Corbin, S., Reed, M., Nobbs, H., & Kedward, M. B. (1985). Acquired hearing loss and psychiatric illness: An estimate of prevalence and co-morbidity in a geriatric setting. *British Journal of Psychiatry, 147,* 552.

Ebrahim, S., Barer, K. D., & Nouri, F. (1987). Affective illness after stroke. *British Journal of Psychiatry, 151,* 52-56.

Edelstein, B., Alberts, G., & Estill, S. (1988). Adult diagnostic interview schedules. In M. Hersen & A. S. Bellack (Eds.), *Dictionary of behavioral assessment techniques.* (pp. 16-17). New York: Pergamon.

Edelstein, B., & Berler, E. (1987). Child behavior problems: Interviewing and report writing. In C. L. Frame & J. L. Matson (Eds.), *Handbook of assessment in childhood psychopathology.* New York: Plenum.

Edelstein, B., Northrop, L., Staats, N., & Packard, N. (1996). Assessment of older adults. In M. Hersen & V. Van Hasselt (Eds.), *Psychological treatment of older adults: An introductory textbook.* New York: Plenum.

Edelstein, B., & Yoman, J. (1991). La entrevista conductual [Behavioral interviewing]. In V. E. Caballo (Ed.), *Manual de tecnicas de terpia y modificación de conducta* (pp. 751-775). Madrid, Spain: Siglo Veintiuno.

Edelstein, B. A., Nygren, M., Northrop, L., Staats, N., & Pool, D. (1993, August). *Assessment of capacity to make financial and medical decisions.* Paper presented at the 101st annual meeting of the American Psychological Association, Toronto, Canada.

Edinger, J. D., Hoelscher, T. J., Marsh, G. R., Lipper, S., & Ionescou-Pioggia, M. (1990). A cognitive-behavioral therapy for sleep-maintenance insomnia. *Psychology and Aging, 7,* 282-289.

Edinger, J. D., Morey, M. C., Sullivan, R. J., Higginbotham, M. B., Marsh, G. R., Dailey, D. S., & McCall, W. V. (1993). Aerobic fitness, acute exercise and sleep in older men. *Sleep, 16,* 351-359.

Egan, M. F, Hyde, T. M., Albers, G. W., Elkashef, A., Alexander, R. C., Reeve, A., Blum, A., Saenz, R. E., & Wyatt, J. R. (1992). Treatment of tardive dyskinesia with vitamin E. *American Journal of Psychiatry, 149,* 773-777.

Ehsani, A. A., Ogawa, T., Miller, T. R., Spina, R. J., & Jilka, S. M. (1991). Exercise training improves left ventricular systolic function in older men. *Circulation, 83,* 96-103.

Eisdorfer, C. (1968). Arousal and performance: Experiments in verbal learning and tentative theory. In G. A. Talland (Ed.), *Human aging and behavior* (pp. 189-217). New York: Academic Press.

Eisdorfer, C., Nowlin, J., & Wilkie, F. (1970). Improvement of learning in the aged by modification of autonomic nervous system activity. *Science, 170,* 1327-1329.

Elias, M. F., Robbins, M. A., Schultz, N. R., Jr., & Pierce, T. W. (1990). Is blood pressure an important variable in research on aging and neuropsychological test performance? *Journal of Gerontology: Psychological Science, 45,* P128-P135.

Elkin, I., Shea, M. T., Watkins, J. T., Imber, S. D., Sotsky, S. M., Collins, J. F., Glass, D. R., Pilkonis, P. A., Leber, W. R., Docherty, J. P., Fiester, S. J., & Parloff, M. B. (1989). NIMH treatment of depression collaborative research program: 1. General effectiveness of treatments. *Archives of General Psychiatry, 46,* 971-983.

Ellison, J. M., Milotsky, J. E., & Ely, E. (1990). Fluoxetine-induced bradycardia and syncope in two patients. *Journal of Clinical Psychiatry, 51,* 385-386.

Emery, O. B. (1985). Language and aging. *Experimental Aging Research, 11,* 3-60.

Endicott, J., & Spitzer, R. L. (1978). A diagnostic interview: The Schedule for Affective Disorders and Schizophrenia. *Archives of General Psychiatry, 35,* 837-844.

Engen, T. (1982). *The perception of odors.* New York: Academic Press.

Engle-Friedman, M., Bootzin, R. R., Hazlewood, L., & Tsao, C. (1992). An evaluation of behavioral treatments for insomnia in the older adult. *Journal of Clinical Psychology, 48,* 77-90.

Epstein, D. R. (1994). *A behavioral intervention to enhance the sleep-wake patterns of older adults with insomnia.* Unpublished doctoral dissertation, University of Arizona, Tucson.

Epstein, L. J. (1976). Depression in the elderly. *Journals of Gerontology, 21,* 278-282.

Erickson, R. C., Eimon, P., & Hebben, N. (1992). A bibliography of normative articles on cognition tests for older adults. *The Clinical Neuropsychologist, 6,* 98-102.

Evans, D. A., Funkenstein, H. H., & Albert, M. S. (1989). Prevalence of Alzheimer's disease in a community population of older persons. *JAMA, 262,* 2551-2556.

Evans, L. K., & Strumpf, N. E. (1990). Myths about elder restraint. *IMAGE: Journal of Nursing Scholarship, 22,* 124-128.

Evans, M. D., Hollon, S. D., De Rubeis, R., Piasecki, J. M., Grove, W. M., Garvey, M. J., & Tuason, V. B. (1992). Differential relapse following cognitive therapy, pharmacotherapy, and combined cognitive-pharmacotherapy for depression. *Archives of General Psychiatry, 49,* 802-808.

Evans, M. E., & Lye, M. (1992). Depression in the elderly physically ill: An open study of treatment with the 5-HT reuptake inhibitor fluoxetine. *Journal of Clinical and Experimental Gerontology, 14,* 297-307.

Evans, W., & Rosenberg, I. (1991). *Biomarkers.* New York: Simon & Schuster.

Everitt, D. E., Fields, D. R., Soumerai, S. S., & Avorn, J. (1991). Residents' behavior and staff distress in the nursing home. *Journal of the American Gerontological Society, 39*(8), 791-798.

Ewing, J. A. (1984). Detecting alcoholism: The CAGE questionnaire. *JAMA, 252,* 1905-1907.

Exton-Smith, A. N. (1977). Malnutrition in the elderly. *Proceedings of the Royal Society of Medicine, 70,* 615-629.

Faber, P., & Heidenreich, J. (1977). Treatment of stress incontinence with estrogens in postmenopausal women. *Urologia International, 32,* 221-223.

Falloon, I. R. H., Boyd, J. L., McGill, C. W., Williamson, M., Razani, J., Moss, H. B., Gilderman, A. M., & Simpson, G. M. (1985). Family management in the prevention of morbidity of schizophrenia: Clinical outcome of a two-year longitudinal study. *Archives of General Psychiatry, 42,* 887-896.

Fantl, J. A., Wyman, J. F., McClish, D. K., Harkins, S. W., Elswick, R. K., Taylor, J. R., & Hadley, E. C. (1991). Efficacy of bladder training in older women with urinary incontinence. *JAMA, 265,* 609-613.

Farmer, M. E., Kittner, S. J., Abbott, R. D., Wolz, M. M., & White, L. R. (1990). Longitudinal measured blood pressure, antihypertensive medication use and cognitive performance: The Framingham study. *Journal of Clinical Epidemiology, 43,* 475-480.

Farmer, M. E., White, L. R., Kittner, S. J., Kaplan, E., Moes, E., McNamara, P., Wolz, M. M., Wolf, P. A., & Feinleib, M. (1987). Neuropsychological test performance in Framingham: A descriptive study. *Psychological Reports, 60,* 1023-1040.

Farmer, P. M., Peck, A., & Terry, R. D. (1976). Correlations among neuritic plaques, neurofibrillary tangles, and the severity of senile dementia. *Journal of Neuropathology and Experimental Neurology, 35,* 367-376.

Farnsworth, M. G. (1989). Evaluation of mental competency. *American Family Physician, 39,* 182-190.

Farrer, L. A., O'Sullivan, D. M., Cupples, L. A., Growdon, J. H., & Myers, R. H. (1989). Assessment of genetic risk for Alzheimer's disease among first-degree relatives. *Annals of Neurology, 25,* 485-493.

Fasey, C. N. (1990). Grief in old age: A review of the literature. *International Journal of Geriatric Psychiatry, 5,* 67-75.

Faulkner, A. O., Heisel, M. A., & Simms, P. (1975). Life strengths and life stresses: Explorations in the measurements of the mental health of the Black aged. *American Journal of Orthopsychiatry, 45*(1), 102-110.

Fava, M., & Rosenbaum, J. F. (1991). Suicidality and fluoxetine: Is there a relationship? *Journal of Clinical Psychiatry, 52,* 108-111.

Fawcett, F. K., & Kravitz, H. (1985). The long-term management of bipolar disorders with lithium, carbamazepine, and antidepressants. *Journal of Clinical Psychiatry, 46,* 58-60.

Feder, R. (1991a). Bradycardia and syncope induced by fluoxetine (letter). *Journal of Clinical Psychiatry, 52,* 139.

Feder, R. (1991b). Reversal of antidepressant activity of fluoxetine by cyrpoheptadine in three patients. *Journal of Clinical Psychiatry, 52,* 163-164.

Federal Council on Aging, U.S. Department of Health and Human Services. (1981). *The need for long term care: Information and issues* (OHDS Publication No. 81-20704). Washington, DC: Government Printing Office.

Feher, E. P., Larrabee, G. J., & Crook. T. J. (1992). Factors attenuating the validity of the geriatric depression scale in a dementia population. *Journal of the American Geriatrics Society, 40,* 906-909.

Feiger, S. M., & Schmitt, M. H. (1979). Collegiality in interdisciplinary health teams: Its measurement and its effects. *Social Science Medicine, 13,* 217-229.

Feighner, J. P., Boyer, W. F., Meredith, C. H., Charles, H., & Hendrickson, G. (1988). An overview of fluoxetine. *British Journal of Psychiatry, 53,* 105-108.

Feighner, J. P., Boyer, W. F., Tyler, D. L., & Neborsky, R. J. (1990). Adverse consequences of fluoxetin-MAOI combination therapy. *Journal of Clinical Psychiatry, 51,* 222-225.

Feighner, J. P., Herbstein, J., & Damlouji, N. (1985). Combined MAOI, TCA and direct stimulant therapy of treatment-resistant depression. *Journal of Clinical Psychiatry, 46,* 206-209.

Feighner, J. P., Pambakian, R., Fowler, R. C., Boyer, W. F., & D'Amillo, M. F. (1989). A comparison of nefazodone, imipramine, and placebo in patients with moderate to severe depression. *Psychopharmacology Bulletin, 25, 219-221.*

Feighner, J. P., Robins, E., Guze, S. B., Woodruff, R. A., Winokur, G., & Rodrigo, M. (1972). Diagnostic criteria for use in psychiatric research. *Archives of General Psychiatry, 26,* 57-63.

Feinberg, I., Koresko, R., & Heller, N. (1967). EEG sleep patterns as a function of normal and pathological aging in man. *Journal of Psychiatric Research, 5,* 107-144.

Feinberg, I., March, J. D., Floyd, T. C., Jimison, R., Bossom-Demitrach, L., & Katz, P. H. (1985). Homeostatic changes during postnap sleep maintain baseline levels of delta EEG. *Electroencephalography and Clinical Neurophysiology, 61,* 134-137.

Feinberg, T., & Goodman, B. (1984). Affective illness, dementia, and pseudodementia. *Journal of Clinical Psychiatry, 45,* 99-103.

Feinson, M. C. (1987). Mental health and aging: Are there gender differences? *The Gerontologist, 27,* 703-711.

Feldt, K. S., & Ryden, M. (1992). Aggressive behavior: Educating nursing assistants. *Journal of Gerontological Nursing, 18*(5), 3-12.

Felson, D. T., Anderson, J. J., Hannan, M. T., Milton, R. C., Wilson, P. W., & Kiel, D. P. (1989). Impaired vision and hip fracture: The Framingham Study. *Journal of the American Geriatrics Society, 37,* 495-500.

Fenske, N. A., & Albers, S. E. (1990). Cosmetic modalities for aging skin: What to tell patients. *Geriatrics, 45*(9), 59-60.

Fernandez, F., Holmes, V. F., Adams, F., & Kavanaugh, J. (1988). Treatment of severe refractory agitation with a haloperidol drip. *Journal of Clinical Psychiatry, 49,* 239-241.

Ferris, S. H., de Leon, M. J., Wolf, A. P., Farkas, T., Christman, D. R., Reisberg, B., Fauler, J. S., MacGregor, R., Goldman, A., George, A. E., & Rampal, S. (1980). Positron emission tomography in the study of aging and senile dementia. *Neurobiology of Aging, 1,* 127-131.

Ferster, C. B. (1979). A laboratory model of psychotherapy: The boundary between clinical practice and experimental psychology. In P. O. Sjoden, S. Bates, & W. S. Dockens (Eds.), *Trends in behavior therapy* (pp. 23-38). New York: Academic Press.

Feuerlein, W., & Reiser, E. (1986). Parameters affecting the course and results of delirium tremens treatment. *Acta Psychiatry Scandanavia, 73,*(Suppl. 329), 120-123.

Fiatarone, M. A., Marks, E. C., Ryan, N. D., & Evans, W. (1992). Strength training in nonagenarians. *JAMA, 63,* 3029-3034.

Fiatarone, M. A., Marks, E. C., Ryan, N. D., Meredith, C. N., Lipsitz, L. A., & Evans, W. J. (1990). High-intensity strength training in nonagenarians: Effects on skeletal muscle. *JAMA, 263,* 3029-3034.

Field, D., & Minkler, M. (1988). Continuity and change in social support between young-old and old-old and very-old age. *Journal of Gerontology, 43,* 100-106.

Field, D., Minkler, M., Falk, R. F., & Leino, E. V. (1993). Influence of health on family contacts and family feelings in advanced old age: A longitudinal study. *Journal of Gerontology, 48,* 18-28.

Figiel, G., Krishnan, K. R., Doraiswamy, P. M. (1990). Subcortical structural changes in ECT-induced delirium. *Journal of Geriatric Psychiatry and Neurology, 3,* 172-176.

File, S. E. (1985). Tolerance to the behavioral actions of benzodiazepines. *Neuroscience and Biobehavioral Reviews, 296,* 603-606.

Fillenbaum, G. G., Hughes, D. C., Heyman, A., George, L. K., & Blazer, D. G. (1988). Relationship of health and demographic characteristics to Mini-Mental State Examination scores among community residents. *Psychological Medicine, 18*(3), 719-726.

Fillmore, K. M. (1987). Prevalence, incidence and chronicity of drinking patterns and problems among men as a function of age: A longitudinal and cohort analysis. *British Journal of Addiction, 82,* 77-83.

Finlayson, R. E., Hurt, R. D., Davis, L. J., & Morse, R. M. (1988). Alcoholism in elderly persons: A study of the psychiatric and psychosocial features of 216 patients. *Mayo Clinic Proceedings, 63,* 761-768.

Fischer, J., & Johnson, M. A. (1990). Low body weight and weight loss in the aged. *Journal of the American Dietetic Association, 90,* 1697-1706.

Fisher, J. E., & Carstensen, L. L. (1990). Behavior management of the dementias. *Clinical Psychology Review, 10,* 611-629.

Fisher, J. E., Goy, E. R., Swingen, D. N., & Szymanski, J. (1994, November). *The functional context of behavioral disturbances in Alzheimer's disease patients.* Paper presented at the meeting of the Association for Advancement of Behavior Therapy, San Diego, CA.

Fisher, J. E., Zeiss, A. M., & Carstensen, L. L. (1993). Psychopathology in the aged. In P. A. Sutker and H. E. Adams (Eds.), *Comprehensive handbook of psychopathology* (2nd ed., pp. 815-842). New York: Plenum.

Fisher, R. F. (1969). Elastic constants of human lens capsule. *Journal of Physiology, 201,* 1-19.

Fisher, R., Ury, W., & Patton, B. (1991). *Getting to YES: Negotiating agreement without giving in.* New York: Penguin.

Fleishman, R., Rosin, A., Tomer, A., & Schwartz, R. (1987). Cognitive impairment and quality of care in long-term care institutions. *Comprehensive Gerontology, 1,* 18-23.

Flint, A. J., Rifat, S. L., & Eastwood, R. (1991). Late-onset paranoia: Distinct from paraphrenia? *International Journal of Geriatric Psychiatry, 6,* 103-109.

Florsheim, M., & Herr, J. (1990). Family counseling with elders. *Generations, 14*(1), 40-42.

Fogel, B. S. (1991). Depression and aging. *Neuropsychiatry, Neuropsychology, and Behavioral Neurology, 4,* 24-35.

Fogelson, D. L., Bystritsky, A., & Pasnau, R. (1992). Buproprion in the treatment of bipolar disorders: The same old story? *Journal of Clinical Psychiatry, 53,* 443-446.

Folkman, S., Lazarus, R. S., Gruen, R., & DeLongis, A. (1986). Appraisal, coping, health status, and psychological symptoms. *Journal of Personality and Social Psychology, 50,* 571-579.

Folstein, M. F. (1983). The Mini-Mental State Examination. In T. Crook, S. Ferris, & R. Bartus (Eds.), *Assessment in geriatric psychopathology* (pp. 47-51). New Canaan, CT: Mark Powley.

Folstein, M. F., & Breitner, J. C. S. (1981). Language disorder predicts familial Alzheimer's disease. *Johns Hopkins Medical Journal, 149,* 145-147.

Folstein, M. F., Folstein, S. E., & McHugh, P. R. (1975). "Mini-Mental state": A practical method for grading the cognitive state of patients for the clinician. *Journal of Psychiatric Research, 12,* 189-198.

Folstein, M. F., & Rabins, P. V. (1991). Replacing pseudodementia. *Neuropsychiatry, Neuropsychology and Behavioral Neurology, 4,* 36-40.

Fong, R. (1992). A history of Asian Americans. In S. M. Furuto, R. Biswas, D. Chung, K. Murase, and F. Ross-Sheriff (Eds.), *Social work practice with Asian Americans.* Newbury Park, CA: Sage.

Fontaine, R., Ontiveros, A., Elie, R., Kensler, T., Roberts, D. I., Kaplita, S., Ecker, J. A., Faludi, G. (1994). A double-blind comparison of nefazodone, imipramine and placebo in major depression. *Journal of Clinical Psychiatry, 55,* 234-241.

Fopma-Loy, J. (1988). Wandering: Causes, consequences, and care. *Journal of Psychosocial Nursing, 26*(5), 8-18.

Ford, M. R., & Widiger, T. A. (1989). Sex bias in the diagnosis of histrionic and antisocial personality disorders. *Journal of Consulting and Clinical Psychology, 57,* 301-305.

Foster, J. R. (1992). Use of lithium in elderly psychiatric patients: A review of the literature. *Lithium, 3,* 77-93.

Fox, B. H. (1989). Depressive symptoms and risk of cancer. *JAMA, 262,* 1231.

Fox, P. C., Heft, M. W., Herrera, M., Bowers, M. R., Mandel, I. D., & Baum, B. J. (1987). Secretion of antimicrobial proteins from the parotid glands of different aged healthy persons. *Journal of Gerontology, 42,* 476-481.

Fozard, J. L. (1985). Psychology of aging-normal and pathological age differences in memory. In J. C. Brocklehurst (Ed.), *Textbook of geriatric medicine and gerontology* (pp. 122-144). Edinburgh: Churchill/Livingstone.

Fozard, J. L. (1990). Vision and hearing in aging. In J. Birren & K. W. Schaie (Eds.), *Handbook of the psychology of aging.* New York: Van Nostrand Reinhold.

572 PRACTICAL HANDBOOK OF CLINICAL GERONTOLOGY

Frank, E., Kupfer, D. J., Perel, J. M., Cornes, C., Jarret, D. B., Mallinger, A. G., Thase, M. E., McEachran, M. S., & Grocholinski, V. J. (1991). Three-year outcomes for maintenance therapies in recurrent depression. *Archives of General Psychiatry, 47,* 1093-1099.

Franzen, M. D., & Rasmussen, P. R. (1990). Clinical neuropsychology and older populations. In A. M. Horton (Ed.), *Neuropsychology across the lifespan* (pp. 81-102). New York: Springer.

Franzen, M. D., Tishelman, A., Smith, S., Sharp, B., & Friedman, A. (1989). Preliminary date regarding the test-retest and parallel-forms reliability of the Randt Memory Test. *The Clinical Neuropsychologist, 3,* 25-28.

Fras, I., Litin, E. M., & Pearson, J. S. (1967). Comparison of psychiatric symptoms in carcinoma of the pancreas with those in some other intra-abdominal neoplasms. *American Journal of Psychiatry, 123,* 1553-1562.

Freed, A. (1992). Discussion: Minority elderly. *Journal of Geriatric Psychiatry, 25*(1), 105-111.

Freeman, C. P., Trimble, M. R., Deubin, J. F., Stokes, T. M., & Ashford, J. J. (1994). Fluooxamine vs. Clomipramine in the treatment of Obsessive Compulsive Disorder: A multicenter, randomized, double-blind parallel group comparison. *Journal of Clinical Psychiatry, 55*(7), 301-305.

Fremouw, W. J., de Perczel, M., & Ellis, T. E. (1990). *Suicide risk: Assessment and responsive guidelines.* New York: Pergamon.

Frewen, W. K. (1978). An objective assessment of the unstable bladder of psychosomatic origin. *British Journal of Urology 50,* 246-249.

Frewen, W. K. (1979). Role of bladder training in the treatment of the unstable bladder in the female. *Urologic Clinics of North America, 6,* 273-277.

Frewen, W. K. (1980). The management of urgency and frequency of micturition. *British Journal of Urology, 52,* 367-369.

Frewen, W. K. (1982). A reassessment of bladder training in detrusor dysfunction in the female. *British Journal of Urology, 54,* 372-373.

Friedman, H. S., & Booth-Kewley, S. (1987). The disease-prone personality: A meta-analytic view of the construct. *American Psychologist, 42,* 539-555.

Friedman, J. H., & Lannson, M. C. (1989). Clozapine in the treatment of psychosis in Parkinson's disease. *Neurology, 39,* 1219-1221.

Friedman, J. H., & Lannson, M. C. (1990). Clozapine-responsive tremor in Parkinson's disease. *Movement Disorders, 5,* 225-229.

Friedman, L., Bliwise, D. L., Yesavage, J. A., & Salom, S. R. (1991). A preliminary study comparing sleep restriction and relaxation treatments for insomnia in older adults. *Journal of Gerontology: Psychological Sciences, 46,* 1-8.

Friedman, L. F., Bliwise, D. L., Tanke, E. D., Salom, S. R., et al. (1992). A survey of self-reported poor sleep and associated factors in older individuals. *Behavior, Health, and Aging, 2*(1), 13-20.

Friend, R. A. (1987). The individual and social psychology of aging: Clinical implications for lesbians and gay men. *Journal of Homosexuality, 14,* 307-331.

Fries, J. (1983). Aging, natural death and the compression of morbidity. *New England Journal of Medicine, 303,* 130-136.

Fries, J. F. (1980). Aging, natural death, and the compression of morbidity. *New England Journal of Medicine, 303,* 130-135.

Fries, J. F., & Crapo, L. M. (1981). *Vitality and aging.* San Francisco: Freeman.

Frieswyk, S. H., Allen, J. G., Colson, D. B., Coyne, L., Gabbard, G. O., Horwitz, L., & Newsom, G. (1986). Therapeutic alliance: Its place as a process and outcome variable in dynamic psychotherapy research. *Journal of Consulting and Clinical Psychology, 54,* 32-38.

Fritz, J., & Stewart J. T. (1990). Lorazepam treatment of resistive aggression in dementia. *American Journal of Psychiatry, 147*(9), 1250.

Frolik, L. A., & Brown, M. C. (1992). *Advising the elderly or disabled client.* Englewood Cliffs, NJ: Rosenfeld Launer.

Fry, P. S. (1986). *Depression, stress, and adaptations in the elderly: Psychological assessment and intervention.* Rockville, MD: Aspen.

Fuld, P. A. (1977). *The Fuld object memory evaluation.* Chicago: Stoelting.

Funkenstein, H. H. (1988). Cerebrovascular disorders. In M. S. Albert & M. B. Moss (Eds.), *Geriatric neuropsychology* (pp. 179-207). New York: Guilford.

Gaffney, J. (1986). Toward a less restrictive environment. *Geriatric Nursing, 7*(2), 94-95.

Gaitz, C. M., & Baer, P. E. (1971). Characteristics of elderly patients with alcoholism. *Archives of General Psychiatry, 24,* 372-378.

Galasko, D., Klauber, M. R., Hofstetter, C. R., Salmon, D. P., Lasker, B., & Thal, L. J. (1990). The Mini-Mental State Examination in the early diagnosis of Alzheimer's disease. *Archives of Neurology, 47,* 49-52.

Gallagher, D. (1979, August). *Behavior group therapy with the elderly.* Paper presented at the meeting of the American Psychological Association, New York.

Gallagher, D. (1986). Assessment of depression by interview methods and psychiatric rating scales. In L. W. Poon (Ed.), *Handbook for clinical memory assessment of older adults* (pp. 205-225). Washington, DC: American Psychological Association.

Gallagher, D., Rose, J., Rivera, P., Lovett, S., & Thompson, L. W. (1989). Prevalence of depression in family caregivers. *The Gerontologist, 29,* 449-456.

Gallagher, D., & Thompson, L. W. (1982). Treatment of major depressive disorder in older adult outpatients with brief psychotherapies. *Psychotherapy, Theory, Research, and Practice, 19,* 482-490.

Gallagher, D. E., Breckinridge, J. N., Thompson, L. W., & Peterson, J. A. (1983). Effects of bereavement on indicators of mental health in elderly widows and widowers. *Journal of Gerontology, 38,* 565-571.

Gallagher-Thompson, D. (1994a). Clinical intervention strategies for distressed caregivers: Rationale and development of psychoeducational approaches. In E. Light, G. Niederehe, & B. D. Lebowitz (Eds.), *Stress effects on family caregivers of Alzheimer's patients: Research and interventions* (pp. 260-277). New York: Springer.

Gallagher-Thompson, D. (1994b). Direct services and interventions for caregivers: A review of extant programs and a look to the future. In M. H. Cantor (Ed.), *Family caregiving: Agenda for the future* (pp. 102-122). San Francisco: American Society on Aging.

Gallagher-Thompson, D., & DeVries, H. (1994). "Coping with Frustration" classes: Development and preliminary outcomes with women who care for relatives with dementia. *The Gerontologist, 34,* 548-552.

Gallagher-Thompson, D., Hanley-Peterson, P., & Thompson, L. W. (1990). Maintenance of gains versus relapse following brief psychotherapy for depression. *Journal of Consulting and Clinical Psychology, 58,* 371-374.

Gallagher-Thompson, D., Lovett, S., Rose, J., & Futterman, A. (1994). *The impact of psychoeducational interventions on distressed family caregivers.* Manuscript submitted for publication.

Gallagher-Thompson, D., & Steffen, A. (1994). Comparative effectiveness of cognitive/behavioral and brief psychodynamic psychotherapies for the treatment of depression in family caregivers. *Journal of Consulting and Clinical Psychology, 62,* 543-549.

Gallagher-Thompson, D., Willis-Shore, J., Steffen, A., Walsh, W., Koin, D., Thompson, L. W. (1994). *A controlled group comparison of the mental and physical health of female dementia caregivers.* Manuscript submitted for publication.

Gallo, J. J. (1990). The effect of social support on depression in caregivers of the elderly. *Journal of Family Practice, 30,* 430-436.

Garb, H. N. (1984). The incremental validity of information used in personality assessment. *Clinical Psychology Review, 4,* 641-655.

Gardner, E. A., & Johnson, J. A. (1985). Buproprion: An antidepressant without sexual pathophysiological action. *Journal of Clinical Psychopharmacology, 5,* 24-29.

Gardos, G. (1980). Disinhibition of behavior by anti-anxiety drugs. *Psychosomatics, 21,* 1025-1026.

Garfinkel, R. (1979). Brief behavioral therapy with an elderly patient. *Journal of Geriatric Psychiatry, 12,* 101-107.

Garnets, L. D., & Kimmel, D. C. (1993). Lesbian and gay male dimensions in the psychological study of human diversity. In L. D. Garnets & D. C. Kimmel (Eds.), *Psychological perspectives on lesbian and gay male experiences* (pp. 1-51). New York: Columbia University Press.

Garrison, J. E. (1978). Stress management training for the elderly: A psychoeducational approach. *Journal of the American Geriatrics Society, 26,* 397-403.

Gaston, L., Marmar, C. R., Gallagher, D., & Thompson, L. W. (1991). Alliance prediction of outcome beyond in-treatment symptomatic change as psychotherapy processes. *Psychotherapy Research, 1,* 104-112.

Gatz, M., & Pearson, C. G. (1988). Ageism revised and provision of psychological services. *American Psychologist, 43,* 184-189.

Gauthier S., Bouchard, R., & Lamontagne, A. (1990). Tetrahydroaminoacridine-lecithin combination treatment in patients with intermediate stage Alzheimer's disease. *New England Journal of Medicine, 322,* 1272-1276.

Gavrilov, L. A., & Gavrilova, N. S. (1991). *The biology of lifespan: A quantitative approach.* Hammond Academic.

Gay, G. (1987). Ethnic identity development and Black expressiveness. In G. Gay & W. L. Baber (Eds.), *Expressively Black: The cultural basis of ethnic identity.* New York: Praeger.

Gelenberg, A. (1994). Buspirone: Seven-year update. *Journal of Clinical Psychiatry, 55,* 222-229.

Gelenberg, A. J., & Katz, M. D. (1993). Antipsychotic agents. In R. Bressler & M. D. Katz (Eds.), *Geriatric pharmacology* (pp. 375-408). New York: McGraw-Hill.

Gelfand, D. E. (1989). Immigration, aging, and intergenerational relationships. *The Gerontologist, 29*(3), 366-372.

Gelfand, D. E., & Baressi, C. M. (1987). *Ethnic dimensions of aging.* New York: Springer.

GenDerm Corporation. (1993). *Capsaicin®* (Product monograph). Lincolnshire, IL: Author.

Genevay, B. (1994). Family issues/family dynamics: A caregiving odyssey to 2001 and beyond. In M. Cantor (Ed.), *Family caregiving: Agenda for the future* (pp. 89-101). San Francisco: American Society on Aging.

George, L. (1988). Social participation in later life: Black-White differences. In J. S. Jackson (Ed.), *The Black American elderly: Research on physical and psychosocial health.* New York: Springer.

George, L. K. (1980). *Role transitions in later life.* Belmont, CA: Wadsworth.

George, L. K. (1992). Gender, age, and psychiatric disorders. In L. Glasse & J. Hendricks (Eds.), *Gender and aging* (pp. 33-43). New York: Baywood.

George, L. K., Blazer, D. G., Winfield-Laird, I., Leaf, P. J., & Fischbach, R. L. (1988). Psychiatric disorders and mental health service use in later life: Evidence from the Epidemiologic Catchment Area Program. In J. Brody & G. L. Maddox (Eds.), *Epidemiology and aging* (pp. 189-219). New York: Springer.

George, L. K., & Weiler, S. J. (1985). Sexuality in middle and late life. In E. Palmore, J. Nowlin, E. Busse, I. Siegler, & G. Maddox (Eds.), *Normal aging* (Vol. 3.). Durham, NC: Duke University Press.

Georgotas, A., & McCue, R. E. (1988). Depressive and manic states of late life: Clinical and research considerations. In A. Georgotas & R. Cancro (Eds.), *Depression and mania* (pp. 592-604). New York: Elsevier.

Georgotas, A., McCue, R. E., Cooper, T. B., Nagachandran, N., & Chang, I. (1988). How effective and safe is continuation therapy in elderly depressed patients? Factors affecting relapse rate. *Archives of General Psychiatry, 45,* 929-932.

Gerber, I., Rusalem, P., Hannon, N., Battin, D., & Arkin, A. (1975). Anticipatory grief of aged widows and widowers. *Journal of Gerontology, 30,* 225-229.

Geringer, E. S., Perlmuter, L. C., Stern, S. A., & Nathan, D. M. (1988). Depression and diabetic neuropathy: A complex relationship. *Journal of Geriatric Psychiatry and Neurology, 1,* 11-15.

German, P. S., Shapiro, S., & Kramer, M. (1986). Nursing home study of the eastern Baltimore catchment area. In M. S. Harper & B. D. Lebowitz (Eds.), *Mental illness in nursing homes: Agenda for research.* Rockville, MD: National Institute of Mental Health.

Gerner, R., Estabrook, W., Steur, J., & Jarvik, L. (1980). Treatment of geriatric depression with trazodone, imipramine and placebo: A double blind study. *Journal of Clinical Psychiatry, 41,* 261-320.

Gersick, C. J. (1989). Marking time: Predictable transitions in task groups. *Academy of Management Journal, 32,* 274-309.

Gerson, S. C., Plotkin, D. A., & Jarvik, L. F. (1988). Antidepressant drug studies, 1964 to 1986: Empirical evidence for aging patients. *Journal of Clinical Psychopharmacology, 8,* 311-322.

Giachello, A. L. (1985). Hispanics and health care. In P. S. J. Cafferty & W. C. McCready (Eds.), *Hispanics in the United States.* New Brunswick, NJ: Transaction Books.

Gibson, A. J., & Kendrick, D. C. (1982). *The Kendrick Cognitive Tests for the Elderly.* Windsor, Berks, UK: NFER-Nelson.

Gibson, R. (1988). The work, retirement, and disability of older Black Americans. In J. S. Jackson (Ed.), *The Black American elderly: Research on physical and psychosocial health* (pp. 304-326). New York: Springer.

Gierl, B., Dysken, M., Davis, J. M., & Lesser, J. M. (1987). Neuroleptic use in the elderly. In N. E. Miller & G. D. Cohen (Eds.), *Schizophrenia and aging* (pp. 259-274). New York: Guilford.

Gilchrest, B. A. (1989). Skin aging and photoaging: An overview. *Journal of the American Academy of Dermatology, 21*(3, Pt. 2), 610-613.

Giles, D. E., Kupfer, D. J., & Roffwarg, H. P. (1990). EEG sleep before and after the first episode of depression. *Sleep Research, 19,* 161.

Giles, D. E., Roffwarg, H. P., Schlesser, M. A., & Rush, A. J. (1986). Which endogenous depressive symptoms relate to REM latency reductions? *Biological Psychiatry, 21,* 473-482.

Gilley, D. W. (1993). Behavioral and affective disturbances in Alzheimer's disease. In R. W. Parks, R. F. Zec, & R. S. Wilson (Eds.), *Neuropsychology of Alzheimer's disease and other dementias* (pp. 112-137). New York: Oxford University Press.

Gilliam, J. H. III. (1990). Pancreatic disorders. In W. R. Hazzard, R. Andres, E. L. Bierman, & J. P. Blass (Eds.), *Principles of geriatric medicine and gerontology* (2nd ed., pp. 640-644). New York: McGraw-Hill.

Gillin, J. C., Duncan, W. C., Murphy, D. L., Post, R. M., Wehr, T. A., Goodwin, F. K., Wyatt, R. J., & Bunney, W. E., Jr. (1981). Age-related changes in sleep in depressed and normal subjects. *Psychiatry Research, 4,* 73-78.

Gilpin, E. A. (1994, September). Smoking initiation rates in adults and minors: United States, 1944-1988. *American Journal of Epidemiology, 140*(6), 535-543.

Giovanni, N. (1994). *Racism 101.* New York: William Morrow.

Given, C. W., Given, B., Stommel, M., Collins, C., King, S., & Franklin, S. (1992). The Caregiver Reaction Assessment (CRA) for caregivers to persons with chronic physical and mental impairments. *Research in Nursing and Health, 15,* 271-283.

Glassman, A. H., Johnson, L. L., Giardina, E. V., Walsh, T., Roose, S. P., Cooper, T. B., & Bigger, J. T. (1983). The use of imipramine in depressed patient with congestive heart failure. *JAMA, 250,* 1997-2001.

Glassman, A. H., Roose, S. P., & Bigger, J. T. (1993). The safety of tricyclic antidepressants in cardiac patients risk-benefit reconsidered. *JAMA, 269*(20), 2673-2675.

Glassman, A. H, Schildkraut, J. J., Orsulak, P. H., Cooper, T. B., Kupfer, D. J., Shader, R. I., Davis, J. M., Carrol, B., Perel, J. M., Klerman, G. L., & Greenblatt, D. J. (1985). Tricyclic antidepressants-blood level measurements and clinical outcome: An APA Task Force report. *American Journal of Psychiatry, 142,* 155-162.

Gleason, R. P., & Schneider, L. S. (1990). Carbamazepine treatment of agitation in Alzheimer's outpatients refractory to neuroleptic. *Journal of Clinical Psychiatry, 51,* 115-118.

Glovinsky, P. B., & Spielman, A. J. (1991). Sleep restriction therapy. In P. Hauri (Ed.), *Case studies in insomnia* (pp. 49-63). New York: Plenum.

Glynn, R. J., Bouchard, S. M., LoCastro, J. S., & Hermos, J. A. (1986). Changes in alcohol consumption behaviors among men. In G. Maddox, L. Robins, & N. Rosenberg (Eds.), *The Normative aging study: The nature and extent of alcohol problems among the elderly* (pp. 101-116). New York: Springer.

Glynn, R. J., Bouchard, G. R., LoCastro, J. S., & Laird, N. M. (1985). Aging and generational effects on drinking behaviors in men: Results from The Normative Aging Study. *American Journal of Public Health, 75,* 1413-1419.

Goetz, C. G., Tannser, C. M., & Kawans, H. L. (1984). Buproprion in Parkinson's disease. *Neurology, 34,* 1092-1094.

Gold, M. S., Herridge, P., & Hapworth, W. E. (1987). Depression and "symptomless" autoimmune thyroiditis. *Psychiatric Annals, 7,* 750-757.

Goldberg, A. P., Andres, R., & Bierman, E. L. (1990). Diabetes mellitus in the elderly. In W. R. Hazzard, R. Andres, E. L. Bierman, & J. P. Blass (Eds.), *Principles of geriatric medicine and gerontology* (2nd ed., pp. 739-758). New York: McGraw-Hill.

Goldberg, A. P., & Hagberg, J. M. (1990). Physical exercise in the elderly. In E. L. Schneider & J. W. Rowe (Eds.), *The handbook of the biology of aging* (3rd ed., pp. 407-428). New York: Academic Press.

Golden, C. J., Purish, A. D., & Hammeke, T. A. (1985). *Luria-Nebraska neuropsychological battery: Forms I and II manual.* Los Angeles: Western Psychological Services.

Golden, R. N., James, S. P., & Sherer, M. A., Rudorfer, M. V., Sack, D. A., & Potter, W. Z. (1985). Psychoses associated with buproprion treatment. *American Journal of Psychiatry, 142,* 1459-1462.

Goldfarb, J. (1985). *Attitudes of gay and heterosexual men towards aging.* Unpublished doctoral dissertation, California School of Professional Psychology, Los Angeles. .

Goldman, A., & Carroll, J. L. (1990). Educational intervention as an adjunct to treatment in erectile dysfunction in older couples. *Journal of Sex and Marital Therapy, 16,* 127-141.

Goldman, L., & Tosteson, A. N. (1991). Uncertainty about postmenopausal estrogen. *New England Journal of Medicine, 325,* 800-802.

Goldstein, M. (1989). Physicians and teams. In R. J. Ham (Ed.), *Geriatric medicine annual* (pp. 256-275). New Jersey: Medical Economics.

Golomb, J., de Leon, M. J., Kluger, A., George, A. E., Tarshish, C., & Ferris, S. H. (1993). Hippocampal atrophy in normal aging. *Archives of Neurology, 50,* 967-973.

Gonyea, J. (1989). Alzheimer's Disease support groups: An analysis of their structure, format and perceived benefits. *Social Work in Health Care, 14,* 61-72.

Goodenough, G. K. (1988). The lack of objectivity of physician evaluations in geriatric guardianship cases. *Journal of Contemporary Law, 14,* 53-59.

Goodman, A., & Siegel, C. (1986). Elderly schizophrenic inpatients in the wake of deinstitutionalization. *American Journal of Psychiatry, 143,* 204-207.

Goodnick, P., & Gershon, S. (1984). Chemotherapy of cognitive disorders in geriatric subjects. *Journal of Clinical Psychiatry, 45,* 196-209.

Goodnick, P. J., & Sandoval, R. (1992). Blood levels and acute response to buproprion. *American Journal of Psychiatry, 149,* 399-400.

Goodwin, F. K., & Jamison, K. R. (1990). *Manic depressive illness.* New York: Oxford University Press.

Goodwin, J. S., Sanchez, C. J., Thomas, P., Hunt, C., Garry, P. J., & Goodwin, J. M. (1987). Alcohol intake in a healthy elderly population. *American Journal of Public Health, 77,* 173-177.

Gordon, L. W. (1980). Southeast Asian refugee migration to the United States. In J. T. Fawcett & B. V. Carino (Eds.), *Pacific bridges: The new immigration from Asia and the Pacific Islands* (pp. 153-173). Staten Island, NY: Center for Migration Studies.

Gordon, T., & Kannel, W. B. (1983). Drinking and its relation to smoking, BP, blood lipids, and uric acid. *Archives of Internal Medicine, 143,* 1366-1374.

Gottesman, I. I. (1991). *Schizophrenia genesis.* New York: Freeman.

Gottesman, I. I., & Shields, J. (1982). *Schizophrenia: The epigenetic puzzle.* Cambridge, UK: Cambridge University Press.

Gottfries, C. G. (1985). Alzheimer's disease and senile dementia: Biochemical characteristics and aspects of treatment. *Psychopharmacology, 86,* 245-252.

Gottfries, C. G., Adolfsson, R., Aquilionius, S. M., Carlsson, A., Eckernas, S., Nordberg, A., Oreland, L., Svennerholm, L., Wiberg, A., & Winblad, B. (1983). Biochemical changes in dementia disorders of Alzheimer's type (AD/SDAT). *Neurobiology of Aging, 4,* 261-271.

Gottfries, C. G., Gottfries, I., & Roos, B. E. (1969). The investigation of homovanillic acid in the human brain and its correlation to senile dementia. *British Journal of Psychiatry, 115,* 563-574.

Gottfries, C. G., Roos, B. E., & Winblad, B. (1976). Monoamine and monamine metabolites in the human brain post mortem in senile dementia. *Aktuelle Gerontologie, 6,* 429-435.

Gottlieb, G. L., & Greenspan, D. (1989). Depression and endocrine disorders. In R. G. Robinson & P. V. Rabins (Eds.), *Depression and coexisting disease* (pp. 83-102). New York: Igaku-Shoin.

Gottlieb, G. L., & Reisberg, B. (1988). Legal issues in Alzheimer's disease. *American Journal of Alzheimer's Care, 3,* 34-36.

Gottman, J. M., & Krokoff, L. J. (1989). The relationships between marital interaction and marital satisfaction: A longitudinal view. *Journal of Consulting and Clinical Psychology, 57,* 47-52.

Gottman, J., Notarius, C., Gonso, J., & Markman, H. (1976). *A couple's guide to communication.* Champaign, IL: Research Press.

Grady, D., Gebretsadik, T., Kerlikowske, K., Ernster, V., & Petitti, D. (1995). Hormone replacement therapy and endometrial cancer risk: A meta-analysis. *Obstetrics and Gynecology, 85,* 304-313.

Graham, K. (1986). Identifying and measuring alcohol abuse among the elderly: Serious problems with existing instrumentation. *Journal of Studies on Alcohol, 47,* 322-326.

Grahame, P. S. (1984). Schizophrenia in old age (late paraphrenia). *British Journal of Psychiatry, 145,* 493-495.

Grambs, J. D. (1989). *Women over forty: Visions and realities.* New York: Springer.

Granger, C., Hamilton, B., Gresham, G., & Kramer, A. (1989). The stroke rehabilitation outcomes study. Part II. Relative merits of the Barthel Index score and a four-item sub-score in predicting patient outcomes. *Archives of Physical Medicine Rehabilitation, 70,* 100-103.

Granger, C. V., Hamilton, B. B., & Fieldler R. D. (1992). Discharge outcome after stroke rehabilitation. *Stroke, 23,* 978-982.

Grant, I. (1987). Alcohol and the brain: Neuropsychological correlates. *Journal of Consulting and Clinical Neuropsychology, 55,* 310-324.

Grant, I., Adams, K. M., & Reed, R. (1984). Aging, abstinence, and medical risk factors in the prediction of neuropsychologic deficit among long-term alcoholics. *Archives of General Psychiatry, 41,* 710-718.

Grant, I., Prigatano, G. P., Heaton, R. K., McSweeney, A. J., Wright, E. C., & Adams, K. M. (1987). Progressive neuropsychological impairment and hypoxemia: Relationship in COPD. *Archives of General Psychiatry, 44,* 999-1006.

Greenberg, D. B. (1989). Depression and cancer. In R. G. Robinson & P. V. Rabins (Eds.), *Depression and coexisting disease* (pp. 103-115). New York: Igaku-Shoin.

Greenberg, R. P., & Bornstein, R. F. (1988a). The dependent personality: 1. Risk for physical disorders. *Journal of Personality Disorders, 2,* 126-135.

Greenberg, R. P., & Bornstein, R. F. (1988b). The dependent personality: 2. Risk for psychological disorders. *Journal of Personality Disorders, 2,* 136-143.

Greenblatt, D. J. (1992). Pharmacology of benzodiazepine hypnotics. *Journal of Clinical Psychiatry, 53*(6, Suppl.), 7-13.

Greenblatt, D. J., Sellers, E. M., & Shader, R. I. (1982). Drug disposition in old age. *New England Journal of Medicine, 306,* 1081-1088.

Greendyke, R. M., & Kanter, D. R. (1986). Therapeutic effects of pindolol on behavior disturbances associated with organic brain disease: A double-blind study. *Journal of Clinical Psychiatry, 47,* 423-426.

Greendyke, R. M., Kanter, D. R., Schuster, D. B., Verstreake, R. N., & Wooton, J. (1986). Propranolol treatment of assaultive patients with organic brain disease: Double-blind crossover placebo-controlled study. *Journal of Nervous and Mental Disorders, 174,* 290-294.

Greene, B. (1994). Lesbian and gay sexual orientations and implications for clinical training and research and practice. In B. Greene & G. M. Herek (Eds.), *Lesbian and gay psychology: Theory, research and clinical applications* (pp. 1-24). Thousand Oaks, CA: Sage.

Greene, M. C., Adelman, R., Charon, R., & Hoffman, S. (1986). Ageism in the medical encounter: An exploratory study of the doctor-elderly interviewee relationship. *Language and Communication, 6,* 113-124.

Greene, V. L., & Monahan, D. (1989). The effect of a support and education program on stress and burden among family caregivers to frail elderly persons. *The Gerontologist, 29,* 472-477.

Greenspan, S. L., Myers, E. R., & Maitland, L. A. (1994). Fall severity and bone mineral density a risk factors for hip fractures vs. ambulatory elderly. *JAMA, 271,* 8-133.

Gregerman, R. I. (1990). Thyroid diseases. In W. R. Hazzard, R. Andres, E. L. Bierman, & J. P. Blass (Eds.), *Principles of geriatric medicine and gerontology* (2nd ed., pp. 719-738). New York: McGraw-Hill.

Grimby, G., & Saltin, B. (1983). The aging muscle. *Clinical Physiology, 3,* 209-218.

Grimsldy, S. R., & Jann, M. W. (1992). Paroxetine, sertraline, and fluvoxamine: New selective serotonin reuptake inhibitors. *Clinical Pharmacology, 11,* 930-957.

Grisso, J. A, Kelsey, J. L., Strom, B. L., Chiu, G. Y., Maisling, G., O'Brien, L. A, Hoffman, S., & Kaplan, F. (1991). Risk factors for falls as a cause of hip fracture in women. *New England Journal of Medicine, 324,* 1326-1331.

Grisso, T. (1986). *Evaluating competencies: Forensic assessments and instruments.* New York: Plenum.

Grisso, T. (1994). Clinical assessments for legal competence of older adults. In M. Storandt & G. Vandenbos (Eds.), *Neuropsychological assessment of dementia and depression in older adults: A clinical guide.* Washington, DC: American Psychological Association.

Grisso, T., & Appelbaum, P. S. (1991). Mentally ill and nonmentally ill patients' abilities to understand informed consent disclosures for medication. *Law and Human Behavior, 15,* 377-388.

Gross, M. D. (1982). Reversal by bethanecol of sexual dysfunction caused by anticholinergic antidepressants. *American Journal of Psychiatry, 139,* 1193-1194.

Grossberg, G. T., Hassan, R., Szwabo, P. A., Morley, J. E., Nakra, B. R. S., Bretscher, C. W., Zimmy, G. H., & Solomon, K. (1990). Psychiatric problems in the nursing home. *Journal of the American Gerontological Society, 38*(8), 907-918.

Grove, G. L. (1989). Physiologic changes in older skin. *Clinics in Geriatric Medicine, 5,* 115-25.

Grzegorczyk, P. B., Jones, S. W., & Mistretta, C. M. (1979). Age-related differences in salt taste acuity. *Journal of Gerontology, 34,* 834-840.

Guilleminault, C., Crowe, L., Quera-Salva, M. A., Miles, L., & Partinen, M. (1988). Periodic leg movement, sleep fragmentation and central sleep apnea in two cases: Reduction with clonazepam. *European Respiratory Journal, 1,* 762-765.

Gur, R. C., Gur, R. E., Obrist, W. D., Skolnick, B. E., & Reivich, M. (1987). Age and regional cerebral blood flow at rest and during cognitive activity. *Archives of Neurology, 44,* 21-33.

Guralnik, J. M., & Simonsick, E. M. (1993). Physical disability in older adults [Special Issue]. *Journal of Gerontology, 48,* 3-10.

Gurian, B., & Miner, J. H. (1991). Clinical presentation of anxiety in the elderly. In C. Salzman & B. D. Lebowitz (Eds.), *Anxiety in the elderly.* New York: Springer.

Gurland, B. (1991). Epidemiology of psychiatric disorders. In J. Sadavoy, L. W. Lazarus, & L. F. Jarvik (Eds.), *Comprehensive review of geriatric psychiatry* (pp. 25-40). Washington, DC: American Psychiatric Press.

Gurland, B., Kuriansky, J., Sharpe, L., Simon, R., Stiller, P., & Birkett, P. (1977-1978). CARE: Rationale, development, and reliability. *International Journal of Aging and Human Development, 8,* 9-42.

Gurland, B. J., & Wilder, D. E. (1984). The CARE interview revisited: Development of an efficient, systematic clinical assessment. *Journal of Gerontology, 39*(2), 129-137.

Gutheil, T. G., & Appelbaum, P. S. (1991). *Clinical handbook of psychiatry and the law* (2nd ed.). New York: McGraw-Hill.

Gutheil, T. G., & Bursztajn, H. (1986). Clinicians' guidelines for assessing and presenting subtle forms of patient incompetence in legal settings. *American Journal of Psychiatry, 143,* 1020-1023.

Gutheil, T. G., Bursztajn, H., Kaplan, A. N., & Brodsky, A. (1987). Participation in competency assessment and treatment decisions: The role of a psychiatrist-attorney team. *Mental and Physical Disability Law Reporter, 11,* 446-449.

Gutmann, D. (1976). Individual adaptation in the middle years: Developmental issues in the masculine mid-life crisis. *Journal of Geriatric Psychiatry, 9,* 41-59.

Gutmann, D. (1987). *Reclaimed powers: Toward a new psychology of men and women in later life.* New York: Basic Books.

Gwenwald, M. (1984). The SAGE model for serving older lesbians and gay men. *Journal of Social Work and Human Sexuality, 2,* 53-61.

Haadem, K., Dahlstrom, J. A., & Ling, L. (1991). Anal sphincter competence in healthy women: clinical implications of age and other factors. *Obstetrics and Gynecology, 78*(5, Pt. 1), 823-827.

Hachinski, V. C., Lassen, N. A., & Marshall, J. (1974). Multi-infarct dementia—A cause of mental deterioration in the elderly. *Lancet, 2,* 207-210.

Hadley, E. C., Ory, M. G., Suzman, R., Weindruch, R., & Fried, L. (Eds.). (1993). Physical frailty: A treatable cause of dependence in old age [Special Issue]. *The Gerontologist, 48,* vii.

Haimov, I., Lavie, P., Laudon, M., Herer, P., Vigder, C., & Zisapel, N. (1995). Melatonin replacement therapy of elderly insomniacs. *Sleep, 18,* 589-598.

Hale, A. S. (1993). New antidepressants: Use in high-risk patients (Symposium on Current Issues in Drug Therapy of Depression). *Journal of Clinical Psychiatry, 54*(8, Suppl.), 61-70.

Haley, W., Brown, L., & Levine, E. (1987). Experimental evaluation of the effectiveness of group interventions for dementia caregivers. *The Gerontologist, 27,* 376-382.

Haley, W. E. (1983). A family-behavioral approach to the treatment of the cognitively impaired elderly. *The Gerontologist, 23,* 18-20.

Hall, M. R. P., MacLennan, W. J., & Lye, M. D. W. (1993). *Medical care of the elderly* (3rd ed.). New York: John Wiley.

Hall, R. C. W., Gardner, E. R., & Popkin, M. K. (1981). Unrecognized physical illness prompting psychiatric admissions: A prospective study. *American Journal of Psychiatry, 138,* 629-635.

Hall, T. C., Miller, A. K. H., & Corsellis, J. A. N. (1975). Variations in the human Purkinje cell population according to age and sex. *Neuropathology and Applied Neurobiology, 1,* 267-292.

Haller, E., Binder, R. L., & McNeil, D. E. (1989). Violence in geriatric patients with dementia. *Bulletin of the American Academy of Psychiatry Law, 17*(2), 183-188.

Hamel, M., Gold, D., Andres, D., Reis, M., Dastoor, D., Grauere, H., & Bergman, H. (1990). Predictors and consequences of aggressive behavior by community-based dementia patients. *The Gerontologist, 30*(2), 206-211.

Hamilton, M. (1960). A rating scale for depression. *Journal of Neurology, Neurosurgery and Psychiatry, 23,* 56-62.

Hamilton, S. A. (1988). Behavioral formulations of verbal behavior in psychotherapy. *Clinical Psychology Review, 8,* 181-193.

Hannappel, M., Calsyn, R. J., & Allen, G. (1993). Does social support alleviate the depression of caregivers of dementia patients? *Journal of Gerontological Social Work, 20,* 35-51.

Hardy, B. G., Shulman, K. I, Mackenzie, S. E, Kutcher, S. P., & Silverberg, J. D. (1987). Pharmacokinetics of lithium in the elderly. *Journal of Clinical Psychopharmacology, 7,* 153-158.

Hare-Mustin, R. T., & Marecek, J. (1990). Beyond difference. In R. T. Hare-Mustin & J. Marecek (Eds.), *Making a difference: Psychology and the construction of gender* (pp. 184-201). New Haven, CT: Yale University Press.

Harford, T. C., & Mills, G. S. (1978). Age-related trends in alcohol consumption. *Journal of Studies on Alcohol, 39,* 207-210.

Harman, D. (1956). Aging: A theory based on free radical and radiation chemistry. *Journal of Gerontology, 11,* 298-300.

Harman, S. M. (1978). Clinical aspects of the male reproductive system. In E. L. Schneider (Ed.), *Aging: 4. The aging reproductive system.* New York: Raven.

Harman, S. M., & Nankin, H. R. (1985). Alterations in reproductive and sexual function: Male. *Principles of geriatric medicine* (pp. 337-353). New York: McGraw-Hill.

Harman, S. M., & Robinson, J. C. (1982). Common problems in reproductive endocrinology. In L. R. Barker, J. R. Burton, & P. D. Zieve (Eds.), *Principles of ambulatory medicine* (pp. 795-796). Baltimore: Williams & Wilkins.

Harman, S. M., & Talbert, G. B. (1985). Reproductive aging. In C. E. Finch & E. L. Schneider (Eds.), *Handbook of the biology of aging* (2nd ed., pp. 457-510). New York: Van Nostrand Reinhold.

Harper, M. S. (1990). Mental health and older adults. In M. O. Hogstel (Ed.), *Geropsychiatric nursing* (pp. 1-37). St. Louis, MO: C. V. Mosby.

Harris, M. J., & Jeste, D. V. (1988). Late-onset schizophrenia: An overview. *Schizophrenia Bulletin, 14,* 39-55.

Harrison, W. M., Rabkin, J. G., Erhardt, A. A., Stewart, J. W., McGrath, P. J., Ross, D., & Quitkin, F. M. (1986). Effects of antidepressant medication on sexual function: A controlled study. *Journal of Clinical Psychopharmacology, 6,* 144-149.

Hart, R. P., Kwentus, J. A., Wade, J. B., & Hamer, R. M. (1987). Digit symbol performance in mild dementia and depression. *Journal of Consulting and Clinical Psychology, 55,* 236-238.

Hart, S., & Semple, J. M. (1990). *Neuropsychology and the dementias.* New York: Taylor & Francis.

Hartley, A. A. (1992). Attention. In F. I. M. Craik & T. A. Salthouse (Eds.), *The handbook of aging and cognition* (pp. 3-50). Hillsdale NJ: Lawrence Erlbaum.

Hartshorn, E. A., & Tatro, D. S. (1991). Principles of drug interaction. In D. S. Tatro (Ed.), *Drug interaction facts* (pp. xix-xxvi). St. Louis, MO: J. B. Lippincott.

Hasher, L., & Zacks, R. T. (1988). Working memory, comprehension, and aging: A review and a new view. In G. H. Bower (Ed.), *The psychology of learning and motivation* (Vol. 22, pp. 193-225). New York: Academic Press.

Haug, H., Barmwater, U., Eggars, R., Fischer, D., Kuhl, S., & Sass, N. L. (1983). Anatomical changes in aging brain: Morphometric analysis of the human prosencephalon. In J. Cervos-Navarro & H. I. Sarkander (Eds.), *Neuropharmacology* (Aging, Vol. 21, pp. 1-12). New York: Raven.

Hauri, P. (1981). Treating psychophysiological insomnia with biofeedback. *Archives of General Psychiatry, 38,* 752-758.

Hauri, P., Chernik, D., Hawkins, D., & Mendels, J. (1974). Sleep of depressed patients in remission. *Archives of General Psychiatry, 31,* 386-391.

Hauri, P., Percy, L., Hellekson, C., Hartmann, E., & Russ, D. (1982). The treatment of psycho-physiologic insomnia: A replication study. *Biofeedback and Self-Regulation, 7,* 223-235.

Hauri, P. J. (1991). Sleep hygiene, relaxation therapy, and cognitive interventions. In P. Hauri (Ed.), *Case studies in insomnia* (pp. 65-84). New York: Plenum.

Hayes, C. (1987). Two worlds in conflict: The elderly Hmong in the United States. In D. E. Gelfand & C. M. Baressi (Eds.), *Ethnic dimensions of aging.* New York: Springer.

Haynes, S. N. (1991). Behavioral assessment. In M. Hersen, A. E. Kazdin, & A. S. Bellack (Eds.), *The clinical psychology handbook* (2nd ed., pp. 430-464). New York: Pergamon.

Haynes, S. N., & Jensen, B. J. (1979). The interview as a behavioral assessment instrument. *Behavioral Assessment, 1,* 97-106.

Healey, E. S., Kales, A., Monroe, L. J., Boxler, E. O., Chamberlin, K., & Soldatos, C. R. (1981). Onset of insomnia: Role of life-stress events. *Psychosomatic Medicine, 43,* 439-451.

Health Care Financing Administration. (1988). *Medicare/Medicaid nursing home information, 1987-1988.* Washington, DC: U.S. Department of Health and Human Services.

Heaton, R. K. (1992). *Comprehensive norms for an expanded Halstead-Reitan Battery: A supplement for the Wechsler Adult Intelligence Scale-Revised.* Odessa, FL: Psychological Assessment Resources.

Heaton, R. K., Chelune, G. J., Talley, J. L., Kay, G. G., & Curtis, G. (1993). *Wisconsin Card Sorting Test manual revised and expanded.* Odessa, FL: Psychological Assessment Resources.

Heaton, R. K., Grant, I., & Matthews, C. G. (1991). *Comprehensive norms for an expanded Halstead-Reitan Battery: Demographic corrections, research findings, and clinical applications.* Odessa, FL: Psychological Assessment Resources.

Heckheimer, E. (1989). *Health promotion of the elderly in the community.* Philadelphia: W. B. Saunders.

Heiby, E. M. (1983). Depression as a function of the interaction of self- and environmentally controlled reinforcement. *Behavior Therapy, 14,* 430-433.

Heidrich, S. M. (1993). The relationship between physical health and psychological well-being in elderly women: A developmental perspective. *Research in Nursing and Health, 16,* 123-130.

Heim, K. M. (1986). Wandering behavior. *Journal of Gerontological Nursing, 12*(11), 4-7.

Heitler, J. B. (1976). Preparatory techniques in initiating expressive psychotherapy with lower class, unsophisticated patients. *Psychological Bulletin, 83,* 339-352.

Helms, J. E. (Ed.). (1990). *Black and White racial identity: Theory, research, and practice.* New York: Greenwood.

Helzer, J. E., & Burnam, A. (1991). Epidemiology of alcohol addiction: United States. In N. S. Miller (Ed.), *Comprehensive handbook of drug and alcohol addiction* (pp. 9-38). New York: Dekker.

Helzer, J. E., Burnam, A., & McEvoy, L. T. (1991). Alcohol abuse and dependence. In L. Robins & D. Reiger (Eds.), *Psychiatric disorders in America: The epidemiologic catchment area study* (pp. 81-115). New York: Free Press.

Hemminki, E., & Heikkila, J. (1975). Elderly people's compliance with prescriptions and quality of medication. *Scandinavian Journal of Social Medicine, 3,* 87-92.

Henderson, G., Tomlinson, B., & Gibson, P. H. (1980). Cell counts in human cerebral cortex in normal adults throughout life using an image analysing computer. *Journal of the Neurological Sciences, 46,* 113-136.

Henderson, J. N., Gutierrez-Mayka, M., Garcia, J., & Boyd, S. (1993). A model for Alzheimer's Disease support group development in African-American and Hispanic populations. *The Gerontologist, 33,* 409-414.

Hendricks, J. (1992). Introduction: Making something of our chromosomes. In L. Glasse & J. Hendricks (Eds.), *Gender and aging* (pp. 1-4). New York: Baywood.

Hendriksen, C., Lund, E., & Stromgard, E. (1984). Consequences of assessment and intervention among elderly people: A three year randomised controlled trial. *British Medical Journal, 29,* 1522-1524.

Herd, D. (1990). Subgroup differences in drinking patterns among black and white men: Results from a national survey. *Journal of Studies on Alcohol, 51,* 221-232.

Herman, J. B., Brotman, A. W., Pollack, M. H., Falk, W. E., Biederman, J., & Rosenbaum, J. F. (1990). Fluoxetine-induced sexual dysfunction. *Journal of Clinical Psychiatry, 51,* 25-27.

Hermanson, B., Omenn, G. S., & Kronmal, R. A. (1988). Beneficial six-year outcome of smoking cessation in older men and women with coronary artery disease. *New England Journal of Medicine, 24,* 1365-1392.

Hernandez, G. G. (1991). Not so benign neglect: Researchers ignore ethnicity in defining family caregiver burden and recommending services. *The Gerontologist, 31*(2), 271-272.

Herr, J. J., & Weakland, J. H. (1979). *Counseling elders and their families.* New York: Springer.

Herrera, C. (1985, November). Treatment of nocturnal agitation in a patient with Alzheimer's disease. *Program of the 38th Annual Scientific Meeting of the Gerontological Society of America* (p. 84). Washington, DC: Gerontological Society of America.

Hersen, M., & Van Hasselt, V. B. (1992). Behavioral assessment and treatment of anxiety in the elderly. *Clinical Psychology Review, 12,* 619-640.

Hersen, M., Van Hasselt, V. B., & Goreczny, A. J. (1993). Behavioral assessment of anxiety in older adults. *Behavior Modification, 17,* 99-112.

Hertzog, C., & Schaie, K. W. (1986). Stability and change in adult intelligence: 1. Analysis of longitudinal covariance structures. *Psychology and Aging, 1,* 159-171.

Hertzog, C., Dixon, R. A., Schulenberg, J. E., & Hultsch, D. F. (1987). On the differentiation of memory beliefs from memory knowledge: The factor structure of the Metamemory in Adulthood Scale. *Experimental Aging Research, 13*(1-2), 101-107.

Herzog, A. R. (1989). Physical and mental health in older women: Selected research issues and data sources. In A. R. Herzog, K. C. Holden, & M. M. Seltzer (Eds.), *Health and economic status of older women* (pp. 35-91). New York: Baywood.

Herzog, A. R., Diokno, A. C., Brown, M. B., Normolle, D. P., & Brock, B. M. (1990). Two-year incidence, remission, and change patterns of urinary incontinence in noninstitutionalized older adults. *Journal of Gerontology: Medical Sciences, 45,* M67-M74.

Herzog, A. R., & Rodgers, W. L. (1989). Age differences in memory performance and memory ratings as measured in a sample survey. *Psychology and Aging, 4,* 173-182.

Hess, T. M., & Slaughter, S. J. (1986). Aging effects on prototype abstraction and concept identification. *Journal of Gerontology, 41,* 214-221.

Heston, L. L. (1976). Alzheimer's disease, trisomy 21, and myeloproliferative disorders: Associations suggesting a genetic diathesis. *Science, 196,* 322-323.

Heston, L. L. (1987). The paranoid syndrome after mid-life. In N. E. Miller & G. D. Cohen (Eds.), *Schizophrenia and aging* (pp. 249-257). New York: Guilford.

Heston, L. L., & Mastri, A. R. (1977). The genetics of Alzheimer's disease: Associations with hematologic malignancy and Down's syndrome. *Archives of General Psychiatry, 34,* 976-981.

Hiatt, L. G. (1980). The happy wanderer. *Nursing Homes, 24*(2), 27-31.

Hickey, T., & Rakowski, W. (1981). Consistency in patients' health and treatment expectations at a geriatric clinic. *Journal of the American Geriatrics Society, 29,* 278-284.

Higatsberger, M. R., Budka, H., & Bernheimer, H. (1982). Neurochemical investigations of aged human brain cortex. In S. Hoyer (Ed.), *The aging brain: Physiological and pathophysiological aspects.* New York: Springer-Verlag.

Higgins, M. W., Enright, P. L., Kronmal, R. A., Schenker, M. B., Anton-Culver, H., & Lyles, M. (1993). The cardiovascular health study. *JAMA, 269,* 2741-2748.

Hikoyeda, N., & Grudzen, M. (Eds.). (1991). *Traditional and non-traditional medication use among ethnic elders* (Working Paper Series, 10). Palo Alto, CA: Stanford Geriatric Education Center.

Hill, C. D., Stoudemire, A., Morris, R., Martino-Saltzman, D., & Markwalter, H. R. (1993). Similarities and differences in memory deficits in patients with primary dementia and depression-related cognitive dysfunction. *Journal of Neuropsychiatry and Clinical Neurosciences, 5,* 277-282.

Hill, R. D., Storandt, M., & Malley, M. (1993). The impact of long-term exercise training on psychological function in older adults. *Journal of Gerontology: Psychological Sciences, 48,* P12-P17.

Hilton, P., & Stanton, S. L. (1981). Algorithmic method for assessing urinary incontinence in elderly women. *British Medical Journal, 282,* 940-942.

Himmelfarb, S., & Murrell, S. A. (1984). The prevalence and correlates of anxiety symptoms in older adults. *Journal of Psychology, 116,* 159-167.

Hing, E. (1987). *Use of nursing homes by the elderly: Preliminary data from the 1985 National Nursing Home Survey. Advance Data from Vital and Health Statistics No. 135* (DHHS Publication No. PHS 87-1250). Hyattsville, MD: Public Health Service.

Hinman, F., Jr. (1979). Urodynamic testing: Alternative to electronics. *Journal of Urology, 121,* 643.

Hipshman, L. (1987). Defining a clinically useful model for assessing competence to consent to treatment. *Bulletin of the American Academy of Psychiatry and Law, 15,* 235-245.

Hirschfeld, R. M., & Cross, C. K. (1982). Epidemiology of affective disorders. *Archives of General Psychiatry, 39,* 35-46.

Hirst, S. T., & Metcalf, B. J. (1989). Whys and whats of wandering. *Geriatric Nursing, 10*(5), 237-238.

Hoch, C. C., Reynolds, C. F., Kupfer, D. J., Berman, S. R., Houck, P. R., & Stack, J. A. (1987). Empirical note: Self-report versus recorded sleep in healthy seniors. *Psychophysiology, 24,* 293-299.

Hoch, C. C., Reynolds, C. F., Kupfer, D. J., Houck, P. R., Berman, S. R., & Stack, J. A. (1987). The superior sleep of healthy elderly nuns. *International Journal of Aging and Human Development, 25,* 1-9.

Hodges, J. R. (1994). *Cognitive assessment for clinicians.* New York: Oxford University Press.

Hodgson, J. (1971). *Age and aerobic capacity of urban midwestern males.* Unpublished thesis. University of Minnesota, St. Paul.

Hoeffer, B., Rader, J., & Siemsen, G. (1987, November). *An observational tool for studying the behavior of cognitively impaired nursing home residents who wander.* Presented at the poster session for the 40th Annual Gerontological Society of America meeting, Washington, DC.

Hoehns, J. D., & Perry, P. J. (1993). Zolpidem: A nonbenzodiazepine hypnotic for treatment of insomnia. *Clinical Pharmacology, 12*(11), 814-828.

Hoelscher, T. J., & Edinger, J. D. (1988). Treatment of sleep-maintenance insomnia in older adults: Sleep period reduction, sleep education, and modified stimulus control. *Psychology and Aging, 3,* 258-263.

Hoffman, S. B. (1987). The "difficult" nursing home patient. *The Gerontologist, 27,* 217A.

Hogarty, G. E., Anderson, C. M., Reiss, D. J., Kornblith, S. J., Greenwald, D. P., Ulrich, R. F., Carter, M., & the Environmental/Personal Indicators in the Course of Schizophrenia (EPICS) Research Group. (1991). Family psychoeducation, social skills training, and maintenance chemotherapy in the aftercare treatment of schizophrenia. *Archives of General Psychiatry, 48,* 340-347.

Holden, K. C. (1989). Economic status of older women: A summary of selected research issues. In A. R. Herzog, K. C. Holden, & M. M. Seltzer (Eds.), *Health and economic status of older women* (pp. 92-130). New York: Baywood.

Holden, N. L. (1987). Late paraphrenia or the paraphrenias? A descriptive study with a 10-year follow-up. *British Journal of Psychiatry, 150,* 635-639.

Holland, J. C., Korzun, A. H., Tross, S., Silberfarb, P., Perry, M., Comis, R., & Oster, M. (1986). Comparative psychological disturbance in patients with pancreatic and gastric cancer. *American Journal of Psychiatry, 143,* 982-986.

Hollon, S. D., De Rubeis, R. J., Seligman, M. E. P. (1992). Cognitive therapy and the prevention of depression. *Applied and Preventive Psychology, 1,* 89-95.

Holmes, C. S. (1990). Neuropsychological sequelae of acute and chronic blood glucose disruption in adults with insulin-dependent diabetes. In C. S. Holmes (Ed.), *Neuropsychological and behavioral aspects of diabetes mellitus* (pp. 122-154). New York: Springer-Verlag.

Holt, P. R. (1991). General perspectives on the aged gut. *Clinics in Geriatric Medicine, 7*(2), 185-189.

Hommel, P. A., Wang, L., & Bergman, J. A. (1990). Trends in guardianship reform: Implications for the medical and legal professions. *Law, Medicine & Health Care, 18,* 213-226.

Hooijer, C., Dinkgreve, M., Jonker, C., & Lindeboom, J. (1992). Short screening tests for dementia in the elderly population: 1. A comparison between AMTS, MMSE, MSQ, and SPMSQ. *International Journal of Geriatric Psychiatry, 7,* 559-571.

Horn, J. (1988). Thinking about human abilities. In J. R. Nesselroade & R. B. Cattell (Eds.), *Handbook of multivariate experimental psychology* (pp. 645-685). New York: Plenum.

Horn, J. L. (1982). The aging of human abilities. In B. B. Wolman (Ed.), *Handbook of developmental psychology* (pp. 847-870). Englewood Cliffs, NJ: Prentice Hall.

Horn, J. L., & Donaldson, G. (1980). Cognitive development in adulthood. In J. Kagan & J. O. G. Brim (Eds.), *Constancy and change in development.* Cambridge, MA: Harvard University Press.

Horowitz, A. (1985). Sons and daughters as caregivers to older parents: Differences in role performance and consequences. *The Gerontologist, 25,* 612-617.

Horvath, T. B., & Davis, K. L. (1990). Central nervous system disorders in aging. In E. L. Schneider & J. W. Rowe (Eds.), *The handbook of the biology of aging* (3rd ed., pp. 306-329). New York: Academic Press.

Houillin, P., & Douge, R. (1989). Treatment by fluvoxamine of elderly patients aged more than 65 years old with a major depressive syndrome. *Psychological Medicine, 21,* 1205-1217.

Howard, R., Castle, D., Wessely, S., & Murray, R. (1993). A comparative study of 470 cases of early-onset and late-onset schizophrenia. *British Journal of Psychiatry, 163,* 352-357.

Howell, T., & Watts, D. T. (1990). Behavioral complication of dementia: A clinical approach for the general internist. *Journal of General Internal Medicine, 5,* 431-437.

Hoyer, W. J. (1985). Aging and the development of expert cognition. In T. M. Schlechter & M. P. Toglia (Eds.), *New directions in cognitive science.* Norwood, NJ: Ablex.

Hsu, J. M., & Smith, J. C., Jr. (1984). B-Vitamins and ascorbic acid in the aging process. In J. M. Ordy, D. Harman, & R. B. Alfin-Slater (Eds.), *Aging: Vol. 26. Nutrition in gerontology* (pp. 87-118). New York: Raven.

Hu, M.-H., & Woollacott, M. H. (1994a). Multisensory training of standing balance in older adults: 1. Postural stability and one-leg stance balance. *Journal of Gerontology: Medical Sciences, 49,* M52-M61.

Hu, M.-H., & Woollacott, M. H. (1994b). Multisensory training of standing balance in older adults: 2. Kinetic and electromyographic postural responses. *Journal of Gerontology: Medical Sciences, 49,* M62-M71.

Hu, T. (1990). Impact of urinary incontinence on healthcare costs. *Journal of the American Geriatrics Society, 38,* 292-295.

Hu, T., Igou, J., Kaltreider, L., Yu, L., Rohner, T., Dennis, P., Craighead, W., Hadley, E., & Ory, M. (1989). A clinical trial of a behavior therapy to reduce urinary incontinence in nursing homes. *JAMA, 261,* 2656-2662.

Hubbard, R. W., Santos, J. F., & Santos, M. A. (1979). Alcohol and older adults: Overt and covert influences. *Social Casework,* 166-170.

Huff, F. J. (1991). Language in normal aging and age-related neurological disease. In F. Boller & J. Grafman (Eds.), *Handbook of neuropsychology* (Vol. 4, pp. 251-264). New York: Elsevier.

Hughes, J. E. (1985). Depressive illness and lung cancer. *European Journal of Surgical Oncology, 11,* 15-20.

Hughes, S. L., Cordray, D. S., & Spiker, V. A. (1984). Evaluation of a long term home care program. *Medical Care, 22,* 460-475.

Hughes, S. L., Edelman, P. L., Singer, R. H., & Chang, R. W. (1993). Joint impairment and self-reported disability in elderly persons. *Journal of Gerontology: Social Sciences, 48,* S84-S92.

Hull, L., Holmes, G. E., & Karst, R. H. (1990). Managing guardianships of the elderly: Protection and advocacy as public policy. *Journal of Elder Abuse and Neglect, 2,* 145-162.

Hunter, N. D., Michaelson, S. E., & Stoddard, T. D. (1992). *The rights of lesbians and gay men: An American Civil Liberties Union handbook.* Carbondale: Southern Illinois University Press.

Hurst, J. W. (1986). *The heart.* New York: McGraw-Hill.

Hurt, R. D., Finlayson, R. E., Morse, R. M., & Davis, L. J., Jr. (1988). Alcoholism in elderly persons: Medical aspects and prognosis of 216 patients. *Mayo Clinic Proceedings, 63,* 753-760.

Husaini, B. A., Moore, S. T., Castor, R. S., Neser, W., Whitten-Stovall, R. (1991). Social density, stressors, and depression: Gender differences among the black elderly. *Journal of Gerontology, 46,* 236-242.

Hussian, R. A. (1981). *Geriatric psychology: A behavioral perspective.* New York: Van Norstrand Reinhold.

Hussian, R. A. (1986). Severe behavioral problems. In L. Teri & P. M. Lewinsohn (Eds.), *Geropsychological assessment and treatment* (pp. 121-143). New York: Springer.

Hussian, R. A. (1987). Wandering disorientation. In L. L. Carlson & B. A. Edelstein (Eds.), *Handbook of clinical gerontology.* New York: Pergamon.

Hussian, R. A., & Brown, D. C. (1985). *Responsive care: Behavioral interventions with elderly persons.* Champaign, IL: Research Press.

Hussian, R. A., & Brown, D. C. (1987). Use of two-dimensional grid patterns to limit hazardous ambulation in demented patients. *Journal of Gerontology, 42,* 558-560.

Huttenlocher, P. (1979). Synaptic density in human frontal cortex— developmental changes and effects of aging. *Brain Research, 163,* 195-205.

Huyck, M. H. (1990). Gender differences in Aging. In J. E. Birren & K. W. Schaie (Eds.), *Handbook of the psychology of aging* (3rd ed., pp. 124-132). New York: Academic Press.

Iber, F. L. (1990). Alcoholism and associated malnutrition in the elderly. In D. Prinsley & H. Sandstead (Eds.), *Nutrition and aging* (pp. 169-178). New York: Alan R. Liss.

In re Schiller, 148 N. J. Super. 168, 372 A. 2d 360 (1977).

Ingevar, D. H. (1983). Cerebral blood flow and cerebral metabolism in Alzheimer's disease: Technical considerations. In B. Reisberg (Ed.), *Alzheimer's disease: The standard reference* (pp. 278-285). New York: Free Press.

Inspector General. (1989). *Medicare drug utilization review* (OAI-01-88-00980). Washington, DC: U.S. Department of Health and Human Services.

Institute of Medicine. (1979). *Sleeping pills, insomnia, and medical practice.* Washington, DC: National Academy of Sciences.

Iruela, L. M., Ibanez-Rojo, V., & Baca, E. (1993). Zolpidem-induced macropsia in an anorexic woman. *Lancet, 342,* 443-444.

Isaacs, B., Gunn, T., McKecham, A., McMillan, J., & Neville, Y. (1971). The concept of pre-death. *Lancet, 1,* 1115-1118.

Isaacs, B., & Walkey, F. A. (1964). A survey of incontinence in the elderly. *Gerontologia Clinica, 6,* 367-376.

Ivnik, R. J., Malec, J. F., Smith, G. E., Tangalos, E. G., Peterson, R. C., Kokmen, E., & Kurland, L. T. (1992a). Mayo's Older Americans Normative Studies: Updated AVLT norms for ages 56-97. *The Clinical Neuropsychologist, 6*(Suppl.), 83-104.

Ivnik, R. J., Malec, J. F., Smith, G. E., Tangalos, E. G., Peterson, R. C., Kokmen, E., & Kurland, L. T. (1992b). Mayo's Older Americans Normative Studies: WAIS-E norms for ages 65-97. *The Clinical Neuropsychologist, 6*(Suppl.), 1-30.

Ivnik, R. J., Malec, J. F., Smith, G. E., Tangalos, E. G., Peterson, R. C., Kokmen, E., & Kurland, L. T. (1992c). Mayo's Older Americans Normative Studies: WMS-R norms for ages 56-97. *The Clinical Neuropsychologist, 6*(Suppl.), 49-82.

Jackson, J. S. (1988). Growing old in Black America: Research on aging Black populations. In J. S. Jackson (Ed.), *The Black American elderly: Research on physical and psychosocial health* (pp. 3-16). New York: Springer.

Jackson, M. E., Drugovich, M. L., Fretwell, M. D., Spector, W. D., Sternberg, J. S., & Rosenstein, R. B. (1989). Prevalence and correlates of disruptive behavior in the nursing home. *Journal of Aging and Health, 1*(3), 349-369.

Jacobsen, F. M. (1992). Fluoxetine-induced sexual dysfunction and an open trial of yohimbine. *Journal of Clinical Psychiatry, 53,* 119-122.

Jacobsson, L., & Ottosson, J. O. (1971). Initial mental disorders in carcinoma of pancreas and stomach. *Acta Psychiatrica Scandinavica, 221*(Suppl.), 120-127.

Jacques, P. F., Sulsky, S., Hartz, S. C., & Russell, R. M. (1989). Moderate alcohol intake and nutritional status in nonalcoholic elderly subjects. *American Journal of Clinical Nutrition, 50,* 875-883.

Janicak, P. G., Davis, J. M., Preskorn, S. H., & Ayd, F. J. (1993). *Principles and practice of psychopharmacological therapy.* Baltimore: Williams & Wilkins.

Janik, S. W., & Dunham, R. G. (1983). A nationwide examination of the need for specific alcoholism treatment programs for the elderly. *Journal of Studies on Alcohol, 44,* 307-317.

Janofsky, J. S., McCarthy, R. J., & Folstein, M. F. (1992). The Hopkins competency assessment test: A brief method for evaluating patients' capacity to give informed consent. *Hospital and Community Psychiatry, 43,* 132-136.

Jarvik, L. F., Mintz, J., Steuer, J., & Gerner, R. (1982). Treating geriatric depression: A 26-week interim analysis. *Journal of the American Geriatrics Society, 30,* 713-717.

Jarvis, G. J. (1981). A controlled trial of bladder drill and drug therapy in the management of detrusor instability. *Journal of Urology, 53,* 565-566.

Jarvis, G. J. (1982). The management of urinary incontinence due to primary vesical sensory urgency by bladder drill. *British Journal of Urology, 54,* 374-376.

Jarvis, G. J., & Miller, D. R. (1980). Controlled trial of bladder drill for detrusor instability. *British Medical Journal, 281,* 1322-1323.

Jefferson, G. W. (1983). Lithium and affective disorder in the elderly. *Comprehensive Psychiatry, 24,* 166-178.

Jefferson, J. (1992). Treatment of depressed patients who have become non-tolerant to antidepressants medication because of cardiovascular effects. *Journal of Clinical Psychiatry Monograph, 10*(1), 66-71.

Jeffreys, R. V., & Wood, M. M. (1978). Adult non-tumourous dementia and hydrocephalus. *Acta Neurochirurgica, 45,* 103-114.

Jenike, M. A. (1989). Sleep disorder in the elderly. In M. A. Jenike (Ed.), *Geriatric psychiatry and psychopharmacology.* Chicago: Year Book Medical.

Jervis, G. K., & Boldt, M. (1980). Suicide in the later years. *Essence, 4,* 144-158.

Jeste, D. V., Harris, M. J., Pearlson, G. D., Rabins, P., Lesser, I. Miller, B., Coles, C., & Yassa, R. (1988). Late-onset schizophrenia: Studying clinical validity. *Psychiatric Annals of North America, 11,* 1-13.

Jeste, D. V., Lacro, J. P., Gilbert, P. L., Kline, J., & Kline, N. (1993). Treatment of late-life schizophrenia with neuroleptics. *Schizophrenia Bulletin, 19,* 817-830.

Jeste, D. V., Lohr, J. B., Clark, K., & Wyatt, R. J. (1988). Pharmacological treatments of tardive dyskinesia in the 1980s. *Journal of Clinical Psychopharmacology, 8,* 385-485.

Jeste, D. V., Manley, M., & Harris, M. J. (1991). Psychoses. In J. Sadavoy, L. W. Lazarus, & L. F. Jarvik (Eds.), *Comprehensive review of geriatric psychiatry* (pp. 353-368). Washington, DC: American Psychiatric Press.

Jeste, D. V., & Wyatt, R. J. (1982). Therapeutic strategies against tardive dyskinesia. *Archives of General Psychiatry, 39,* 803-816.

Jeste, D. V., & Wyatt, R. J. (1987). Aging and tardive dyskinesia. In N. E. Miller & G. D. Cohen (Eds.), *Schizophrenia and aging* (pp. 275-286). New York: Guilford.

Jick, S. S., Jick, H., Knauss, T. A., & Dean, A. D. (1992). Antidepressants and convulsions. *Journal of Clinical Psychopharmacology, 12,* 241-245.

Jinks, M. J., & Raschko, R. R. (1990). A profile of alcohol and prescription drug abuse in a high-risk community-based elderly population. *DICP, The Annals of Pharmacotherapy, 24,* 971-975.

Jirovec, M. M. (1991). The impact of daily exercise on the mobility, balance and urine control of cognitively impaired nursing home residents. *International Journal of Nursing Studies, 28,* 145-151.

Joffe, R. T., Rubinow, D. R., Denicoff, K. D., Maher, M., & Sindelar, W. F. (1986). Depression and carcinoma of the pancreas. *General Hospital Psychiatry, 8,* 241-245.

John, R. (1985). Service needs and support networks of elderly Native Americans: Family, friends, and social service agencies. In W. A. Peterson & S. Quadagno (Eds.), *Social bonds in later life: Aging and interdependence.* Beverly Hills, CA: Sage.

Johnson, M. J., & Werner, C. (1982). We had no choice—a study of familial guilt feelings surrounding nursing home care. *Journal of Gerontological Nursing, 8,* 631-645.

Johnsson, L. G., & Hawkins, J. E., Jr. (1972). Sensory and neural degeneration with aging, as seen in micro-dissections of the human inner ear. *Annals of Otolaryngology, Rhinology, and Laryngology, 81,* 179-193.

Johnston, J. A., Laneberry, C. G., Ascher, J. A., Davidson, J., Khayrallah, M. A., Feighner, J. P., & Stark, P. (1991). 102-center prospective study of seizure in association with buproprion. *Journal of Clinical Psychiatry, 52,* 450-456.

Joint National Committee on Detection, Evaluation, and Treatment of High Blood Pressure. (1993). *Archives of Internal Medicine, 153,* 154-183.

Jolliffe, N. (1963). *Reduce and stay reduced on the prudent diet.* New York: Simon & Schuster.

Jones, B. N., Teng, E. L., Folstein, M. F., & Harrison, K. S. (1993). A new bedside test of cognition for patients with HIV infection. *Annals of Internal Medicine, 119,* 1001-1004.

Jonsen, A., Siegler, M., & Winslade, W. (1992). *Clinical ethics* (3rd. ed.). New York: Macmillan.

Judge, T. G. (1969). The use of quinestradol in elderly incontinent women: Preliminary report. *Gerontologia Clinica, 11,* 159-164.

Junjinger, J., & Ditto, B. (1984). Multitreatment of obsessive-compulsive checking in a geriatric patient. *Behavior Modification, 8,* 379-390.

Kahn, A., Fabre, L. F., & Rudolph, R. (1991). Venlafaxine in depressed outpatients. *Psychopharmacology Bulletin, 27,* 141-144.

Kahn, D., Stevenson, E., & Douglas, C. J. (1988). Effect of sodium valproate in three patients with organic brain syndrome. *American Journal of Psychiatry, 145,* 1010-1011.

Kahn, R. J., McNair, D. M., Lipman, R. S., Covi, L., Rickels, K., Downing, R., Fisher, S., & Frankenthaler, L. M. (1986). Imipramine and chlordiazepoxide in depressive and anxiety disorders: II. Efficacy in anxious out-patients. *Archives of General Psychiatry, 43,* 79-85.

Kalayam, B., Alexopoulos, G. S., Merrell, H. B., & Young, R. C. (1991). Patterns of hearing loss and psychiatric morbidity in elderly patients attending a hearing clinic. *International Journal of Geriatric Psychiatry, 6*(3), 131-136.

Kales, J. D. (1975). Aging and sleep. In R. Goldman & M. Rockstein (Eds.), *Symposium on the physiology and pathology of aging.* New York: Academic Press.

Kales, J., Tan, T., Swearingen, C., & Kales, A. (1971). Are over-the-counter sleep medications effective? All-night EEG studies. *Current Therapeutic Research, 13,* 143-151.

Kalish, R. A., & Moriwaki, S. (1973). The world of the elderly Asian American. *Journal of Social Issues, 29*(2), 187-209.

Kamocka, D. (1970). Cytological studies of parotid gland secretion in people over 60 years of age. *Excerpta Medica, Section 20, 13,* 412.

Kane, J. M., Carpenter, W. T., Kendler, K. S., Lieberman, J. S., Csernansky, J. G., Addington, D. E., & Marder, S. R. (1993). Understanding and treating psychoses: Advances in research and therapy. *Journal of Clinical Psychiatry, 54,* 445-452.

Kane, J. M., Cole, K., Sarantakes, S., Howard, A., & Borenstein, M. (1983). Safety and efficacy of buproprion in elderly patients: Preliminary observations. *Journal of Clinical Psychiatry, 44,* 134-136.

Kane, J. M., Honingfeld, G., Singer, J., Meltzer, H., & the Clozaril Collaborative Study Group. (1989). Clozapine for the treatment resistent schizophrenic: Results of a U.S. multi-center trial. *Psychopharmacology, 99,* S60-S63.

Kane, R. (1989). Sensory Impairment. In *Essentials of clinical geriatrics* (2nd ed., pp. 301-320). New York: McGraw-Hill.

Kane, R. A., & Kane, R. L. (1984). *Assessing the elderly: A practical guide to measurement.* Lexington, MA: Lexington Books.

Kanfer, F., & Schefft, B. (1988). *Guiding the process of therapeutic change.* Champaign, IL: Research Press.

Kannel, W. B. (1987). Epidemiology and prevention of cardiac failure: Framingham Study insights. *European Heart Journal, 8*(Suppl. F), 23-29.

Kaplan, E. F., Goodglass, H., & Weintraub, S. (1983). *The Boston naming test* (2nd ed.). Philadelphia: Lea & Febiger.

Kaplitz, S. E. (1975). Withdrawn, apathetic geriatric patients responsive to methylphenidate. *Journal of the American Geriatric Society, 23,* 271-276.

Kapp, M. B. (1990). Evaluating decision making capacity in the elderly: A review of recent literature. *Journal of Elder Abuse and Neglect, 2,* 15-29.

Kapp, M. B. (1992). *Geriatrics and the law: Patient rights and professional responsibilities* (2nd ed.). New York: Springer.

Karacan, I., Williams, R. L., Thornby, J. I., & Salis, P. J. (1975). Sleep-related penile tumescence as a function of age. *American Journal of Psychiatry, 132,* 932-937.

Karajgi, B., Rifkin, A., & Doddi, S. (1990). The prevalence of anxiety disorders in patients with chronic obstructive pulmonary disease. *American Journal of Psychiatry, 147,* 200-201.

Karpman, R. (1987). Orthopedic issues in the elderly. In L. L. Carstensen & B. A. Edelstein (Eds.), *Handbook of clinical gerontology* (pp. 144-151). New York: Pergamon.

Kasch, F., Boyer, J., Van Camp, S., Swerty, L., & Wallace, S. (1990). The effect of physical activity and inactivity on aerobic power in older men: A longitudinal study. *Physician and Sports Medicine, 18,* 73-83.

Kashner, T. M., Rodell, D. E., Ogden, S. R., Guggenheim, F. G., & Karson, C. N. (1992). Outcomes and costs of two VA inpatient treatment programs for older alcoholic patients. *Hospital and Community Psychiatry, 43,* 985-989.

Kastenbaum, R., & Candy, S. E. (1973). The 4% fallacy: A methodological and empirical critique of extended care facility population statistics. *International Journal of Aging and Human Development, 4,* 15-21.

Kaszniak, A. W. (1987). Neuropsychological consultation to geriatricians: Issues in the assessment of memory complaints. *The Clinical Neuropsychologist, 1,* 35-46.

Kaszniak, A. W. (1990). Psychological assessment of the aging individual. In J. E. Birren & K. W. Schaie (Eds.), *Handbook of the psychology of aging* (3rd ed., pp. 427-445). New York: Academic Press.

Kaszniak, A. W., & Allender, J. (1985). Psychological assessment of depression in older adults. In G. M. Chaisson-Stewart (Ed.), *Depression in the elderly: An interdisciplinary approach* (pp. 107-160). New York: John Wiley.

Katch, F., & Katch, V. (1991). *Exercise physiology: Energy, nutrition and human performance.* Philadelphia: Lee & Febiger.

Katon, W. (1984). Depression : Relationship to somatization and chronic medical illness. *Journal of Clinical Psychiatry, 45,* 4-11.

Katon, W., & Raskind, M. (1980). Treatment of depression in the medically ill elderly with methylphenidate. *American Journal of Psychiatry, 137,* 963-965.

Katona, C. L. E. (1994). Approaches to the management of depression in old age. Satellite Symposium: Depression in the elderly: Clinical considerations and therapeutic approaches (1993, Berlin, Germany). *Gerontology, 40*(Suppl. 1), 5-9.

Katz, G. P., & Blaivas, J. C. (1983). A diagnostic dilemma: When urodynamic findings differ from the clinical impression. *Journal of Urology, 129,* 1170-1174.

Katz, I. R. (1993). Drug treatment of depression in the frail elderly: Discussion of the NIH Consensus Development Conference on the Diagnosis and Treatment of Depression in Late Life. 32nd Annual Meeting of the New Clinical Drug Evaluation Unit: Symposium on diagnosis and treatment of depression in late life (1992, Boca Raton, Florida). *Psychopharmacology Bulletin, 29,* 101-108.

Katz, I. R., Curlik, S., & Nemetz, P. (1988). Functional psychiatric disorders in the elderly. In L. S. Lazarus (Ed.), *Essentials of geriatric psychiatry* (pp. 113-136). New York: Springer.

Katz, R. J., Landau, P. S., Lot M., Bystritsky, A., Diamond, B., Hoehn-Saric, R., Rosenthal, M., & Weise, C. (1993). Serotonergic (5-HT2) mediation of anxiety: Therapeutic effects of serazapine in generalized anxiety disorder. *Biological Psychiatry, 34,* 41-44.

Katz, S., Branch, L. G., Branson, M., Papsidero, J., Beck, J., & Green, D. (1983). Active life expectancy. *New England Journal of Medicine, 309,* 1218-1224.

Katz, S., Ford, A. B., Moskowitz, R. W., Jackson, B. A., & Jaffe, M. W. (1963). Studies of illness in the aged. The index of ADL: A standardized measure of biological and psychological function. *JAMA, 185,* 914-919.

Kaufman, M. W., Cassem, N. H., Murray, G., & MacDonald, D. (1984). The use of methylphenidate in depressed patients after cardiac surgery. *Journal of Clinical Psychiatry, 45,* 82-84.

Kausler, D. H. (1982). *Experimental psychology and human aging.* New York: John Wiley.

Kausler, D. H. (1991). *Experimental psychology, cognition, and human aging.* New York: Springer-Verlag.

Kay, D. W. K., Beamish, P., & Roth, M. (1964). Old age mental disorders in Newcastle upon Tyne. *British Journal of Psychiatry, 110,* 146-158.

Kay, D. W. K., Cooper, H. F., Garside, R. F., & Roth, M. (1976). The differentiation of paranoid from affective psychoses by patients' premorbid characteristics. *British Journal of Psychiatry, 129,* 207-215.

Kay, D. W. K., & Roth, R. (1961). Environmental and hereditary factors in the schizophrenias of old age (late paraphrenia) and their bearing on the general problem of causation in schizophrenia. *Journal of Mental Science, 107,* 649-686.

Kayser-Jones, J. (1992). Culture, environment, and restraints: A conceptual model for research and practice. *Journal of Gerontological Nursing, 18,* 13-20.

Keck, P. E., & McElroy, S. L. (1993). Current perspectives on treatment of bipolar disorder with lithium. *Psychiatric Annals, 23,* 64-69.

Kegel, A. H. (1948). Progressive resistance exercise in the functional restoration of the perineal muscles. *American Journal of Obstetrics and Gynecology, 56,* 238-248.

Kegel, A. H. (1956). Stress incontinence of urine in woman: Physiologic treatment. *Journal of the International College of Surgeons, 25,* 487-499.

Kehoe, M. (1986). Lesbians over 65: A triple invisible minority. *Journal of Homosexuality, 12*(3-4), 267-275.

Kehoe, M. (1989). Lesbians over 60 speak for themselves [Special issue]. *Journal of Homosexuality, 16*(3-4), 1-111.

Keller, M. (1960). Definition of alcoholism. *Quarterly Journal on Studies of Alcohol, 21,* 125-134.

Kelley, K., & Streeter, D. (1992). The roles of gender in organizations. In K. Kelley (Ed.), *Issues, theory, and research in industrial/organizational psychology* (pp. 285-337). New York: Elsevier.

Kellner, M. B., & Noher, F. (1991). A first episode of mania after age 80: A case report. *Canadian Journal of Psychiatry, 36,* 607-608.

Kelly, P. J., Nguyen, T., Hopper, J., Pocock, N., Sambrook, P., & Eisman, J. (1993). Changes in axial bone density with age: A twin study. *Journal of Bone Mineral Research, 8,* 11-17.

Kelsey, J. L., & Hoffman, S. (1987). Risk factors for hip fracture. *New England Journal of Medicine, 316,* 404-406.

Kemp, B. (1993). Psychologic care of the older rehabilitation patient. *Clinics in Geriatric Medicine, 9,* 841-857.

Kemp, B. J., Staples, F., & Lopez-Aqueres, W. (1987). Epidemiology of depression and dysphoria in an elderly Hispanic population: Prevalence and correlates. *Journal of the American Geriatrics Society, 35,* 920-926.

Kendig, H. L., Coles, R., Pittelkow, Y., & Wilson, S. (1988). Confidants and family structure of old age. *Journal of Gerontology, 43,* 31-40.

Kennedy, G., Kelman, H. R., Thomas, C., Wisniewski, W., Metz, H., & Bijur, P. (1989). Hierarchy of characteristics associated with depressive symptoms in an urban elderly sample. *American Journal of Psychiatry, 146,* 220-225.

Kenney, A. R. (1989). *Physiology of aging* (2nd ed.). Chicago: Year Book Medical.

Kermis, M. D. (1986). The epidemiology of mental disorder in the elderly: A response to the senate/AARP report. *The Gerontologist, 26,* 482-487.

Kessler, R. C., Brown, R. L., and Broman, C. L. (1981). Sex differences in psychiatric help-seeking: Evidence from four large-scale surveys. *Journal of Health and Social Behavior, 22,* 49-64.

Kessler, R. C., McGonagle, K. A., Shanyang, Z., Nelson, C. B., Hughes, M., Eshleman, S., Wittchen, H. U., & Kendler, K. (1994). Lifetime and 12-month prevalence of *DSM-III-R* psychiatric disorders in the United States. *Archives of General Psychiatry, 51,* 8-19.

Khan, T. A., Shragge, B. W., Crispin, J. S., & Lind, J. F. (1977). Esophageal motility in the elderly. *American Journal of Digestive Diseases, 22,* 1049-1054.

Kiecolt-Glaser, J. K., Glaser, R., Williger, D., Stout, J., Messick, G., Sheppard, S., Ricker, D., Romisher, S. C., Briner, W., Bonnel, G., & Donnerberg, R. (1985). Psychosocial enhancement of immunocompetence in a geriatric population. *Health Psychology, 4,* 25-41.

Kiernan, R. J., Mueller, J., Langston, J. W., & Van Dyke, C. (1987). The Neurobehavioral Cognitive Status Examination: A brief but quantitative approach to cognitive assessment. *Annals of Internal Medicine, 107,* 481-485.

Kindermann, T. (1986). *Entwicklungsbedingungen selbständigen und unselbständigen Verhaltens im der frühen Kindheit: Sozial-Ökologische Analyse alltäglicher Mutter Kind-Interaktionen* [Environmental conditions of dependent and independent behaviors: An ecological analysis of everyday mother-toddler interactions]. Unpublished doctoral dissertation, Freie Universität Berlin.

King, P., & Barrowclough, C. (1991). A clinical pilot study of cognitive-behavioural therapy for anxiety disorders in the elderly. *Behavioural Psychotherapy, 19,* 337-345.

King, T., & Mallet, L. (1991). Brachial plexus palsy with the use of haloperidol and a geriatric chair. *DICP, Annals of Pharmacotherapy, 25,* 1072-1074.

Kirchmeyer, C., & Cohen, A. (1992). Multicultural groups: Their performance and reactions with constructive conflict. *Group & Organization Management, 17,* 153-170.

Kirmayer, L., Robbins, J. M., Dworkind, M., & Yaffe, M. J. (1993). Somatization and the recognition of depression and anxiety in primary care. 144th Annual Meeting of the American Psychiatric Association. *American Journal of Psychiatry, 150,* 734-741.

Kitzman, D. W., & Edwards, W. D. (1990). Age-related changes in the anatomy of the normal human heart. *Journal of Gerontology: Medical Sciences, 45,* M33-M39.

Klatsky, A. L., & Armstrong, A. (1993). Alcohol use, other traits, and risk of unnatural death: A prospective study. *Alcohol Clinical & Experimental Research, 17,* 1156-1162.

Kleinman, A. (1986). *Social origins of distress and disease: Depression, neurasthenia, and pain in modern China.* New Haven, CT: Yale University Press.

Kleinsmith, D. M., & Perricone, N. V. (1989). Common skin problems in the elderly. *Clinics in Geriatric Medicine, 5*(1), 189-211.

Kleitman, N. (1963). *Sleep and wakefulness.* Chicago: University of Chicago Press.

Kligman, A. M. (1989). Psychological aspects of skin disorders in the elderly. *Cutis, 43,* 498-501.

Kline, C. (1991). *Counseling our own: Lesbian/gay subculture meets the mental health system.* Renton, WA: Publication Service.

Klisz, D. (1978). Neuropsychological evaluation in older persons. In M. Storandt, I. D. Stiegler, & M. F. Elias (Eds.), *The clinical psychology of aging* (pp. 71-98). New York: Freeman.

Knapp, P. H., & Mathe, A. A. (1985). Psychophysiologic aspects of bronchial asthma. In E. B. Weiss, M. S. Segal, & M. Stein (Eds.), *Bronchial asthma: Mechanisms and therapeutics* (2nd ed.). Boston: Little, Brown.

Knight, B. (1978-79). Psychotherapy change in non-institutionalized aged. *International Journal of Aging and Human Development, 9,* 221-236.

Knight, B. G., Lutzky, S., & Macofsky-Urban, F. (1993). A meta-analytic review of interventions for caregiver distress: Recommendations for future research. *The Gerontologist, 33,* 240-248.

Knight, R. G. (1992). *The neuropsychology of degenerative brain diseases.* Hillsdale, NJ: Lawrence Erlbaum.

Knopman, D. S., & Sawyer-DeMaris, S. (1990). Practical approach to managing behavioral problems in dementia patients. *Geriatrics, 45*(4), 27-35.

Knupfer, G., Fink, R., Clark, W. B., & Goffman, A. S. (1963). *Factors related to amount of drinking in an urban community: California drinking practices study* (Report No. 6). Berkeley, CA: California State Department of Public Health, Division of Alcoholic Rehabilitation.

Knupfer, G., & Room, R. (1964). Age, sex, and social class as factors in amount of drinking in a metropolitan community. *Social Problems, 12,* 224-240.

Kobata, F. S., Lockery, S. A., & Moriwaki, S. Y. (1990). Minority issues in mental health and aging. In J. E. Birren & R. B. Sloane (Eds.), *Handbook of mental health and aging* (2nd ed.). San Diego, CA: Academic Press.

Koenig, H. G., & Blazer, D. G. (1992a). Epidemiology of geriatric affective disorders. *Clinics in Geriatric Medicine, 8,* 235-251.

Koenig, H. G., & Blazer, D. G. (1992b). Mood disorders and suicide. In J. E.Birren, R. B. Sloane, & G. D. Cohen (Eds.), *Handbook of mental health and aging* (pp. 380-407). San Diego, CA: Academic Press.

Koenig, H. G., & Breitner, J. C. (1990). Use of antidepressants in medically ill older patients. *Psychosomatics, 31,* 22-32.

Koenig, H. G., & Studenski, S. (1988). Post-stroke depression in the elderly. *Journal of General Internal Medicine, 3,* 508-517.

Koenig, H. G., Meador, K. G., Cohen, H. J., & Blazer, D. G. (1988). Depression in elderly hospitalized patients with medical illness. *Archives of Internal Medicine, 148,* 1929-1936.

Koenig, H. G., Meador, K. G., Shelp, F., Goli, V., Cohen, H. J., & Blazer, D. G. (1991). Major depressive disorder in hospitalized medically ill patients: An examination of young and elderly male veterans. *Journal of the American Geriatrics Society, 39,* 881-890.

Koewler, J. H. (1982). Differences between elderly and non-elderly alcoholics in treatments: Referral source, compliance, service provision and improvement. *Dissertation Abstracts International,* 313-B.

Kofoed, L. L., Tolson, R. L., Atkinson, R. M., Toth, R. L., & Turner, J. A. (1987). Treatment compliance of older alcoholics: An elder-specific approach is superior to "mainstreaming." *Journal of Studies on Alcohol, 48,* 47-51.

Koin, D., Rinki, M., Willis-Shore, J., Steffen, A., Gallagher-Thompson, D., & Thompson, L. W. (1994). *Stress and cardiovascular risk in female caregivers of dementia patients.* Manuscript submitted for publication.

Kolb, B., & Whishaw, I. Q. (1985). *Fundamentals of human neuropsychology* (2nd ed.). New York: Freeman.

Kolcaba, K., & Miller, C. A. (1989). Geropharmacology treatment: Behavioral problems extend nursing responsibility. *Journal of Gerontological Nursing, 15,* 29-35.

Kongstvedt, S. J., & Sime, W. (1992). Diagnosis of depression in early- and late-onset geriatric depression: An evaluation of commonly used self-assessment measures. *Behavior, Health, and Aging, 2,* 133-148.

Korzeniowski, S. (1994). Reproductive history and prognosis in patients with operable breast cancer. *Cancer, 74*(5), 1591-1594.

Kosnik, W., Winslow, L., Kline, D., Rasinski, K., & Sekuler, R. (1988). Visual changes in daily life throughout adulthood. *Journal of Gerontology: Psychological Sciences, 43,* P63-P70.

Kraepelin, E. (1919). *Dementia praecox and paraphrenia* (R. M. Barclay, Trans.). Edinburgh: E. S. Livingstone.

Kraft, L., & Vraa, C. W. (1975). Sex composition of groups and pattern of self-disclosure by high school females. *Psychological Reports, 37,* 733-734.

Kral, V. A. (1958). Neuro-psychiatric observations in an old people's home: Studies of memory dysfunction in senescence. *Journal of Gerontology, 13,* 169-176.

Krall, E. A., & Dawson-Hughes, B. (1993). Heritable and life-style determinants of bone mineral density. *Journal of Bone Mineral Research, 8,* 1-9.

Kramer, S. I., & Reifler, B. V. (1992). Depression, dementia, and reversible dementia. *Clinics in Geriatric Medicine, 8,* 289-297.

Krasik, M. K. (1989). The lights of science and experience: Historical perspectives on legal attitudes toward the role of medical expertise in guardianship of the elderly. *American Journal of Legal History, 33,* 201-240.

Kraupl-Taylor, F. (1972). Loss of libido in depression (letter). *British Medical Journal, 1,* 305.

Kraus, H., & Raab, W. (1961). *Hypokinetic disease: Diseases produced by the lack of exercise.* Springfield, IL: Charles C Thomas.

Krauthammer, C., & Klerman, G. (1978). Secondary mania. *Archives of General Psychiatry, 35,* 1333-1339.

Krmpotic-Nemanic, J. (1969). Presbycusis and retrocochlear structures. *International Audiology, 8,* 210-220.

Kukull, W. A., Koepsell, T. D., Inui, T. S., Borson, S., Okimoto, J., Raskind, M. A., & Gale, J. A. (1986). Depression and physical illness among elderly general medical clinic patients. *Journal of Affective Disorders, 10,* 153-162.

Kukull, W. A., & Larson, E. B. (1989). Distinguishing Alzheimer's disease from other dementias: Questionnaire responses of close relatives and autopsy results. *Journal of the American Geriatrics Society, 37,* 521-527.

Kunik, M. E., Yudofsky, S. C., Silver, J. M., & Hales, R. E. (1994). Pharmacologic approach to management of agitation associated with dementia. *Journal of Clinical Psychiatry, 55*(2, Suppl.), 13-17.

Kunitz, S. J., & Levy, J. E. (1989). Aging and health among Navajo Indians. In K. S. Markides (Ed.), *Aging and health* (pp. 211-246). Newbury Park, CA: Sage.

Kupfer, D. J., Frank, E., Perel, J. M., Cornes, C., Mallinger, A. G., Thase, M. E., McEachran, A. B., & Grocholinski, V. J. (1992). Five-year outcome for maintenance therapies in recurrent depression. *Archives of General Psychiatry, 49,* 769-773.

Kuriansky, J. B., Gurland, B. J., & Fleiss, J. L. (1976). The assessment of self-care capacity in geriatric psychiatric patients by objective and subjective methods. *Journal of Clinical Psychology, 32*(1), 95-102.

Kurtze, J. F. (1985). Epidemiology of cerebrovascular disease. In F. H. McDowell & L. R. Caplan (Eds.), *Cerebrovascular survey report (1985)* (For the National Institute of Neurological and Communicative Disorders and Stroke). Washington, DC: National Institutes of Health, Public Health Service.

Kyomen, H. H., Nobel, K. W., & Wei, J. Y. (1991). The use of estrogen to decrease aggressive physical behavior in elderly men with dementia. *Journal of the American Geriatric Society, 39,* 1110-1112.

LaBarge, E., Edwards, D., & Knesevich, J. W. (1986). Performance of normal elderly on the Boston Naming Test. *Brain and Language, 27,* 380-384.

Lacey, J. I. (1967). Somatic response patterning and stress: Some revisions of activation theory. In M. H. Appley & R. Trumball (Eds.), *Psychological stress.* New York: Appleton-Century-Crofts.

Lachman, J. L., Lachman, R., & Thronesberry, C. (1979). Metamemory throughout the adult life span. *Developmental Psychology, 15,* 543-551.

Lachs, M. S., Becker, M., Siegal, A. P., Miller, R. P., & Tinetti, M. E. (1992). Delusions and behavioral disturbances in cognitively impaired elderly persons. *Journal of the American Gerontological Society, 40,* 768-773.

Lack, L., & Wright, H. (1993). The effect of evening bright light in delaying the circadian rhythms and lengthening the sleep of early morning awakening insomniacs. *Sleep, 16,* 436-443.

Lacks, P., & Morin, C. M. (1992). Recent advances in the assessment and treatment of insomnia. *Journal of Consulting and Clinical Psychology, 60,* 586-594.

LaForge, R. G., Spector, W. D., & Sternberg, J. (1992). The relationship of vision and hearing impairment to one-year mortality and functional decline. *Journal of Aging and Health, 4,* 126-148.

Lair, T., & Lefkowitz, D. (1990). *Mental health and functional status of residents of nursing and personal care homes* (DHHS Publication No. PHS 90-3470, National Medical Expenditure Survey Research Findings 7, Agency for Health Care Policy and Research). Rockville, MD: U.S. Public Health Service.

Lakatta, E. G. (1987). Why cardiovascular function may decline with age. *Geriatrics, 42,* 84-94.

Lamberty, G. J., & Bieliauskas, L. A. (1993). Distinguishing between depression and dementia in the elderly: A review of neuropsychological findings. *Archives of Clinical Neuropsychology, 8,* 149-170.

Lamy, P. P. (1988). Actions of alcohol and drugs in older people. *Generations, 12*(4), 9-13.

Lane, J. (1994, December). Sarcoma and other tumors in Paget's disease. *Paget Foundation Newsletter.*

Langsley, D. G., & Hollender, M. H. (1982). The definition of a psychiatrist. *American Journal of Psychiatry, 139,* 81-85.

Lapierre, S., Pronovost, J., Dube, M., & Delisle, I. (1992). Risk factors associated with suicide in elderly persons living in the community. *Canada's Mental Health, 40,* 8-12.

Laporte, R. E., Kuller, C. H., Kupfer, D. J., McPartland, R. J., Matthews, G., & Caspersen, C. (1979). An objective measure of physical activity for epidemiologic research. *American Journal of Epidemiology, 109*(2), 158-167.

Larrabee, G. J., & Crook, T. H. (1989). Dimensions of everyday memory in age-associated memory impairment. *Psychological Assessment: A Journal of Consulting and Clinical Psychology, 1,* 92-97.

Larrabee, G. J., Youngjohn, J. R., Sudilovsky, A., & Crook, T. H. (1993). Accelerated forgetting in Alzheimer-type dementia. *Journal of Clinical and Experimental Neuropsychology, 15,* 701-712.

Larsen, R. J. (1973). *The Puerto Ricans in America.* Minneapolis, MN: Lerner.

Larson, E. B., Kukull, W. A., Buchner, D., & Reifler, B. V. (1987). Adverse drug reactions associated with global cognitive impairment in elderly persons. *Annals of Internal Medicine, 107,* 169-173.

LaRue, A. (1992). *Aging and neuropsychological assessment.* New York: Plenum.

LaRue, A., Dessonville, C., & Jarvik, L. F. (1985). Aging and mental disorders. In J. E. Birren & K. W. Schaie (Eds.), *Handbook of the Psychology of Aging* (2nd ed., pp. 664-702). New York: Van Nostrand Reinhold.

LaRue, A., Goodman, S., & Spar, J. E. (1992). Risk factors for memory impairment in geriatric depression. *Neuropsychiatry, Neuropsychology, and Behavioral Neurology, 5,* 178-184.

LaRue, A., Watson, J., & Plotkin, D. A. (1992). Retrospective accounts of dementia symptoms: Are they reliable? *The Gerontologist, 32,* 240-245.

Lawton, M. P., & Brody, E. M. (1969). Assessment of older people: Self-maintaining and instrumental activities of daily living. *The Gerontologist, 9,* 179-186.

Lazarus, L. W., Winemiller, D. R., & Lingarn, V. R. (1992). Efficacy and side effects of methylphenidate for post-stroke depression. *Journal of Clinical Psychiatry, 53,* 447-449.

Lazarus, R. S., & Folkman, S. (1984). *Stress, appraisal, and coping.* New York: Springer.

Leaf, A. (1984). Dehydration in the elderly. *New England Journal of Medicine, 311,* 791-795.

Leaf, P. J., Berkman, C. S., Weissman, M. M., Holzer, C. E., Tischler, G. L., & Myers, J. K. (1988). The epidemiology of late-life depression. In J. Brody & G. Maddox (Eds.), *Epidemiology and aging.* New York: Springer.

Lebo, C. P., & Reddell, R. C. (1972). The presbycusis component in occupational hearing loss. *Laryngoscope, 82,* 1399-1409.

Lee, G. R. (1992). Gender differences in family caregiving: A fact in search of a theory. In J. W. Dwyer & R. T. Coward (Eds.), *Gender, families, and elder care* (pp. 120-131). Newbury Park, CA: Sage.

Lee, G. R., Dwyer, J. W., & Coward, R. T. (1993). Gender differences in parent care: Demographic factors and same-gender preferences. *Journal of Gerontology, 48,* S9-S16.

Lee, I. M., Paffenbarger, R., & Hsieh, C. (1992). Physical activity and risk of prostate cancer among college alumni. *American Journal of Epidemiology, 135,* 169-172.

Lee, J. (1986). Asian American elderly: A neglected minority group [Special issue: Ethnicity and gerontological social work]. *Journal of Gerontological Social Work, 9*(4), 103-116.

Lehmann, H. E. (1982). Affective disorders in the aged. In L. F. Jarvik & G. W. Small (Eds.), *The psychiatric clinics of North America* (pp. 537-553). Philadelphia: W. B. Saunders.

Lehmann, J. F., DeLateur, B. J., Fowler, R. S., Warren, C. G., Arnhold, R., Schertzer, G., Hurka, R., Whitmore, J. J., Masock, A. J., & Chambers, K. H. (1975). Stroke: Does rehabilitation affect outcome? *Archives of Physical Medicine Rehabilitation, 56,* 375-382.

Leiblum, S., & Bachman, G. (1987). The sexuality of the climacteric woman. In B. Eskin (Ed.), *The menopause: Comprehensive management* (pp. 165-180). New York: Yearbook Publications.

Leiblum, S. R., & Segraves, R. T. (1989). Sex therapy with aging adults. In S. R. Leiblum & R. C. Rosen (Eds.), *Principles and practice of sex therapy: Update for the 1990's* (pp. 352- 381). New York: Guilford.

Leon, A. C., Klerman, G. L., & Wickramaratne, P. (1993). Continuing female predominance in depressive illness. *American Journal of Public Health, 83,* 754-757.

Leonard, B. E. (1993). The comparative pharmacology of new antidepressants. *Journal of Clinical Psychiatry, 45*(8, Suppl.), 3-15.

Leslie, L. A. (1992). The role of informal support networks in the adjustment of Central American immigrant families. *Journal of Community Psychology, 20,* 243-256.

Leslie, L. A., & Leitch, M. L. (1989). A demographic profile of recent Central American immigrants: Service and clinical implications. *Hispanic Journal of Behavioral Sciences, 11,* 315-329.

Leuchter, A. F., & Spar, J. E. (1985). The late-onset psychoses: Clinical and diagnostic features. *Journal of Nervous and Mental Disease, 173,* 488-494.

Leung, S. N., & Orrell, M. W. (1993). A brief cognitive behavioural therapy group for the elderly: Who benefits? *International Journal of Geriatric Psychiatry, 8,* 593-598.

Levenson, R. W., Carstensen, L. L., & Gottman, J. M. (1994). Influence of age and gender on affect, physiology, and their interrelations: A study of long-term marriages. *Journal of Personality and Social Psychology, 67,* 56-68.

Levey, A. B., Aldaz, J. A., Watts, F. N., & Coyle, K. (1991). Articulatory suppression and the treatment of insomnia. *Behaviour Research and Therapy, 29,* 85-89.

Levine, S., Napoliello, M. J., & Domantay, A. G. (1989). Open study of buspirone in octogenarians with anxiety. *Human Psychopharmacology, 4,* 51-53.

Lewinsohn, P. M. (1974). A behavioral approach to depression. In R. J. Friedman & M. M. Katz (Eds.), *The psychology of depression: Contemporary theory and research* (pp. 157-178). New York: Winston-Wiley.

Lewinsohn, P. M., Duncan, E. M., Stanton, A. K., & Hautzinger, M. (1986). Age at first onset for nonbipolar depression. *Journal of Abnormal Psychology, 95,* 378-383.

Lewinsohn, P., Sullivan, J. M., & Grosscup, S. (1982). Behavioral therapy: Clinical applications. In A. J. Rush (Ed.), *Short-term psychotherapies for depression* (pp. 50-87). New York: Guilford.

Lewis, T. Z. (1975). A syndrome of depression and mutism in the Oglala Sioux. *American Journal of Psychiatry, 132,* 753-755.

Lichstein, K. L., & Johnson, R. S. (1993). Relaxation for insomnia and hypnotic medication use in older women. *Psychology and Aging, 8,* 103-111.

Lichstein, K. L., & Riedel, B. W. (1994). Behavioral assessment and treatment of insomnia: A review with an emphasis on clinical application. *Behavior Therapy, 25,* 659-688.

Lichtenberg, P. (1994). *A guide to psychological practice in geriatric long-term care.* New York: Haworth.

Lichtenberg, P., & Barth, J. (1990). Depression in elderly caregivers: A longitudinal study to test Lewinsohn's model of depression. *Medical Psychotherapy: An International Journal, 3,* 147-156.

Lichtenberg, P., Strzepek, D., & Zeiss, A. (1990). Bringing psychiatric aides into the treatment team: An application of the Veterans Administration's ITTG model. *Gerontology and Geriatrics Education, 10,* 63-73.

Lieberman, A. (1974). Parkinson's disease: A clinical review. *American Journal of Medical Science, 267,* 66-80.

Lieberman, J. A., Saltz, B. L., Johns, C. A., Pollack, S., Borenstein, M., & Kane, J. (1991). The effects of clozapine on tardive dyskinesia. *British Journal of Psychiatry, 158,* 503-510.

Light, K. E., & Spirduso, W. W. (1990). Effects of aging on the movement complexity factor of response programming. *Journal of Gerontology, 45,* P107-P109.

Light, L. L. (1988). Language and aging: Competence versus performance. In J. E. Birren & V. L. Bengtson (Eds.), *Emergent theories of aging.* New York: Springer.

Light, L. L. (1992). The organization of memory in old age. In F. I. M. Craik & T. A. Salthouse (Eds.), *The handbook of aging and cognition* (pp. 111-165). Hillsdale NJ: Lawrence Erlbaum.

Lin, K. M., & Kleinman, A. M. (1988). Psychopathology and clinical course of schizophrenia: A cross-cultural perspective. *Schizophrenia Bulletin, 14,* 555-568.

Lin, K. M., Poland, R. E., & Lesser, I. M. (1986). Ethnicity and psychopharmacology. *Culture, Medicine, and Psychiatry, 10,* 151-165.

Lind, K. (1982). Synthesis of studies on stroke rehabilitation. *Journal of Chronic Disease, 351,* 133-149.

Lindenberger, U., & Baltes, P. B. (1994). Sensory functioning and intelligence in old age: A strong connection. *Psychology and Aging, 9,* 339-355.

Lipinski, J. F., Mallya, G., Zimmerman, P., & Pope, H. G. (1989). Fluoxetine-induced akathesia: Clinical and theoretical implications. *Journal of Clinical Psychiatry, 50,* 339-342.

Lipinski, J. F., Zubenko, G. S., Cohen, B. M., & Barreira, P. J. (1984). Propranolol and the treatment of neuroleptic-induced akathesia. *American Journal of Psychiatry, 141,* 412-415.

Lipowski, Z. J. (1980). *Delirium: Acute brain failure in man.* Springfield, IL: Charles C Thomas.

Lipowski, Z. J. (1983). Transient cognitive disorders in the elderly. *American Journal of Psychiatry, 140,* 1426-1436.

Lipowski, Z. J. (1990). *Acute confusional states.* New York: Oxford University Press.

Lipsey, J. R., & Parikh, R. M. (1989). In R. K. Robinson & P. Rabins (Eds.), *Depression and coexisting disease* (pp. 186-201). New York: Igaku-Shoin.

Lipsitz, L. A., Jonsson, P. V., Kelley, M. M., & Koestner, J. S. (1991). Causes and correlates of recurrent falls in ambulatory frail elderly. *Journal of Gerontology: Medical Sciences, 46,* M114-M122.

Liptzin, B. (1991). The treatment of depression in older suicidal persons. *Journal of Geriatric Psychiatry, 24,* 203-215.

Liptzin, B. (1992). Treatment of mania. In C. Salzman (Ed.), *Clinical geriatric psychopharmacology* (2nd ed., pp. 172-188). Baltimore: Williams & Wilkins.

Lishman, W. A. (1987). *Organic psychiatry. The psychological consequences of cerebral disorder* (2nd ed.). Oxford, UK: Blackwell.

Little, K. Y. (1993). D-Amphetamine versus methylphenidate effect in depressed individuals. *Journal of Clinical Psychiatry, 54,* 349-355.

Litwack, L., & Whedon, G. (1959). The effect of physical conditioning on glucose tolerance. *Clinical Research, 7,* 143-144.

Lloyd, G. G., & Cawley, R. H. (1983). Distress or illness? A study of psychological symptoms after myocardial infarction. *British Journal of Psychiatry, 142,* 120-125.

Lopez, A., Bocellari, A., & Hall, K. (1988). Posttraumatic stress disorder in a Central American refugee. *Hospital and Community Psychiatry, 39,* 1309-1311.

Lopez, S. R. (1989). Patient variable biases in clinical judgment: Conceptual overview and methodological considerations. *Psychological Bulletin, 106,* 184-203.

LoPiccolo, J. (1991). Counseling and therapy for sexual problems in the elderly. *Clinics in Geriatric Medicine, 7,* 161-179.

Lord, S. R., Clark, R. D., & Webster, I. W. (1991a). Physiological factors associated with falls in an elderly population. *Journal of the American Geriatrics Society, 39*(12), 1194-1200.

Lord, S. R., Clark, R. D., & Webster, I. W. (1991b). Postural stability and associated physiological factors in a population of aged persons. *Journal of Gerontology: Medical Sciences, 46,* M69-M76.

Lovelace, E. A., & Marsh, G. A. (1985). Prediction and evaluation of memory performance by young and old adults. *Journal of Gerontology, 40,* 192-197.

Lovell, M. R., & Nussbaum, P. D. (1994). Neuropsychological assessment of the geriatric patient. In C. E. Coffey, J. L. Cummings, M. R. Lovell, & G. Pearlson (Eds.), *Textbook of geriatric neuropsychiatry* (pp. 129-144). Washington, DC: American Psychiatric Press.

Lovett, S., & Gallagher, D. (1988). Psychoeducational interventions for family caregivers: Preliminary efficacy data. *Behavior Therapy, 19,* 321-330.

Lowe, C. F., & Chadwick, P. D. J. (1990). Verbal control of delusions. *Behavior Therapy, 21,* 461-479.

Luangpraset, K. (1989). *Laos culturally speaking.* San Diego, CA: San Diego State University, Multifunctional Resource Center.

Lubben, J. E., & Becerra, R. M. (1987). Social support among Black, Mexican, and Chinese elderly. In D. E. Gelfand & C. M. Baressi (Eds.), *Ethnic dimensions of aging.* New York: Springer.

Lubben, J. L., Weiler, P. G., & Chi, I. (1989). Gender and health differences in the health practices of the elderly poor. *Journal of Clinical Epidemiology, 42,* 725-733.

Luborsky, M. R., & Rubenstein, R. L. (1990). Ethnic identity and bereavement in later life: The case of older widowers. In J. Sokolovsky (Ed.), *The cultural context of aging.* New York: Bergin & Garvey.

Luecht, R. M., Madsen, M. K., Taugher, M. P., & Petterson, B. J. (1990). Assessing professional perceptions: Design and validation of an interdisciplinary education perception scale. *Journal of Allied Health, 19,* 181-191.

Lum, D. (1983). Asian Americans and their aged. In R. L. McNeely & J. L. Colen (Eds.), *Aging in minority groups.* Beverly Hills, CA: Sage.

Lum, D., Cheung, L. Y. S., Cho, E. R., Tang, T. Y., & Yau, H. B. (1980). The psychosocial needs of the Chinese elderly. *Social Casework,* 100-105.

Lund, D. A., Caserta, M. S., & Dimond, M. F. (1986). Gender differences through two years of bereavement among the elderly. *The Gerontologist, 26,* 314-320.

Lustig, J., Ross, A., Davis, D., Old Elk, J. (1979). *The needs of elderly Indians in Phoenix, Arizona: Recommendations for services.* Unpublished report. Phoenix, AZ: Affiliation of American Indian Centers.

Lustman, P. J., Griffith, L. S., & Clouse, R. E. (1988). Depression in adults with diabetes: Results of 5-year follow-up study. *Diabetes Care, 11,* 605-612.

Lustman, P. J., Griffith, L. S., Clouse, R. E., & Cryer, P. E. (1986). Psychiatric illness in diabetes mellitus: Relationship to symptoms and glucose control. *Journal of Nervous and Mental Disease, 174,* 736-742.

Lustman, P. J., Harper, G. W., Griffith, L. S., & Clouse, R. E. (1986). Use of the Diagnostic Interview Schedule in patients with diabetes mellitus. *Journal of Nervous and Mental Disease, 174,* 743-746.

Lyles, K. W. (1990). Hyperparathyroidism in the elderly. In W. R. Hazzard, R. Andres, E. L. Bierman, & J. P. Blass (Eds.), *Principles of geriatric medicine and gerontology* (2nd ed., pp. 837-842). New York: McGraw-Hill.

Lynch, S. R., Finch, C. A., Monsen, E. R., & Cook, J. D. (1982). Iron status of elderly Americans. *American Journal of Clinical Nutrition, 36,* 1032-1045.

Lyness, J. M., Conwell, Y., & Nelson, J. C. (1992). Suicide attempts in elderly psychiatric inpatients. *Journal of the American Geriatrics Society, 40,* 320-324.

Maccoby, E. (1988). Gender as a social category. *Developmental Psychology, 24,* 755-765.

MacDonald, J. B. (1985). The role of drugs in the elderly. *Clinics in Geriatric Medicine, 1,* 621-636.

Mace, N. L. (1990). *Dementia care: Patient, family, and community.* Baltimore: Johns Hopkins University Press.

MacInnes, W. D., Gillen, R. W., Golden, C. J., Graber, B., Cole, J. K., Uhl, H. S., & Greenhouse, A. J. (1983). Aging and performance on the Luria-Nebraska Neuropsychological Battery. *International Journal of Neuroscience. 19,* 179-190.

Madden, D. J., Allen, P. A., Blumenthal, J. A., & Emery, C. F. (1989). Improving aerobic capacity in healthy older adults does not necessarily lead to improved cognitive performance. *Psychology and Aging, 4,* 307-320.

Madson, J. (1991). The study of wandering in persons with senile dementia. *The American Journal of Alzheimer's Care and Related Disorders & Research, 6*(1), 21-24.

Magaziner, J., Simonsick, E. M., Kashner, T. M., Hebel, J. R., & Kenzora, J. (1990). Predictors of functional recovery one year following hospital discharge for hip fracture: A prospective study. *Journal of Gerontology, 45*(3), M101-M107.

Magni, G., & DeLeo, D. (1984). Anxiety and depression in geriatric and adult medical patients. *Psychological Reports, 55,* 607-612.

Magruder-Habib, K., Saltz, C. C., & Barron, P. M. (1986). Age-related patterns of alcoholism among veterans in ambulatory care. *Hospital and Community Psychiatry, 37,* 1251-1255.

Mahard, R. E. (1989). Elderly Puerto Rican women in the continental United States. In C. T. Garcia Coll & M. Mattei (Eds.), *The psychosocial development of Puerto Rican women.* New York: Praeger.

Mahler, J., & Perry, S. (1988). Assessing competency in the physically ill: Guidelines for psychiatric consultants. *Hospital and Community Psychiatry, 39,* 856-861.

Mahurin, R. K., Feher, E. P., Nance, M. L., Levy, J. K., & Pirozzolo, F. J. (1993). Cognition in Parkinson's Disease and related disorders. In R. W. Parks, R. F. Zec, & R. S. Wilson (Eds.), *Neuropsychology of Alzheimer's disease and other dementias* (pp. 308-349). New York: Oxford University Press.

Maki, B. E., Holliday, P. J., & Topper, A. K. (1991). Fear of falling and postural performance in the elderly. *Journals of Gerontology, 46*(4), M123-M131.

Maki, B. E., Holliday, P. J., & Topper, A. K. (1994). A prospective study of postural balance and risk of falling in an ambulatory and independent elderly population. *Journal of Gerontology: Medical Sciences, 49,* M72-M84.

Maldondo, D. (1975). The Chicano aged. *Social Work, 20*(8), 213-216.

Maldondo, D. (1985). The Hispanic elderly: A socio-historical framework for public policy [Special issue: Aging and ethnicity]. *Journal of Applied Gerontology, 4*(1), 18-27.

Malec, J. F., Ivnik, R. J., & Smith, G. E. (1993). Neuropsychology and normal aging: The clinician's perspective. In R. W. Parks, R. F. Zec, & R. S. Wilson (Eds.), *Neuropsychology of Alzheimer's disease and other dementias* (pp. 81-111). New York: Oxford University Press.

Malec, J. F., Richardson, J. W., Sinaki, M., & O'Brien, M. W. (1990). Types of affective response to stroke. *Archives of Physical Medicine and Rehabilitation, 71,* 278-284.

Maletta, G. J. (1988). Management of behavior problems in elderly patients with Alzheimer's disease and other dementias. *Clinics in Geriatric Medicine, 4*(4), 719-747.

Maletta, G. J. (1992). Treatment of behavioral symptomatology of Alzheimer's disease, with emphasis on aggression: Current clinical approaches. *International Psychogeriatrics, 4*(1), 117-130.

Malone, M. L., Thompson, L., & Goodwin, J. S. (1993). Aggressive behaviors among institution-alized elderly. *Journal of the American Geriatric Society, 41,* 853-856.

Mandell, A. L., Knoefel, J. E., & Albert, M. L. (1994). Mental status examination in the elderly. In M. L. Albert & J. E. Knoefel (Eds.), *Clinical neurology of aging* (2nd ed., pp. 277-313). New York: Oxford University Press.

Mann, D. M. (1991). Is the pattern of nerve cell loss in aging and Alzheimer's disease a real, or only an apparent, selectivity? [comment]. *Neurobiology of Aging, 12,* 340-343.

Manning, D. W., Markowitz, J. C., & Frances, A. J. (1992). A review of combined psychotherapy and pharmacotherapy in the treatment of depression. *Journal of Psychotherapy Practice and Research, 1,* 103-116.

Manton, K. (1982). Changing concepts of morbidity and mortality in the elderly population. *Milbank Memorial Fund Quarterly Health & Society, 60,* 183-244.

Manton, K. G., Cordero, L. S., & Stallard, E. (1993). Estimates of change in chronic disability and institutional incidence and prevalence rates in the U.S. elderly populations from the 1982, 1984 and 1989 National Long Term Care Survey. *Journal of Gerontology, 48,* S153-S156.

Marcus, R. (1982). The relationship of dietary calcium to the maintenance of skeletal integrity in man: An interface of endocrinology and nutrition. *Metabolism, 31,* 93-95.

Marder, S. R., & Meibach, R. C. (1994). Risperidone in the treatment of schizophrenia. *American Journal of Psychiatry, 151,* 825-835.

Marengo, J. (1994). Classifying the courses of schizophrenia. *Schizophrenia Bulletin, 3*(20), 519-536.

Marengo, J., Harrow, M., Sands, J., & Galloway, C. (1991). European versus U.S. data on the course of schizophrenia. *American Journal of Psychiatry, 148,* 606-611.

Marin, D. B., & Greenwald, B. S. (1989). Carbamazepine for aggressive agitation in demented patients during nursing care. *American Journal of Psychiatry, 146,* 805.

Marin, G., Sabogal, F., Marin, B., Otero-Sabogal, R., & Perez-Stable, E. J. (1987). Development of a short acculturation scale for Hispanics. *Hispanic Journal of Behavioral Sciences, 9,* 183-205.

Markides, K. S., Martin, H. W., & Sizemore, M. (1980). Psychological distress among elderly Mexican Americans and Anglos. *Ethnicity, 7,* 298-309.

Markides, K. S., & Mindel, C. (1987). *Aging and ethnicity.* Newbury Park, CA: Sage.

Markovitz, P. J. (1993). Treatment of anxiety in the elderly. *Journal of Clinical Psychiatry, 54*(Suppl.), 64-68.

Marmor, M. F. (1980). Clinical physiology of the retina. In G. A. Reyman, D. R. Sanders, & M. F. Goldberg (Eds.), *Principles and practice of opthalmology* (Vol. 2, pp. 823-856). Philadelphia: W. B. Saunders.

Marneros, A., & Deister, A. (1984). The psychopathology of "late schizophrenia." *Psychopathology, 17,* 264-274.

Marsiglio, W., & Donnelly, D. (1991). Sexual relations in later life: A national study of married persons. *Journal of Gerontology: Social Sciences, 46,* S338-S344.

Martin-Buro, I. (1989). Political violence and war as causes of psychosocial trauma in El Salvador. *International Journal of Mental Health, 18,* 3-20.

Martinez, C., Jr. (1988). Mexican Americans. In L. Comas-Diaz & E. E. H. Griffith (Eds.), *Clinical guidelines in cross-cultural mental health.* New York: John Wiley.

Martino-Salzman, D., Blasch, B., Morris, R. D., & McNeal, L. W. (1991). Travel behavior of nursing home residents perceived as wanderers and nonwanderers. *The Gerontologist, 31*(5), 666-672.

Marx, M. S., Cohen-Mansfield, J., & Werner, P. (1990). A profile of the aggressive nursing home resident. *Behavior, Health and Aging, 1*(1), 65-73.

Marx, M. S., Werner, P., & Cohen-Mansfield, J. (1989). Agitation and touch in the nursing home. *Psychological Reports, 64,* 1019-1026.

Mash, E. J. (1985). Some comments on target selection in behavior therapy. *Behavioral Assessment, 7,* 63-78.

Masoro, E. (1993). Dietary restrictions and aging. *Journal of the American Geriatrics Society, 41,* 994-999.

Masters, W. H., & Johnson, V. E. (1966). *Human sexual response.* Boston: Little, Brown.

Masters, W. H., & Johnson, V. E. (1970). *Human sexual inadequacy.* Boston: Little, Brown.

Masur, D. M., Sliwinski, M., Lipton, R. B., Blau, A. D., Crystal, H. A. (1994). Neuropsychological prediction of dementia and the absence of dementia in healthy elderly persons. *Neurology, 44,* 1427-1432.

May, P. R. A., Tuma, A. H., & Dixon, W. J. (1981). Schizophrenia: A follow-up study of the results of five forms of treatment. *Archives of General Psychiatry, 38,* 776-784.

Mayer, J. (1953). Decreased activity and energy balance in hereditary obese diabetic syndrome of mice. *Science, 11,* 504-505.

Mayer, J. (1968). *Overweight: Causes, cost and control.* Englewood Cliffs, NJ: Prentice Hall.

Mayeux, R. (1982). Depression and dementia in Parkinson's disease. In C. C. Marsden & S. Fahn (Eds.), *Movement disorders* (pp. 75-95). London: Butterworth.

Mayeux, R. (1989). A current analysis of behavioral problems in patients with idiopathic Parkinson's disease. *Movement Disorders, 4,* 48-56.

Mayeux, R., Foster, A., & Williamson, B. (1978). The psychological and social effects of myocardial infarction on wives. *British Medical Journal, 1,* 699-701.

Mayeux, R., Sano, M., Chen, J., Tatemichi, T., & Stern, Y. (1991). Risk of dementia in first-degree relatives of patients with Alzheimer's disease and related disorders. *Archives of Neurology, 48,* 269-273.

Mayeux, R., Stern, Y., Cote, L., & Williams, J. B. W. (1984). Altered serotonin metabolism in depressed patients with Parkinson's disease. *Neurology, 31,* 645-650.

Mayeux, R., Stern, Y., Rosen, J., & Leventhal, J. (1981). Depression, intellectual impairment, and Parkinson's disease. *Neurology, 31,* 645-650.

Mayeux, R., Stern, Y., Williams, J. B. W., Cote, L., Frantz, A., & Dyrenfurth, I. (1986). Clinical and biochemical features of depression in Parkinson's disease. *American Journal of Psychiatry, 143,* 756-759.

McArdle, W. D., Katch, F. I., & Katch, V. L. (1991). *Exercise physiology: Energy, nutrition, and human performance* (3rd ed.). Philadelphia: Lea & Ferbiger.

McAuley, E., Lox, C., & Duncan, T. E. (1993). Long-term maintenance of exercise, self-efficacy, and physiological change in older adults. *Journal of Gerontology: Psychological Sciences, 48,* P218-P224.

McCabe, M., & Cuellar, J. (1994). *Aging and health: American Indian/Alaska Native Elders* (2nd ed., Working Paper Series, No. 6.). Palo Alto, CA: Stanford Geriatric Education Center.

McCalden, R. W., McGeough, J. A., Barker, M. B., & Court-Brown, C. M. (1993). Age-related changes in the tensile properties of cortical bone: The relative importance of changes in porosity, mineralization, and microstructure. *Journal of Bone and Joint Surgery in America, 75*(8), 1193-1205.

McCarthy, P. R., Katz, I. R., & Foa, E. B. (1991). Cognitive-behavioral treatment of anxiety in the elderly: A proposed model. In C. Salzman & B. D. Lebowitz (Eds.), *Anxiety in the elderly: Treatment and research* (pp. 197-214). New York: Springer.

McCay, C. (1935). The effect of retarded growth upon the length of lifespan and upon the ultimate body size. *Journal of Nutrition, 10,* 63-73.

McConnell, A. K., & Davies, C. T. M. (1992). A comparison of the ventilatory responses to exercise of elderly and younger humans. *Journal of Gerontology, 47,* B137-B141.

McCormicks, O. J., & Brotman, A. W. (1990). Reversal of fluoxetine-induced anorgasmia by cyproheptadine in two patients. *Journal of Clinical Psychiatry, 51,* 383-384.

McCue, M., Goldstein, G., & Shelly, C. (1989). The application of a short form of the Luria-Nebraska Neuropsychological Battery to discriminate between dementia and depression in the elderly. *International Journal of Clinical Neuropsychology, 11,* 21-29.

McCusker, J., Cherubin, C. E., & Zimberg, S. (1971). Prevalence of alcoholism in a general municipal hospital population. *New York State Journal of Medicine, 71,* 751-754.

McDowd, J. M., & Filion, D. L. (1992). Aging, selective attention, and inhibitory processes: A psychophysiological approach. *Psychology and Aging, 7*(1), 65-71.

McDowell, B. J., Burgio, K. L., Dombrowski, M., Locher, J. L., & Rodriguez, E. (1992). Interdisciplinary approach to the assessment and behavioral treatment of urinary incontinence in geriatric outpatients. *Journal of the American Geriatrics Society, 40,* 370-374.

McElroy, S. L., Keck, P. E., Jr., Pope, H. G., Jr., & Hudson, J. I. (1989). Valproate in psychiatric disorders: Literature review and clinical guidelines. *Journal of Clinical Psychiatry, 50*(3, Suppl.), 23-29.

McEntee, W. J., & Crook, T. H. (1990). Age-associated memory impairment: A role for catecholamines. *Neurology, 40,* 526-530.

McEntee, W. J., & Crook, T. H. (1991). Serotonin, memory, and the aging brain. *Psychopharmacology, 103,* 143-149.

McEntee, W. J., & Crook, T. H. (1992). Cholinergic function in the aged brain: Implications for treatment of memory impairments associated with aging. *Behavioral Pharmacology, 3,* 327-336.

McEntee, W. J., & Crook, T. H. (1993). Glutamate: Its role in learning, memory, and the aging brain. *Psychopharmacology, 111,* 391-401.

McEntee, W. J., Crook, T. H., Jenkyn, L. R., Petrie, W., Larrabee, G. J., & Coffey, D. J. (1991). Treatment of age-associated memory impairment with guanfacine. *Psychopharmacology Bulletin, 27,* 41-46.

McFarland, B. H., Miller, M. R., & Straumfjord, A. A. (1990). Valproate use in the older manic patient. *Journal of Clinical Psychiatry, 51,* 479-481.

McFarland, R. A., Domey, R. G., Warren, A. B., & Ward, D. C. (1960). Dark adaptation as a function of age: 1. A statistical analysis. *Journal of Gerontology, 15,* 149-154.

McGarvey, B., Gallagher, D., Thompson, L. W., & Zelinsky, E. (1982). Reliability and factor structure of the Zung Self-Rating Depression scale in three age groups. *Essence, 5,* 141-153.

McGinty, D., Littner, M., Beahm, E., Ruiz-Primo, E., Young, E., & Saver, J. (1982). Sleep related to breathing disorders in older men: A search for underlying mechanisms. *Neurobiology of Aging, 3,* 337-350.

McGlashan, T. H. (1988). A selective review of recent North American long-term followup studies of schizophrenia. *Schizophrenia Bulletin, 14,* 515-542.

McGlone, J., Gupta, S., Humphrey, D., Oppenheimer, S., Mirsen, T., & Evans, D. R. (1990). Screening for early dementia using memory complaints from patients and relatives. *Archives of Neurology, 47,* 1189-1193.

McGlynn, S. M., & Schacter, D. L. (1989). Unawareness of deficits in neuropsychological syndromes. *Journal of Clinical and Experimental Neuropsychology, 11,* 143-205.

McGrowder-Lin, R., & Bhatt, A. (1988). A wanderer's lounge program for nursing home residents with Alzheimer's disease. *The Gerontologist, 28*(5), 607-609.

McGuire, M. H., & Rabins, P. V. (1994). Mood disorders. In C. E. Coffey & J. L. Cummings (Eds.), *Textbook of geriatric neuropsychiatry* (pp. 244-260). Washington, DC: American Psychiatric Press.

McInnis, K. (1991). Practice forum: Ethnic sensitive work with Hmong refugee children. *Child Welfare, 70,* 571-580.

McIntosh, J. L. (1992). Epidemiology of suicide in the elderly. *Suicide and Life Threatening Behavior 22,* 15-35.

McKhann, G., Drachman, D., Folstein, M., Katzman, R., Price, D., & Stadlan, E. M. (1984). Clinical diagnosis of Alzheimer's disease: Report of the NINCDS-ADRDA Work Group under the auspices of the Department of Health and Human Services Task Force on Alzheimer's Disease. *Neurology, 34,* 939-944.

McKnight, D. L., Nelson, R. O., Hayes, S. C., & Jarrett, R. B. (1984). Importance of treating individually assessed response classes in the amelioration of depression. *Behavior Therapy, 15,* 315-335.

McMurdo, M. E., & Gaskell, A. (1991). Dark adaptation and falls in the elderly. *Gerontology, 37*(4), 221-224.

McSweeny, A. J., Grant, I., Heaton, R. K., Adams, K. M., & Timms, R. M. (1985). Relationship of neuropsychological status to everyday functioning in healthy and chronically ill persons. *Journal of Clinical Experimental Neuropsychology, 7,* 281-291.

Mechanic, D. (1962). Sources of power of lower participants in complex organizations. *Administrative Science Quarterly, 7,* 349-364.

Meddaugh, D. I. (1987). Aggressive and nonaggressive nursing home patients [Special Issue]. *The Gerontologist, 27,* 127A.

Meeks, S., Carstensen, L. L., Staffor, P. B., Brenner, L. L., Weathers, F., Welch, R., & Oltmanns, T. F. (1990). Mental health needs of the chronically mentally ill elderly. *Psychology and Aging, 5,* 163-171.

Meier, M. S., & Ribera, F. (1993). *Mexican Americans/American Mexicans: From conquistadors to Chicanos.* New York: Hill & Wang.

Mellinger, G. D., Balter, M. B., & Uhlenhuth, E. H. (1985). Insomnia and its treatment: Prevalence and correlates. *Archives of General Psychiatry, 42,* 225-232.

Mellstrom, D., Nilsson, A., Oden, A., Rundgren, A., & Svanborg, A. (1982). Mortality among the widowed in Sweden. *Scandinavian Journal of Social Medicine, 10,* 33-41.

Melton, G. B., Petrila, J., Poythress, N. G., & Slobogin, C. (1987). *Psychological evaluations for the courts: A handbook for mental health professionals and lawyers.* New York: Guilford.

Meltzer, H. Y. (1993). Serotonin-dopamine interactions and atypical antipsychotic drugs. *Psychiatric Annals, 23,* 193-200.

Meltzer, H. Y., & Luchins, D. J. (1984). Effect of clozapine in severe tardive dyskinesia: A case report. *Journal of Clinical Psychopharmacology, 4,* 286-287.

Mendels, J., Johnston, R., Mattes, J., & Reisenberg, R. (1993). Efficacy and safety of b.i.d. doses of venlafaxine in a dose-response study. *Psychopharmacology Bulletin, 29,* 169-174.

Mendels, J., Reimherr, F., Marcus, R. N., Roberts, D. C., Francis, R. J., & Anton, S. F. (1995). A double-blind, placebo-controlled trial of two dose ranges of nefazodone in the treatment of depressed outpatients. *Journal of Clinical Psychiatry, 56*(Suppl. 6), 30-36.

Mentes, J. C., & Ferraro, J. (1989). Calming aggressive reactions: A preventive program. *Journal of Gerontological Nursing, 15*(2), 22-27.

Meredith, C. N., Frontera, W. R., Fisher, E. C., Hughes, V. A., Herland, J. C., Edwards, J., & Evans, W. J. (1989). Peripheral effects of endurance training in young and old subjects. *Journal of Applied Physiology, 66,* 2844-2849.

Metter, E. J., & Wilson R. S. (1993). Vascular dementia. In R. W. Parks, R. F. Zec, & R. S. Wilson (Eds.), *Neuropsychology of Alzheimer's disease and other dementias* (pp. 416-437). New York: Oxford University Press.

Meyer, J., Schalock, R., & Genaidy, H. (1991). Aggression in psychiatric hospitalized geriatric patients. *International Journal of Geriatric Psychiatry, 6,* 589-592.

Meyer, T. J., Miller, M. L., Metzger, R. L., & Borkovec, T. D. (1990). Development and validation of the Penn State Worry Questionnaire. *Behavioural Research and Therapy, 28,* 487-495.

Meyerhoff, B. (1987). A symbol perfected in death: Continuity and ritual in the life and death of an elderly Jew. In B. Meyerhoff & A. Simic (Eds.), *Life's career—Aging: Cultural variations on growing old.* Newbury Park, CA: Sage.

Mick, C. (1983). *A profile of American Indian nursing homes* (Working paper). Tucson: University of Arizona, Long-term Care Gerontology Center.

Miles, L. E., & Dement, W. C. (1980). Sleep and aging. *Sleep, 3,* 119-122.

Milke, D. L. (1988). Wandering in dementia: behavioral observations [Special Issue]. *The Gerontologist, 28,* 47.

Miller, B., & Cafasso, L. (1992). Gender differences in caregiving: Fact or artifact? *The Gerontologist, 32,* 498-507.

Miller, B. L., Benson, D. F., Cummings, J. L., & Neshkes, R. (1986). Late-life paraphrenia: An organic delusional syndrome. *Journal of Clinical Psychiatry, 47,* 204-207.

Miller, B. L., & Lesser, I. M. (1988). Late-life psychosis and modern neuroimaging. *Psychiatric Clinics of North America, 2,* 33-45.

Miller, N. E., & Cohen, G. D. (1987). *Schizophrenia and Aging.* New York: Guilford.

Miller, P., & Ingham, J. (1976). Friends, confidants, and symptoms. *Social Psychiatry, 11,* 51-58.

Miller, W., & Rollnick, S. (1991). *Motivational interviewing: Preparing people to change addictive behavior.* New York: Guilford.

Milligan, W. L., Powell, A., Harley, C., & Furchtgott, E. (1984). A comparison of physical health and psychosocial variables as predictors of reaction time and serial learning performance. *Journal of Gerontology, 39,* 704-710.

Minaker, K. L., & Rowe, J. W. (1982). Gastrointestinal system. In J. W. Rowe & R. W. Besdine (Eds.), *Health and disease in old age.* Boston: Little, Brown.

Mindell, E., & Vernon, M. (1987). *They grow in silence* (2nd ed.). San Diego: College-Hill.

Mindham, R. H. S. (1970). Psychiatric symptoms in parkinsonism. *Journal of Neurology, Neurosurgery, and Psychiatry, 33,* 188-191.

Mirchandani, I. C., & Young, R. C. (1993). Management of mania in the elderly: An update. *Annals of Clinical Psychiatry, 5,* 67-77.

Mishara, B. L., & Kastenbaum, R. (1973). Self-injurious behavior and environmental change in the institutionalized elderly. *International Journal of Aging and Human Development, 4,* 133-145.

Mishkin, B. (1989). Determining the capacity for making health care decisions. *Advances in Psychosomatic Medicine, 19,* 151-166.

Mitchell, C. O. (1982). Malnutrition in the elderly. *American Journal of Clinical Nutrition, 35,* 398-409.

Mittenberg, W., Seidenberg, M., O'Leary, D. S., & DiGiulio, D. V. (1989). Changes in cerebral functioning associated with normal aging. *Journal of Clinical and Experimental Neuropsychology, 11,* 918-932.

Moak, G. S. (1990). Characteristics of demented and nondemented geriatric admissions to a state hospital. *Hospital and Community Psychiatry, 41*(7), 799-801.

Mogan, K., Gilleard, C. J., & Reive, A. (1982). Hypnotic usage in residential homes for the elderly: A prevalence and longitudinal analysis. *Age and Aging, 11,* 229-234.

Mohr, E., Schlegel, J., & Fabbgrini, G. (1989). Clonidine treatment of Alzheimer's disease. *Archives of Neurology, 46,* 376-378.

Mohs, R. C., Rosen, W. G., Greenwald, B. S., & Davis, K. L. (1983). Neuropathologically validated scales for Alzheimer's disease. In T. Crook, S. Ferris, & R. Bartus (Eds.), *Assessment in geriatric psychopathology* (pp. 37-46). New Canaan, CT: Mark Powley.

Moisey, C. U., Stephenson, T. P., & Brendler, C. B. (1980). The urodynamic and subjective results of treatment of detrusor instability with oxybutynin chloride. *British Journal of Urology, 52,* 472-475.

Molgaard, C. A., Nakamura, C. M., Stanford, E. P., Peddecord, K. M., & Morton, D. J. (1990). Prevalence of alcohol consumption among older persons. *Journal of Community Health, 15,* 239-251.

Mollica, R. F., & Lavelle, J. P. (1988). Southeast Asian refugees. In L. C. Comas-Diaz & E. E. H. Griffith (Eds.), *Clinical guidelines in cross-cultural mental health.* New York: John Wiley.

Monsour, N., & Robb, S. S. (1982). Wandering behavior in old age: A psychosocial study. *Social Work, 27*(5), 411-416.

Montgomery, R. J. V., & Kosloski, K. (1994). Outcomes of family caregiving: Lessons from the past and challenges for the future. In M. Cantor (Ed.), *Family caregiving: Agenda for the future* (pp. 123-136). San Francisco: American Society on Aging.

Montgomery, S. A. (1990). Depression in the elderly: Pharmacokinetics of antidepressants and death from overdose. *International Clinical Psychopharmacology, 5*(Suppl. 3), 67-76.

Montgomery, S. A. (1993). Venlafaxine: A new dimension in antidepressant pharmacology. *Journal of Clinical Psychiatry, 54,* 119-126.

Moore, L. M., Nielsen, C. R., & Mistretta, C. M. (1983). Sucrose taste thresholds: Age-related differences. *Journal of Gerontology, 37,* 64-69.

Moore, N. C. (1981). Is paranoid illness associated with sensory defects in the elderly? *Psychosomatic Research, 25,* 69-74.

Moos, R. H., & Lemke, S. (1985). Specialized living environments for older people. In J. E. Birren & K. W. Schaie (Eds.), *Handbook of the psychology of aging* (2nd ed., pp. 864-889). New York: Van Nostrand Reinhold.

Moos, R. H., Lemke, S., & David, T. G. (1987). Priorities for design and management in residential settings for the elderly. In V. Regnier & J. Pynos (Eds.), *Housing the aged: Design directions and policy considerations* (pp. 179-205). New York: Elsevier.

Morey, M. C., Cowper, P. A., Feussner, J. R., DiPasquale, R. C., Crowley, G. M., & Sullivan, R., Jr. (1991). Two-year trends in physical performance following supervised exercise among community-dwelling older veterans. *Journal of the American Geriatrics Society, 39,* 549-554.

Morgan, K. (1987). *Sleep and aging: A research-based guide to sleep in later life.* Baltimore: John Hopkins University Press.

Morganroth, J., & Goin, J. E. (1991). Quinide-related mortality in the short-to-medium term treatment of ventricular arrhythmias: A meta-analysis. *Circulation, 84,* 1977-1983.

Morin, C. M. (1993). *Insomnia: Psychological assessment and management.* New York: Guilford.

Morin, C. M., & Azrin, N. H. (1987). Stimulus control and imagery training in treating sleep-maintenance insomnia. *Journal of Consulting and Clinical Psychology, 2,* 260-262.

Morin, C. M., & Azrin, N. H. (1988). Behavioral and cognitive treatments of geriatric insomnia. *Journal of Consulting and Clinical Psychology, 56,* 748-753.

Morin, C. M., Culbert, J. P., & Schwartz, S. M. (1995). Nonpharmacological interventions for insomnia: A meta-analysis of treatment efficacy. *American Journal of Psychiatry, 151,* 1172-1180.

Morin, C. M., Gaulier, B., Barry, T., & Kowatch, R. A. (1992). Patient's acceptance of psychological and pharmacological therapies for insomnia. *Sleep, 15,* 302-305.

Morin, C. M., & Gramling, S. E. (1989). Sleep patterns and aging: Comparison of older adults with and without insomnia complaints. *Psychology and Aging, 4,* 290-294.

Morin, C. M., Kowatch, R., Berry, T., & Walton, E. (1993). Cognitive-behavior therapy for late-life insomnia. *Journal of Consulting and Clinical Psychology, 61,* 137-146.

Morin, C. M., Kowatch, R. A., & O'Shanick, G. (1990). Sleep restriction for the inpatient treatment of insomnia. *Sleep, 13,* 183-186.

Morin, C. M., Kowatch, R. A., & Wade, J. B. (1989). Behavioral management of sleep disturbances secondary to chronic pain. *Journal of Behaviour Therapy & Experimental Psychiatry, 20,* 295-302.

Morin, C. M., & Kwentus, J. A. (1988). Behavioral and pharmacological treatments for insomnia. *Annals of Behavioral Medicine, 10,* 91-100.

Morin, C. M., Stone, J., Trinkle, D., Mercer, J., & Remsberg, S. (1992). Dysfunctional beliefs and attitudes about sleep among older adults with and without insomnia complaints. *Psychology and Aging, 8,* 463-467.

Morioka-Douglas, N., & Yeo, G. (1990). *Aging and health: Asian/Pacific Island American elders* (Working Paper Series, 3). Palo Alto, CA: Stanford Geriatric Education Center.

Morley, J. E., & Kaiser, F. E. (1990). Unique aspects of diabetes mellitus in the elderly. *Clinics in Geriatric Medicine, 6,* 693-702.

Morley, J. E., & Reese, S. S. (1989). Clinical implications of the aging heart. *American Journal of Medicine, 86,* 77-86.

Morley, J. E., Silver, A., Fiatarone, M., & Mooradian, A. D. (1986). Geriatric grand rounds: Nutrition in the elderly. *Journal of the American Geriatrics Society, 34,* 823-827.

Morowitz, H. J. (1987). *Cosmic joy and local pain: Musings of a mystic scientist.* New York: Scribner.

Morris, J. C., & McManus, D. Q. (1991). The neurology of aging: Normal versus pathologic change. *Geriatrics, 46*(8), 47-48.

Morris, J. C., Rubin, E. H., Morris, E. J., & Mandel, S. A. (1987). Senile dementia of the Alzheimer's type: An important risk factor for serious falls. *Journal of Gerontology, 42*(4), 412-417.

Morris, P. L., Robinson, R. G., & Raphael, B. (1990). Prevalence and course of depressive disorders in hospitalized stroke patients. *International Journal of Psychiatry in Medicine, 20,* 349-364.

Morris, P. L., Robinson, R. G., Raphael, B., &, Bishop, D. (1991). The relationship between the perception of social support and post-stroke depression in hospitalized patients. *Psychiatry, 54,* 306-316.

Morris, R., Craik, F. I. M., & Glick, M. (1990). Age differences in working memory tasks: The role of secondary memory and the central executive system. *Quarterly Journal of Experimental Psychology, 42A,* 67-86.

Morse, J. M., Tylko, S. J., & Dixon, H. A. (1987). Characteristics of the fall-prone patient. *The Gerontologist, 27*(4), 516-522.

Morse, R. M. (1988). Substance abuse among the elderly. *Bulletin of the Menninger Clinic, 52,* 259-268.

Mortimer, J. A. (1983). Alzheimer's disease and senile dementia: Prevalence and incidence. In B. Reisburg (Ed.), *Alzheimer's disease: The standard reference* (pp. 141-148). New York: Free Press.

Moses, R. A. (1981). Accommodation. In R. A. Moses (Ed.), *Adler's physiology of the eye.* St. Louis, MO: C. V. Mosby.

Mosher-Ashley, P. B. (1986/87). Procedural and methodological parameters in behavioral-gerontological research: A review. *International Journal of Aging and Human Development, 24,* 189-229.

Mosqueda, L. M. (1993). Assessment of rehabilitation potential. *Clinics in Geriatric Medicine, 9,* 689-703.

Moss, A. J. (1986). Prolonged QT interval syndromes. *JAMA, 256,* 2985-2987.

Moss, L. E., Neppe, V. M., & Drevets, W. C. (1993). Buspirone in the treatment of tardive dyskinesia. *Journal of Clinical Psychopharmacology, 13,* 204-209.

Mouritzen Dam, A. (1979). The density of neurons in the human hippocampus. *Neuropathology and Applied Neurobiology, 5,* 249-264.

Mukherjee, S., Sackheim, H. A., & Schnur, D. B. (1994). Electroconvulsive therapy of acute manic episodes: A review of 50 years' experience. *American Journal of Psychiatry, 151,* 169-176.

Mulford, H. A. (1964). Drinking and deviant drinking, U. S. A., 1963. *Quarterly Journal of Studies on Alcohol, 25,* 634-650.

Mulford, H. A., & Fitzgerald, J. L. (1992). Elderly versus younger problem drinker profiles: Do they indicate a need for special programs for the elderly? *Journal on Studies of Alcohol, 53,* 601-610.

Muller, O. F., Goodman, N., & Bellet, S. (1961). The hypotensive effect of imipramine hydrochloride on inpatients with cardiovascular disease. *Clinical Pharmacology and Therapeutics, 2,* 300-307.

Mungas, D., Weiler, P., Franzi, C., & Henry, R. (1989). Assessment of disruptive behavior associated with dementia: The Disruptive Behavior Rating Scales. *Journal of Geriatric Psychiatry and Neurology, 2*(4), 196-202.

Murdock, S. H., & Schwartz, D. F. (1978). Family structure and the use of agency services: An examination of patterns among elderly Native Americans. *The Gerontologist, 18,* 475-481.

Murphy, C. (1983). Age-related effects on the threshold, psychophysiological function, and pleasantness of menthol. *Journal of Gerontology, 38,* 217-222.

Murphy, C., & Gilmore, M. M. (1989). Quality-specific effects of aging on the human taste system. *Perceptual Psychophysiology, 45*(2), 121-128.

Murphy, E. (1982). Social origins of depression in old age. *British Journal of Psychiatry, 141,* 135-142.

Murphy, G. E. (1988). Prevention of suicide. In A. J. Francis & R. E. Hales (Eds.), *Review of psychiatry* (Vol. 7). Washington, DC: American Psychiatric Press.

Murphy, J. (1992). Dysmobility and immobility. In R. Ham (Ed.), *Primary care geriatrics* (2nd ed., pp. 313-335). St. Louis, MO: Mosby Year Book.

Murphy, J. R. (1991). Older clients of questionable competency: Making accurate competency determinations through the utilization of medical professionals. *Georgetown Journal of Legal Ethics, 4,* 899-918.

Murrell, S. A., Himmelfarb, S., & Wright, K. (1983). Prevalence of depression and its correlates in older adults. *American Journal of Epidemiology, 117,* 173-185.

Murtagh, D. R. R., & Greenwood, K. M. (1995). Identifying effective psychological treatments for insomnia: A meta-analysis. *Journal of Consulting and Clinical Psychology, 63,* 79-89.

Musetti, L., Perugi, G., Soriani, A., Rossi, V. M., Cassano, G. B., & Akiskal, H. S. (1989). Depression before and after age 65: A reexamination. *British Journal of Psychiatry, 155,* 330-336.

Mutch, W. J. (1992). Parkinsonism and other movement disorders. In J. C. Brocklehurst, R. C. Tallis, & H. M. Fillit (Eds.), *Textbook of geriatric medicine and gerontology* (pp. 423). London: Churchill Livingstone.

Myers, A. M., & Huddy, L. (1985). Evaluating physical capabilities in the elderly: The relationship between ADL self-assessments and basic abilities. *Canadian Journal of Aging, 4,* 189-200.

Myers, A. R., Goldman, E., Hingson, R., Scotch, N., & Mangione, T. (1984). Evidence for cohort or generational differences in the drinking behavior of older adults. *International Journal of Aging and Human Development, 14,* 31-44.

Myers, J. K., Weissman, M. M., Tischler, G. L., Holzer, C. E., Leaf, P. J., Orvaschel, H., Anthony, J. C., Boyd, J. H., Burke, J. D., Kramer, M., & Stolzman, R. (1984). Six month prevalence of psychiatric disorders in three communities: 1980-1982. *Archives of General Psychiatry, 41,* 959-967.

Myerson, J., Hale, S., Wagstaff, D., Poon, L. W., & Smith, G. A. (1990). The information-loss model: A mathematical theory of age-related cognitive slowing. *Psychological Review, 97,* 475-487.

Namazi, K. H., Rosner, T. T., & Calkins, M. P. (1989). Visual barriers to prevent patients from exiting through an emergency door. *The Gerontologist, 29*(5), 699-702.

Napoliello, M. J. (1986). An interim multicenter report on 677 anxious geriatric out-patients treated with buspirone. *British Journal of Clinical Practice, 40,* 71-73.

National Cancer Institute. (1978). *Surveillance, Epidemiology and End Results (SEER) Program, 1973-1977.* Bethesda, MD: Author.

National Indian Council on Aging. (1981). *American Indian elderly: A national profile.* Albuquerque, NM: Author.

National Institute of Mental Health. (1985). *Annual survey of patient characteristics—1985 state and county mental hospital inpatient services.* Rockville, MD: Author, Division of Biometry and Applied Science.

National Institutes of Health. (1983). *Consensus development conference summary: Drugs and insomnia* (Vol. 4, No. 10). Bethesda, MD: Author, Office of Medical Applications of Research.

National Institutes of Health Consensus Development Conference. (1985). Lowering blood cholesterol to prevent heart disease. *Arteriosclerosis, 5,* 404-410.

Negley, E. N., Molla, P. M., & Obenchain, J. (1990). No exit: The effects of an electronic security system on confused patients. *Journal of Gerontological Nursing, 16*(8), 21-25.

Neils, J., Newman, C. W., Hill, M., & Weiler, E. (1991). The effects of rate, sequencing, and memory on auditory processing in the elderly. *Journals of Gerontology, 46*(2), 71.

Nelson, M. E. (1994). Effects of high-intensity strength training on multi-risk factors for osteoporotic fractures: A randomized controlled trial. *JAMA, 272*(24), 1909-1914.

Nelson, R., & Franci, L. (1992). Nutrition. In R. Ham (Ed.), *Primary care geriatrics* (2nd ed., pp. 162-193). St. Louis, MO: Mosby Year Book.

Neumann, E. M., Zank, S., Tzschätzsch, K., & Baltes, M. M. (1993). Selbständigkeit im Alter. Ein Trainingsmanual für Pflegende [Independence in old age: A training manual for caregivers]. Bern, Switzerland: Huber.

Neundorfer, M. M. (1991a). Coping and health outcomes in spouse caregivers of persons with dementia. *Nursing Research, 40,* 260-265.

Neundorfer, M. M. (1991b). Family caregivers of the frail elderly: Impact of caregiving on their health and implications for interventions. *Family and Community Health, 14,* 48-58.

Nevitt, M. C., Cummings, S. R., & Hudes, E. S. (1991). Risk factors for injurious falls: A prospective study. *Journal of Gerontology: Medical Sciences, 46,* M164-M170.

Nicholson, A. N. (1994). Hypnotics: Clinical pharmacology and therapeutics. In M. H. Kryger, T. Roth, & W. C. Dement (Eds.), *Principles and practice of sleep medicine* (2nd ed., pp. 355-363). Philadelphia: W. B. Saunders.

Nicholson, A. N., & Pascoe, P. A. (1986). Hypnotic activity of an imidazopyridine (Zolpidem). *British Journal of Clinical Pharmacology, 21,* 205-211.

Nietzel, M. T., Bernstein, D. A., & Russell, R. L. (1988). Assessment of anxiety and fear. In A. S. Bellack & M. Hersen (Eds.), *Behavioral assessment: A practical handbook* (3rd ed., pp. 280-312). New York: Pergamon.

Nightingale, S. L. (1993). Treatment IND for MS drug, from FDA. *JAMA, 269,* 974.

Nilsson, K., Palmstierna, B., & Wistedt, B. (1988). Aggressive behavior in hospitalized psychogeriatric patients. *Acta Psychiatric Scandinavia, 78,* 172-175.

Nolan, B. S. (1984). Functional evaluation of the elderly in guardianship proceedings. *Law, Medicine & Health Care, 12,* 210-218.

Nolan, B. S. (1990). A judicial menu: Selecting remedies for the incapacitated elder. *Journal of Elder Abuse and Neglect, 2,* 73-88.

Nolen-Hoeksema, S. (1987). Sex differences in unipolar depression: Evidence and theory. *Psychological Bulletin, 101,* 259-282

Nolen-Hoeksema, S. (1991). Responses to depression and their effects on the duration of depressive episodes. *Journal of Abnormal Psychology, 100,* 569-582.

Norcross, J., Prochaska, J. O., & Gallagher, K. M. (1989). Clinical psychologists in the 1980s: II. Theory, research, and practice. *The Clinical Psychologist, 42,* 45-53.

Norman, T. R. (1993). Pharmacokinetic aspects of antidepressant treatment in the elderly. *Progress in Neuro-Psychopharmacology and Biological Psychiatry, 17,* 329-344.

Norris, J. T. (1987). Assessment of depression in geriatric medical outpatients. *Journal of the American Geriatric Society, 35,* 989-995.

Norris, M. L., & Cunningham, D. R. (1981). Social impact of hearing loss in the aged. *Journal of Gerontology, 36,* 727-729.

Notelowitz, M. (1990). Management of the changing vagina [Special Issue]. *Clinical Practice in Sexuality, 1,* 16-17.

Nussbaum, P. D. (1994). Pseudodementia: A slow death. *Neuropsychology Review, 4,* 71-90.

Nussbaum, P. D., & Sauer, L. (1993). Self-report of depression in elderly with and without progressive cognitive deterioration. *The Clinical Gerontologist, 13,* 69-80.

Nuti, R., & Martini, G. (1993). Effects of age and menopause on bone density of entire skeleton in healthy and osteoporotic women. *Osteoporosis International, 3,* 59-65.

O'Connor, D. W., Pollitt, P. A., Roth, M., Brook, P. B., & Reiss, B. B. (1990). Memory complaints and impairment in normal, depressed, and demented elderly persons identified in a community survey. *Archives of General Psychiatry, 47,* 224-227.

O'Donoghue, M. N. (1991). Cosmetics for the elderly. *Dermatology Clinics, 9*(1), 29-34.

Ogden, J. A. (1991). Spatial abilities and deficits in aging and age-related disorders. In F. Boller & J. Grafman (Eds.), *Handbook of neuropsychology* (Vol. 4). New York: Elsevier.

Okawa, A., Mishima, K., Hishikawa, Y., Hozumi, S., Hori, H., & Takahashi, K. (1991). Circadian rhythm disorders in sleep-waking and body temperature in elderly patients with dementia and their treatment. *Sleep, 14,* 478-485.

Okun, M. (1976). Adult age and cautiousness in decision: A review of the literature. *Human Development, 19,* 220-233.

Olson, J. S., & Wilson, R. (1984). *Native Americans in the Twentieth century.* Provo, UT: Brigham Young University Press.

Omnibus Budget Reconciliation Act of 1987, Pub. L. No. 100-203, Subtitle C: Nursing Home Reform.

Ordy, J. M., Brizzee, K. R., Beavers, T., & Medart, P. (1979). Age differences in the functional and structural organization of the auditory system in man. In J. M. Ordy & K. R. Brizzee (Eds.), *Aging: Vol 10. Sensory systems and communication in the elderly* (pp. 153-166). New York: Raven.

Ordy, J. M., Brizzee, K. R., & Johnson, H. A. (1982). Cellular alterations in visual pathways and the limbic system: Implications for vision and short-term memory. In R. Sekuler, D. Kline, & K. Dismukes (Eds.), *Aging and human visual function.* New York: Alan R. Liss.

Oreland, L., & Gottfries, C. G. (1986). Brain and brain monoamine oxidase in aging and dementia of Alzheimer's type. *Progress in Neuro-Psychopharmacology and Biological Psychiatry, 10,* 533-540.

Orlinsky, D. E., & Howard, K. I. (1987). A generic model of psychotherapy. *Journal of Integrative and Ecclectic Psychotherapy, 6,* 6-27.

Orne, M. T., & Wender, P. H. (1968). Anticipatory socialization for psychotherapy: Method and rationale. *American Journal of Psychiatry, 124,* 1201-1212.

Ory, M. G., Abeles, R. P., & Lipman, P. D. (1992). Introduction: An overview of research on aging, health, and behavior. In M. G. Ory, R. P. Abeles, & P. D. Lipman (Eds.), *Aging, health, and behavior* (pp. 1-23). Newbury Park, CA: Sage.

Osato, S. S., Yang, J., & LaRue, A. (1993). The Neurobehavioral Cognitive Status Examination in an older psychiatric population: An exploratory study of validity. *Neuropsychiatry, Neuropsychology, and Behavioral Neurology, 6,* 98-102.

Osgood, N. (1985). *Suicide in the elderly.* Rockville, MD: Aspen.

Osgood, N. (1991). Prevention of suicide in the elderly. *Journal of Geriatric Psychology, 24,* 293-306.

Osgood, N. J. (1992). Suicide assessment in the elderly: Etiology and assessment. *International Review of Psychiatry, 4,* 217-223.

Osterweis, M. (1985). Bereavement and the elderly. *Aging, 348,* 8-13.

Ostrow, A. C., & Dzewaltowski, D. A. (1986). Older adults perceptions of physical activity participation based on age-role and sex-role appropriateness. *Research Quarterly for Exercise and Sport, 57,* 167-169.

Ouslander, J. G. (1981). Drug therapy in the elderly. *Annals of Internal Medicine, 94,* 711-722.

Ouslander, J. G., & Abelson, S. (1990). Perceptions of urinary incontinence among elderly outpatients. *The Gerontologist, 30*(3), 369-372.

Ouslander, J. G., Kane, R. L., & Abrass, I. B. (1982). Urinary incontinence in elderly nursing home patients. *JAMA, 248,* 1194-1198.

Ouslander, J. G., Zarit, S. H., Orr, N. K., & Muira, S. A. (1990). Incontinence among elderly community-dwelling dementia patients: Characteristics, management, and impact on caregivers. *Journal of the American Geriatrics Society, 38,* 440-445.

Owsley, C., Ball, K., Sloane, M. E., Roenker, D. L., & Bruni, J. R. (1991). Visual/cognitive correlates of vehicle accidents in older drivers. *Psychology and Aging, 6*(3), 403-415.

Oxman, T. E., Barrett, J. E., Barrett, J., & Gerber, P. (1987). Psychiatric symptoms in the elderly in a primary care practice. *General Hospital Psychiatry, 9,* 167-173.

Oxman, T. E., Barrett, J. E., Barrett, J., & Gerber, P. (1990). Symptomatology of late-life minor depression among primary care patients. *Psychosomatics, 31,* 174-180.

Paffenbarger, R. S., Hyde, R. T., Wing, A. L., & Steinmetz, C. H. (1984). A natural history of athleticism and cardiovascular health. *JAMA, 252,* 491-492.

Pahkala, K. (1990). Social and environmental factors and atypical depression in old age. *International Journal of Geriatric Psychiatry, 5,* 99-113.

Palinkas, L. A., Wingard, D. L., & Barrett-Connor, E. (1990). Chronic illness and depressive symptoms in the elderly: A population-based study. *Journal of Clinical Epidemiology, 43,* 1131-1141.

Palmstierna, T., & Wistedt B. (1987). Staff Observation Aggression Scale, SOAS: Presentation and evaluation. *Acta Psychiatrica Scandinavia, 76,* 657-663.

Panek, P. E., Barrett, G. V., Sterns, H. L., & Alexander, R. A. (1977). A review of age changes in perceptual information ability with regard to driving. *Experimental Aging Research, 3,* 387-449.

Park, D. (1992). Applied cognitive aging research. In F. I. M. Craik & T. A. Salthouse (EdS.), *The handbook of aging and cognition* (pp. 449-494). Hillsdale, NJ: Lawrence Erlbaum.

Parkes, C. M. (1992). Bereavement and mental health in the elderly. *Reviews in Clinical Gerontology, 2,* 45-51.

Parkinson, J. (1817). *An essay on the shaking palsy.* London: Whittingham & Rowland.

Parkinson Study Group. (1989). Parkinson Study Group DATA TOP: A multicenter controlled clinical trial in early Parkinson's disease. *Archives of Neurology, 46,* 1052-1060.

Parmalee, P. A., Katz, I. R., & Lawton, M. P. (1989). Depression among institutionalized aged: Assessment and prevalence estimation. *Journal of Gerontology: Medical Sciences, 44,* M22-M29.

Parmalee, P. A., Katz, I. R., & Lawton, M. P. (1992). Incidence of depression in long-term care settings. *Journal of Gerontology: Medical Sciences, 47,* M189-M196.

Parmalee, P. A., & Lawton, M. P. (1990). The design of special environments for the aged. In J. E. Birren & K. W. Schaie (Eds.), *The handbook of the psychology of aging* (3rd ed., pp. 464-488). New York: Academic Press.

Parsons, O. A., & Nixon, S. J. (1993). Neurobehavioral sequelae of alcoholism. *Neurologic Clinics, 11,* 205-218.

Patel, V., & Hope, R. A. (1992a). Aggressive behavior in elderly psychiatric inpatients. *Acta Psychiatric Scandinavia, 85*(2), 131-135.

Patel, V., & Hope, R. A. (1992b). A rating scale for aggressive behavior in the elderly—the RAGE. *Psychological Medicine, 22,* 211-221.

Patel, V., & Hope, T. (1993). Aggressive behavior in elderly people with dementia: A review. *International Journal of Geriatric Psychiatry, 8,* 457-472.

Paterson, C. A. (1979). Crystalline lens. In R. E. Records (Ed.), *Physiology of the human eye and visual system.* New York: Harper & Row.

Patterson, R. L. (1988). Anxiety in the elderly. In C. G. Last & M. Hersen (Eds.), *Handbook of anxiety disorders* (pp. 541-551). New York: Pergamon.

Pearlin, L., Mullan, J., Semple, S., & Skaff, M. (1990). Caregiving and the stress process: An overview of concepts and their measures. *The Gerontologist, 30,* 583-591.

Pearlson, G., & Rabins, P. (1988). The late-onset psychoses: Possible risk factors. *Psychiatric Clinics of North America, 11,* 15-32.

Pearlson, G. D., Kreger, L., Rabins, P. V., Chase, G. A., Cohen, B., Wirth, J. B., Schlaepfer, T. B., & Tune, L. E. (1989). A chart review study of late-onset and early-onset schizophrenia. *American Journal of Psychiatry, 146,* 1568-1574.

Pendergast, D. R., Fisher, N. M., & Calkins, E. (1993). Cardiovascular, neuromuscular, and metabolic alterations with age leading to frailty [Special Issue]. *Journal of Gerontology, 48,* 61-70.

Penn, P. E., & Bootzin, R. R. (1990). Behavioural techniques for enhancing alertness and performance in shift work. *Work & Stress, 4,* 213-226.

Pepeu, G., & Spignoli, G. (1990). Neurochemical actions of "nootropic drugs." *Advances in Neurology, 51,* 247-252.

Perdue, C. W., & Gurtman, M. W. (1990). Evidence for the automaticity of ageism. *Journal of Experimental Social Psychology, 26*(3), 199-216.

Perlmuter, L. C., Goldfinger, S. H., Shore, A. R., & Nathan, D. M. (1990). Cognitive function in non-insulin-dependent diabetes. In C. S. Holmes (Ed.), *Neuropsychological and behavioral aspects of diabetes mellitus* (pp. 222-238). New York: Springer-Verlag.

Perlmutter, M. (1978). What is memory aging the aging of? *Developmental Psychology, 14,* 330-345.

Perlmutter, M., Metzger, R., Miller, K., & Nazworski, T. (1980). Memory of historical events. *Experimental Aging Research, 6,* 47-60.

Perlmutter, M., & Mitchell, D. B. (1982). The appearance and disappearance of age differences in adult memory. In F. I. M. Craik & S. Trehub (Eds.), *Aging and cognitive processes* (pp. 127-144). New York: Plenum.

Perry, E. K., Perry, R. H., Blessed, G., & Tomlinson, B. E. (1977). Necropsy evidence of central cholinergic deficits in senile dementia. *Lancet, 1,* 189.

Perry, P. (1994, November-December). Breakthrough for emphysema patients. *Saturday Evening Post.*

Persson, G., & Svanborg, A. (1992). Marital coital activity in men at the age of 75: Relation to somatic, psychiatric, and social factors at the age of 70. *Journal of the American Geriatrics Society, 40,* 439-444.

Petrich, J., & Holmes, T. H. (1980). Psychiatric presentations of pulmonary disorders. In R. C. W. Hall (Ed.), *Psychiatric presentations of medical illness: Somatopsychic disorders* (pp. 177-189). New York: S. P. Scientific and Medical.

Petrie, W. M., & Ban, T. A. (1981). Propranolol in organic agitation. *Lancet, 1,* 324.

Petrie, W. M., Lawson, E. C., & Hollender, M. H. (1982). Violence in geriatric patients. *JAMA, 248*(4), 443-444.

Pettinati, H. M., & Bonner, K. M. (1984). Cognitive functioning in depressed geriatric patients with a history of ECT. *American Journal of Psychiatry, 141,* 49-52.

Pfeifer, E. (1980). The psychosocial evaluation of the elderly interviewee. In E. W. Busse & D. G. Glazer (Eds.), *Handbook of geriatric psychiatry* (pp. 275-284). New York: Van Nostrand.

Pfeiffer, E. (1976). A short portable mental status questionnaire for the assessment of organic brain deficit in elderly patients. *Journal of the American Geriatrics Society, 2,* 433-437.

Phifer, J. F., & Murrell, S. A. (1986). Etiologic factors in the onset of depressive symptoms in older adults. *Journal of Abnormal Psychology, 95,* 282-291.

Phillips, C. J., & Henderson, A. S. (1991). The prevalence of depression among Australian nursing home residents: Results using draft ICD-10 and DSM-III-R criteria. *Psychological Medicine, 21,* 739-748.

Phillips, P. A., Bretherton, M., Johnston, C. I., & Gray, L. (1991). Reduced osmotic thirst in healthy elderly men. *American Journal of Physiology, 261*(1, Pt. 2), R166-R171.

Phillips, S., & Elledge, R. (1989). *The team-building sourcebook.* San Diego, CA: University Associates.

Pickett, P., Masand, P., & Murray, G. B. (1990). Psychostimulant treatment of geriatric depressive disorders secondary to medical illness. *Journal of Geriatric Psychiatric Neurology, 3,* 146-151.

Pillon, B., Dubois, B., Bonnet, A. M., Esteguy, M., Guimaraes, J., Vigouret, J. M., Lhermitte, F., & Agid, Y. (1989). Cognitive slowing in Parkinson's disease fails to respond to levodopa treatment: The 15-objects test. *Neurology, 39,* 762-768.

Pinkston, E., & Linsk, N. (1984). *Care of the elderly: A family approach.* New York: Pergamon.

Pinner, E., & Rich, C. L. (1988). Effects of trazodone on aggressive behavior in seven patients with organic mental disorders. *American Journal of Psychiatry, 145*(10), 1295-1296.

Pleak, R. R., & Appelbaum, P. S. (1985). The clinician's role in protecting patients' rights in guardianship proceedings. *Hospital and Community Psychiatry, 36,* 77-79.

Plein, J. B., & Plein, E. M. (1981). Aging and drug therapy. In C. Eisdorfer (Ed.), *Annual review of geronotology and geriatrics* (p. 211). New York: Springer-Verlag.

Plude, D. J., & Doussard-Roosevelt, J. A. (1989). Aging, selective attention, and feature integration. *Psychology and Aging, 4*(1), 98-105.

Plude, D. J., & Doussard-Roosevelt, J. A. (1990). Aging and attention: Selectivity, capacity, and arousal. In E. A. Lovelace (Ed.), *Aging and cognition: Mental processes, self-awareness, and interventions* (pp. 97-133). Amsterdam: North-Holland.

Plude, D. J., & Hoyer, W. J. (1986). Age and selectivity of visual information processing. *Experimental Aging Research, 12,* 221-225.

Pokorny, A. D., Miller, B. A., & Kaplan, H. B. (1972). The brief MAST: A shortened version of the Michigan Alcoholism Screening Test. *American Journal of Psychiatry, 129,* 342-345.

Polakoff, S. A., Forgi, P. J., & Ratey, J. J. (1986). The treatment of impulsive and aggressive behavior with nadolol. *Journal of Clinical Psychopharmacology, 6,* 125-126.

Polich, J. M., Armor, S. J., & Braiker, H. B. (1981). *The course of alcoholism: Four years after treatment.* New York: John Wiley.

Pollack, C. P., & Perlick, D. (1987). Sleep problems and institutionalization of the elderly. *Sleep Research, 16,* 407.

Pollack, C. P., Perlick, D., Linser, J. P., Wenston, J., & Hsieh, F. (1990). Sleep problems in the community elderly as predictors of death and nursing home placement. *Journal of Community Health, 15,* 123-135.

Pollack, M. H., & Rosenbaum, J. F. (1987). Management of antidepressant-induced side effects: A practical guide for the clinician. *Journal of Clinical Psychiatry, 48,* 3-8.

Pollak, M., Foster, C., Knapp, D., Rod, J. L., & Schmidt, D. H. (1987). Effects of age and training on aerobic capacity and body composition of master athletes. *Journal of Applied Physiology, 62,* 725-731.

Poon, L. W. (1985). Differences in human memory with aging: Nature, causes, and clinical implications. In J. E. Birren & K. W. Schaie (Eds.), *Handbook of the psychology of aging* (2nd ed., pp. 427-462). New York: Van Nostrand Reinhold.

Poon, L. W., Rubin, D. C., & Wilson, B. A. (1989). *Everyday cognition in adulthood and late life.* Cambridge, UK: Cambridge University Press.

Pope, H. G., Jr., Mc Elroy, S. L., Keck, P. E., Jr., & Hudson, J. I. (1991). Valproate in the treatment of acute mania: A placebo-controlled study. *Archives of General Psychiatry, 48,* 62-68.

Popkin, M. K. (1989). Depression and patients with diabetes mellitus. In R. G. Robinson & P. V. Rabins (Eds.), *Depression and coexisting disease* (pp. 73-82). New York: Igaku-Shoin.

Popkin, M. K., Callies, A. L., Lentz, R. D., Colon, E. A., & Sutherland, D. E. (1988). Prevalence of major depression, simple phobia, and other psychiatric disorders in patients with long-standing Type I diabetes mellitus. *Archives of General Psychiatry, 45,* 64-68.

Posner, B. M., Jette, A., Smigelski, C., Miller, D., & Mitchell, P. (1994). Nutritional risk in New England elders. *Journal of Gerontology: Medical Sciences, 49,* M123-M132.

Post, F. (1966). *Persistent persecutory states of the elderly.* Oxford, UK: Pergamon.

Post, F. (1989). Schizophrenia and delusional disorders. In H. I. Kaplan & B. J. Sadock (Eds.), *Comprehensive textbook of psychiatry* (Vol. 2., pp. 2026-2028). Baltimore: Williams & Wilkins.

Post, R. M. (1993). Issues in the long-term management of bipolar affective illness. *Psychiatric Annals, 23,* 86-93.

Poulin, M., Paterson, D. H., Govindasamy, D., & Cunningham, D. A. (1988). Endurance training of elderly men: Responses to submaximal exercise. *Canadian Journal of Sport Sciences, 13,* 78P-79P.

Power, C., & Hachinski, V. (1990). Stroke in the elderly. In W. R. Hazzard, R. Andres, E. L. Bierman, & J. P. Blass (Eds.), *Principles in geriatric medicine and gerontology* (2nd ed., pp. 926-933). New York: McGraw-Hill.

Powers, J. K., & Powers, E. A. (1978). Hearing problems of elderly persons: Social consequences and prevalence. *American Speech and Hearing Association, 20,* 79-83.

President's Commission for the Study of Ethical Problems in Medicine and Biomedical and Behavioral Research. (1982). *Making health care decisions: The ethical and legal implications of informed consent in the patient-practitioner relationship.* Washington, DC: Government Printing Office.

Preskorn, S. H. (1993). Pharamacokinetics of antidepressants: Why and how they are relevant to treatment. *Journal of Clinical Psychiatry, 54*(9, Suppl.), 14-34.

Preskorn, S. H., & Jorkovich, G. S. (1990). Central nervous system toxicity of tricyclic antidepressants: Pharmacology, course risk factors, and role of therapeutic drug monitoring. *Journal of Clinical Psychopharmacology, 10,* 88-95.

Price, D. L. (1986). New perspectives on Alzheimer's disease. *Annual Review of Neuroscience, 9,* 489-512.

Price, D. L., Whitehouse, P. J., Struble, R. G., Clark, A. W., Coyle, J. T., De Long, M. R., & Hedreen, J. C. (1982). Basal forebrain cholinergic systems in Alzheimer's disease and related dementias. *Neuroscience Commentaries, 1,* 84-92.

Price, J. L., Davis, P. B., Morris, J. C., & White, D. L. (1991). The distribution of tangles, plaques and related immunohistochemical markers in healthy aging and Alzheimer's disease. *Neurobiology of Aging, 12*(4), 295-312.

Price, T. R. P., & McAllister, T. (1989). Safety and efficacy of ECT in depressed patients with dementia: A review of clinical experience. *Convulsive Therapy, 5,* 61-74.

Prien, R. F., & Gelenberg, A. J. (1989). Alternatives to lithium for preventive treatment of bipolar disorder. *American Journal of Psychiatry, 146,* 840-848.

Prigogine, I., & Stengers, I. (1984). *Order out of chaos: Man's new dialogue with nature.* New York: Bantam.

Prinz, P. (1977). Sleep patterns in the healthy aged: Relationship with intellectual function. *Journal of Gerontology, 32,* 179-186.

Prinz, P., Obriest, W., & Wang, H. (1975). Sleep patterns in healthy elderly subjects: Individual differences as related to other neurological variables. *Sleep Research, 4,* 132.

Prinz, P., Peskind, E. R., Vitaliano, P. P., Raskind, M. A., Eisdorfer, C., Zemcuznikov, N., & Gerber, C. J. (1982). Changes in the sleep and waking EEGs of nondemented and demented elderly subjects. *Journal of the American Geriatrics Society, 30,* 86-93.

Prinz, P., & Raskind, M. (1978). Aging and sleep disorders. In R. Williams & I. Karacan (Eds.), *Sleep disorders: Diagnosis and treatment.* New York: John Wiley.

Prinz, P. N., Dustman, R. E., & Emmerson, R. (1990). Electrophysiology and aging. In J. E. Birren & K. W. Schaie (Eds.), *Handbook of the psychology of aging (3rd ed.).* San Diego: Academic Press.

Prinz, P. N., Vitiello, M. V., Raskind, M. A., & Thorpy, M. J. (1990). Geriatrics: Sleep disorders and aging. *New England Journal of Medicine, 323*(8), 520-526.

Puder, R., Lacks, P., Bertelson, A. D., & Storandt, M. (1983). Short-term stimulus control treatment of insomnia in older adults. *Behavior Therapy, 14,* 424-429.

Puryear, D. A., Lovitt, R., & Miller, D. A. (1991). Characteristics of elderly persons seen in an urban psychiatric emergency room. *Hospital and Community Psychiatry, 42,* 802-807.

Quadagno, J., & Myer, M. H. (1993). Gender and public policy. In L. Glasse & J. Hendricks (Eds.), *Gender and aging* (pp. 121-128). New York: Baywood.

Qualls, S., & Czirr, R. (1988). Geriatric health teams: Classifying models of professional and team functioning. *The Gerontologist, 28,* 372-376.

Qualls, S. H. (1988). Problems in families of older adults. In N. Epstein, S. E. Schlesinger, & W. Dryden (Eds.), *Cognitive-behavioral therapy with families* (pp. 215-253). New York: Brunner/Mazel.

Quam, J. K., & Whitford, G. S. (1992). Adaptation and age-related expectations of older gay and lesbian adults. *The Gerontologist, 32,* 367-374.

Rabbitt, P. (1982). Development of methods to measure changes in activities of daily living in the elderly. In S. Corkin, K. L. Davis, J. H. Growdon, E. Usdin, & R. J. Wurtman (Eds.), *Alzheimer's disease: A report of progress.* New York: Raven.

Rabbitt, P., & McInnis, L. (1989). Do clever old people have earlier and richer first memories? *Psychology and Aging, 3,* 338-341.

Rabins, P., Pauker, S., & Thomas, J. (1984). Can schizophrenia begin after age 44? *Comprehensive Psychiatry, 25,* 290-293.

Rabins, P. V. (1983). Reversible dementia and the misdiagnosis of dementia: A review. *Hospital and Community Psychiatry, 34,* 830-835.

Rabins, P. V. (1991, September). *Wandering.* Paper presented at the Alzheimer's Association Annual Scientific Meeting, Chicago, IL.

Rabins, P. V., & Folstein, M. F. (1982). Delirium and dementia: Diagnostic criteria and fatality rates. *British Journal of Psychiatry, 140,* 149-153.

Rabins, P. V., Harvis, K., & Koven, S. (1985). High fatality rates of late-life depression associated with cardiovascular disease. *Journal of Affective Disorder, 9,* 165-167.

Rabins, P. V., Mace, N. L., & Lucas, M. J. (1982). The impact of dementia on the family. *JAMA, 248,* 333-335.

Rachman, S. J. (1977). The conditioning theory of fear acquisition: A critical examination. *Behaviour Research and Therapy, 15,* 375-387.

Rader, H., Doan, J., & Schwab, M. (1985). How to decrease wandering, a form of agenda behavior. *Geriatric Nursing, 6*(4), 196-199.

Rader, J. (1987). A comprehensive staff approach to problem wandering. *The Gerontologist, 27*(6), 756-760.

Radloff, I. S. (1977). The CES-D scale: A self-report depression scale for research in the general population. *Applied Psychological Measurement, 1,* 385.

Raisz, L. G. (1990). Disorders of mineral metabolism. In W. Abrams & R. Berkow (Eds.), *The Merck manual of geriatrics* (pp. 815-831). Rahway, NJ: Merck.

Raj, B. A., Corvea, M. H., & Dagon, E. M. (1993). The clinical characteristics of panic disorder in the elderly: A retrospective study. *Journal of Clinical Psychiatry, 54,* 150-155.

Randolph, C., Goldberg, T. E., & Weinberger, D. R. (1993). The neuropsychology of schizophrenia. In K. E. Heilman & E. Valenstein (Eds.), *Clinical neuropsychology* (3rd ed., pp. 499-522). New York: Oxford University Press.

Randt, C. T., & Brown, E. R. (1979). *The Randt Memory Test*. Bayport, NY: Life Science.

Rao, S. M. (1993). White matter dementias. In R. W. Parks, R. F. Zec, & R. S. Wilson (Eds.), *Neuropsychology of Alzheimer's disease and other dementias* (pp. 438-456). New York: Oxford University Press.

Raphael, S. M., & Robinson, M. K. (1980). The older lesbian. *Alternative Lifestyles, 3,* 207-229.

Rapp, S. R., Parisi, S. A., & Walsh, D. A. (1988). Psychological dysfunction and physical health among elderly medical inpatients. *Journal of Consulting and Clinical Psychology, 56,* 851-855.

Raskin, S. A., Borod, J. C., & Tweedy, J. R. (1990). Neuropsychological aspects of Parkison's disease. *Neuropsychology Review, 1,* 185-221.

Raskind, M., Alvarez, C., & Herlin, S. (1979). Fluphenazine enanthate in the outpatient treatment of late paraphrenia. *Journal of the American Geriatrics Society, 27,* 459-463.

Raskind, M., & Peskind, E. R. (1992). Alzheimer's disease and other dementing disorders. In J. E. Birren, R. B. Sloane, & R. D. Cohen (Eds.), *Handbook of mental health and aging* (2nd ed.). San Diego, CA: Harcourt Brace Jovanovich.

Ratcliffe, G., & Saxton, J. (1994). Age-associated memory impairment. In C. E. Coffey & J. L. Cummings (Eds.), *Textbook of geriatric neuropsychiatry* (pp. 146-158). Washington, DC: American Psychiatric Press.

Rathbone-McCuan, E., Lohn, H., Levenson, J., & Hsu, J. (1976). *Community survey of aged alcoholics and problem drinkers* (Publication No. PB 259 625). Springfield, VA: U.S. Department of Commerce.

Rauch, R. K., & Jenike, M. A. (1984). Digoxin toxicity possibly recipitated by trazodone. *Pscyhosomatics, 25,* 334-335.

Ray, W. A., Griffin, M. R., & Downdy, W. (1989). Benzodiazepines of long and short term elimination half-life and the risk of hip fracture. *JAMA, 262,* 3303-3307.

Ray, W. A., Griffin, M. R., Schattner, W., Baugh, D. K., & Melton, L. J. (1987). Psychotropic drug and the risk of hip fracture. *New England Journal of Medicine, 316,* 363-369.

Ray, W. A., Griffin, M. R., & Shorr, R. I. (1990). Adverse drug reaction and the elderly. *Health Affairs, 9,* 114-122.

Ray, W. A., Taylor, J. A., Lichtenstein, M. J., & Meador, K. G. (1992). The Nursing Home Behavior Problem Scale. *Journal of Gerontology, 47*(1), M9-M16.

Red Horse, J. (1980). American Indian elders: Unifiers of families. *Social Casework,* 491-493.

Reddan, W. G. (1981). Respiratory system and aging. In E. L. Smith & R. C. Serfass (Ed.), *Exercise and aging: The scientific basis* (pp. 89-107). Hillside, NJ: Enslow.

Rediehs, M. H., Reis, J. S., & Creason, N. S. (1990). Sleep in old age: Focus on gender differences. *Sleep, 13,* 410-424.

Reed, H. B. C., & Reitan, R. M. (1963). Changes in psychological test performance associated with the normal aging process. *Journal of Gerontology, 18,* 271-274.

Regier, D. A., Boyd, J. H., Burke, J. D., Jr., Rae, D. S., Myers, J. K., Kramer, M., Robins, L. N., George, L. K., Karno, M., & Locke, B. Z. (1988). One-month prevalence of mental disorders in the United States: Based on five epidemiologic catchment area sites. *Archives of General Psychiatry, 45,* 977-986.

Rehm, L. P., Kaslow, N. J., & Rabin, A. S. (1987). Cognitive and behavioral targets in a self-control therapy program for depression. *Journal of Consulting and Clinical Psychology, 55,* 60-67.

Reichert, M. (1993). *Hilfeverhalten gegenüber alten Menschen: eine experimentelle überprüfung der Rolle von Erwartungen* [Helping behavior towards elderly people: An experimental analysis of expectations]. Essen, Germany: Blau Eule.

Reifler, B. V. (1986). Mixed cognitive-affective disturbances in the elderly: A new classification. *Journal of Clinical Psychiatry, 47,* 354-356.

Reifler, B. V. (1992). Depression versus dementia in the elderly. In M. Bergener, K. Hasegawa, S. I. Finkel, & T. Nishimura (Eds.), *Aging and mental disorders* (pp. 83-90). New York: Springer.

Reifler, B. V., Larson, E., & Hanley, R. (1982). Coexistence of cognitive impairment and depression in geriatric outpatients. *American Journal of Psychiatry, 139,* 623-626.

Reifler, B. V., Larson, E., Teri, L., & Poulsen, M. (1986). Dementia of the Alzheimer's type and depression. *Journal of the American Geriatrics Society, 34,* 855-859.

Reimherr, F. W., Chouinard, G., Cohn, C. K., Cole, J. O., Itil, T. M., LaPierre, Y. D., Masco, H. L., & Mendels, J. (1990). Antidepressant efficacy of sertraline: A double-blind placebo-and amitriptyline-controlled multicenter comparison study in outpatients with major depression. *Journal of Clinical Psychiatry, 51*(12, Suppl.), 18-27.

Reisberg, B. (1983). The brief cognitive rating scale and global deterioration scale. In T. Crook, S. Ferris, & R. Bartus (Eds.), *Assessment in geriatric psychopathology* (pp. 19-35). New Canaan, CT: Mark Powley.

Reisberg, B., Borenstein, J., Salob, S. P., Ferris, S. H., Franssen, E., & Georgotas, A. (1987). Behavioral symptoms in Alzheimer's disease: Phenomenology and treatment. *Journal of Clinical Psychiatry, 48*(5, Suppl.), 9-15.

Reisberg, B., Ferris, S. H., de Leon, M. J., & Crook, T. (1982). The global deterioration scale for assessment of primary degenerative dementia. *American Journal of Psychiatry, 139,* 1136-1139.

Reiss, I. L., & Lee, G. R. (1988). *Family systems in America* (4th ed.). New York: Holt, Rinehart & Winston.

Reitan, R. M. (1967). Psychologic changes associated with aging and cerebral damage. *Mayo Clinic Proceedings, 42,* 653-673.

Reitan, R. M., & Wolfson, D. (1985). *The Halstead-Reitan neuropsychological test battery: Theory and clinical interpretation.* Tucson, AZ: Neuropsychology Press.

Renshaw, T. (1988). Sexuality in the later years. *Geriatric Sexual Counseling Medi-Guide to Aging, 3,* 1-6.

Resnick, N. (1987). Detrusor hyperactivity with impaired contractile function. *JAMA, 257,* 3076-3081.

Resnick, N. M., Baumann, M., Scott, M., Laurino, E., & Yalla, S. V. (1988). Risk factors for incontinence in the nursing home: A multivariate study. *Neurourology and Urodynamics, 7,* 274-276.

Resnick, N. M., Yalla, S. V., & Laurino, E. (1989). The pathophysiology and clinical correlates of established urinary incontinence in frail elderly. *New England Journal of Medicine, 320,* 1-7.

Reynolds, C. F. III. (1989). Sleep in affective disorders. In M. H. Kryger, T. Roth, & W. C. Dement (Eds.), *Principles and practice of sleep medicine* (pp. 413-415). Philadelphia: W. B. Saunders.

Reynolds, C. F. III. (1992). Treatment of depression in special populations. *Journal of Clinical Psychiatry, 53,* 45-53.

Reynolds, C. F. III, Hoch, C. C., Kupfer, D. J., Buysse, D. J., Stack, J. A. & Campbell, D. W. (1988). Bedside differentiation of depressive pseudodementia from dementia. *American Journal of Psychiatry, 145,* 1099-1103.

Reynolds, C. F. III, Kupfer, D. J., Hoch, C. C., Strack, J. A., Houck, P. R., & Sewitch, D. E. (1986). Two year follow-up of elderly patients with mixed depression and dementia: Clinical electroencephalographic sleep findings. *Journal of the American Geriatrics Society, 34,* 793-799.

Reynolds, C. F. III, Kupfer, D. J., Taska, L. S., Hoch, C. C., Sewitch, D. E., & Spiker, D. G. (1985). Sleep of healthy seniors: A revisit. *Sleep, 8,* 20-29.

Reynolds, C. F. III, Kupfer, D. J., Thase, M. E., Frank, E., Jarrett, D. B., Coble, P. A., Hoch, C. C., Buysse, D. J., & Houck, P. R. (1990). Sleep, sex, and depression: An analysis of gender effects on the electroencephalographic sleep of 302 depressed outpatients. *Sleep Research, 19,* 173.

Reynolds, C. F. III, Monk, T. H., Hoch, C. C., Jennings, J. R., Buysse, D. J., Houck, P. R., Jarrett, D. B., & Kupfer, D. J. (1991). Electroencephalographic sleep in the healthy "old old": A comparison with the "young old" in visually scored and automated measures. *Journal of Gerontology: Medical Sciences, 46,* M39-M46.

Ribeiro, J., & Smith, S. R. (1985). Evaluation of urinary catheterization and urinary incontinence in a general nursing home population. *Journal of the American Geriatrics Society, 33,* 479-482.

Riccio, D. C., & Sylvestri, R. (1973). Extinction of avoidance behavior and the problem of residual fear. *Behavior Research and Therapy, 11,* 1-9.

Richards, O. W. (1977). Effects of luminance and contrast on visual acuity ages 16 to 90 years. *American Journal of Optometry and Physiological Optics, 54,* 178-184.

Richardson, J. (1990). *Aging and health: Black American elders* (Working Paper Series, 4). Palo Alto, CA: Stanford Geriatric Education Center.

Richardson, R., Lowenstein, S., & Weissberg, M. (1989). Coping with the suicidal elderly: A physician's guide. *Geriatrics, 44,* 43-51.

Rickels, K., Case, W. G., Schweizer, E. E., Swenson, C., Reita, B., & Fridman, B. S. (1986). Low-dose dependence in chronic benzodiazepine users: a preliminary report on 119 patients. *Psychopharmacology Bulletin, 22,* 407-415.

Rickels, K., Jay, D., Amsterdam, J. D., Clary, C., Puzzoli, G., & Schweizer, E. (1991). Buspirone in major depression: A controlled study. *Journal of Clinical Psychiatry, 52,* 34-38.

Rikli, R. E., & McManis, B. G. (1990). Effects of exercise on bone mineral content in post-menopausal women. *Research Quarterly in Exercise of Sport, 61,* 243.

Risse, S. C., & Barnes, R. (1986). Pharmacologic treatment of agitation associated with dementia. *Journal of the American Geriatric Society, 34*(5), 368-376.

Robbins, L. N., Helzer, J. E., Croughan, J., & Ratcliff, K. S. (1981). National Institute of Mental Health Diagnostic Interview Schedule: Its history, characteristics, and validity. *Archives of General Psychiatry, 38,* 381-389.

Robbins, M. A., Elias, M. F., & Schultz, N. R. (1990). The effects of age, blood pressure, and knowledge of hypertensive diagnosis on anxiety and depression. *Experimental Aging Research, 16,* 199-207.

Roberto, K. A., & Kimboko, P. J. (1989). Friendships in later life: Definitions and maintenance patterns. *International Journal of Aging and Human Development, 28,* 9-19.

Robine, J. M., Labbe, M., Serouss, M. C., & Colvez, A. (1989). The upper Normandy longitudinal survey on disability in the aged 1978-1985. *Revue D'Epidemiologie et de Sante Publique, 37,* 37-48.

Robins, L. N., & Regier, D. A. (Eds.). (1991). *Psychiatric disorders in America: The Epidemiological Catchment Area Study.* New York: Free Press.

Robins, L. N., Helzer, J. E., Croughan, J., & Ratcliff, K. S. (1981). National Institute of Mental Health Diagnostic Interview Schedule: Its history, characteristics and validity. *Archives of General Psychiatry, 38,* 381-389.

Robins, L. N., Helzer, J. E., Weissman, M. M., Orvaschel, H., Gruenberg, E., Burke, J. D., & Regier, D. A. (1984). Lifetime prevalence of specific psychiatric disorder in three sites. *Archives of General Psychiatry, 41,* 949-958.

Robinson, D., Napoliello, M. J., & Schenk, J. (1988). The safety and usefulness of buspirone as an anxiolytic drug in elderly vs. young patients. *Clinical Therapy, 10,* 740-746.

Robinson, L. A., Berman, J. S., & Neimeyer, R. A. (1990). Psychotherapy for the treatment of depression: A comprehensive review of controlled outcome research. *Psychological Bulletin, 108,* 30-49.

Robinson, N., Fuller, J. H., & Edmeades, S. P. (1988). Depression and diabetes. *Diabetic Medicine, 5,* 268-274.

Roche Laboratories. (1994). *Bactrisin®* (Product monograph). Nutly, NJ: Author.

Rockwell, E., Lam, R. W., & Zisook, S. (1988). Antidepressant drug studies in the elderly. *Psychiatric Clinics of North America, 11,* 215-233.

Rodeheaver, D. (1990). Ageism. In I. A. Parham, L. W. Poon, & I. C. Siegler (Eds.), *Access: Aging curriculum content for education in the social-behavioral sciences* (pp. 7.1-7.43). New York: Springer.

Rodeheaver, D., & Datan, N. (1988). The challenge of double jeopardy: Toward a mental health agenda for aging women. *American Psychologist, 43,* 648-654.

Rodeheaver, D., & Stohs, J. (1991). The adaptive misperception of age in older women: Sociocultural images and psychological mechanisms of control [Special Issue: Women, education, and aging]. *Educational Gerontology, 17,* 141-156.

Rodgers, W. L., & Herzog, A. R. (1987). Interviewing older adults: The accuracy of factual information. *Journal of Gerontology, 42*(4), 387-394.

Rodin, G., Craven, J., & Littlefield, C. (1993). *Depression in the medically ill.* New York: Brunner/Mazel.

Rodin, G., & Voshcart, K. (1986). Depression in the medically ill: An overview. *American Journal of Psychiatry, 143,* 696-705.

Rodin, J., & Langer, E. J. (1977). Long-term effects of a control-relevant intervention with the institutionalized aged. *Journal of Personality and Social Psychology, 35,* 897-902.

Rodriguez, J. G., Sattin, R. W., & Waxweiler, R. J. (1989). Incidence of hip fractures. *American Journal of Preventive Medicine, 5,* 175-181.

Roehrs, T., Zorick, F., Sicklesteel, J., Wittig, R., & Roth, T. (1983). Age-related sleep-wake disorders at a sleep disorders center. *Journal of the American Geriatrics Society, 31,* 364-369.

Roman, D. D., Edwall, G. E., Buchanan, R. J., & Patton, J. H. (1991). Extended norms for the Paced Auditory Serial Addition Task. *The Clinical Neuropsychologist, 5,* 33-40.

Roman, G. C., Tatemichi, T. K., Erkinjuntti, T., Cummings, J. L., Masdeu, J. C., Garcia, J. H., Amaducci, L., Orgogozo, J. M., Brun, A., Hofman, A., Moody, D. M., O'Brien, M. D., Yamaguchi, T., Grafman, J., Drayer, B. P., Bennett, D. A., Fisher, M., Ogata, J., Kokmen, E., Bermejo, F., Wolf, P. A., Gorelick, P. B., Bick, K. L., Pajeau, A. K., Bell, M. A., DeCarli, C., Culebras, A., Korczyn, A. D., Bogusslavsky, J., Hartmann, A., & Scheinberg, P. (1993). Vascular dementia; diagnostic criteria for research studies (Report of the NINDS-AIREN International Workshop). *Neurology, 43,* 250-260.

Ron, M. A. (1977). Brain damage in chronic alcoholism: A neuropathological, neuroradiological and psychological review. *Psychologic Medicine, 7,* 103-112.

Roose, S. P., Dalack, G. W., Glassman, A. H., Woodring, S., Walsh, B. T., & Giardina, E. G. (1991). Cardiovascular effects of buproprion in depressed patients with heart disease. *American Journal of Psychiatry, 148,* 512-561.

Roose, S. P., Glassman, A. H., Giardina, E. G., Johnson, L. L., Walsh, B. T., Woodring, S., & Bigger, J. T. (1986). Nortriptyline in depressed patients with left ventricular impairment. *JAMA, 256,* 3253-3257.

Roose, S. P. Glassman, A. H., Giardina, E. G., Walsh, B. T., Woodring, S., & Bigger, J. T. (1987). Tricyclic antidepressants in depressed patients with cardiac conduction disease. *Archives of General Psychiatry, 44,* 273-275.

Roose, S. P., Glassman, A. H., Siris, S. G., Walsh, B. T., Bruno, R. L., & Wright, L. B. (1981). Comparison of imipramine and nortriptyline-induced orthostatic hypotension: a meaningful difference. *Journal of Clinical Psychopharmacology, 1,* 316-319.

Rosberger, Z., & MacLean, J. (1983). Behavioral assessment and treatment of "organic" behaviors in an institutionalized geriatric patient. *International Journal of Behavioral Geriatrics, 1*(4), 33-46.

Rosen, H. D., & Giacomo, J. N. (1978). The role of physical restraint in the treatment of psychiatric illness. *Journal of Clinical Psychiatry, 39,* 228-232.

Rosen, J., Burgio, L., Kollar, M., Cain, M., Allison, M., Fogleman, M., Michael, M., Zubenko, G. S. (1994). The Pittsburgh Agitation Scale: A user-friendly instrument for rating agitation in dementia patients. *The American Journal of Geriatric Psychiatry, 2*(1), 52-59.

Rosenberg, G. M. (1980). Neuropsychiatric manifestations of cardiovascular disease in the elderly. In A. J. Levenson & R. C. W. Hall (Eds.), *Neuropsychiatric manifestations of physical disease in the elderly* (pp. 29-40). New York: Raven.

Rosenbloom, C. A., & Whittington, F. J. (1993). The effects of bereavement on eating behaviors and nutrient intakes in elderly widowed persons. *Journal of Gerontology: Social Sciences, 48,* S223-S229.

Rosenfeld, I. (1991, February). Stroke—A major killer on the wane. *Cardiovascular Reviews & Reports, 12,* 15-16, 77.

Rosenfield, S. (1982). Sex roles and societal reactions in mental illness: The labeling of deviant deviance. *Journal of Health and Social Behavior, 23,* 18-24.

Rosenhall, U., & Rubin, W. (1975). Degenerative patterns in the aging human vestibular neuroepithelia. *Acta Otolaryngolica, 76,* 208-220.

Rossi, A. S. (1986). Sex and gender in the aging society. In A. J. Pifer & L. Bronte (Eds.), *Our aging society* (pp. 111-139). New York: W. W. Norton.

Rosswurm, M. A., Zimmerman, S. L., Schwartz-Fulton, J., & Norman, G. A. (1986). Can we manage wandering behavior? *Journal of Long-Term Care Administration, 14,* 5-8.

Roth, L. H., Meisel, A., & Lidz, C. (1977). Tests of competency to consent to treatment. *American Journal of Psychiatry, 134,* 279-283.

Roth, M. (1987). Late paraphrenia: Phenomenology and etiological factors and their bearing upon problems of the schizophrenic family of disorders. In N. E. Miller & G. D. Cohen (Eds.), *Schizophrenia and aging* (pp. 259-274). New York: Guilford.

Roth, M., Tym, E., Mountjoy, C. Q., Huppert, F. A., Hendrie, F. A., Verma, S., & Goddard, R. (1986). A standardised instrument for the diagnosis of mental disorder in the elderly with special reference to the early detection of dementia. *British Journal of Psychiatry, 149,* 698-709.

Rothblum, E. D. (1994). "I only read about myself on bathroom walls": The need for research on the mental health of lesbians and gay men. *Journal of Consulting and Clinical Psychology, 62,* 213-220.

Rothschild, A. J., & Locke, C. A. (1991). Re-exposure to fluoxetine after serious suicide attempts by three patients: The role of akathesia. *Journal of Clinical Psychiatry, 52,* 491-493.

Rovner, B. W., Kafonek, S., Filipp, L., Lucas, M. J., & Folstein, M. F. (1986). Prevalence of mental illness in a community nursing home. *American Journal of Psychiatry, 143,* 1446-1449.

Rowan, V. C., Holborn, S. W., Walker, J. K., & Siddiqui, A. (1984). A rapid multi-component treatment for an obsessive-compulsive disorder. *Journal of Behavior Therapy and Experimental Psychiatry, 15,* 347-352.

Rowe, J. W. (1982). Renal function and aging. In M. E. Reff & E. L. Schneider (Ed.), *Biological markers of aging* (Publication Number 82-2221). Bethesda, MD: National Institutes of Health.

Rowe, J. W. (1985). Health care of the elderly. *New England Journal of Medicine, 312,* 827-835.

Rowe, J. W., & Ahronheim, J. C. (Eds.). (1992). *Annual review of gerontology and geriatrics: Vol. 12. Focus on medications and the elderly.* New York: Springer.

Rowe, J. W., & Kahn, R. L. (1987). Human aging: Usual and successful. *Science, 237,* 143-149.

Rubenstein, L., Wieland, D., English, P., Josephson, K., Sayre, J., & Abrass, I. (1984). The Sepulveda VA Geriatric Evaluation Unit: Data on four-year outcomes and predictors of improved patient outcomes. *Journal of the American Geriatrics Society, 32,* 503-512.

Rubenstein, L. Z., Schairer, C., Wieland, G. D., & Kane, R. (1984). Systematic biases in functional status assessment of elderly adults: Effects of different data sources. *Journal of Gerontology, 39*(6), 686-691.

Rubin, E. H., Drevets, W. C., & Burke, W. J. (1988). The nature of psychotic symptoms in senile dementia of the Alzheimer type. *Journal of Geriatric Psychiatric Neurology, 1,* 16-20.

Rubinstein, M. L., Rothenberg, S. A., Maheswaran, S., Tsai, J. S., Zozula, R., & Spielman, A. J. (1990). Modified sleep restriction therapy in middle-aged and elderly chronic insomniacs. *Sleep Research, 19,* 276.

Ruff, C. B., Trinkhaus, E., Walter, A., & Larsen, C. (1993). Postcranial robusticity in homo: Temporal trends and mechanical interpretations. *American Journal of Physiological Anthropology, 91,* 21-53.

Rundall, T. C. (1992). Health services for an aging society (editorial). *Medical Care Review, 49,* 3-18.

Rush, M. (Ed.). (1985). *Feminist therapy with the woman over 50.* New York: Springer.

Ryan, A. S., Craig, L. D., & Finn, S. C. (1992). Nutrient intakes and dietary patterns of older Americans: A national study. *Journal of Gerontology: Medical Sciences, 47,* M145-M150.

Ryan, C. M. (1990). Neuropsychological consequences and correlates of diabetes in childhood. In C. S. Holmes (Ed.), *Neuropsychological and behavioral aspects of diabetes mellitus* (pp. 58-84). New York: Springer-Verlag.

Ryden, M. B. (1988). Aggressive behavior in persons with dementia living in the community. *Alzheimer's Disease and Associated Disorders: International Journal, 2*(4), 342-355.

Ryden, M. B., & Feldt, K. S. (1992). Goal-directed care: Caring for aggressive nursing home residents with dementia. *Journal of Gerontological Nursing, 18*(11), 35-42.

Ryden, M., & Bossenmaier, M. (1988). Aggressive behavior in cognitively impaired nursing home residents [Special Issue]. *The Gerontologist, 28,* 179A.

Sager, M. A., Dunham, N. C., Schwantes, A., Mecum, L., Halverson, K., & Harlowe, D. (1992). Measurement of activities of daily living in hospitalized elderly: A comparison of self-report and performance-based methods, *Journal of the American Geriatrics Society, 40,* 457-462.

Sakayue, K. M., Camp, C. J., & Ford, P. A. (1993). Effects of buspirone on agitation associated with dementia. *American Journal of Geriatric Psychiatry, 1,* 82-84.

Sakayue, K. (1992). The elderly Asian patient. *Journal of Geriatric Psychiatry, 25*(1), 105-111.

Saks, E. (1991). Competency to refuse treatment. *North Carolina Law Review, 69,* 945-999.

Salamon, M. J., & Charytan, P. (1984). Sexuality workshop program for the elderly. *The Clinical Gerontologist, 2,* 25-35.

Salmon, D. P., Butters, N., & Heindel, W. C. (1993). Alcoholic dementia and related disorders. In R. W. Parks, R. F. Zec, & R. S. Wilson (Eds.), *Neuropsychology of Alzheimer's disease and other dementias* (pp. 193-221). New York: Oxford University Press.

Salthouse, T. A. (1985). Speed of behavior and its implications for cognition. In J. E. Birren & K. W. Schaie (Eds.), *Handbook of the psychology of aging* (pp. 400-426). New York: Van Nostrand Reinhold.

Salthouse, T. A. (1990a). Cognitive competence and expertise in aging. In J. E. Birren & K. W. Schaie (Eds.), *Handbook of the psychology of aging* (3rd ed., pp. 311-319). San Diego, CA: Academic Press.

Salthouse, T. A. (1990b). Influence of experience on age differences in cognitive functioning. *Human Factors, 32,* 551-570.

Salthouse, T. A. (1991). Mediation of adult age differences in cognition by reduction in working memory and speed of processing. *Psychological Science, 2,* 179-183.

Salthouse, T. A., Babcock, R. L., & Shaw, R. J. (1991). Effects of adult age on structural and operational capacities in working memory. *Psychology and Aging, 6,* 118-127.

Salthouse, T. A., & Coon, V. E. (1993). Influence of task-specific processing speed on age differences in memory. *Journal of Gerontology: Psychological Sciences, 48,* P245-P255.

Salthouse, T. A., & Prill, K. A. (1987). Inferences about age impairments in inferential reasoning. *Psychology and Aging, 2,* 43-51.

Salthouse, T. A., Rogan, J. D., & Prill, K. A. (1984). Division of attention: Age differences on a visually presented memory task. *Memory and Cognition, 12,* 613-620.

Salthouse, T. A., & Somberg, B. L. (1982). Isolating the age deficit in speeded performance. *Journal of Gerontology, 37,* 59-63.

Saltin, B., & Grimby, G. (1968). Physiologic analysis of middle age and old former athletes. *Circulation, 38,* 1104-1115.

Saltz, B. L., Kane, J. M., Woerner, M. G., & Lieberman, J. (1989). Prospective study of tardive dyskinesia in the elderly. *Psychopharmacology Bulletin, 25,* 52-56.

Saltz, C. (1992). The interdisciplinary team in geriatric rehabilitation [Special Issue: Geriatric Social Work Education]. *Journal of Gerontological Social Work, 18,* 133-142.

Salvio, M. (1992). *Sleep disorders and sedative/hypnotic use in elderly nursing home residents.* Unpublished dissertation, University of Arizona, Tucson.

Salzman, C. (1990a). Anxiety in the elderly; Treatment strategies. *Journal of Clinical Psychiatry, 51*(10, Suppl.), 18-21.

Salzman, C. (1990b). Principles of psychopharmacology. In D. Bienenfeld (Ed.), *Verwoerdt's clinical geropsychiatry* (3rd ed., pp. 234-244). Baltimore: Williams & Wilkens.

Salzman, C. (1991a). The APA task force report on benzodiazepine dependence, toxicity and abuse. *American Journal of Psychiatry, 148, 1,* 51-152.

Salzman, C. (1991b). Pharmacological treatment of the anxious elderly patient. In C. Salzman & B. D. Lebowitz (Eds.), *Anxiety in the elderly: Treatment and research* (pp. 149-173). New York: Springer.

Salzman. C. (1992). *Clinical geriatric psychopharmacology* (2nd ed.). Baltimore: Williams & Wilkins.

Salzman, C. (1993). Pharmacologyogic treatment of depression in the elderly. *Journal of Clinical Psychiatry, 54*(2, Suppl.), 23-28.

Salzman, C., Schneider, L., & Lebowitz, B. (1993). Antidepressant treatment of very old patients. *American Journal of Geriatric Psychiatry, 1,* 21-29.

Salzman, C., & Shader, R. I. (1978). Depression in the elderly: 1. Relationships between depression, psychological defense mechanisms, and illness. *Journal of the American Geriatrics Society, 20,* 215-221.

Sammons, F. (1994). *Your complete source for orthopedic and ADL products* (Product brochure). Author.

Sanavio, E., Vidotto, G., Bettinardi, O., Rolletto, T., & Zorzi, M. (1990). Behaviour therapy for DIMS: Comparison of three treatment procedures with follow-up. *Behavioural Psychotherapy, 18,* 151-167.

Sanchez, C. (1992). Mental health issues: The elderly Hispanic. *Journal of Geriatric Psychiatry, 253*(1), 105-111.

Sanchez, R., & Bootzin, R. R. (1985). A comparison of white noise and music: Effects of predictable and unpredictable sounds on sleep. *Sleep Research, 14,* 121.

Sanchez-Ayendez, M. (1989). Puerto Rican elderly women: The cultural dimension of social support networks. *Women & Health, 14*(3-4), 239-252.

Sanford, I. R. A. (1975). Tolerance of debility in elderly dependents by supports at home: Its significance for hospital practice. *British Medical Journal, 3,* 471-473.

Santamaria, J., Tolosa E., & Valles, A. (1986). Parkinson's disease with depression: A possible subgroup of idiopathic parkinsonism. *Neurology, 36,* 1130-1133.

Satel, S. L., & Nelson, J. C. (1989). Stimulants in the treatment of depression; A critical overview. *Journal of Clinical Psychiatry, 50,* 241-249.

Satlin, A., Volicer, L., Ross, V., Herz, L., & Campbell, S. (1992). Bright light treatment of behavioral and sleep disturbances in patients with Alzheimer's disease. *American Journal of Psychiatry, 149,* 1028-1032.

Sawicki, P. T. (1993). Behaviour therapy versus doctors' anti-smoking advice in diabetic patients. *Journal of Internal Medicine, 234*(4), 407-409.

Sawyer, J. C., & Mendlovitz, A. A. (1982, November). *A management program for ambulatory institutionalized patients with Alzheimer's disease and related disorders.* Paper presented at the Annual Scientific Meeting of the Gerontological Society of America, Boston, MA.

Saxton, J., McGonigle-Gibson, K. L., Swihart, A. A., Miller, V. J., & Boller, F. (1990). Assessment of the severely-impaired patient: Description and validation of a new neuropsychological test batter. *Psychological Assessment: A Journal of Consulting and Clinical Psychology, 2,* 298-303.

Sbordone, R. J., & Sherman, L. T. (1983). The psychologist as a consultant in a nursing home: Effect on staff morale and turnover. *Professional Psychology, 14,* 240-250.

Schaie, K. W. (1988). Ageism in psychological research. *American Psychologist, 43,* 179-184.

Schaie, K. W. (1990). Intellectual development in adulthood. In J. E. Birren & K. W. Schaie (Eds.), *Handbook of the psychology of aging* (3rd ed., pp. 291-310). San Diego: Academic Press.

Schaie, K. W., & Willis, S. L. (1986). *Adult development and aging.* Glenview, IL: Scott, Foresman.

Scharf, M. B., Fletcher. K., & Graham, J. P. (1988). Comparative amnestic effects of benzodiazepines hypnotic agents. *Journal of Clinical Psychiatry, 49,* 34-137.

Scharf, M. B., Mayleben, D. W., Kaffeman, M., Krall, R., & Ochs, R. (1991). Dose response effects of zolpidem in normal geriatric subjects. *Journal of Clinical Psychiatry, 52,* 77-83.

Scharf, M. B., Roth, T., Vogel, G. W., & Walsh, J. K. (1994). A multicenter, placebo-controlled study evaluating zolpidem in the treatment of chronic insomnia. *Journal of Clinical Psychiatry, 55*(5), 192-99.

Schatt, M. R., Fawcett, J., & Zajecka, J. M. (1993). Divalproex sodium in the treatment of refractory attentive disorders. *Journal of Clinical Psychiatry, 54,* 380-384.

Schatzberg, A. F, & Cole, J. O. (1991). *Manual of Clinical Psychopharmacology* (2nd ed.). Washington, DC: American Psychiatric Press.

Schear, J. M. (1984). Neuropsychological assessment of the elderly in clinical practice. In P. E. Logue & J. Shear (Eds.), *Clinical neuropsychology: A multidisciplinary approach* (pp. 199-237). Springfield, IL: Charles C Thomas.

Scheibel, A. B. (1982). Age-related changes in the human forebrain. *Neurosciences Research Progress Bulletin, 20,* 577-583.

Scheie, H. G., & Albert, D. M. (1977). *Textbook of opthalmology* (9th ed.). Philadelphia: W. B. Saunders.

Schemper, T., Voss, S., & Cain, W. S. (1981). Odor identification in young and elderly persons: Sensory and cognitive limitations. *Journal of Gerontology, 36,* 446-452.

Schiavi, R. C., & Schreiner-Engel, P. (1988). Nocturnal penile tumescence in healthy aging men. *Journal of Gerontology, 43,* M146-M150.

Schiff, I., & Wilson, E. (1978). Clinical aspects of aging of the female reproductive system. In E. L. Schneider (Ed.), *Aging: Vol. 4. The aging reproductive system.* New York: Raven.

Schiffer, R. B., Kurlan, R., Rubin, A., & Boer, S. (1988). Evidence for atypical depression in Parkinson's disease. *American Journal of Psychiatry, 145,* 1020-1022.

Schiffman, S. (1977). Food recognition by the elderly. *Journal of Gerontology, 32,* 586-592.

Schiffman, S. S., & Warwick, Z. S. (1989). Use of flavor-amplified foods to improve nutritional status in elderly patients. *Annals of the New York Academy of Science, 561,* 267-276.

Schlenoff, D. (1989). Assessment of older persons with motor disabilities. In T. Hunt & C. J. Lindley (Eds.), *Testing older adults: A reference guide for geropsychological assessments* (pp. 122-134). Austin, TX: PRO-ED.

Schmall, V. L., & Pratt, C. C. (1989). Family caregiving and aging: Strategies for support. *Journal of Psychotherapy and the Family, 5,* 71-87.

Schneekloth, U., & Potthoff, P. (1993). Möglichkeiten und Grenzen selbständiger Lebensführung. Endbericht Forschungsprojekt im Auftrag des Bundeministeriums für Familie und Senioren [Potential and limits of independent living. Research project initiated and funded by the German Ministry of Family and Senior Citizens]. Stuttgart, Germany: Kohlhammer.

Schneider, E., & Reed, J. (1985). Life extension. *New England Journal of Medicine, 312,* 1159-1168.

Schneider, E. L., & Rowe, J. W. (1990). *Handbook of the biology of aging.* San Diego: Academic Press.

Schneider, E. L., Vining, E. L., Handley, E. C., & Farnum, S. A. (1986). Recommended dietary allowances and the health of the elderly. *New England Journal of Medicine, 314,* 157-165.

Schneider, L. S., & Sobin, P. B. (1992). Non-neuroleptic treatment of behavioral symptoms in agitation in Alzheimer's disease and other dementias. *Psychopharmacology Bulletin, 28,* 771-790.

Schneider, L. S., Pollock, V. E., & Lyness, S. A. (1990). Meta-analysis of controlled trials of neuroleptic treatment in dementia. *Journal of the American Geriatric Society, 38,* 553-563.

Schnelle, J. F. (1990). Treatment of urinary incontinence in nursing home patients by prompted voiding. *Journal of the American Geriatrics Society, 38,* 356-360.

Schnelle, J. F., Traughber, B., Morgan, D. B., Embry, J. E., Binion, A. F., & Coleman, A. (1983). Management of geriatric incontinence in nursing homes. *Journal of Applied Behavior Analysis, 16,* 235-241.

Schnelle, J. F., Traughber, B., Sowell, V. A., Newman, D. R., Petrilli, C. O., & Ory, M. (1989). Prompted voiding treatment of urinary incontinence in nursing home patients: A behavior management approach for nursing home staff. *Journal of the American Geriatrics Society, 37,* 1051-1057.

Schoenborn, C. A., & Cohen, B. H. (1986). *Trends in smoking, alcohol consumption, and other health practices among U.S. adults, 1977 and 1983* (Publication No. 86-1250). Hyattsville, MD: U.S. Department of Health and Human Services.

Scholtes, P. R. (1988). *The team handbook: How to use teams to improve quality.* Madison, WI: Joiner.

Schon, M. (1984). Long-lasting neurological sequelae after lithium intoxication. *Acta Psychiatrica Scandinavica, 70,* 594-602.

Schonfeld, L. S., & Dupree, L. W. (1991). Antecedents of drinking for early and late-life onset elderly alcohol abusers. *Journal of Studies on Alcohol, 52,* 587-592.

Schover, L., & Jensen, S. (1988). *Sexuality and chronic illness.* New York: Guilford.

Schuckit, M. A., & Miller, P. L. (1975). Alcoholism in elderly men: A survey of a general medical ward. *Annals of the New York Academy of Science, 37,* 558-571.

Schulz, R., & Williamson, G. M. (1991). A 2-year longitudinal study of depression among Alzheimer's caregivers. *Psychology and Aging, 6,* 569-578.

Schulz, R., Visintainer, P., & Williamson, G. (1990). Psychiatric and physical morbidity effects of caregiving. *Journal of Gerontology, 45,* 181-191.

Schweizer, E., Weise, C., Clary, C., Fox, I., & Rickels, K. (1991). Placebo-controlled trial of venlafaxine for the treatment of major depression. *Journal of Clinical Psychopharmacology, 11,* 233-236.

Scogin, F., & Perry, J. (1986). Guardianship proceedings with older adults: The role of functional assessment and gerontologists. *Law & Psychology Review, 10,* 123-128.

Scogin, F., Rickard, H. C., Keith, S., Wilson, J., & McElreath, L. (1992). Progressive and imaginal relaxation training for elderly persons with subjective anxiety. *Psychology and Aging, 7,* 419-424.

Segraves, R. T. (1992). Sexual dysfunction complicating the treatment of depression. *Journal of Clinical Psychiatry Monograph, 10*(1), 75-79.

Seligman, M. E. P. (1975). *Helplessness: On depression, development, and death.* San Francisco: Freemann.

Seltzer, M. L. (1971). The Michigan Alcoholism Screening Test: The questionnaire for a new diagnostic instrument. *American Journal of Psychiatry, 127,* 1653-1658.

Settle, E. C. (1992). Antidepressant side effects: Issues and options. *Journal of Clinical Psychiatry Monograph, 10*(1), 48-61.

Shader, R. I., & Greenblatt, D. J. (1982). Management of anxiety in the elderly: The balance between therapeutic and adverse effects. *Journal of Clinical Psychiatry, 43,* 8-16.

Shahtahmasebi, S., Davies, R., & Wenger, G. C. (1992). A longitudinal analysis of factors related to survival in old age. *The Gerontologist, 32,* 404-413.

Shamoian, C. A. (1991). What is anxiety in the elderly? In C. Salzman & B. D. Lebowitz (Eds.), *Anxiety in the elderly: Treatment and research* (pp. 3-15). New York: Springer.

Shaper, A. G. (1990). Alcohol and mortality: A review of prospective studies. *British Journal of Addiction, 85,* 837-847.

Shapiro, S., Skinner, E. A., Kessler, L. G., Von Korff, M., German, P. S., Tischler, G. L., Leaf, P. J., Benham, L., Cottler, L., & Regier, D. A. (1984). Utilization of health and mental health services. *Archives of General Psychiatry, 41,* 971-982.

Shaw, S. H., Carson, H., & Coquelin, J. P. (1992). A double blind comparative study of zolpidem and placebo in the treatment of insomnia in the elderly psychiatric in-patients. *Journal of International Medical Research, 20,* 150-161.

Shea, S. C. (1990). Contemporary psychiatric interviewing: Integration of DSM-III-R, psychodynamic concerns, and mental status. In G. Goldstein & M. Hersen (Eds.), *Handbook of psychological assessment* (2nd ed.). New York: Pergamon.

Sheehan, D. V., & Sheehan, K. H. (1982). The classification of phobic disorders. *International Journal of Psychiatry in Medicine, 12*(4), 243-266.

Sheikh, J. J. (1991). Anxiety rating scales in the elderly. In C. Salzman & B. D. Lebowitz (Eds.), *Anxiety in the elderly: Treatment and research* (pp. 251-265). New York: Springer.

Shekelle, R. B., Raynor, W. J., Ostfeld, A. M., Garron, D. C., Biliauskas, L. A., Liu, S. C., Maliza, C., & Paul, O. (1981). Psychological depression and 17-year risk of death from cancer. *Psychosomatic Medicine, 43,* 117-125.

Shephard, R. J. (1978). *Physical activity and aging.* Chicago: Yearbook Medical.

Shepherd, A. M., Montgomery, E., & Anderson, R. S. (1983). Treatment of genuine stress incontinence with a new perineometer. *Physiotherapy, 69,* 113.

Sherbourne, C. D., & Meredith, L. S. (1992). Quality of self-report data: A comparison of older and younger chronically ill interviewees. *Journal of Gerontology, 47,* S204-S211.

Sherlock, S. (1984). Nutrition and the alcoholic. *Lancet, 1,* 436-439.

Sherman, B. M., West, J. H., & Korenmann, S. G. (1976). The menopausal transition: Analysis of LH, FSH, estradiol, and progesterone concentrations during menstrual cycles of older women. *Journal of Clinical Endocrinology and Metabolism, 42,* 629-636.

Shindell, S. (1989). Assessing the visually impaired older adult. In T. Hunt & C. J. Lindley (Eds.), *Testing older adults: A reference guide for geropsychological assessments* (pp. 135-149). Austin, TX: PRO-ED.

Ship, J. A., Patton, L. L., & Tylenda, C. A. (1991). An assessment of salivary function in healthy premenopausal and postmenopausal females. *Journal of Gerontology: Medical Sciences, 46,* M11-M15.

Shock, N. W., Greulich, R. C., Andres, R., Arenberg, D., Cost, P., Lakatta, E., & Tobin, J. (Eds.). (1984). *Normal human aging: The Baltimore longitudinal study of aging* (NIH Publication No. 84-2450). Washington, DC: Government Printing Office.

Shoham, V., Bootzin, R. R., Rohrbaugh, M., & Urry, H. (1995). Paradoxical versus relaxation treatment for insomnia: The moderating role of reactance. *Sleep Research, 24a,* 365.

Shoham-Salomon, V., & Rosenthal, R. (1987). Paradoxical interventions: A meta-analysis. *Journal of Consulting and Clinical Psychology, 55,* 22-28.

Shomaker, D. M. (1981). Navajo nursing homes: Conflict of philosophies. *Journal of Gerontological Nursing, 7*(9), 531-536.

Shriqui, C. L., Bradwejn, J., Annable, L., & Jones, B. D. (1992). Vitamin E in the treatment of tardive dyskinesia: A double-blind placebo-controlled study. *American Journal of Psychiatry, 149,* 3391-3393.

Shulman, K. I. (1993). Mania in the elderly. *International Review of Psychiatry, 5,* 445-453.

Shulman, K. I., Tohen, M., Satlin, A., Mallya, G., &, Kalunian, D. (1992). Mania compared with unipolar depression in old age. *American Journal of Psychiatry, 149,* 341-345.

Siassi, I., Crocetti, G., & Spiro, H. R. (1973). Drinking patterns and alcoholism in a blue-collar population. *Quarterly Journal of Studies on Alcohol, 34,* 917-926.

Sidney, K. H., & Shephard, R. J. (1976). Attitudes toward health and physical activity in the elderly: Effects of a physical training program. *Medicine and Science in Sports and Exercise, 246,* 246-252.

Sifton, D. W. (1988). *PDR drug interactions and side effects index.* Oradell, NJ: Medical Economics.

Silberfeld, M., Nash, C., & Singer, P. A. (1993). Capacity to complete an advance directive. *Journal of the American Geriatrics Society,* 41, 1141-1143.

Silberman, E. K., Reus, V. I., Jimerson, D. C., Lynott, A. M., & Post, R. M. (1981). Heterogeneity of amphetamine response in depressed patients. *American Journal of Psychiatry, 138,* 1302-1307.

Silver, H. M. (1987). Alzheimer's disease: Ethical and legal decisions. *Medicine and Law, 6,* 537-551.

Silverman, J. M., Breitner, J. C. S., Mohs, R. C., & Davis, K. L. (1986). Reliability of the family history method in genetic studies of Alzheimer's disease and related dementias. *American Journal of Psychiatry, 143,* 1279-1282.

Silverstein, M., & Bengtson, V. L. (1991). Do close parent-child relations reduce the mortality risk of older parents? *Journal of Health and Social Behavior, 32,* 382-395.

Silverstone, B., Williams, T. F. (1984). *Social aspects of rehabilitation in the aging.* New York: Raven.

Silverstone, P. H. (1987). Depression and outcome in acute myocardial infarction. *British Medical Journal, 294,* 645.

Simic, A. (1987). Ethnicity as a career for the elderly: The Serbian-American case. *Journal of Applied Gerontology, 6*(1), 113-126.

Simon, A., Epstein, L. J., & Reynolds, L. (1968). Alcoholism in the geriatric mentally ill. *Geriatrics, 23,* 125-131.

Simons, J. (1985). Does incontinence affect your client's self-concept? *Journal of Gerontological Nursing, 11,* 37-42.

Simpson, D. M., & Foster, D. (1986). Improvement in organically disturbed behavior with trazodone treatment. *Journal of Clinical Psychiatry, 47,* 191-193.

Sines, L. K. (1959). The relative contribution of four kinds of data to accuracy in personality assessment. *Journal of Consulting Psychology, 23,* 483-492.

Singer, V.I., Tracz, S., & Dworkin, S. (1991). Reminiscence group therapy: A treatment modality for older adults. *Journal for Specialists in Group Work, 16,* 167-171.

Sinha, D., Zemlan, F. P., Nelson, S., Bienenfeld, D., Thienhaus, O., Ramaswamy, G., & Hamilton, S. (1992). A new scale for assessing behavioral agitation in dementia. *Psychiatry Research, 41,* 73-88.

Sinnott, J. D. (1977). Sex-role inconstancy, biology, and successful aging. *The Gerontologist, 17,* 459-463.

Sjogren, T., Sjogren, H., & Lindgren, A. G. H. (1952). Morbus Alzheimer and morbus Pick [Alzheimer's disease and Pick's disease]. *Acta Psychiatrica Scandinavica, 82,* 68-108.

Skolnick, A. (1986). *The psychology of human development.* San Diego, CA: Harcourt Brace Jovanovich.

Smart, R. G., & Adlaf, E. M. (1988). Alcohol and drug use among the elderly: Trends in use and characteristics of users. *Canadian Journal of Public Health, 79,* 236-242.

Smith, A. L., & Weissman, M. M. (1992). Epidemiology. In E. S. Paykel (Ed.), *Handbook of affective disorders* (pp. 111-129). New York: Guilford.

Smith, C. K., Barish, J., Correa, J., & Williams, R. H. (1972). Psychiatric disturbance in endocrinologic disease. *Psychosomatic Medicine, 34,* 69-86.

Smith, C. M., & Reynard, A. M. (1992). *Textbook of pharmacology*. Philadelphia: W. B. Saunders.

Smith, D. W. (1990). The biology of gender and aging. *Generations, 14,* 1-8.

Smith, D. W. (1992). The biology of gender and aging. In L. Glasse & J. Hendricks (Eds.), *Gender and aging* (pp. 5-14). New York: Baywood.

Smith, D. W., & Warner, H. R. (1989). Does genotypic sex have a direct effect on longevity? *Experimental Gerontology, 24,* 277-288.

Smith, E. L. (1981). Physical activity: A preventive and maintenance modality for bone loss with age. In F. J. Nagle & H. J. Montoye (Ed.), *Exercise in health and disease* (pp. 196-202). Springfield IL: Charles C Thomas.

Smyer, M. A. (1989). Nursing homes as a setting for psychological practice. *American Psychologist, 44,* 1307-1314.

Smyer, M. A., Cohn, M. D., & Brannon, D. (1988). *Mental health consultation in nursing homes.* New York: New York University Press.

Smyer, M. A., Zarit, S., & Qualls, S. (1990). Psychological intervention with the aging individual. In J. E. Birren & K. W. Schaie (Eds.), *Handbook of the psychology of aging* (3rd ed., pp. 375-403). San Diego, CA: Academic Press.

Snowden, J. (1991). A retrospective case-note study of bipolar disorder in old age. *British Journal of Psychiatry, 158,* 485-490.

Snyder, L. H., Rupprecht, P., Pyrek, J., Brekhus, S., & Moss, T. (1978). Wandering. *The Gerontologist, 18*(3), 272-280.

Sogbein, S. K., & Awad, S. A. (1982). Behavioral treatment for urinary incontinence in geriatric patients. *Canadian Medical Association Journal, 127,* 863-864.

Solnick, R. L., & Birren, J. E. (1977). Age and male erectile responsiveness. *Archives of Sexual Behavior, 6,* 1-9.

Solomon, K. (1981). The masculine gender role and its implications for the life expectancy of older men. *Journal of the American Geriatrics Society, 29,* 297-301.

Solomon, R. (1982). Gerontological social work practice in long-term care: Serving families of the institutionalized aged: The four crises. *Journal of Gerontological Social Work, 5,* 83-96.

Spaner, D., Bland, R. C., Newman, S. C. (1994). Major depressive disorder. *Acta Psychiatrica Scandinavica, 89,* 7-15.

Spar, J. E., & LaRue, A. (1990). *Geriatric Psychiatry.* Washington, DC: American Psychiatric Press.

Spar, J. E., Ford, C. V., & Liston, E. H. (1979). Bipolar affective disorder in aged patients. *Journal of Clinical Psychiatry, 40,* 504-507.

Spar, J. E., LaRue, A., Hewes, C., & Fairbanks, L. (1987). Multivariate prediction of falls in elderly inpatients. *International Journal of Geriatric Psychiatry, 2*(3), 185-188.

Spector, A. (1982). Aging of the lens and cataract formation. In R. Sekuler, D. Kline, & K. Dismukes (Eds.), *Aging and human visual function.* New York: Alan R. Liss.

Speer, D., & Bates, K. (1992). Comorbid mental and substance disorders among older psychiatric patients. *Journal of the American Geriatric Society, 40,* 886-890.

Spencer, G. (1989, January). *Projections of the population of the United States, by age, sex, and race: 1988 to 2080* (Series P-25, No. 1018). Washington, DC: U.S. Department of Commerce.

Spielberger, C. D., Gorsuch, R. L., Lushene, R., Vagg, P. R., & Jacobs, G. A. (1983). *Manual for the State-Trait Anxiety Inventory.* Palo Alto, CA: Consulting Psychologists Press.

Spielman, A., Saskin, P., & Thorpy, M. J. (1987). Treatment of chronic insomnia by restriction of time in bed. *Sleep, 10,* 45-56.

Spirduso, W. W. (1980). Physical fitness, aging, and psychomotor speed. *Journal of Gerontology, 35,* 850-865.

Spitze, G., & Logan, J. (1989). Gender differences in family support: Is there a payoff? *The Gerontologist, 29,* 108-113.

Spitzer, R. L., & Endicott, J. (1977). *Schedule for affective disorders and schizophrenia—Lifetime version (SADS-L).* New York: New York State Psychiatric Institute.

Spitzer, R. L., Fleiss, J. L., Burdock, E. I., & Hardesty, A. S. (1964). The Mental Status Schedule: Rational, reliability and validity. *Comprehensive Psychiatry, 5,* 384-395.

Spitzer, R. L., Williams, J. B. W., Gibbon, M., & First, M. B. (1987). *Structured Clinical Interview for DSM III-R (SCID).* Washington, DC: American Psychiatric Press.

Spitzer, R. L., Williams, J. B., Gibbon, M., & First, M. B. (1992). The Structured Clinical Interview for DSM-III-R (SCID). I: History, rationale, and description. *Archives of General Psychiatry, 49,* 624-629.

Spitzform, M. (1982). Normative data in the elderly on the Luria-Nebraska Neuropsychological Battery. *Clinical Neuropsychology, 4,* 103-105.

Spreen, O., & Strauss, E. (1991). *A compendium of neuropsychological tests: Administration, norms, and commentary.* New York: Oxford University Press.

Stahl, S. M. (1992). Serotonin neuroscience discoveries usher in a new era of novel drug therapies for psychiatry. *Psychopharmacology Bulletin, 28,* 3-9.

Stall, R. (1986). Change and stability in quantity and frequency of alcohol use among aging males: A 19-year follow-up study. *British Journal of Addiction, 81,* 537-544.

Stam, H. J., & Bultz, B. D. (1986). The treatment of severe insomnia in a cancer patient. *Journal of Behavior Therapy & Experimental Psychiatry, 17,* 33-37.

Stambrook, M., Cardoso, E. R., Hawryluk, G. A., Erikson, P., Piatek, D., & Sicz, G. (1988). Neuropsychological changes following the neurosurgical treatment of normal pressure hydrocephalus. *Archives of Clinical Neuropsychology, 3,* 323-330.

Stambrook, M., Gill, D. D., Cardoso, E. R., & Moore, A. D. (1993). Communicating (normal-pressure) hydrocephalus. In R. W. Parks, R. F. Zec, & R. S. Wilson (Eds.), *Neuropsychology of Alzheimer's disease and other dementias* (pp. 283-307). New York: Oxford University Press.

Stamey, T. A. (1983). Screening for prostate cancer, should we or shouldn't we? (letter). *JAMA, 269,* 2212.

Stamey, T. A. (1983). Cancer of the prostate: An analysis. *1982 Monographs in Urology, 3,* 67.

Stamford, B. A. (1988). Exercise in the elderly. In K. B. Pandolf (Ed.), *Exercise and sports sciences reviews* (Vol. 16). New York: Macmillan.

Stamler, J. (1993). MRFIT Trial data, and blood pressure, systolic and diastolic, and cardiovascular risks: U.S. population data. *Archives of Internal Medicine, 153,* 598-615.

Stampfer, M. J., & Colditz, G. A. (1991). Estrogen replacement therapy and coronary heart disease: A quantitative assessment of the epidemiologic evidence. *Preventive Medicine, 20,* 47-63.

Stanford, E. P., & DuBois, B. C. (1992). Gender and ethnicity patterns. In J. E. Birren, R. B. Sloane, & G. D. Cohen (Eds.), *Handbook of mental health and aging* (pp. 99-117). San Diego, CA: Academic Press.

Stanley, M. A., Beck, J. G., Barron, M., & Wagner, A. L. (1994, November). *Treatment of generalized anxiety disorder in older adults: Examination of outcome predictors.* Paper resented at the 28th annual meeting of the Association for Advancement of Behavior Therapy, San Diego, CA.

Stanley, M. A., Beck, J. G., DeWitt, J. A., Deagle, E. A., & Zebb, B. J. (1994, November). *Generalized anxiety in older adults: Treatment with cognitive-behavioral and supportive approaches.* Presented at the annual meeting of the Association for Advancement of Behavior Therapy, San Diego, CA.

Starker, S., & Hasenfled, R. (1976). Daydream styles and sleep disturbance. *Journal of Nervous and Mental Disease, 163,* 391-400.

Starkstein, S. E., Cohen, B. S., Fedoroff, P., Parikh, R. M., Price, T. R., & Robinson, R. G. (1990). Relationship between anxiety disorders and depressive disorders in patients with cerebrovascular injury. *Archives of General Psychiatry, 47,* 246-251.

Starkstein, S. E., & Mayberg, H. S. (1993). Depression in Parkinson's disease. In S. E. Starkstein & R. G. Robinson (Eds.), *Depression in neurologic disease* (pp. 97-116). Baltimore: Johns Hopkins.

Starkstein, S. E., Preziosi T. J., Bolduc, P. L., & Robinson, R. G. (1990). Depression in Parkinson's disease. *Journal of Nervous and Mental Disorders, 178,* 27-31.

Starkstein, S. E., & Robinson, R. G. (1989). Depression and Parkinson's disease. In R. G. Robinson & P. V. Rabins (Eds.), *Depression and coexisting disease* (pp. 213-225). New York: Igaku-Shoin.

Starkstein, S. E., & Robinson, R. G. (1992). Neuropsychiatric aspects of cerebral vascular disease. In S. C. Yudofsky & R. E. Hales (Eds.), *The American Psychiatric Press textbook of neuropsychiatry* (2nd ed., pp. 449-472). Washington, DC: American Psychiatric Press.

Starkstein, S. E., & Robinson, R. G. (1993). Depression in cerebrovascular disease. In S. E. Starkstein & R. G. Robinson (Eds.), *Depression in neurologic disease* (pp. 28-49). Baltimore: Johns Hopkins.

Starkstein, S. E., Robinson, R. G., Berthier, M. L., Parikh, R. M., & Price, T. R. (1988). Differential mood changes following basal ganglia vs. thalamic lesions. *Archives of Neurology, 45,* 725-730.

Starkstein, S. E., Robinson, R. G., & Price, T. R. (1987). Comparison of cortical and subcortical lesions in the production of poststroke mood disorders. *Brain, 110,* 1045-1059.

Starr, B. D. (1985). Sexuality and aging. In M. P. Lawton & G. I. Maddox (Eds.), *Annual review of gerontology and geriatrics* (pp. 97-112). New York: Springer.

Starr, B. D., & Weiner, M. B. (1981). *The Starr-Weiner report on sex and sexuality in the mature years.* New York: McGraw-Hill.

Starrett, R. A., Decker, J. T., Araujo, A., Walters, G. (1989). The Cuban elderly and their service use. *Journal of Applied Gerontology, 8*(1), 69-85.

Starrett, R. A., Todd, A. M., & DeLeon, L. (1989). A comparison of the social service utilization behavior of the Cuban and Puerto Rican elderly. *Hispanic Journal of Behavioral Sciences, 11*(4), 341-353.

Staudinger, U. M., Marsiske, M., & Baltes, P. B. (1993). Resilience and levels of reserve capacity in later adulthood: Perspectives from life-span theory. *Development and Psychopathology, 5,* 541-566.

Stein, L. I., & Test, M. A. (1982). Community treatment of the young adult patient. In B. Pepper & H. Ryglewicz (Eds.), *New directions for mental health services: The young adult chronic patient* (pp. 57-67). San Francisco: Jossey-Bass.

Stein, M. B., Heuser, I. J., Juncos, J. L., & Uhde, T. W. (1990). Anxiety disorders in patients with Parkinson's disease. *American Journal of Psychiatry, 147,* 217-220.

Stelmach, G. E., Amrhein, P. C., & Goggin, N. L. (1988). Age differences in bimanual coordination. *Journal of Gerontology, 43,* P18-P23.

Stelmach, G. E., Goggin, N. L., & Garcia-Colera, A. (1987). Movement specification time with age. *Experimental Aging Research, 13,* 39-46.

Stepansky, E., Lamphere, J., Badia, P., Zorick, F., & Roth, T. (1984). Sleep fragmentation and daytime sleepiness. *Sleep, 7,* 18-26.

Stern, M. J., Pascale, L., & Ackerman, A. (1977). Life adjustment postmyocardial infarction: Determining predictive variables. *Archives of Internal Medicine, 137,* 1680-1685.

Sternberg, J., Whelihan, W. M., Fretwell, M. D., Biellecki, C. A., & Murray, S. L. (1989). Disruptive behaviors in the elderly: Nurses' perceptions. *The Clinical Gerontologist, 8*(3), 43-56.

Stevens, J. C. (1989). Food quality reports from noninstitutionalized aged. *Annals of the New York Academy of Science, 561,* 87-93.

Stevens, J. C., & Cain, W. S. (1987). Old-age deficits in the sense of smell as gauged by thresholds, magnitude matching, and odor identification. *Psychology and Aging, 2*(1), 36-42.

Stevens, J. C., Cain, W. S., Demarque, A., & Ruthruff, A. M. (1991). On the discrimination of missing ingredients: Aging and salt flavor. *Appetite, 16*(2), 129-40.

Stevenson, J. S., & Topp, R. (1990). Effects of moderate and low intensity long-term exercise by older adults. *Research in Nursing and Health, 13,* 209-213.

Stine, E. A. L., & Wingfield, A. (1990). The assessment of qualitative age differences in discourse processing. In T. M. Hess (Ed.), *Aging and cognition: Knowledge organization and utilization* (pp. 33-92). Amsterdam: North Holland.

Stoller, E. P. (1990). Male as helpers: The role of sons, relatives and friends. *The Gerontologist, 30,* 228-235.

Stone, K. (1989). Mania in the elderly. *British Journal of Psychiatry, 155,* 220-224.

Stone, R., Cafferata, G. L., & Sangl, J. (1987). Caregivers of the elderly: a national profile. *The Gerontologist, 27,* 616-631.

Storandt M. (1991). Longitudinal studies of aging and age-associated dementias. In F. Boller & J. Grafman (Eds.), *Handbook of neuropsychology* (Vol. 4, pp. 349-364). New York: Elsevier.

Storandt, M. (1994). General principles of assessment of older adults. In M. Storandt & G. Vandenbos (Eds.), *Neuropsychological assessment of dementia and depression in older adults: A clinician's guide* (pp. 7-31). Washington, DC: American Psychological Association.

Storandt, M., Siegler, I. C., & Elias, M. F. (Eds.). (1978). *The clinical psychology of aging.* New York: Plenum.

Stoudemire, A., & Moran, M. G. (1993). Psychopharmacologyogic treatment of anxiety in the medically ill elderly patient: Special considerations. *Journal of Clinical Psychiatry, 54*(5, Suppl.), 27-33.

Strandness, D. E. (1993). Carotid endarterectomy: Current status, and effects of clinical trials. *Cardiovascular Surgery, 1*(4), 311-316.

Strasburger, L. H., & Welpton, S. (1991). Elderly suicide: Minimizing risk for patient and professional. *Journal of Geriatric Psychiatry, 24,* 235-259.

Strauss, P. J., Wolf, R., & Shilling, D. (1990). *Aging and the law.* Chicago: Commerce Clearing House.

Strub, R. C., & Black, F. W. (1988). *Neurobehavioral disorders: A clinical approach.* Philadelphia: F. A. Davis.

Strub, R. L., & Black, F. W. (1993). *The mental status examination in neurology* (3rd ed.). Philadelphia: F. A. Davis.

Strupp, H. H., & Bloxom, A. L. (1973). Preparing lower-class clients for group psychotherapy: Development and evaluation of a role-induction film. *Journal of Consulting and Clinical Psychology, 41,* 373-384.

Suarez-Orozco, M. M. (1990). Speaking of the unspeakable: Toward a psychosocial understanding of responses to terror. *Ethos, 18,* 353-383.

Sudilovsky, A., Croog, S., Crook, T., Turnbull, B., Testa, M., Levine, S., & Klerman, G. L. (1989). Differential effects of antihypertensive medications on cognitive functioning. *Psychopharmacology Bulletin, 25,* 133-138.

Sue, D. W., & Sue, D. (1990). *Counseling the culturally different: Theory and practice* (2nd ed.). New York: John Wiley.

Sue, S. (1977). Community mental health services to minority groups: Some optimism, some pessimism. *American Psychologist, 32,* 616-624.

Sughandabhirom, B. (1986). Experiences in a first asylum country: Thailand. In C. L. Williams & J. Westermeyer (Eds.), *Refugee mental health in resettlement countries* (pp. 81-96). New York: Hemisphere.

Sullivan, G. (1988). Increased libido in three men treated with trazodone. *Journal of Clinical Psychiatry, 49,* 202-203.

Sulsky, S. I., Jacques, P. F., Otradovec, C. L., Hartz, S. C., & Russell, R. M. (1990). Descriptors of alcohol consumption among noninstitutionalized nonalcoholic elderly. *Journal of the American College of Nutrition, 9,* 326-331.

Summers, W. K., Majovski, L. V., & Marsh, G. M. (1986). Oral tetrahydroaminoacridine in long-term treatment of senile dementia, Alzheimer type. *New England Journal of Medicine, 16,* 145-153.

Sunderland, A., Watts, K., Baddeley, A. D., & Harris, J. E. (1986). Subjective memory assessment and test performance in elderly adults. *Journal of Gerontology, 41*(3), 376-384.

Sunderland, T. (1987). Neurotransmission in the aging central nervous system. In C. Salzman (Ed.), *Clinical geriatric psychopharmacology* (2nd ed., pp. 41-59). Baltimore: Williams & Wilkins.

Sunderland, T., Cohn, R. M., Molchan, S., Lawlor, B. A., Mello, A. M., Newhouse, P. A., Tariot, P. N., Mueller, E. A., & Murphy, D. L. (1994). High-dose selegiline in treatment-resistant older depressive patients. *Archives of General Psychiatry, 51,* 607-615.

Sussman, N. (1994). The potential benefits of serotonin receptor-specific agents. *Journal of Clinical Psychiatry, 55*(2, Suppl.), 45-51.

Suzman, R. M., Willis, D. P., & Manton, K. G. (1992). *The oldest old.* New York: Oxford University Press.

Svanborg, A. (1988). The health of the elderly population: Results from the longitudinal studies with age-cohort comparisons. In D. Evered & J. Whelan (Eds.), *Research and the aging population.* Chichester, UK: Wiley.

Swartz, M., Landerman, R., George, L. K., Melville, M. L., Blazer, D., & Smith, K. (1991). Benzodiazepine anti-anxiety agents: Prevalence and correlates of use in a southern community. *American Journal of Public Health, 81,* 592-596.

Swartzman, L., & Teasell, R. W. (1993). Psychological consequences of stroke. *Physical Medicine and Rehabilitation, 7,* 179-193.

Swearer, J. M., Drachman, D. A., O'Donnell, B. F., & Mitchell, A. L. (1988). Troublesome and disruptive behaviors in dementia: Relationships to diagnosis and disease severity. *Journal of the American Geriatrics Society, 36,* 784-790.

Sweet, J. J., Newman, P., & Bell, B. (1992). Significance of depression in clinical neuropsychological assessment. *Clinical Psychology Review, 12,* 21-45.

Szapocznik, J., Scopetta, M. A., Kurtines, W., & de los Angeles Arande, M. (1978). Theory and measurement of acculturation. *Interamerican Journal of Psychology, 12,* 113-130.

Szinovacz, M., & Washo, C. (1992). Gender differences in exposure to life events and adaptation to retirement. *Journal of Gerontology, 467,* 191-196.

Szuba, M. P., Bergman, K. S., Baxter, L. R., & Guze, B. H. (1992). Safety and efficacy of high-dose droperidol in agitated patients. *Journal of Clinical Psychopharmacology, 12,* 144-145.

Szuba, M. P., & Leuchter, A. F. (1992). Falling backward in two elderly patients taking buproprion. *Journal of Clinical Psychiatry, 53,* 157-159.

Szymanksi, S., Munne, R., Gordon, M. F., & Lieberman, J. (1993). A selective review of recent advances in the management of tardive dyskinesia. *Psychiatric Annals, 23,* 209-215.

Takaki, R. (1989). *Strangers from a different shore: A history of Asian Americans.* Boston: Harcourt Brace Jovanovich.

Takamura, J. (1985). Introduction: Health teams. In L. J. Campbell & S. Vivell (Eds.), *Interdisciplinary team training for primary care in geriatrics: An educational model for program development and evaluation* (pp. II:64-II:67). Washington, DC: Government Printing Office.

Takamura, J., Bermost, L., & Stringfellow, L. (1979). *Health team development.* Honolulu: University of Hawaii, John A. Burns School of Medicine.

Tankersley, C. G., Smolander, J., Kenney, W. L., & Fortney, S. M. (1991). Sweating and skin blood flow during exercise: Effects of age and maximal oxygen uptake. *Journal of Applied Physiology, 71,* 236-242.

Tappy, L., Randin, J. P., Schwed, P., Wertheimer, J., & Lemarchand-Beraud, T. (1987). Prevalence of thyroid disorders in psychogeriatric inpatients. *Journal of American Geriatrics Society, 35,* 526-531.

Tarter, R. E., & Edwards, K. L. (1985). Neuropsychology of alcoholism. In R. Tarter & D. Van Thiel (Eds.), *Alcohol and the brain: Chronic effects.* New York: Plenum.

Tarter, R. E., Hays, A. L., & Carra, J. (1988). Sjogren's syndrome: Its contributions to neuropsychiatric syndrome in patients with primary biliary cirrhosis. *Journal of Family Practice, 30,* 430-436.

Tarter, R. E., & Ryan, C. M. (1983). Neuropsychology of alcoholism: Etiology, phenomenology, process and outcome. In M. Galanter (Ed.), *Recent developments in alcoholism* (Vol. 1). New York: Plenum.

Tavris, C. (1992). *The mismeasure of women.* New York: Simon & Schuster.

Taylor, F. K. (1988). The damnation of benzodiazepines. *British Journal of Psychiatry, 154,* 697-704.

Taylor, R. J. (1988). Aging and supportive relationships among Black Americans. In J. S. Jackson (Ed.), *The Black American elderly: Research on physical and psychosocial health* (pp. 259-281). New York: Springer.

Teasdale, J. D., & Barnard, P. J. (1993). *Affect cognition and change: Remodelling depressive thought.* Sussex, UK: Lawrence Erlbaum.

Teicher, M. H., Gold, C., & Cole, J. O. (1990). Emergence of intense suicidal preoccupation during fluoxetine treatment. *American Journal of Psychiatry, 147,* 207-210.

Temple, M. T., & Leino, E. V. (1989). Long-term outcomes of drinking: A 20-year longitudinal study of men. *British Journal of Addiction, 84,* 889-899.

Tennstedt, S., Cafferata, G. L., & Sullivan, L. (1992). Depression among caregivers of impaired elders. *Journal of Aging and Health, 4,* 58-76.

Teresi, J. A., Golden, R. R., & Gurland, B. J. (1984). Concurrent and predictive validity of indicator scales developed for the comprehensive assessment and referral evaluation interview schedule. *Journal of Gerontology, 39,* 158-165.

Teri, L. (1982). Effects of sex and sex-role style on psychiatric diagnosis. *Journal of Nervous and Mental Disease, 47,* 349-353.

Teri, L., & Gallagher, D. G. (1991). Cognitive-behavioral interventions for treatment of depression in Alzheimer's patients. *The Gerontologist, 21,* 413-416.

Teri, L., & Keller, L. (1987). Multimodal assessment of the cognitively impaired older adult. In E. Borgatta (Ed.), *Alzheimer's caregivers: Strategies for support* (pp. 40-64). Seattle: University of Washington Press.

Teri, L., Larson, E. B., & Reifler, B. V. (1988). Behavioral disturbance in dementia of the Alzheimer's type. *Journal of the American Geriatrics Society, 36*(1), 1-6.

Teri, L., & Lewinsohn, P. M. (1986). *Gerontological assessment and treatment: Selected topics.* New York: Springer.

Teri, L., & Logsdon, R. (1991). Identifying pleasant activities for individuals with Alzheimer's disease: The Pleasant Events Schedule-AD. *The Gerontologist, 31,* 124-127.

Teri, L., & Uomoto, J. (1991). Reducing excess disability in dementia patients: Training caregivers to manage patient depression. *The Clinical Gerontologist, 10*(4), 49-63.

Terman, M. (1994). Light therapy. In M. H. Kryger, T. Roth, & W. C. Dement (Eds.), *Principles and practice of sleep medicine* (2nd ed., pp. 1012-1029). Philadelphia: W. B. Saunders.

Terry, L. C., & Halter, J. B. (1990). Aging of the endocrine system. In W. R. Hazzard, R. Andres, E. L. Bierman, & J. P. Blass (Eds.), *Principles of geriatric medicine and gerontology* (2nd ed., pp. 705-718). New York: McGraw-Hill.

Tesar, G. E., Murray, G. B., & Cassem, E. H. (1985). Use of high-dose intravenous haloperidol in the treatment of agitated cardiac patients. *Journal of Clinical Psychopharmacology, 5,* 344-347.

Test, M. A., and Stein, L. I. (1980). Alternative to mental hospital treatment: 3. Social cost. *Archives of General Psychiatry, 37,* 409-412.

Thaysen, P., Bjerre, M., Kragh-Sprensen, P., Moller, M., Petersen, O. L., Kristensen, C. B., & Gram, L. F. (1981). Cardiovascular effects of imipramine and nortriptyline in elderly patients. *Psychopharmacology, 74,* 360-364.

Thienhaus, O. J. (1988). Practical overview of sexual functioning and advancing age. *Geriatrics, 43,* 63-67.

Thomas, J. L. (1986). Gender differences in satisfaction with grandparenting. *Psychology and Aging, 1,* 215-219.

Thompson, L. W., & Gallagher-Thompson, D. (1991, November). *Comparison of desipramine and cognitive/behavioral therapy in the treatment of late-life depression.* Paper presented at the Gerontogical Society of America Meetings, San Francisco, CA.

Thompson, L. W., Gallagher, D., & Breckenridge, J. S. (1987). Comparative effectiveness of psychotherapies for depressed elders. *Journal of Consulting and Clinical Psychology, 55,* 385-390.

Thompson, L. W., Gallagher-Thompson, D., Futterman, A., Gilewski, M. J., & Peterson, J. (1991). Effects of late-life spousal bereavement over a 30-month interval. *Psychology and Aging, 6,* 434-441.

Thompson, P. (1979). Death during jogging or running. *JAMA, 242,* 1265-1267.

Thompson, S. C., Bundek, N. I., & Sobolew-Shubin, A. (1990). The caregivers of stroke patients: An investigation of factors associated with depression. *Journal of Applied Social Psychology, 20,* 115-129.

Thompson, T. L., Moran, M. G., & Nies, A. S. (1983). Psychotropic drug use in the elderly. *New England Journal of Medicine, 308,* 134-135.

Thyer, B. A. (1981). Prolonged in vivo exposure therapy with a 70-year-old woman. *Journal of Behavior Therapy and Experimental Psychiatry, 12,* 69-71.

Tinetti, M. E. (1988). Risk factors for falls among elderly persons. *New England Journal of Medicine, 319,* 1701-1707.

Tinetti, M. E., & Powell, L. (1993). Fear of falling and low self-efficacy: A cause of dependence in elderly persons [Special Issue]. *Journals of Gerontology, 48,* 35-58.

Tinetti, M. E., Richman, D., & Powell, L. (1990). Falls efficacy as a measure of fear of falling. *Journals of Gerontology, 45*(6), 239.

Tinetti, M. E., Speechley, M., & Ginter, S. F. (1988). Risk factors for falls among elderly persons living in the community. *New England Journal of Medicine, 319*(26), 1701-1707.

Tjosvold, D. (1991). *The conflict-positive organization: Stimulate diversity and create unity.* Reading, MA: Addison-Wesley.

Tobias, C. R., Lippmann, S., Pary, R., Oropilla, T., & Emrby, C. K. (1989). Alcoholism in the elderly: How to spot and treat a problem the patient wants to hide. *Postgraduate Medicine, 86,* 67-79.

Tobis, J. S., Nayak, L., & Hoehler, F. (1981). Visual perception of verticality and horizontality among elderly fallers. *Archives of Physical Medicine and Rehabilitation, 62,* 619-622.

Todes, C. J., & Lee, A. J. (1985). The pre-morbid personality of patients with Parkinson's disease. *Journal of Neurological and Neurosurgical Psychiatry, 48,* 97-100.

Toglia, J. U. (1975). Dizziness in the elderly. In W. Fields (Ed.), *Neurological and sensory disorders in the elderly.* New York: Grune & Stratton.

Tohen, M., Shulman, K. I., & Satlin, A. (1994). First-episode mania in late life. *American Journal of Psychiatry, 151,* 130-132.

Tollefson, G. D. (1990). Short-term effects of the calcium channel blocker nimodipine in the management of primary degenerative dementia. *Biological Psychiatry, 27,* 1133-1142.

Tollefson, G. D., Rampey, A. H., Potvin, J. H., Jenicke, M. A., Rush, A. J., Kominguez, R. A., Koran, L. M., Shear, M. K., Goodman, W., & Genduso, L. (1994). A multicenter investigation of fixed dose fluoxetine in the treatment of obsessive-compulsive disorder. *Archives of General Psychiatry, 51,* 559-567.

Tomlinson, B. E., Blessed, G., & Roth, M. (1970). Observations on the brains of demented old people. *Journal of the Neurological Sciences, 11,* 205-242.

Toseland, R., Rossiter, C., & Labrecque, M. (1989). The effectiveness of peer-led and professionally-led groups to support family caregivers. *The Gerontologist, 29,* 465-471.

Travis, C. B. (1988). *Women and health psychology: Mental health issues.* Hillsdale, NJ: Lawrence Erlbaum.

Troll, L. E. (1987). Gender differences in cross-generation networks. *Sex Roles, 11-12,* 751-766.

Trzepacz, P. T., McCue, M., Klein, I., & Levey, G. S. (1988). A psychiatric and neuropsychological study of patients with untreated Graves' disease. *General Hospital Pshychiatry, 10*(1), 49-55.

Tsuang, M. M., Lu, L. M., Stotsky, B. A., & Cole, J. O. (1971). Haloperidol versus thioridazine for hospitalized psycho-geriatric patients: Double-blind study. *Journal of the American Geriatrics Society, 19,* 593-600.

Tsuang, M. T., Woolson, R. F., & Fleming, J. A. (1979). Long-term outcome of major psychosis. *Archives of General Psychiatry, 39,* 1295-1301.

Tuckman, B. W. (1965). Developmental sequence in small groups. *Psychological Bulletin, 64,* 384-399.

Tully, C. T. (1983). *Social support systems of a selected sample of older women.* Doctoral dissertation, Virginia Commonwealth University, Richmond.

Turner, R. J., & Noh, S. (1988). Physical disability and depression: A longitudinal analysis. *Journal of Health and Social Behavior, 29,* 23-37.

Turner, S. M., Hersen, M., Bellack, A. S., & Wells, K. C. (1979). Behavioral treatment of obsessive-compulsive neurosis. *Behaviour Research and Therapy, 17,* 95-106.

Twiss, G., Hengel, F., & Mercier, S. (1989). *Elderly needs assessment of the elderly on the Rosebud reservation* (Indian Health Service Leadership Projects 1989). Aberdeen Area: Indian Health Service Community Health Service Program and Dakota Plains Geriatric Education Center.

U.S. Bureau of the Census. (1992a). *Population projections of the United States by age, sex, race, and Hispanic origin: 1992-2050* (Current Population Reports, Series 25-1092). Washington, DC: Government Printing Office.

U.S. Bureau of the Census. (1992b). *Marital status and living arrangments* (Current Population Reports. Series P20-468). Washington, DC: Government Printing Office.

U.S. Bureau of the Census. (1992c). *Sixty-five plus in America* (Current Population Reports, Special Studies, P23-1787RV). Washington, DC: Government Printing Office.

U.S. Bureau of the Census. (1993a). Racial and ethnic diversity of America's elderly population. *Profiles of America's elderly, No. 3.* Washington, DC: Government Printing Office.

U.S. Bureau of the Census. (1993b). *Statistical abstract of the United States: 1993* (113th ed.). Washington, DC: Government Printing Office.

U.S. Department of Health and Human Services. (1988). *Surgeon General's report on nutrition and health.* Washington, DC: Government Printing Office.

U.S. National Center for Health Statistics. (1985). *Vital statistics in the United States, 1980: Vol. 2. Mortality* (DHHS publication PHS 85-1102). Washington, DC: Government Printing Office.

U.S. National Center for Health Statistics. (1994). *Current estimates from the National Health Interview Survey, 1992* (DHHS Publication No. PHS 94-1517, Series 10, No. 189). Washington, DC: Government Printing Office.

U.S. Public Health Service. (1976). *Physician's drug prescribing patterns in skilled nursing facilities.* Washington, DC: U.S. Department of Health, Education, and Welfare.

Umberson, D., Wortman, C. B., & Kessler, R. C. (1992). Widowhood and depression: Explaining long-term gender differences in vulnerability. *Journal of Health and Social Behavior, 33,* 10-24.

Vaccaro, F. J. (1988a). Application of operant procedures in a group of institutionalized aggressive geriatric patients. *Psychology and Aging, 3*(1), 22-28.

Vaccaro, F. J. (1988b). Successful operant conditioning procedures with an institutionalized aggressive geriatric patient. *International Journal of Aging and Human Development, 26*(1), 71-79.

Valle, R. (1989). Cultural and ethnic issues in Alzheimer's disease family research. In E. Light & B. Lebowitz (Eds.), *Alzheimers's disease treatment and family stress: Directions for research* (Publication No. ADM 89-1569, pp. 122-154). Washington, DC: U.S. Department of Health and Human Services.

van Gorp, W. G., Satz, P., Kiersch, M. E., & Henry, R. (1986). Normative data on the Boston Naming Test for a group of normal older adults. *Journal of Clinical and Experimental Neuropsychology, 8,* 702-705.

van Gorp, W. G., Satz, P., & Mitrushina, M. (1990). Neuropsychological processes associated with normal aging. *Developmental Neuropsychology, 6,* 279-290.

Van Nostrand, J. F., Zappolo, A., Hing, E., Bloom, B., Hirsch, B., & Foley, D. J. (1979). *The national nursing home survey: 1977 summary for the United States* (National Center for Health Statistics, Vital and Health Statistics Series 13, No. 43, Publication No. PHS 79-1794). U.S. Department of Health, Education, and Welfare.

Van-Rooij, J. C., & Plomp, R. (1990). Auditive and cognitive factors in speech perception by elderly listeners: II. Multivariate analyses. *Journal of the Acoustical Society of America, 88*(6), 2611-2624.

Van-Rooij, J. C., & Plomp, R. (1992). How much do working memory deficits contribute to age differences in discourse memory? [Special Issue: Cognitive gerontology]. *Journal of the Acoustical Society of America, 91*(2), 1028-1033.

Vandervoort, A. A., Chesworth, B. M., Cunningham, D. A., Paterson, D. H., Rechnitzer, P. A., & Koval, J. J. (1992). Age and sex effects on mobility of the human ankle. *Journal of Gerontology: Medical Sciences, 47*, M17-M21.

Varghese, R., & Medinger, F. (1979). Fatalism in response to stress among the minority aged. In D. E. Gelfand & A. J. Kutzik (Eds.), *Ethnicity and aging: Theory, research, and policy.* New York: Springer.

Varni, J. W. (1980). Behavioral treatment of disease-related chronic insomnia in a hemophiliac. *Journal of Behavior Therapy and Experimental Psychiatry, 11*, 143-145.

Vaux, A. (1985). Variations in social support associated with gender, ethnicity, and age. *Journal of Social Issues, 41*, 89-110.

Verbrugge, L. M. (1989). Gender, aging and health. In K. S. Markides (Ed.), *Aging and health: Perspectives on gender, race, ethnicity, and class* (pp. 23-78). Newbury Park, CA: Sage.

Verbrugge, L. M. (1990). The twain meet: Empirical explanation of sex differences in health and mortality. In M. G. Ory & H. R. Warner (Eds.), *Gender, health, and longevity* (pp. 159-200). New York: Springer.

Verhaeghen, P., Marcoen, A., & Goossens, L. (1993). Facts and fiction about memory aging: A quantitative integration of research findings. *Journal of Gerontology: Psychological Sciences, 48*, P157-P171.

Vernon, M. (1989). Assessment of persons with hearing disabilities. In T. Hunt & C. J. Lindley (Eds.), *Testing older adults: A reference guide for geropsychological assessments* (pp. 150-162). Austin, TX: PRO-ED.

Vernon, M., Griffin, D. H., & Yoken, C. (1981). Hearing loss. *Journal of Family Practice, 12*(6), 1053-1058.

Verwoerdt, A. (1980). Anxiety, dissociative disorders, and personality disorders in the elderly. In E. W. Busse & D. G. Blazer (Eds.), *Handbook of geriatric psychiatry* (pp. 368-380). New York: Van Norstrand Reinhold.

Vestal, R. E. (1990). Clinical pharmacology. In W. R. Hazzard, R. Andres, E. L. Bierman, & J. P. Blass (Eds.), *Principles of geriatric medicine and gerontology* (2nd ed., pp. 201-211). New York: McGraw-Hill.

Vestal, R. E., & Dawson, G. W. (1985). Pharmacology and aging. In C. E. Finch & E. L. Schneider (Eds.), *Handbook of the biology of aging* (2nd ed., pp. 744-819). New York: Van Nostrand Reinhold.

Vetter, N. J., & Ford, D. (1989). Anxiety and depression scores in elderly fallers. *International Journal of Geriatric Psychiatry, 4*(3), 159-163.

Victor, M. (1993, August). Persisitent altered mentation due to ethanol. *Neurologic Complications of Drug and Alcohol Abuse, 11*, 639.

Villardita, C., Cultrera, S., Cupone, V., & Meija, R. (1985). Neuropsychological test performances and normal aging. *Archives of Gerontology and Geriatrics, 4*, 311-319.

Vitaliano, P. P., Maiuro, R., Ochs, H., & Russo, J. (1989). A model of burden in caregivers of DAT patients. In E. Light & B. D. Lebowitz (Eds.), *Alzheimer's disease treatment and family stress: Directions for research* (Publication No. ADM 89-1569, pp. 267-291). Washington, DC: U.S. Department of Health and Human Services.

Vitiello, M. V., Bliwise, D. L., & Prinz, P. N. (1992). Sleep in Alzheimer's disease and the sundown syndrome. *Neurology, 42*(Suppl. 6), 83-94.

Vitiello, M. V., Schwartz, R. S., Davis, M. W., Ward, R. R., Ralph, D. D., & Prinz, P. N. (1992). Sleep quality and increased aerobic fitness in healthy aged men: Preliminary findings. *Journal of Sleep Research, 1*(Suppl.), 245.

Volavka, J. (1985). Late-onset schizophrenia: A review. *Comprehensive Psychiatry, 26,* 148-156.

Volavka, J., & Cancro, R. (1986). The late onset schizophrenic disorders. In E. Busse (Ed.), *Aspects of Aging.* Philadelphia: Smith Kline & Frank Laboratories.

Wahl, H. W. (1991). Dependence in the elderly from an interactional point of view: Verbal and observational data. *Psychology and Aging, 6,* 238-246.

Wahl, H. W. (1993). Kompetenzeinbussen im Alter: eine Auswertung der Literatur zu "Activities of Daily Living" und Pflegebedürftigkeit [Competence loss in old age: An analysis of the literature on "Activities of Daily Living" and basic care needs]. *Zeitschrift für Gerontologie, 26,* 366-377.

Wahl, H. W., & Baltes, M. M. (1990). Die soziale Umwelt alter Menschen: Entwicklungsanregende oder-hemmende Pflegeinteraktionen? [The social environment of the elderly: Development-enhancing or inhibiting care interactions?]. *Zeitschrift für Entwicklungspsychologie und Pädagogische Psychologie, 22,* 266-283.

Waldstein, S. R., Manuck, S. B., Ryan, C. M., & Muldoon, M. F. (1991). Neuropsychological correlates of hypertension: Review and methodological considerations. *Psychological Bulletin, 110,* 451-468.

Walker, A. J. (1992). Conceptual perspectives on gender and family caregiving. In J. W. Dwyer & R. T. Coward (Eds.), *Gender, families, and elder care* (pp. 34-46). Newbury Park, CA: Sage.

Walker, A. J., & Allen, K. R. (1991). Relationships between caregiving daughters and their elderly mothers. *The Gerontologist, 31*(3), 389-396.

Walker, P. W., Cole, J. O., & Gardner, E. A., Hughes, A. R., Johston, J. A., Batey, S. R., & Lineberry, C. G. (1993). Improvement in fluoxetine-associated sexual dysfunction in patients switched to buproprion. *Journal of Clinical Psychiatry, 54,* 459-465.

Wallace, C. J. (1984). Community and interpersonal functioning in the course of schizophrenic disorders. *Schizophrenia Bulletin, 10,* 233-257.

Wallace, C. J., & Liberman, R. P. (1985). Social skills training for patients with schizophrenia: A controlled clinical trial. *Psychiatry Research, 15,* 239-245.

Walter, S., Wolf, H., Barlebo, H., & Jenson, H. K. (1978). Urinary incontinence in postmenopausal women treated with estrogens. *Urologia Internationalis, 33,* 135-143.

Wantz, M. S., & Gay, J. E. (1981). *The aging process: A health perspective.* Cambridge, MA: Winthrop.

Ward, H. W., Ramsdell, J. W., Jackson, J. E., Renvall, M., Swart, J. A., & Rockwell, E. (1990). Cognitive function testing in comprehensive geriatric assessment: A comparison of cognitive test performance in residential and clinical settings. *Journal of the American Geriatrics Society, 38,* 1088-1092.

Ware, C. J. G., Fairburn, C. G., & Hope, R. A. (1990). A community-based study of aggressive behavior in dementia. *International Journal of Geriatric Psychiatry, 5,* 337-342.

Watkins, S. C., Menken, J. A., & Bongaarts, J. (1987). Demographic foundations of family change. *American Sociological Review, 52,* 346-358.

Watson, G., & Williams, J. (1992). Feminist practice in therapy. In J. M. Ussher & P. Nicolson (Eds.), *Gender issues in clinical psychology* (pp. 212-236). London: Routledge.

Wattis, J. P. (1990). Diagnostic issues in depression in old age. *International Clinical Psychopharmacology, 5*(Suppl. 3), 1-6.

Weale, R. A. (1963). *The aging eye.* London: H. K. Lewis.

Webb, W. B. (1982). The measurement and characteristics of sleep in older persons. *Neurobiology of Aging, 3,* 311-319.

Webb, W. B., & Campbell, S. S. (1980). Awakenings and the return to sleep in an older population. *Sleep, 3,* 41-66.

Webb, W. B., & Drebow, L. M. (1982). A modified method for scoring slow-wave sleep of older subjects. *Sleep, 5,* 195-199.

Webb, W. B., & Levy, C. M. (1982). Age, sleep deprivation and performance. *Psychophysiology, 19,* 372-276.

Webb, W. B., & Swinburne, H. (1971). An observational study of sleep in the aged. *Perceptual and Motor Skills, 32,* 895-898.

Webster, J. R., & Kadah, H. (1991). Unique aspects of respiratory disease in the aged. *Geriatrics, 46,* 31-34.

Wechsler, D. (1981). *Wechsler Adult Intelligence Scale—Revised.* New York: Psychological Corporation.

Wechsler, D. (1987). *Wechsler Memory Scale—Revised Manual.* San Antonio, TX: Psychological Corporation.

Wechsler, H., Demone, H. W., & Gottlieb, N. (1978). Drinking patterns of greater Boston adults: Subgroup differences on the QFV Index. *Journal of Studies on Alcohol, 39,* 1158-1165.

Weg, R. B. (1983). *Sexuality in the later years.* New York: Academic Press.

Weg, R. B. (1991). Sensuality, sexuality, and intimacy in ageing. In M. S. J. Pathy (Eds.), *Principles and practice in geriatric medicine* (pp. 231-51). New York: John Wiley.

Wehr, T. A., & Sack, D. A. (1988). The relevance of sleep research to affective illness. In W. P. Koella, F. Obal, H. Schulz, & P. Visser (Eds.), *Sleep '86* (pp. 207-211). New York: Gustav Fisher Verlag.

Weiffenbach, J. M., & Bartoshuk, L. M. (1992). Taste and smell. *Clinics in Geriatric Medicine, 8*(3), 543-555.

Weiler, K. (1991). Functional assessment in the determination of the need for a substitute decision maker. *Journal of Professional Nursing, 7,* 328.

Weiler, P. G., Mungas, D., & Bernick, C. (1988). Propranolol for the control of disruptive behavior in senile dementia. *Journal of Geriatric Psychiatry and Neurology, 1,* 226-230.

Weinberger, D. R. (1987). Implications of normal brain development for the pathogenesis of schizophrenia. *Archives of General Psychiatry, 44,* 660-669.

Weiner, R. D. (1984). Does electroconvulsive therapy cause brain damage? *Behavioral and Brain Sciences, 7,* 1-53.

Weingartner, H. (1986). Automatic and effort-demanding cognitive processes in depression. In L. Poon (Ed.), *Handbook for clinical memory assessment of older adults* (pp. 218-225). Washington, DC: American Psychological Association.

Weingartner, H., & Silberman, E. (1982). Models of cognitive impairment: Cognitive changes in depression. *Psychopharmacology Bulletin, 90,* 187-196.

Weinstein, W. S., & Khanna, P. (1986). *Depression in the elderly: Conceptual issues and psychotherapeutic intervention.* New York: Philosophical Library.

Weisfeldt, M. L., & Gerstenblith, G. (1986). Cardiovascular aging and adaptation to disease. In J. W. Hurst (Ed.), *The heart.* New York: Macmillan.

Weiss, K. J. (1994). Management of anxiety and depression syndromes in the elderly. *Journal of Clinical Psychiatry, 55*(2, Suppl.), 5-12.

Weiss, K. S., & Rosenberg, D. J. (1984). Prevalence of anxiety disorder among alcoholics. *Journal of Clinical Psychiatry, 46,* 3-5.

Weissman, M. M., Bruce, M. L., Leaf, P. J., Florio, L. P., & Holzer, C., III. (1991). Affective disorders. In L. Robins & D. Regier (Eds.), *Psychiatric disorders in America* (pp. 53-81). New York: Free Press.

Weissman, M. M., Leaf, P. J., Bruce, M. L., & Florio, L.P. (1988a). The epidemiology of dysthymia in five communities: Rates, risks, comorbidity, and treatment. 140th Annual Meeting of the American Psychiatric Association (1987, Chicago, Illinois). *American Journal of Psychiatry, 145,* 815-819.

Weissman, M. M., Leaf, P., Tischler, G., Blazer, D., Karno, M., Bruce, M., & Florio, L. (1988b). Affective disorders in five United States communities. *Psychological Medicine, 18,* 141-153.

Wells, C. E. (1980). The differential diagnosis of psychiatric disorders in the elderly. In J. O. Cole & J. E. Barrett (Eds.), *Psychopathology in the aged.* New York: Raven.

Wells, K. B., Golding, J. M., Burnam, M. A. (1988). Psychiatric disorder in a sample of the general population with and without chronic medical conditions. *American Journal of Psychiatry, 145,* 976-981.

Wells, T. J., Brink, C. A., Diokno, A. D., Wolfe, R., & Gillis, G. L. (1991). Pelvic muscle exercise for stress urinary incontinence in elderly women. *Journal of the American Geriatrics Society, 39,* 785-791.

Welsh, K., Butters, N., Hughes, J., Mohs, R., & Heyman, A. (1991). Detection of abnormal memory decline in mild cases of Alzheimer's disease using CERAD neuropsychological measures. *Archives of Neurology, 48,* 278-281.

Welsh, K. A., Butters, N., Hughes, J. P., Mohs, R. C., & Heyman, A. (1992). Detection and staging of dementia in Alzheimer's Disease. *Archives of Neurology, 49,* 448-452.

Wengel, S. P., Burke, W. J., Ranno, A. E., & Roccaforte, W. H. (1993). Use of benzodiazepines in the elderly. *Psychiatric Annals, 23,* 325-331.

Wenger, N. K. (1992, October). Cardiovascular disease in the elderly. *Current Problems in Cardiology,* 651-660.

Werch, C. H. (1989). Quantity-frequency and diary measures of alcohol consumption for elderly drinkers. *The International Journal of the Addictions, 24,* 859-865.

Werner, P., Cohen-Mansfield, J., Braub, J., & Marx, M. S. (1989). Physical restraints and agitation in nursing home residents. *Journal of the American Geriatrics Society, 37,* 1122-1126.

Wesner, R. B., & Winokur, G. (1989). The influence of age on the natural history of unipolar depression when treated with ECT. *European Archives of Psychiatry and Neurological Science, 238,* 149-154.

Wessler, R., Rubin, M., & Sollberger, A. (1976). Circadian rhythm of activity and sleep-wakefulness in elderly institutionalized patients. *Journal of Interdisciplinary Cycle Research, 7,* 333.

West, R. L. (1986). Everyday memory and aging. *Developmental Neuropsychology, 2,* 323-344.

Westbrook, M. T., & Mitchel, R. A. (1979). Changes in sex-role stereotypes from health to illness. *Social Science and Medicine, 13,* 297-302.

Westermeyer, J. F. (1993). Schizophrenia. In P. Tolan & B. Cohler (Eds.), *Handbook of clinical research and practice with adolescents* (pp. 359-385). New York: John Wiley.

Westermeyer, J. F., & Harrow, M. (1984). Prognosis and outcome using broad (DSM-II) and narrow (DSM-III) concepts of schizophrenia. *Schizophrenia Bulletin, 10,* 624-637.

Westermeyer, J. F., & Harrow, M. (1988). Course and outcome in schizophrenia. In M. Tsuang & J. C. Simpson (Eds.), *Handbook of schizophrenia. Vol. 3: Nosology, epidemiology and genetics* (pp. 205-244). New York: Elsevier.

Westermeyer, J. F., Harrow, M., & Marengo, J. T. (1991). Risk for suicide in schizophrenia and other psychotic and nonpsychotic patients. *Journal of Nervous and Mental Disease, 179,* 259-266.

Whipple, R. H., Wolfson, L. I., & Amerman, P. M. (1987). The relationship of knee and ankle weakness to falls in nursing home residents: An isokinetic study. *Journal of the American Geriatrics Society, 35,* 13-20.

Whitbourne, S. K. (1976). Test anxiety in elderly and young adults. *International Journal of Aging and Human Development, 7,* 201-210.

Whitbourne, S. K. (1986). *The aging individual: Physiological and psychological perspectives.* New York: Springer.

Whitbourne, S. K. (1986). *Adult development.* New York: Praeger.

Whitbourne, S. K. (1987). Personality development in adulthood and old age: Relationships among identity style, health, and well-being. In K. W. Schaie (Ed.), *Annual review of gerontology and geriatrics* (pp. 189-216). New York: Springer.

Whitbourne, S. K., & Wills, K.-J. (1993). Psychological issues in institutional care of the aged. In S. B. Goldsmith (Ed.), *Long-term care administration handbook* (pp. 19-32). Gaithersburg, MD: Aspen.

White, S., & Edelstein, B. (1991). Behavioral assessment and investigatory interviewing. *Behavioral Assessment, 13,* 245-264.

Whitehead, M. I. (1989). Sexual problems in the elderly: Men's vs. women's: A geriatrics panel discussion. *Geriatrics, 44,* 75-86.

Whitehead, W. E., Burgio, K. L., & Engel, B. T. (1984). Behavioral methods in the assessment and treatment of urinary incontinence. In J.C. Brocklehurst (Ed.), *Urology in the elderly.* New York: Churchill Livingstone.

Whitehouse, P. J., Price, D. L., Struble, R. G., Clark, W. W., Coyle, J. T., & DeLong, M. R. (1982). Alzheimer's disease and senile dementia: Loss of neurons in the basal forebrain. *Science, 215,* 1237-1239.

Whitlatch, C., Zarit, S. H., & von Eye, A. (1991). Efficacy of interventions with caregivers: A reanalysis. *The Gerontologist, 31,* 9-14.

Wiebel-Orlando, J. (1989). Elders and elderlies: Well-being in Indian old age. *American Indian Culture and Research Journal, 13*(3&4), 75-87.

Wieman, H. (1992). Nursing home care. In R. Ham (Ed.), *Primary care geriatric* (pp. 675-703). St. Louis, MO: Mosby Year Book.

Wiens, A. N., Mensutik, C. E., Miller, S. I., & Schmitz, R. E. (1982). Medical-behavioral treatment of the older alcoholic patient. *American Journal of Drug and Alcohol Abuse, 9,* 461-475.

Williams, R. L., Karacan, I., & Hursch, C. J. (1974). *EEG of human sleep: Clinical applications.* New York: John Wiley.

Williams, T. (1987). The future of aging. *Archives of Physical Medicine Rehabilitation, 68,* 335-338.

Williamson, G. M., & Schulz, R. (1992a). Pain, activity restriction, and symptoms of depression among community-residing adults. *Journal of Gerontology: Psychological Sciences, 47,* P367-P372.

Williamson, G. M., & Schulz, R. (1992b). Physical illness and symptoms of depression among elderly outpatients. *Psychology and Aging, 7,* 343-351.

Willington, F. L. (1980). Urinary incontinence: A practical approach. *Geriatrics, 35,* 41-48.

Willis, S. L., Jay, G. M., Diehl, M., & Marsiske, M. (1992). Longitudinal change and prediction of everyday task competence in the elderly. *Research on Aging, 14,* 68-91.

Willis, S. L., & Schaie, K. W. (1994). Cognitive training in the normal elderly. In F. Boller (Ed.), *Cerebral plasticity in human aging.* New York: Springer-Verlag.

Wilson, T. S. (1948). Incontinence of urine in the aged. *Lancet, II,* 374-377.

Wing. J. L., Birley, J. L. T., Cooper, J. W., Graham, P., & Isaacs, A. (1967). Reliability of a procedure for measuring and classifying "Present Psychiatric State." *British Journal of Psychiatry, 113,* 499-515.

Wingard, D. L. (1982). The sex differential in mortality rates, *American Journal of Epidemiology, 115,* 205-216.

Winger, J., Schirm, V., & Stewart, D. (1987). Aggressive behavior in long-term care. *Journal of Psychosocial Nursing, 25*(4), 28-33.

Winokur, A., Maislin, G., Phillips, J. L., & Amsterdam, J. D. (1988). Insulin resistance after oral glucose tolerance testing in patients with major depression. *American Journal of Psychiatry, 145,* 325-330.

Wise, M. G., & Rieck, S. O. (1993). Diagnostic considerations and treatment approaches to underlying anxiety in the medically ill. *Journal of Clinical Psychiatry, 54*(2, Suppl.), 22-26.

Wise, M. G., & Rundell, J. R. (1988). *Consultation psychiatry.* Washington, DC: American Psychiatric Press.

Wisocki, P. A. (1988). Worry as a phenomenon relevant to the elderly. *Behavior Therapy, 19,* 369-379.

Wistedt, B., Rasmussen, A., Pedersen, L., Malm, U., Trakman-Bendz, L., Wakelin, J., & Bech, P. (1990). The development of an observer-scale for measuring social dysfunction and aggression. *Pharmacopsychiatry, 23,* 249-252.

Wolf, E. (1960). Glare and age. *Archives of Ophthalmology, 64,* 502-514.

Wolf, E., & Gardiner, J. S. (1965). Studies on the scatter of light in the dioptric media of the eye as a basis of visual glare. *Archives of Ophthalmology, 74,* 338-345.

Wolf, P. A., D'Agostino, R. B., Belanger, A. J., & Kannel, W. B. (1991). Probability of stroke: A risk profile from the Framingham Study. *Stroke, 22,* 312-318.

Wolfe, S. M., & Hope, R. (1993). *Worst pills, best pills II: The older adult's guide to avoiding drug-induced death or illness.* Washington, DC: Public Citizen Health Research Group.

Wolin, L. H. (1969). Stress incontinence in young, healthy nulliparous female subjects. *Journal of Urology, 101,* 545-549.

Wolk, R. L., & Goldfarb, A. I. (1967). The response to group psychotherapy of aged recent admission compared with long-term mental hospital patients. *American Journal of Psychiatry, 123,* 1251-1257.

Wolk, S. I., & Douglas, C. J. (1992). Clozapine treatment of psychosis in Parkinson's disease: A report of five consecutive cases. *Journal of Clinical Psychiatry, 53,* 373-376.

Wolpe, J. (1973). *The practice of behavior therapy* (2nd ed.). New York: Pergamon.

Wood, P., Stefanich, M., Williams, P. T., & Haskell, W. L. (1991). The effect on plasma lipoprotein of a prudent weight-reducing diet, with or without exercise in overweight men and women. *New England Journal of Medicine, 325,* 461-466.

Woods, J. H, Katz, J. L., & Winger, G. (1987). Abuse liability of benzodiazepines. *Pharmacology Reviews, 39,* 251-413.

Woods, R. T., & Britton, P. G. (1985). *Clinical psychology with the elderly.* Rockville, MD: Aspen.

Woods, S. W., Tesar, G. E., Murray, G. B., & Cassem, N. H. (1986). Psychostimulant treatment of depressive disorders secondary to medical illness. *Journal of Clinical Psychiatry, 47,* 12-15.

Woolf, S. H., Kamerow, D. B., Lawrence, R. S., Medalie, J. H., & Estes, E. H. (1990). The periodic health examination of older adults: The recommendations of the U.S. Preventive Services Task Force. *Journal of the American Geriatrics Society, 38,* 933-942.

Woollacott, J. H. (1993). Age-related changes in posture and movement [Special Issue]. *Journal of Gerontology, 48,* 56-60.

World Health Organization. (1980). *International classification of impairment, disability, and handicaps.* Geneva, Switzerland: Author.

World Health Organization. (1988). *World health statistics annual* (Vols 1982-1985, 1987, 1988). Geneva, Switzerland: Demographic Yearbook.

Wragg, R., & Jeste, D. V. (1989). An overview of depression and psychosis in Alzheimer's disease. *American Journal of Psychiatry, 146,* 577-587.

Wu, A. J., Atkinson, J. C., Fox, P. C., Baum, B. J., & Ship, J. A. (1992). Cross-sectional and longitudinal analyses of stimulated parotid salivary constituents in healthy, different-aged subjects. *Journal of Gerontology: Medical Sciences, 48,* M219-M224.

Wyman, J. F., Harkins, S. W., & Fantl, J. A. (1990). Psychosocial impact of urinary incontinence in the community-dwelling population. *Journal of the American Geriatrics Society, 38*(3), 282-288.

Yabusaki, A. (1993, March 8). *Working with Japanese Americans: Impact of the internment.* Paper presented at the University of California, Berkeley School of Social Welfare.

Yamagata, A. (1965). Histopathological studies of the colon in relation to age. *Japanese Journal of Gastroenterology, 62,* 229-235.

Yarnell, J. W. G., & St. Legar, A. S. (1979). The prevalence, severity, and factors associated with urinary incontinence in a random sample of the elderly. *Age and Aging, 8,* 81-85.

Yassa, R. (1991). Late-onset schizophrenia. In E. Walker (Ed.), *Schizophrenia: A life-course developmental perspective.* (pp. 243-255). New York: Academic Press.

Yassa, R., Naiv, N.P.V., & Iskandar, H. (1988.). Late onset bipolar disorder in psychosis and depression in the elderly. *Psychiatry Clinics of North America, 11,* 117-131.

Yassa, R., Natase, C., Dupont, D., & Thibeau, M. (1992). Tardive dyskinesia in elderly psychiatric patients: A 5-year study. *American Journal of Psychiatry, 149,* 1206-1211.

Yassa, R., & Suranyi-Cadotte, B. (1993). Clinical characteristics of late-onset schizophrenia and delusional disorder. *Schizophrenia Bulletin, 19,* 701-708.

Yellowlees, P. M., Alpers, J. H., & Bowden, J. J. (1987). Psychiatric morbidity in patients with chronic airflow obstruction. *Medical Journal of Australia, 146,* 305-307.

Yeo, G., & Hikoyeda, N. (1992). *Cohort analysis as a clinical and educational tool in ethnogeriatrics: Historical profiles of Chinese, Filipino, Mexican, and African American elders* (Working Paper Series, 12). Palo Alto, CA: Stanford Geriatric Education Center.

Yeo, G., & Hikoyeda, N. (in press). Asian and Pacific Islander American elders. In G. Maddox (Ed.), *The encyclopedia of aging* (2nd ed.). New York: Springer.

Yesavage, J. A. (1986). The use of self-rating depression scales in the elderly. In L. Poon, T. Crook, B. J. Gurland, K. L. Davis, A. W. Kaszniak, C. Eisdorfer, & L. W. Thompson (Eds.), *Handbook for clinical memory assessment for older adults* (pp. 213-217). Washington, DC: American Psychological Association.

Yesavage, J. A., Brink, T. L., Rose, T. L., & Aday, M. (1983a). Development and validation of a geriatric depression screening scale: A preliminary report. *Journal of Psychiatraic Research, 17,* 37-49.

Yesavage, J., Brink, T. L., Rose, L. R., & Aday, M. (1983b). The Geriatric Depression Rating Scale: Comparison with other self-report and psychiatric rating scales. In T. Crook, S. Ferris, & R. Bartus (Eds.), *Assessment in geriatric psychopharmacology* (pp. 153-167). New Canaan, CT: Mark Powley.

Ying, Y. (1993, March). *Southeast Asians: Vietnamese, Cambodians, and Lao Mien—War, escape/migration trauma, cultural conflicts.* Paper presented at the University of California, Berkeley School of Social Welfare.

Yinger, J. M. (1986). Intersecting strands in the theorization of race and ethnic relations. In J. Rex & D. Mason (Eds.), *Theories of race and ethnic relations.* Cambridge, UK: Cambridge University Press.

Young, R. C. (1991). Hydroxylated metabolites of antidepressants. *Psychopharmacy Bulletin, 27,* 521-532.

Young, R. C., & Klerman, G. L. (1992). Mania in late life: Focus on age at onset. *American Journal of Psychiatry, 149,* 867-876.

Young, R. C., & Meyers, B. S. (1991). Psychopharmacology. In J. Sadavoy, L. W. Lazarus, & L. F. Jarvik (Eds.), *Comprehensive review of geriatric psychiatry* (pp. 435-467). Washington, DC: American Psychiatric Press.

Young, S. H., Muir-Nash, J., & Ninos, M. (1988). Managing nocturnal wandering behavior. *Journal of Gerontological Nursing, 14*(5), 7-12.

Young, V. D., Munro, H. N., & Fukayama, N. (1989). Protein and functional consequences of deficiency in nutrition in the elderly. In H. Horowitz, D. A. MacFadgen, H. Munro, N. S. Scrimshaw, D. Stern, & T. F. Williams (Eds.), *Motivation in the elderly.* Oxford, UK: Oxford University Press.

Youngjohn, J. R., Beck, J., Jogerst, G., & Caine, C. (1992). Neuropsychological impairment, depression, and Parkinson's disease. *Neuropsychology, 6,* 149-158.

Youngjohn, J. R., & Crook, T. H. (1993a). Learning, forgetting, and retrieval of everyday material across the adult life span. *Journal of Clinical and Experimental Neuropsychology, 15,* 447-460.

Youngjohn, J. R., & Crook, T. H. (1993b). Stability of everyday memory in age-associated memory impairment: A longitudinal study. *Neuropsychology, 7,* 406-416.

Youngjohn, J. R., Larrabee, G. J., & Crook, T. H. (1992). Discriminating age-associated memory impairment from Alzheimer's disease. *Psychological Assessment: A Journal of Consulting and Clinical Psychology, 4,* 54-59.

Youngjohn, J. R., Larrabee, G. J., & Crook, T. H. (1993). New adult age- and education-correction norms for the Benton Visual Retention Test. *The Clinical Neuropsychologist, 7,* 155-166.

Yu, L. C. (1987). Incontinence Stress Index: Measuring psychological impact. *Journal of Gerontological Nursing, 13*(7), 18-25.

Yu, L., Rohner, T., Kaltreider, D., Hu, T., Igou, J., & Dennis, P. (1990). Profile of urinary incontinent elderly in long-term care institutions. *Journal of the American Geriatrics Society, 38,* 433-439.

Yudofsky, S. C., Silver, J. M., & Hales, R. E. (1990). Pharmacologic management of aggression in the elderly. *Journal of Clinical Psychiatry, 51*(10, Suppl.), 22-28.

Yudofsky, S. C., Silver, J. M., Jackson, W., Endicott, J., & Williams, D. (1986). The Overt Aggression Scale: An operational rating scale for verbal and physical aggression. *American Journal of Psychiatry, 143,* 35-39.

Yudofsky, S., Williams, D., & Gorman, J. (1981). Propranolol in the treatment of rage and violent behavior in patients with chronic brain syndrome. *American Journal of Psychiatry, 138,* 218-220.

Zacks, R. T., & Hasher, L. (1988). Capacity theory and the processing of inferences. In L. L. Light & D. M. Burke (Eds.), *Language, memory, and aging* (pp. 154-170). New York: Cambridge University Press.

Zajecka, J. (1993). Pharmacology, pharmacokinetics, and safety issues of mood-stabilizing agents. *Psychiatric Annals, 23,* 79-85.

Zallen, E. M., Hooks, L. B., & O'Brien, K. (1990). Salt taste preferences and perceptions of elderly and young adults. *Journal of the American Dietary Association, 90,* 947-950.

Zank, S., & Baltes, M. M. (in press). Psychologische Interventionsmöglichkeiten im Altenheimen [Psychological intervention possibilities in nursing homes]. In A. Kruse & H. W. Wahl (Eds.), *Altern und Wohnen im Heim.* Bern, Switzerland: Huber.

Zarit, S., Anthony, C., & Boutselis, M. (1987). Interventions to caregivers of dementia patients: Comparison of two approaches. *Psychology and Aging, 2,* 225-232.

Zarit, S. H. (1989). Issues and directions in family intervention research. In E. Light & B. D. Lebowitz (Eds.), *Alzheimer's disease and family stress: Directions for research* (Publication No. ADM 89-1569, pp. 458-486). Washington, DC: U.S. Department of Health and Human Services.

Zarit, S. H., Johansson, B., & Berg, S. (1993). Functional impairment and co-disability in the oldest-old: A multidimensional approach. *Journal of Aging and Health, 5,* 291-305.

Zavaroni, I., & Reaven, G. M. (1994). Hyperinsulinemia, obesity and syndrome x. *Journal of Internal Medicine, 235*(1), 51-56.

Zawadski, R. T., & Eng, C. (1988). Case management in capitated long-term care. *Health Care Financing Review*(Annual Suppl.), 75-81.

Zec, R. (1993). Neuropsychological functioning in Alzheimer's disease. In R. W. Parks, R. F. Zec, & R. S. Wilson (Eds.), *Neuropsychology of alzheimer's disease and other dementias* (pp. 1-80). New York: Oxford University Press.

Zec, R. F., Landreth, E. S., Vicari, S. K., Belman, J., Feldman, E., Andrise, A., Robbs, R., Becker, R., & Kumar, V. (1992). Alzheimer's Disease Assessment Scale: A subtest analysis. *Alzheimer's Disease and Associated Disorders, 6,* 164-181.

Zeiss, A. (1992, November). *What behavior therapy has to offer older adults.* Workshop presented at meeting of the Association for Advancement of Behavior Therapy. Boston, MA.

Zeiss, A. M., & Lewinsohn, P. M. (1986). Adapting behavioral treatment for depression to meet the needs of the elderly. *The Clinical Psychologist, 39,* 98-100.

Zeiss, A. M., Lewinsohn, P. M., & Muñoz, R. F. (1979). Nonspecific improvement effects in depression using interpersonal skills training, pleasant activity schedules, and cognitive training. *Journal of Consulting and Clinical Psychology, 47,* 427-439.

Zeiss, A. M., & Okarma, T. (1985). Effects of interdisciplinary health care teams on elderly arthritic patients: A randomized prospective trial of alternative team models. *Proceedings of the Sixth Annual Conference on Interdisciplinary Health Team Care* (pp. 21-35). Hartford: University of Connecticut, School of Allied Health Professions, Nursing, Pharmacy, & Medicine.

Zelinski, E. M., Gilewski, M., & Schaie, K. W. (1993). Individual differences in cross-sectional and 3-year longitudinal memory performance across the adult life span. *Psychology and Aging, 8,* 176-186.

Zelinski, E. M., Gilewski, M. J., & Thompson, L. W. (1980). Do laboratory tests relate to self-assessment of memory ability in the young and old? In L. W. Poon, J. L. Fozard, L. S. Cermak, D. Arenberg, & L. W. Thompson (Eds.), *New directions in memory and aging: Proceedings of the George A. Talland memorial conference.* Hillsdale, NJ: Lawrence Erlbaum.

Zepelin, H. (1973). A survey of age differences in sleep patterns and dream recall among well-educated men and women. *Sleep Research, 2,* 81.

Zepelin, H., McDonald, C. S., & Zammit, G. K. (1984). Effects of age on auditory awakening thresholds. *Journal of Gerontology, 39,* 294-300.

Zhdanova, I. V., Wurtman, R. J., Lynch, H. L., Morabito, C., & Matheson, J. (1995). Sleep inducing effects of low melatonin doses. *Sleep Research, 24,* 66.

Zifa, E., & Fillion, F. (1992). 5-Hydroxtyriptamine receptors. *Pharmacological Reviews, 44,* 410-460.

Zimbardo, P. G., Andersen, S. M., & Kabat, L. G. (1981). Induced hearing deficit generates experimental paranoia. *Science, 212,* 1529-1531.

Zimberg, S. (1987). Alcohol abuse among the elderly. In L. L. Carstensen & B. A. Edelstein (Eds.), *The handbook of clinical gerontology.* New York: Pergamon.

Zimmer, J., Eggert, G., & Schiverton, P. (1990). Individual versus team case management in optimizing community care for chronically ill patients with dementia. *Journal of Aging and Health, 2,* 357-372.

Zimmer, J. G., Watson, N., & Treat, A. (1984). Behavioral problems among patients in skilled nursing facilities. *American Journal of Public Health, 74*(10), 1118-1121.

Zimmerman, B. R. (1990). Non-insulin-dependent (Type II) diabetes: Medical overview. In C. S. Holmes (Ed.), *Neuropsychological and behavioral aspects of diabetes* (pp. 177-183). New York: Springer-Verlag.

Zis, A. P., & Goodwin, F. K. (1979). Major affective disorder as a recurrent illness. *Archives of General Psychiatry, 36,* 835-839.

Zivkovic, B., Perrault, G., Morel, E., et al. (1981). Comparative pharmacology of zolpidem and other hypnotics and sleep inducers. In J. P. Sauvanet, S. Z. Kanger, & P. L. Morselli (Eds.). (1981). *Imidazopyridines in sleep disorders: A novel experimental and therapeutic approach* (LERS Monograph Series, Vol. 6, pp. 97-109). New York: Raven.

Zola, I. K. (1979). "Oh where, oh where has ethnicity gone?" In D. E. Gelfand & A. J. Kutzik (Eds.), *Ethnicity and aging: Theory, research, and policy.* New York: Springer.

Zubin, J., & Spring, B. (1977). Vulnerability—A new view of schizophrenia. *Journal of Abnormal Psychology, 86,* 103-126.

Zung, W. (1967). Depression in the normal aged. *Psychosomatics, 8,* 287-292.

Zung, W. (1983). Self-rating scales for psychopathology. In T. Crook, S. Ferris, & R. Bartus (Eds.), *Assessment in geriatric psychopathology* (pp. 145-151). New Canaan, CT: Mark Powley.

Zung, W. W. K. (1965). A self-rating depression scale. *Archives of General Psychiatry, 12,* 63-70.

Zung, W. W. K. (1971). A rating instrument for anxiety disorders. *Psychosomatics, 12,* 371-379.

Zwick, R., & Attkisson, C. C. (1984). The use of reception checks in client pretherapy orientation research. *Journal of Clinical Psychology, 40,* 446-452.

Index

Wilson, B. A., 156, 195
Wilson, E., 19
Wilson, J., 319, 320
Wilson, P. W., 9, 134
Wilson, R., 96, 97
Wilson, R. S., 201, 202, 205
Wilson, S., 115, 116
Wilson, T. S., 366
Winblad, B., 248, 487
Winemiller, D. R., 510
Winfield-Laird, I., 62, 276, 277, 291
Wing, A. L., 41
Wing. J. L., 159
Wingard, D. L., 111, 337
Winger, G., 514
Winger, J., 385, 389
Wingfield, A., 31
Winokur, A., 231
Winokur, G., 293, 294, 337, 510
Winslade, W., 183
Winslow, L., 25
Wirth, J. B., 264, 267
Wisconsin Card Sorting Test, 196, 209, 211, 215
Wise, M. G., 307, 314, 315, 512, 514, 535, 536
Wisniewski, W., 282
Wisocki, P. A., 305
Wistedt, B., 386, 387, 389, 390, 392
Witheridge, T. F., 262
Wittchen, H. U., 305, 306, 308
Wittig, R., 410
Woerner M. G., 526
Wolf, A. P., 248
Wolf, E., 24
Wolf, H., 353
Wolf, P. A., 124, 134, 191, 192, 193, 200, 201
Wolf, R., 180
Wolfe, R., 364
Wolfe, Rachel, 274-303
Wolfe, S. M., 293
Wolfson, D., 212
Wolfson, L. I., 9
Wolfson, Michele A., 374-397
Wolin, L. H., 352
Wolk, R. L., 297
Wolk, S. I., 529
Wolpe, J., 419
Wolz, M. M., 191, 192, 193, 205
Women

antipsychotic side effects in, 528
mental illness rates among ethnic, 101
sexism against, 168
sexuality in, 112-113
urinary incontinence in, 13
See also Gender differences
Wood, J. M., 415-416
Wood, M. M., 252
Wood, P., 42
Woodbury, M., 124
Woodring, S., 317, 495, 500
Woodruff, R. A., 510
Woods, J. H, 514
Woods, S. W., 510
Woolf, S. H., 424
Woollacott, J. H., 9
Woollacott, M. H., 27
Woolson, R. F., 260
Wooton, J., 539
Word knowledge, 193
Working memory, 172, 173
World Health Organization, 111, 121, 469
Worrying, 305-306. See also Anxiety
Wortman, C. B., 121-122
Wragg, R., 522
Wright, E. C., 222
Wright, H., 409
Wright, K., 221
Wright, L. B., 497, 501
Wu, A. J., 15
Wurtman, R. J., 407
Wyatt, J. K., 410, 411
Wyatt, J. R., 526
Wyatt, R. J., 263, 268, 411, 526, 527
Wyman, J. F., 14, 349, 366
Wynder, E. L., 42

Yabusaki, A., 89, 103
Yaffe, M. J., 277, 286
Yalla, S. V., 355, 361
Yamagata, A., 15
Yamaguchi, T., 200, 201
Yang, J., 211
Yarnell, J. W. G., 352
Yassa, R., 264, 265, 266, 267, 268, 271, 526, 529-530
Yau, H. B., 80
Yellowlees, P. M., 308
Yeo, G., 79, 80, 83, 84, 85, 86, 87, 88, 90, 91, 92, 94, 95, 101, 103

About the Editors

Laura L. Carstensen, Ph.D., is Associate Professor of Psychology at Stanford University. She is past president of the Society for a Science of Clinical Psychology. Her research, supported by the National Institute on Aging, focuses on social and emotional development in adulthood and old age. She is a Fellow of the Gerontological Society of America.

Barry A. Edelstein, Ph.D., is Professor of Psychology at West Virginia University. He has served on the editorial boards of 13 journals, as Associate Editor of 2 journals,, and on the Executive Boards of the American Psychological Association divisions of Clinical Psychology and Adult Development and Aging. His current research addresses older adult decision making and the antecedents and psychological consequences of falls among older adults.

Laurie Dornbrand, M.D., M.P.H., is a Geriatrician and Clinical Assistant Professor of Medicine at Stanford University Medical Center. She directs the Geriatric Clinic at the Palo Alto VA Health Care System and codirects the Andrology Clinic.

About the Contributors

Matt Dane Baker, PA-C, M.S., is Program Director of the Physician Assistant Program and Assistant Professor at the Philadelphia College of Textiles and Science. He is also an adjunct faculty member in the Physician Assistant Program at Hahnemann University Medical College of Pennsylvania. His expertise is in cardiac rehabilitation, physical fitness, and family medicine.

Margret M. Baltes, Ph.D., is Professor of Psychology and Gerontopsychiatry at the Free University Berlin and head of the Research Unit for Psychological Gerontology. She has published extensively on the effect of social ecology on the aging processes and has investigated dependency, everyday competence, and early dementia. She has also written extensively about successful aging. She is a Fellow of the Gerontological Society of America.

Eric Bickel, B.A., was a Research Assistant at the Research Institute of the Hebrew Home of Greater Washington who worked with Dr. Jiska Cohen-Mansfield.

Richard R. Bootzin, Ph.D., is Professor of Psychology at the University of Arizona. He is also Director of the Insomnia Clinic of the University of Arizona Sleep Disorders Center. He is coauthor of *Abnormal Psychology: Current Perspectives,* in its seventh edition. His publications and research interests focus on sleep and sleep disorders.

Walter M. Bortz II, M.D., is Clinical Associate Professor of Medicine at Stanford University Medical Center and a practicing physician at the Palo Alto Medical Clinic. He is past president of the American Geriatrics Society. His research interests focus on aging, exercise, frailty, and quality of life. In addition to numerous journal articles, he recently authored *We Live Too Short and Die Too Long* and *Dare to be 100.*

Sharon Stewart Bortz, M.S., is a registered dietitian who is in private practice in Ukiah, California. She has a master's degree in Applied Physiology and Nutrition from Columbia University and has collaborated on the Human Nutrition Research Center on Aging study at Tufts University. Her research interests concern the effects of strength training and weight loss in post-menopausal women.

Kathryn Larsen Burgio, Ph.D., is Associate Professor and Co-Director of the Behavioral Sciences Section in the Division of Gerontology and Geriatric Medicine at the University of Alabama at Birmingham (UAB). She is Director of the UAB Continence Program and Scientist in the UAB Center for Aging. She has authored numerous articles and chapters on behavioral interventions for urinary incontinence and other age-associated problems.

Jiska Cohen-Mansfield, Ph.D., is Professor of Psychiatry at Georgetown University Medical Center and Director of the Research Institute of the Hebrew Home of Greater Washington. In addition to her doctorate in clinical psychology, she completed a postdoctoral fellowship in rehabilitation medicine. She has published numerous articles on agitation and related issues, such as sleep and physical restraints, in nursing home residents. Her research has been funded by the National Institute of Mental Health, the National Institute on Aging, and the National Center for Health Services Research. She is a Fellow in the Gerontological Society of America.

Thomas H. Crook III, Ph.D., is President of Memory Assessment Clinics, Inc., based in Bethesda, Maryland. He was formerly a clinical research psychologist at the National Institute of Mental Health and Director of the Institute's geriatric psychopharmacology program. He is author of numerous journal articles and book chapters on the assessment and treatment of late-life memory disorders.

William J. Culpepper II, M.A., was a Research Associate at the Research Institute of the Hebrew Home of Greater Washington. He currently is Project Director of Clinical Hip Studies at the Anderson Orthopaedic Research Institute and a doctoral candidate in experimental psychology at Bowling Green State University.

Mindy Engle-Friedman, Ph.D., is Assistant Professor of Psychology at Baruch College at City University of New York. Her research interests focus on health psychology including the assessment and treatment of insomnia.

Dana Epstein, Ph.D., R.N., is a postdoctoral fellow at the Veterans Administration (VA) Postdoctoral Nurse Fellowship Program and is located at the Tucson VA Medical Center. Her doctoral dissertation focused on the behavioral treatment of insomnia in older adults. Her research interests are in geriatrics and the treatment of sleep disorders.

Jane E. Fisher, Ph.D., is Associate Professor of Psychology at the University of Nevada. A clinical psychologist by training, her research addresses the assessment and treatment of behavioral disturbance in Alzheimer's disease, learning and aging, social behavior in late life, and psychological distress and coping across the life span. She is the recipient of the prestigious First Independent Research Support and Transition Award from the National Institute on Aging.

Michael D. Franzen, Ph.D., is Director of Neuropsychology and Associate Professor in the Department of Psychiatry and the Allegheny Neuropsychiatric Institute, Medical College of Pennsylvania. He completed a postdoctoral fellowship in clinical neuropsychology at the University of Nebraska Medical school and served on the faculty at West Virginia University for several years before assuming his current position. His research interests include the development of screening procedures for cognitive dysfunction, psychometric properties of neuropsychological assessment instruments for the elderly, and psychotropic treatment of cognitive decline in dementing conditions.

Deborah W. Frazer, Ph.D., is Director of Clinical Psychology and Training Director for the Postdoctoral Fellowship Program of the Philadelphia Geriatric Center. She consults to the Philadelphia Corporation for Aging, the American Society on Aging, and the National Institute of Mental Health. Her research interests include the interaction of medical and psychological disorders in the elderly and psychotherapy with the frail elderly.

Barbara L. Fredrickson, Ph.D., is Assistant Professor of Psychology at the University of Michigan. She completed a postdoctoral research fellowship at the University of California, Berkeley, where she studied psychophysiological aspects of emotion. She also served for 3 years on the faculty at Duke University. Her research centers on emotions, particularly the psychophysiological functions of positive emotions, as well as on age and gender differences in emotion experience.

Dolores Gallagher-Thompson, Ph.D., is a clinical psychologist at the Veteran's Affairs Palo Alto Health Care System and the Stanford Geriatric Education Center. In these roles, she is responsible for training interns and postdoctoral fellows in clinical geropsychology. She has published extensively in the area of clinical geropsychology, with a particular emphasis on depression and family caregiving. Most recently, she has been investigating cultural differences in caregiving distress in Hispanic American and European American caregivers. She is a Fellow of the Gerontological Society of America.

Margaret Gatz, Ph.D., is Professor of Psychology at the University of Southern California. For the past 15 years, she has led the specialization track in aging within USC's clinical psychology training program. Her scholarly and research interests encompass genetic and environmental factors in the etiology and manifestation of dementia, age-related change in depressive symptoms, integration of prevention with life span developmental theories, and evaluation of the effects of intervention. She has served as the Associate Editor of *Psychology and Aging* and coeditor of the third and fourth editions of the *Handbook of the Psychology of Aging.*

Ann L. Horgas, Ph.D., R.N., is Assistant Professor of Gerontology and Nursing at Wayne State University. She was a recent postdoctoral research fellow at the Free University Berlin where she collaborated on a multidisciplinary study of the old and oldest-old. Her early work focused on staff training of nursing home caregivers to manage mental health problems of residents. More recently, she has been studying the effect of medication use and chronic pain on everyday competence and depression.

Marshall B. Kapp, J.D., M.P.H., is Professor and Director of Geriatric Medicine and Gerontology at Wright State University and holds an adjunct faculty appointment at the University of Dayton School of Law. He has authored numerous books, journal articles, and chapters on legal and ethical aspects of health care for the elderly. Professor Kapp is also founding editor of the *Journal of Ethics, Law and Aging.* In 1987-88 he was a Robert Wood

Johnson Faculty Fellow in Health Care Finance. He is a Fellow of the Gerontological Society of America.

Martin L. Leicht, M.D., is Associate Medical Director of the Philadelphia Geriatric Center, Medical Director of Senior Health Associates, a multi-specialty geriatric medical practice in northeast Philadelphia, and Assistant Professor of Medicine at Temple University Medical School. He is board certified in Internal Medicine and Geriatrics. He provides primary care for an elderly community population and works as part of a task force to facilitate continuity of care for the frail elderly across multiple sites. He also has a strong interest in medical ethics.

Joseph G. Liberto, M.D., is Chief of the Substance Abuse Treatment Program at the Baltimore Veterans Administration and Assistant Professor of Psychiatry at the University of Maryland School of Medicine. Through his work with older patients, he has developed special expertise in the diagnosis and management of substance use disorders in the elderly. He has authored articles and book chapters on the topic of addiction in the elderly and has been involved in clinical trial studies with older addicts as the medical director of a geriatric substance abuse clinic at the Baltimore VA.

Julie L. Locher, M.A., is a Research Associate in the Division of Gerontology and Geriatric Medicine and the Continence Program at the University of Alabama at Birmingham (UAB). She is an Associate in the UAB Center for Aging and a doctoral student in the Medical Sociology program. Her research interests include incontinence and nutrition in older adults.

Joanne Marengo, Ph.D., is Associate Professor of Clinical Psychiatry and Behavioral Sciences at Northwestern University Medical School and is on the Attending Scientific Staff of Michael Reese Medical Center in Chicago, Illinois. She has a full-time private practice in Chicago. She has been a collaborator on the Chicago Follow-up Study, a longitudinal study of schizophrenia and related psychiatric illnesses, at Michael Reese Medical Center funded by the National Institute of Mental Health. Her research focuses on the evolutions of cognitive symptoms in schizophrenia and classification of the courses of illness across individuals.

Roy C. Martin, Ph.D., is Assistant Professor in the Department of Neurology at the Epilepsy Center at the University of Alabama at Birmingham. He is director of the neuropsychology service for the Epilepsy Center. His current research interests include the neuropsychological correlates of temporal lobe epilepsy and neuropsychological psychosocial outcome of temporal lobectomy.

Jannay Morrow, Ph.D., is Assistant Professor of Psychology at Vassar College, where she teaches courses in abnormal, social, and health psychology. Her research focuses on individual, social, and cognitive factors involved in coping with depression and stressful events. Recent work examines the effect of coping styles on evaluations of and reactions to social interactions, self-perception of social skills, and social effectiveness, social preferences, and interaction styles.

Laura Mosqueda, M.D., is Director of Geriatrics at St. Luke Medical Center in Pasadena, California and Assistant Professor of Clinical Family Medicine, Director of Geriatrics in the Department of Family Medicine at the University of Southern California School of Medicine. She is board certified in both family medicine and geriatrics. She lectures and publishes extensively about geriatrics. Her specific research and teaching interests include geriatric rehabilitation, assessment, and bioethics.

James P. Noll, M.A., is a doctoral candidate in the clinical psychology program at Northern Illinois University. He recently completed his clinical internship at the Veteran's Affairs Medical Center in Lexington, Kentucky. Specializing in gerontological research, his dissertation focuses on the spatial and temporal properties of wandering in dementia patients. More broadly, his research interests include behavioral disturbances in dementia patients, operant learning in pathological and normal aging, and the behavioral assessment and treatment of elderly individuals.

David W. Oslin, M.D., is a fellow in geriatric psychiatry at the University of Pennsylvania. His career focuses on bridging the areas of addiction and geriatric psychiatry. His research interests include impairment in activities of daily living and health-related quality of life associated with excessive alcohol use in late life. He is also engaged in prevention and treatment trials for older alcohol-dependent adults as well as developing models for alcohol-related cognitive impairments.

Tara Rose, B.A., is a doctoral student in clinical psychology at the University of Southern California. Her research interests include clinicians' attitudes and behaviors toward older clients and the psychological well-being of people in nontraditional families.

Paul E. Ruskin, M.D., is Chief of Geriatric Psychiatry at the Baltimore VA and Associate Professor of Psychiatry at the University of Maryland School of Medicine. He is founder and director of the University of Maryland/VA geriatric psychiatry fellowship. He has conducted research in the areas of schizophrenia and depression in the elderly. Additionally, he has edited a book on posttraumatic stress disorder in the elderly and has written articles and book chapters on substance abuse in the elderly.

Marie-Anne Salvio, Ph.D., is a psychologist in private practice in Connecticut. She does individual and group psychotherapy in nursing homes and extended-care facilities. She also consults to nursing homes regarding staff education and medication management in geriatrics.

Jeanette Schneider, Ph.D., M.D., is Director of the Geriatric Psychiatry Clinic at the Palo Alto Veterans Administration Medical Center. She holds a Ph.D. in biochemistry from John Hopkins University and an M.D. from Stanford University School of Medicine. She completed her residency and fellowship in geropsychiatry at Stanford, and is now board certified in psychiatry with added qualifications in geriatric psychiatry.

Eleanor S. Segal, M.D., is Clinical Professor of Medicine at Stanford University and a core faculty member of the Stanford Geriatric Education Center. She is board certified in family medicine and holds a Certificate of Added Qualifications in Geriatric Medicine. A family physician and geriatrician for over 25 years, she teaches physician-patient communication and develops medical school curricula that promote culturally sensitive assessment of ethnic minority elderly. She is a Fellow of the American Academy of Family Practice.

Elizabeth M. Semenchuk, Ph.D., is Assistant Professor of Clinical Psychology at Bowling Green State University, Associate Director of the Behavioral Medicine Department at St. Francis Health Care Center, and Adjunct Assistant Professor in the Department of Behavioral Medicine and Psychiatry at the Medical College of Ohio. Her research interests include chronic pain syndromes, recurrent headache, and cardiovascular risk factors and disorders.

Ann M. Steffen, Ph.D., is Assistant Professor of Psychology at the University of Missouri—St. Louis. She teaches Geropsychology to health care professionals through the Gerontology Program and supervises therapists in the treatment of older adults. Her research interests include family caregiving of dementia patients, cognitive behavioral interventions, and prevention of mental health problems in later life.

Larry W. Thompson, Ph.D., is a clinical psychologist at the Veteran's Affairs Palo Alto Health Care System and Stanford University School of Medicine. He is Director of the postdoctoral training program in gerontological research and a member of the core faculty in the predoctoral clinical geropsychology training program. He has investigated clinical electrophysiology, clinical neuropsychology, and geriatric mental health. His current research interests focus on the effectiveness of various forms of nonpharmacologic treatment for late-life depression. He is a Fellow of the Gerontological Society of America.

Jeanne L. Tsai, M.A., is currently a predoctoral Psychology Fellow in the Public Service and Minority Cluster at the University of California, San Francisco, Clinical Psychology Training Program and a doctoral candidate in clinical psychology at the University of California, Berkeley. Her research interests include the influences of age and culture on the physiological, subjective, and behavioral aspects of emotional responding. Her clinical interests include working with ethnic minority elderly and underserved populations.

Susan Turk-Charles, M.A., is a doctoral student in clinical psychology at the University of Southern California. Her research interests include older adults' attitudes and decision-making processes regarding health behaviors. She is also interested in how people cope with chronic illness across the adult life span.

Perla Werner, M.A., is a doctoral candidate at the University of Maryland and a Senior Research Associate at the Research Institute of the Hebrew Home of Greater Washington. Prior to entering the program, she obtained a master's degree in sociology and anthropology from Bar Ilan University in Tel Aviv. For several years, she researched home health care and support programs for caregivers of disabled elderly at the Research Department of the National Insurance Institute in Israel. Her current research interests focus on agitation, sleep disturbance, effects of the removal of physical restraints, and psychotropic medication use in nursing home residents.

Hans-Werner Wahl, Ph.D., is psychologist and senior scientist at the Institute of Gerontology at the University of Heidelberg. He has been affiliated with a major research project on the social origins of dependency in old age at the Free University Berlin. His current research interests are in environmental gerontology, rehabilitation, coping with severe chronic disabilities, and visual loss.

Jerry F. Westermeyer, Ph.D., is Associate Dean of Clinical Training at the Adler School of Professional Psychology in Chicago. For 7 years, he directed the Chicago Follow up Study, a long-term study of schizophrenia, depression, and other major mental disorders through Michael Reese Hospital in Chicago.

Currently, he serves as teacher, clinical supervisor, and administrator at the Adler School.

Susan Krauss Whitbourne, Ph.D., is Professor of Psychology at the University of Massachusetts at Amherst. She is past president of the American Psychological Association's Division 20 (Adult Development and Aging) and is author of numerous books and articles that address gerontology. She teaches award-winning courses on the psychology of aging. Her current research investigates the effects of age-related changes in physical and cognitive functioning on identity development in later adulthood. She is a Fellow of the Gerontological Society of America.

Rachel Wolfe, M.A., is a doctoral student in the clinical psychology program at Duke University. Her research interests include the psychology of women, aging, and health; effects of exercise on mental health; psychological sequelae of osteoporosis; and the neuropsychological consequences of cardiac surgery.

Michele A. Wolfson, B.A., was formerly a research assistant at the Research Institute of the Hebrew Home of Greater Washington. She is currently a graduate student at St. John's University.

James R. Youngjohn, Ph.D., is a clinical neuropsychologist in independent practice in Scottsdale, Arizona. He is a Diplomate in Clinical Neuropsychology from the American Board of Clinical Neuropsychology and the American Board of Professional Psychology. He is past director of the Neuropsychological Testing Laboratory at the National Rehabilitation Hospital and past director of neuropsychological research at Memory Assessments Clinics, Inc. His research interests include memory disorders, age-related neuropsychological changes, brain injury, and forensic issues.

Antonette M. Zeiss, Ph.D., is Director of the Interdisciplinary Team Training Program at the Palo Alto Veteran's Administration Health Care System and is Clinical Lecturer at the Stanford University School of Medicine. A clinical psychologist by training, she supervises interns and postdoctoral fellows in Geropsychology. She teaches an interdisciplinary seminar on the basic theory of interdisciplinary teams and provides training to teams throughout the national Veteran's Administration system. She is president-elect of the Association for Advancement of Behavior Therapy. Her research interests include depression, caregiving, and sexuality in the elderly.